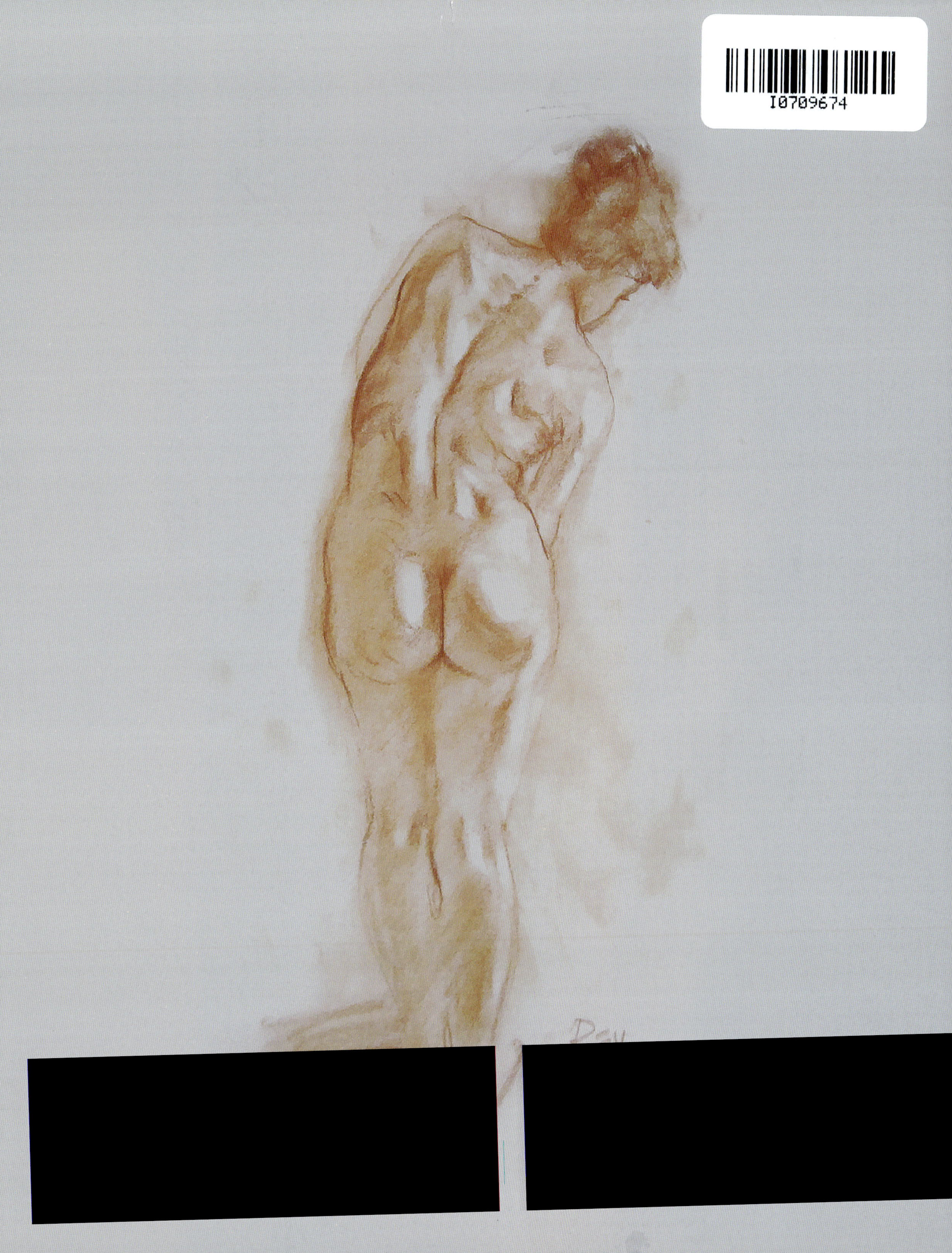

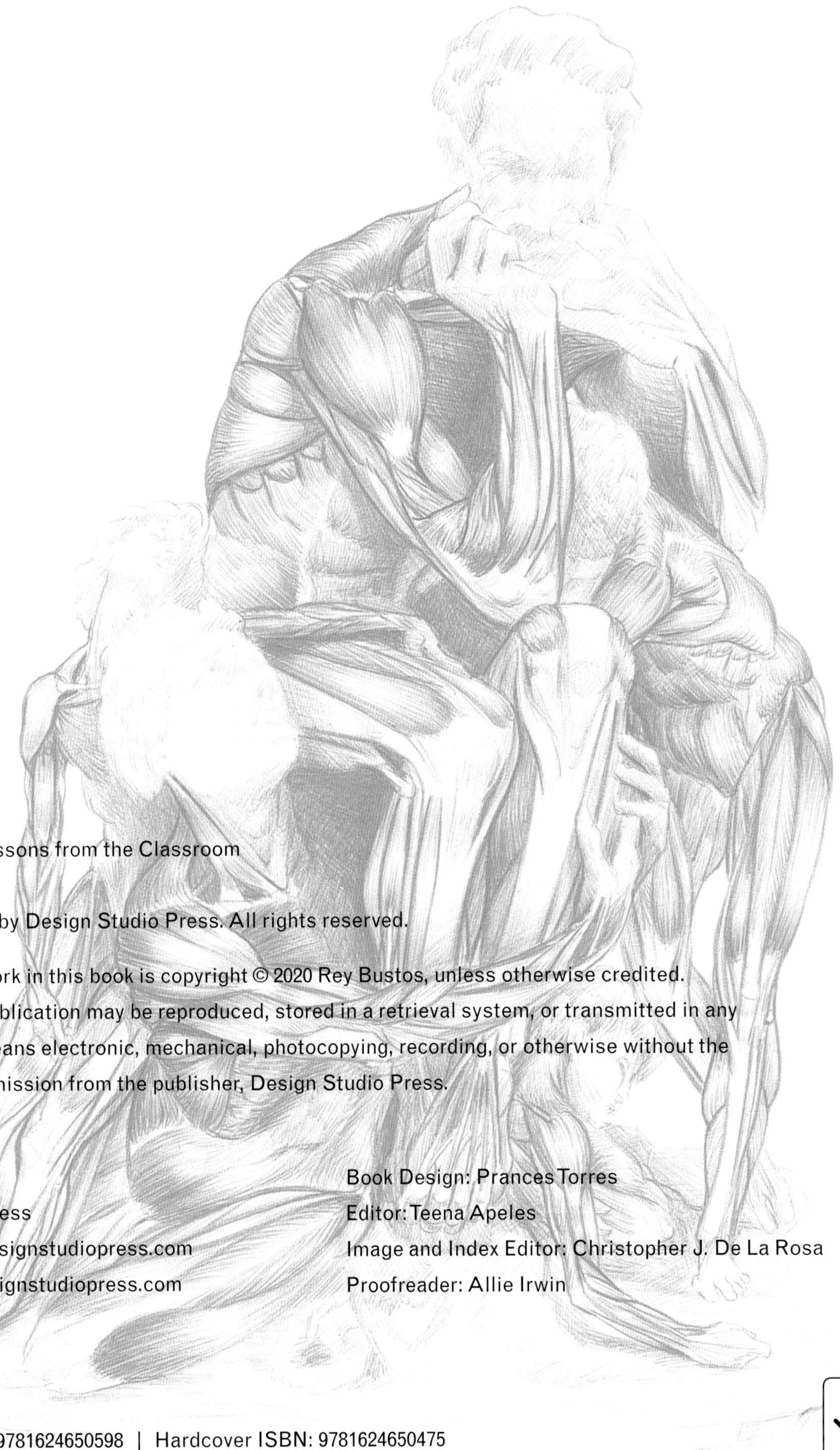

Rey's Anatomy

Figurative Art Lessons from the Classroom

Copyright © 2020 by Design Studio Press. All rights reserved.

All text and artwork in this book is copyright © 2020 Rey Bustos, unless otherwise credited.
No part of this publication may be reproduced, stored in a retrieval system, or transmitted in any
form or by any means electronic, mechanical, photocopying, recording, or otherwise without the
prior written permission from the publisher, Design Studio Press.

Published by
Design Studio Press
Website: www.designstudiopress.com
E-mail: info@designstudiopress.com

Book Design: Prances Torres
Editor: Teena Apeles
Image and Index Editor: Christopher J. De La Rosa
Proofreader: Allie Irwin

Printed in China
10 9 8 7 6 5 4 3 2 1
Softcover ISBN: 9781624650598 | Hardcover ISBN: 9781624650475
Library of Congress Control Number: 2020948693

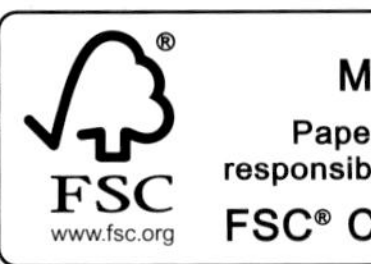

REY'S ANATOMY

Figurative Art Lessons from the Classroom

by Rey Bustos

CONTENTS

FOREWORD 07

INTRODUCTION 08

TERMINOLOGY 11

TOOLS OF THE TRADE 14

PART I: ANATOMY EXPLORED

THE SKELETON 18
What Gives Us Shape 18
The Axial and Appendicular Skeletons 21
Drawing a Skeleton 22

THE LEG AND FOOT 25
The Leg 25
The Foot 27
Identifying the Forms 29
Drawing the Feet 30

THE THIGH AND GLUTEAL AREA 33
The Quadriceps 33
Four Views of the Knee 34
The Adductors 35
The Flexors 36
The Gluteals 37
Analysis of Form in Four Steps 38

THE TORSO 43
The Front Torso 43
How to Draw the Front Torso 45
The Pelvis 47
The Back Torso and Shoulder 48
On Aging 50
Three Movements of the Scapula 51

THE ARM 54
Upper Arm 55
Arm Skeleton 56
Forearm 59

THE HAND 62
Handedness 62
Male and Female Characteristics 63
The Anatomical Snuffbox 64
Drawing Techniques 65

THE HEAD AND NECK 67
Facial Expressions 68
Temporalis 69
Orbicularis Oris and the Mentalis Group 70
The Masseter 70
The Neck 71
What Can You Tell from a Skull? 74

FACIAL FEATURES 77
The Eyes 78
The Nose 80
Nose Construction 81
Mouth Construction 82
The Mouth 83
The Ears 83
Drawing the Head and Face:
The Globe Method 85

PANNICULUS ADIPOSUS 89
Subcutaneous Fat and Visceral Fat 90

THE ART OF ÉCORCHÉ 92

THE HUMAN MUSCULAR SYSTEM 94

PART II: ANATOMY APPLIED

FIGURATIVE ART   105

Literal/Classical and Interpretive Approaches   105

Finding Your Style   105

Is Copying Ever Okay?   107

HOW TO MAINTAIN PROPORTIONS   108

Depicting Different Body Types   110

DRAWING FROM CADAVERS   111

PUTTING THE "LIFE" IN LIFE DRAWING   113

To Commit or Not to Commit to a Pose?   115

Tutorial: Analytical to Gestural Drawing   116

PART III: MORE ANATOMY EXERCISES

EXERCISE DAILY   122

Draw a Tree   122

Switch Drawing Hands   123

Draw from TV: Control Your Model   124

FOCUS ON BODY PARTS   125

Tutorial: Female vs. Male Standing Figure   126

Capturing the Main Frame   127

Drawing Skeletal Armature   128

Origin & Insertion: The Drumstick Form   129

Constellation Drawing   130

Proportion Check   131

CREATING SILHOUETTES   132

Quick Thumbnails   132

Cutting vs. Drawing   133

Drawing with a Chamois   134

APPLYING SHADOWS   135

MASTERING POSES: CHOOSING YOUR REFERENCE   137

Tutorial: Standing Poses   138

Tent Drawing   140

Tutorial: Reclining Poses   142

ANIMATING THE BODY   144

THE "LAST-PAGE" TIP   145

GALLERY   146

CREDITS   205

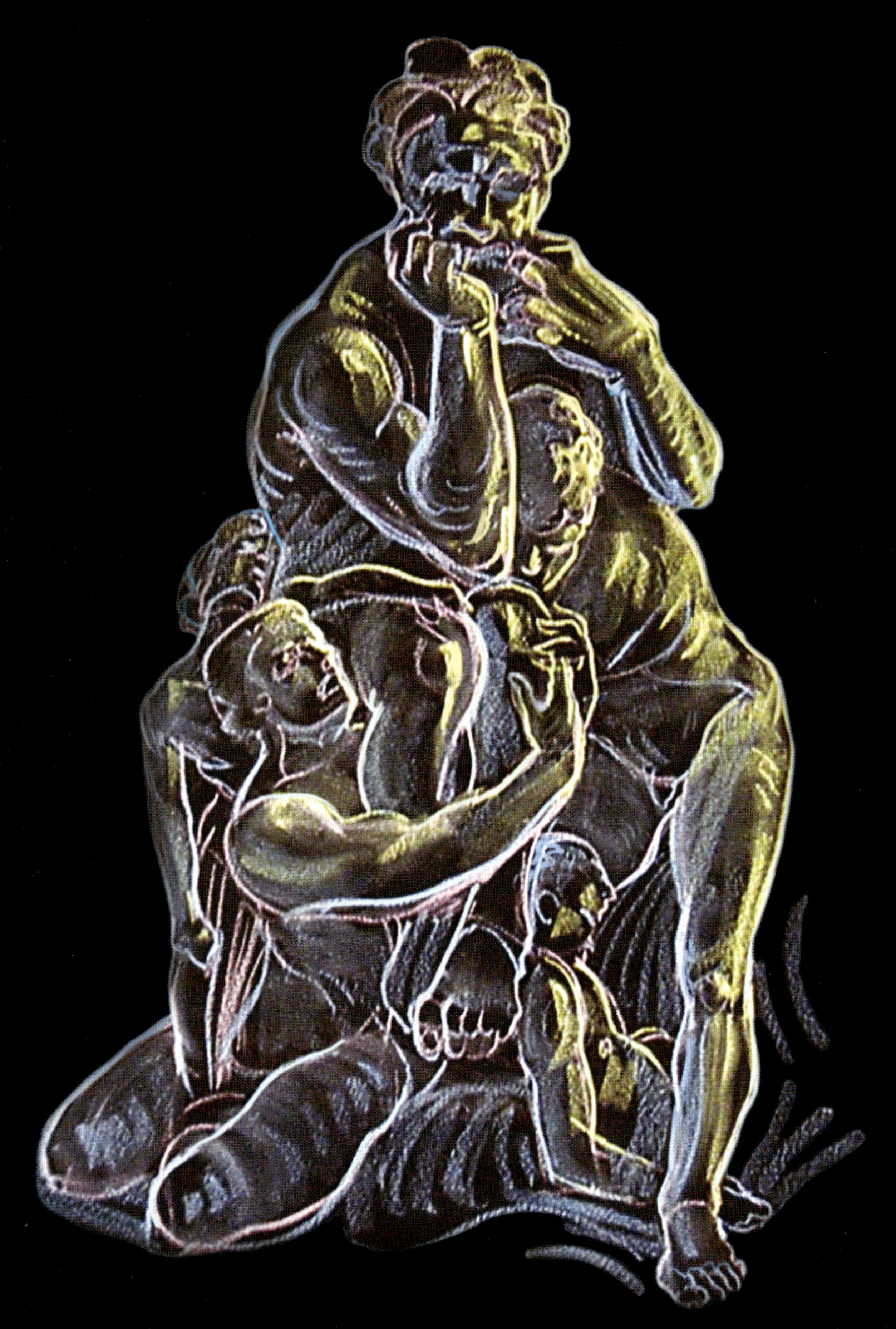

FOREWORD

Anatomy for artists is a descriptive science. Traditionally, we explore and memorize the elements that create or influence surface form. We seek an understanding of each structure's form, and how it contributes to overall complex form. We can think of an analogy in language: when we first learn the individual letters of the alphabet, then how they form words, how words create sentences, then paragraphs, and so on. Then, with all this knowledge, we assemble our words, sentences, and paragraphs into literature. Likewise, we must first understand the form of every component of the human body in order to use them to create accurate figurative art.

This is the hierarchy of the study of artistic anatomy: we traditionally learn each bone and muscle, assemble the skeleton, and clothe it with muscles, fat, and skin. After, we develop the various regions (limbs, torso, etc.) and then finally build a complete figure. Whether it is a drawing, painting, or sculpture, we ultimately hope to transcend the sum of the parts, and transform nature into art. Here we leave science and enter the realm of creativity, inspiration, and expression.

Rey Bustos—teacher extraordinaire—has presented his take on artistic anatomy in this incredible book to a level I have not seen before. In a word, he has electrified every aspect of the study of artistic anatomy with *vitality*. He brings anatomy to life. In the extraordinary presentations he has developed over many years of teaching, he brings not only accuracy to his teaching, but energy and excitement; clever, original presentations will engage the reader. His expertise comes from his own intense study of classic paintings, drawings, and sculptures by the great masters of the figure, along with direct anatomical studies of cadavers. This valuable information is the core of the book.

Once the basics of anatomy are covered, Rey goes into the changes that take place in the body during motion and in various poses. And the emphasis is on *form*, so beautifully illustrated in his drawings and tutorials, his students' drawings, and his analysis of Old Master artwork. His system of color-coding the anatomy yields a welcome clarity to the subject. Neighboring structures (and therefore forms) are easily identifiable. His magnificent blackboard drawings and clear, accessible text make one feel as though they are in the classroom watching and listening to Rey in action. The book concludes with an invaluable section on drawing techniques.

Rey's sensitivity to all aspects of figurative creativity makes this book appropriate both as a first text for the beginner and a sophisticated reference for the seasoned artist. It teaches how anatomy can be used to create classic art, contemporary art, and everything in between. It is an excellent guide to basic anatomy as well as a course on how to use anatomy in art. *Rey's Anatomy* is a significant contribution to the study of artistic anatomy.

Eliot Goldfinger

INTRODUCTION

The beauty and precision of pre-20th-century figurative art made it clear to me that in-depth anatomical knowledge was once mandatory for the artist. When Claude Monet laid the foundation for Impressionism, he broke with academic traditions such as the popular ateliers that were in vogue in the 1800s, including the work of William-Adolphe Bouguereau who epitomized the realism that had rarely ever been achieved and was heralded in his life but reviled by the avant-garde Impressionists. Breaking with that tradition was a new breed of artists dedicated to finding ways of expression less committed to superrealism and more concerned with the deeper meaning behind what we perceive to be real. Monet and these radical thinkers paved the way for a newfound freedom of emotional and unique expression. Regardless of worldly gain or popular acceptance, this development was necessary for artists, and helped them to reach beyond the cerebral to find their hearts. But it was a trail blazed by highly educated artists who understood that their artistic voice was enhanced by their classical instruction.

Although artists in Europe enjoyed their freedom from the confinements of academic realism and the tight rules that governed them, something was also lost in the century that followed. Many felt that they did not need to know foundational necessities such as anatomy and perspective. New artists may have thought that they had found a shortcut to creating art, but expression without hard work does not produce quality art. While some of my favorite artists lived during this period of the early 1900s—Marcel Duchamp, Piet Mondrian, Georges Braque, and Pablo Picasso—and we needed that courageous exploration, in my opinion that exploration was misinterpreted by some artists as a medium in which to indulge without the integrity that one needs to be a true artist, or, at least, to be true to oneself as an artist. True artists understood why art had to take this course away from realism. They were not creating images that looked less real than before because they couldn't do traditional work, it was because they wanted to find the significance of art and life rather than to copy the world that their eyes saw.

It is no coincidence that Impressionism happened at the same time as the invention of the camera. What better way to capture what is "real" than a camera? Then what would become of the portrait painter or landscape painter? They had to find something more than what is observable. The other major factor that changed the history of Western art was the introduction of prints from the Far East. The Impressionists were astounded that the way Japanese and Chinese artists were working was completely different than they had ever seen. The great Japanese artist Ando Hiroshige, for example, was creating block prints of Edo (now Tokyo) that had large areas of white and seemingly no focus on linear perspective, yet the images created were astoundingly complex and stunningly beautiful and impactful. We now know these to be of the *ukiyo-e* genre of Japanese art or "images of the floating world." It is this genre and the "feeling" of the drawing, which are at the core of my philosophy of art and figure drawing.

There is no one way to depict the human figure. From Leonardo and Michelangelo to Egon Schiele and Dean Cornwell to Richmond Barthé and Ernie Barnes (I was inspired to create my own art and attend ArtCenter College of Design after I framed some of his inspiring artwork), the contrast between their representations is great, but each artist's strokes are loud and clear just as the voices of Luciano Pavarotti, Janis Joplin, Joan Baez, and John Lennon are unique and identifiable but emotionally conjoined. The sincerity and passion of these artists shine through and communicate to the audience in a way that allows the spirit of art to connect us to one another. Communication is the essence and the common denominator of all the arts. This is our gift to the world.

My family came to the United States from Colombia when I was six years old. I have no memories of drawing until we came here. I did not know English and had a hard time in this strange new world. I now realize that is why I started to draw. It was my way of communicating, and my needed equalizer among the other kids. I discovered through my classmates' reactions to my work that I was better at art than they were. So if I think about it, I am not sure if I was born an artist, but I am sure that I made myself an artist, and that is why I truly feel that I gravitated toward becoming an educator.

Rey's Anatomy: Figurative Art Lessons from the Classroom is intended to be the ultimate resource for an art anatomy student. This book gathers my most valuable anatomy lessons and drawing approaches developed over three decades of teaching at ArtCenter College of Design, two decades at Los Angeles Academy of Figurative Art, and a myriad of other places past and present, including online classes for New Masters Academy and Computer Graphics Masters Academy (CGMA). With all my students, I assure them from the onset that their means of expression will not suffer with anatomical or historical knowledge. Nonrepresentational or highly stylized artwork is valid as long as they understand why they are doing it and what they are trying to communicate.

I created this book to teach artists *how* to see, and also how to *understand* what they are seeing—not just the surface of skin but the depths of the body. While I do go over how to view and block a model and share ways to start a figure drawing, this is not a "how-to-draw" book. To learn how to draw a figure, anatomy is not enough. Anatomy is only one way to develop your capacity to see in order to draw. The body is and has always been the most challenging subject for the artist to depict, because of its intricate complexity and movement. This is proven when we try to draw the human form without the discipline of study. When I look at my students' drawings of a figure at the start of class, I can see the talent, but I also see that they do not know the subject, the human body. There is little evidence of a skeletal structure, of the interplay between the bones and the muscles and tendons; basically there is no "life" to their life drawings. Art students must constantly hone their skills in line quality, form, and composition. These combined skills provide the qualities that breathe life into figurative art.

We are all—artists and people alike—intimately familiar with the human body; we are of the body and the body is of us. Therefore, even the average person may not know anything about the anatomy of the hand, but will easily notice a flaw in the depiction of a hand in a piece of art. For this reason alone, the figurative artist will benefit from knowing the mechanical, anatomical aspects of the hand and how to compose and arrange it. The master artist, steeped in anatomy, can depict the human form to emote an

"I created this book to teach artists *how* to see, and also how to *understand* what they are seeing—not just the surface of skin but the depths of the body."

emotional and creative artistic statement. The novice often can only see parts of the body—not the more important aspects which lie beneath them.

Ultimately the aim of this book is to help an artist create without being slowed down by the process or the intellect, because only through serious education and sheer pencil mileage can an artist obtain enough knowledge and skill to transcend human anatomy and engage in intuitive fluidity. To do this, I have included works from the great masters

to help you understand how an artist can take the same anatomical knowledge and express it so differently and personally. These masters signed each and every stroke with their own unique flair. References to the masters appear throughout the book, which is organized by chapters that follow a logical order as you move up the body, from feet, to legs, thighs, and so on. I will teach you what the body is, but it is up to you to explore your own expression. The exercises I provide are designed to facilitate this personal journey.

Anatomical knowledge will help you "see" what you cannot readily observe due to bad lighting, your position in the room with a model, or any other myriad of things. You will know the knowledge has entered your soul when you find yourself relying less and less on looking at the model, and more and more on your inner eye. You can start to alter the reality of the human figure because you know what that reality is made from.

We all learn best when we feel joy rather than frustration, so I wrote *Rey's Anatomy: Figurative Art Lessons from the Classroom* with the intention to make this journey toward acquiring anatomical knowledge a pleasant and approachable one for anyone, at any level.

I hope I have succeeded.

Rey Bustos
Altadena, California

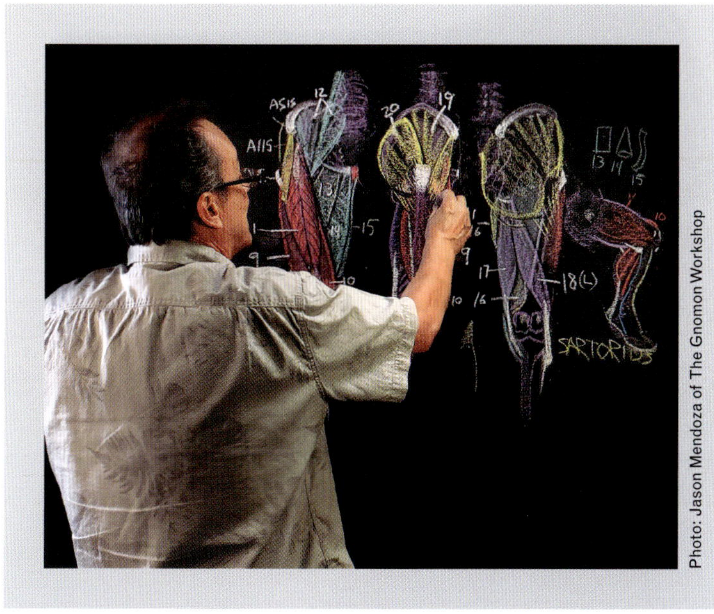

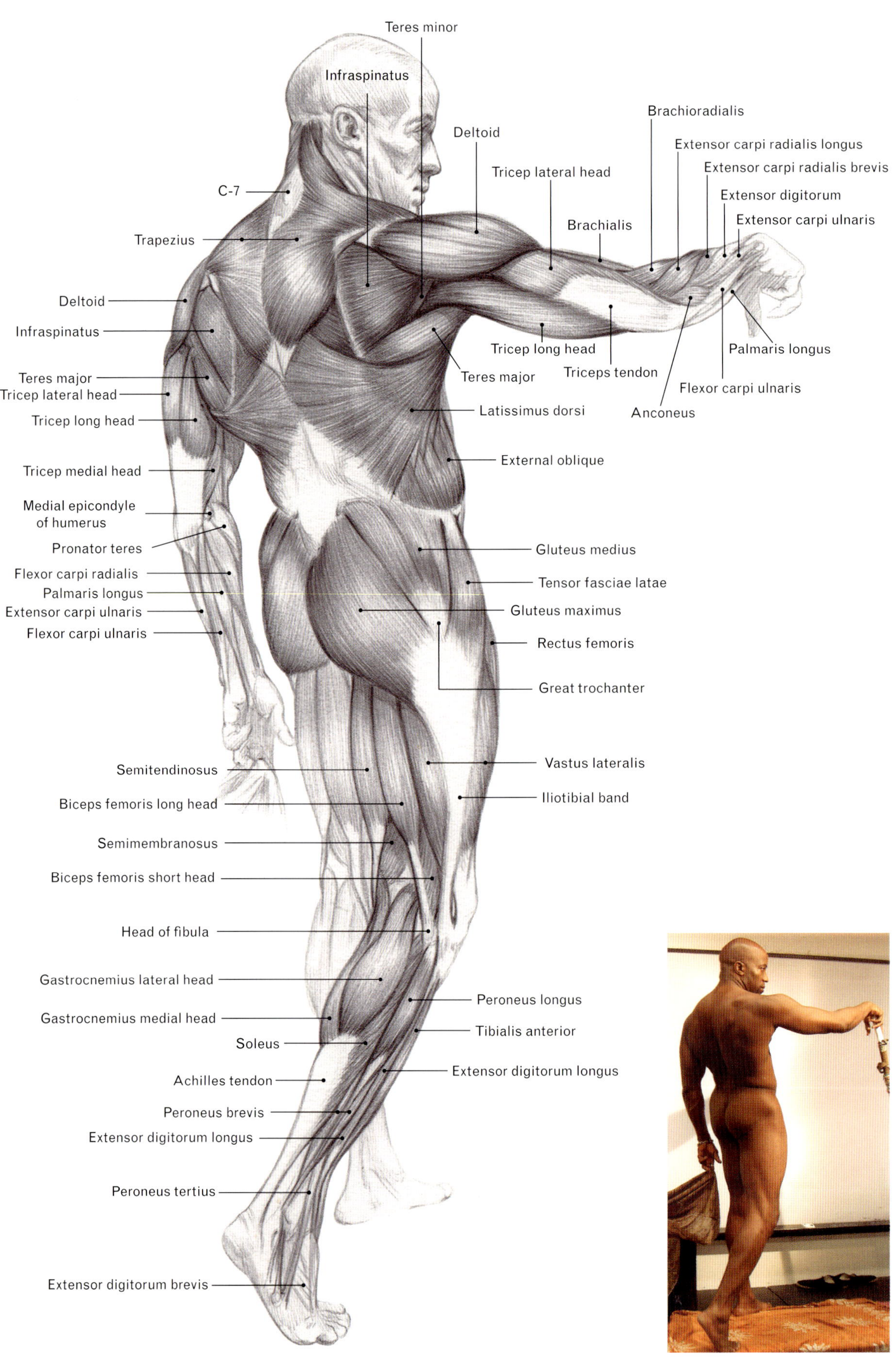

Teres minor
Infraspinatus
Deltoid
Tricep lateral head
Brachialis
Brachioradialis
Extensor carpi radialis longus
Extensor carpi radialis brevis
Extensor digitorum
Extensor carpi ulnaris
C-7
Trapezius
Deltoid
Infraspinatus
Teres major
Tricep lateral head
Tricep long head
Tricep medial head
Medial epicondyle of humerus
Pronator teres
Flexor carpi radialis
Palmaris longus
Extensor carpi ulnaris
Flexor carpi ulnaris
Tricep long head
Teres major
Triceps tendon
Latissimus dorsi
Palmaris longus
Flexor carpi ulnaris
Anconeus
External oblique
Gluteus medius
Tensor fasciae latae
Gluteus maximus
Rectus femoris
Great trochanter
Semitendinosus
Biceps femoris long head
Semimembranosus
Biceps femoris short head
Head of fibula
Gastrocnemius lateral head
Gastrocnemius medial head
Soleus
Achilles tendon
Peroneus brevis
Extensor digitorum longus
Peroneus tertius
Extensor digitorum brevis
Vastus lateralis
Iliotibial band
Peroneus longus
Tibialis anterior
Extensor digitorum longus

TERMINOLOGY

There are key words that come up when studying anatomy. They are primarily of Greek or Latin origin and learning these words will help you decipher what you are reading as if you had a code book. I pair one set of anatomical directions with its opposite to help you commit them to memory. It is important to know all these terms because much of anatomy—like muscles and bones—are named for either their shape (the deltoid is shaped like the Greek letter delta, which is a triangle), their function or action (extensors, for example), their size (major, minor, longus, brevis), and lastly, their location (posterior, anterior, superior, inferior).

Some of the words are the names of limbs or of objects that reminded the people who named them of something that was familiar to them: the acetabulum (socket on the pelvis for your femur) means "vinegar cup" in Greek, is one such instance, and another is brachium, which means "arm," so many of the arm muscles have that in their name (biceps brachii and triceps brachii). In all of my classes, learning basic anatomy terminology has been an essential part of my students' training, and time and time again I get much gratitude for demystifying the process of learning it.

Anatomical Directions

abduction/adduction: moving away from/moving toward the midline of the body

anterior/posterior: front/back

dorsal/ventral: referring to back/underneath or belly of an animal

internal/external: inside/outside

inversion/eversion: foot turned inward/foot turned outward

lateral/medial: further from/closer to midline

longitudinal: long axis, imaginary center line

oblique: slanted

plantar flexion/dorsiflexion: foot pointed/foot turned upward

proximal/distal: closer to origin/further from origin of limb

superior (supra)/inferior (infra): higher or closer to the head/lower or closer to the foot

supination/pronation: palm up ("begging for soup")/palm down

transverse: at right angles to the long axis

Pertaining to Muscle

My students sometimes ask, "Why couldn't they have just called that muscle 'arm muscle,' instead of biceps brachii?" I answer, "They did." By acquainting yourself with the terms below, it will be easier for you to understand the language of anatomy. Biceps brachii, for example, refers to *bi*/two, *cep*/head and *brachii*/arm: "two-headed muscle of the arm." Voilà!

abductor: draws away from midline

action: movement accomplished by a muscle

adductor: draws toward midline

aponeurosis: flat, sheet-like tendon

belly: fleshy aspect of a muscle

bi: two

brachii: arm, or of the arm

cep: head

corrugator: creases skin into wrinkles, like the forehead

depressor: lowers

erector: pulls upright

extensor: causes straightening

fascia: sheath that envelops muscle structures

femoral: thigh, or of the thigh

flexor: causes bending

insertion: endpoint of a muscle, where the movement or action takes place

levator: raises

muscle: contractile tissue capable of creating force and motion

origin: beginning of muscle attachment, anchor point

rotator: causes to revolve

sphincter: closes an aperture

tendon: fibrous tissue attaching muscle to bone

tensor: pulls tight

Pertaining to Bone

As artists, continuing to learn about the inner workings of our bodies will lead us to creating better art and a more rewarding experience while depicting it. The following terms pertain mainly to the skeletal system.

articulation or joint: connection between bones

bone: strong but light structure creating the skeleton

capitulum: ball-shaped joint on the humerus

cartilage: substance from which bone ossifies

condyle: polished, round prominence at the distal end of a bone at an articulation point

crest: ridge

eminence: small convexity on the surface such as on the forehead

epicondyle: bony protuberance by a condyle

foramen: opening or hole in a bone

fossa: shallow depression

head: rounded end of a bone

ligament: fibrous tissue attaching bone to bone

neck: the area between the head of a bone and its shaft

process: bony bump often seen or felt on the surface

shaft: the body of a long bone

spine: pointy, bony projection or projections

symphysis: the border between two halves, such as the pubic symphysis

trochlea: spool-shaped joint, hinge

tuberosity: bony bump where often there is a ligament or tendon attached

Etymology of Bone Terms

These terms are used throughout the book to identify the bones that make up the skeleton. Each word is followed by its translation and origin: Latin (L), Greek (G), or both (LG).

calcaneus: heel (L)

carpi: wrist (LG)

cervical: neck (L)

clavicle: key (L)

coccyx: cuckoo's beak (G)

condyle: knuckle (G)

coracoid: raven's beak (G)

epicondyle: small knuckle (G)

femur: thigh (L)

fibula: clasp (L)

fossa: small depression (G)

glenoid: socket (G)

humerus: shoulder (L)

ilium: flank (L)

ischium: hip bone (G)

lumbar: loin (L)

meta: beyond (G)

olecranon: elbow head (G)

patella: a small pan (L)

pelvis: basin (L)

phalanx: a row of soldiers (G)

radius: wheel spoke (L)

sacrum: sacred bone (L)

scapula: shoulder blade (L)

sternum: breastbone (L)

thorax: chest (G)

tibia: flute (L)

trochanter: to run (G)

ulna: elbow (L)

vertebra: turning joint (L)

xiphoid: sword (G)

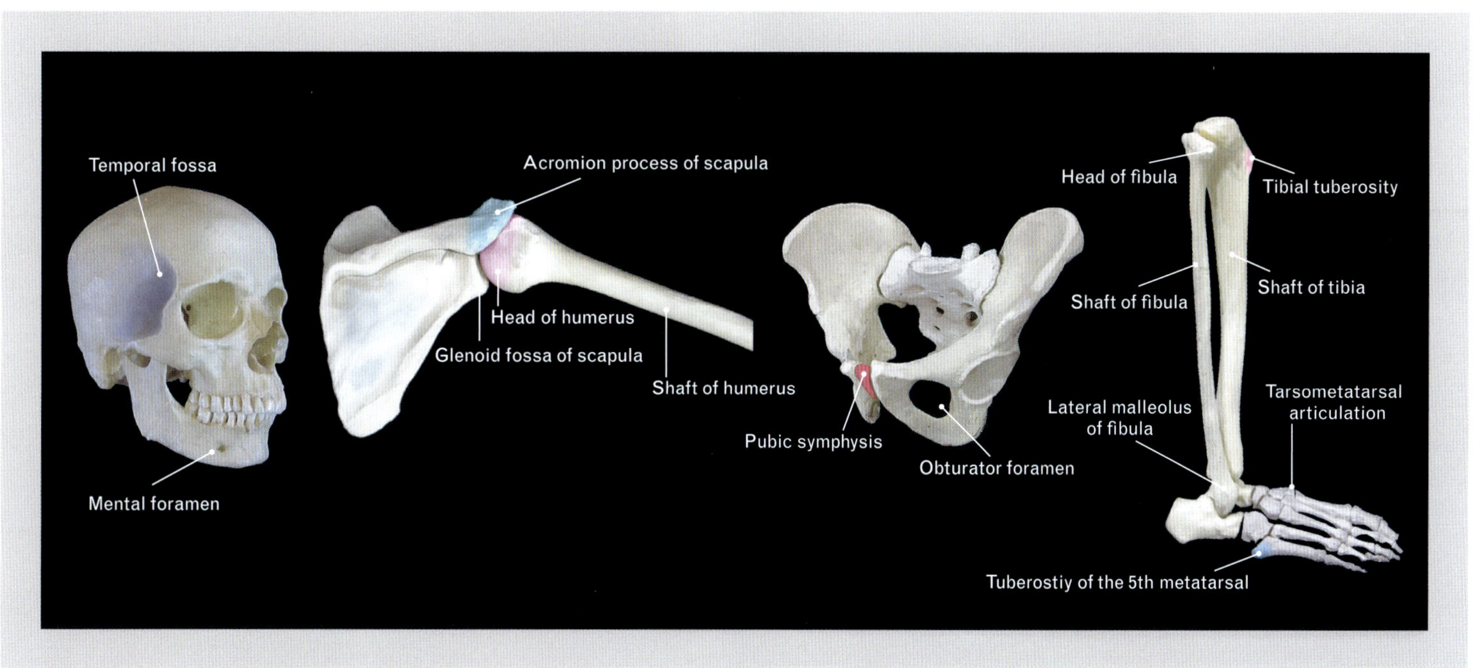

TOOLS OF THE TRADE

This book features a variety of artwork ranging from quick how-to sketches I did on the blackboard in class to detailed skeleton anatomies by my students and my own figurative drawings. The following list includes the majority of materials that we used to produce this work. The tools you choose can make a huge difference in your work. I have known guitarists who can talk for hours about different guitar brands, the various sounds they produce, and why one may be preferred over another for a particular song or expression. This is also true of pencils and papers for a draftsperson.

Drawing is about exploration; every artist should try different materials and explore what works best for his or her particular drawing or objective. This includes using newer technologies to refine your work. I, like my students, utilize digital tools such as Photoshop and a Wacom Cintiq tablet in addition to the following tools.

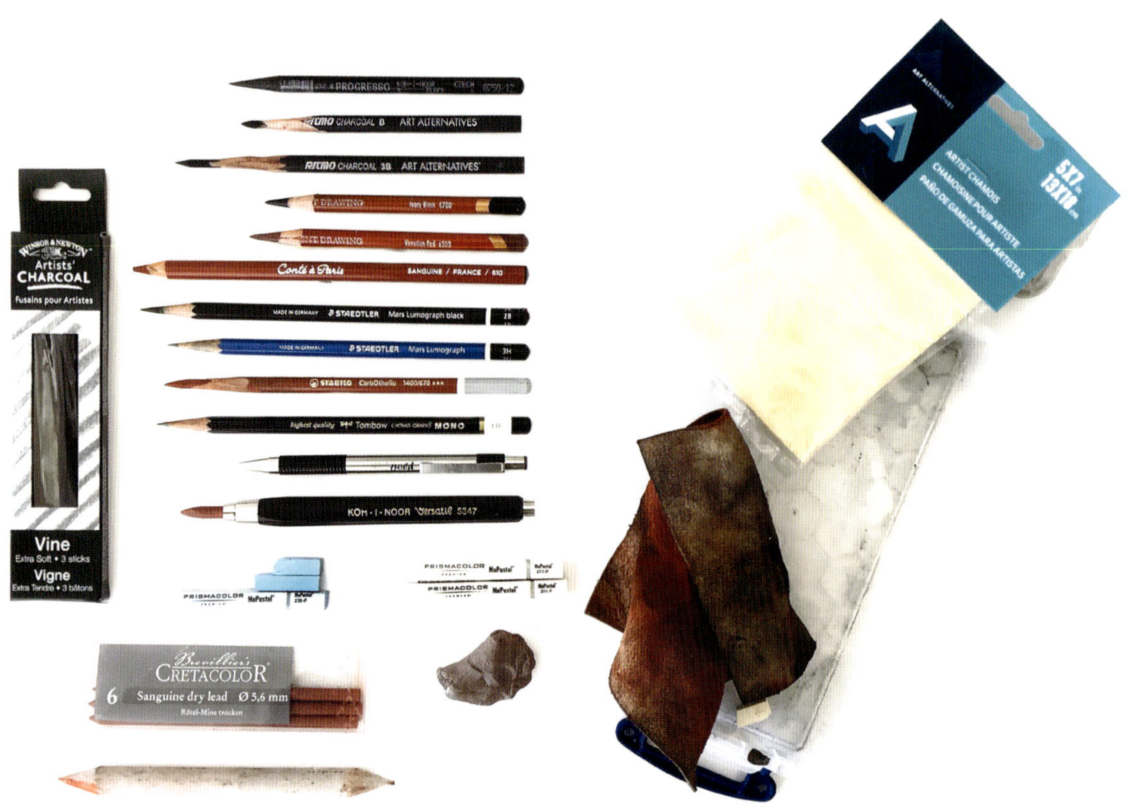

Materials

Faber-Castell Pitt Pastel Pencil #190

soft or very soft vine charcoal

Progresso woodless pencil

graphite pencils: 2H and/or 4H, HB, 2B, and/or 3B and 6B

Derwent drawing pencil: black and Venetian red

Derwent or Prismacolor white pencil, or other brand

ivory and light blue Nupastel

Zebra F-301 retractable 0.7mm black ballpoint pen

chamois

kneaded eraser

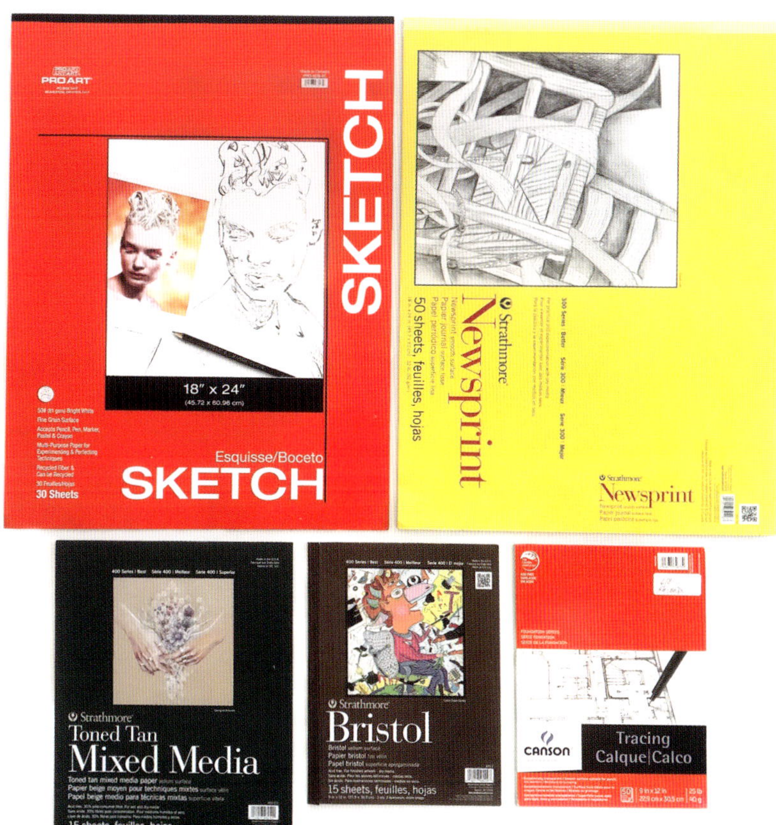

Paper

Strathmore "Bristol" vellum paper, 9 x 12 inch

Canson "Calque" tracing paper

White drawing paper, 18 x 24 inch

Newsprint pad, 18 x 24 inch

Toned Tan "Mixed Media" paper

When to Use Them

- **20-minute figure sketches:** ivory and light blue Nupastel on toned paper

- **40-minute to hour-long drawing sessions:** graphite pencils (4H, 2H, and HB) for blocking or "searching" and the softer graphite pencils (2B, 3B, and 6B) for small accents or very dark spots, using white 18 x 24 inch sketchpads

- **Realistic and organic, sometimes referred to as gestural:** Progresso or Derwent pencil

- **Smaller, more rendered drawings, including muscle illustrations:** graphite pencils and ballpoint pen on Bristol paper

- **Tracing paper:** HB and 2H graphite pencils

- **Detailed analytical drawings:** Zebra ballpoint pen on Bristol paper

- **More organic drawings:** soft pencils on soft paper, such as rough newsprint pads or single sheets of Strathmore charcoal paper over an open pad of newsprint

- **Smoky silhouettes:** use chamois or even a soft paper towel to spread medium

- **Every occasion:** vine charcoal is very effective in searching for what you need whether it is the line between light and shadow or blocking in a figure. It is easy to manipulate and to push around even with a finger. It is easy to correct and can create a more painterly look to your work.

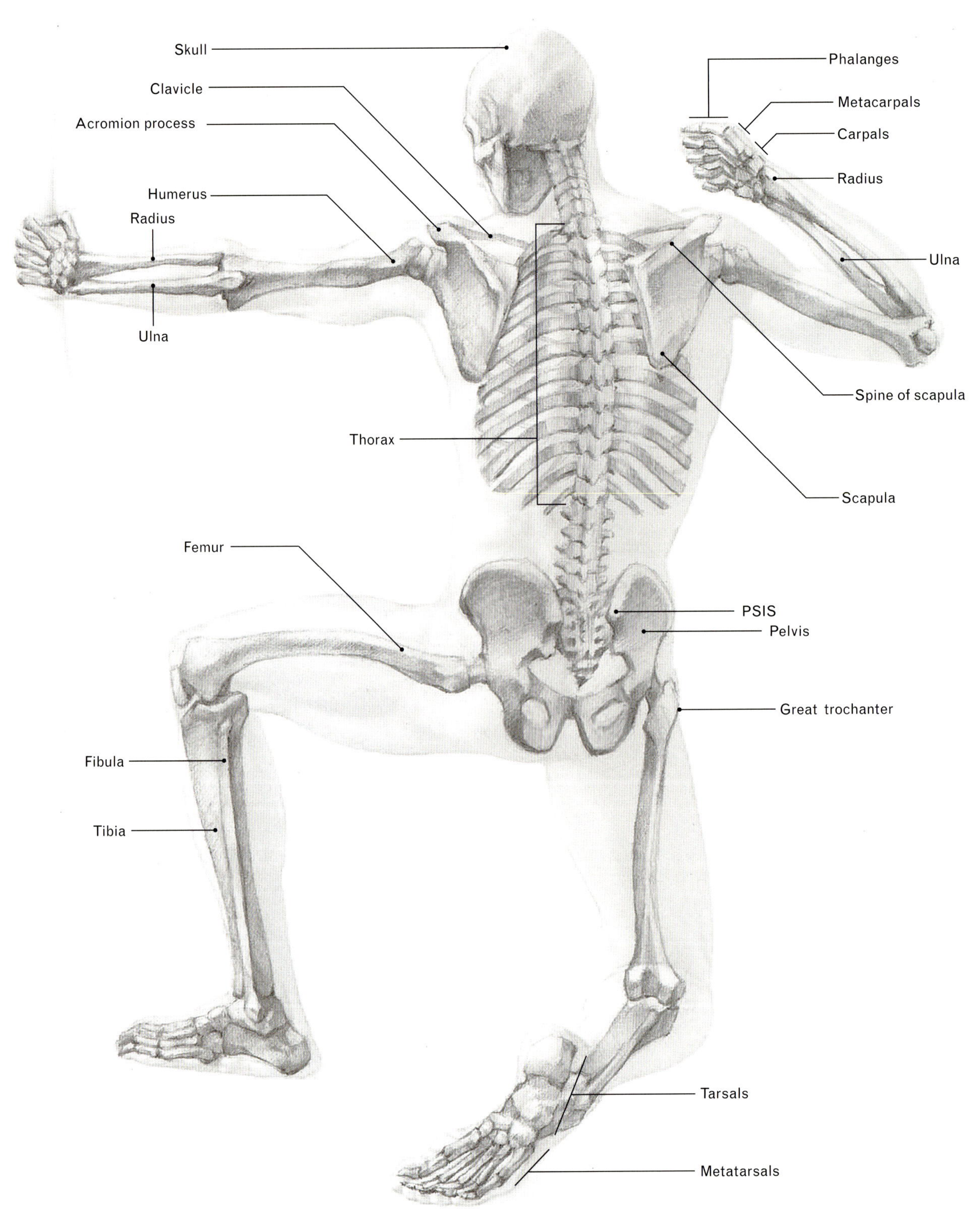

Skull
Clavicle
Acromion process
Humerus
Radius
Ulna
Phalanges
Metacarpals
Carpals
Radius
Ulna
Spine of scapula
Thorax
Scapula
Femur
PSIS
Pelvis
Great trochanter
Fibula
Tibia
Tarsals
Metatarsals

PART I
ANATOMY EXPLORED

"Learn the rules like a pro, so that you can break them like an artist."

—Pablo Picasso

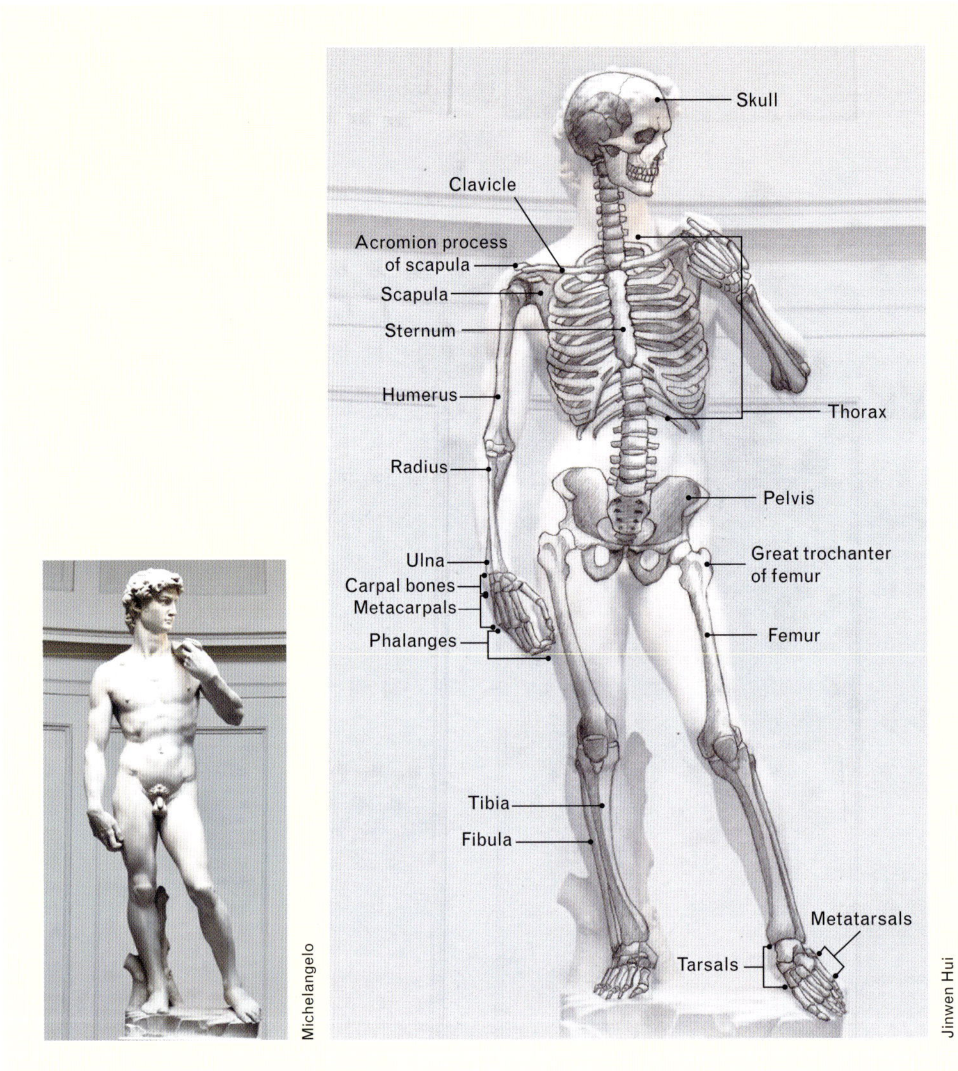

"The greatest figurative art gives you the impression that there is a living skeleton inside the body."

A local newspaper once asked me, "What is the most important aspect of figurative art?" Without really thinking, I responded, "The skeleton." I then pointed to a chair in the room that had a coat draped over it. I told the reporter that the coat would have no shape without the chair. The chair was the foundation that gave the coat a form. Likewise, the human body, with all of its muscles, tendons, fat, and skin, conforms to the primary source of its shape, the skeleton. The greatest figurative art gives you the impression that there is a living skeleton inside the body.

For instance, during my first visit to Florence, Italy, I was struck with the powerful appearance of the country's most famous sculptures. From the magnificent *David* by Michelangelo to *Perseus* by Cellini, or any of the myriad works around, I noticed that each suggested the skeleton beneath its form. With sculpture, it is imperative that artists know the human body so well that they are able to work from the outside in, with solid knowledge of where and how the skeleton manifests itself on the surface of their subject.

Did you know that when you were born, you had more bones in your body than you do as an adult? Actual numbers vary from person to person, but on average, a baby is born with 270 bones, and that number drops to around 206 as bones fuse together as one approaches adulthood. These are among the many wonders of the human skeleton.

I advise all of my students to know the skeleton well and to be able to animate it in many positions. By doing so, they will see it better in the living form. This section features several drawings from my students of skeletons in various poses so you can become acquainted with its structure. These incredibly detailed drawings are by artists ranging in age from 18 to 22, and on average took them approximately three hours to do. All the skeletons in this section are of men because we used Old Master drawings and sculptures as reference. (It is easier to see many of the muscles and bony landmarks of men in art pieces.) Some specific skeletal details that apply to women will be reviewed later in the book.

While all the bones are depicted, only select ones are labeled. This is because of the fact that some are seen as a group on the living form, such as the eight carpal bones that make up the wrist and the seven that make up the ankle and heel. For artists, the determining factor as to which bones are essential is if we can see them with our eyes on most individuals—or simply that if one of them was missing, such as your femur, it would be obvious. The bony landmarks may also be used to help in placing the muscles and their relative positions. Even the bony protrusions where ligaments or tendons insert may not be as obvious or may even be hidden, but knowing where they are, such as the deltoid and tibial tuberosities, will always create a more realistic drawing of the shoulder. This is also how we know where to place muscles on animals that we have never seen alive, such as dinosaurs.

"For artists, the determining factor as to which bones are essential is if we can see them with our eyes on most individuals..."

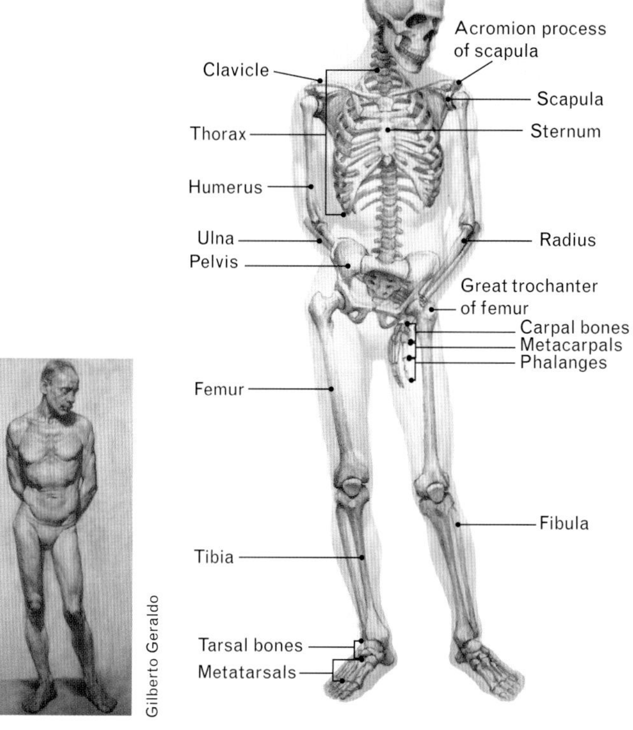

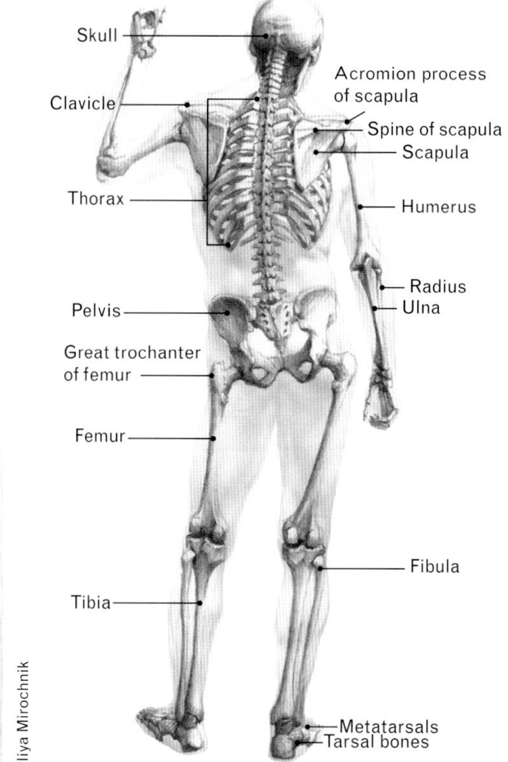

Every time that I teach human anatomy, the skeleton is the first lecture; it is the foundation of the entire form and should be evident inside that form, regardless of the medium used. Artists can change or customize their art, it is almost a requirement; but at first, it is necessary to know the rules before they are changed to suit an artist's need or personal expression. As seen on my blackboard, I start with a proportional guide of an 8-head-tall figure, then have the students take that image and animate it on paper. I tell my students that it is like taking a doll out of the box and then making it move, posing it at will. Although it is easy to find limitless reference of all sorts on the Internet, I always have a full-scale skeleton in the classroom and bring examples from my studio. I also suggest apps such as L'Ecorché that allow you to rotate a skeleton and also view muscles. For more skeletal reference, see pages 27, 35, 47, 51, 54, and 74.

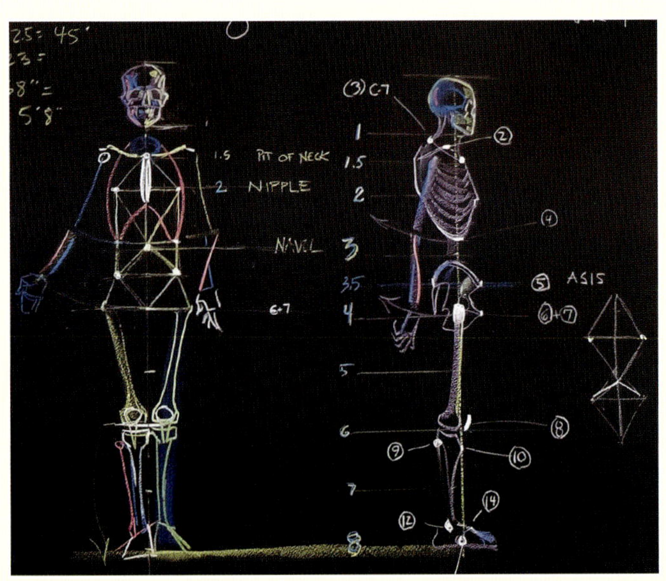

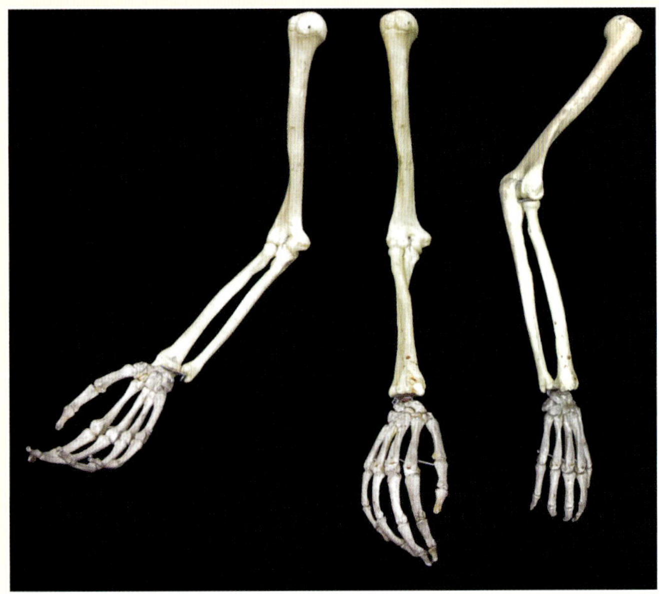

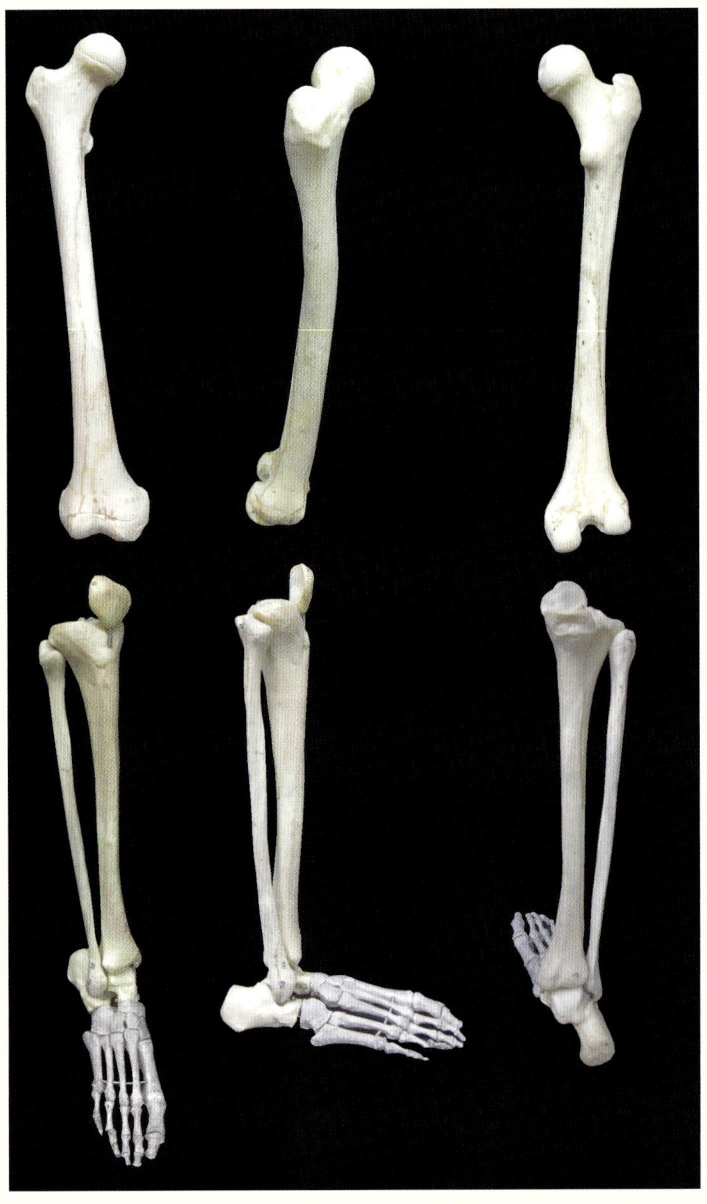

The Axial and Appendicular Skeletons

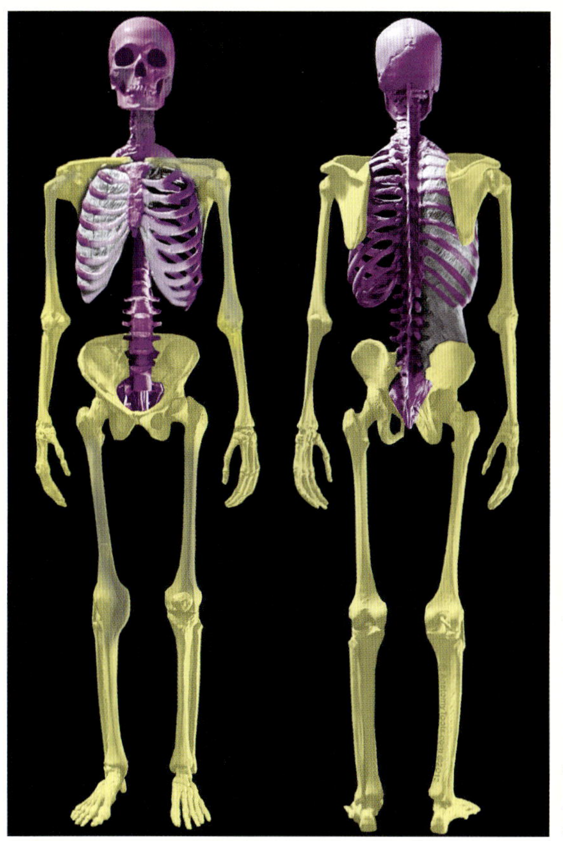

The skeleton is made up of two groups of bones: the **axial** (in violet) and the **appendicular** (in yellow).

The axial is the central axis or support of the body and also the protector of the internal organs.

The appendicular group is comprised of the bones that make up the appendages (the upper and lower limbs).

The white area at the chest is the costal cartilage that bridges the area between the ribs and the sternum. They are there to allow the thorax (rib cage) to expand and contract.

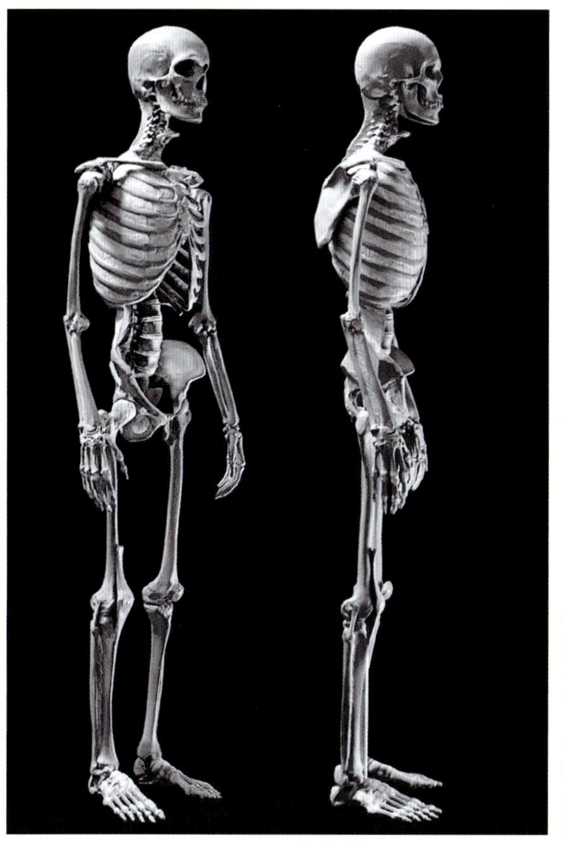

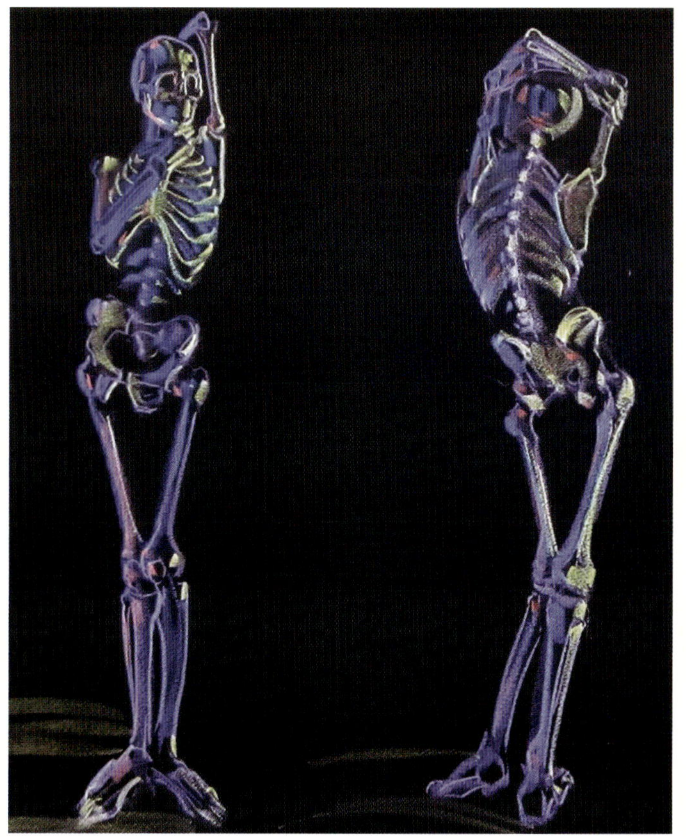

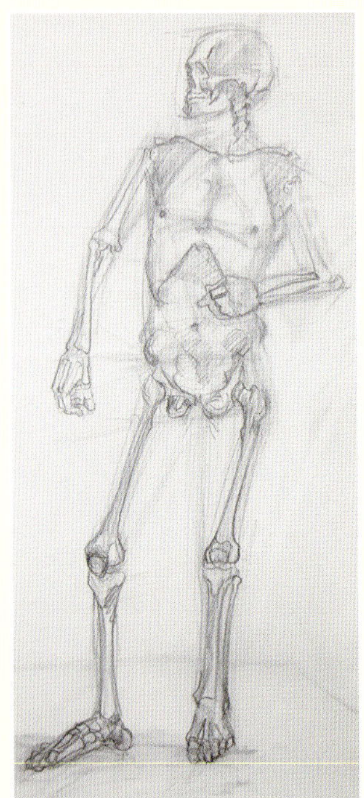 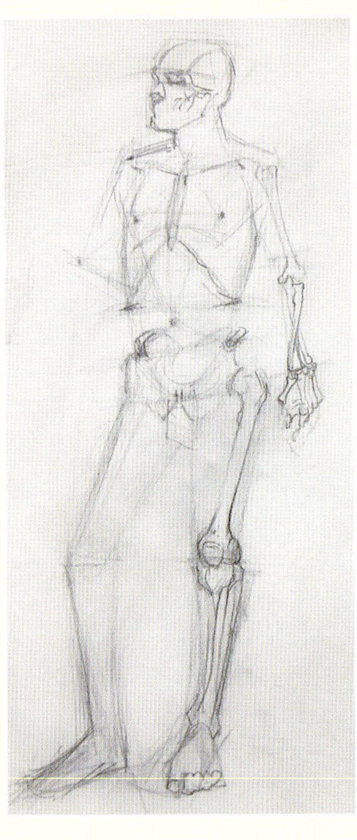 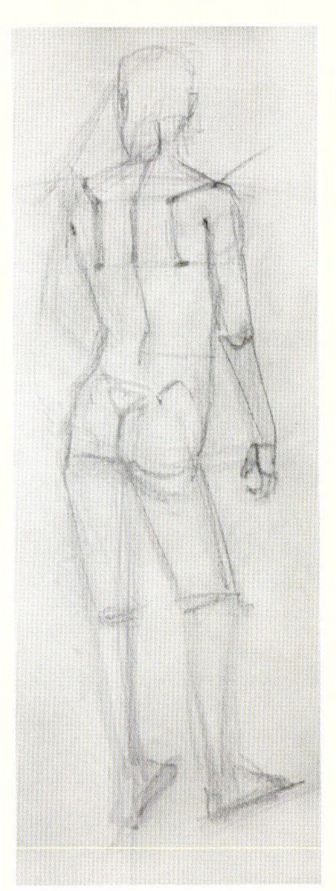

THE 20-MINUTE POSE

One simple exercise we do in class is to try to capture the skeletal frame of a model in 20 minutes. This trains you to draw the essential shapes and lines of a person's frame quickly.

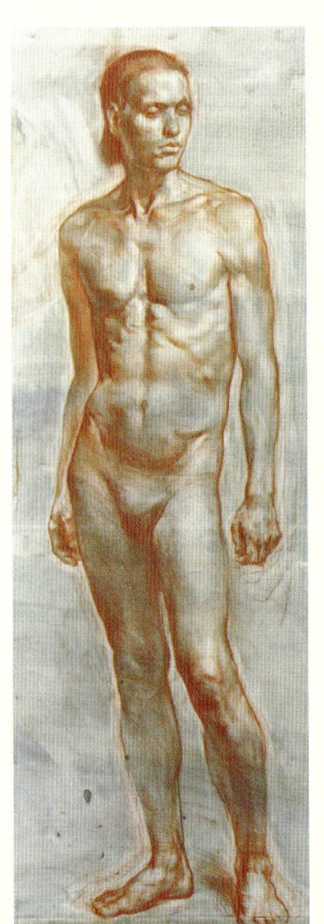

Iliya Mirochnik

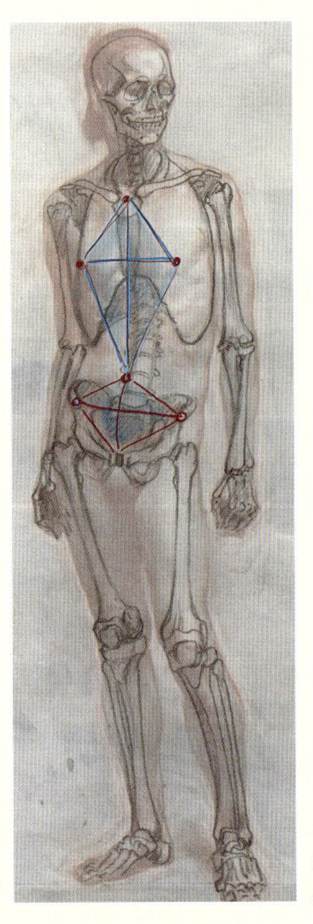

Rey Bustos

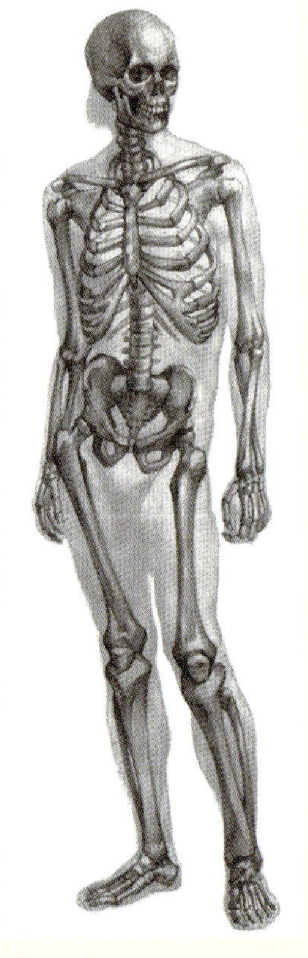

Allie Irwin

DRAW IN A FOG

Use photo reference of your choice, open in Photoshop, and bring down the opacity of the image so that the body looks as if it's in a fog. Print the image on matte photo paper and draw the skeleton directly onto the paper. I like using a ballpoint pen for this, but if that is not comfortable for you to commit ink to paper, you can try graphite pencils or another drawing implement that can be used on matte paper. See page 45 for the "kite" technique.

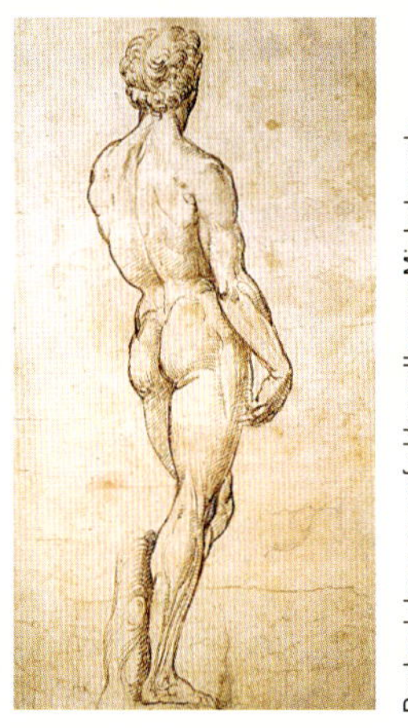

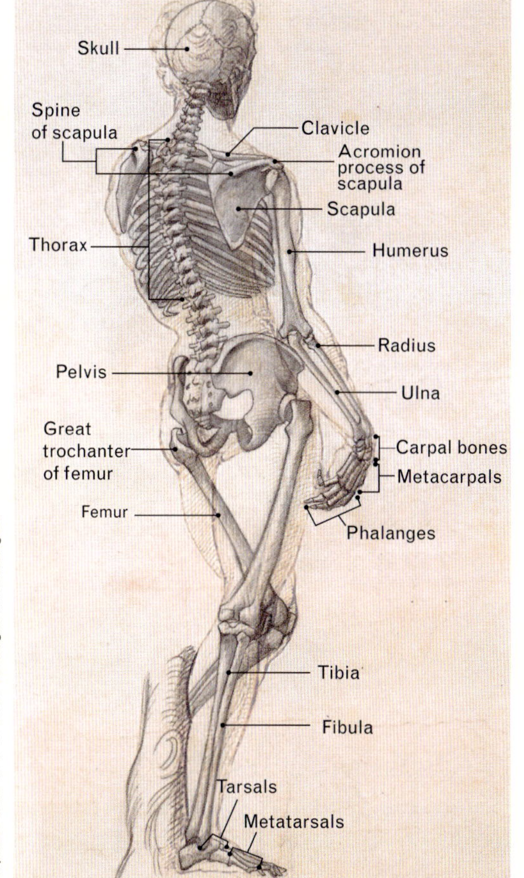

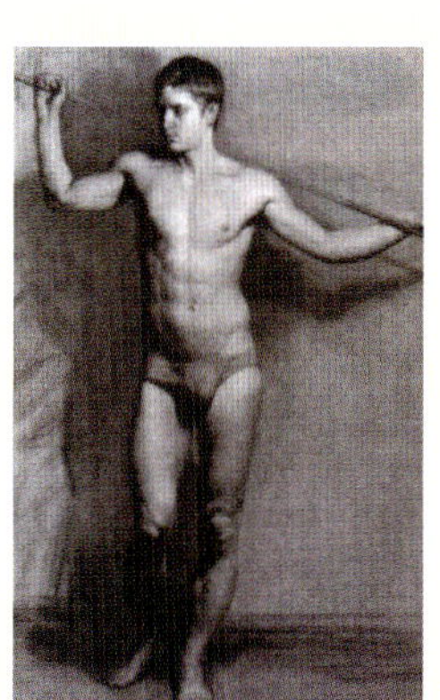

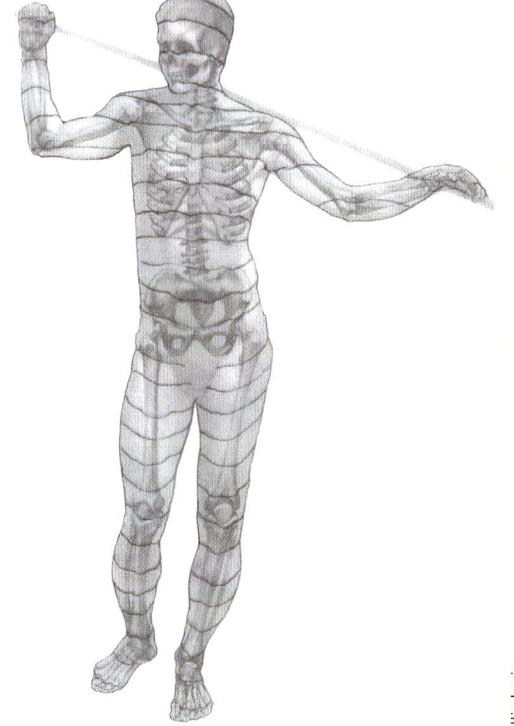

SKETCH A MASTER

Place tracing paper over an existing master drawing, photo of a sculpture, or any work from your favorite art book, and sketch the skeleton. This is the easiest way to study the skeleton. Or, as in the examples shown, my student created an overlay using Photoshop, and then drew the skeleton separately. See page 29 for section slices technique.

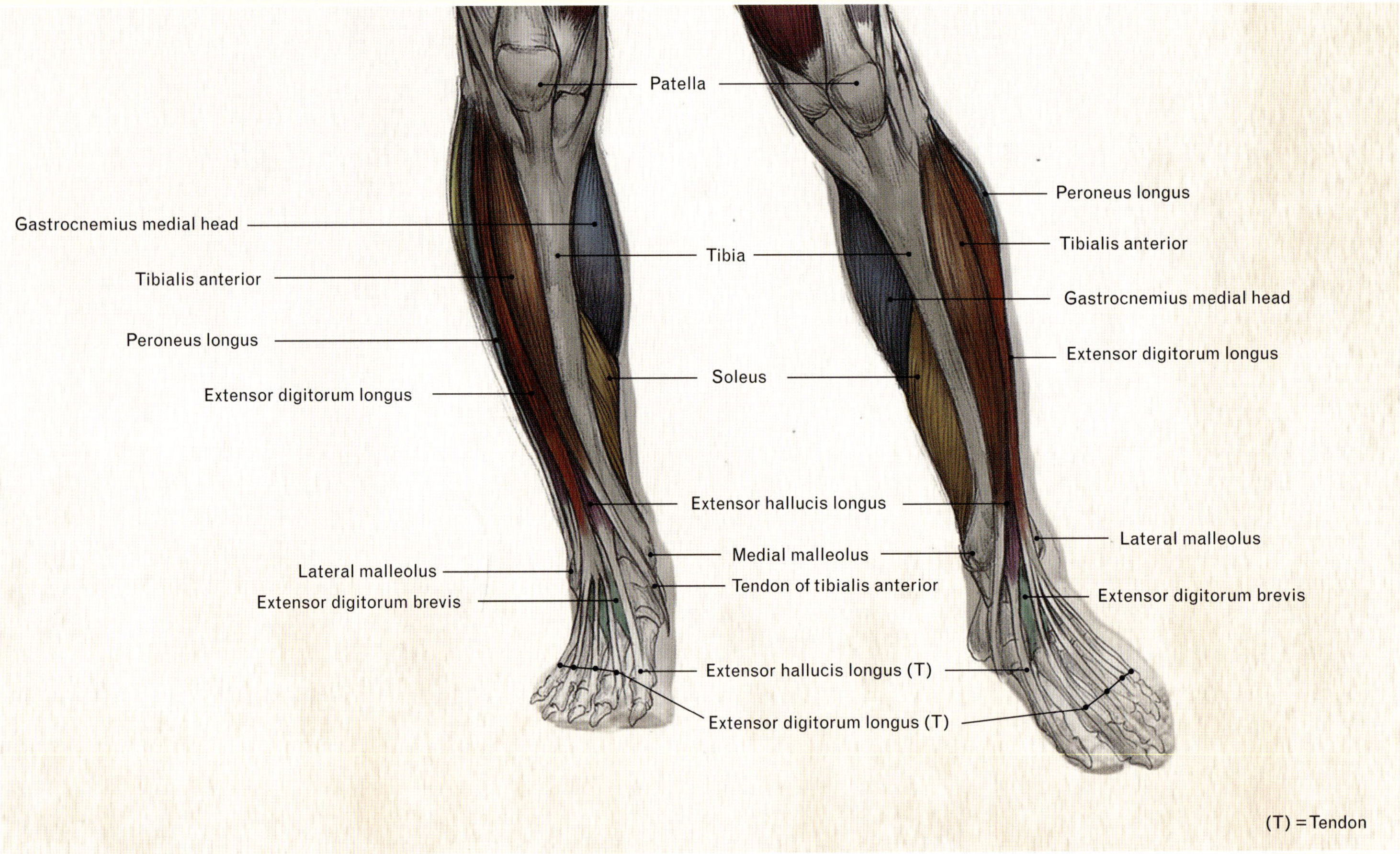

Patella
Gastrocnemius medial head
Tibialis anterior
Peroneus longus
Extensor digitorum longus
Tibia
Soleus
Peroneus longus
Tibialis anterior
Gastrocnemius medial head
Extensor digitorum longus
Extensor hallucis longus
Medial malleolus
Lateral malleolus
Tendon of tibialis anterior
Lateral malleolus
Extensor digitorum brevis
Extensor digitorum brevis
Extensor hallucis longus (T)
Extensor digitorum longus (T)
(T) = Tendon

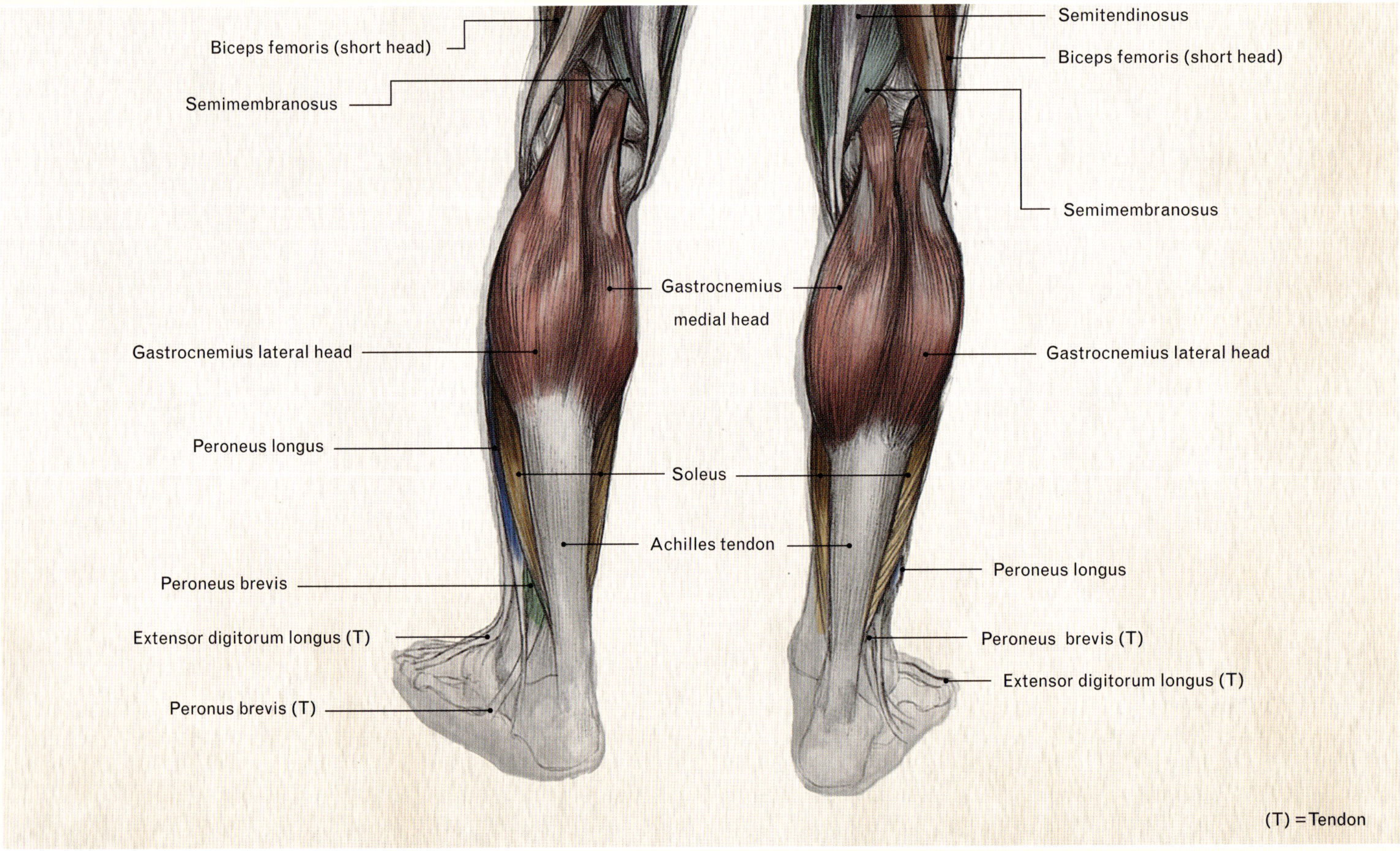

Biceps femoris (short head)
Semimembranosus
Semitendinosus
Biceps femoris (short head)
Semimembranosus
Gastrocnemius lateral head
Gastrocnemius medial head
Gastrocnemius lateral head
Peroneus longus
Soleus
Achilles tendon
Peroneus longus
Peroneus brevis
Extensor digitorum longus (T)
Peroneus brevis (T)
Peronus brevis (T)
Extensor digitorum longus (T)
(T) = Tendon

THE LEG AND FOOT

I cover the leg and foot as one section in my classes to more effectively illustrate their mutual relationship and use. In anatomy, the leg is generally considered the area between the knee and the foot; in common conversation it would be what we refer to as the shin. The leg has a few hidden muscles that are not seen easily by casual observation but with guidance and study they can be. Being able to identify them will help artists greatly in depicting the leg onto the foot.

The Leg

For the artist, I have pared down the lower leg to six essential muscles grouped in sets of two: **peroneus brevis** with **peroneus longus**, **soleus** with **gastrocnemius** (calf), and the **extensor digitorum longus** with the **tibialis anterior**.

The peroneus brevis and peroneus longus ride the length of the fibula, right on top of the bone shaft, and are relatively easy to find but often overlooked by artists. The peroneus brevis starts roughly at the halfway point of the fibula, but in most cases, is barely noticeable to virtually invisible on many people, especially women. When it is visible, it is only at the lower aspect, by the ankle (lateral malleolus). The tendon of the peroneus brevis, however, is quite visible on most people, especially when the foot is either everted (turned outward), when the side of the foot is pulled up toward the outside of the body, or when one is on tiptoe. At times, you can also see the tendon turn toward its ultimate insertion at the tuberosity of the fifth metatarsal (the bump on the side of the foot), roughly halfway between the heel and the little toe. The tendon uses the **lateral malleolus** like a pulley. This starts at the head of the fibula and rides down the fibular shaft until it overlaps slightly atop the peroneus brevis (see page 27). The peroneus longus creates a dimple at its inferior aspect, usually when contracted as explained in the example of the peroneus brevis.

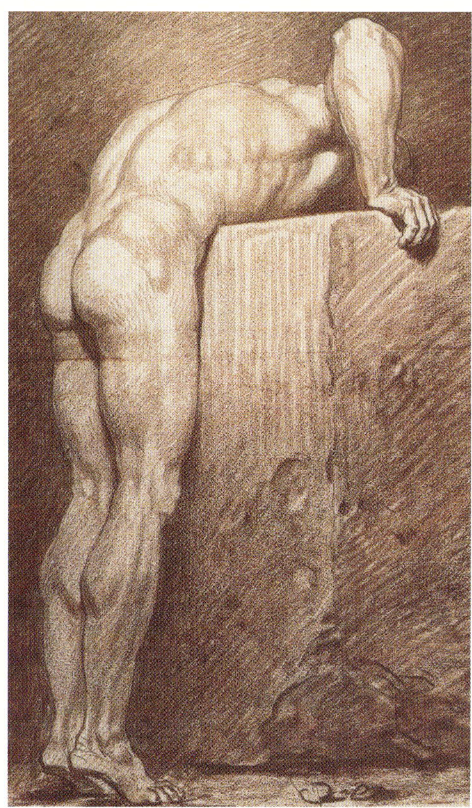

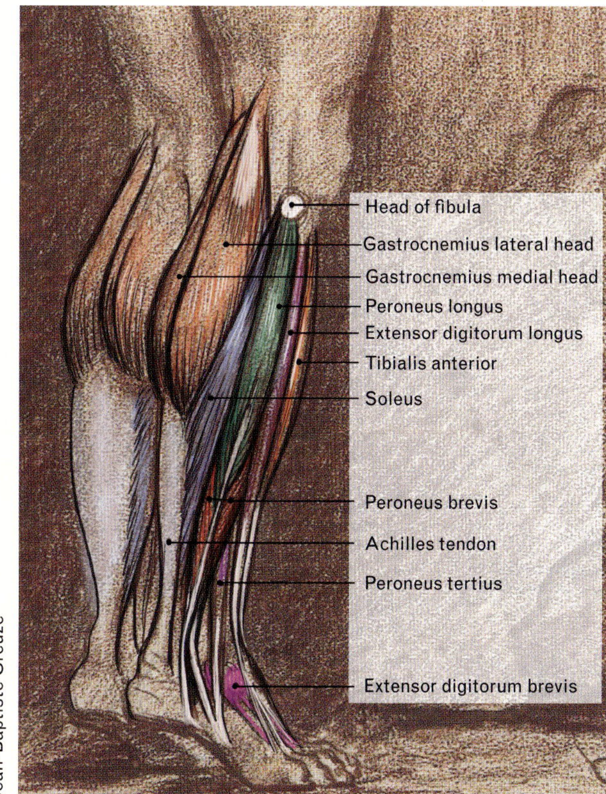

The second set of muscles is the **soleus** and the **gastrocnemius**. The soleus touches the head of the fibula and from behind is roughly triangular in shape as it tapers down, ending with the Achilles tendon at the heel. From the side, it is wedge-shaped and appears squeezed between the **peroneals** and the great gastrocnemius heads, which are commonly known as the calf muscles. The gastrocnemius is made up of two teardrop-shaped heads: the medial head and the lateral head. The medial head is lower and very pronounced when the inside of the leg is visible. The lateral head is higher and thinner when viewing the side of the leg. The medially slanted line of these heads, if continued, would meet with the upward slant of the ankles at the medial and lateral malleolus.

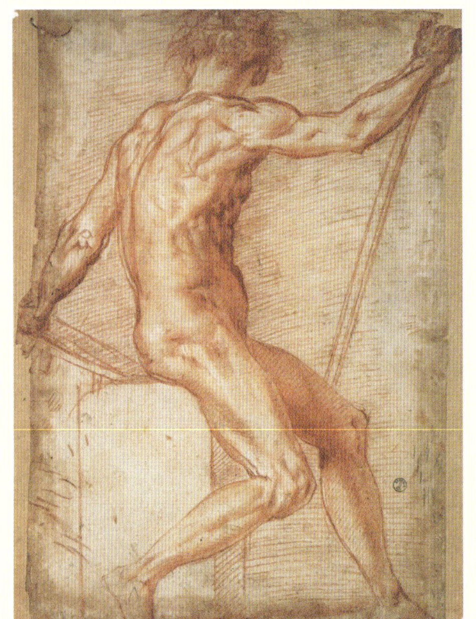

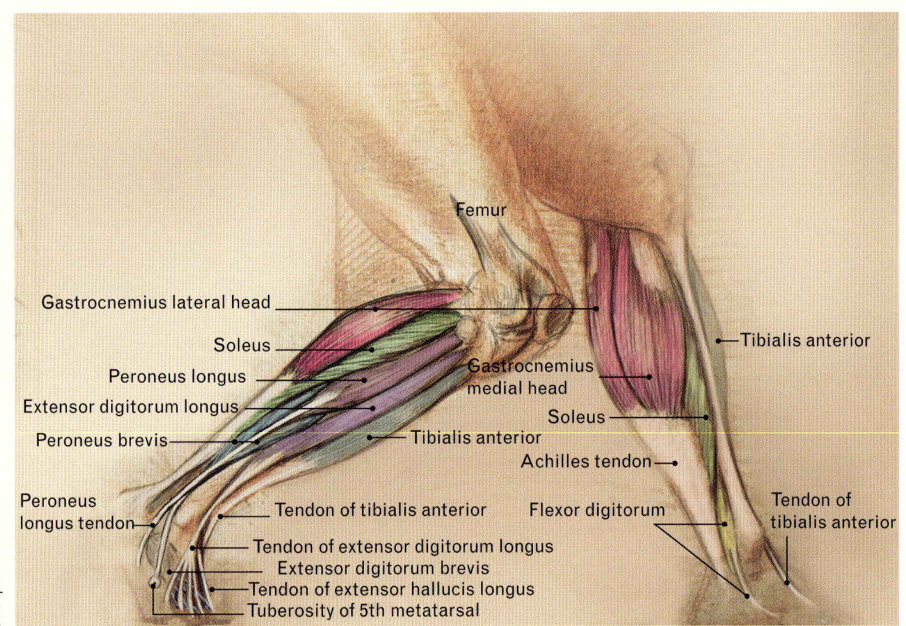

The third couple is made up of the **extensor digitorum** and the **tibialis anterior**. These are rarely seen as two separate muscles. You are able to see each one on athletic people such as marathon runners and bicyclists, and even then, it's most obvious when the muscles are activated. The extensor digitorum is long and narrow and its most important physical manifestation is its tendon, which appears at the beginning of the foot, slightly outside of center, and it splits into four tendons. Each of the split tendons goes to a toe, excluding the big toe. The tibialis anterior is a contour muscle, which creates a front contour on the lower leg when viewed from the side. The muscle is long, large, tapered, and about three-quarters down the lower leg. The tendon becomes prominent as it crosses medially (in the middle), disappearing at the inside arch of the foot. This muscle can be flexed by pulling the foot up toward the head. With this contraction, its tendon becomes highly visible and appears as if it were a cable at the top and slightly inside part of the foot.

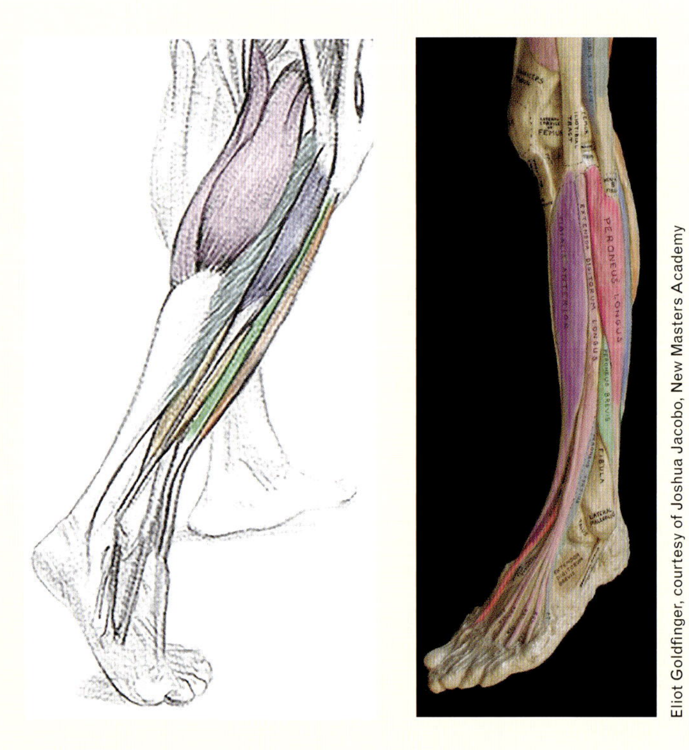

The Foot

To understand the foot, one must understand its skeleton, which is composed of 26 bones. The foot bones are generally divided into three segments: the tarsal bones (7), the metatarsals (5) and the phalanges or toe bones (14). The **calcaneus**, or heel, is the most obvious member of the tarsal group, and the rest make up part of the arch and the beginnings of the top of the foot. There is a bone called the **navicular,** at the arch of the foot which can be quite visible and should be noted. The foot takes a slight change of direction at the top and just in front of the lower leg. This is the joint between the tarsal and metatarsal bones (tarsometatarsal articulation). This slight change of contour can easily be seen in the stretched-out foot as it points away from the body as a ballet dancer would. This change of contour is roughly at the midpoint between the back of the heel and the end of the big toe.

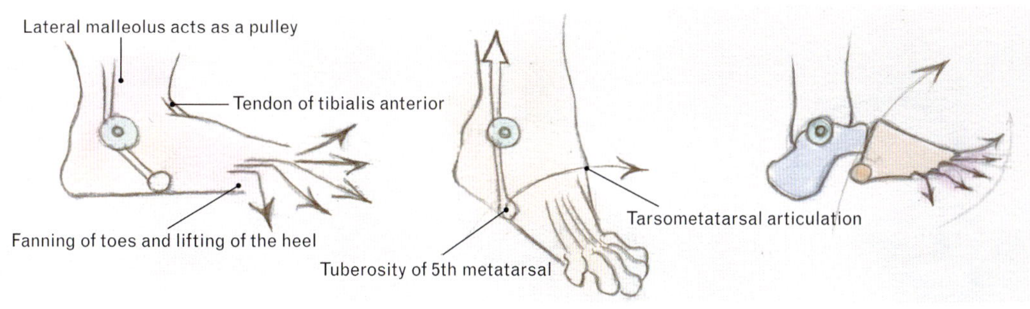

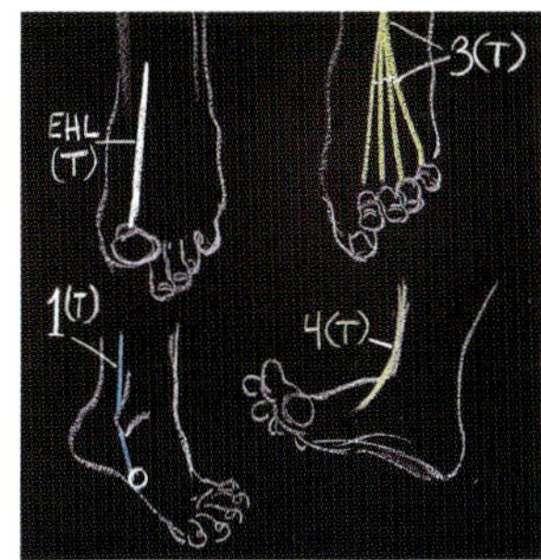

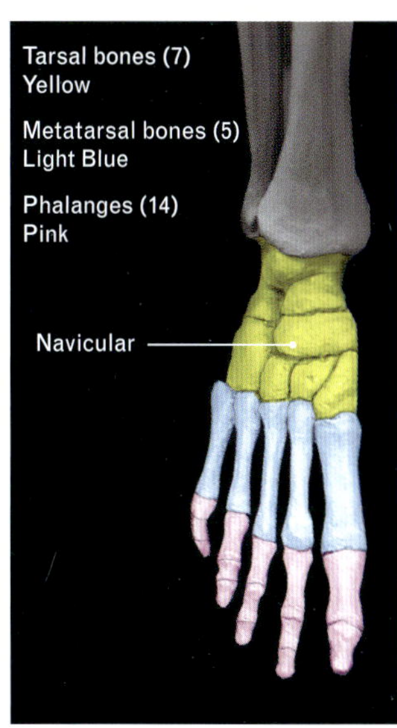

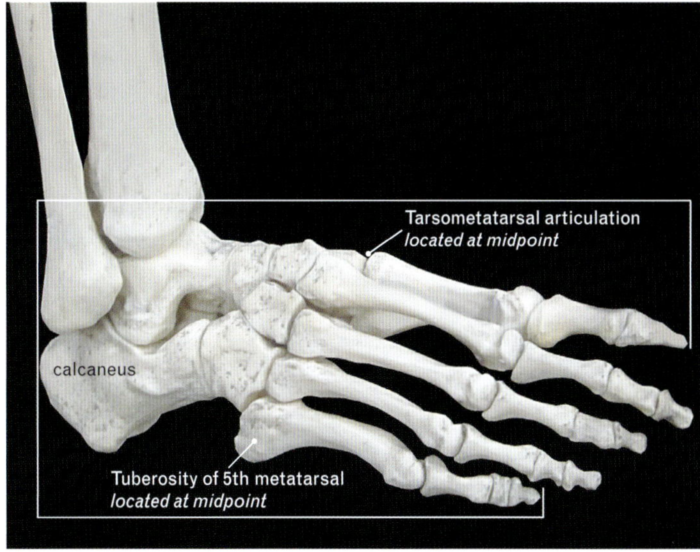

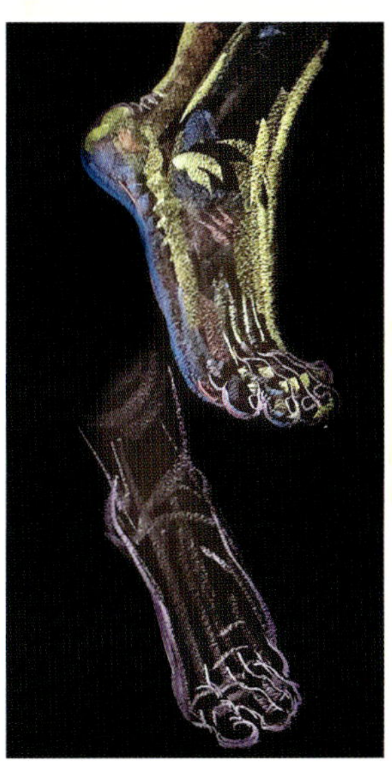

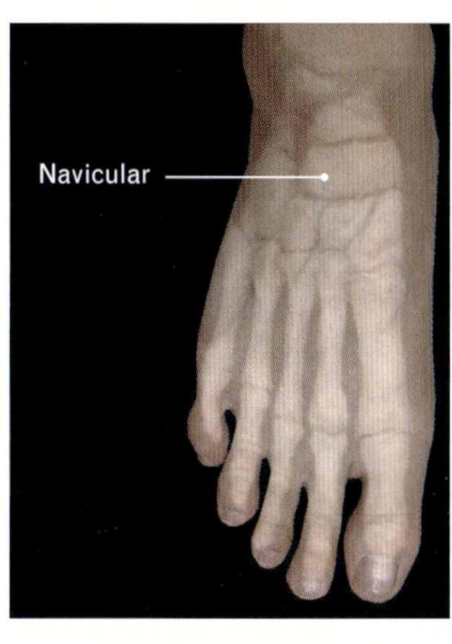

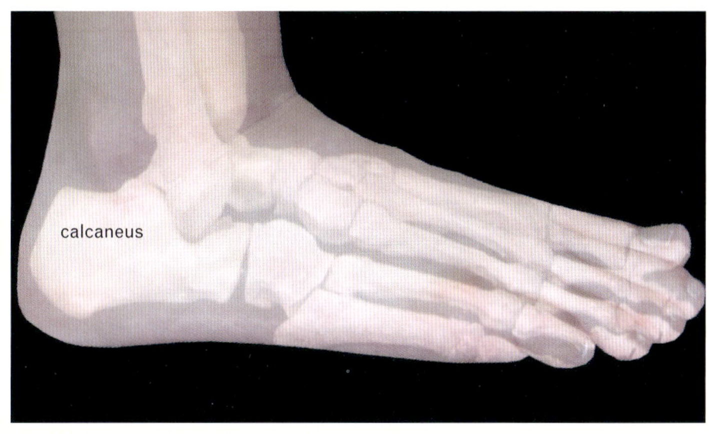

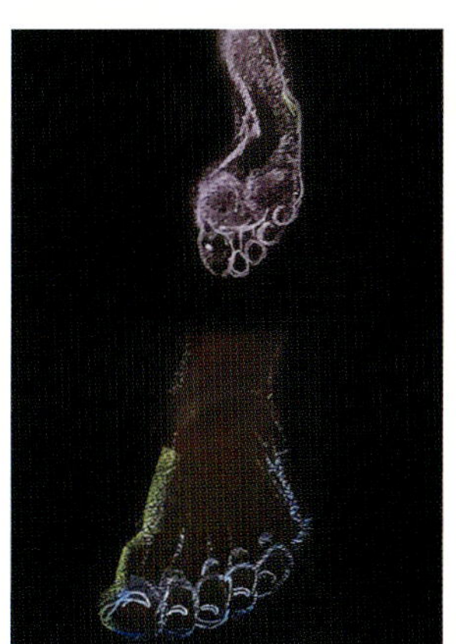

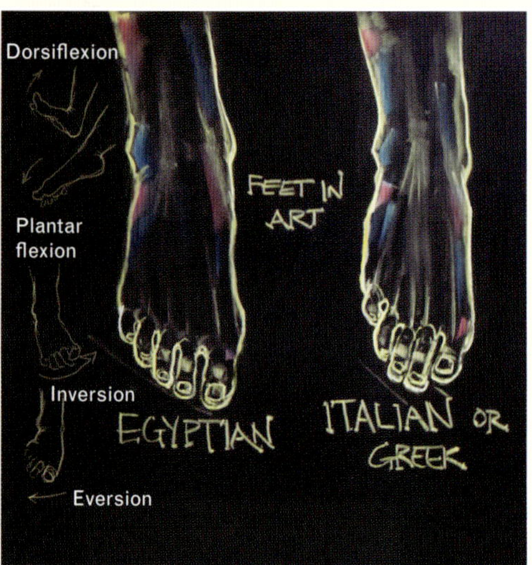

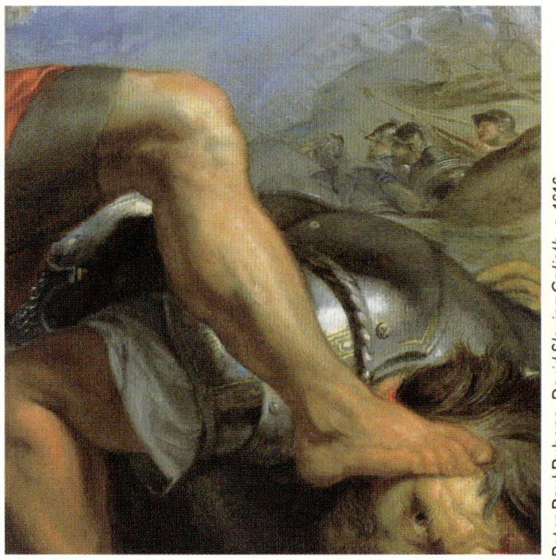
Peter Paul Rubens, *David Slaying Goliath*, c. 1616

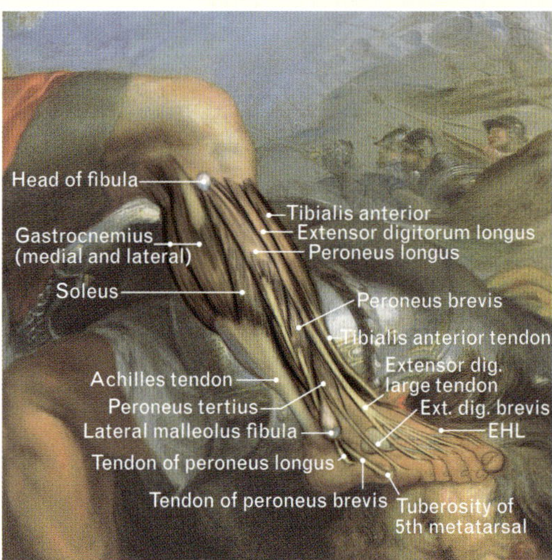

"The foot is more noble than the shoe," wrote the great Michelangelo. Besides the face and hands, the feet are areas chock-full of possibilities for great expression. Look at any exposed foot by any of the great masters and you will see an amazing array of drama and dynamism with the foot and toes.

Traditionally European and Western artists have classified two types of feet: the Egyptian and the Greek or Italian foot. To put it quite simply, the difference is determined by the length of the second toe. In the Egyptian foot, so called because of the way that all classic Egyptian feet were depicted, the second toe is always shorter than the big toe.

The Greek foot by contrast is quite different.

In most Italian and Italian-inspired art from the Renaissance on, the exposed foot was always depicted with the second toe being longer and, in some cases, much longer to the point where even the middle toe is as long as or even longer than the big toe. These artists elongated the toes to create more dynamism in their works, more drama so that when you take in the entire composition, the body pulls you through a rhythm that ends with the tips of the toes. They can be fanned or bent in a feeling of weight. All of this to create the drama with which the Old Masters were so, well, masterful.

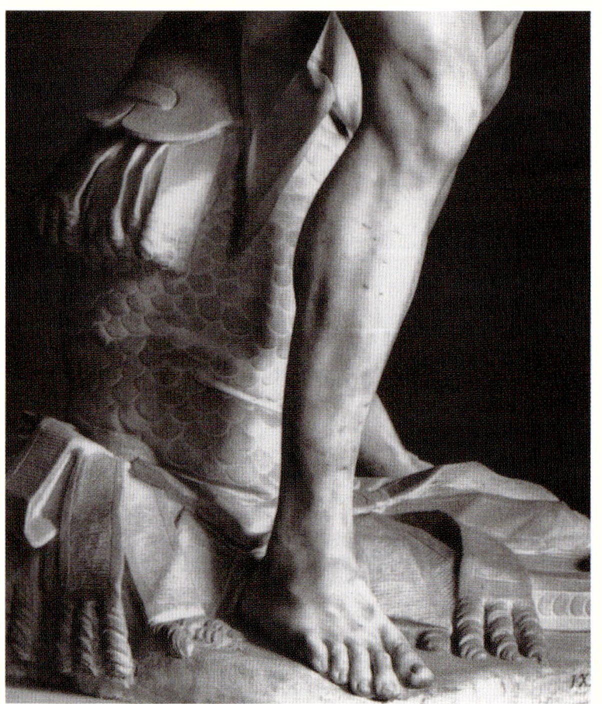
Gian Lorenzo Bernini, *David*, 1624

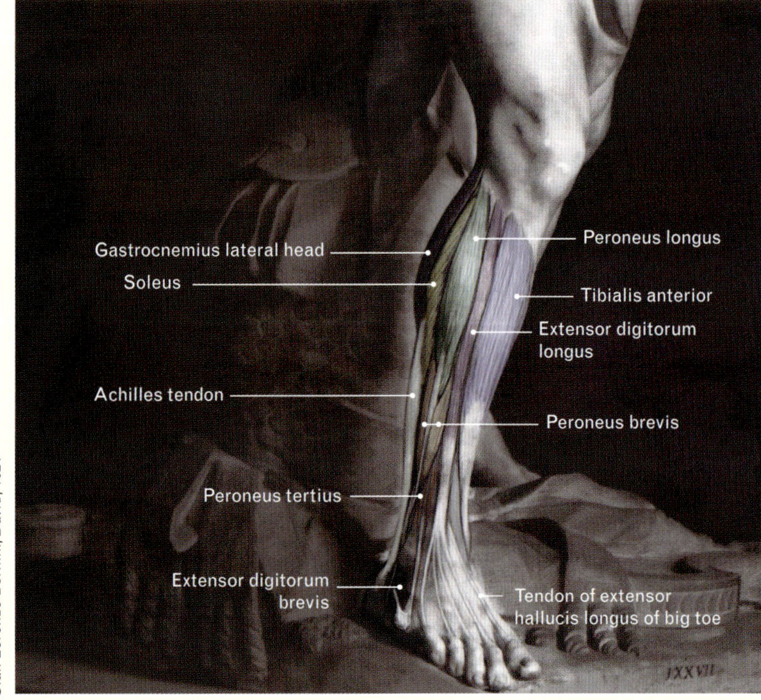

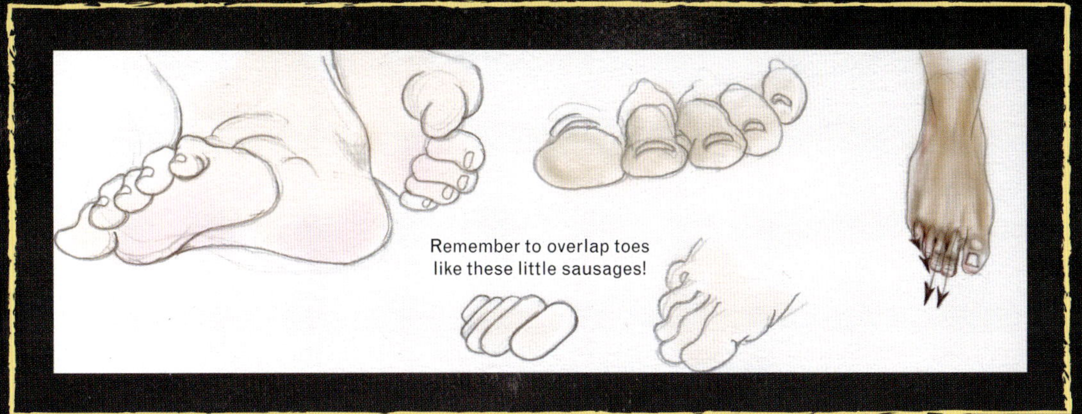

On the lateral view, or outside little-toe view, there is a landmark halfway between the end of the heel and the tip of the little toe and that is the tuberosity of the fifth metatarsal. This is a bony bump which is very visible on some individuals and may be a bit redder due to friction against tight shoes. The **peroneus brevis tendon** is attached to it and is often visible. Between this tuberosity and the lateral malleolus, outside ankle on the bottom of the fibula, is a little bulbous muscle called the **extensor digitorum brevis** which often appears greenish in people with fair skin. These tendons reach out to all the toes except the little toe, as opposed to the tendons above them called **extensor digitorum longus** which go to all except the big toe.

The tendons of the foot play a major role and should be studied. More often than not these tendons are best pulled out in the masculine foot. The **extensor hallucis longus tendon** is easily seen when raising the big toe (hallux means "greater toe"). The extensor digitorum longus, already mentioned, are seen when raising all of the toes toward the face. The **tibialis anterior** is the largest and is very visible when pulling the entire foot towards the head. The peroneus brevis mentioned earlier is visible when the foot is pulled laterally, away from the centerline of the body, or when the heel is lifted as when elevating on tiptoes.

Exercise: I have my students draw section slices over their reference, which can be from any source, art or photography. Place tracing paper over the image and visualize the forms on the feet, or any object for that matter. This is a great way to get better at seeing the multitudes of forms within forms that may be missed by casual observation.

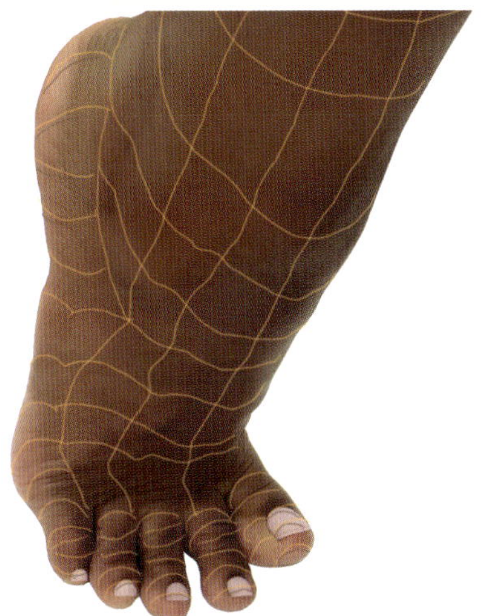

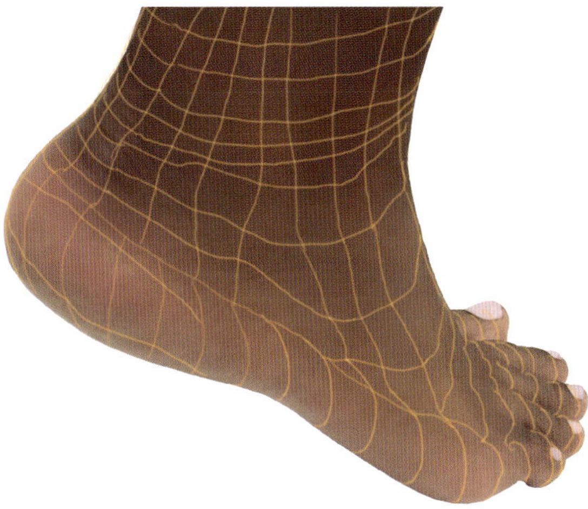

DRAWING THE FEET

In drawing the feet, I often tell my students to remember the three aspects of the foot introduced on page 27: 1) the tarsal section, which includes the heel, 2) the metatarsal, the top of the foot; and then, of course, 3) the toes. These three sections bend. While you may be aware of this fact, note that at the tarsometatarsal joint, the area where the tarsals meet the top of the foot, there is a slight bending ability there as well. Picture a woman's foot inside a transparent high-heeled shoe in profile.

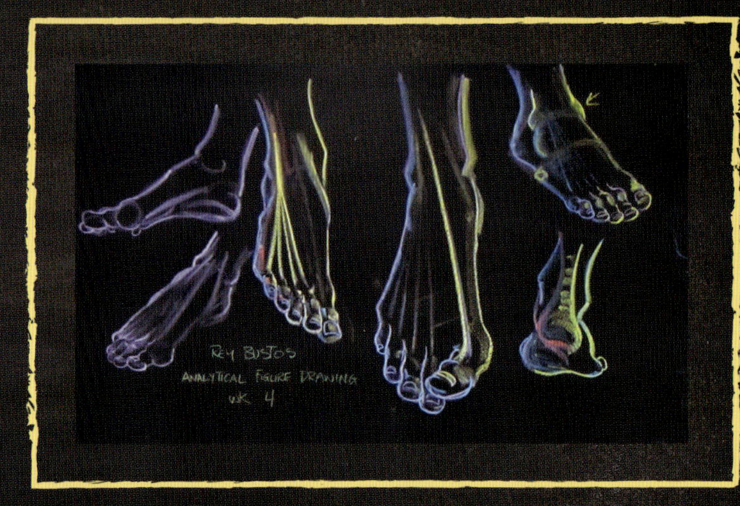

LOOK FOR THE ARCADE

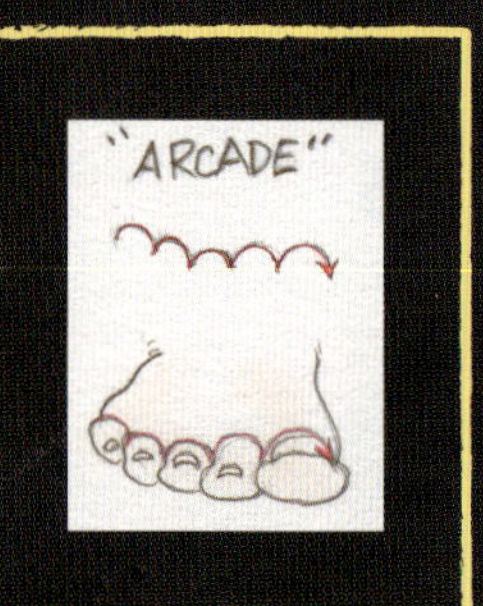

When drawing the front, foreshortened view of the foot I talk about the "arcade." The arcade is a simple way of seeing how the toes look as they face you. As you can see from my drawings, it is an effective and easy way to draw what can be an awkward angle. I use this for hands as well. The other aspect that creates the illusion of foreshortening is the toenail of each toe. Arc it to further illustrate the effect of the toe and toes coming at you. In profile with the little toe closest to your view, the toes, as I teach them, have a fanning effect. This does not have anything to do with how the model's toes are in reality; the way that I teach is less about reality than about perceived reality and making this look better. The toes therefore fan out and the way they do is like taking five playing cards from a deck. Hold them at one corner and fan. So, in the case of the toes, the little toe is facing down, followed by the next toe at a 45-degree angle, then a bit straighter for the middle toe, then the toe next to the big toe, being the straightest, most horizontal, and finally the big toe kicked up a bit.

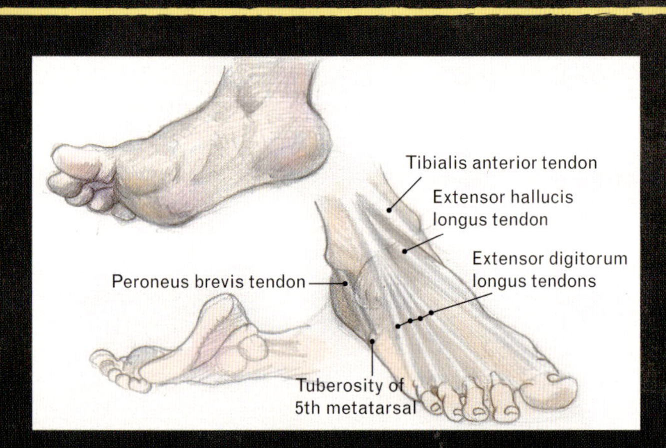

START WITH THE FOOTPRINT

Drawing the underside of the foot can be awkward. What I tell my class is to simply draw the footprint of the foot. One thing that you might now notice is the tuberosity of the fifth metatarsal and how clear it is. It pushes outward and can create a definite angle change between the heel and the front half of the foot. Note the many wrinkles and be sure to use them to express movement and dynamic directional flow. One notable muscle not included is the **peroneus tertius** whose tendon can at times be visible on some individuals on the outer side of the foot, by the ankle (lateral malleolus of fibula), attaching itself to the area of the tuberosity of the fifth metatarsal, just in front of the peroneus brevis tendon.

If you want to study toes in art, my suggestion is to look at the work of William-Adolphe Bouguereau (1825–1905); his paintings are chock-full of feet, hundreds of feet, and all are magnificently executed by one of the greatest painters ever. He also painted many feet that have the "peasant toe," where the little toe is off the ground. The great anatomist and sculptor Dr. Paul Richer attributes this interesting trait to the fact that peasants often did not wear shoes, therefore the little toe floated off the ground because the feet were not bound to the confines of shoes. While I do not agree with this, that is how this toe got its name.

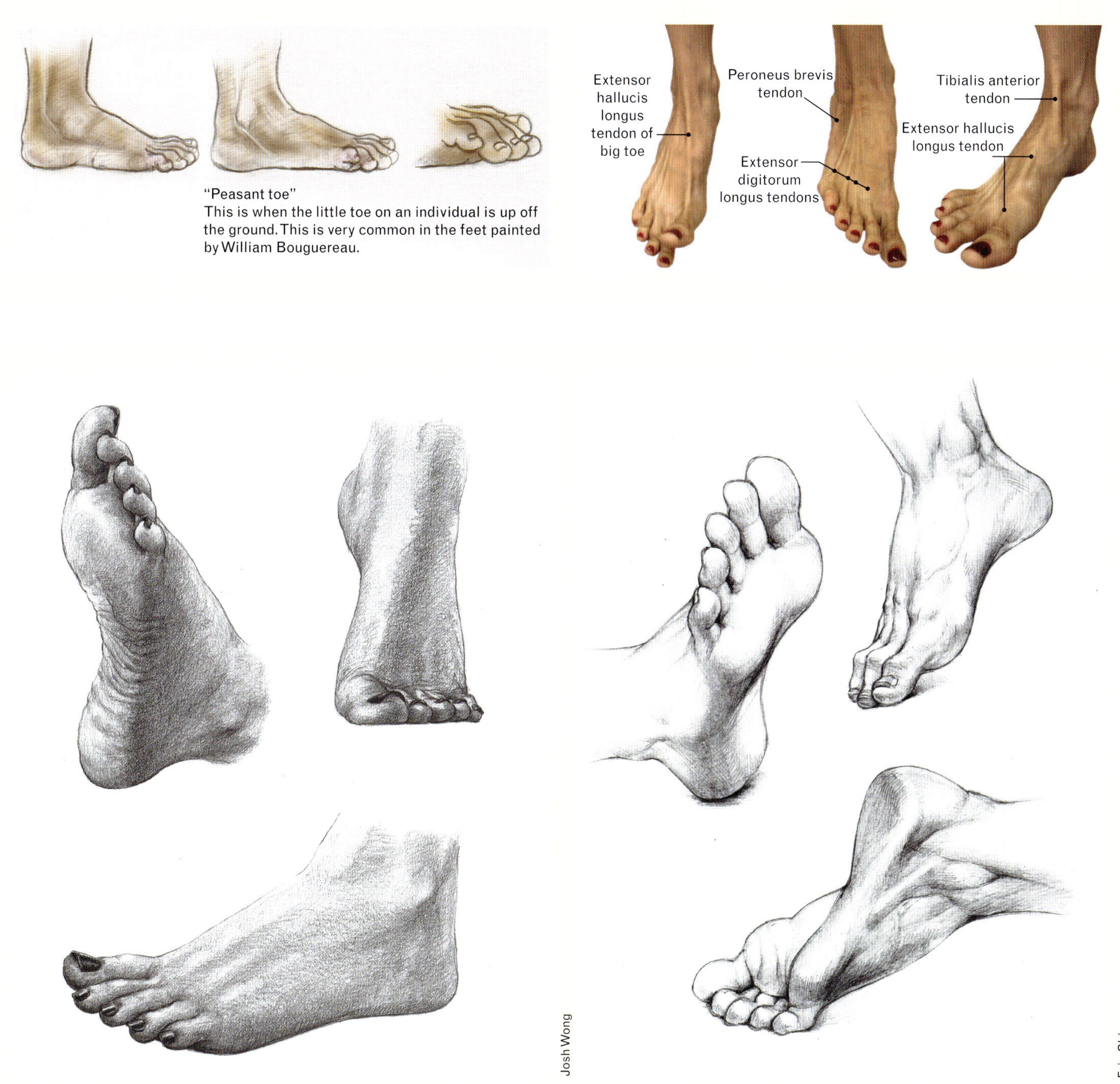

"Peasant toe"
This is when the little toe on an individual is up off the ground. This is very common in the feet painted by William Bouguereau.

My students are often amazed as to how little they knew of their own feet. In summer, when many of my students wear sandals, it is funny to see how many of them look down at their own feet, moving them to and fro, wiggling toes and even checking out each other's feet.

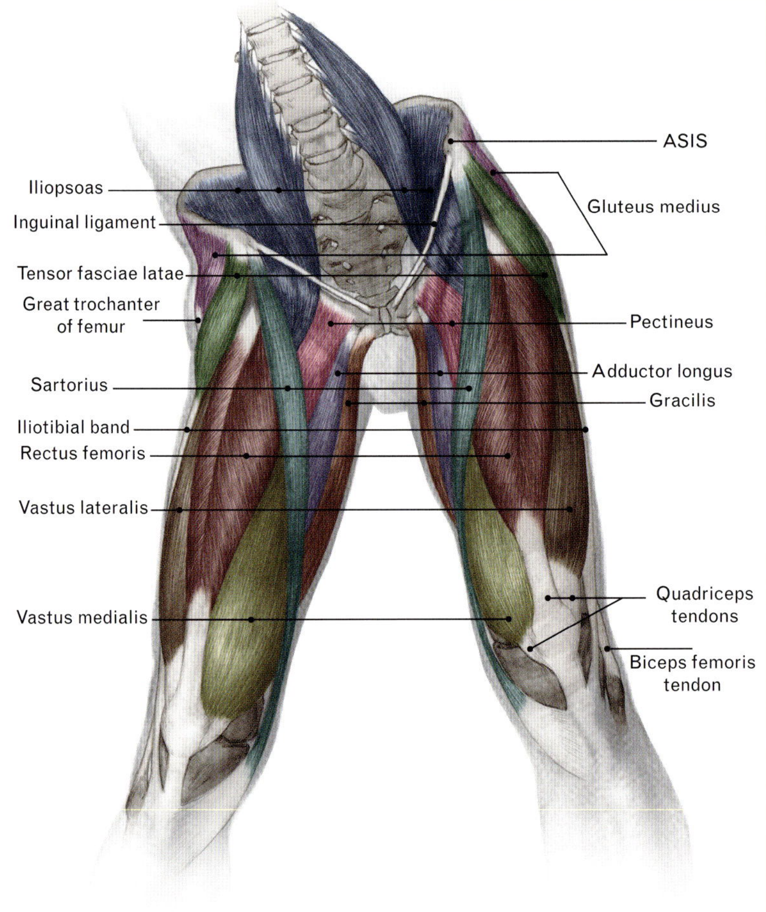

ASIS
Gluteus medius
Iliopsoas
Inguinal ligament
Tensor fasciae latae
Great trochanter of femur
Pectineus
Sartorius
Adductor longus
Gracilis
Iliotibial band
Rectus femoris
Vastus lateralis
Vastus medialis
Quadriceps tendons
Biceps femoris tendon
Hetian Duan

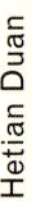

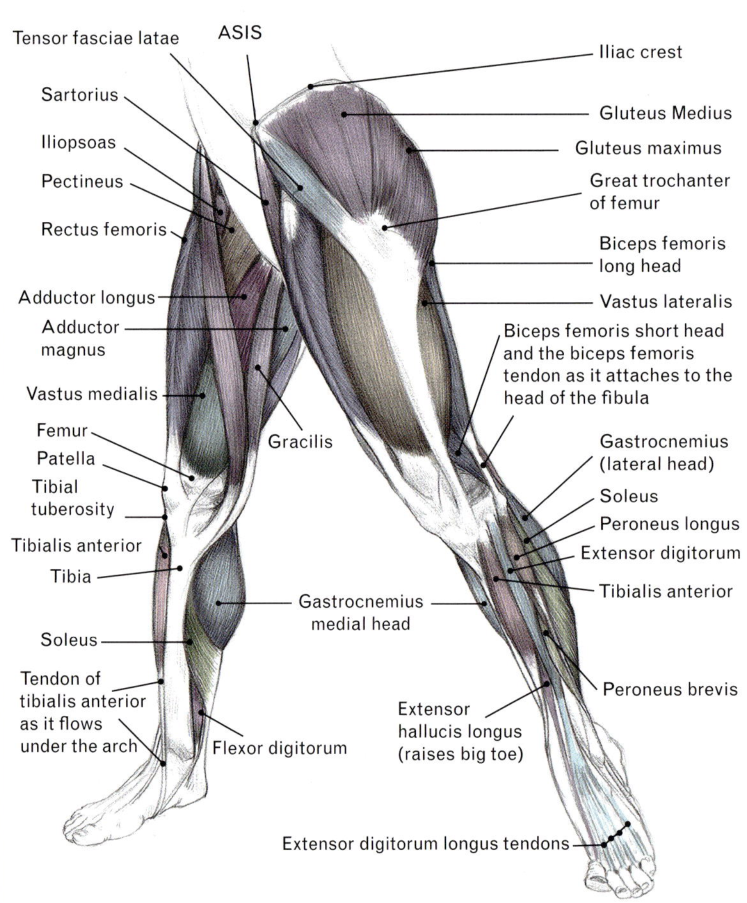

Tensor fasciae latae
ASIS
Iliac crest
Sartorius
Gluteus Medius
Iliopsoas
Gluteus maximus
Pectineus
Great trochanter of femur
Rectus femoris
Biceps femoris long head
Adductor longus
Vastus lateralis
Adductor magnus
Biceps femoris short head and the biceps femoris tendon as it attaches to the head of the fibula
Vastus medialis
Gracilis
Gastrocnemius (lateral head)
Femur
Patella
Soleus
Tibial tuberosity
Peroneus longus
Extensor digitorum
Tibialis anterior
Tibialis anterior
Tibia
Gastrocnemius medial head
Soleus
Tendon of tibialis anterior as it flows under the arch
Peroneus brevis
Flexor digitorum
Extensor hallucis longus (raises big toe)
Extensor digitorum longus tendons

THE THIGH AND GLUTEAL AREA

I have the number of essential muscles of the thigh down to 15. They are broken down into four groups: the **quadriceps** (three), the **adductors** (five), the **flexors** (four), and the **gluteals** (three). My students draw these details in order to see them on the live model better. At first, they do not see them as clearly as their teacher but experience will hone their eyes; soon, they will see the subtle changes in the underlying muscles revealed by shadows. In this way, the entire purpose of knowing anatomy is not to merely draw all of the anatomy that we know, but to know what to put in and what to leave out as a personal choice. It is about editing as one would a textbook.

The Quadriceps

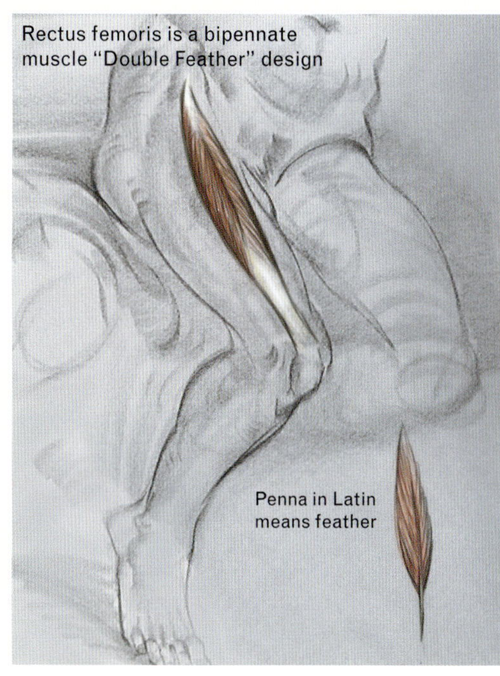

Rectus femoris is a bipennate muscle "Double Feather" design

Penna in Latin means feather

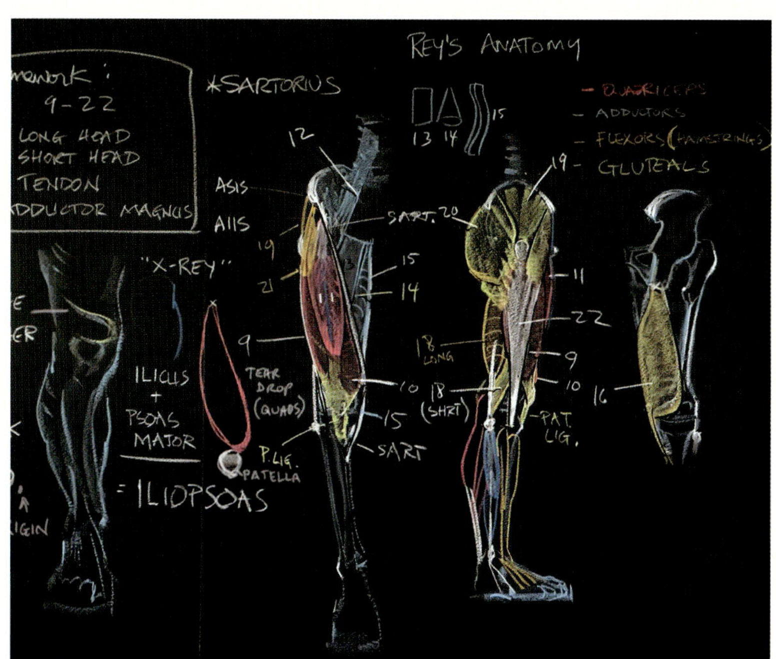

Photo: Jason Mendoza of The Gnomon Workshop

The quadriceps consist of four muscles, the **vastus medialis**, **vastus lateralis**, **rectus femoris**, and the **vastus intermedius**. Generally, the fourth quadriceps muscle, the vastus intermedius, is not visible since it is under the **rectus femoris**, which is the only quadriceps that is attached to the pelvis. The rectus femoris originates at the anterior inferior iliac spine of the pelvis, right in front of the thigh. The rectus femoris is flanked by the vastus medialis on the inside of the thigh and knee area, and the vastus lateralis, which is on the outer thigh and knee area. The rectus femoris is fish-shaped and has a furrow down the center with muscle fibers arranged in an upward slant toward the center furrow, making it look like a feather when seen on a cadaver. Sometimes the rectus femoris can appear to look like two muscles, such as on a bodybuilder or heavily muscled athlete. This type of muscle is called

bipennate or "double feather." I call it the "Captain America" muscle since it is depicted very prominently on every superhero and action figure. If you can picture a feather with the spine down the middle and the feather hairs on either side, it gives you an image of the rectus femoris.

The vastus lateralis is broad and is a major part of the side of the thigh and as it turns to the front, the knee area. The vastus lateralis approaches the **patella** (kneecap) and shares a common tendon, the quadriceps tendon, with the other quadriceps.

When we are born, our patellas are little pieces of cartilage, just like small coins. As we grow, so do the patellas, and eventually these knees develop the protruding forms that we recognize on adults to be our kneecaps.

FOUR VIEWS OF THE KNEE

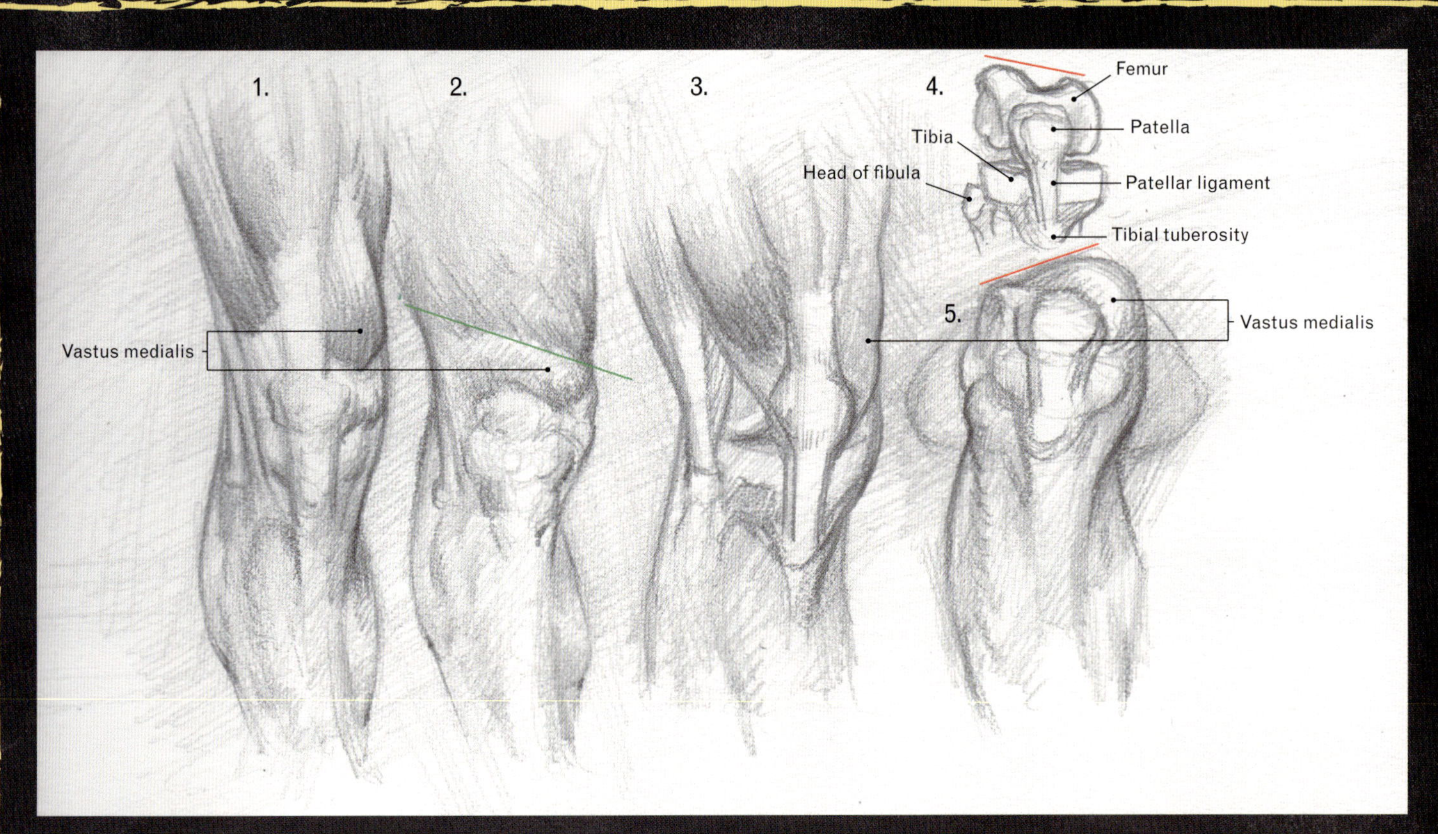

1. **Tensed knee**: You can often see the three distinct muscles that make up the quadriceps.

2. **Relaxed knee**: Shows how the band of Richer (green line) cuts along the lower portion of the vastus medialis. This band is an offshoot of the iliotibial band.

3. **A 3/4 view of knee**: In this view with the femur and tibia visible behind the patella, the biceps femoris tendon and the patellar ligament are prominent.

4. **Femur**: This is the femur as it articulates with the tibia and the connection of the patella to the tibial tuberosity.

Notice also the angle of the bone end of the femur, it is higher laterally, but on the muscled illustration, 5, the muscle creates a higher peak medially (red lines).

The vastus medialis is tear-shaped and is seen on the inside and front of the lower thigh and appears to rest on the patella. Therefore, the vastus medialis is lower than the vastus lateralis creating a medial slant just above the knee. The band of Richer is an offshoot of the iliotibial band, which crosses at a downward slant, medially and when the leg is relaxed it cuts into the lower aspect of the vastus medialis creating a bubble that rests on the patella.

The Adductors

The **adductor** muscles are the inner-thigh muscles, which is the area that you would use to ride a horse. They pull your legs together; they adduct, and keep your knees tightly pressed together.

This basic group includes the **pectineus**, **adductor longus**, **adductor magnus**, and **gracilis**. I see the adductors as a group since they appear as a bubble separated from the quadriceps by the longest muscle of the body, the belt-like **sartorius**. This natural border muscle originates at the **anterior superior iliac spine** and inserts at the tibia, just inside the **tibial tuberosity**. Until a baby reaches 18 months this area appears to cut the little person's inside thigh in half, and gives them a delightful doughboy look. I named this crease the sartorial crease. You will see this in life and in many baby depictions in art history.

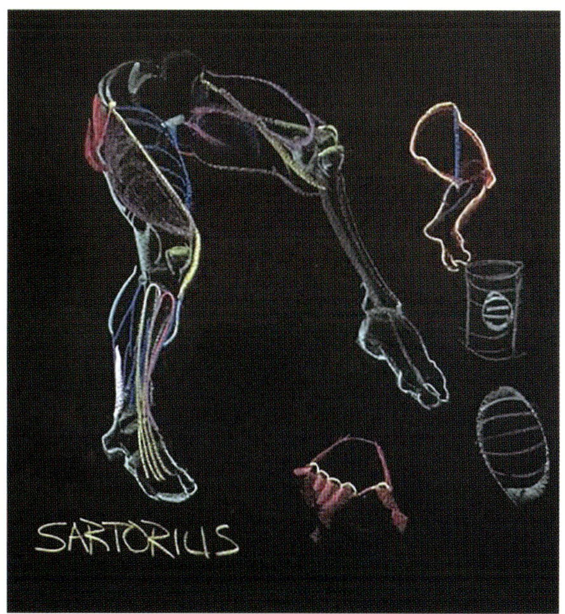

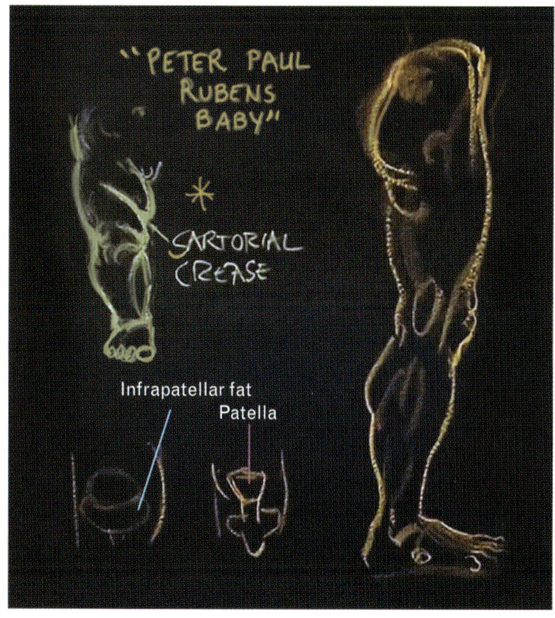

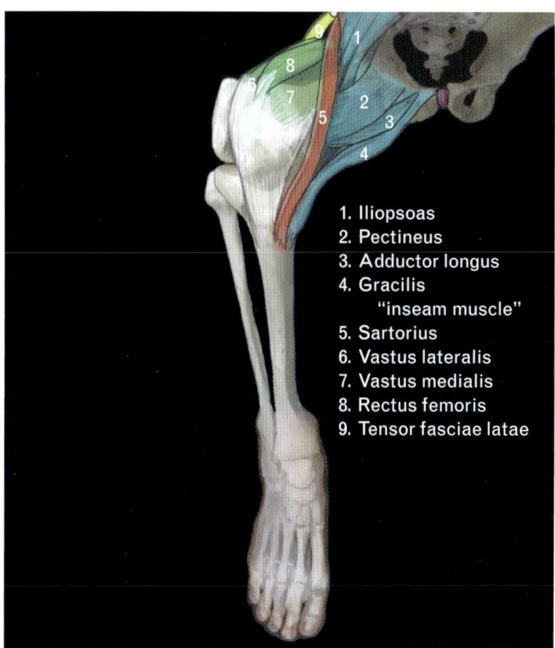

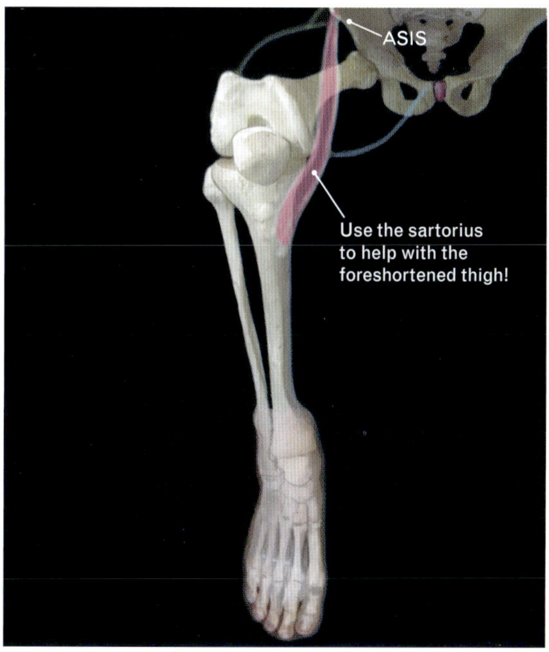

The Flexors

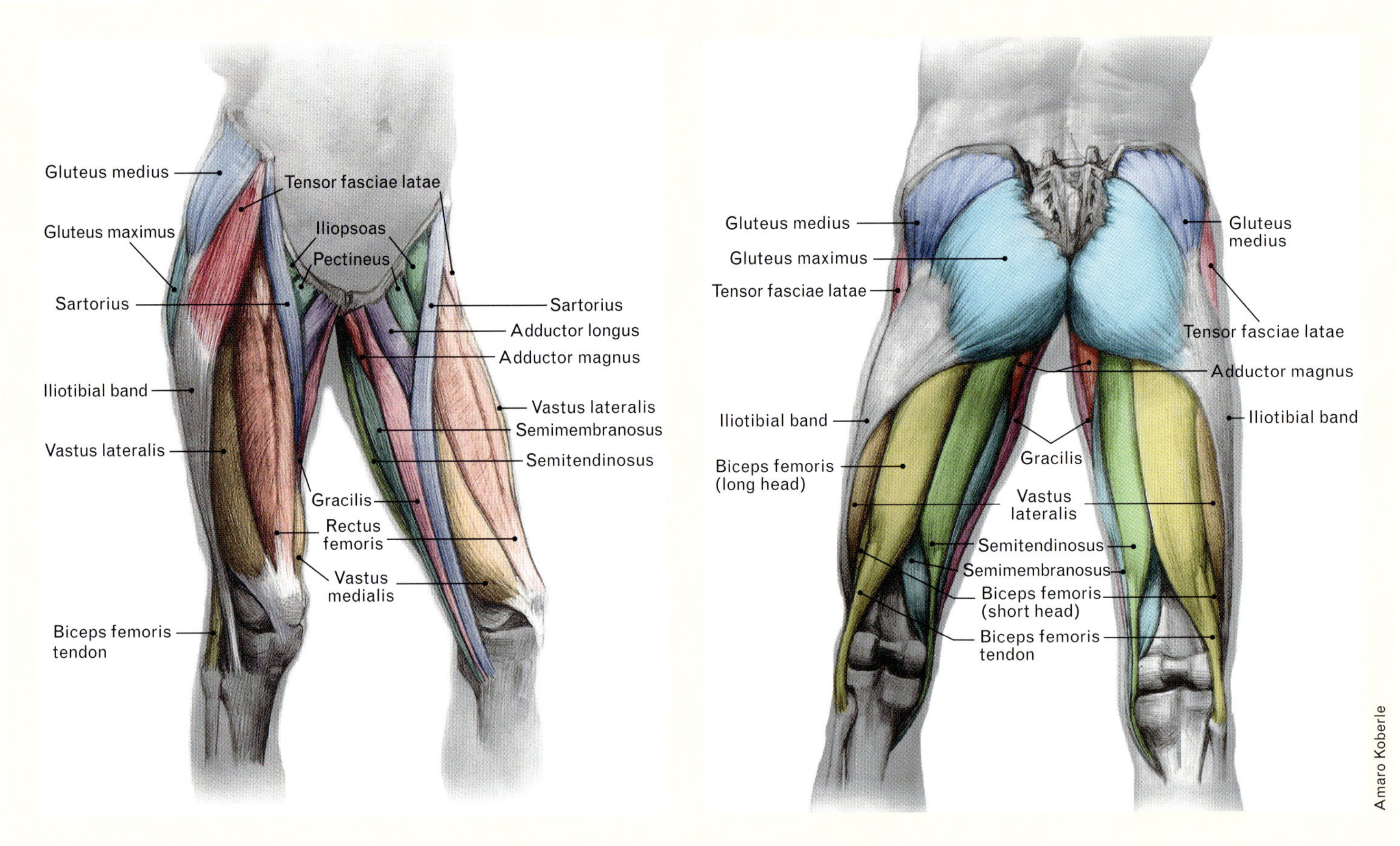

The flexors (also called the hamstrings) that the artist needs to know are the **semimembranosus**, **semitendinosus,** and the **biceps femoris long head** and **short head**. These combine to create the bulk of the forms of the back of the thigh. When the knee is bent back these muscles can approximate the look of the biceps of the arm as the muscles bunch up in contraction. These particular flexors of the back of the thigh originate at the ischial tuberosity or the "sit bone." They flow out from under the gluteus maximus and are up against the vastus lateralis. The semitendinosus and the biceps femoris long head appear to be one singular form in most people, while on athletic individuals, the two appear to split one quarter of the way up from the bend of the knee.

There is a smaller part of the biceps femoris long head that lies underneath, the biceps femoris short head. This muscle is under the long head, originates on the femur, and shares the tendon with the biceps femoris long head as they insert on the head of the fibula.

When the knee, seen from the side or back, is bent at 90 degrees from the vertical thigh, the two tendons from each of these muscles pop out and can be quite dramatic in appearance. The muscles ride up in unison roughly emulating the biceps brachii of the upper arm.

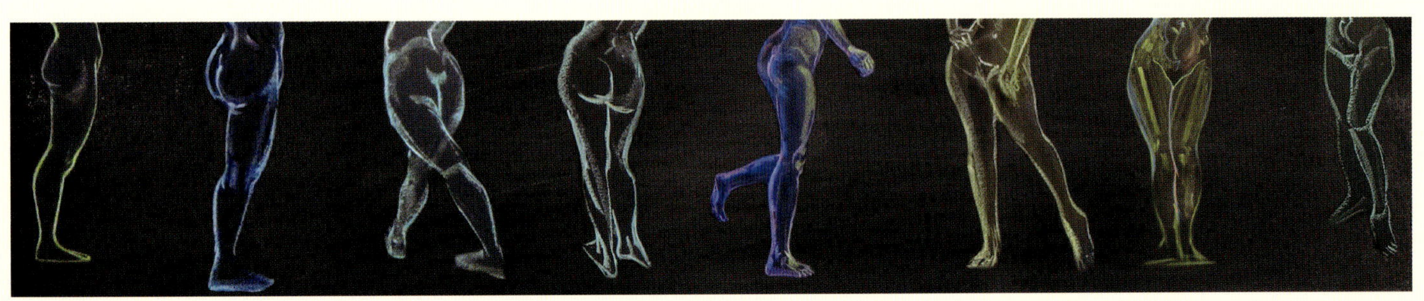

The Gluteals

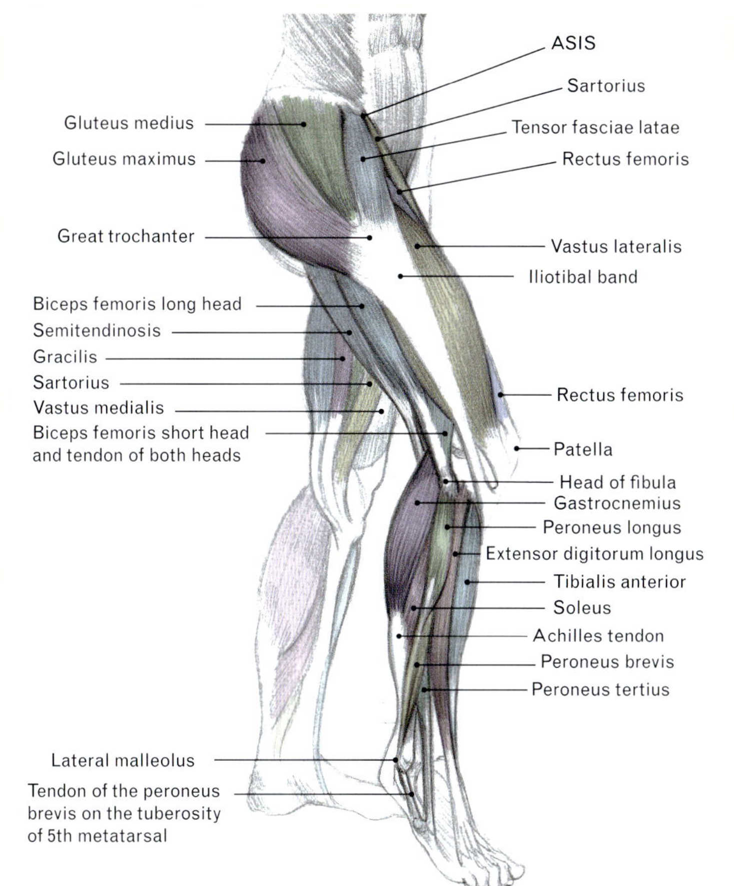

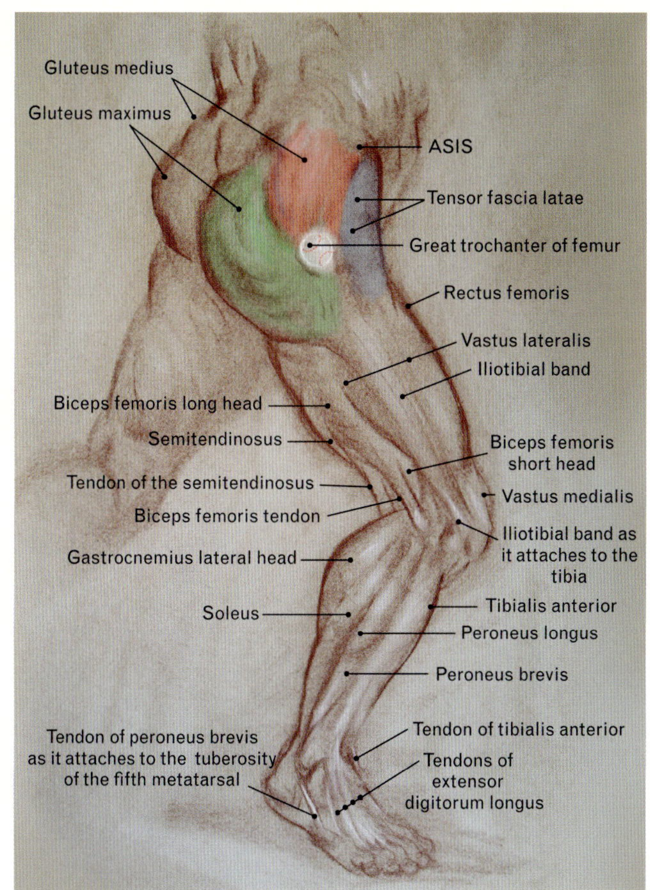

I include the **tensor fasciae latae** muscle with the **gluteus medius** and **gluteus maximus** as part of the gluteal muscles because these three muscles make a very tightly fitting group. The gluteus maximus, the butt, is a large, round muscle that is impossible to miss. On humans, it is prominent since we walk upright. The muscle surrounds the back aspect of the great trochanter of the femur and is further attached to the sacrum on the back and even a bit on the upper shaft of the femur. It has a strap, the gluteal strap, which pulls it up, giving us the familiar round butt shape at the rear. As one ages that strap and surrounding fasciae (covering sheath) will cease to be able to hold that area up. That, as well as loss of subcutaneous fat, will make that area less round.

The gluteus medius is a large abductor muscle and its contraction pulls your leg away from your body. This muscle is fan-shaped and takes up the entire area of the ilium and inserts at the great trochanter. The gluteus maximus covers a good deal of this muscle on a cadaver; I have noticed that in some individuals you do see a wee sliver of the gluteus medius. This is contrary to most artistic anatomy books, which often show much more of this muscle, including my own drawings of this area. I believe that this is due to the artists' visual representations and what we see on living models. The form of the gluteus medius pushes through the large form of the gluteus maximus. From the back, this area can look like a butterfly on lean males.

The tensor fasciae latae has a teardrop shape, originating at the anterior superior iliac spine (ASIS), and along with the gluteus maximus is attached to the iliotibial band that goes all the way down the side of the leg to the lateral aspect of the tibia. The tensor fascia drops down to approximately the same point as the gluteal strap. In a simplified form, these three muscles look like a first baseman's mitt. The gluteus maximus are the combined fingers of the mitt, the gluteus medius its pocket and the tensor fasciae latae the thumb.

ANALYSIS OF FORM IN FOUR STEPS

Exercise: Take an image, an artwork or photograph, and draw the skeleton from the waist down. (This can be done with any area of the body, or even the entire body.) In class, this is done after extensive study of all of the limbs. With this assignment, students are asked to utilize all the knowledge they have learned so far, from the skeleton through the muscles of the leg, thigh, and the gluteal group.

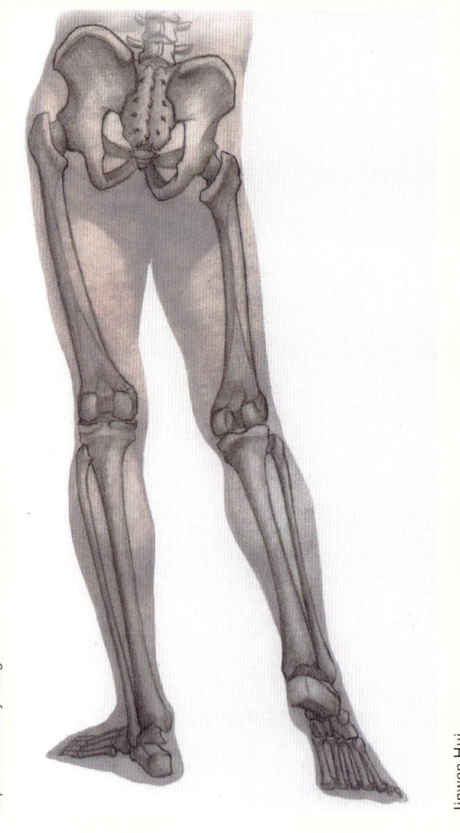

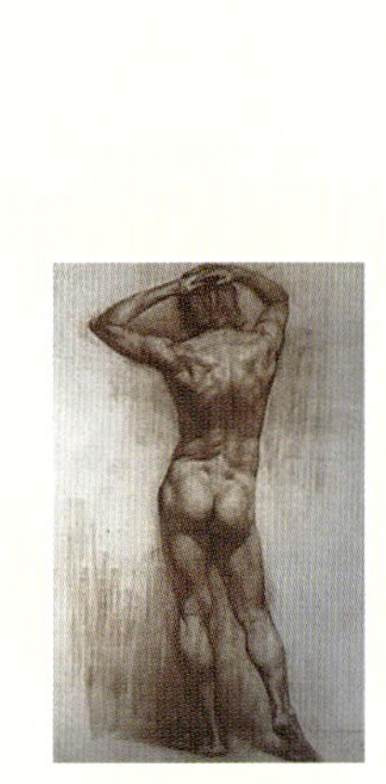

Jinwen Hui

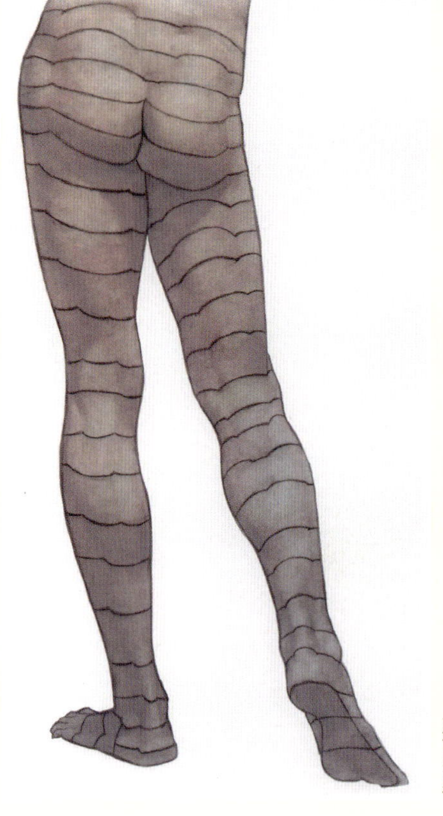

Jinwen Hui

STEP 1: SKELETON OVERLAY

Take a sheet of tracing paper and place it over your reference, drawing to the best of your ability the skeleton from the waist down as seen here. These examples were done in this way. Watch for the tilt and rotation of the pelvis, femurs, leg bones, and feet. Have as much reference of the skeleton as possible to help with this. Some of my students use online skeletal reference and some have a skeleton model to help them as well. (Optional: Placing the reference with the tracing overlay onto a scanner, scan and print it out for your study on one sheet of paper.)

STEP 2: SLICED OVERLAY

Replace the tracing paper with a new sheet. In this overlay you will now draw the section lines as if slicing the body or imagining the body with horizontally pinstriped tights. Carefully visualize the form as you draw around the entire form of the body. Go in and out of the peaks and valleys. Remember how we identified the forms of the foot on page 29.

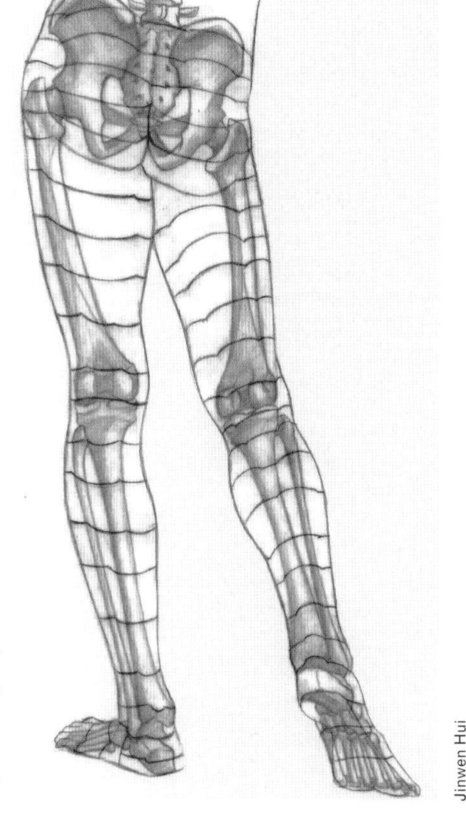

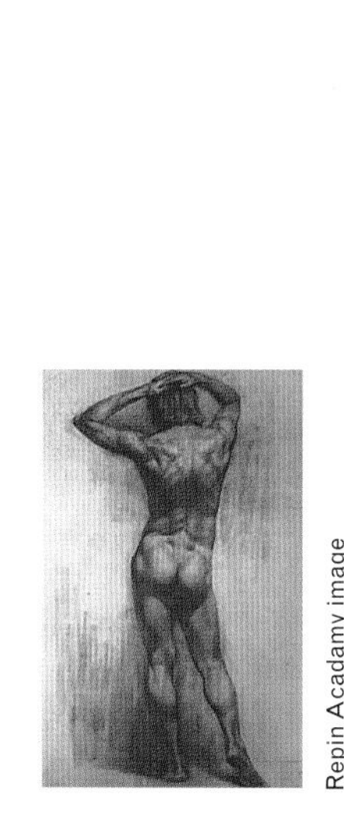

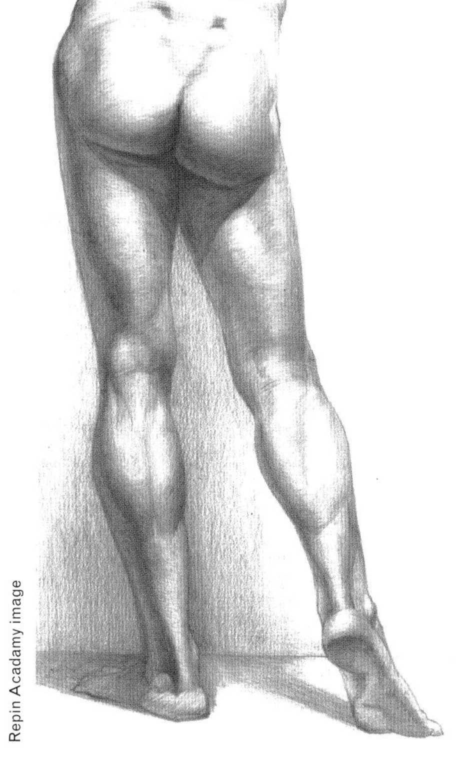

STEP 3: MERGED OVERLAYS

This is the easiest step because all that you do here is take the two tracings, the skeleton and the section lines, and photocopy them together. While an easy step, there's a valuable lesson learned: you can clearly see the structure, skeleton, and the form of the body as it floats over the skeleton *without* the reference.

STEP 4: INTERPRETED DRAWING

Lastly, I ask each student to redraw the reference. This means that it should be reinterpreted, not copied as if you were a forger. Redrawing in this case means to draw it as if it was your original artwork. Try not to look at the original reference too often; use it only as an aid.

This is one of my students' favorite assignments and is always an eye-opening exercise that helps them when viewing a live model thereafter.

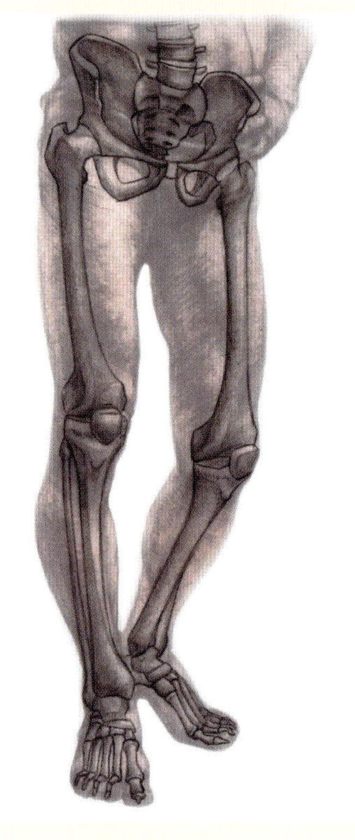
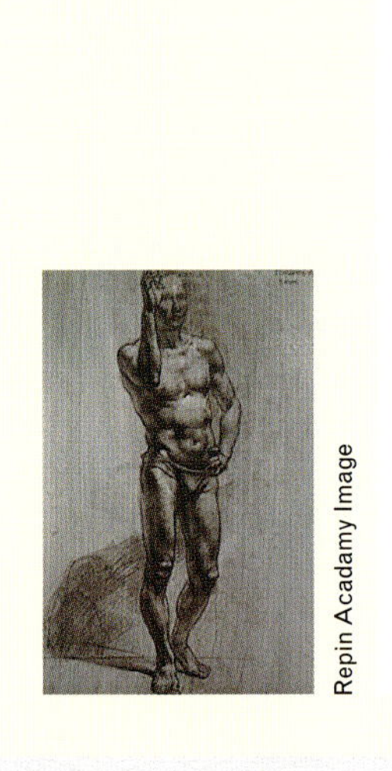
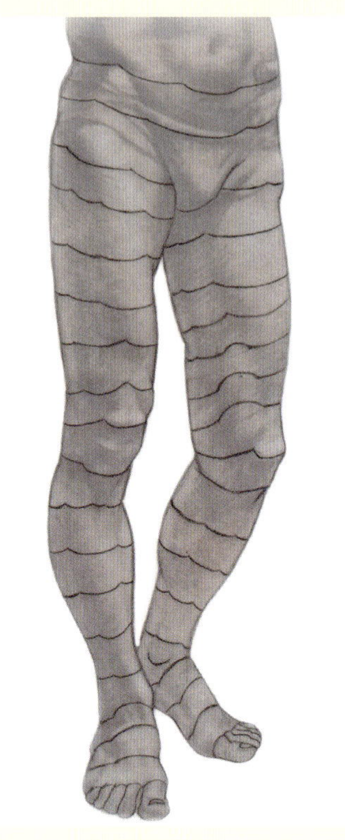

Repin Acadamy Image

Jinwen Hui

STEP 1: SKELETON OVERLAY

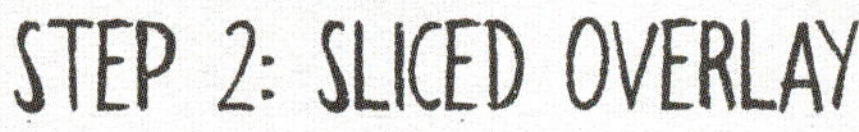

STEP 2: SLICED OVERLAY

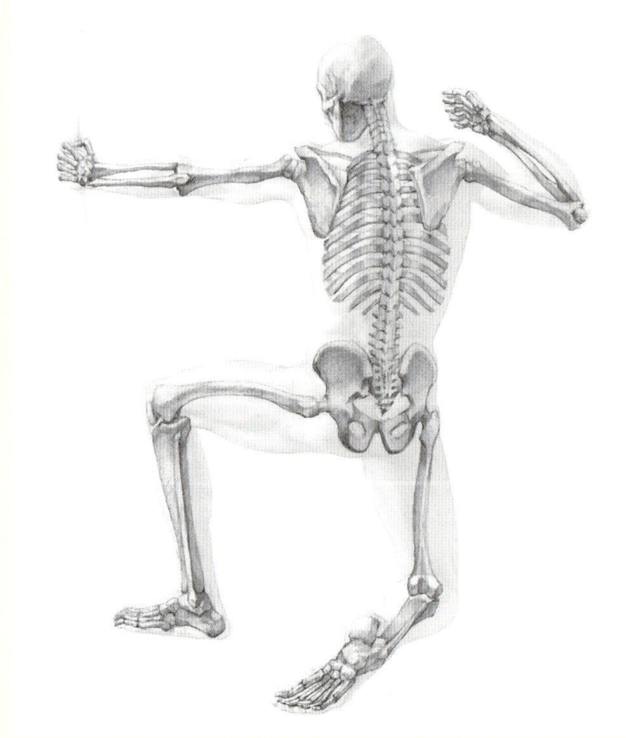
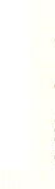

Allie Irwin

STEP 1: SKELETON OVERLAY

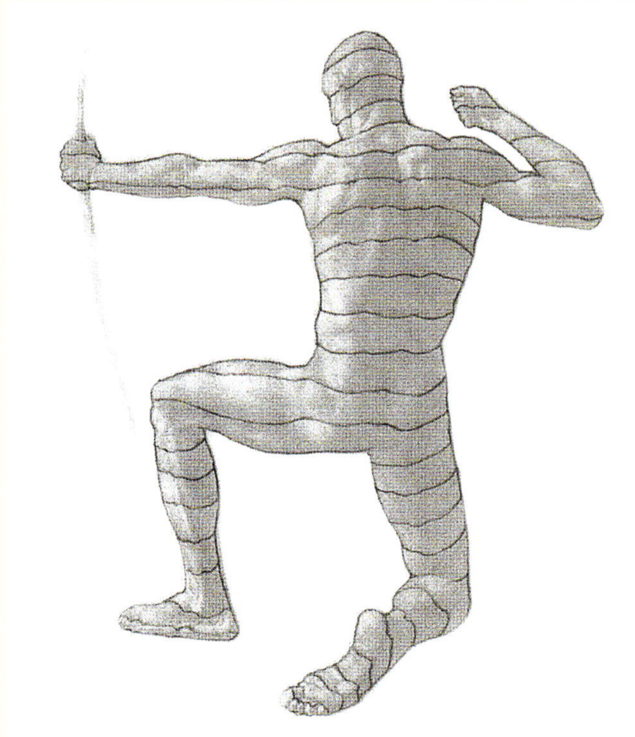

Allie Irwin

STEP 2: SLICED OVERLAY

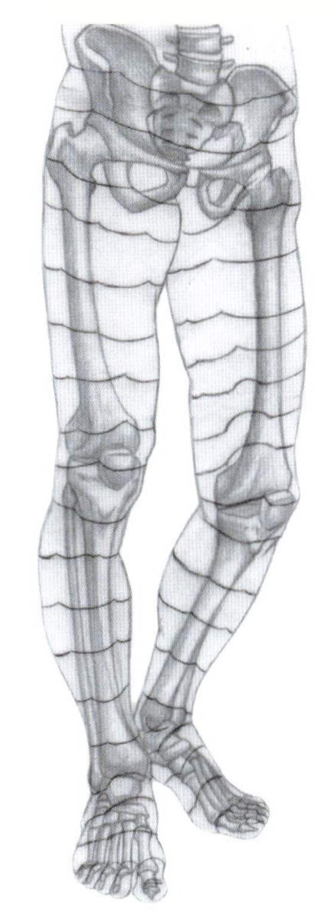
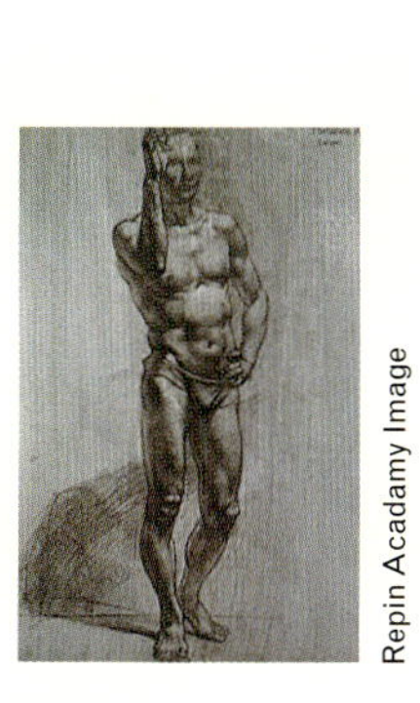

STEP 3: MERGED OVERLAYS

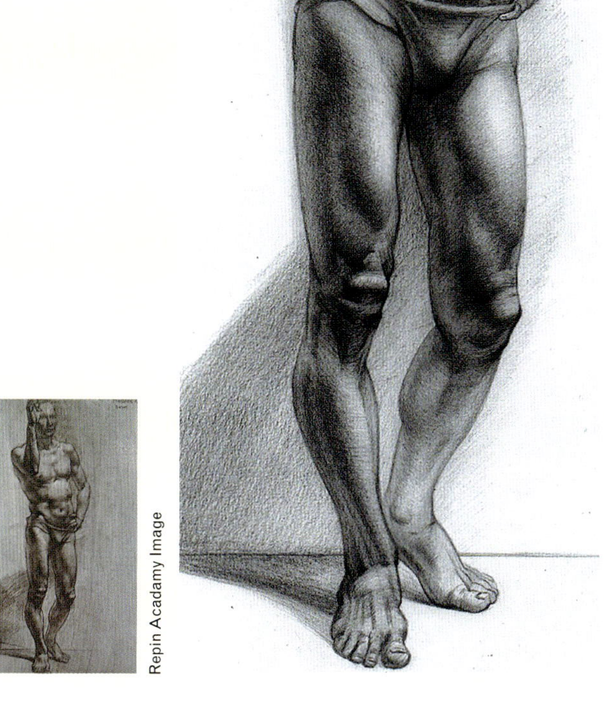

STEP 4: INTERPRETED DRAWING

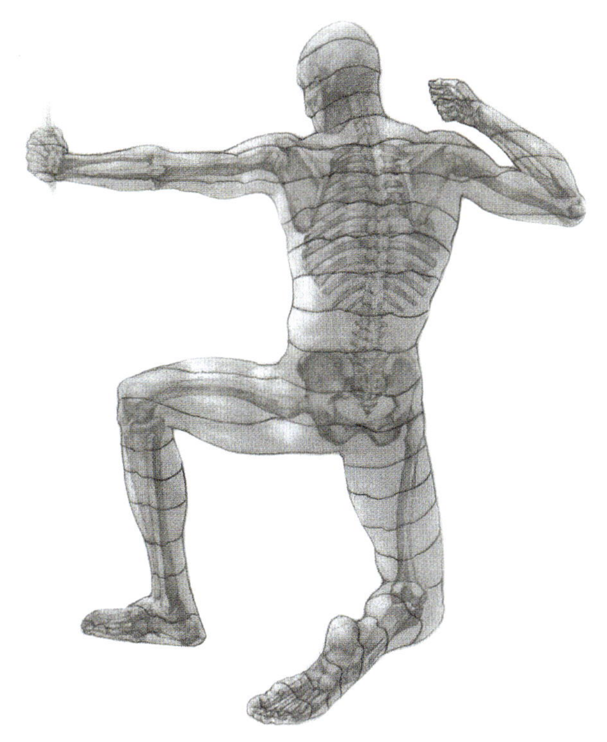

STEP 3: MERGED OVERLAYS

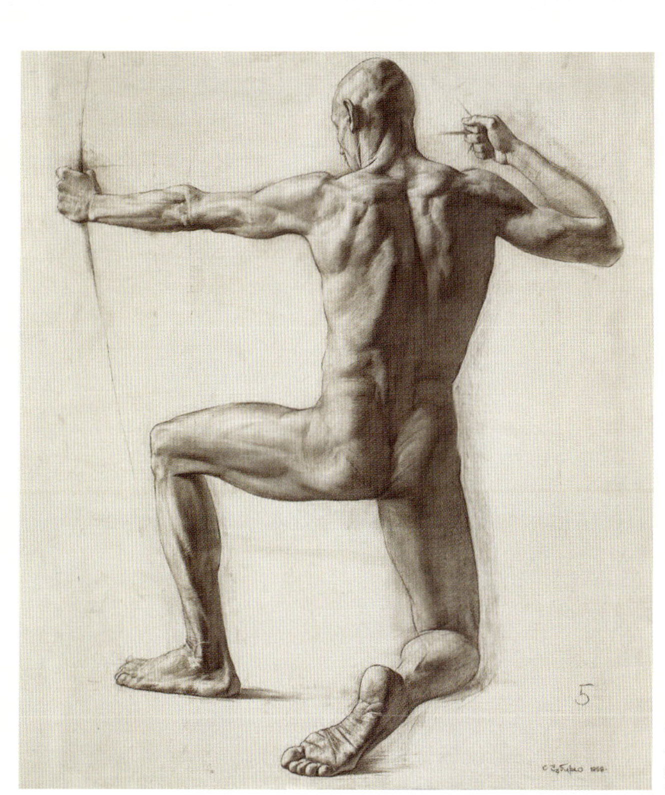

ORIGINAL MASTER REFERENCE

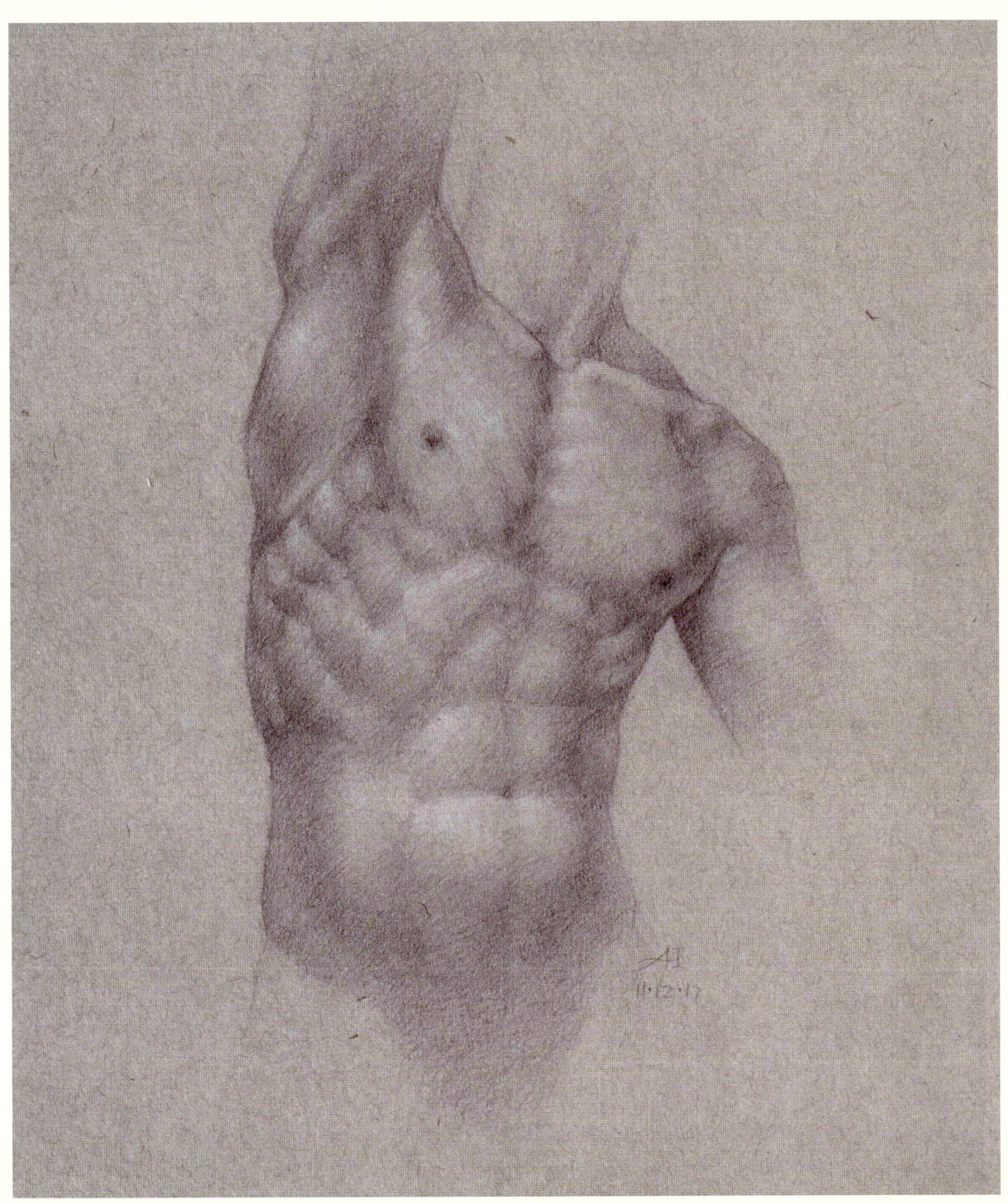

Allie Irwin

THE TORSO

The torso (or trunk) is the area of the body, human or animal, that consists of everything except the head, legs, and arms. This area is so central, literally and figuratively, that in many cases in art history it has even been depicted as finished art. The torso can twist, bend, extend, and fold, move backward, forward, and side to side. All that you need to do is go to a dance studio or a gym and watch gymnastics or a basketball game to see just how dynamic the torso is. The movement of the torso can whip the arms and throw the legs to and fro. It is such an important part of dynamic drawing that every artist will learn many methods as to how to better lay this in, by blocking or some other organic method. In this book I have used the **main frame** and interlocking forms to quickly draw the rhythm of the figures (see page 45). It would be a good idea to draw many torsos on a page just to focus on this critical mass of the body.

The Front Torso

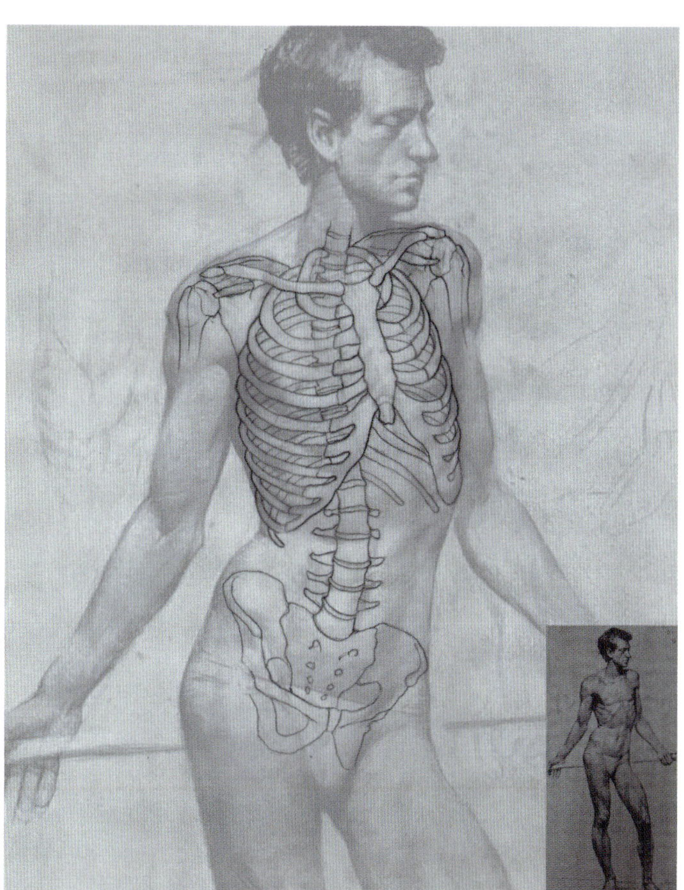

Russian Academy of Art image, draw over by Leon Lee

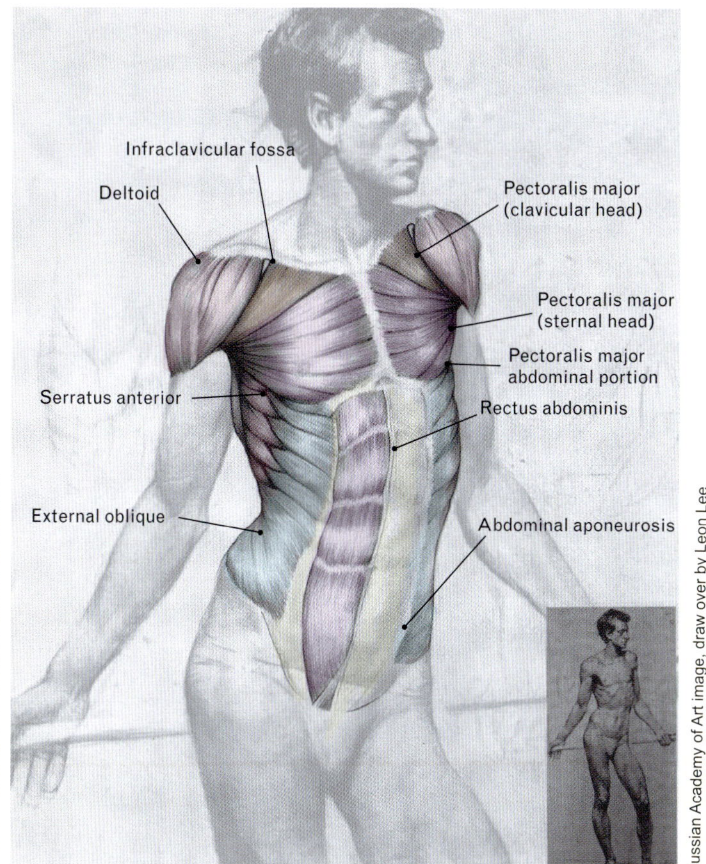

Russian Academy of Art image, draw over by Leon Lee

Starting from the top of the front torso is the **pectoralis major**, which is made up of the sternal portion and the clavicular portion. Just below these muscles in the center are the **rectus abdominis** muscles, or the "six-pack" group, which are flanked on each side by the **external oblique** muscles. It is very important to note that the pectoralis major sternal portion and the external obliques are attached to an **aponeurosis** or sheath that covers the rectus abdominis. That is why when viewing my student's work, note that they had to "cut" away one side of this sheath to show the rectus abdominis underneath. There is the pectoralis major abdominal portion as well that can be seen as a muscle bump under the male nipple, next to the sternal portion, and butted up against the top section of the rectus abdominis.

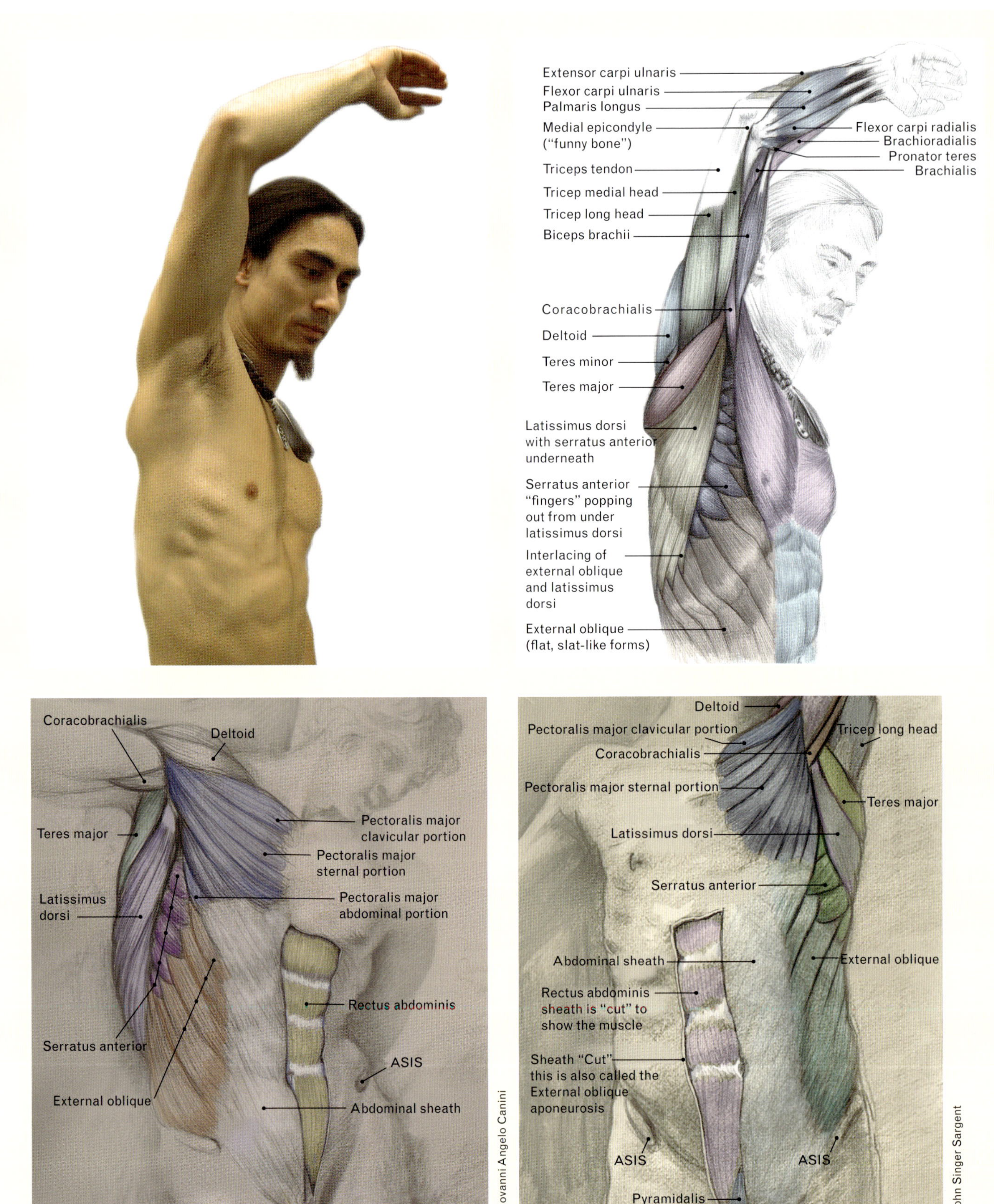

The only other important muscles to know for drawing the front torso actually wrap around from the back. These are the **serratus anterior** muscles, which originate at the medial border of the **scapulae**. When viewed from the front torso this muscle creates a very interesting visual effect, like fingertips that appear to be interwoven with the **external oblique** muscles.

HOW TO DRAW THE FRONT TORSO

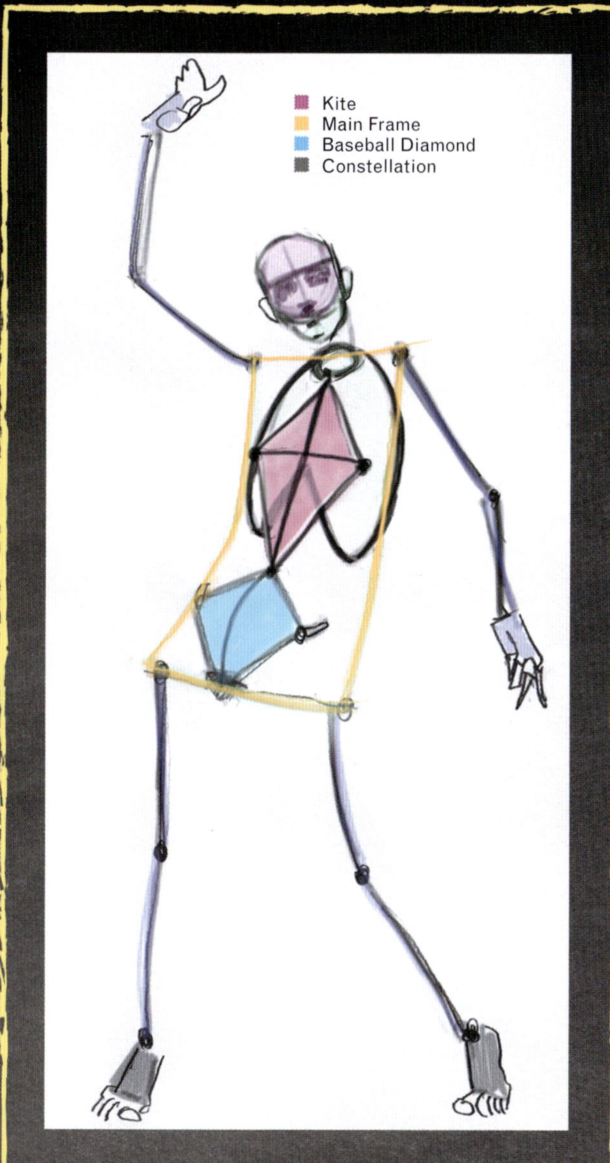

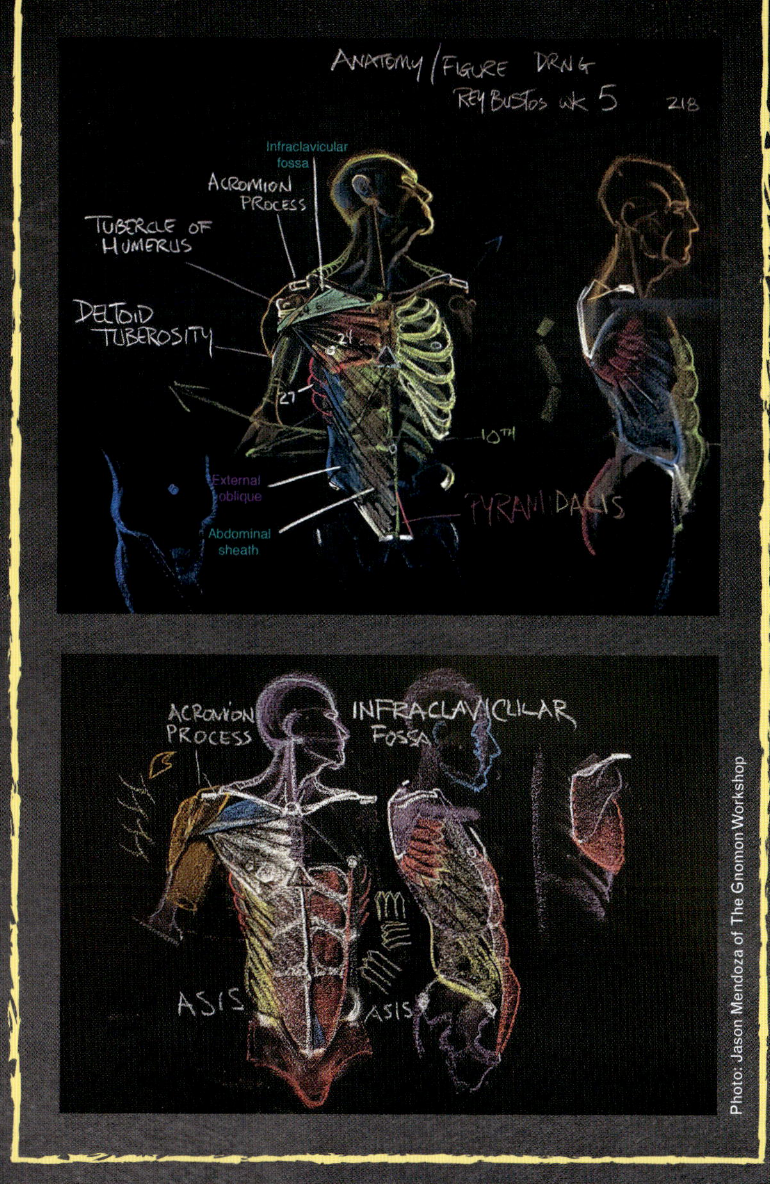

When drawing the front torso, I draw a line from the acromion process through the nipple to the navel. This method is effective especially when I am making up figures and want to capture the proportions quickly. I also tell my students to look for several triangulations. There is one between the nipples and navel, another between the nipples and pit of the neck. Combined, these create what I call the "kite" of the front torso. The kite is formed by the points of the pit of the neck to each nipple and from the nipples to the navel.

The third triangulation is between the navel and the anterior superior iliac spines (ASIS). The ASIS are the points on the pelvis right on the belt line. The last triangle is from the

ASIS points to the pubic bone. These points form what I call the "baseball diamond." Looking at the model from the front, the right ASIS is first base, the navel is second base, the left ASIS is third base, and finally the pubic bone is home plate.

You can also draw a structure line or arc from the pit of the neck downward through the nipples, and this structure line will hit the exposed ends of the digitation of the **serratus anterior**. Note: Usually only four or five of the serratus anterior digitations pop out from under the **latissimus dorsi**. These can be seen more easily when the model raises his or her arm and seen on the mid to lower part of the side, appearing to look like big fingers holding the body, hugging the torso.

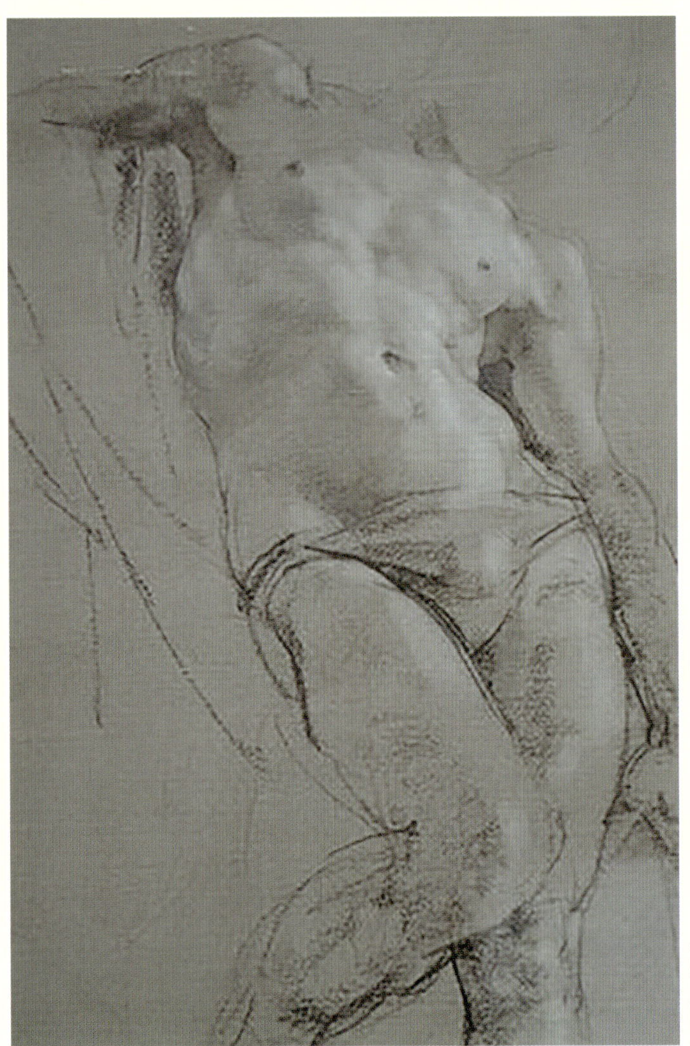

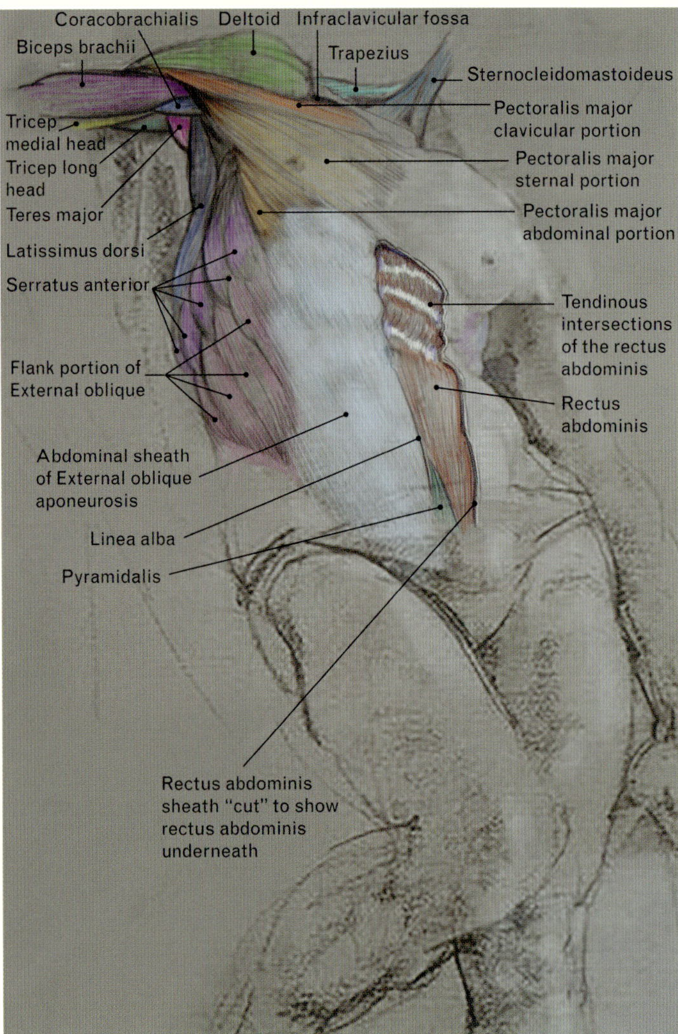

Peter Paul Rubens

The **external oblique** (slanted) group is mostly made up of flat, slat-like muscle forms. In the classroom, I draw a picket fence without gaps on the blackboard, and then I draw it again but at a slant (obliquely). The points of the "fence" intermesh tightly with the digitation of the serratus anterior. As with the serratus anterior, the external oblique segments are attached to the ribs. The lower portion, the area of your waist without ribs, is where the external oblique fleshes fully, creating the meaty flank portion, or love-handle area of the waist.

On fit models, more often on men, this muscle can be very angular and boxy; on women it is more often softer and less prominent. As already mentioned above, the external oblique attaches along with the pectoralis major sternal head onto the abdominal aponeurosis (sometimes called the external oblique aponeurosis), which then attaches to the center of the body, the **linea alba**, from the pit of the stomach down to the pubic bone. Note: There is a **pectoralis minor** (completely hidden by pectoralis major) but is of little form value for artists.

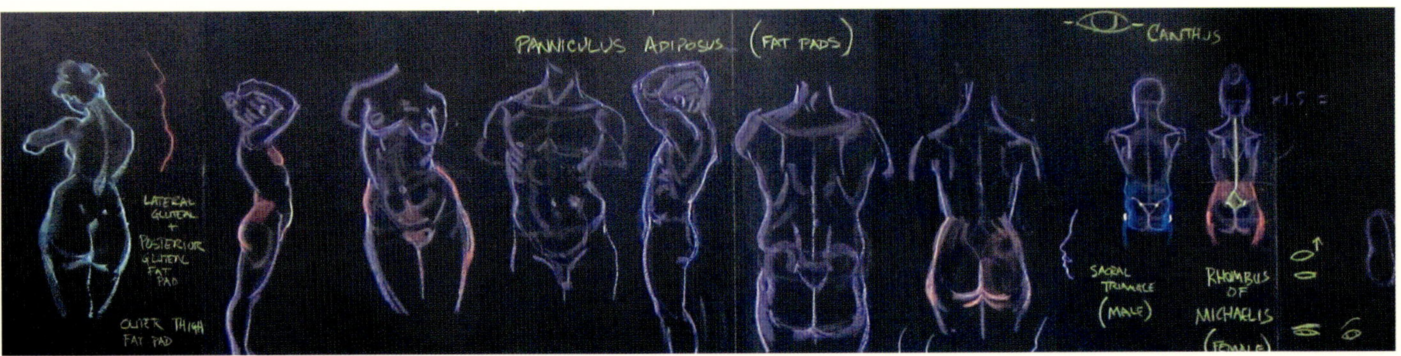

The Pelvis

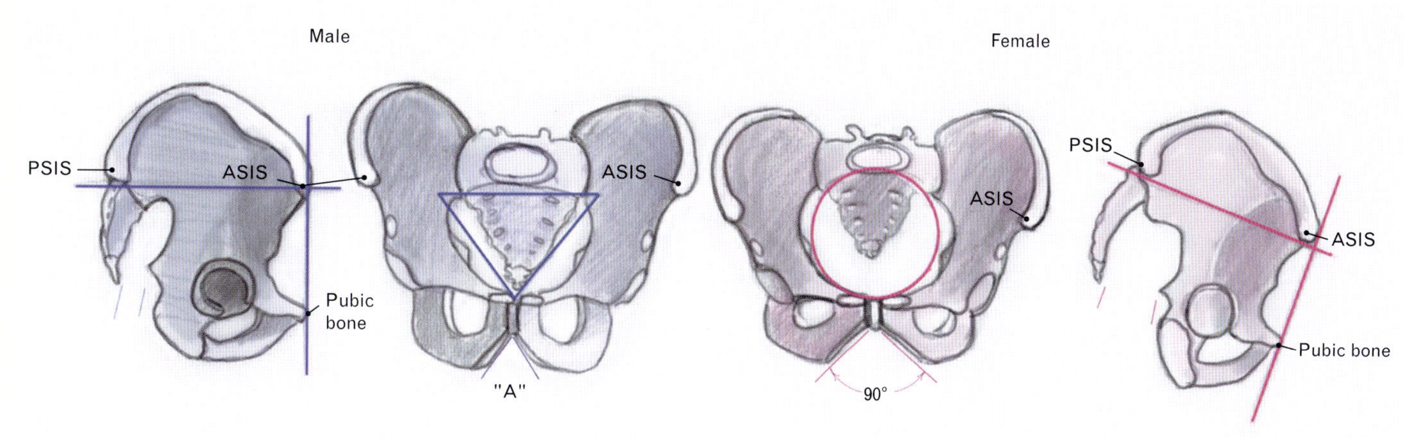

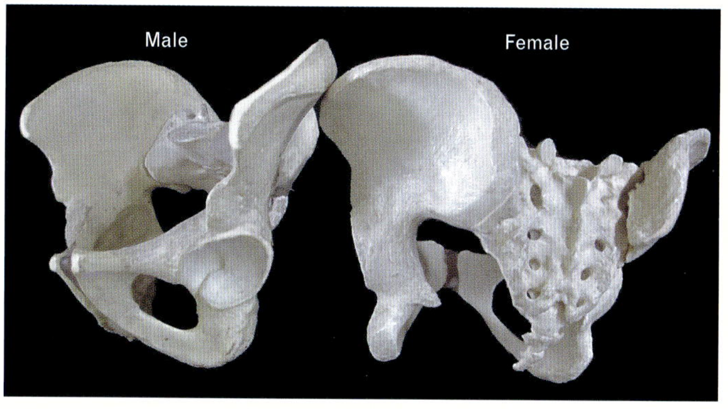

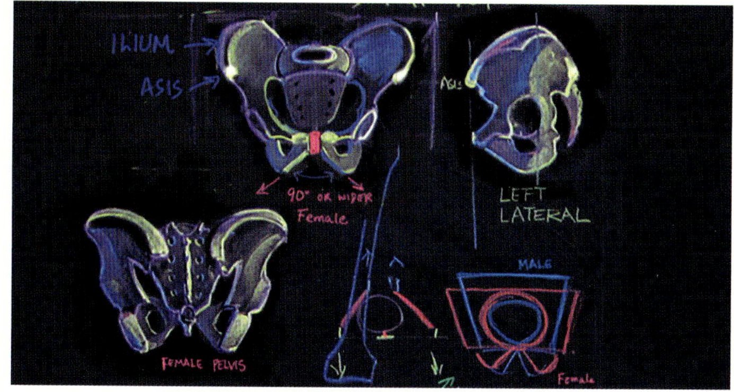

Male and Female Characteristics

There are clear differences between the male and female pelvis. The pubic arch is 90 degrees or wider on women and more like a capital "A" on men. The medical-lab class, easy-to-remember way is to take your hand and look at the space between your thumb and index finger, spread apart: that span represents the female. The index finger and middle finger when spread apart represents the male pubic arch!

The female pelvis is also tipped forward so that the anterior superior iliac spine (ASIS) points are positioned further than the pubic cone. This is important because it makes it easier for women to have better posture.

The small area in red is made of cartilage; it is the pubic symphysis of the pelvis. These pelvises are male.

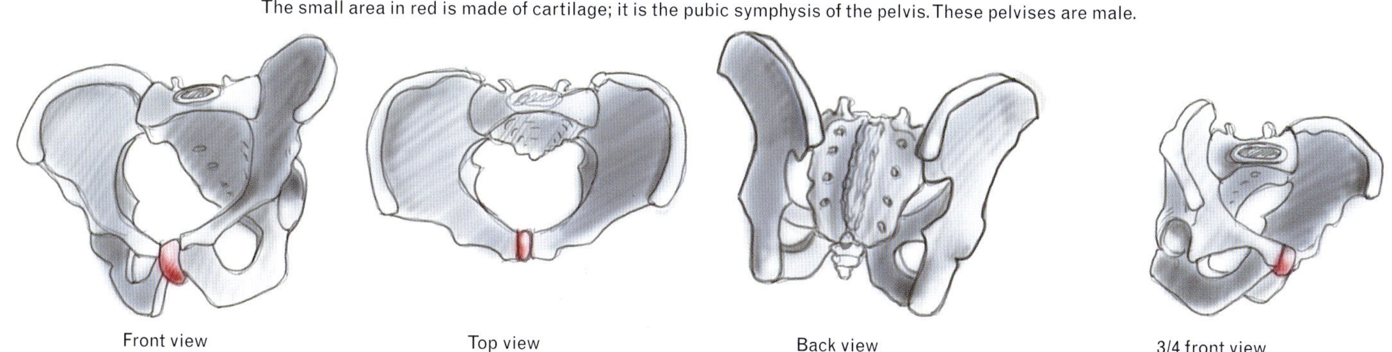

Front view   Top view   Back view   3/4 front view

The Back Torso and Shoulder

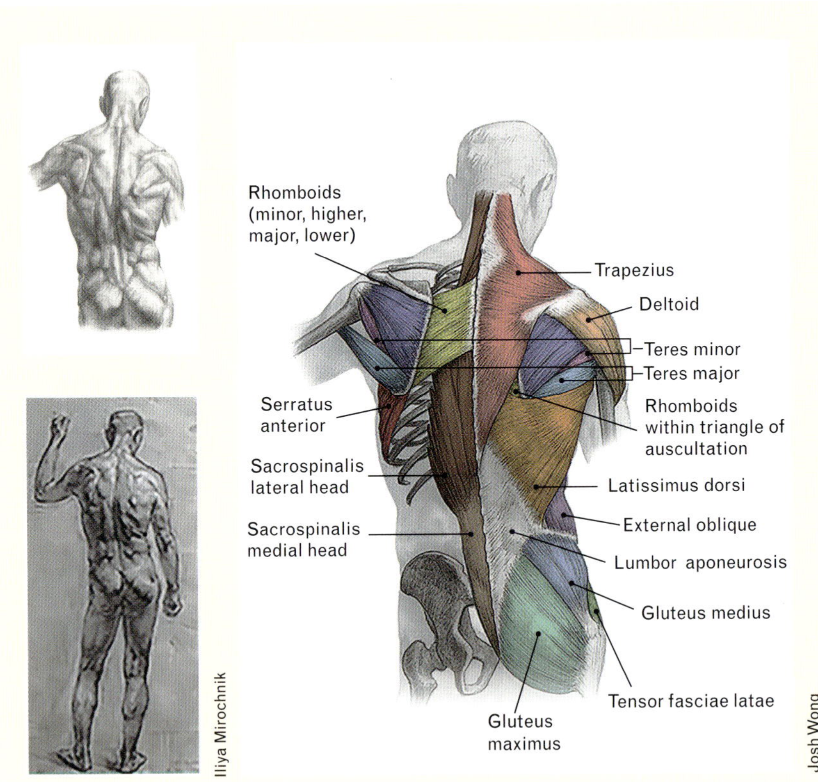

Without thoroughly learning the muscles of the back, it becomes one of the most confusing regions of the body for most artists. The back has some of the most beautiful and elegant combinations of muscle and skeleton than any other region of the body. The scapulae are very helpful bones to use to orient the proportions when drawing the back. The muscles that are on, above, and drape from each scapula create many forms of the back and shoulder. There are two prominent bony aspects of each scapula: one is the medial border, which at rest is somewhat parallel with the vertebra and the other, the spine of the scapula, the distal end of which articulates with the distal end of the clavicle at the top of the shoulder. On the end of the spine of the scapula is the acromion process. On the right, this points to 2 o'clock and on the left, it points to 10 o'clock (see page 127).

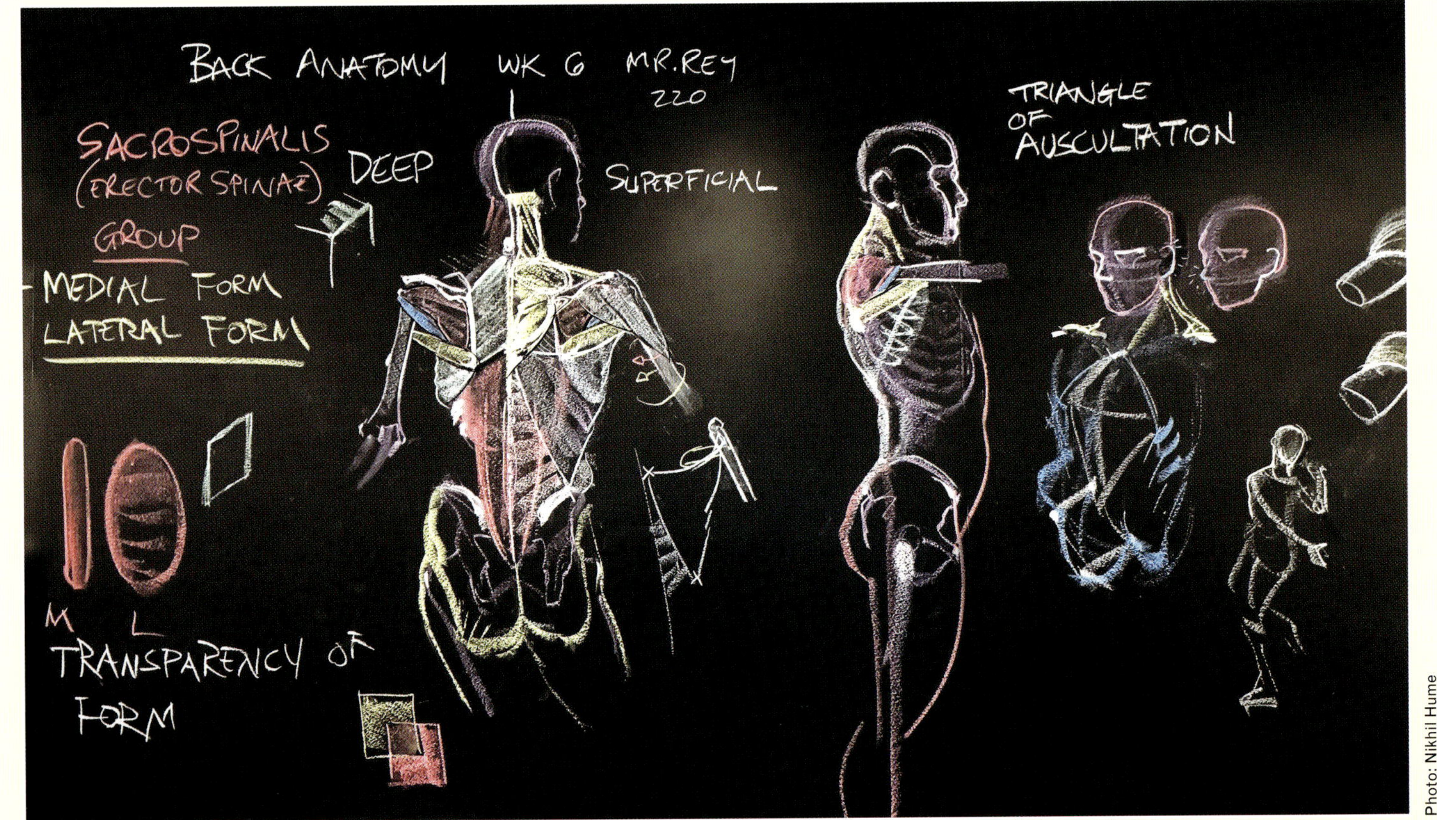

"Without thoroughly learning the muscles of the back, it becomes one of the most confusing regions of the body for most artists."

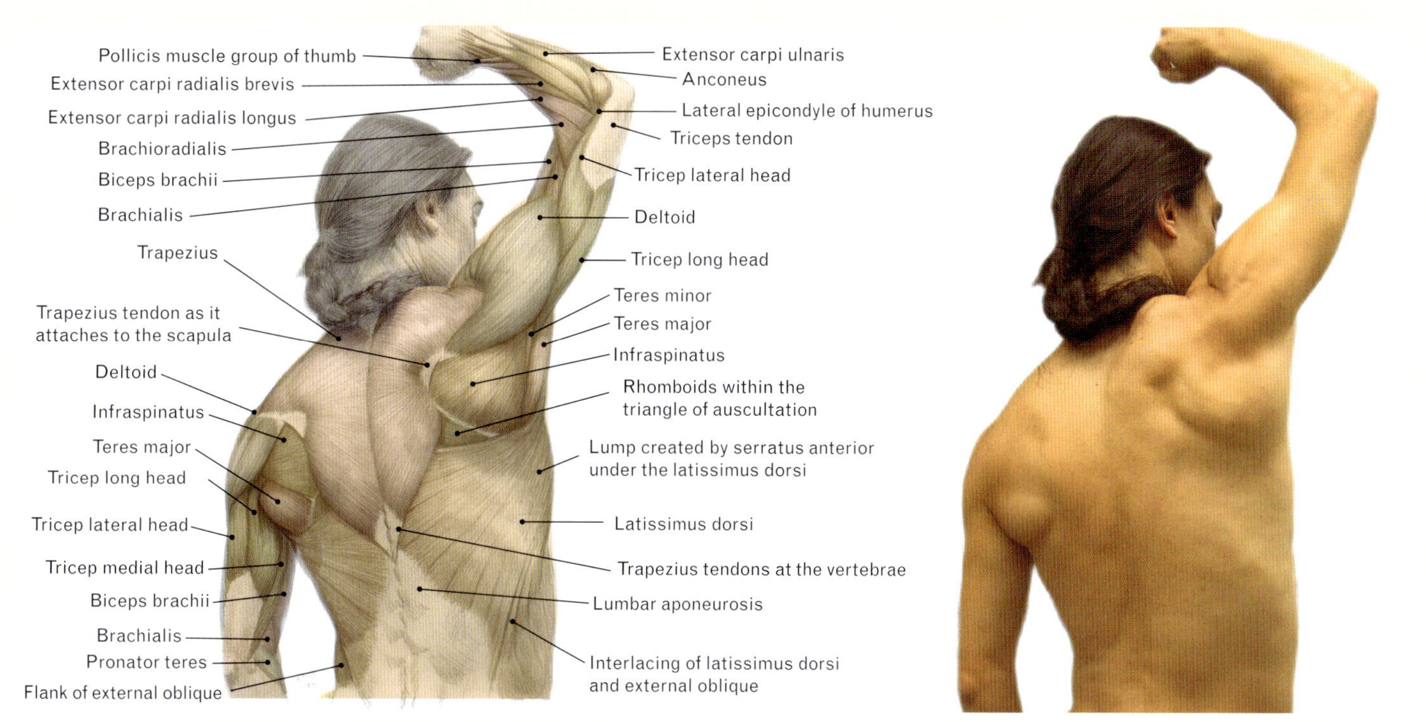

Maybe because I was born in South America, I have always thought that each scapula resembles the continent; this really works to help my students visualize these very important landmark bones of the back and shoulders.

Below is an image of South America as it is on a map or globe. The left scapula is this shape, the right scapula is flipped horizontally. At the lowest tip of the South American–shaped scapula is what I call the "Tierra del Fuego," named for the Argentine province.

This lovely landmark is visible when a model reaches back, places a wrist at the small of the back and then slowly moves the hand upward as if trying to scratch in between the scapulae. In this position, the Tierra del Fuego pops out and away from the thorax (rib cage). Note: You will also see the drapery of the serratus anterior of the Tierra del Fuego moving forward, hugging the side of the thorax and popping out anteriorly in finger-like forms.

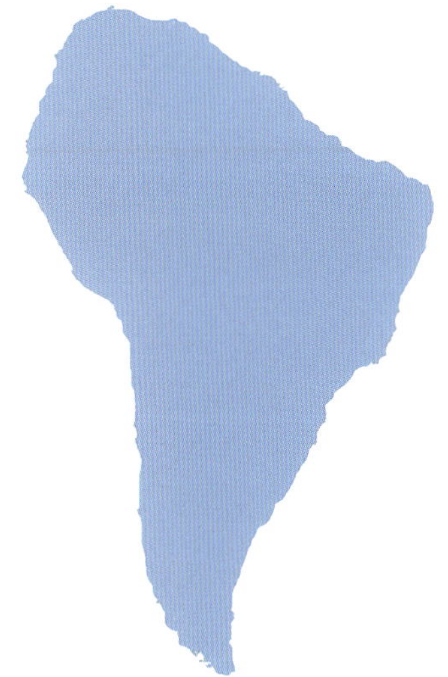

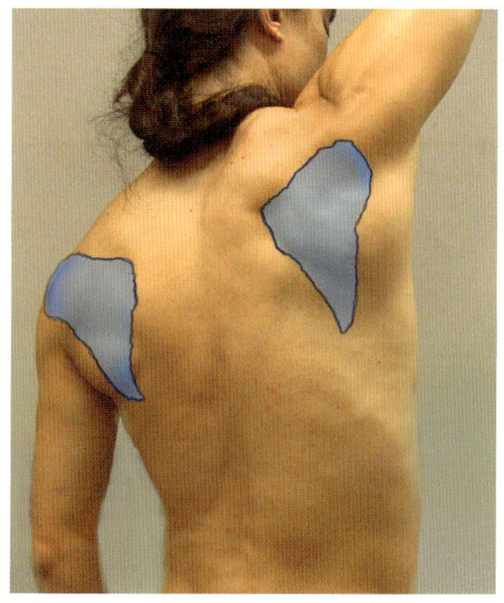

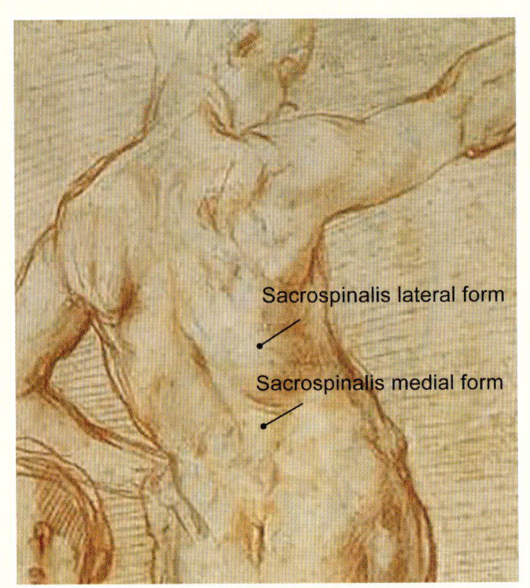

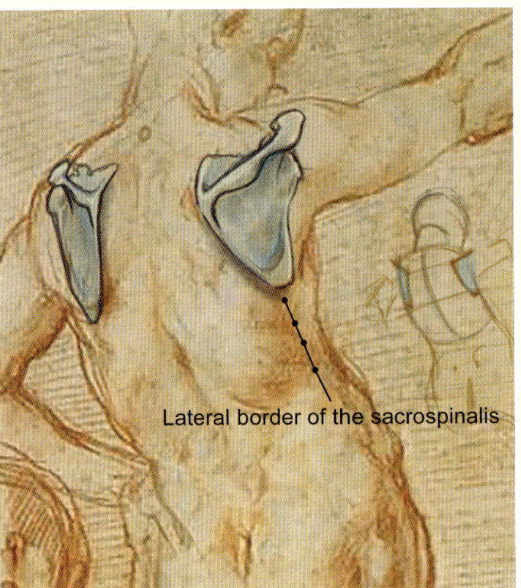

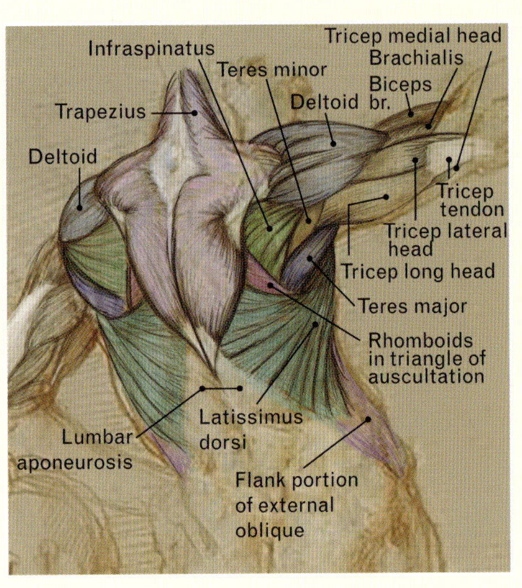

The **sacrospinalis** muscles are the deepest muscles of the back and yet are often the most visible. Sometimes called the erector spinae, this group of muscles rides the length of the vertebral column. They originate at the sacrum and are squeezed in between each **posterior superior iliac spine** (**PSIS**), thus creating two cylindrical forms (the lower lumbar and the thoracic) that become more bulbous as they approach the lower aspect of the thorax.

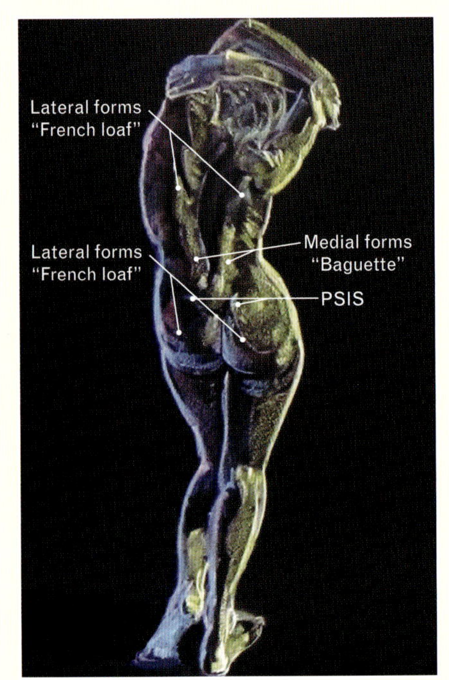

I liken the lower-lumbar medial form (sacrospinalis muscles) to a baguette and the thoracic lateral form to a big French bread loaf. Flanking and covering this group of muscles is the **latissimus dorsi** that ends in a tendinous tissue called the **lumbar aponeurosis**. The sheet-like thinness of the latissimus dorsi, including the aponeurosis, allows the sacrospinalis muscles to visually dominate the back. As the sacrospinalis goes up the vertebra it seems to disappear at the lower points of each scapula. Note: You will not see any evidence of ribs on the back until they clear the lateral border of the sacrospinalis. Exceptions are seen, but rarely, and usually when someone is emaciated.

On Aging

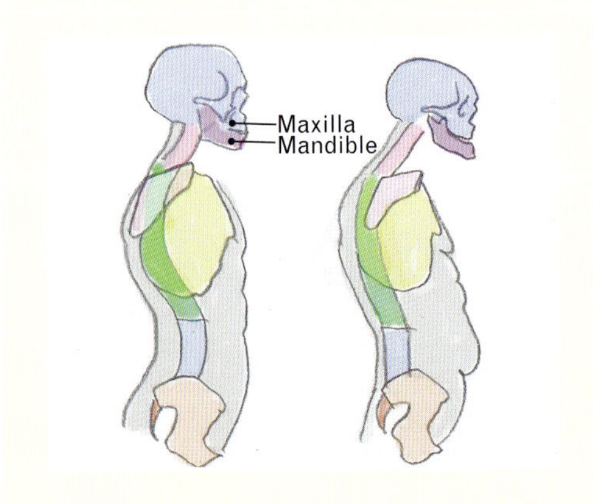

As we age our bodies begin to break down. The spine curves, and arms that were held up in youth by strong muscles begin to droop downward. Loss of teeth is common, and without dentures the mouth collapses and the mandible comes up to meet the maxilla, but with a slight jutting forward effect. The scapulae push toward the front, and the skin that was once taut and full sags as gravity takes its toll. If you were 5'8" as a 30-year-old, by 80 you may be 5'4" or shorter, due to the fact that it is easy to lose 1/8 of an inch of cartilage thickness by compression alone. An 1/8 of an inch times 24 vertebrae = 3 inches. My illustration shows this progression.

THREE MOVEMENTS OF THE SCAPULA

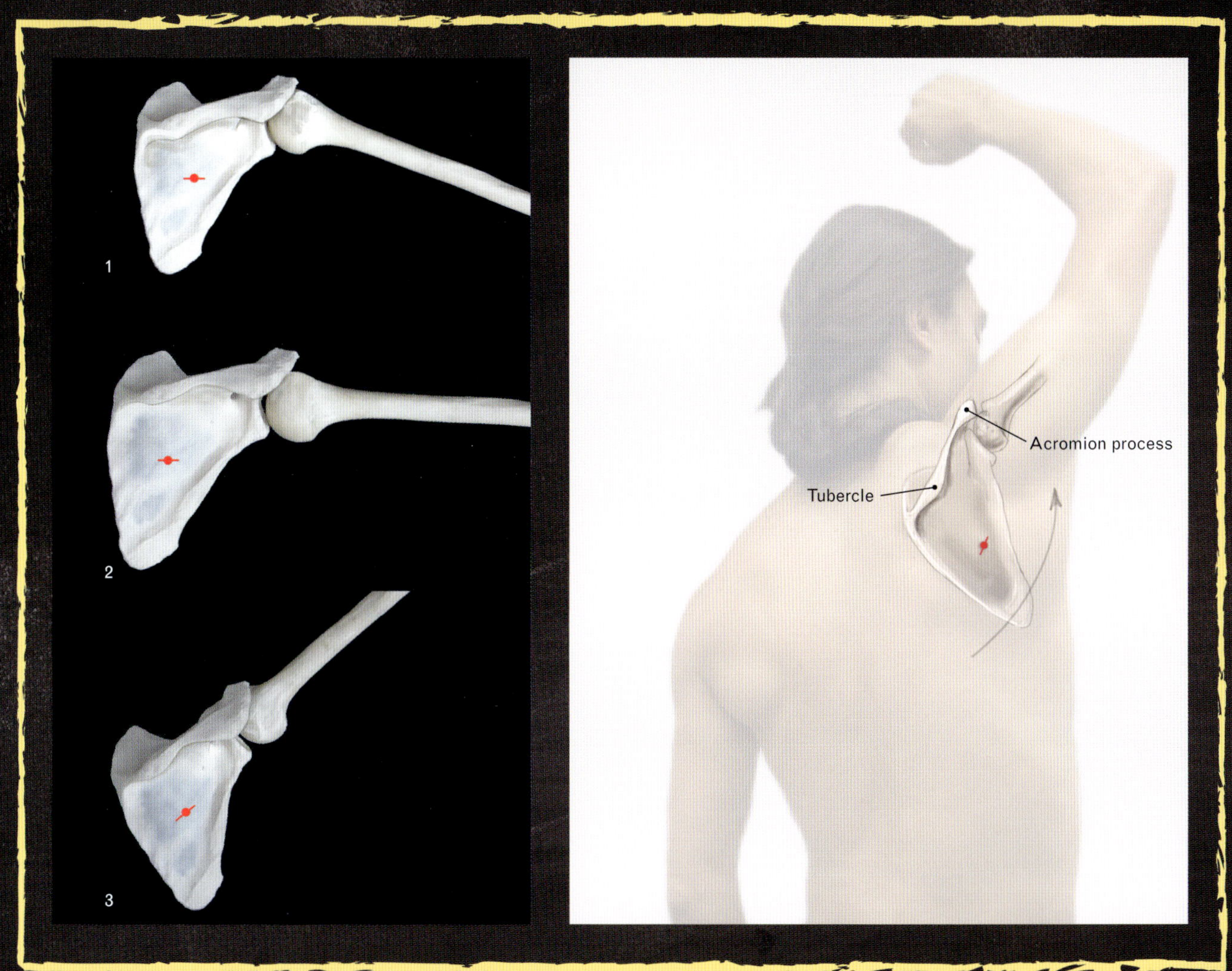

1. The scapula here is in a neutral position as if it were relaxed on its side, or starting to move away, abducting, from the body. The red dot approximates the scapula's pivot point, as if it were a pin.

2. Though still neutral, the scapula is ready to start rotating, in this case, counterclockwise as the humerus continues to move upward. As you may see, the tubercle or bump on the humerus is close to hitting the acromion process. Once the arm hits its horizontal position, the scapula starts its movement.

3. Finally the scapula is put into action so as not to have the two bony aspects, the tubercle of the humerus and the acromion process, hit each other. The scapula rotates from the pivot point and the lower tip pushes out, often pushing the latissimus dorsi creating a bulge on the side contour of the body.

Understanding all of this adds life to your work. It doesn't matter what the media is. I see this information as more critical than ever since many of my students and the industry are creating more digitized art. It is even more important that the artist makes the work more human, more alive rather than doll-like or plastic and artificial in

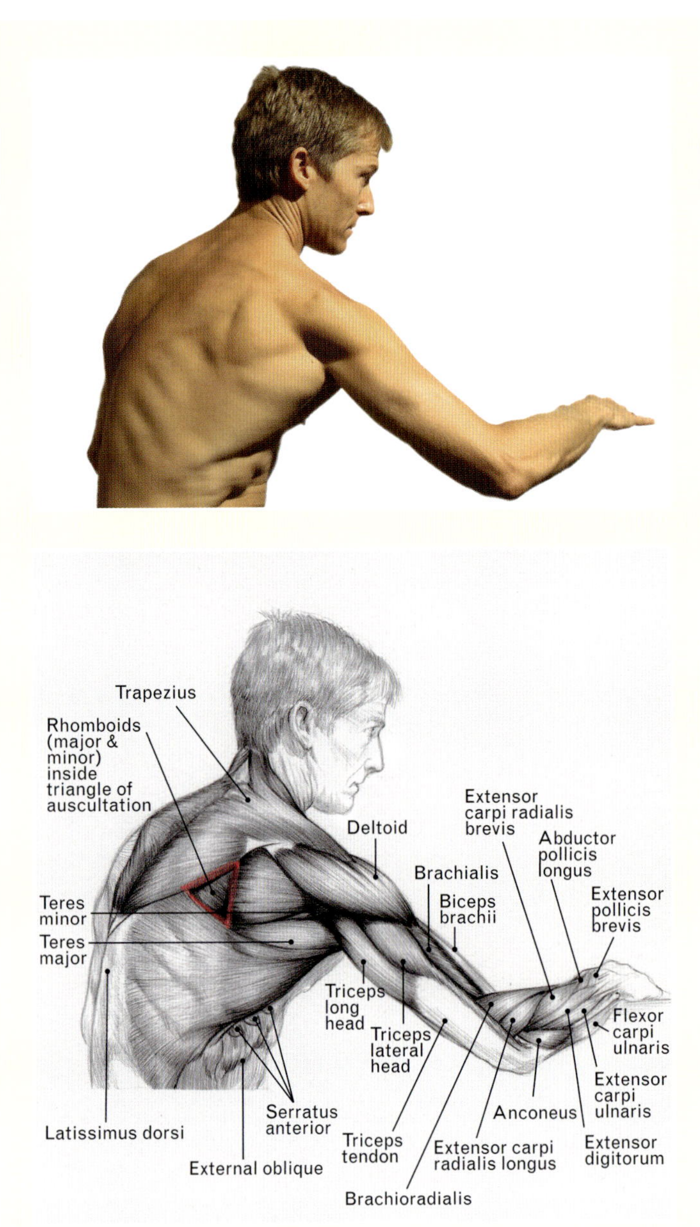

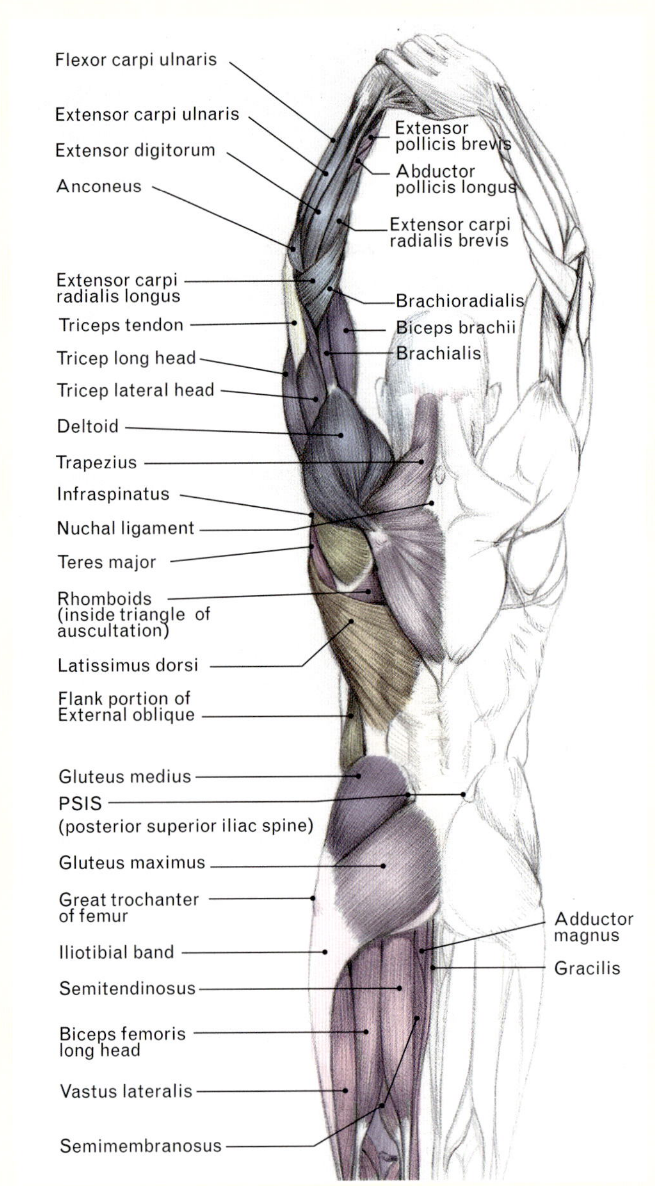

The final helpful point of interest when drawing the back is the **triangle of auscultation,** which was known as far back as 130 AD by the Greek physician Galen. He was one of the first to recognize many physiological aspects of the body. He found that if he put his ear to the back, he could hear whether the patient had a respiratory, circulatory, or gastrointestinal issue because there was a "window," a depression on the back, made bigger by having the patient put their arms forward. This window is the coming together of three forms: the medial border of the scapula, the **trapezius,** and the top part of the latissimus dorsi. To this day doctors place a stethoscope in this triangle, and for us artists it is a great way to navigate the back.

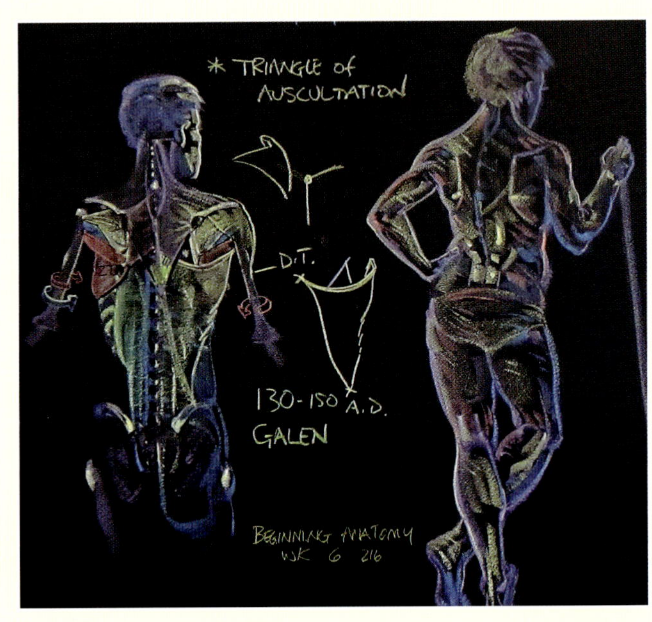

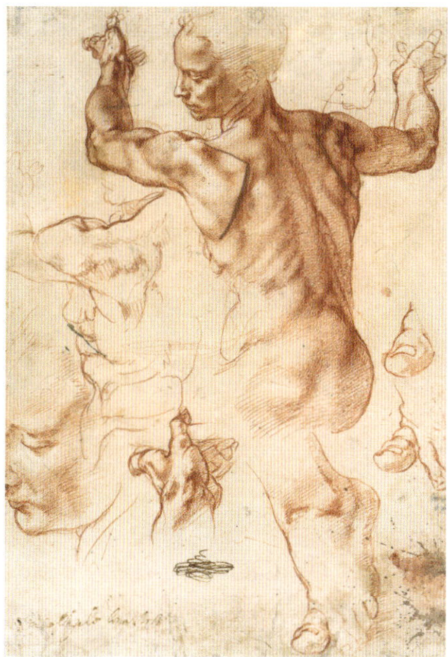
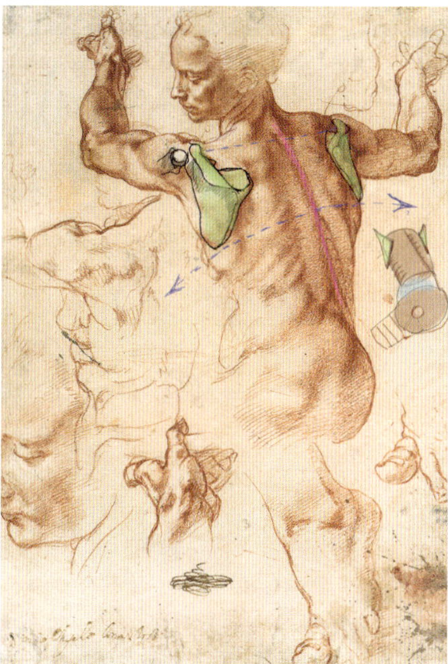
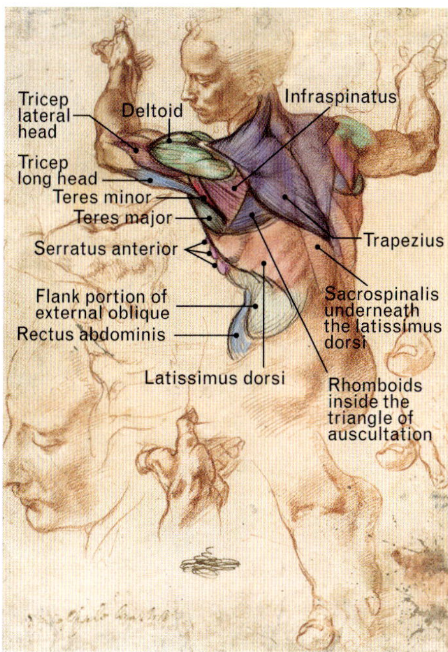

When I was a young student in artist and educator Burne Hogarth's class, I remember how desperately I wanted to learn the back. It was by far the most confusing part of any of the many lectures he had given us. I decided that I would use an old technique from when I was young and trying to learn all the states of America. I started by choosing my "favorite state"—I picked Kansas—and then I learned a bit about that state, its capital, its state flower, etc. I grew fond of Kansas and the next logical step was to know the states bordering it, and then the states that bordered those, and so on.

Well, I did the same with the back muscles. I picked the **teres major** of the back shoulder as my "favorite muscle." (It still is, by the way!) I then learned the muscles that also lie on the scapula, the **teres minor** and the **infraspinatus**, and then the muscles bordering it, the latissimus dorsi, trapezius and the draping of the serratus anterior at the bottom tip of the scapula. I also remembered how I likened the scapula to South America (specifically the lower tip as the Tierra Del Fuego) and made up a story about how before the Panama Canal was put in allowing ships to cut across the narrow isthmus between North and South America, ships would have to go all the way down and around. In class I call that long trip "The Latissimus Dorsi Pass." You can now imagine the latissimus dorsi swooping through that tip of the scapula on its voyage to the humerus. I radiated out in my exploration until the back became so familiar to me that it would never again be a mystery to fear. We fear only what we do not know. The back is now and has been for a long time, my favorite area to draw on any figure.

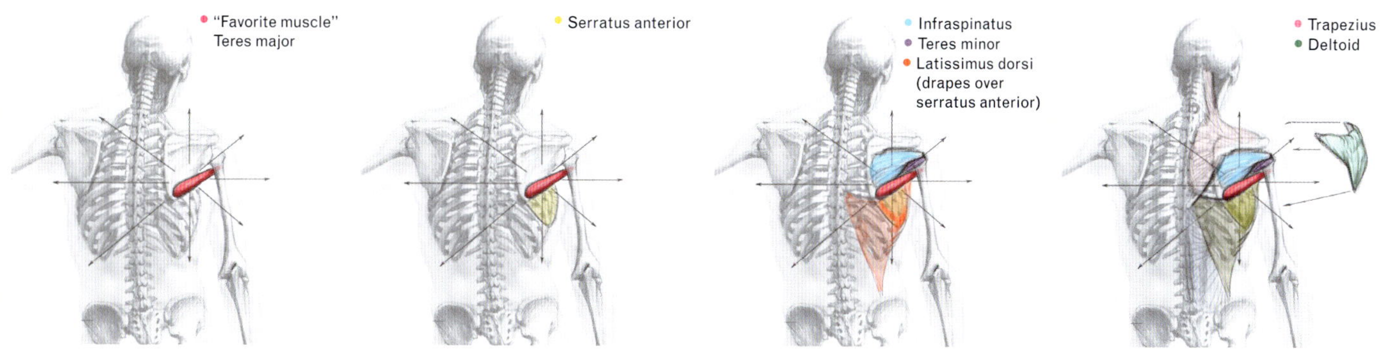

THE ARM

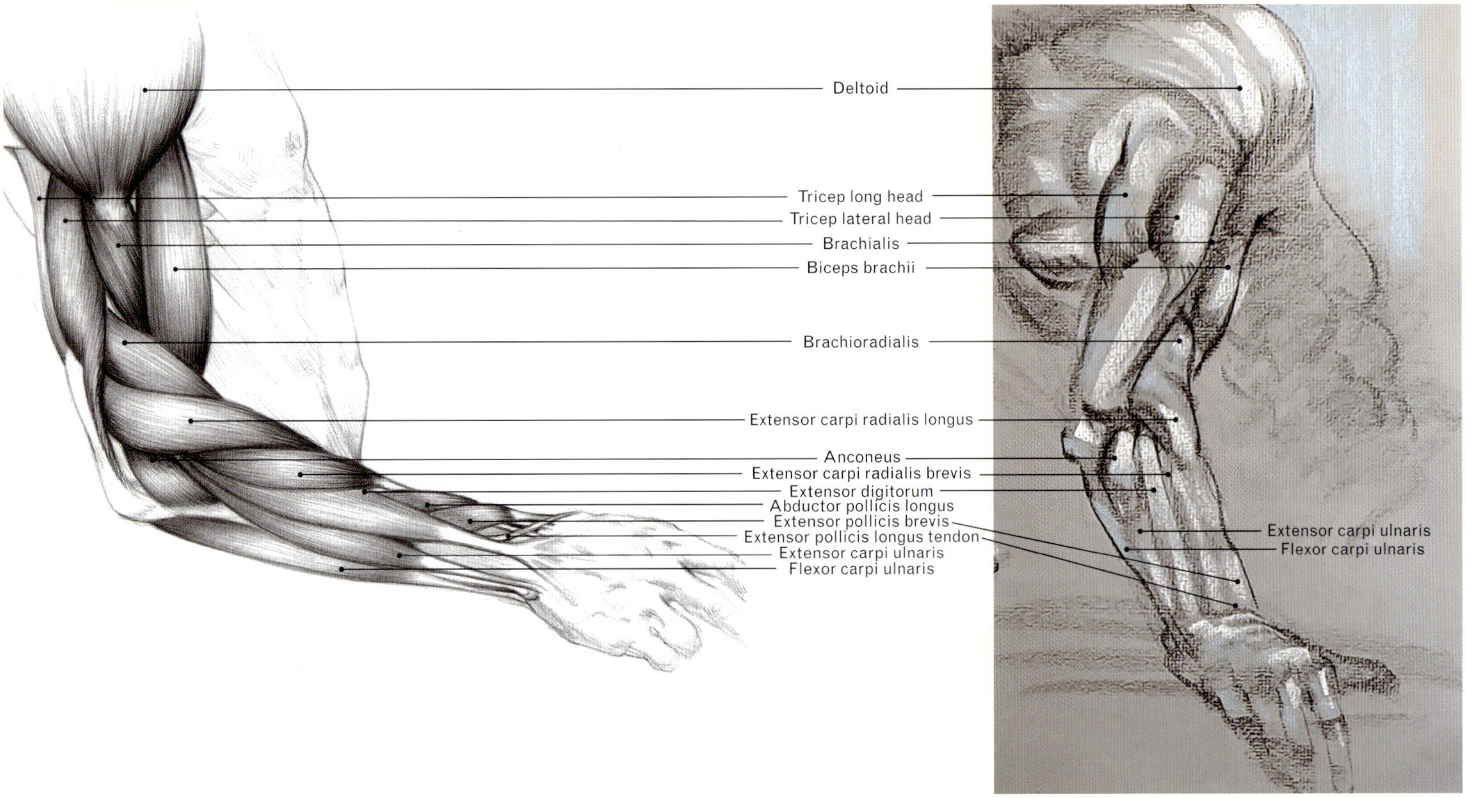

Photo: Jason Mendoza of The Gnomon Workshop

It is obvious to most artists that the hand is extremely important in good figurative art. It is expressive, dynamic, and a focal point in many art pieces. It adds drama and action; it often supports many other aspects of the composition and its numerous parts. The arm as a whole therefore holds the same importance; interconnected with the dynamism of the hand is the highly mobile arm.

From shoulder to wrist the arm extends beyond the body and branches out on its own to add to every aspect of the full-figure composition. The arm is the only part of the body that the model can instantly turn upside down, twist to and fro. Plus, remember, there are two of them!

My lecture on the arms is what many of my students are most afraid of and the consequent homework that follows. But it is also anticipated with fascination and a nervous excitement. I personally love seeing how the Old Masters such as Peter Paul Rubens and Michelangelo depicted arms. They were drawn with power and grace, and rhythm and force in their hands. You can often see studies by many of these great masters of bodies drawn in action and surrounded by many alternate positions of the arms and hand to create just the right look for that composition, whether it be painted or sculpted in the finished work.

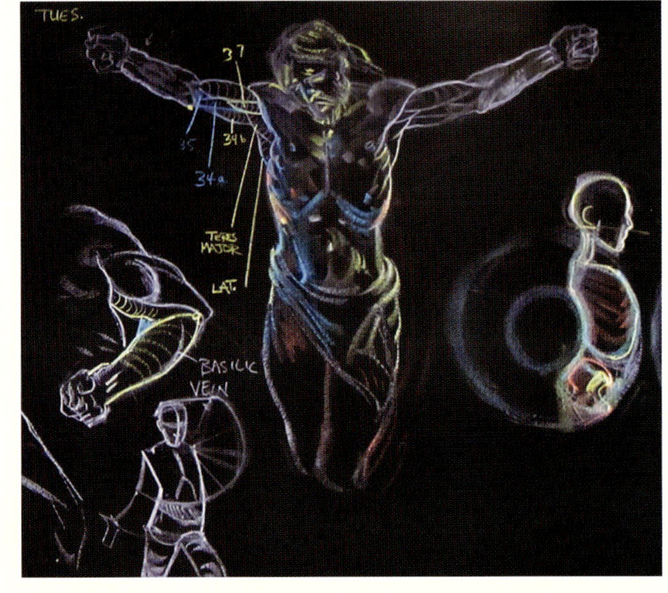

Upper Arm

The upper arm has many muscles that contain the root word "brachium," which means arm. Therefore, you'll see variations of this throughout the muscles of the arm. As mentioned on page 11, biceps brachii, for instance, just refers to "double-headed" muscle of the arm: "bi" (two), "cep" (head), and "brachii" (arm). See? It's easy once you have a Rosetta Stone type of teacher. This distinguishes the biceps brachii from the biceps femoris, which means "double-headed muscle of the thigh." So, I can use the word simply as biceps if the conversation is about the arm, no need to use the "last name" brachii, but if I am talking in general, then I have to be specific, biceps brachii or biceps femoris. It's like having two friends named Susie. To distinguish one from the other you would refer to them as Susie Smith or Susie Gutierrez to make it clear as to which Susie you are referring to.

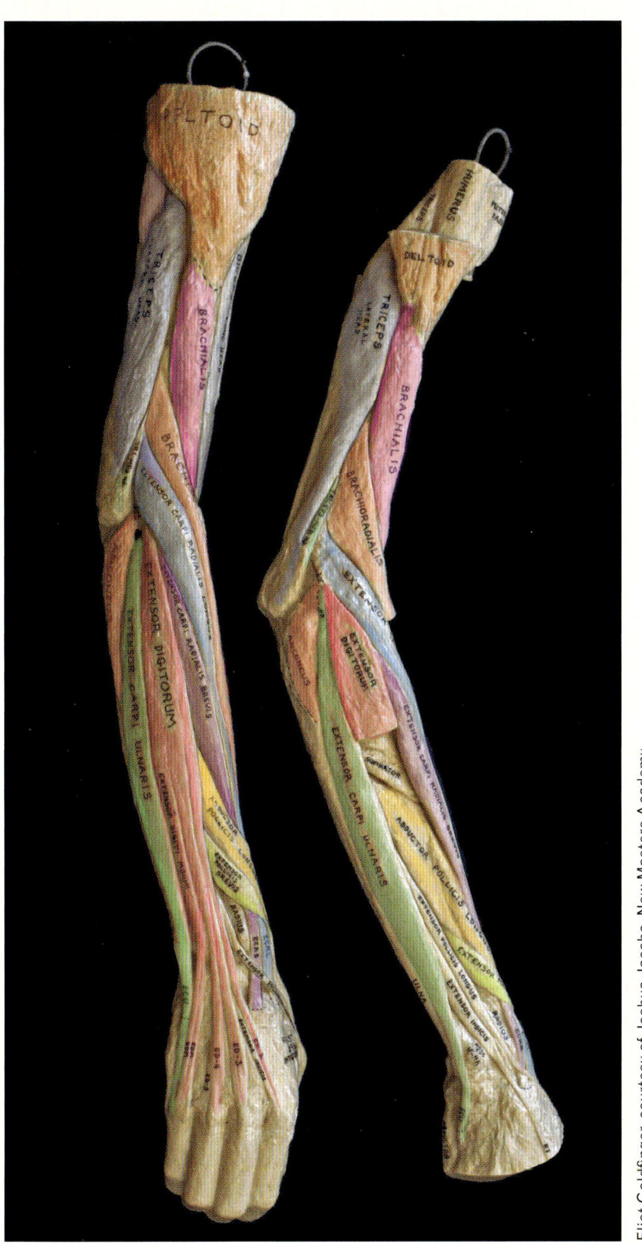

Eliot Goldfinger, courtesy of Joshua Jacobo, New Masters Academy

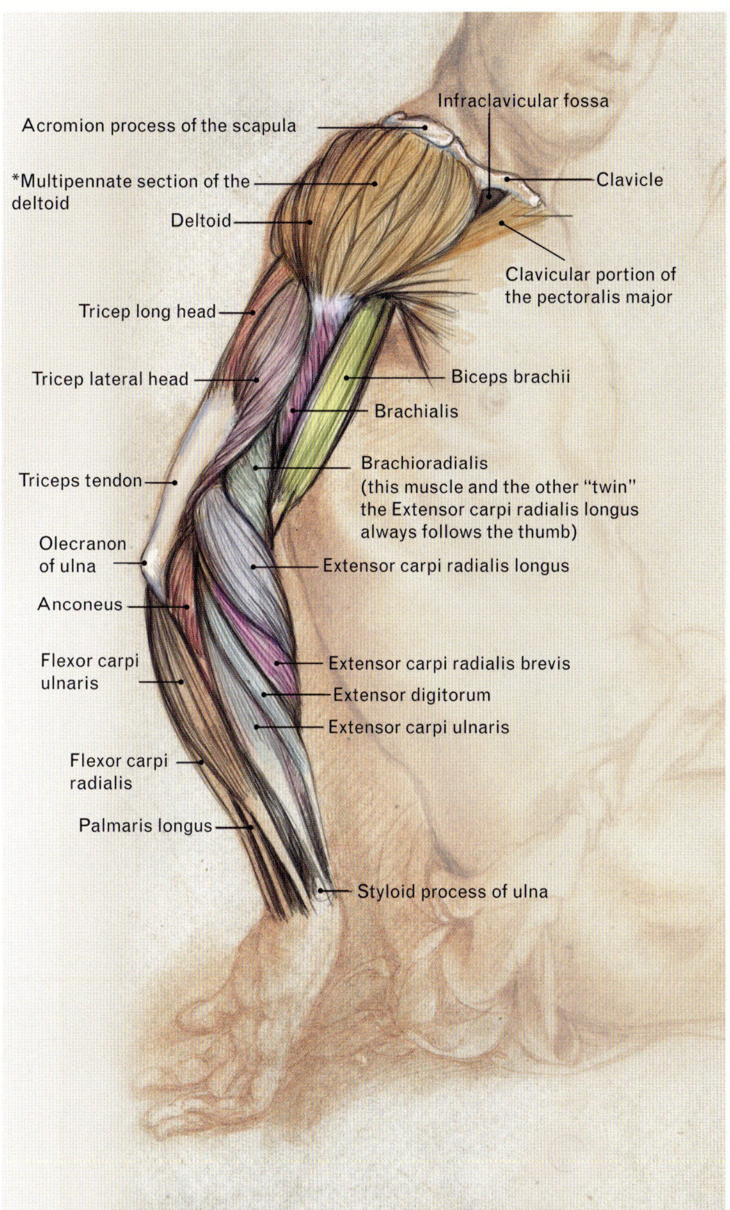

*Pennate refers to the feather-like design of the center section of the deltoid. See how it looks like feathers? This adds strength to the muscle since the center section abducts the arm, and does not have many other muscles to help with that action.

Arm Skeleton

Front

The radius always follows the thumb.
The ulna follows the pinky finger.

This is important when rotating the
arms on the live model.

Back

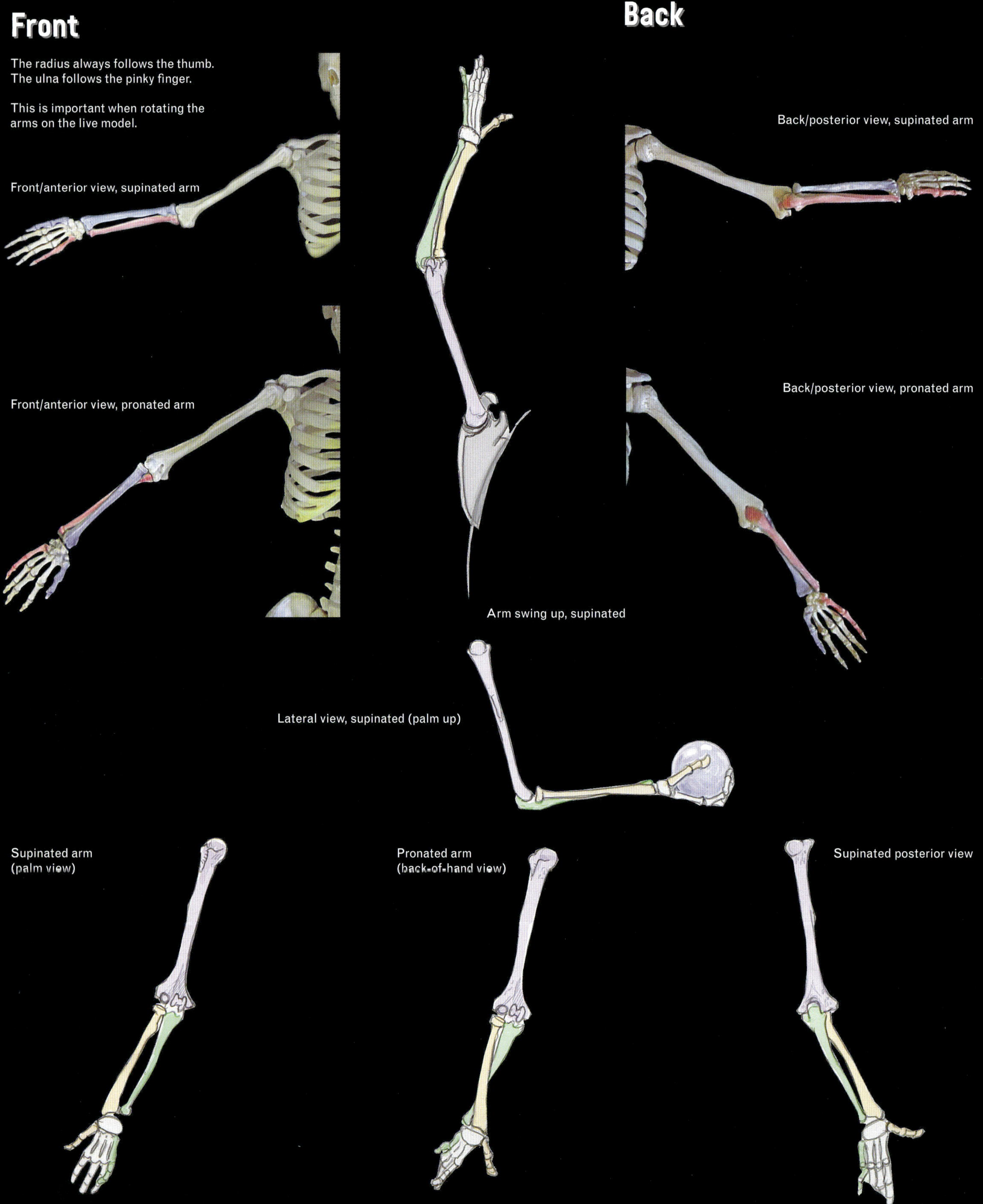

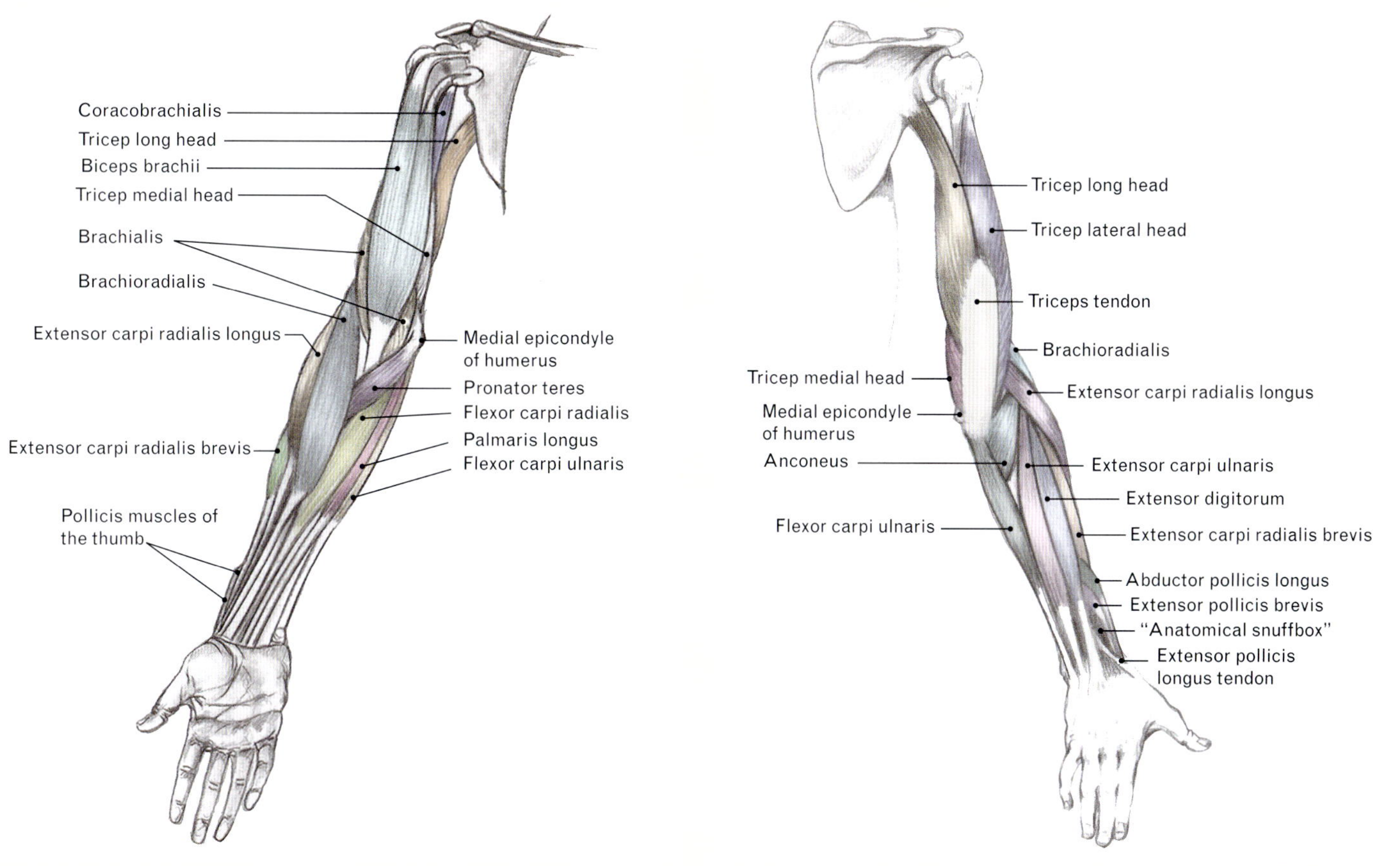

Coracobrachialis
Tricep long head
Biceps brachii
Tricep medial head
Brachialis
Brachioradialis
Extensor carpi radialis longus
Extensor carpi radialis brevis
Pollicis muscles of the thumb
Medial epicondyle of humerus
Pronator teres
Flexor carpi radialis
Palmaris longus
Flexor carpi ulnaris
Tricep long head
Tricep lateral head
Triceps tendon
Brachioradialis
Tricep medial head
Medial epicondyle of humerus
Anconeus
Flexor carpi ulnaris
Extensor carpi radialis longus
Extensor carpi ulnaris
Extensor digitorum
Extensor carpi radialis brevis
Abductor pollicis longus
Extensor pollicis brevis
"Anatomical snuffbox"
Extensor pollicis longus tendon
EPL (t) = Extensor pollicis longus (tendon) 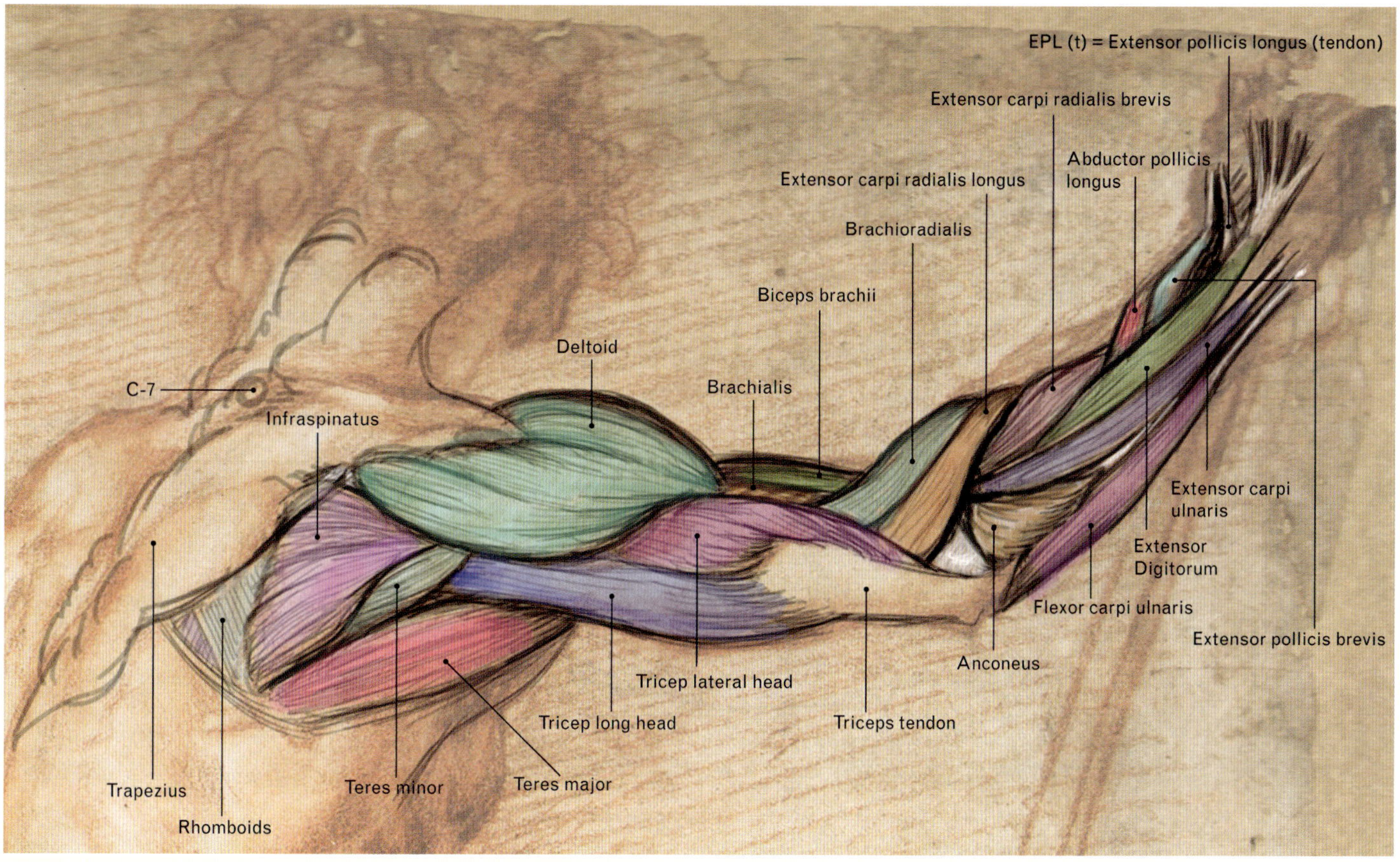
Extensor carpi radialis brevis
Extensor carpi radialis longus
Abductor pollicis longus
Brachioradialis
Biceps brachii
Deltoid
Brachialis
C-7
Infraspinatus
Extensor carpi ulnaris
Extensor Digitorum
Flexor carpi ulnaris
Extensor pollicis brevis
Anconeus
Trapezius
Rhomboids
Teres minor
Teres major
Tricep long head
Tricep lateral head
Triceps tendon

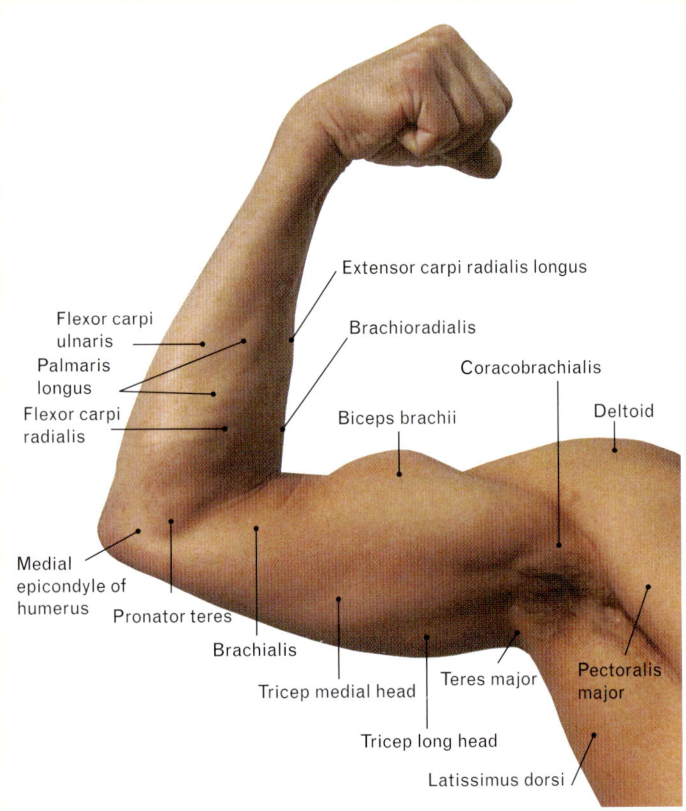

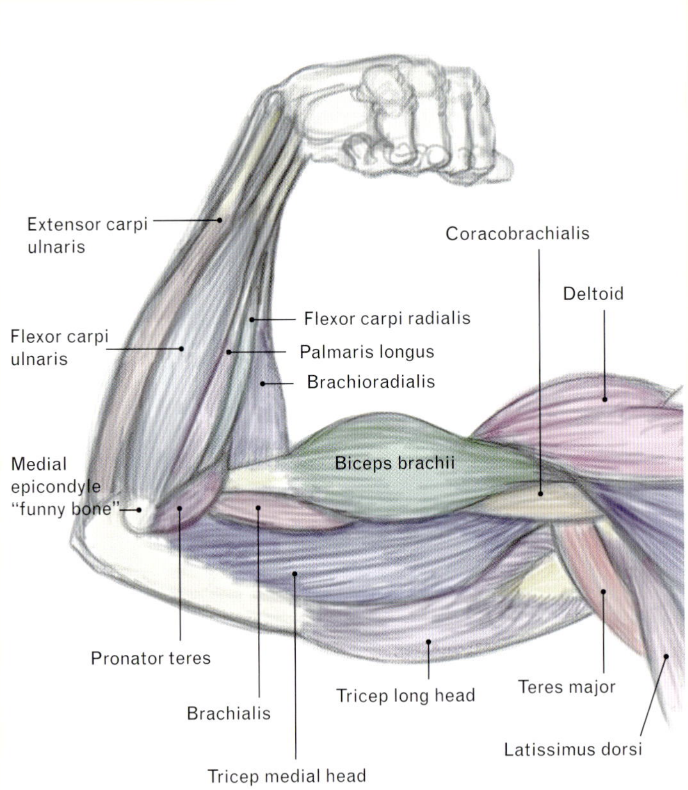

The following is a list of the upper arm muscles essential to every artist: **biceps brachii**, **brachioradialis**, **brachialis**, **tricep medial head**, **tricep long head**, **tricep lateral head**, **coracobrachialis**, and the **deltoid**. These are the muscles that create the look of the arm, all of the peaks and valleys that are seen on all of us: young, old, male, and female. The study of these muscles will better enable the artist to create from the imagination more expressive and believable arms, especially in dynamic poses. It also facilitates drawing from pure observation of a live model, or to augment the live model to better express oneself, which is often an artist's ultimate goal.

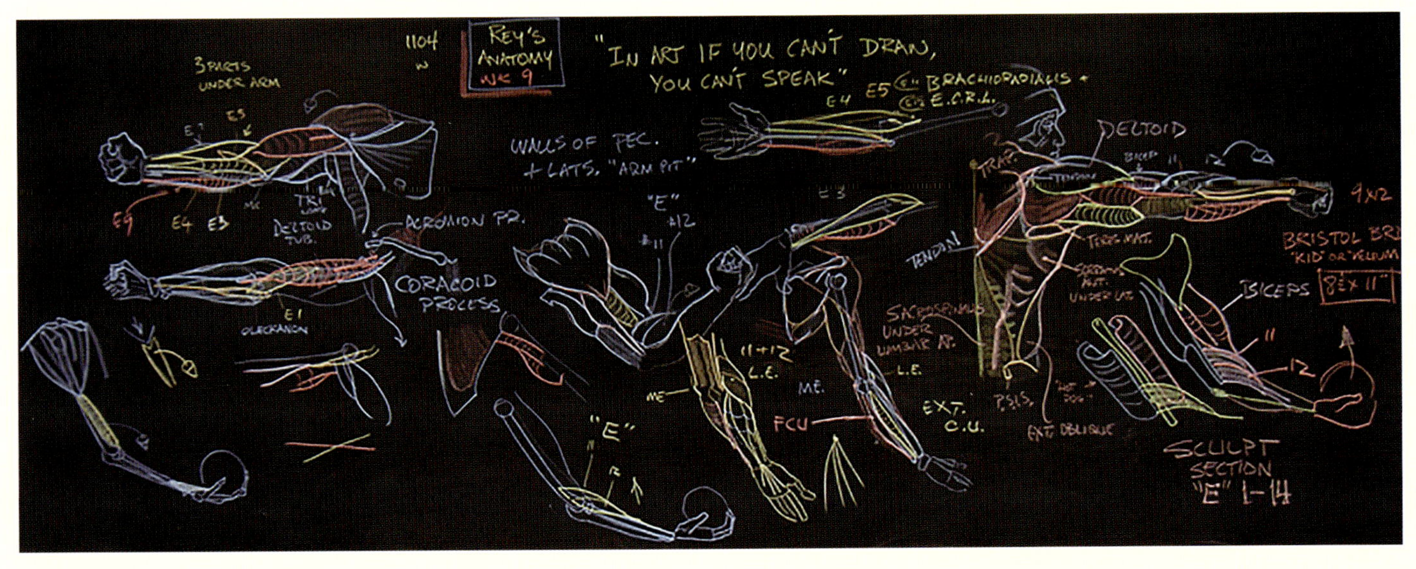

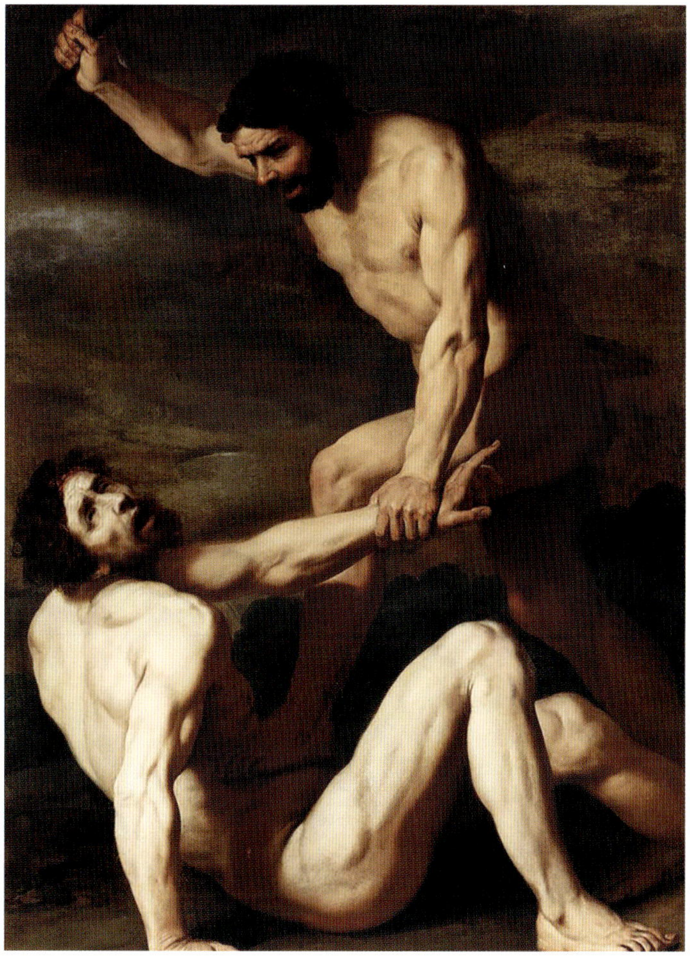

Daniele Crespi, *Cain Killing Abel*, c. 1618

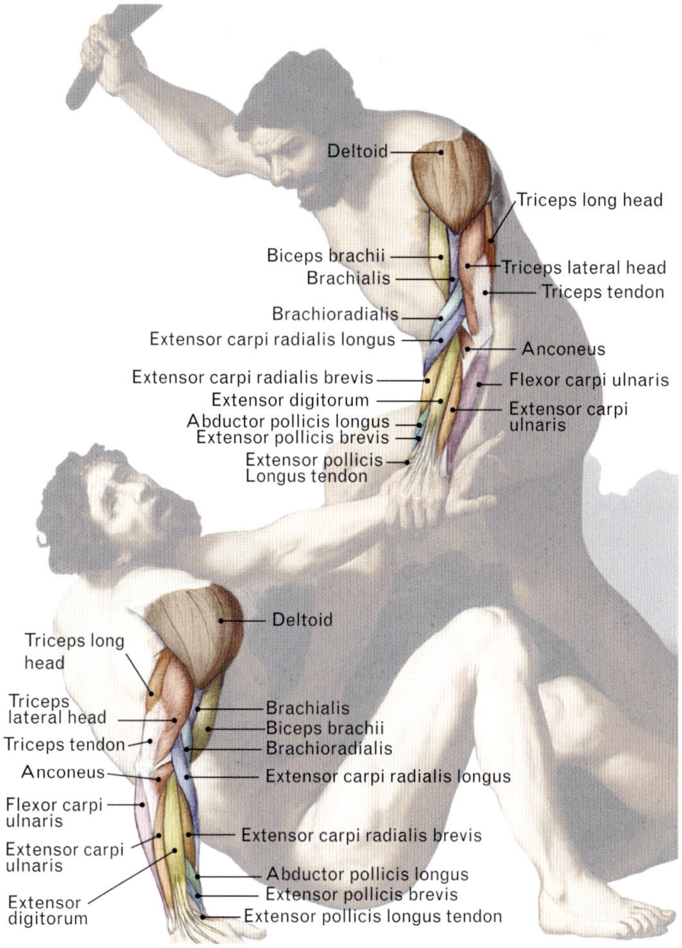

The forearm muscles often give anatomy students a headache and understandably so. The forearms contain many of the complicated muscles that allow us to activate not only our arms but more significantly, they are the power source for the most amazing mechanical objects on the planet: the human hands. I have learned to reduce these forearm muscles to the ones that most significantly create the shape of the arm structure, the morphology.

As complicated as these muscles are, the lower-arm muscles can be separated into four simple visible groups: the **flexors**, the **extensors**, the **"twins,"** and finally the **"mini twins."**

As artists, we only need to concern ourselves with the few muscles that define the external form. I have reduced these important muscles to the four flexor muscles on the **palmar aspect of the forearm: palmaris longus, flexor carpi radialis, pronator teres** and the **flexor carpi ulnaris.**

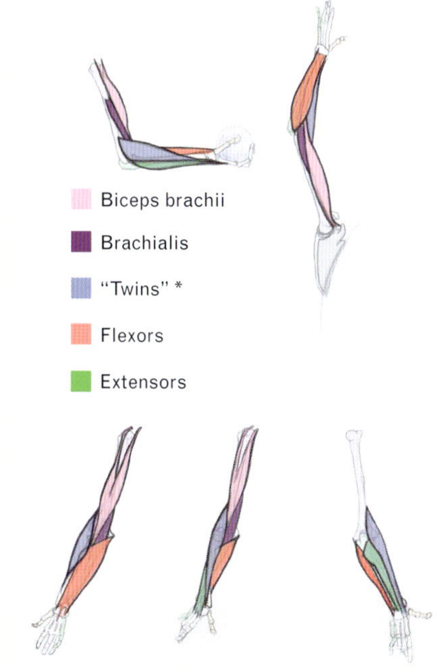

These are the four major tendons of the distal arm.
Most tendons do not have their own names like the Achilles tendon;
instead, they get the name of the muscle.

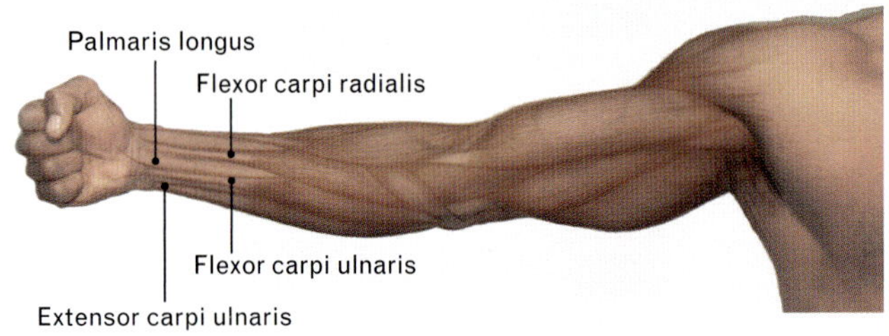

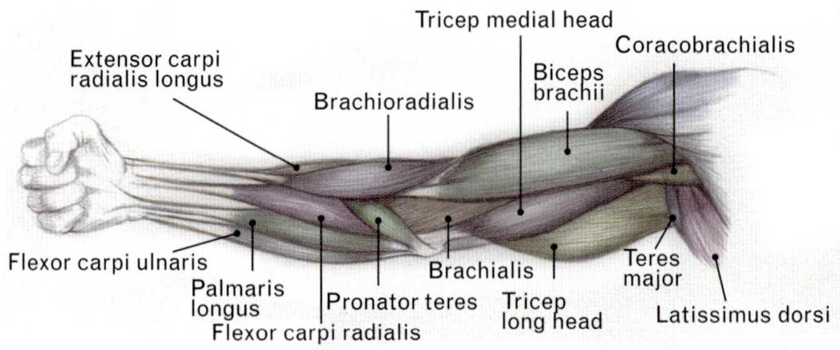

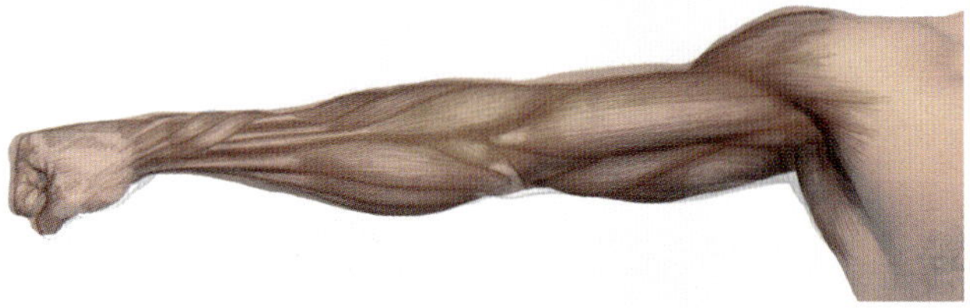

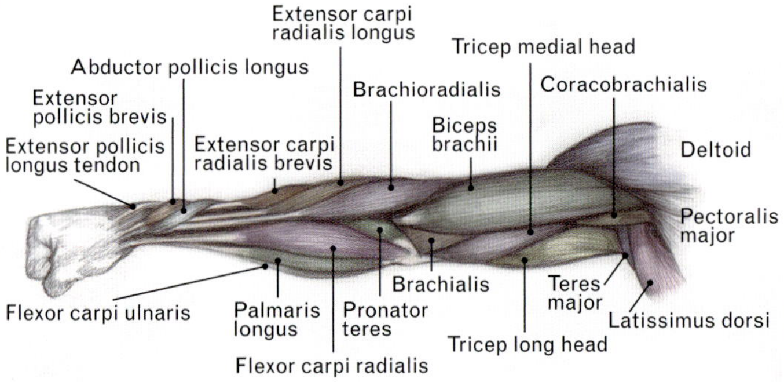

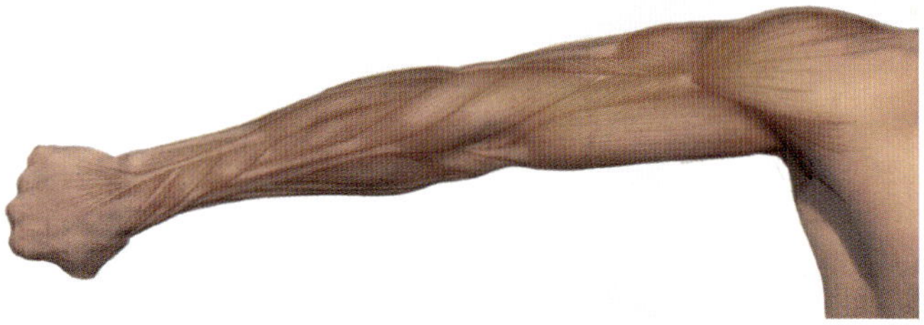

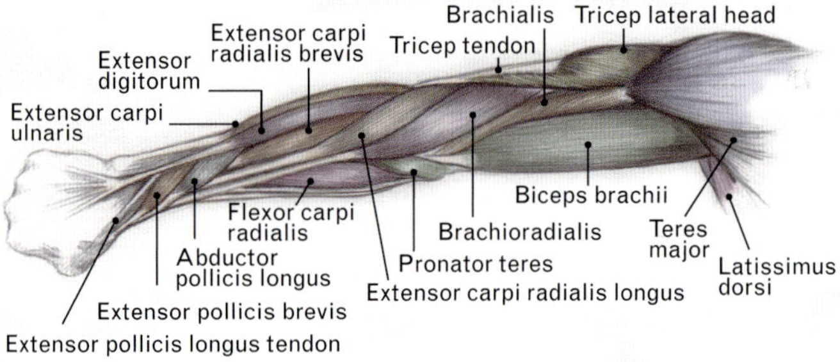

All of these originate in the same general area of the arm, the **medial epicondyle** (a.k.a. the funny bone) and radiate out onto the arm toward the hand.

As far as the extensors are concerned, to even things out I have also reduced these to four essential muscles: **extensor digitorum, extensor carpi radialis brevis, extensor carpi ulnaris** and the triangular in shape **anconeus**. These all originate in the general area of the **lateral epicondyle** and spread out toward the back of your hand. The separator or border between the flexors and extensors is the crest of the ulna. This same exact border is also called the **ulnar furrow** on the living form.

Along with the flexors and the extensors are the **brachioradialis** and the **extensor carpi radius longus**, which I call "twins" because they look so similar to each other. These muscles originate on the lateral and lower aspect of the humerus splitting the **biceps** and the **triceps** and roughly following the thumb. They are seen as one form except in very lean and defined individuals. The other set of muscles are thumb muscles that I call the "mini twins," the **abductor pollicis longus,** and the **extensor pollicis brevis**, because of their resemblance to the larger twins.

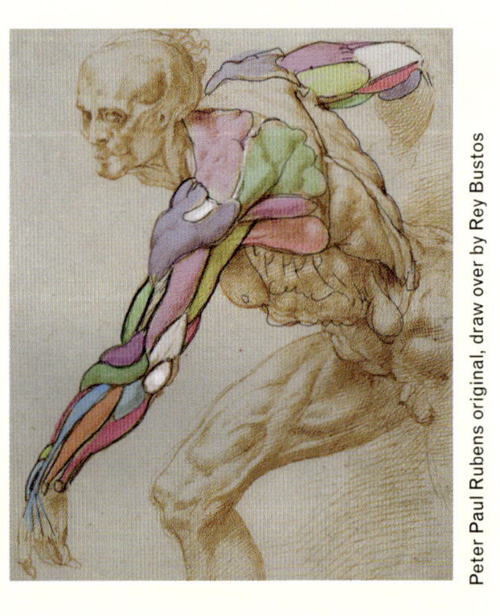

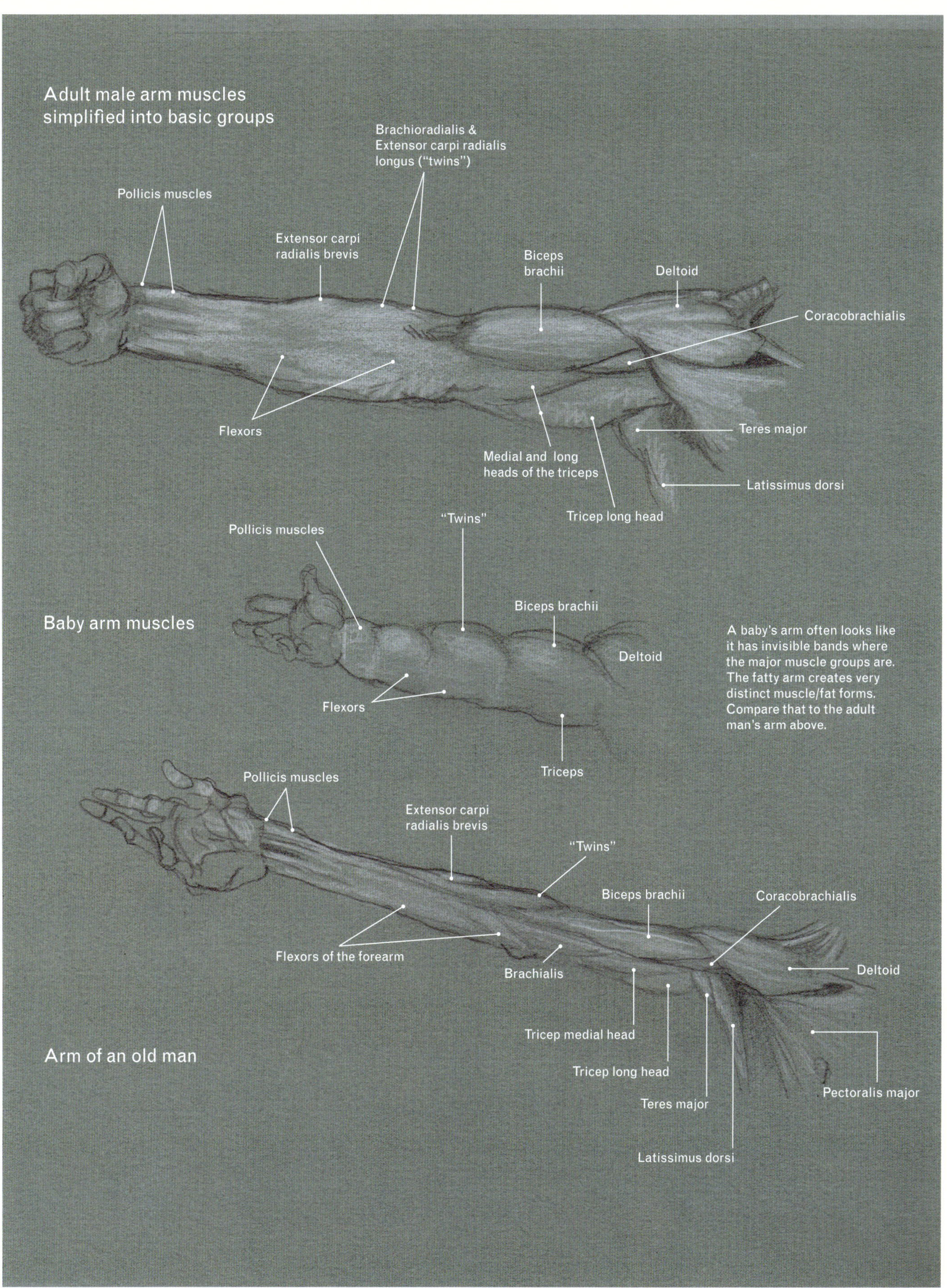

Adult male arm muscles
simplified into basic groups

Pollicis muscles

Brachioradialis &
Extensor carpi radialis
longus ("twins")

Extensor carpi
radialis brevis

Biceps
brachii

Deltoid

Coracobrachialis

Flexors

Medial and long
heads of the triceps

Tricep long head

Teres major

Latissimus dorsi

Baby arm muscles

Pollicis muscles

"Twins"

Biceps brachii

Deltoid

Flexors

A baby's arm often looks like
it has invisible bands where
the major muscle groups are.
The fatty arm creates very
distinct muscle/fat forms.
Compare that to the adult
man's arm above.

Triceps

Pollicis muscles

Extensor carpi
radialis brevis

"Twins"

Biceps brachii

Coracobrachialis

Flexors of the forearm

Brachialis

Deltoid

Tricep medial head

Tricep long head

Teres major

Pectoralis major

Latissimus dorsi

Arm of an old man

THE HAND

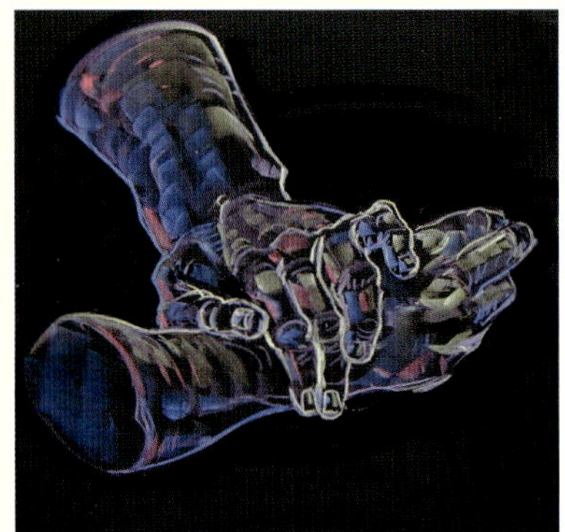

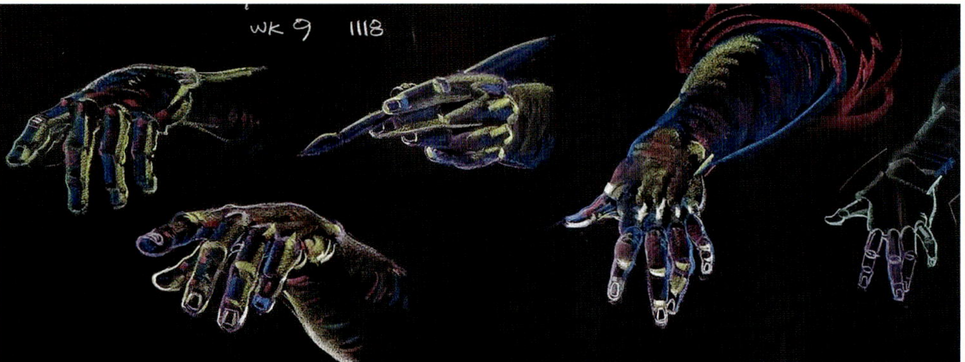

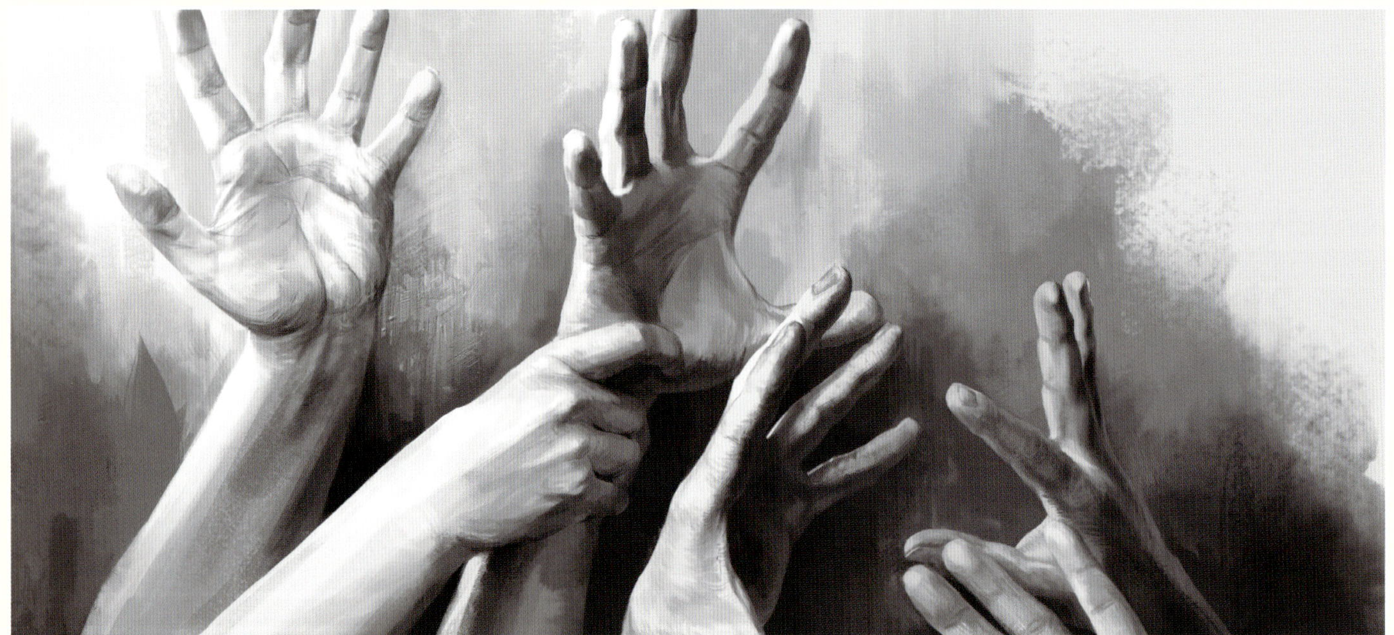

Minji Kim

Handedness

A characteristic that can often be determined by studying bones is that when you have the entire skeleton, you can measure bones and determine the handedness of an individual. Quite simply, you can measure the thickness of each humerus, for example, and its deltoid tuberosity, where the deltoid muscle is attached, and see that one side is bigger than the other. If the thicker, heavier bones are on the right side, well then, that person was right-handed.

On a living person, you can often see that one clavicle is slightly larger than the other, as well as the hand itself. I am right-handed, and it shows: my right hand looks thicker, veiny, and slightly larger than my left.

This extends to the arm too: one arm, in my case, my right, is larger in musculature.

The human hand is an engineering marvel. The hand is made up of 27 bones, eight **carpal** (wrist), five **metacarpal** (palm), and 14 **phalanges** (fingers). The human fingers contain some of the densest areas of nerves anywhere in the body making them the greatest source of tactile feedback. We first experience the world as babies with our little hands. We touch and are touched with hands and we never lose the desire to examine and feel everything from our pets to a loved one's face. The hand is prehensile, which means that it is capable of grasping. With an opposable thumb we are able to perform an amazing array of functions.

Male and Female Characteristics

Did you know that men generally have longer ring fingers than index fingers? Women by contrast tend to have longer index fingers than their ring fingers. This is due to the level of exposure to sex hormones while in utero. Look and see for yourself. You'll be amazed how often this digit ratio happens. In my classroom it often holds true and provides a moment of levity and laughter as my students examine each other's hands.

In depicting hands, I have often seen that in many cases the Old Masters would draw men's hands in a more aggressive manner with more exposed tendons and veins due to the fact that men have less subcutaneous fat on the top of their hands. The fingers are thicker and squarer along with the fingernails. Women's hands would be more graceful with tapered fingers and longer, more narrow fingernails; less tendon and vein detail, unless it is of an older woman.

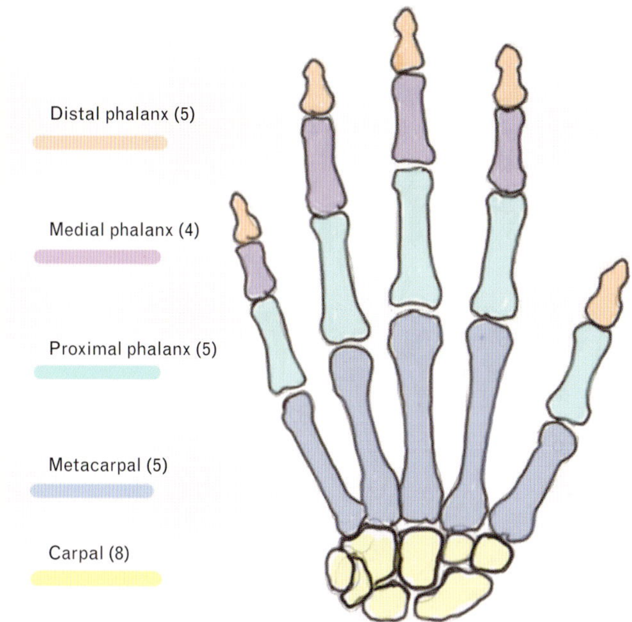

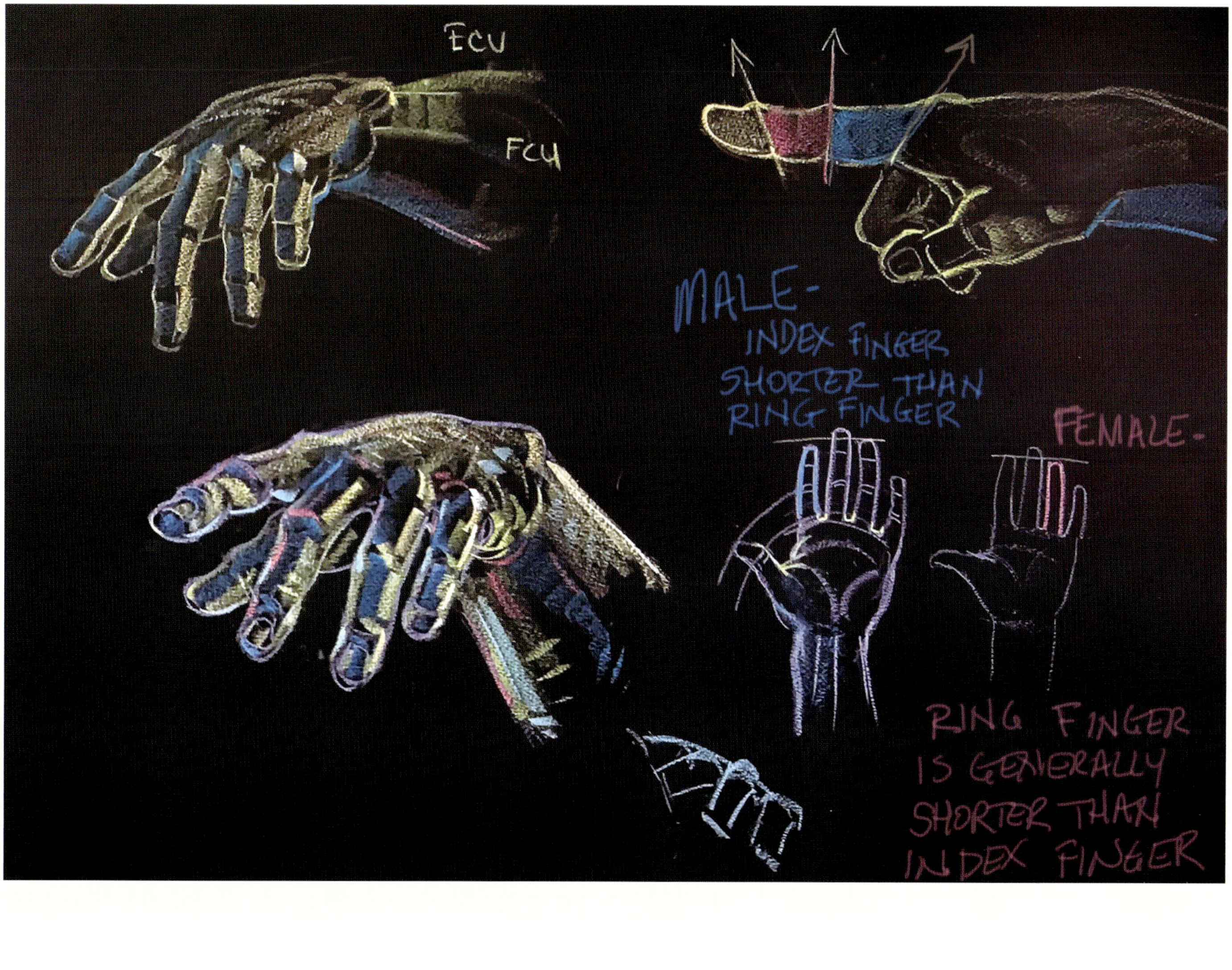

THE ANATOMICAL SNUFFBOX

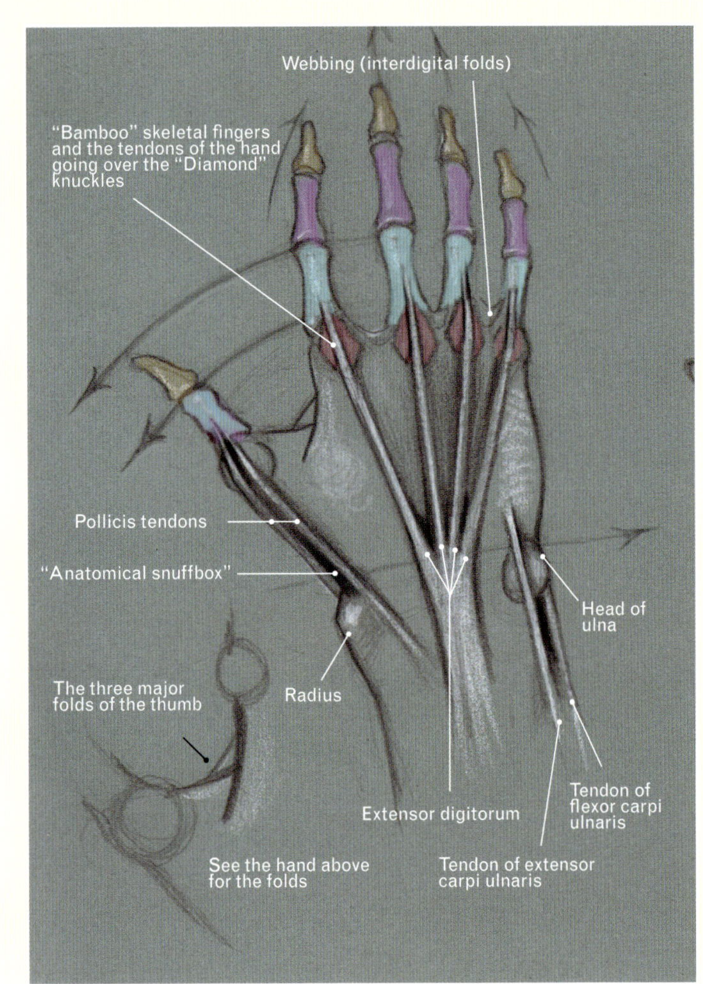

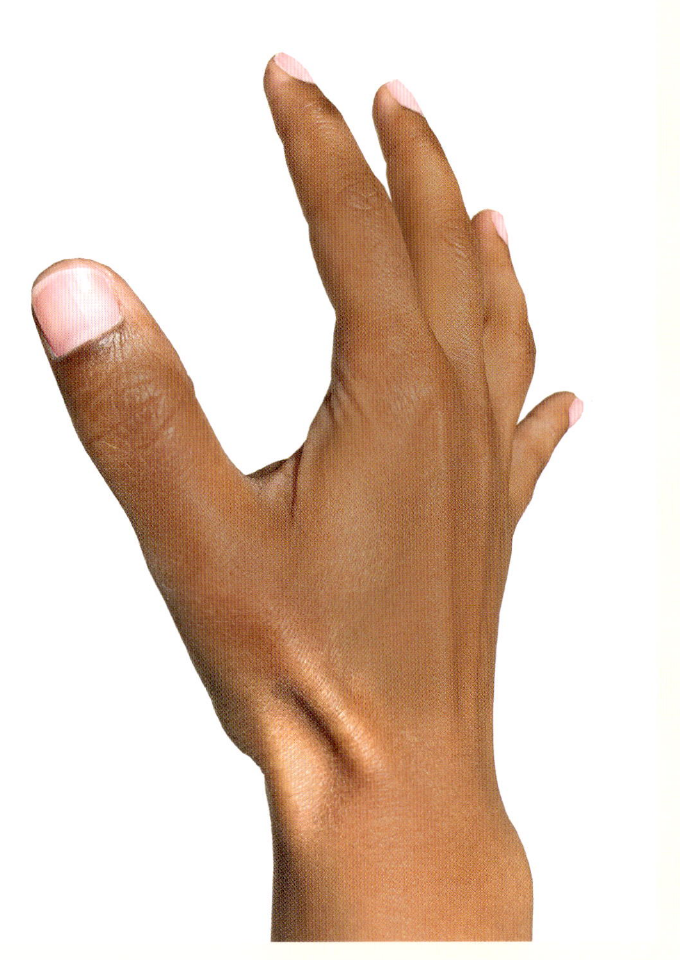

You may have noticed how a hollow is created when you both extend and abduct your thumb, like a hitchhiker would. This depression is what is known as the "anatomical snuffbox." The origin of its name stretches back to the 16th and 17th centuries, when snuff, a powdered version of tobacco that was inhaled or dipped, became ubiquitous in Europe as it was less expensive than regular tobacco. People placed their snuff in this depression in the hand—created by the twins (**brachioradialis** and **extensor carpi radius**), the mini twins (**longus, pollicis longus** and **extensor pollicis brevis**), and the tendon of the **extensor pollicis longus** (see pages 57 and 59)—and inhaled it from there. That is how the hollow became known as the anatomical snuffbox.

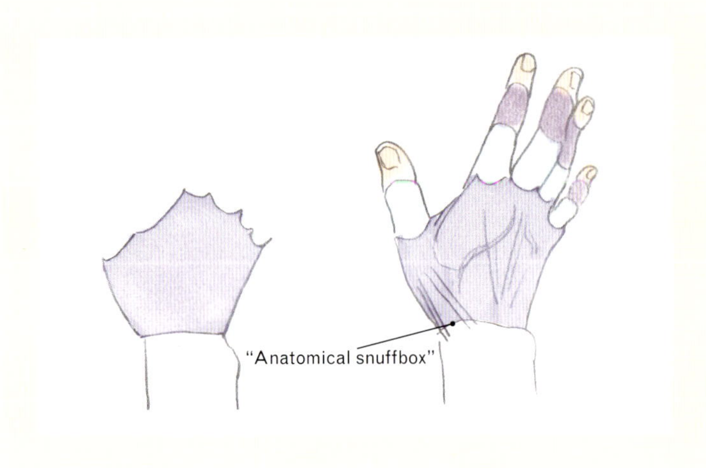

DRAWING TECHNIQUES

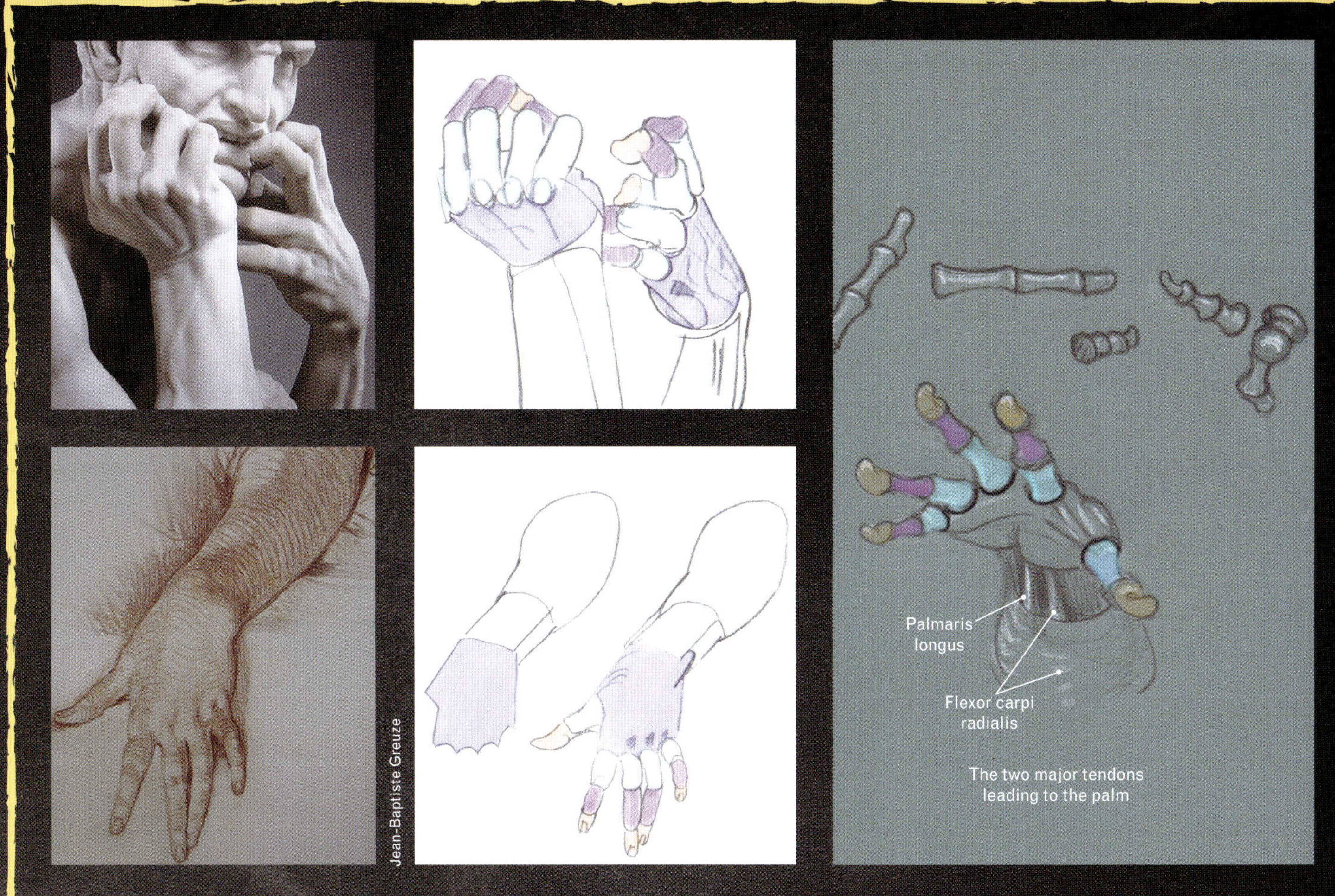

I teach a variety of ways to draw hands, including copying a model's hands, imagining them, or a combination of the two. When I am drawing the hand, I visualize the hand without the fingers or thumb, specifically like the back of a glove with the fingers cut off. It is easier to see the variations of movement, foreshortening and such, if you simply visualize this fingerless glove. Once you draw this in a variety of positions, add the proximal phalanges, then medial, and finally the distal or end of each finger. Place the webbing (interdigital folds), knuckles, and shading if you like.

There are many methods of drawing the hand and each artist has to learn which one works best for his or her own purposes. If you are drawing gesturally, you want to draw each finger as a dynamic line of action.

If your intent is to draw more representationally, then you must slow down and carefully study the many forms that make up this complex object.

The Bamboo Approach: Notice how your digit bones look like bamboo shoots. Practice drawing bamboo fingers to help train yourself to draw human fingers. My students find this exercise helpful.

The "Arcade" Method (from page 30): This is an amazingly simple and effective way to draw hands in any position as well. Try it with a live model and also while sketching hands from your imagination. Remember to only look at the body of the hand, then each finger. Always start with the finger closest to your vision. Focus on the body before moving out to the fingers.

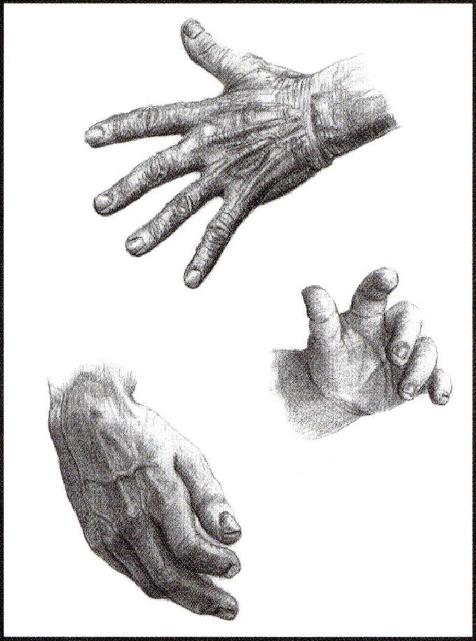

The S Strokes: When I draw hand demonstrations for my students, specifically the back of the hand, I draw straight lines toward the fingers. As they radiate from the wrist they read as tendons. This is part of how we humans see things as symbols. When I then draw random wavy "S" strokes they read as veins. This always gets my students to smile.

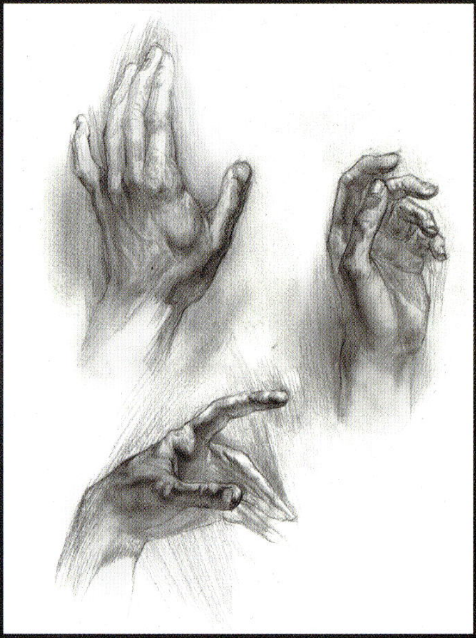

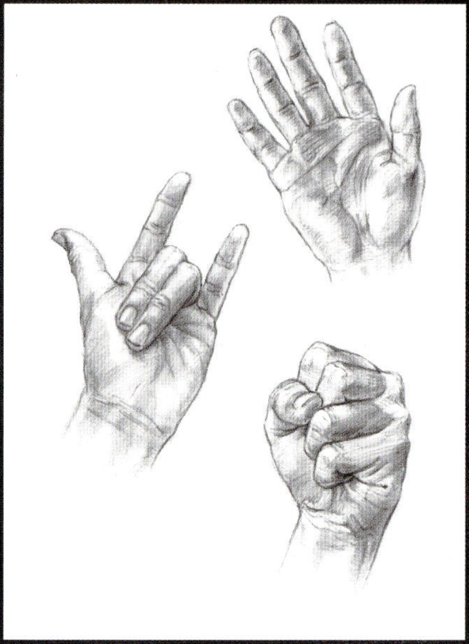

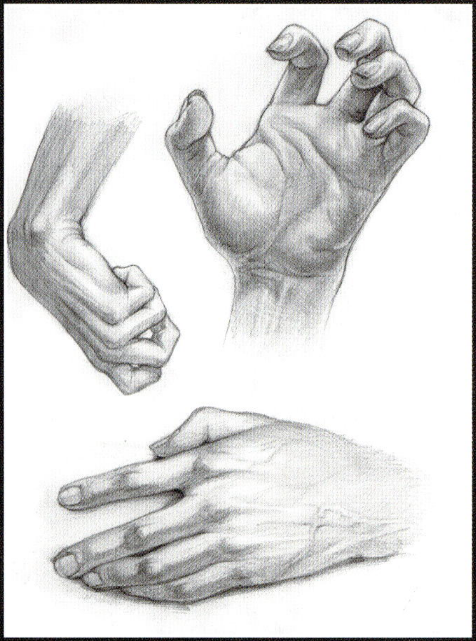

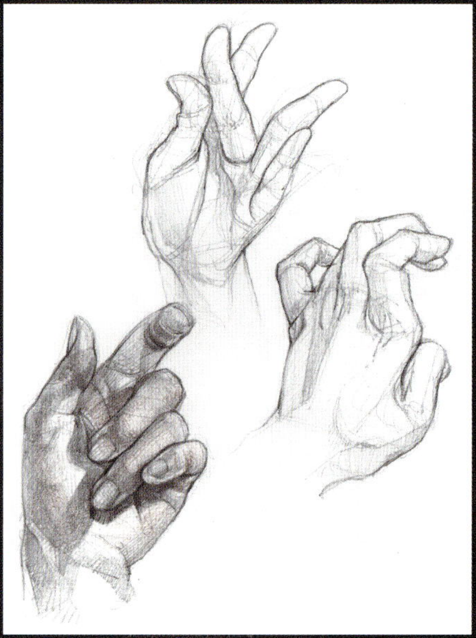

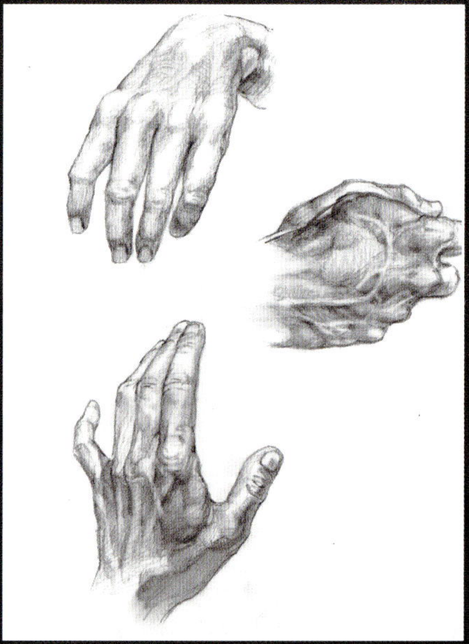

My students did the hand illustrations above. When drawing hands from life, one of the best sources is your own hand. I also encourage students to draw an elderly person's or a child's hand for variety and experience.

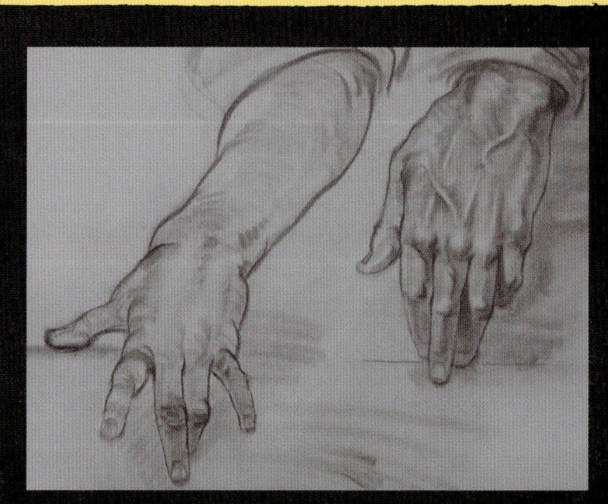

In most cases, when artists say, "head," we mean the face. I have scaled down the face muscles to what I call the "Essential Five" necessary for drawing it. These are the **masseter** and **temporalis** (muscles that raise the lower jaw in chewing), **orbicularis oris** (mouth and lip area), the **frontalis** (forehead), and the **mentalis** (chin group).

The face contains more than 40 muscles and is the only region that consists mainly of muscles that don't move levers; rather they move each other and the skin on top of them. Human beings have the most sophisticated facial muscles in the animal kingdom, which allow us to create a multitude of facial expressions. The variety of expressions gives us the extraordinary ability to communicate nonverbally with one another in subtle and not- so-subtle ways.

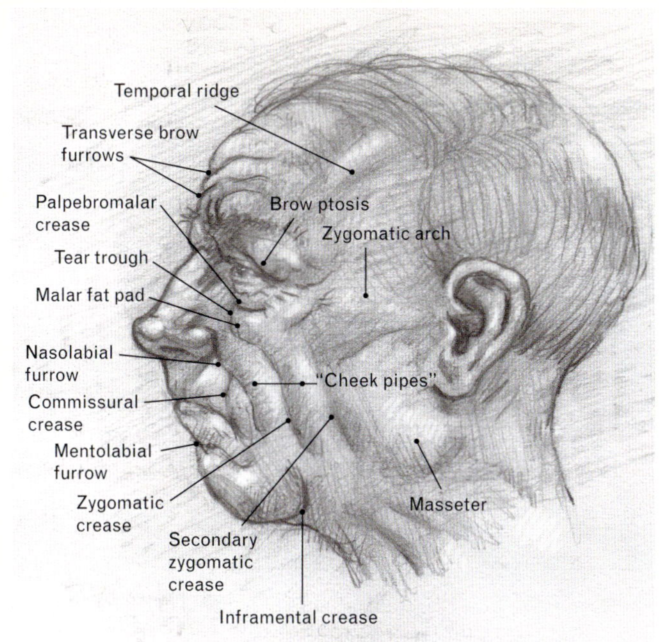

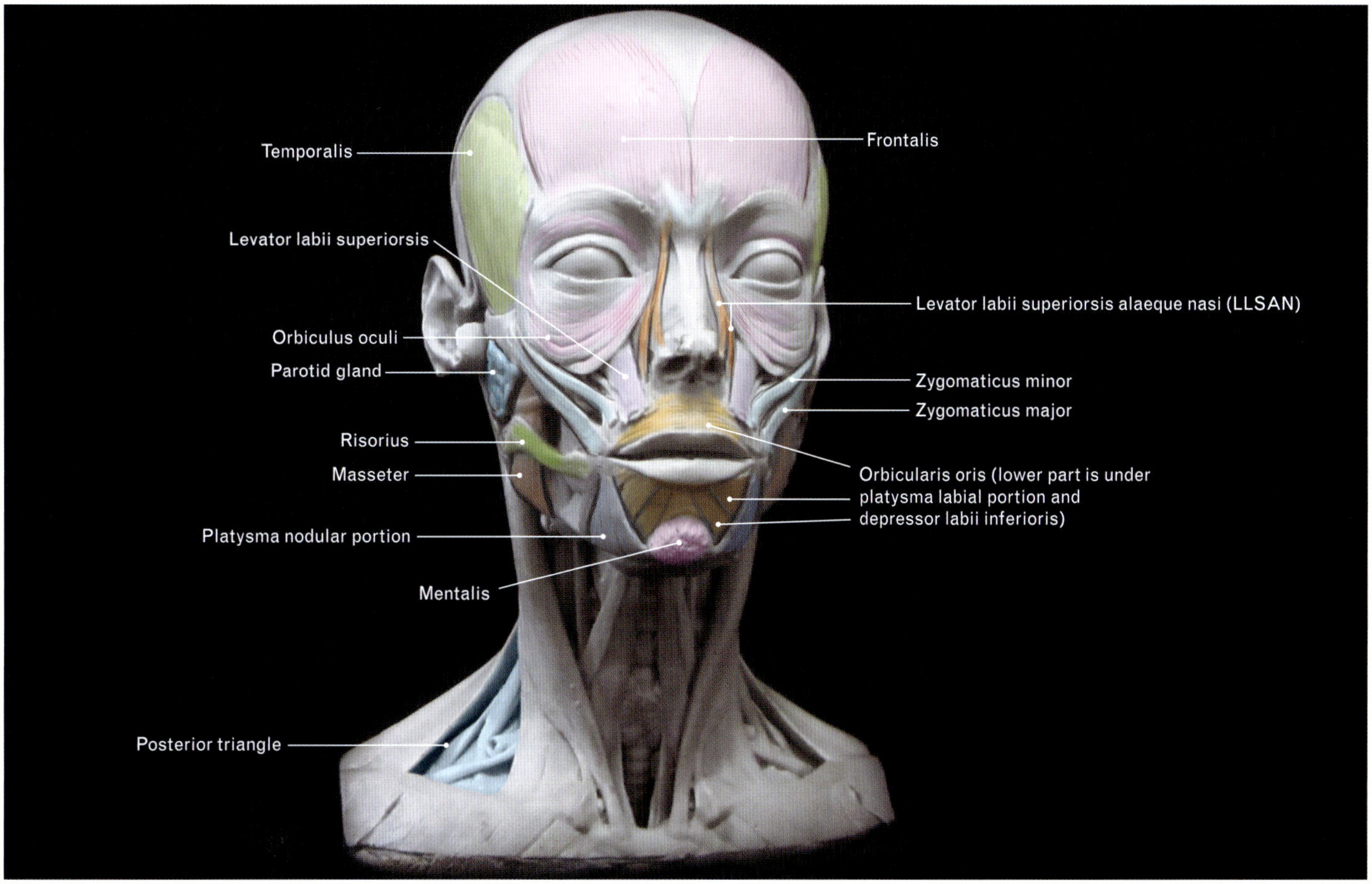

FACIAL EXPRESSIONS

Here are some common facial expressions followed by the primary muscles involved in each.

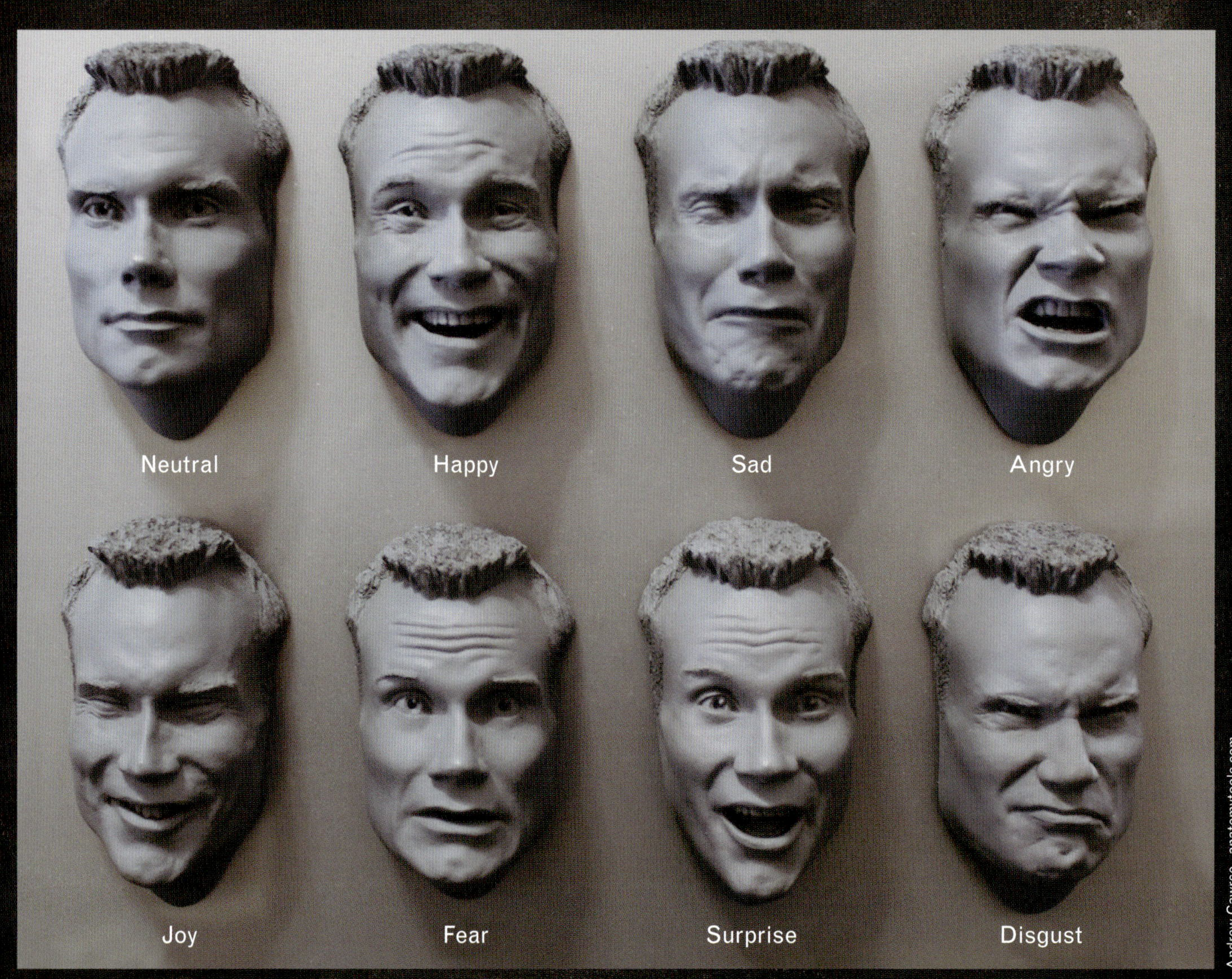

Happy: corrugator, orbicularis oculi, procerus, levator anguli oris, levator labii superioris, zygomaticus minor, zygomaticus major

Sad: frontalis, corrugator, orbicularis oculi, depressor labii inferior, depressor anguli oris, platysma

Angry: corrugator, orbicularis oculi, procerus, levator labii, depressor anguli oris, zygomaticus major and minor

Joy: frontalis, orbicularis oculi, levator labii superioris, zygomaticus major and minor

Fear: frontalis, corrugator, orbicularis oculi, levator palpebrae, risorius, buccinator and platysma

Surprise: frontalis, orbicularis oculi, levator anguli oris, orbicularis oris

Disgust: corrugator, procerus, orbicularis oculi, levator labii superioris, depressor anguli oris, mentalis, levator labii superioris alaeque nasi (LLSAN)

The countless contractions created by the muscles underneath our skin produce the expressive wrinkles on our face, which over time become permanent. For example, the two muscles on the forehead, the **frontalis** muscles, raise the eyebrows. When one or both contract (shorten), they do so vertically since their muscle fibers run vertically. The skin on the forehead therefore is pulled and compressed resulting in accordion-like wrinkles that create the familiar furrows that run horizontally across the forehead, or perpendicular to the muscle fibers of the frontalis. Intimate knowledge of the facial muscles and their directional pull is fundamentally important for the artist in order to bring life and character into their figurative art. Even very subtle shifts in muscle tension will create a whole different experience for the viewer and capturing this in the artist's media of choice is what distinguishes the great portrait artists.

"Intimate knowledge of the facial muscles and their directional pull is fundamentally important for the artist in order to bring life and character into their figurative art."

Temporalis

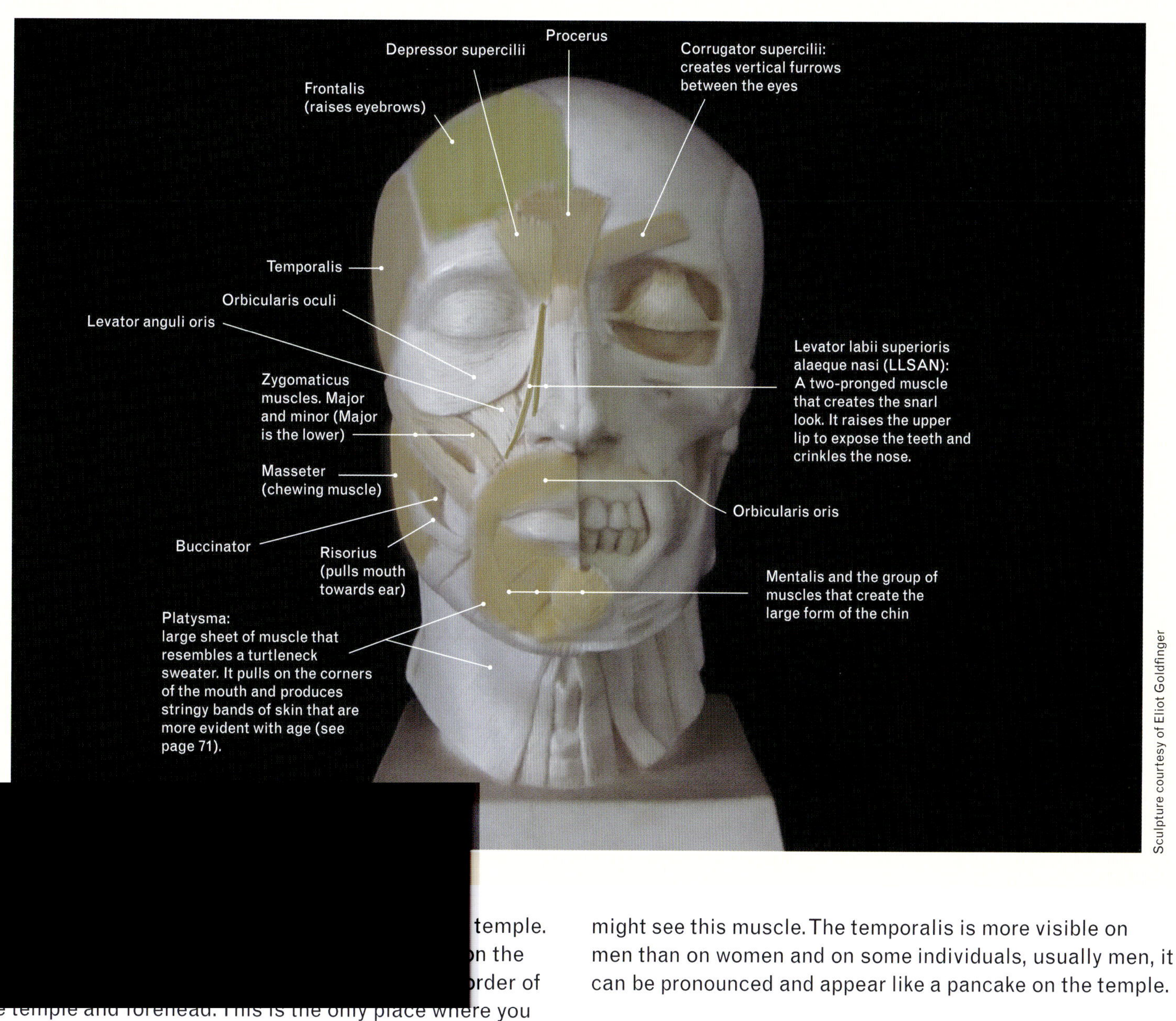

Sculpture courtesy of Eliot Goldfinger

temple. might see this muscle. The temporalis is more visible on men than on women and on some individuals, usually men, it can be pronounced and appear like a pancake on the temple. on the rder of the temple and forehead. This is the only place where you

Orbicularis Oris and the Mentalis Group

The **orbicularis oris** is the flat ovoid area that surrounds the mouth and the membranous tissue that we call the lips. Just below this is the chin, which is made up of several muscles that surround the **mentalis** (see page 69). This is why I call this the mentalis group. The mentalis by itself is a funny muscle that attaches to the chin, as a projection of tubular-like muscle fibers starting at the anterior aspect of the mandible, our chin bone, and it inserts into the soft protruding part of the chin. Since this muscle is in two parts, in some individuals it produces a cleft or dimple.

If you suck on a lemon, you might also see the mentalis in that it creates the dimply look of the chin when puckering. What I want you to visualize is the orbicularis oris and the mentalis group as two bubble shapes. The orbicularis oris will appear softer than the chin group. Now, imagine forcing the firmer chin group form up and into the softer orbicularis oris form that surrounds your mouth. What you will see is a shape that resembles the handlebars of a bike or the "pout" of the lower lip area (see page 82).

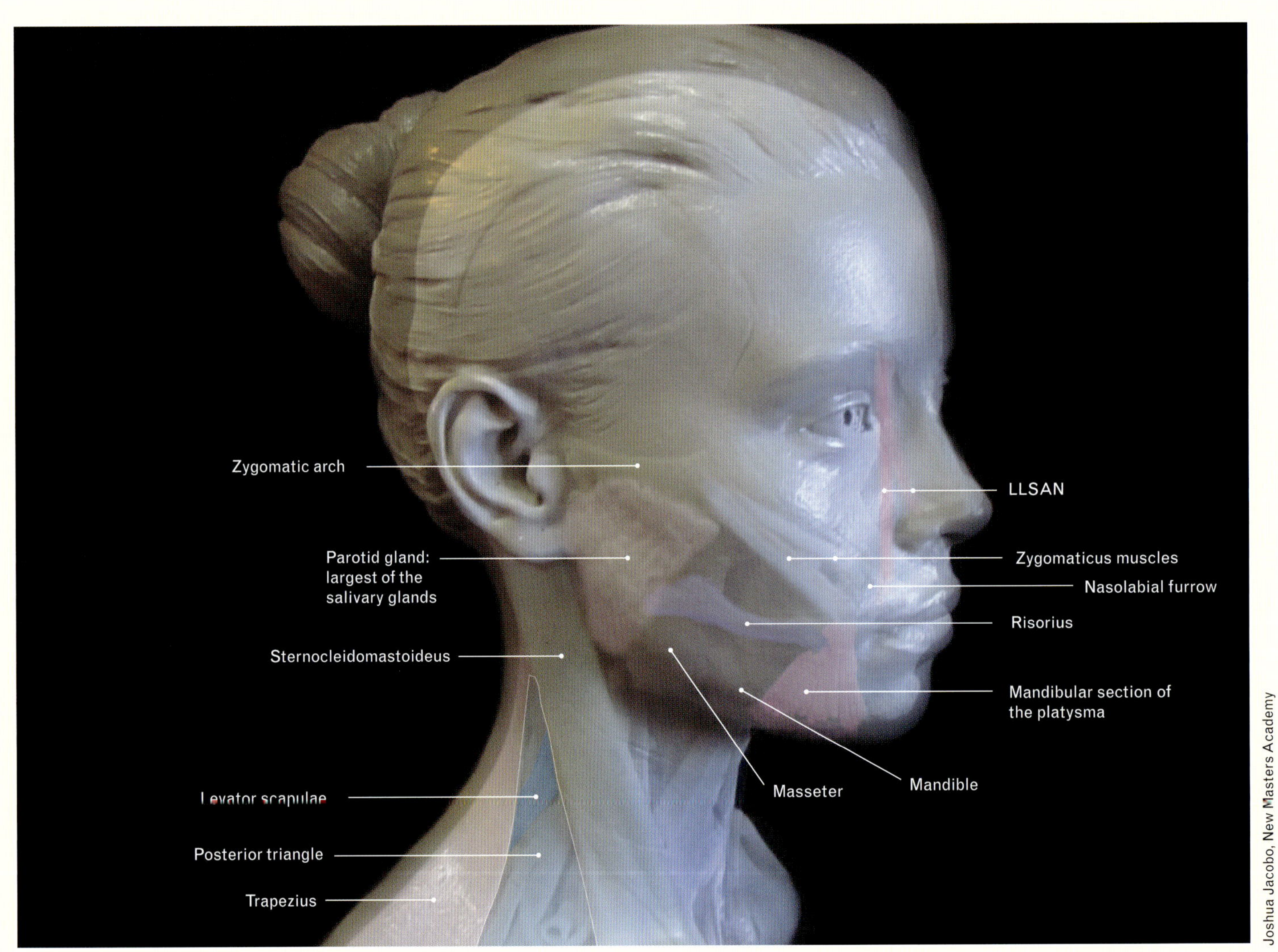

The Masseter

The **masseter** is the most visible of all the facial muscles. Fit human beings have a good deal of fat on their faces, which softens and gives us a healthy look and character. Even a thin person has a healthy mask of luscious fat.

The one muscle that is often visible, even with all the stores of the fat layer, is the chewing muscle, or masseter. It is anchored on the inferior (lower) aspect of the **zygomatic arch.** On the side of the skull the masseter inserts on the mandible, (jaw) in the area roughly below the molars. The masseter drops down slightly lower than the lowest line of the back of the jaw. As the zygomatic arch approaches the face and moves under the eye socket, it changes from a side form or facet to a front facet (front of the cheek). This facet is slanted toward 2 o'clock and on the right profile creates a visually elegant line from bone to muscle. This long form is visible on many individuals.

The cheek area has a deep crease called the **nasolabial furrow** (nasal = nose, labial = lip) that flanks the wings of the nose and flows behind each node at the corner of the mouth. This area between the masseter and the orbicularis oris and just behind the nasolabial furrow is also the space that would occupy dimples as well as character lines.

These lines can run up the whole cheek area to the base of the eye area. I have noticed that there is piping that occurs just behind the nasolabial furrow and the area mentioned above, which I call the "cheek pipe."

There are other notable creases that have their own names and these are very much a part of an individual's personal characteristics. An offshoot of the nasolabial furrow is a crease that cuts through the corner of the mouth called the **commissural crease**, which appears as one ages (see page 67). Creases are so much a part of us. We inherit a lot of what makes our face age with lines and furrows along with the natural flexing of a life full of expression. Sometimes our lives are etched on our faces. This reminds me of a quote by the great British writer George Orwell: "At 50, everyone gets the face he deserves."

The Neck

The neck doesn't get enough attention from most artists in life-drawing classes and workshops. Too often the neck is lumped in with the head, but I have found that it is important enough to be considered a separate region. The neck is the bridge from the head to the torso and there are a few essential aspects for the artist to know. First, there is a sheet of thin and stringy muscle called the **platysma**. The platysma covers the front of the neck from jaw to chest and shoulders as if the person were wearing a turtleneck sweater. You can see the platysma when you use it to pull down the corners of your mouth, exposing the lower teeth. The platysma hides many muscles underneath it until movement forces them to the surface.

The main muscle of the neck for artists to pay attention to is the **sternocleidomastoideus**, which is sometimes called the **sternomastoid** or **sternocleidomastoid**. I prefer using its entire name because it reminds me of the three main contact points of this graceful muscle: the sternum, the clavicle, and the bony mastoid process of the skull located just behind the ear. This triadic muscle helps turn the head and becomes very visible with an extreme turn to the left or the right. With an extreme turn of the head the sternocleidomastoideus becomes vertical, and produces a straight vertical line from the ear to the pit of the neck. It is very dynamic and often used by illustrators such as J. C. Leyendecker, who created strong, heroic-looking yet

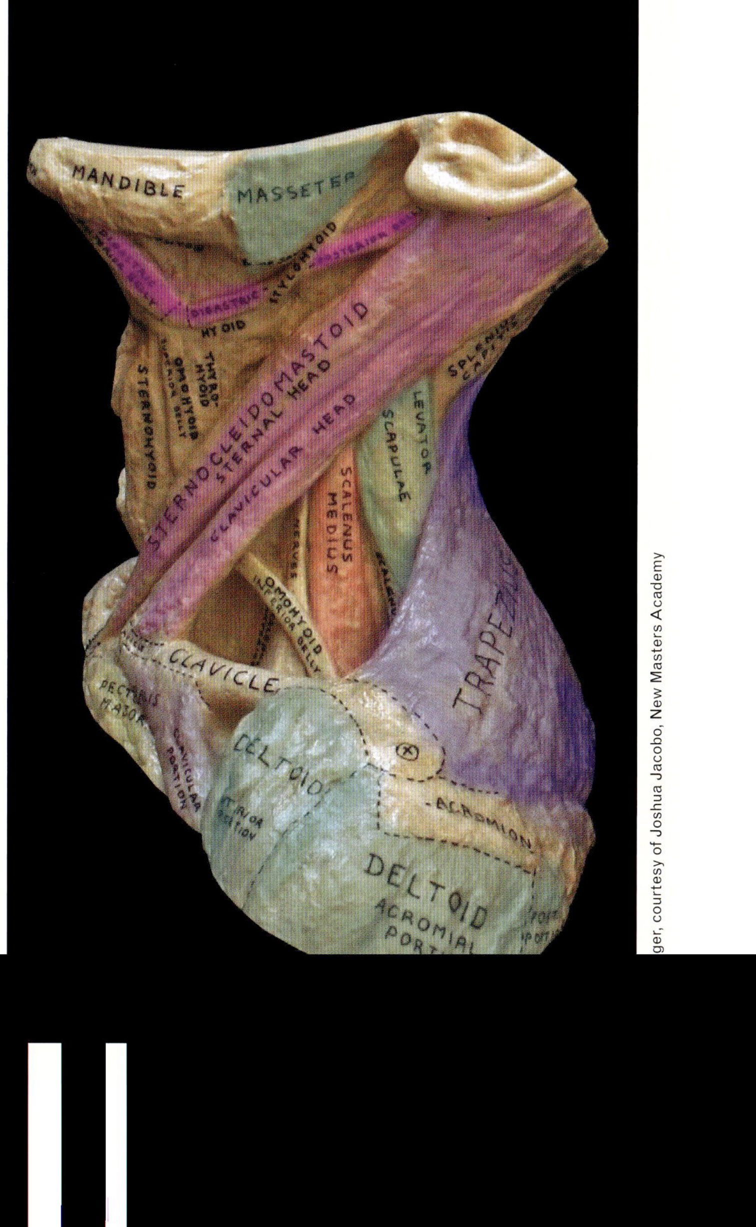

I have often seen the neck drawn as if it were a coffee can because the artist neglects what is underneath the skin. Even though there are many muscles in the neck, there are only a few that an artist really needs to know to correct the coffee-can look. First is the trapezius, the large kite-shaped muscle of the back, which runs up to the back of the skull and is a very important bridge between the back and the neck, and the contour of the neck to the shoulder. On pages 67 and 70, you can see that in between the trapezius and the sternocleidomastoideus is a hollow area called the **posterior triangle**. Within this hollow, which is often more visible on women, there is a muscle that pops up with a certain position, the **levator scapulae**.

Secondly, there is the **hyoid bone**, a small horseshoe-shaped bone located deep inside your neck. This small bone lies roughly a couple of inches behind the chin and is not visible but is helpful to know about; it is what makes the contour of your silhouette change, starting from the chin, moving under the jaw, and following the angle down to the pit of the neck. The hyoid bone is an important hub of activity. It is small, U-shaped, and would roughly fit around a bottle cap. There are many muscles attached to it, and the **trachea** (windpipe) lies behind it. The hyoid bone is the insertion point of the tongue. There is a muscle attached to the hyoid bone called the **digastric** that helped me learn to draw under the jawline.

As a student at ArtCenter College of Design, I took Burne Hogarth's anatomy class. I always sat in the front row but that meant I was at a lower point of view. I had to look up at the model from the drawing benches that lined the front row. I had trouble drawing the jaw to the neck and it often looked awkward. Years later as a teacher in the same classroom I started teaching my students about this little-known muscle called the digastric. The digastric is helpful because it leaves a trail from the chin to the hyoid bone. The trail continues to the back of the hyoid bone, or roughly at the vertical line of the sternocleidomastoideus, and then follows the sternocleidomastoideus to its origin at the mastoid process, the bony bump at the base of the skull. The line of the digastric, along with the jawline creates what is called the canopy. This canopy is the facet that is the bridge between the head and the neck. Visualize an imaginary line drawn from underneath the chin to the hyoid bone and up to the ear area, on both sides of the neck. Now picture a line that starts underneath the chin, moves to the hyoid bone and down to the pit of the neck. This will forever simplify drawing under the jaw, making it much easier.

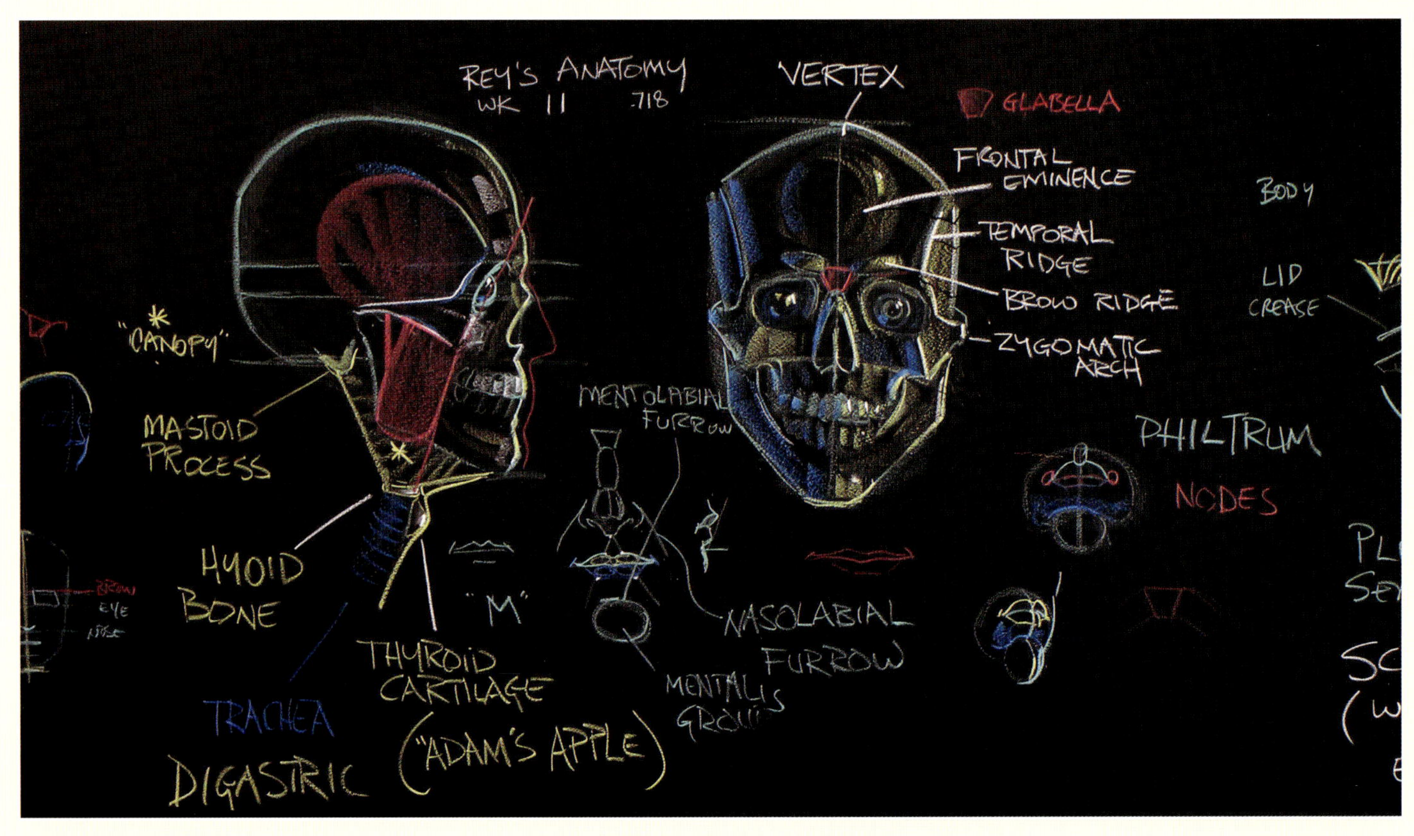

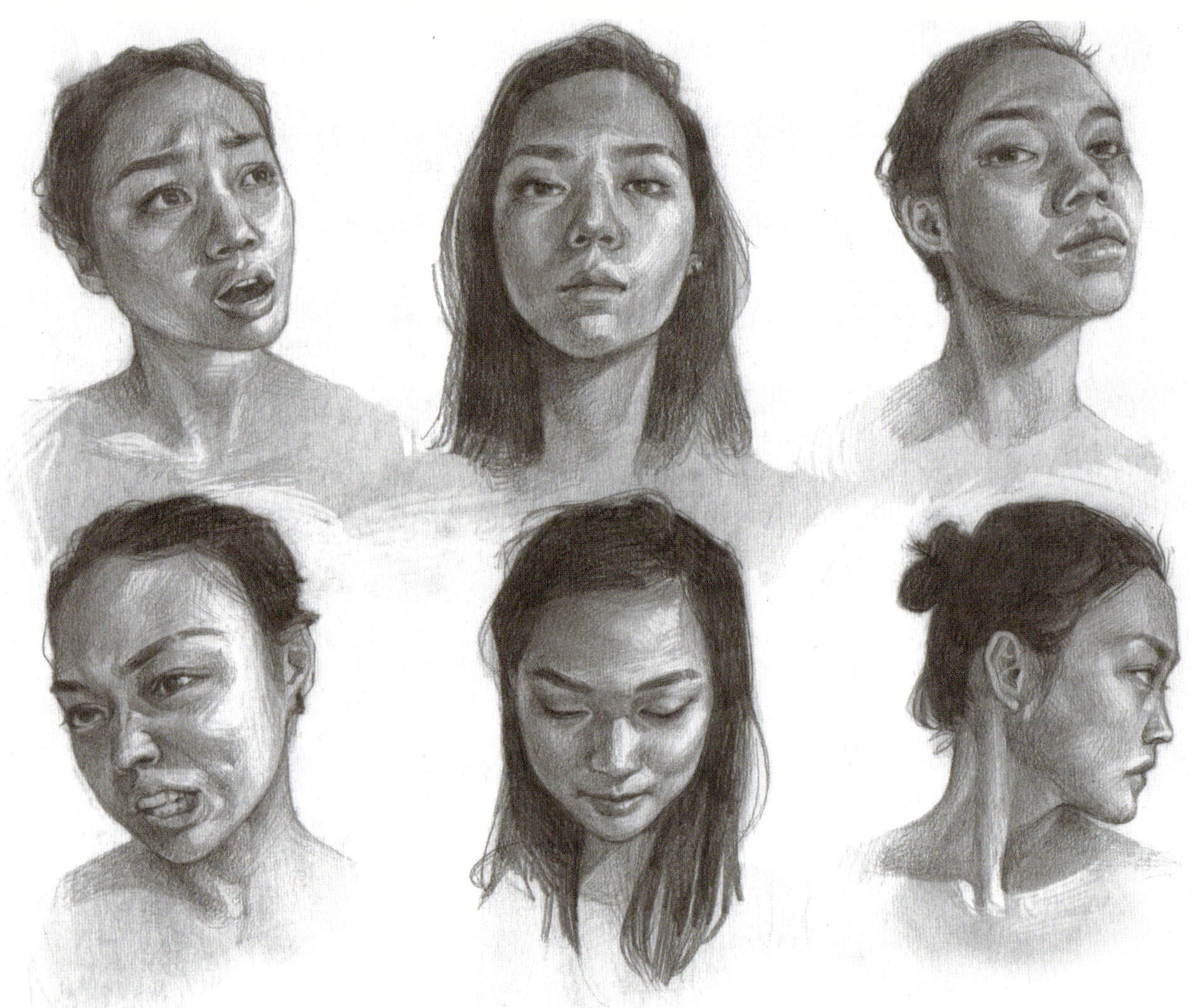

On males, there is an additional form: the thyroid cartilage or Adam's apple. Women have it as well but it is small and rarely seen. This protruding form is just below the hyoid bone and it creates a peak poking forward and can be very pronounced and pointed on some individuals. Whether you can see the Adam's apple or not, it is an important reference point, the middle form, between the chin and the pit of the neck.

Lastly, depending on the age and the character lines of the person posing, there are three forms the jawline takes that need to be considered. In the prime of life, the **masseter** and the **mental protuberance** on the chin are lower than

everyday wear and tear become etched on our faces. There is an area between the masseter and the **orbicularis oris** that is relatively void of strong muscular forms, the cheek area.

As anyone knows, our identity is in our face, our method of recognizing one another. Because so much of ourselves is our face it is also one of the most critical areas of any figurative art. A good face can offset many little errors in one's drawings of the human body. Conversely, a well-drawn body can be seen as not good when topped with a badly drawn head and face. Scale and emotion are established by the head more often than not. It will always be important to

WHAT CAN YOU TELL FROM A SKULL?

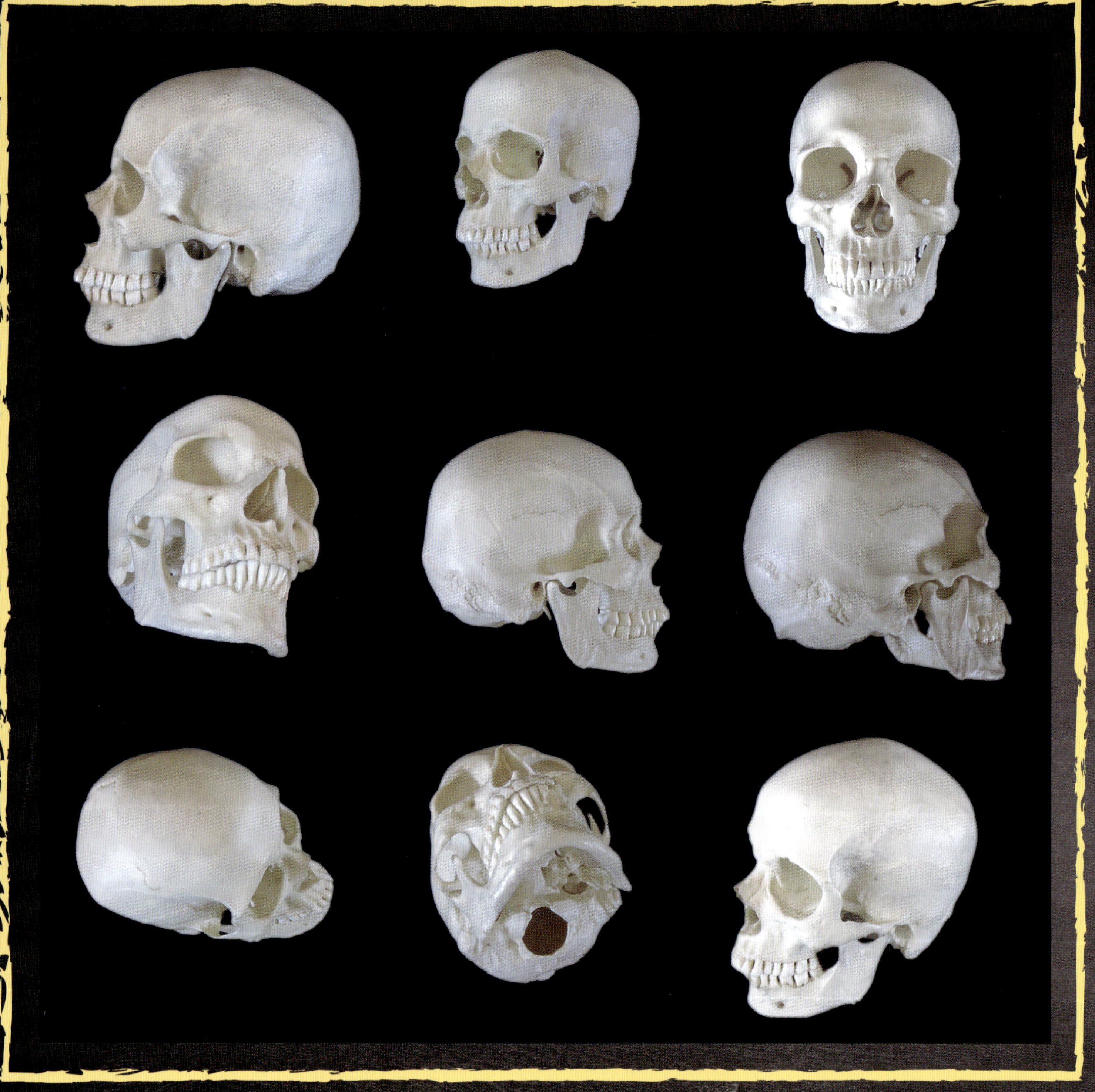

An anatomy expert can tell you many things about an individual based on his or her skeletal remains: gender, height, and, in some cases, even weight. The skull, in particular, can reveal a lot, even someone's gender. The brow ridges above the eyes of a female are less prominent and the skull overall tends to be smaller. Aspects of the skull can also indicate race.

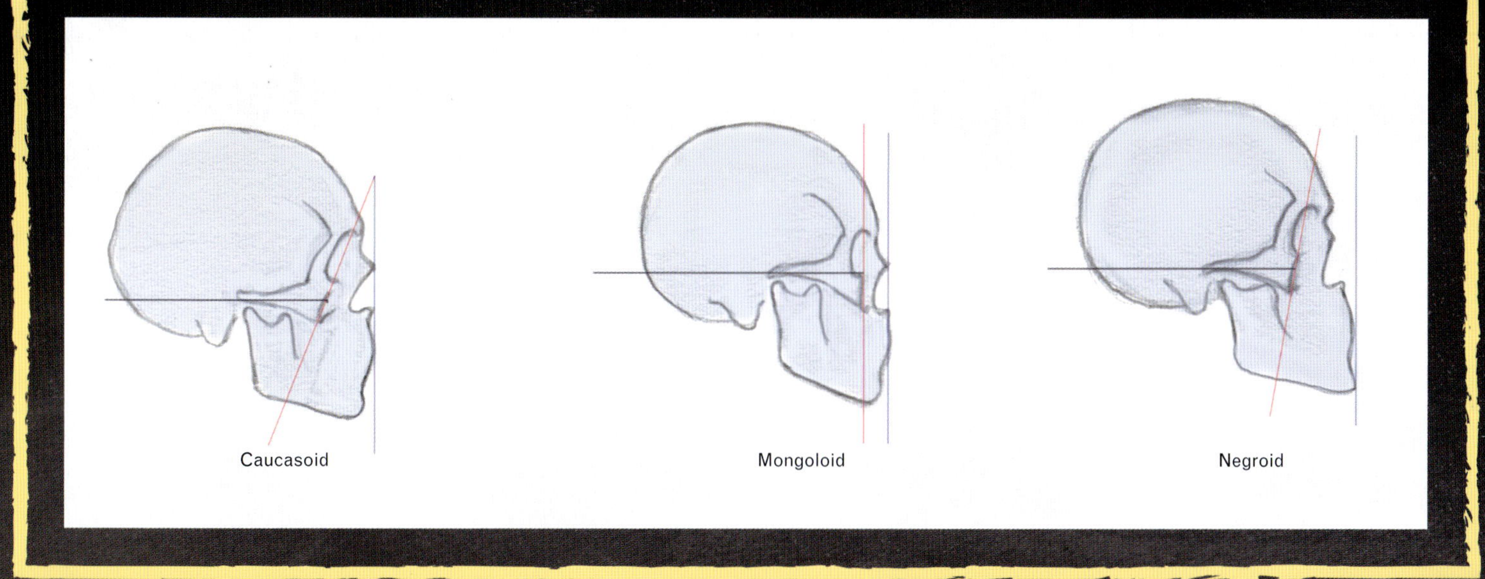

The three most common skull shapes are called Caucasoid, Mongoloid, and Negroid. Generally speaking, the nasal opening of each is different. The nasal width is the narrowest in the Caucasoid skull, in the shape of an isosceles triangle. The Mongoloid skull is a little wider than the Caucasoid skull. The Negroid skull has the widest opening with an aperture closer to being equilateral.

The nasal opening is important because it determines the width of the nose. The angles of the nasal bones from profile are different. The Caucasoid nose is at a greater degree moving closer to being horizontal than the other two, which can lead to a recognizable bump on the nose.

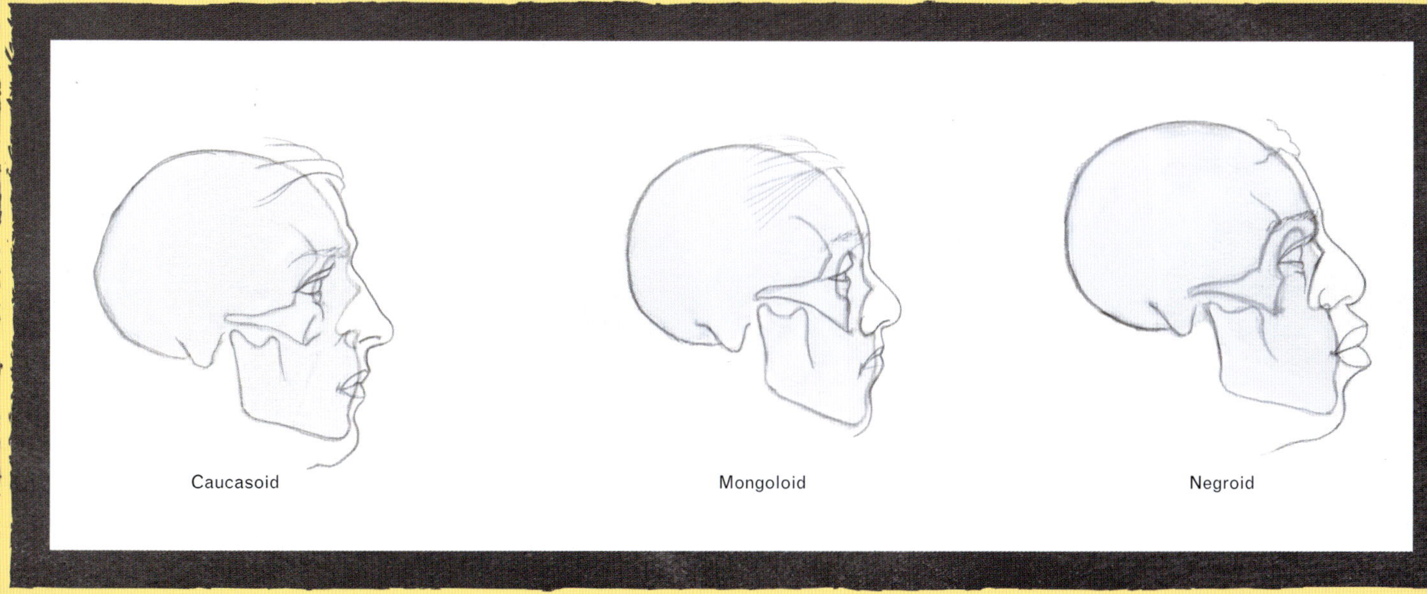

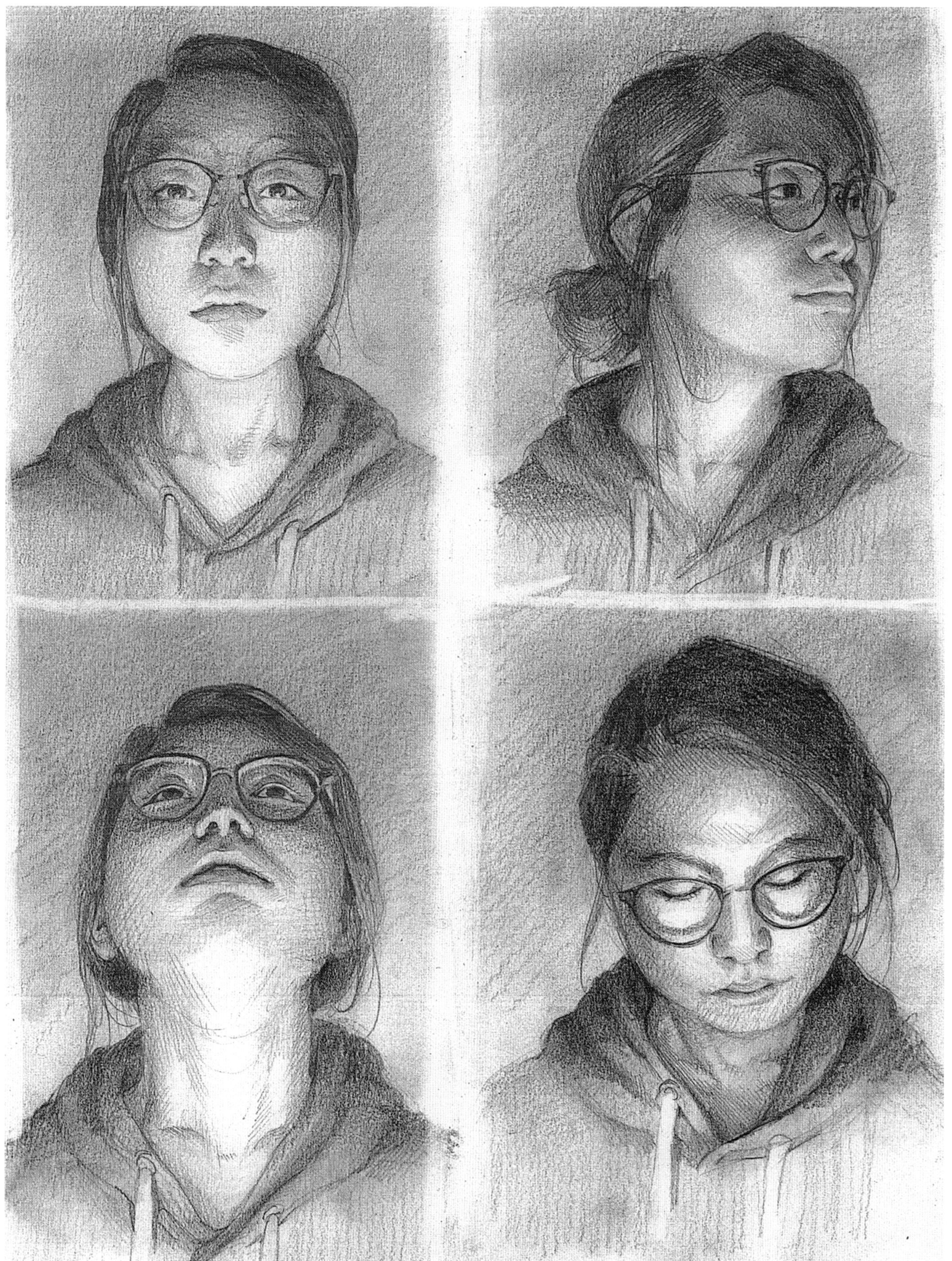

Erin Shin

FACIAL FEATURES

The features of the face need to be discussed separately from the head and neck simply because they are the most important aspects of our identity. We recognize others and ourselves by our faces. Each part of our features, especially the eyes, nose and mouth are so unique to us it is hard to fathom how many variations there have been of each. Think about it, no one looks exactly like you. Even twins can't fool their loved ones. This is why I so admire colleagues who do portraits well. If an artist portrays someone it is the ultimate challenge to capture that "something" that makes that person "that" person.

The history of portraiture is a rich one; artists throughout history are plenty but revered are those who had that special ability to capture the most elusive of all representational art: the portrait. I have three colleagues that I admire greatly for their abilities to capture the likeness of a person, but more than that, they capture the essence too. They are Sean Cheetham, Nathan Fowkes, and Daniel Bilmes. They are different from one another but geniuses in their power to convey the deeper aspects of the human spirit. Rembrandt had this before them. John Singer Sargent and Henry Raeburn had it. There are too many people to list, of course, but just the thought of their work reminds me as to why I live humbly alongside their immense talent.

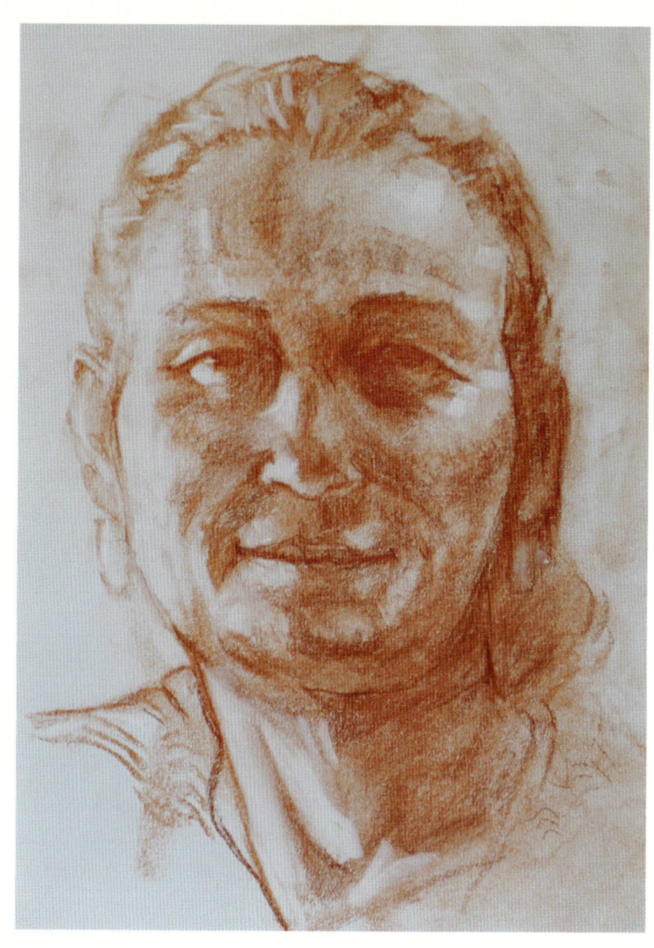

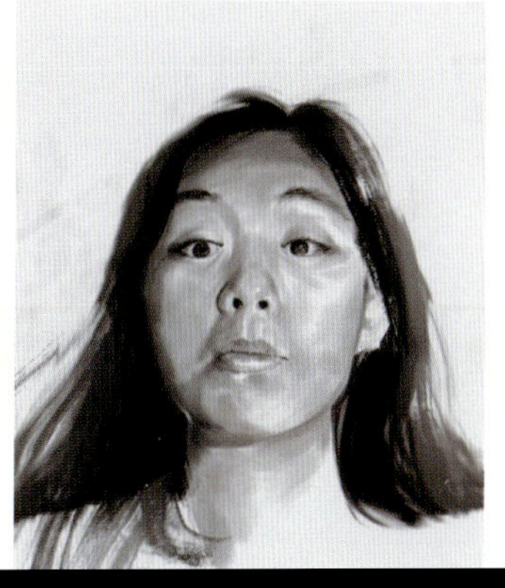

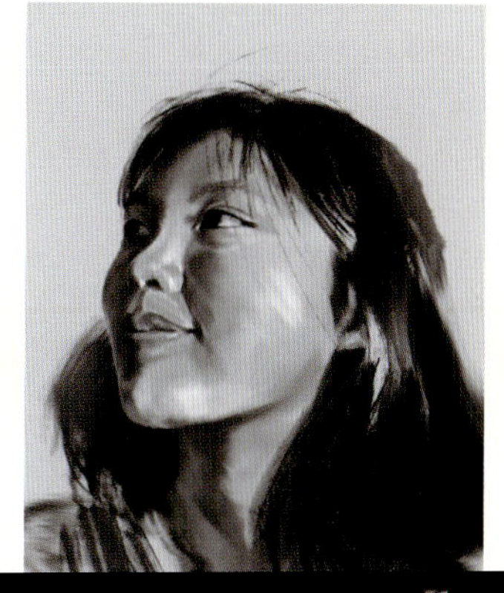

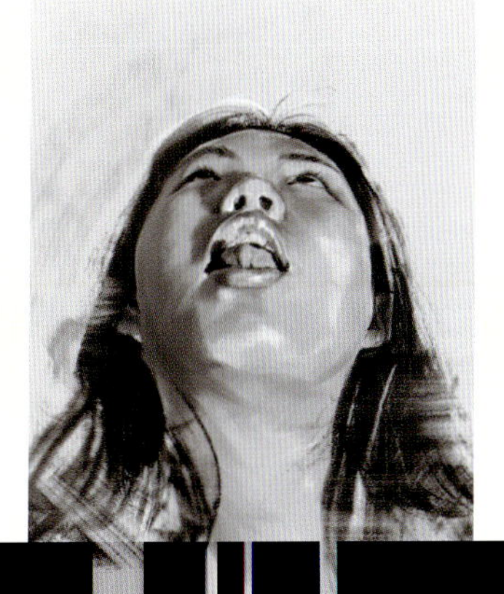

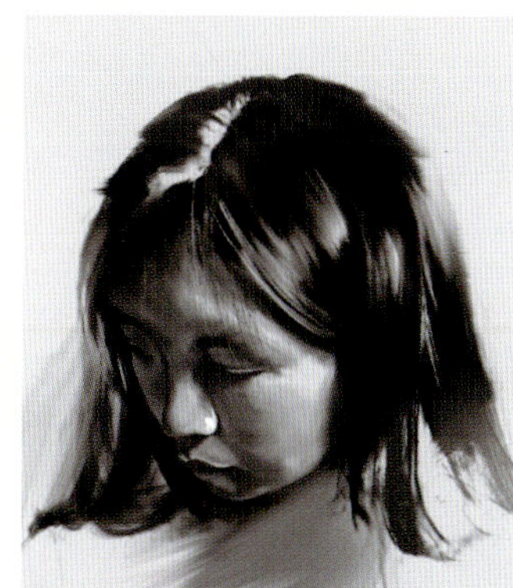

The Eyes

We have all heard the saying, "The eyes are the windows to the soul." The reason we believe this is obvious: the eyes carry with them our emotions, our thoughts, our ancestors, our age, and even our condition and health. Structurally our eyes are aspheric, or almost spherical. They are elongated if viewed from the side. But for simplicity we can call them spheres or orbs. Our eye sockets are conical like the inside of a child's party hat. A little fat pad is nestled behind the eyeball. It resembles a Hershey's Kiss pointing inward, creating a protective cushion. Therefore, on a blind person, since they do not use their eye muscles, that fat dissolves away creating the sunken look of the eyes. Eyelids are thick, and when I explain this thickness in class, I draw an orange with its thick rind cut in an eye shape and taken out. You can see the thickness of the rind and the spherical orange inside. This is a great way to learn how to visualize the eye and lid in rotation.

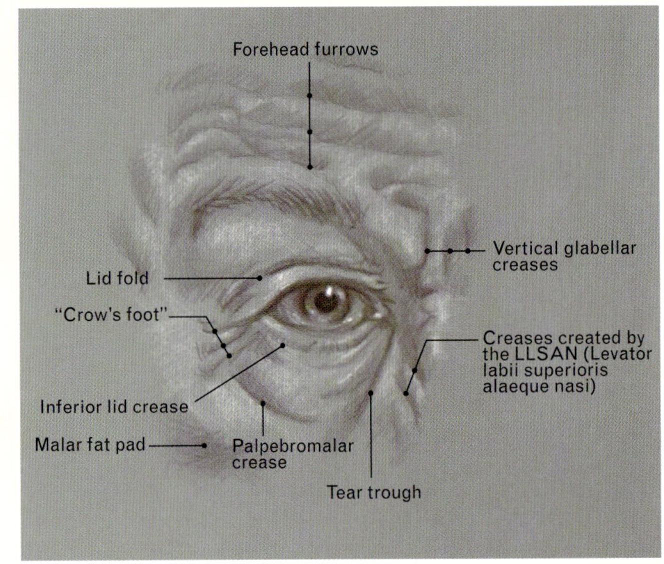

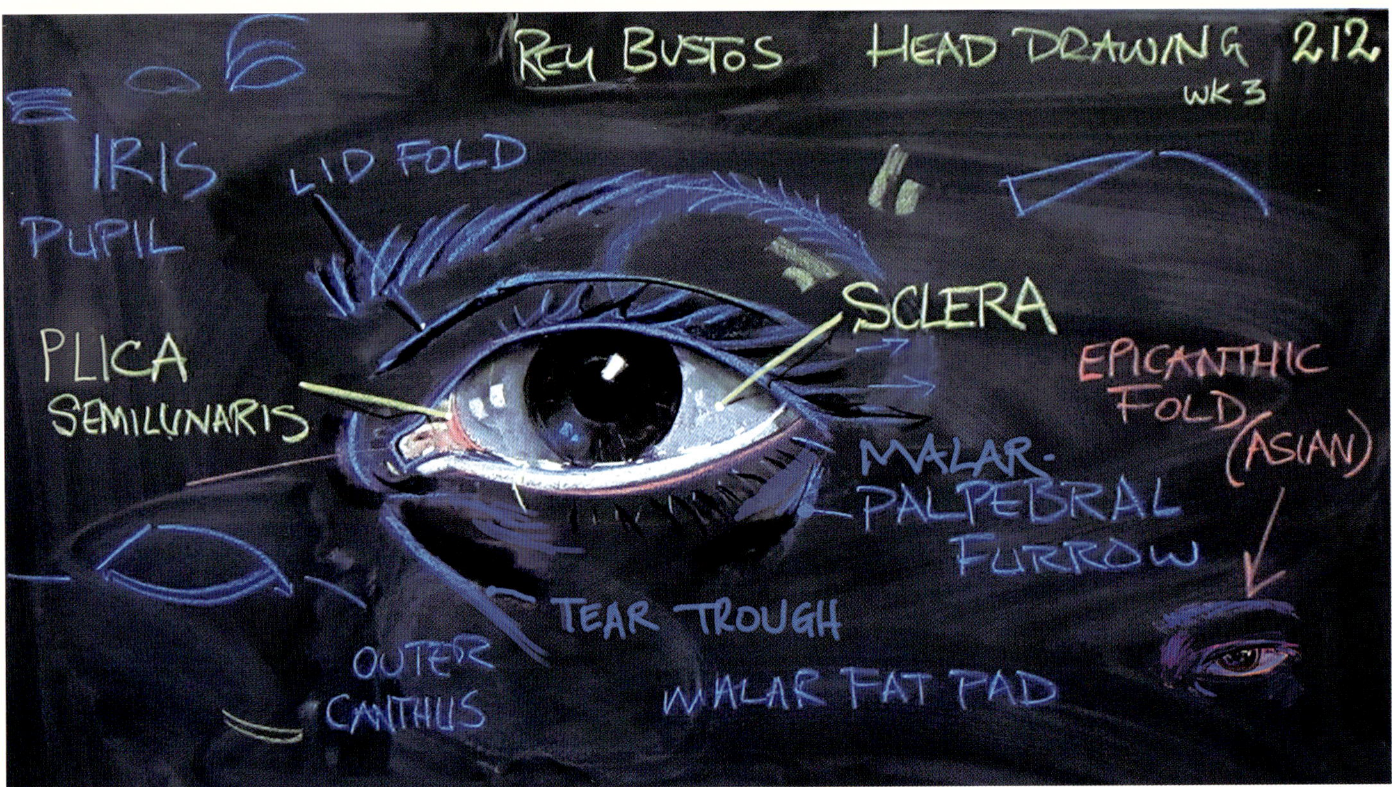

The eyes are very wet and therefore shiny. It is important to note that the **sclera**, the white of the eye, is not a pure white but a darker value. Otherwise, you would not be able to add the white highlight necessary to make the white of the eye look shiny as well as the iris. You cannot put a white highlight on a white area. In movies and TV shows, if detectives examine an open-eyed "corpse" and the eyes are still shiny, that is not accurate. A dead person's eyes would be dull and dry.

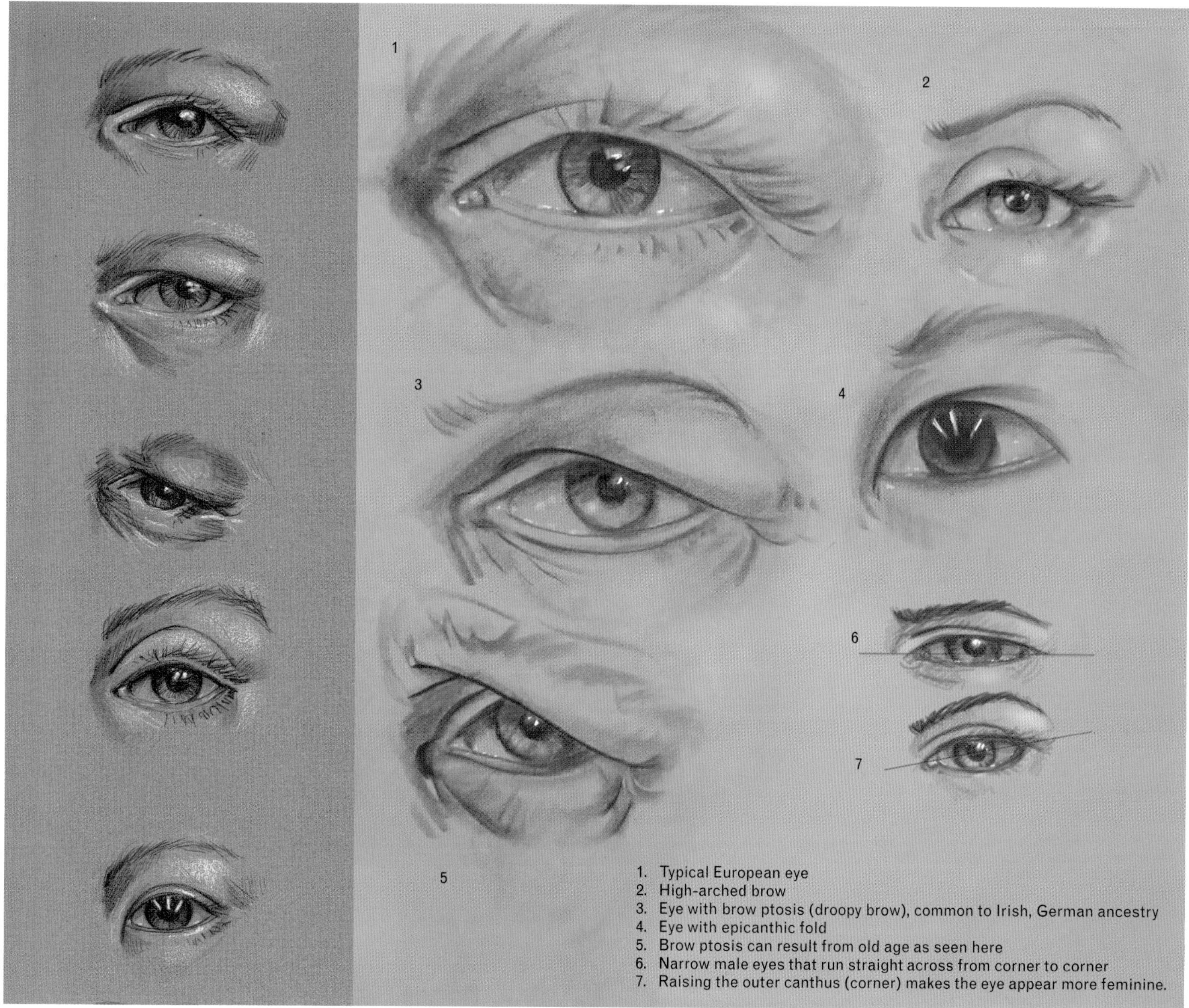

1. Typical European eye
2. High-arched brow
3. Eye with brow ptosis (droopy brow), common to Irish, German ancestry
4. Eye with epicanthic fold
5. Brow ptosis can result from old age as seen here
6. Narrow male eyes that run straight across from corner to corner
7. Raising the outer canthus (corner) makes the eye appear more feminine.

The eyelids are a feature that distinguishes one individual's eyes from another's as much as eye color. There is too much to cover on this particular feature to delve into it too deeply—the variances are great and interesting to study—but for the purposes of this book, I will describe aspects of the eyelids in very basic terms. Above are certain lid types that I draw when addressing my students on this subject:

The Caucasian eyelid: the lid is generally off the aperture of the eye creating an open look that is referred to in art as the European eye.

Brow ptosis: when the top portion of the eyelid fold drops down, over and into the eye area itself. I call this the "Kennedy"

The Nose

The nose is basically made of three parts: the bony bridge, the middle cartilage, and the tip cartilages and fatty pads of the wings of the nose. On babies, there is not enough bone or skin to see any of these separate forms, thus we refer to a baby's nose as a button. As the child grows, the nose elongates and the age of the child starts manifesting itself in that aspect. On a five-year-old, the nose in profile is smooth; by around seven years old the three parts can be seen, subtle but apparent. Finally, in the adult nose the three parts can be very evident and very identifiable as that person's nose. There are far too many variations to consider them all here. This overview is in the most general sense.

Ancestry may determine many of these forms, from the bump on the nose to its width.

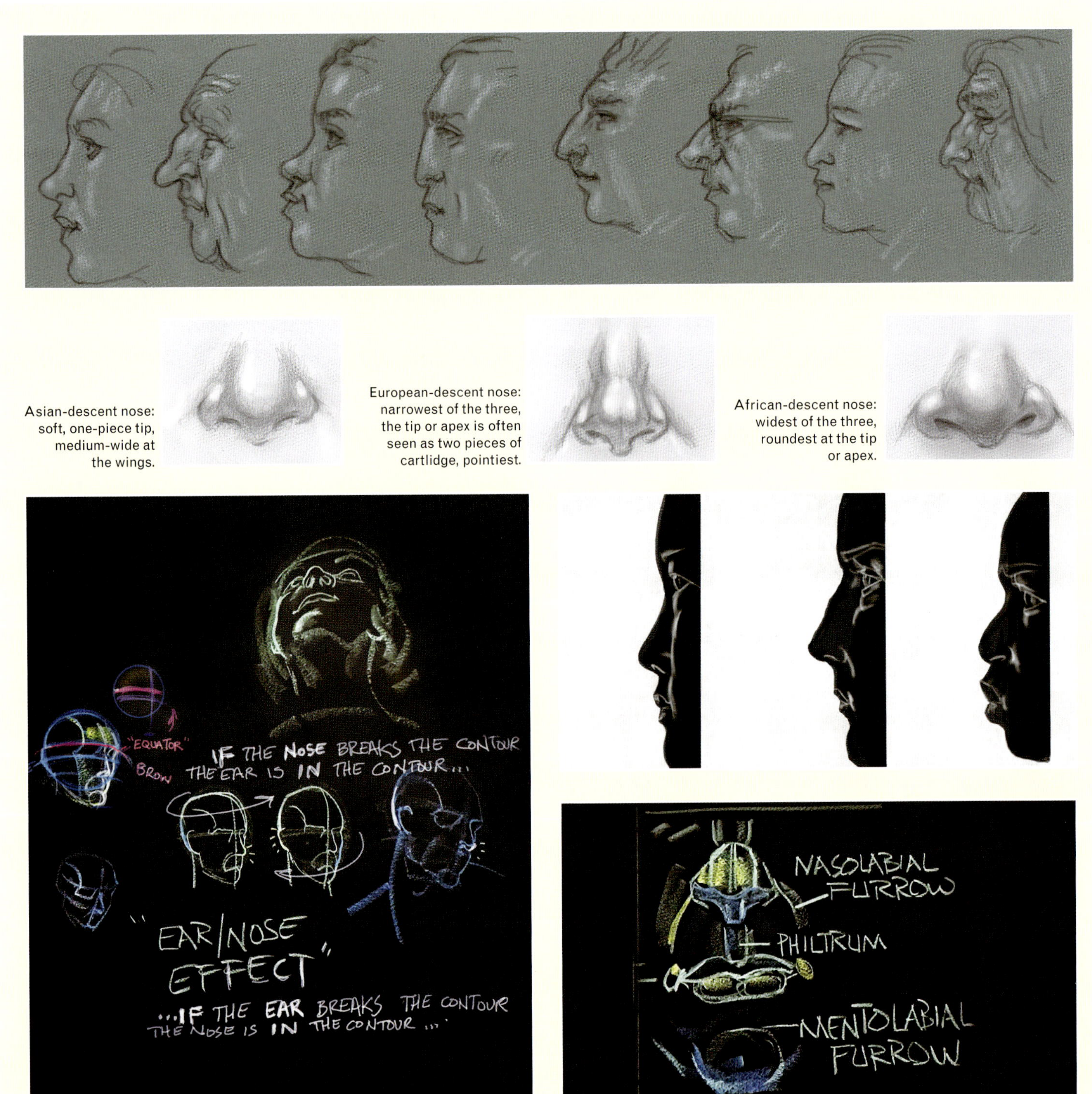

Asian-descent nose: soft, one-piece tip, medium-wide at the wings.

European-descent nose: narrowest of the three, the tip or apex is often seen as two pieces of cartlidge, pointiest.

African-descent nose: widest of the three, roundest at the tip or apex.

NOSE CONSTRUCTION

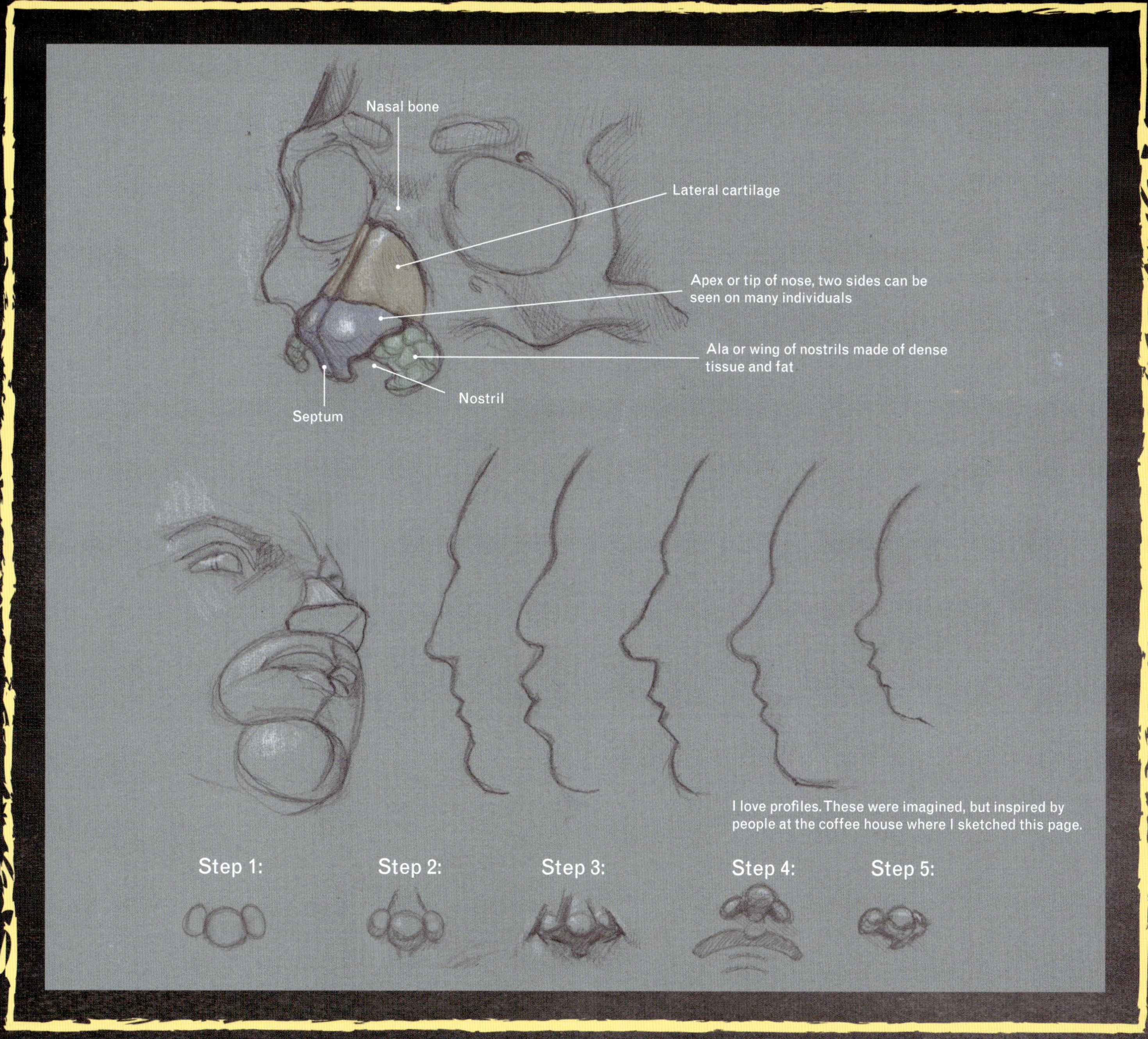

STEP 1:

Start with three bubbles: one for the tip, two jelly-bean

STEP 2:

Add a line above each wing for the bridge, and two lines

MOUTH CONSTRUCTION

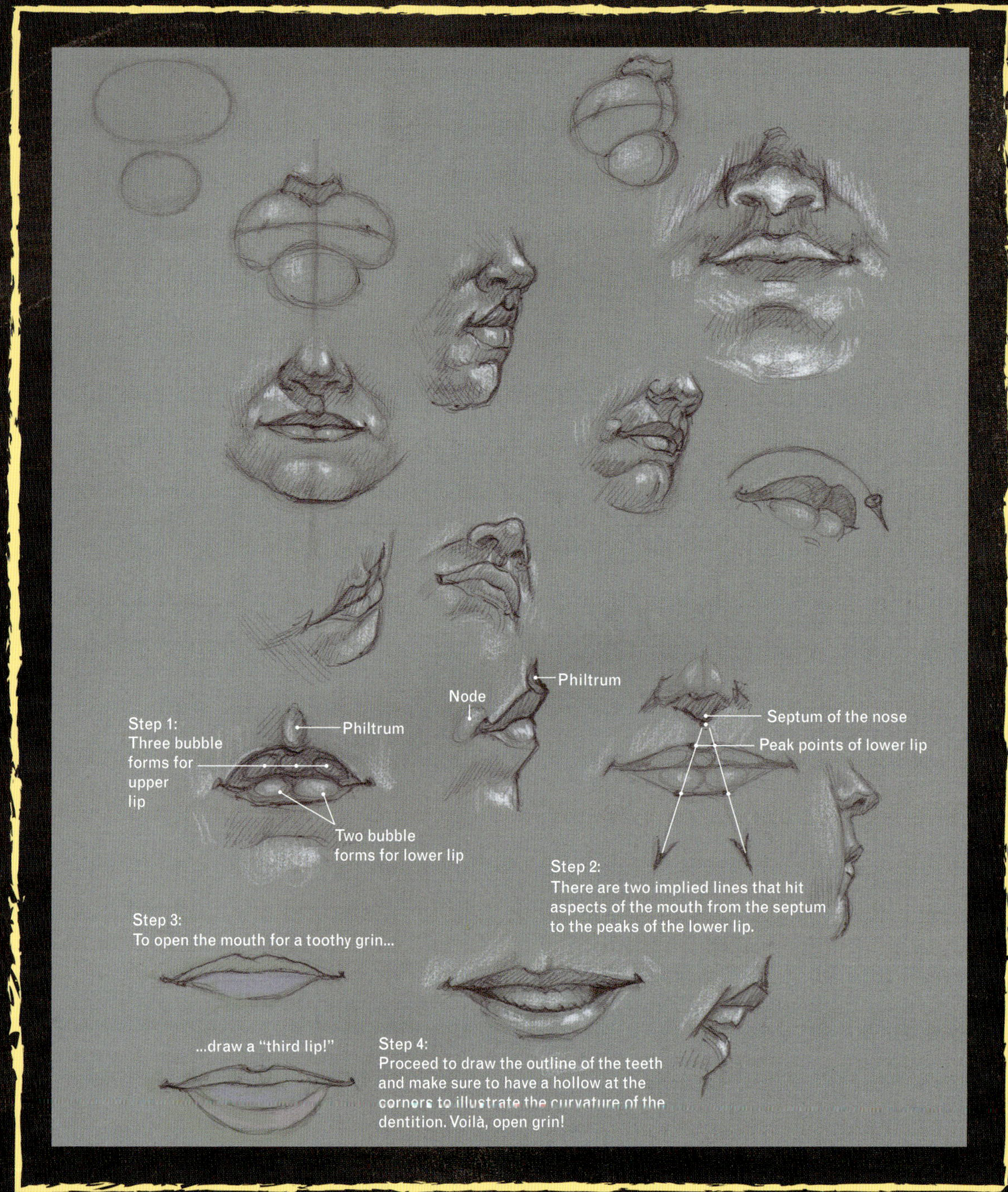

STEP 1:

Place three bubble forms for the upper lip and two bubble forms for the lower lip, as shown above.

STEP 2:

Lightly mark the two implied lines that hit aspects of the mouth from the septum to the peaks of the lower lip.

STEP 3:

Leave closed, or draw a "third lip" for a toothy grin.

STEP 4:

For a toothy grin, proceed to draw the outline of the teeth

The Mouth

The mouth is the last of the features that we know well on each other and ourselves: the thickness or thinness, the width of it and the symmetry or lack of it. Does the upper lip protrude out further than the lower lip as with most people, or does the lower lip? Or are they even? Is the top lip thin and the lower lip full, the inverse, or are they equal?

To draw lips, squeeze three little bubbles into the upper lip and two fuller oblong bubbles inside the lower lip. The two on the lower lip are easily seen on many people without having to imagine them. It is good to note that we have two little jelly-bean-shaped forms at each corner of our mouths. Sometimes you can see the full bean, but often you will see a little flap of skin that adds a pleasant and natural look to the corners of the mouth. When we are developing in the womb, we have a split at the center of the lip; this is evident in life by a little trough between the septum (separator) of the nostrils and the top-center of the upper lip. This little ravine is called the **philtrum**. An individual's philtrum can be deep and angular or very soft and gentle. Around the lips often you can see a little piping or rim that can be very beautiful when added to the area surrounding the mouth. I think of Michelangelo's *David* when talking about this rim (piping). What I would suggest when viewing an individual is to look for any of these seemingly little things that added together create big things, and better art.

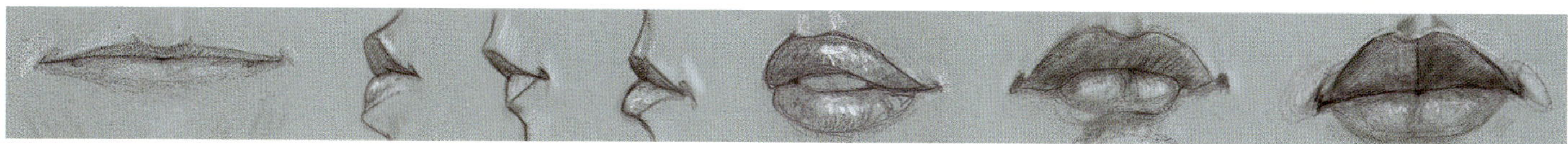

The Ears

It is difficult to identify one's ears if they were in a "lineup" with other ears unless you have an obvious variance (piercings, for instance) or some extreme distinguishing feature. But in the ear's defense, it is a fascinating and complex engineering marvel. It catches sound waves and helps in how we experience the world around us. Its many folds are designed and formed to help facilitate how we hear and how waves of sound travel into our auditory canal onto the eardrum and beyond. Each fold and hollow has a name; that is how important and well-designed our ears are.

Do yourself a favor and study these marvels, what I call the "unmade beds," to better add reality and character to your work. There are more named forms on an ear than most people would imagine. The outer part is very tubular, like a bike tire, which is the **helix**. One interesting aspect of the helix is a form that seems to be bulbous: like a snake with a rodent inside its body. Many people have this; sometimes it's at the very top and sometimes just behind that apex. So that means that the best way to draw an ear is to depict an imperfect bike tire, varying it in thickness as it arcs back and down toward the **earlobe**. The wrinkly inner part that splits

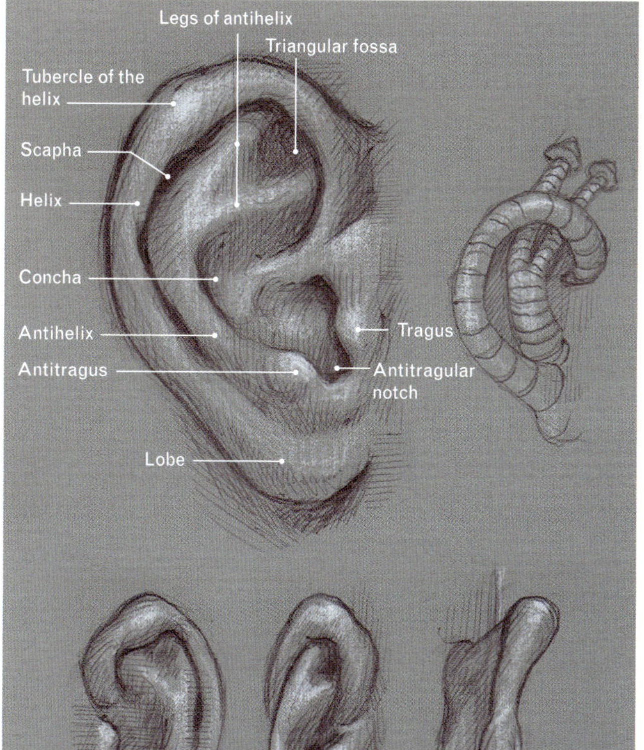

DRAWING THE HEAD AND FACE: GLOBE METHOD

One of the most basic guides artists use to draw a head and face is a globe.

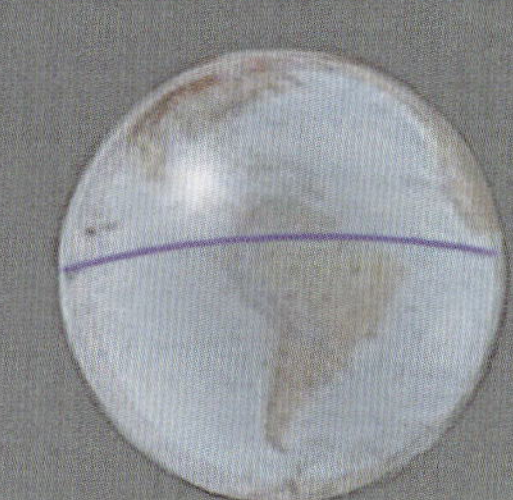

Equator = Brow line

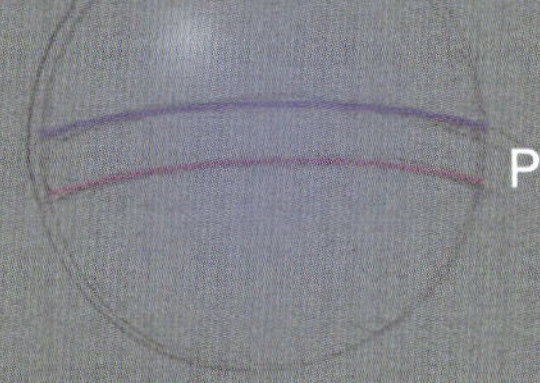

Place the next line just below for the eye line (red)

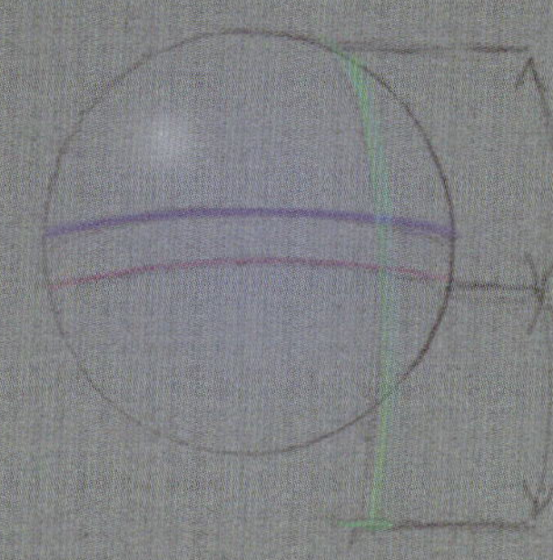

Take the distance from the top of the head to the eye line and double it to get the bottom of the chin.

Depending on what angle the person is facing, decide on vertical center and draw a line (green). This is the line of symmetry for the face.

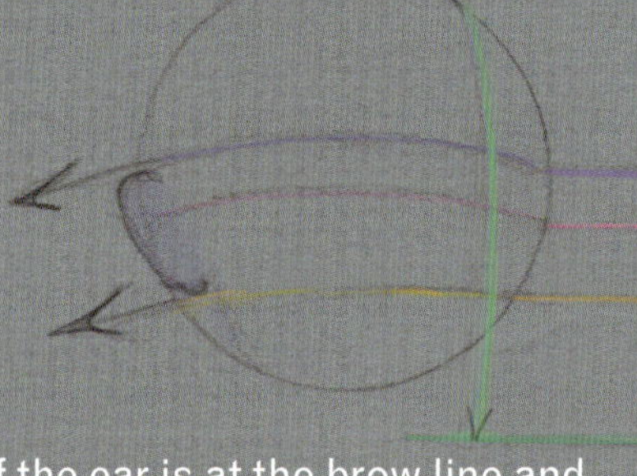

Halfway between the brow and the chin, draw a line (yellow) to find the bottom of the nose. This is also how to find the bottom of the ear.

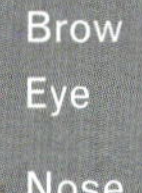

The top of the ear is at the brow line and the bottom is at the nose line.

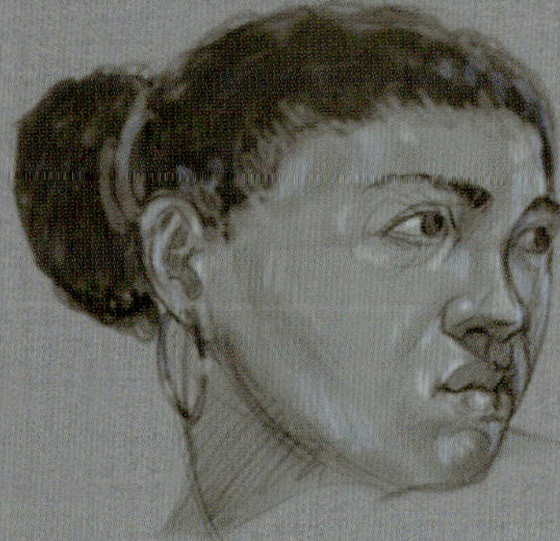

The base of the skull falls on the same line as the bottom of the nose.

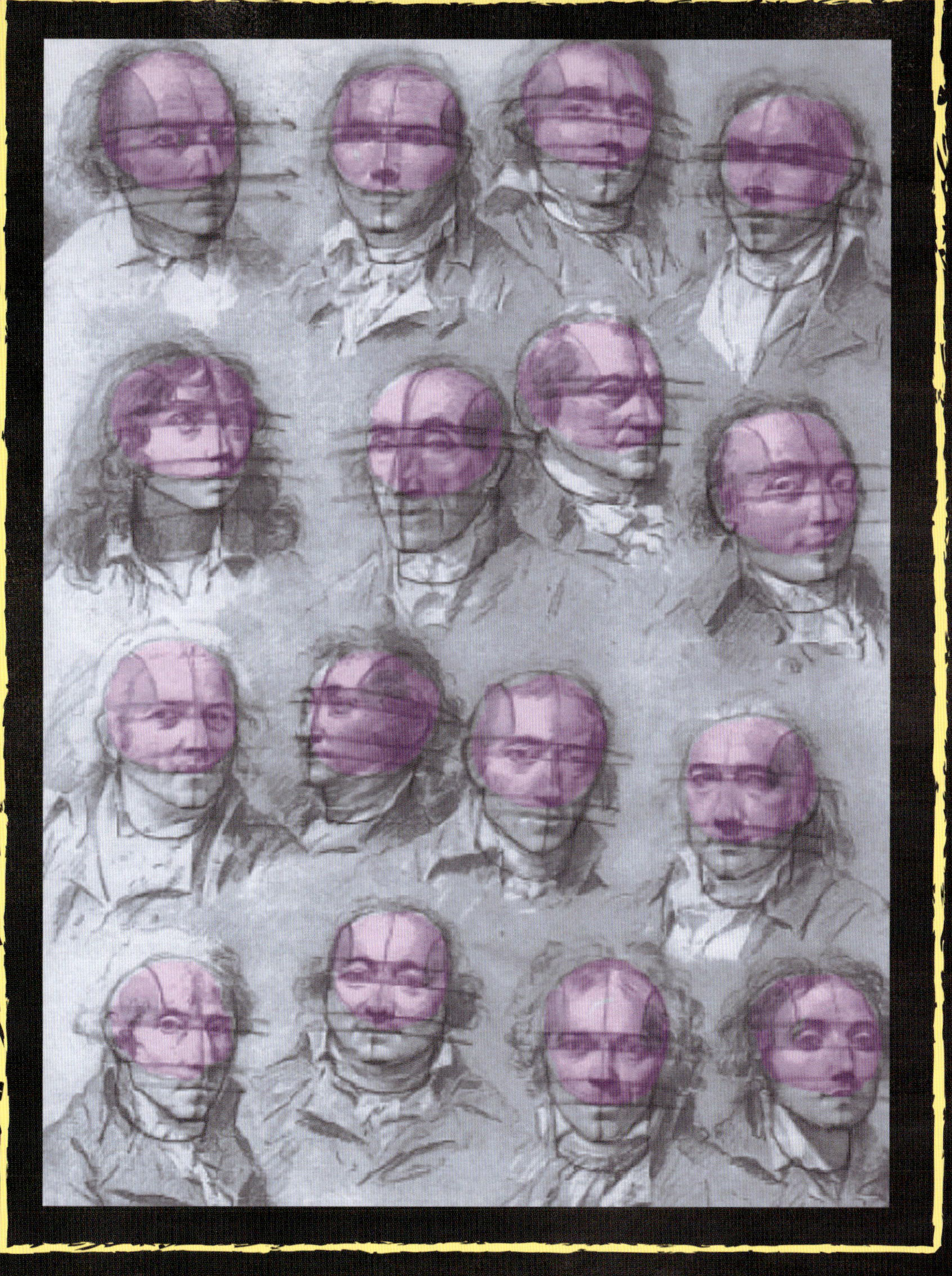

Using the drawings of Louis-Léopold Boilly, I implemented the Globe Method to help my students place facial

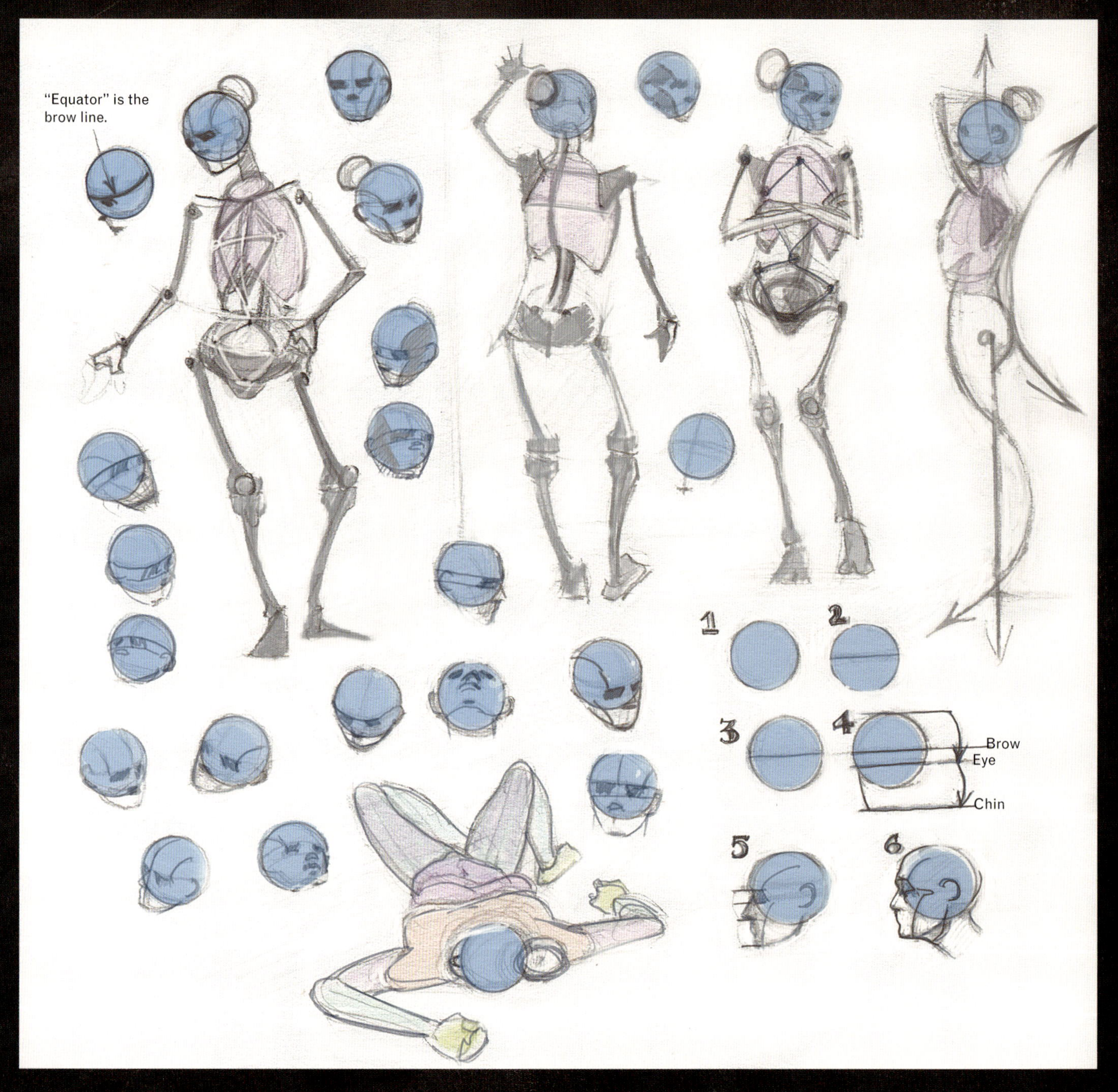

Practice figures from imagination to fine-tune proportions and rhythms. Note the random spheres for heads in all positions you can think of. The more you use these lines as a guide, the better you will get at depicting people's faces in realistic positions.

"Always carry your sketchbook. Copy from life, from reference, from anything as long as you are putting in your daily pencil mileage."

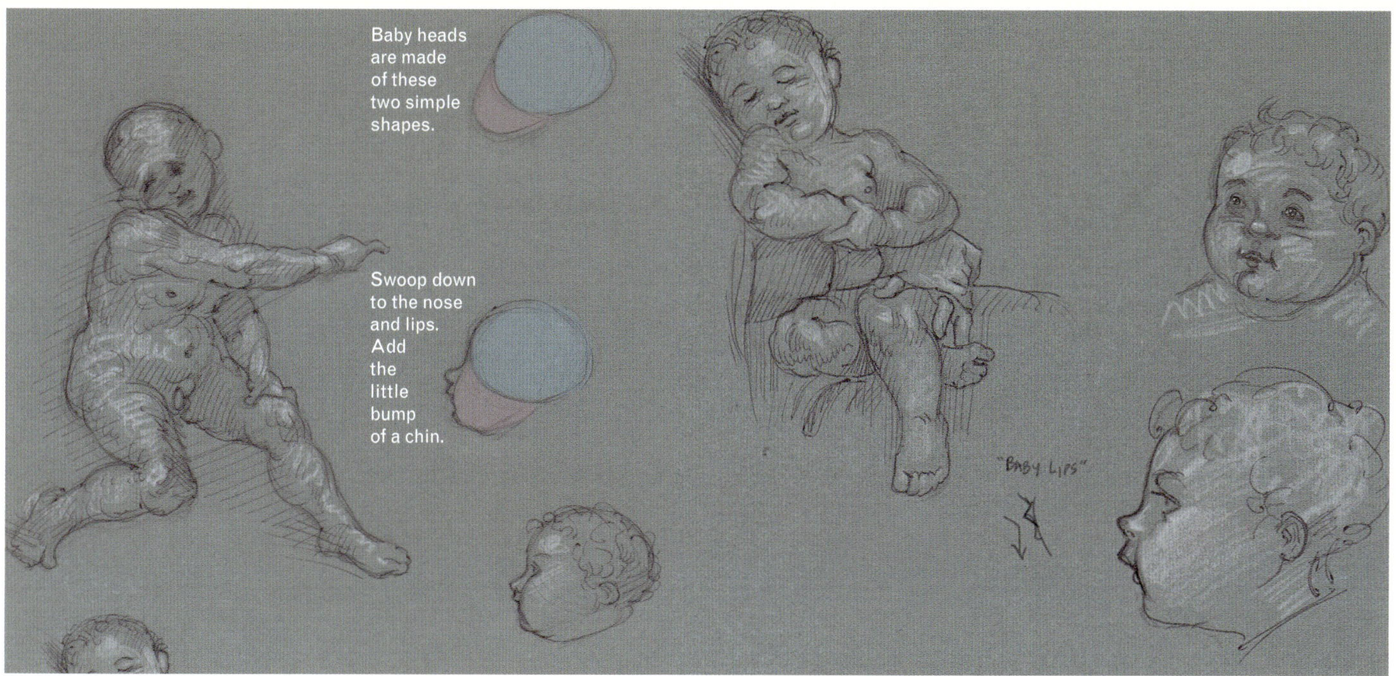

There are countless babies in art history! Use them to practice, then make some up from imagination.

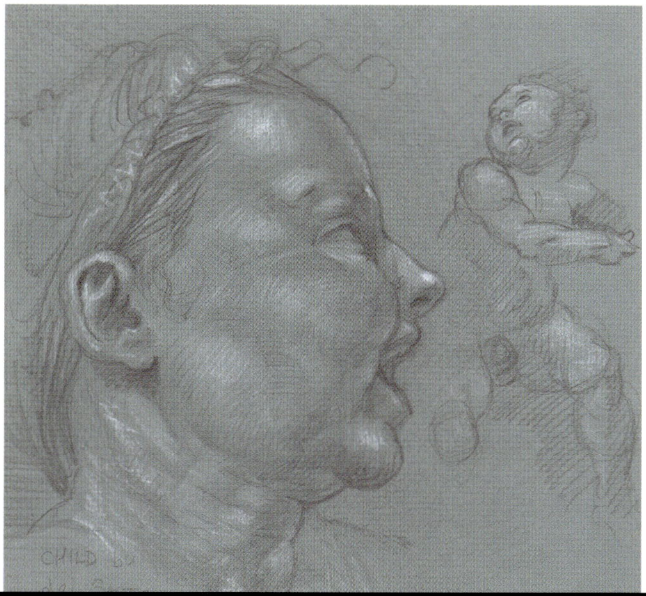

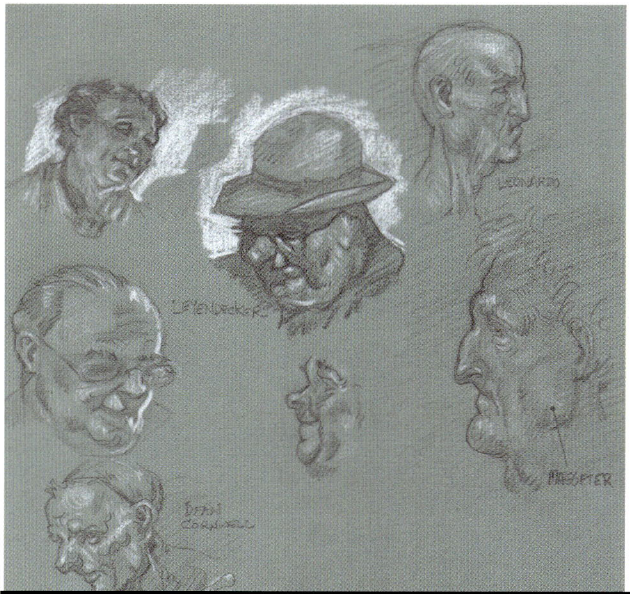

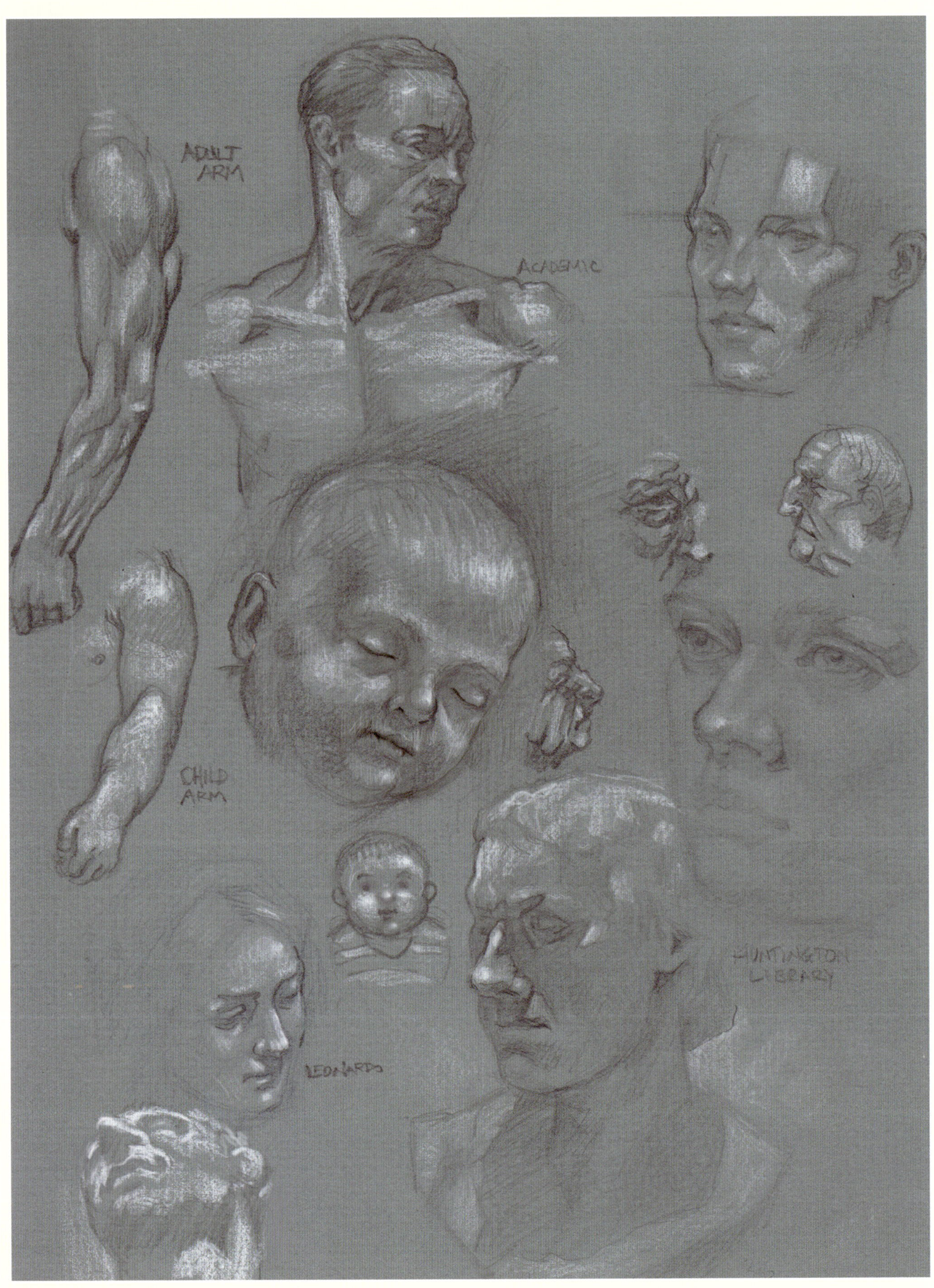

ADULT ARM
ACADEMIC
CHILD ARM
LEONARDO
HUNTINGTON LIBRARY

PANNICULUS ADIPOSUS

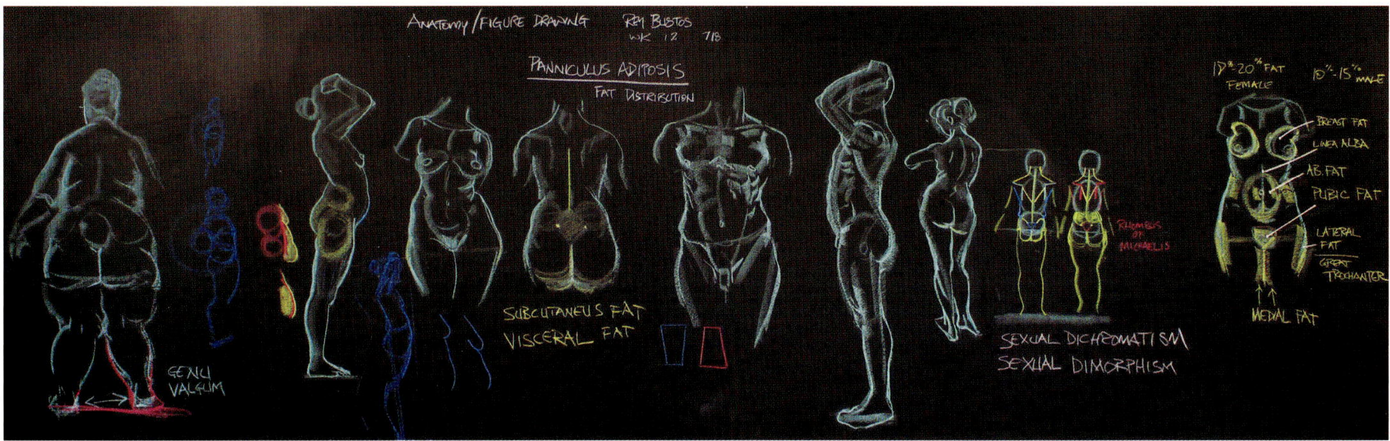

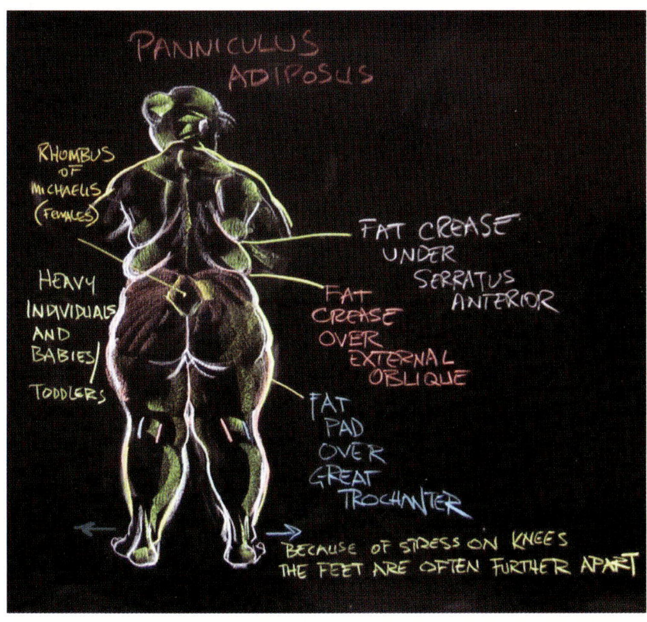

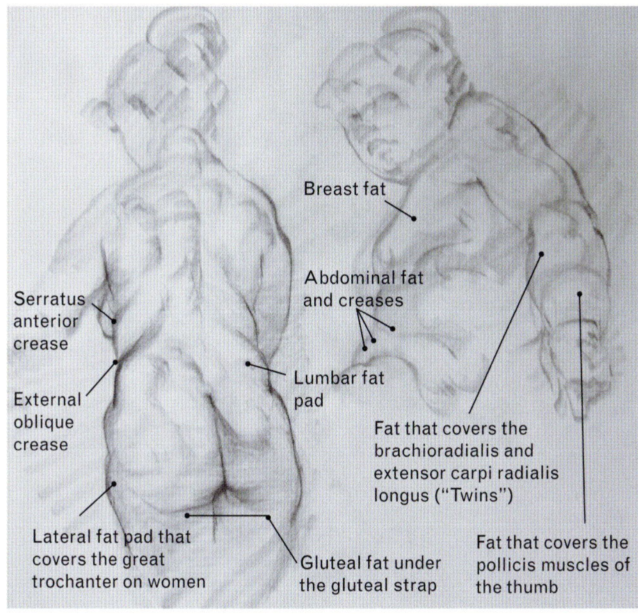

Panniculus adiposus is the fancy name for the suit of fat that all of us wear. Here too, I will give an overview to address the most important aspects of this. Fat varies from person to person, especially from male to female. On males, the fatty area over the sacrum is referred to as the

It is critical that every artist have some familiarity with the fat pads of the body, especially on women. The healthy fat that covers the body when added to a piece of art adds the humanity needed to connect with the viewer. Notice how low the gluteus maximus is below the gluteal strap. Add

Subcutaneous Fat and Visceral Fat

Fat cells are throughout our bodies. As adults we have between 10 to 30 billion fat cells in our bodies. In this book, I wanted to mention fat because knowing the skeleton and the muscles well is not enough to explain the myriad of forms and differences in the outer appearance of the human body. I do not want to get into too much physiology, you can delve into that as interest dictates, but I must explain two very important types of fat: **subcutaneous** and **visceral fat**.

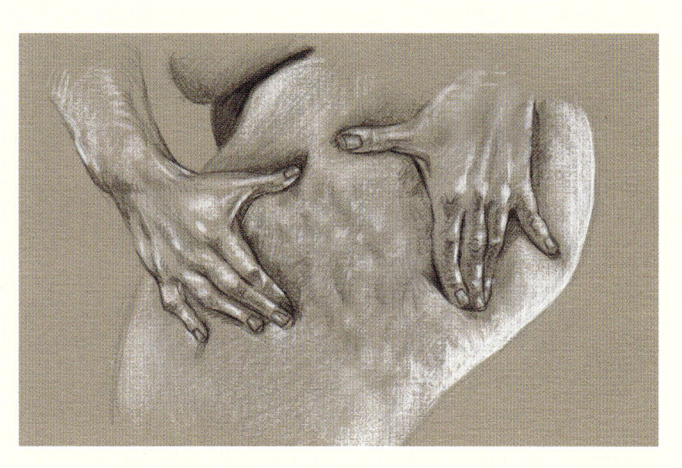

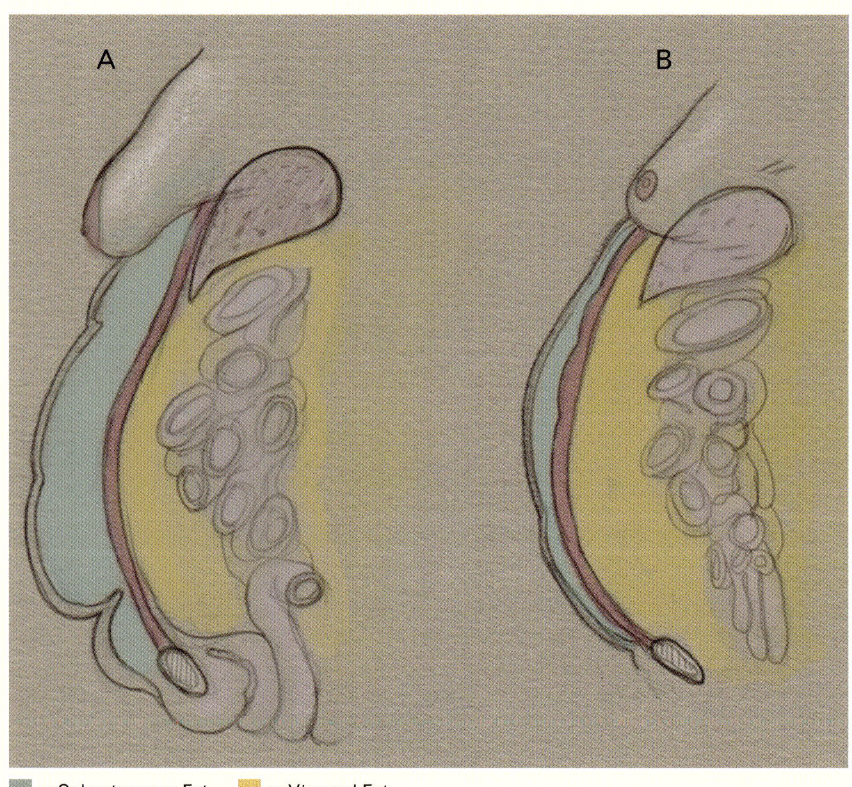

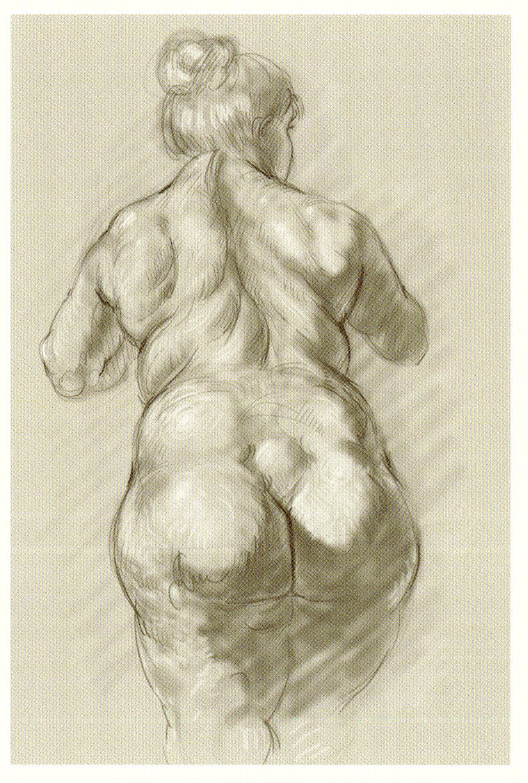

In the female illustration (A) depicting the stomach area, the blue area is subcutaneous fat over the abdominal muscles and is generally soft and often pulled down by gravity. This is more common with women. The yellow is visceral fat that is behind the abdominal muscle and surrounds the organs and intestines. In the male example (B), the proportions are reversed. Here, the subcutaneous fat has less volume and the visceral fat is dominant, therefore pushing the abdominal muscle out, giving the appearance of a hard, round belly. This is more typical of men and very unhealthy. This form is reminiscent of a pregnant woman in one way, that the baby is behind the abdominal muscle, pushing out the abdomen and creating the firm, big belly of a soon-to-be mother.

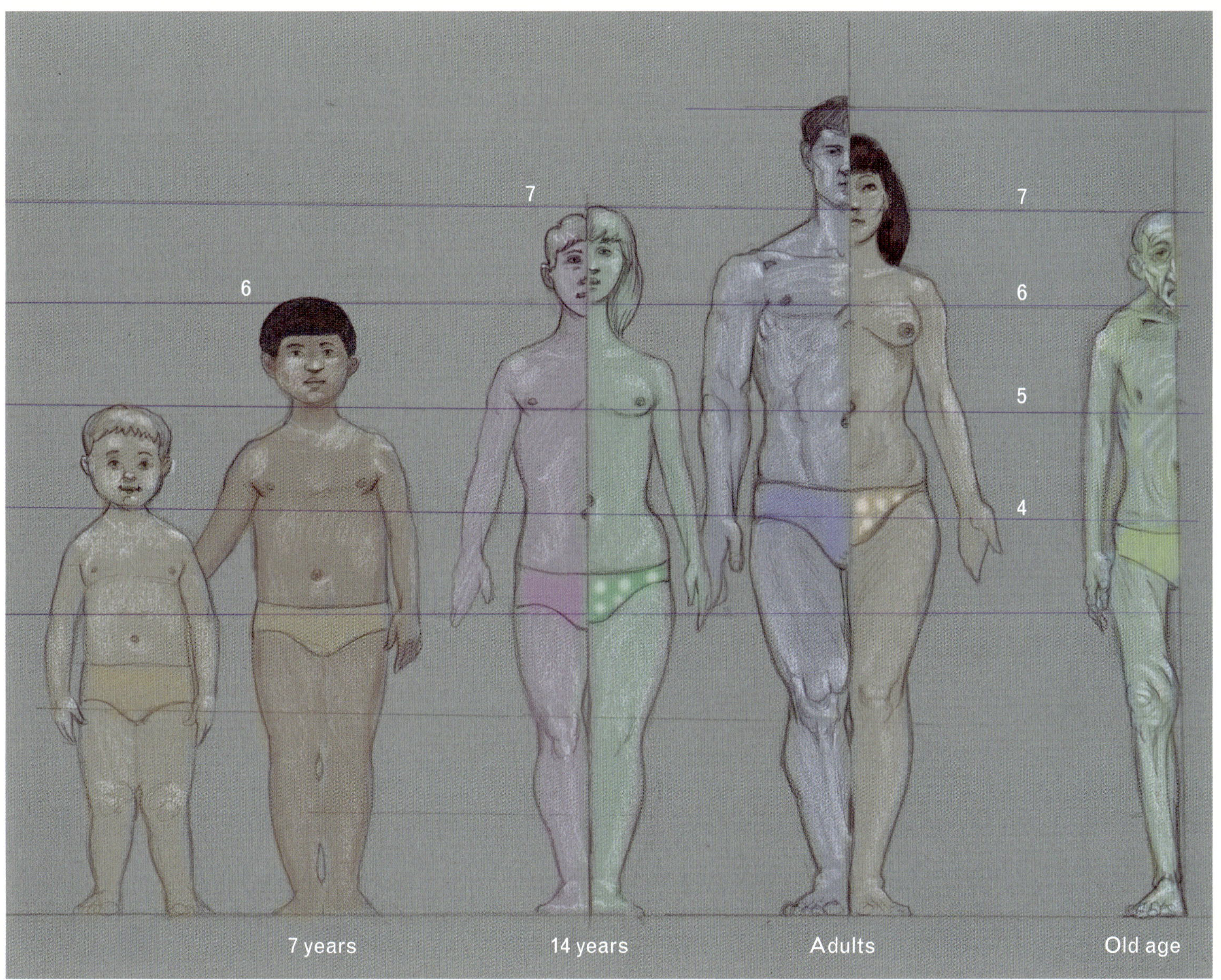

With age, factors such as loss of cartilage and curvatures of the skeleton decrease subcutaneous fat and overall height.

THE ART OF ÉCORCHÉ

Écorché (ay-kor-shay) is a French word that means flayed. It is an age-old method of learning anatomy by drawing or sculpting the body without the skin. This technique reveals the interplay between the muscle groups and the skeletal framework directly; undisguised by the layering of the skin, which allows the student to cultivate a more intimate knowledge of the body.

In my écorché class, students make sculptures using polymer clay. I have found that this way of teaching is a highly effective way for any art student to learn anatomy. My écorché images are included in this book because of the clarity and elegance that is revealed so uniquely through the use of three dimensionality.

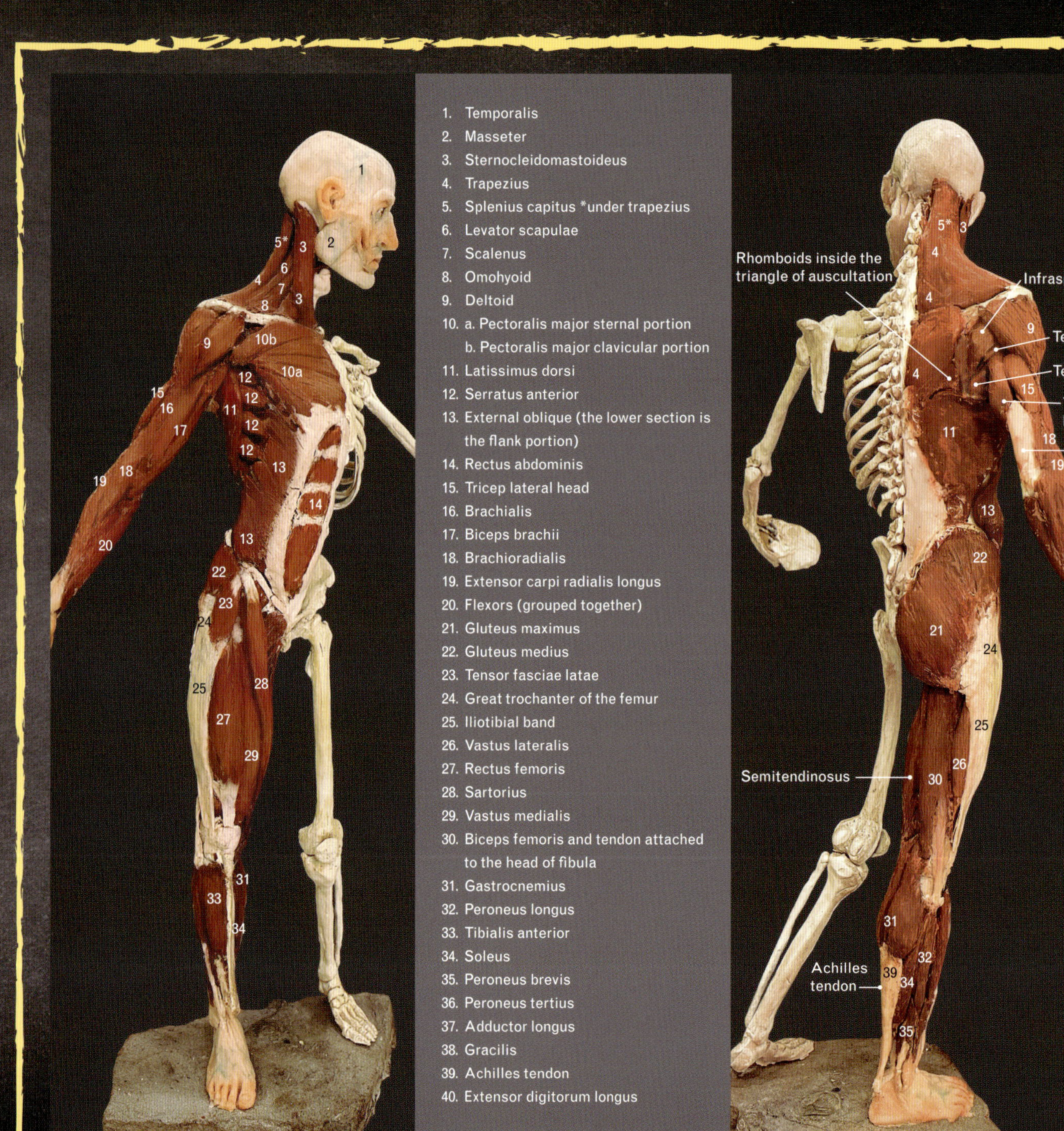

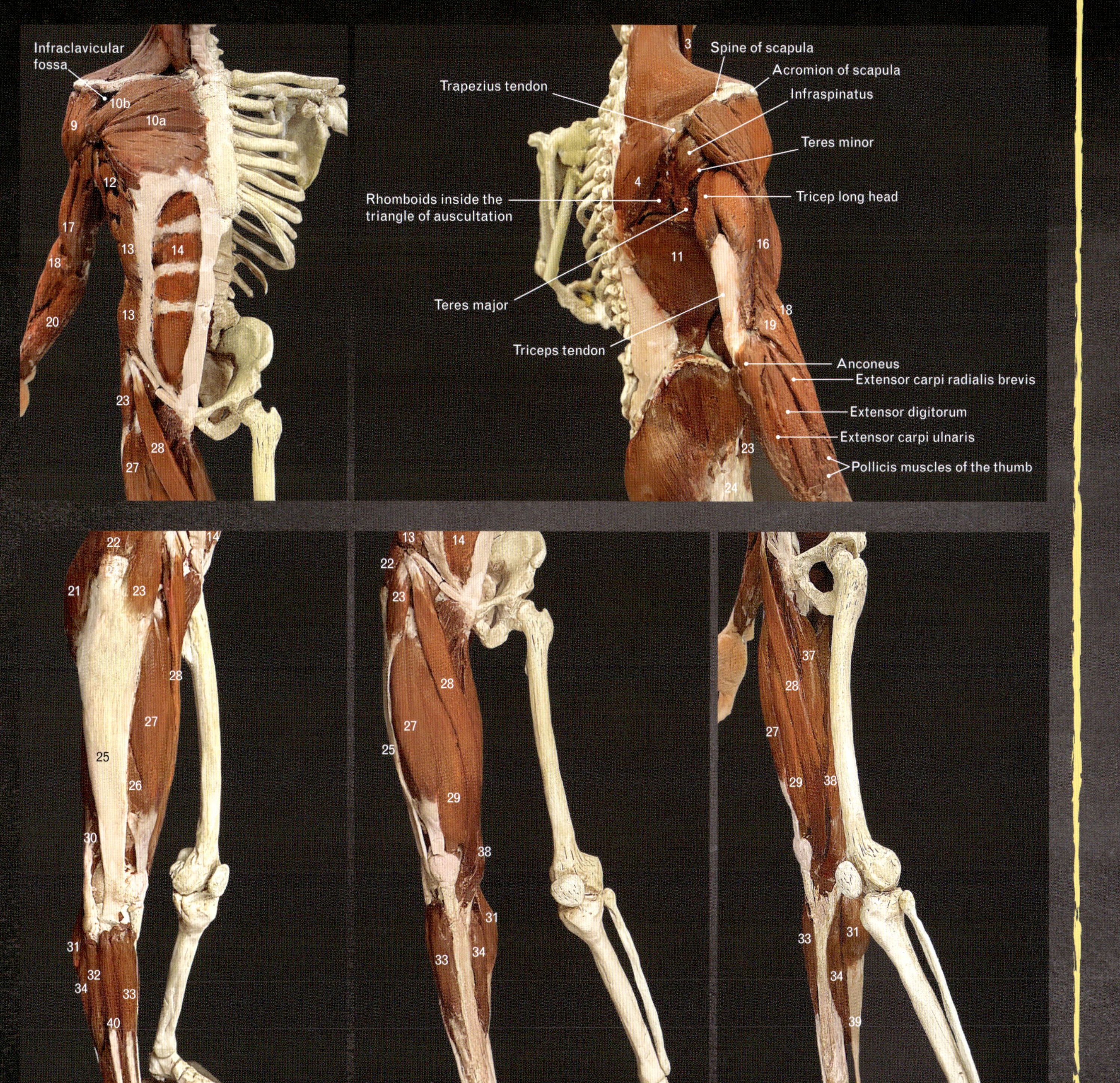

Infraclavicular fossa
10b
9
10a
12
17
13
18
14
13
20
13
23
28
27
Spine of scapula
Acromion of scapula
Trapezius tendon
Infraspinatus
Teres minor
Rhomboids inside the triangle of auscultation
Tricep long head
4
11
16
Teres major
18
19
Triceps tendon
Anconeus
Extensor carpi radialis brevis
Extensor digitorum
23
Extensor carpi ulnaris
Pollicis muscles of the thumb
24
22
14
21
23
28
27
25
26
30
31
32
34
33
40
13
14
22
23
28
27
25
29
38
31
33
34
37
28
27
29
38
33
31
34
39

THE HUMAN MUSCULAR SYSTEM

Now that we have reviewed the essential bones and muscles of the human body that any artist should know, I've provided several illustrations that depict the entire human muscular system.

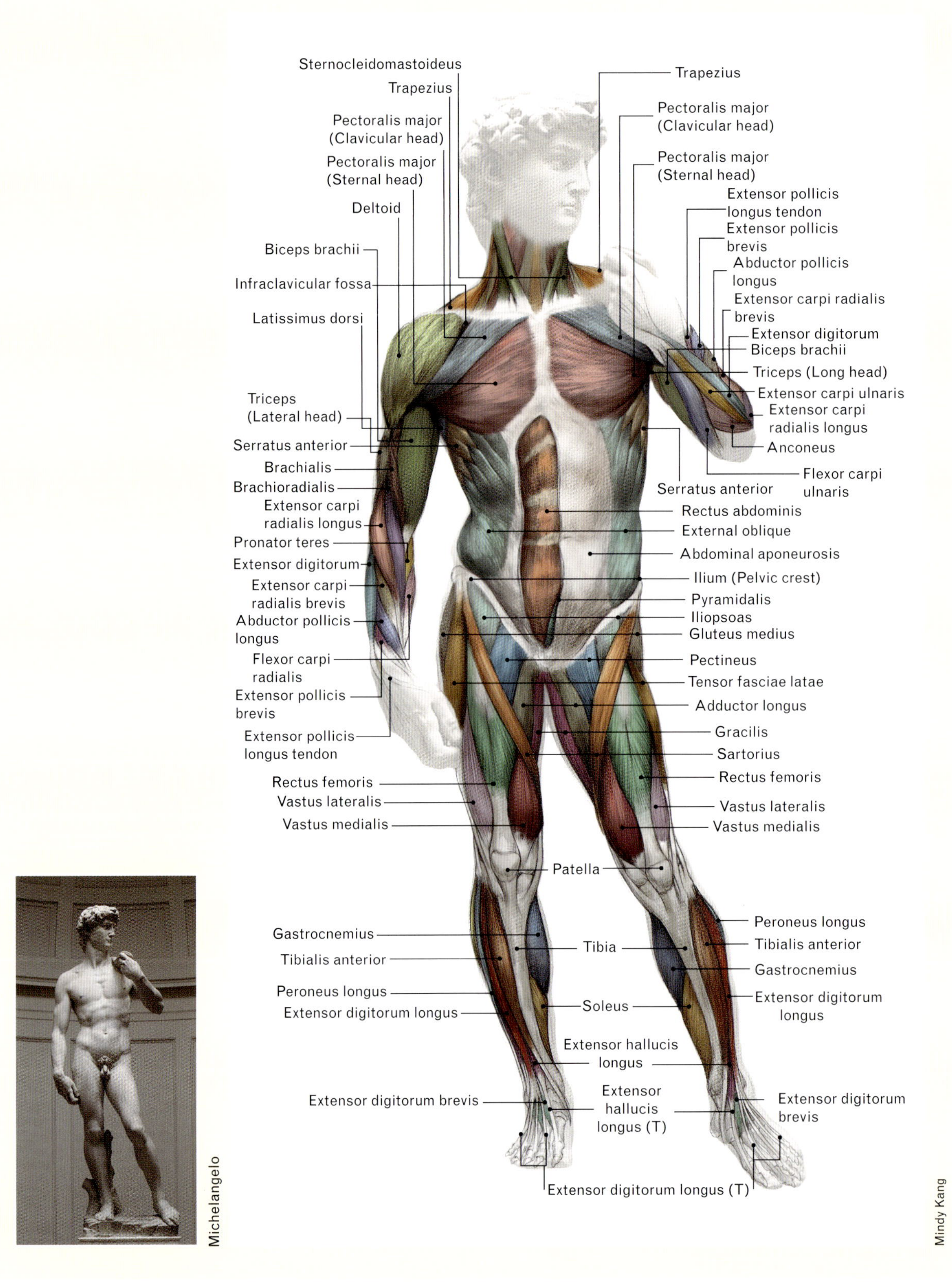

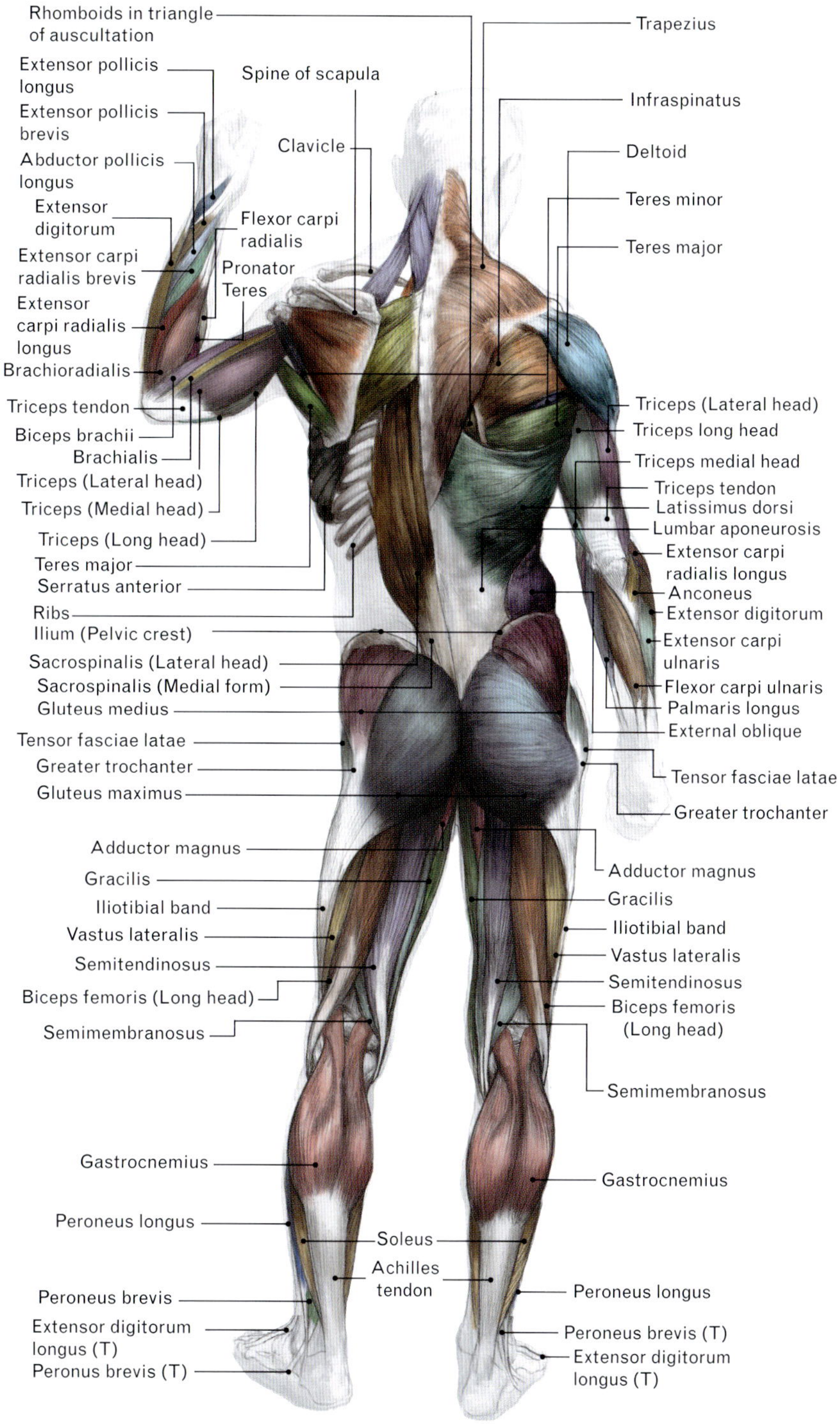

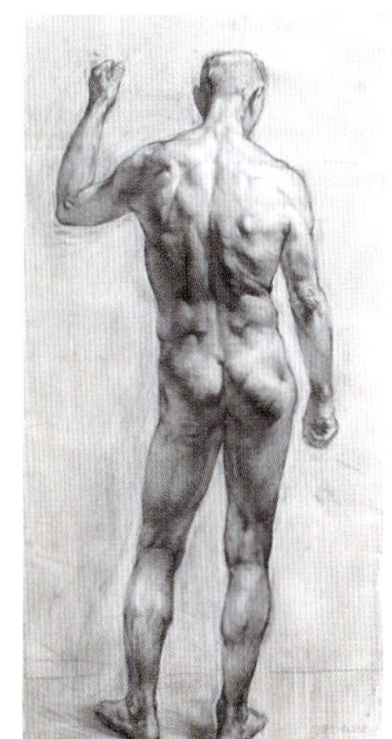

Rhomboids in triangle of auscultation
Extensor pollicis longus
Extensor pollicis brevis
Abductor pollicis longus
Extensor digitorum
Extensor carpi radialis brevis
Extensor carpi radialis longus
Brachioradialis
Triceps tendon
Biceps brachii
Brachialis
Triceps (Lateral head)
Triceps (Medial head)
Triceps (Long head)
Teres major
Serratus anterior
Ribs
Ilium (Pelvic crest)
Sacrospinalis (Lateral head)
Sacrospinalis (Medial form)
Gluteus medius
Tensor fasciae latae
Greater trochanter
Gluteus maximus
Adductor magnus
Gracilis
Iliotibial band
Vastus lateralis
Semitendinosus
Biceps femoris (Long head)
Semimembranosus
Gastrocnemius
Peroneus longus
Peroneus brevis
Extensor digitorum longus (T)
Peronus brevis (T)
Spine of scapula
Clavicle
Flexor carpi radialis
Pronator Teres
Soleus
Achilles tendon
Trapezius
Infraspinatus
Deltoid
Teres minor
Teres major
Triceps (Lateral head)
Triceps long head
Triceps medial head
Triceps tendon
Latissimus dorsi
Lumbar aponeurosis
Extensor carpi radialis longus
Anconeus
Extensor digitorum
Extensor carpi ulnaris
Flexor carpi ulnaris
Palmaris longus
External oblique
Tensor fasciae latae
Greater trochanter
Adductor magnus
Gracilis
Iliotibial band
Vastus lateralis
Semitendinosus
Biceps femoris (Long head)
Semimembranosus
Gastrocnemius
Peroneus longus
Peroneus brevis (T)
Extensor digitorum longus (T)
Iliya Mirochnik
Mindy Kang

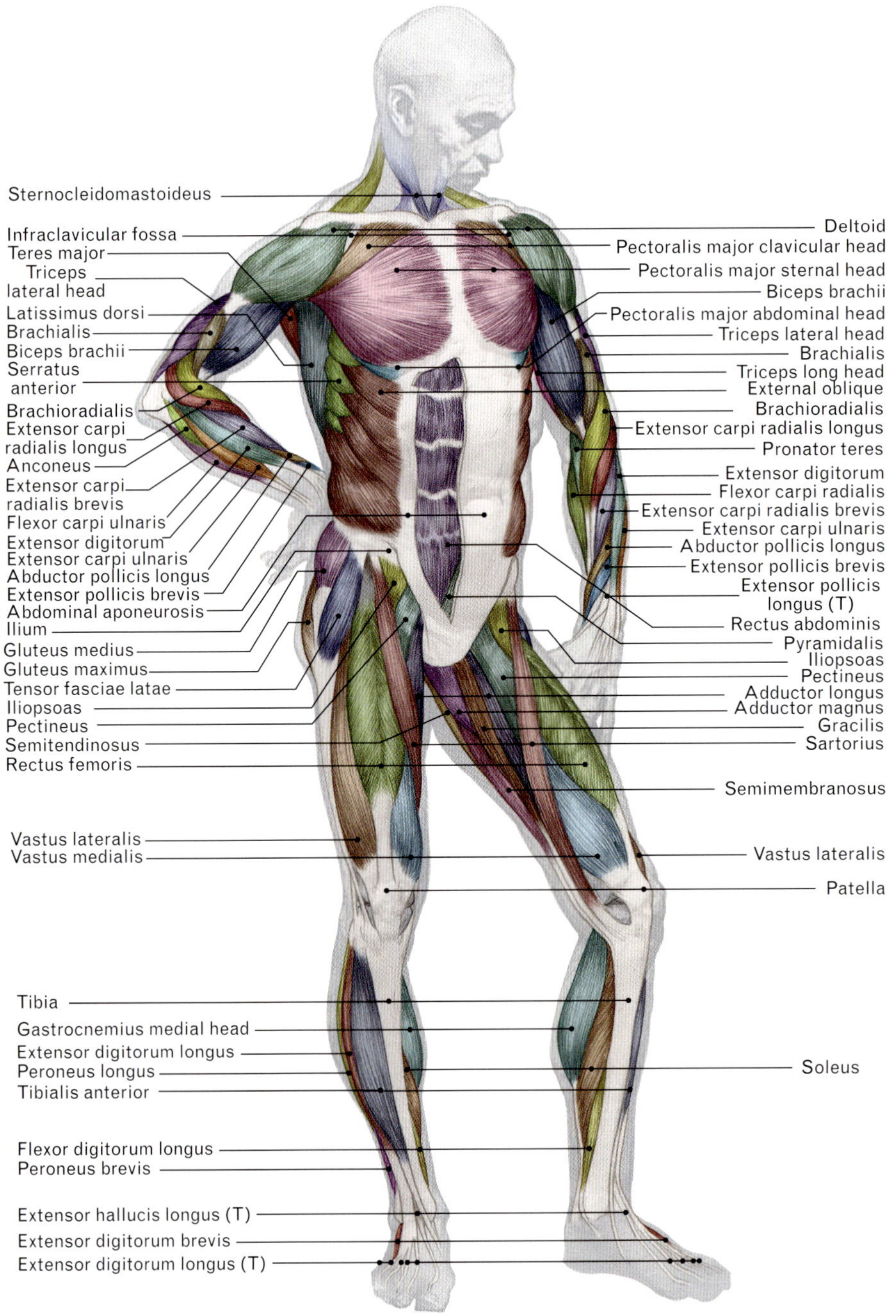

Sternocleidomastoideus
Infraclavicular fossa
Teres major
Triceps lateral head
Latissimus dorsi
Brachialis
Biceps brachii
Serratus anterior
Brachioradialis
Extensor carpi radialis longus
Anconeus
Extensor carpi radialis brevis
Flexor carpi ulnaris
Extensor digitorum
Extensor carpi ulnaris
Abductor pollicis longus
Extensor pollicis brevis
Abdominal aponeurosis
Ilium
Gluteus medius
Gluteus maximus
Tensor fasciae latae
Iliopsoas
Pectineus
Semitendinosus
Rectus femoris
Vastus lateralis
Vastus medialis
Tibia
Gastrocnemius medial head
Extensor digitorum longus
Peroneus longus
Tibialis anterior
Flexor digitorum longus
Peroneus brevis
Extensor hallucis longus (T)
Extensor digitorum brevis
Extensor digitorum longus (T)
Deltoid
Pectoralis major clavicular head
Pectoralis major sternal head
Biceps brachii
Pectoralis major abdominal head
Triceps lateral head
Brachialis
Triceps long head
External oblique
Brachioradialis
Extensor carpi radialis longus
Pronator teres
Extensor digitorum
Flexor carpi radialis
Extensor carpi radialis brevis
Extensor carpi ulnaris
Abductor pollicis longus
Extensor pollicis brevis
Extensor pollicis longus (T)
Rectus abdominis
Pyramidalis
Iliopsoas
Pectineus
Adductor longus
Adductor magnus
Gracilis
Sartorius
Semimembranosus
Vastus lateralis
Patella
Soleus
Repin Acadamy Image
Hetiam Duan

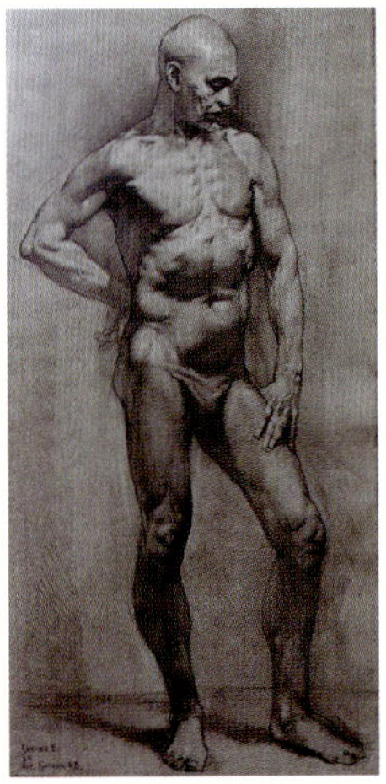

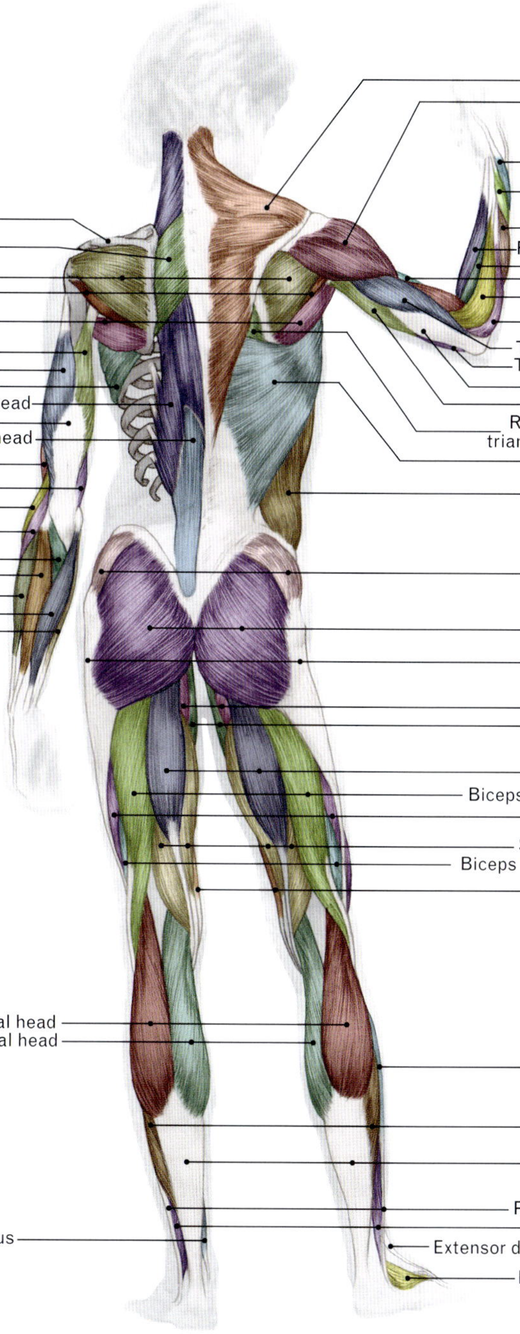

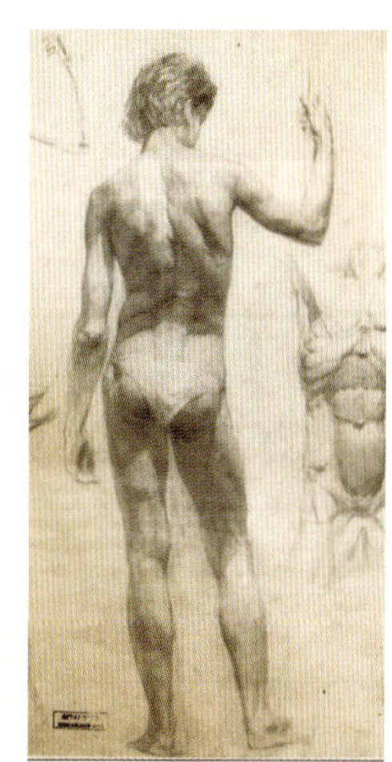

Iliya Mirochnik

Trapezius
Deltoid
Extensor pollicis brevis
Abductor pollicis longus
Extensor carpi radialis brevis
Flexor carpi radialis
Pronator teres
Biceps brachii
Brachioradialis
Extensor carpi radialis longus
Triceps lateral head
Triceps medial head
Triceps tendon
Triceps long head
Rhomboid within the triangle of auscultation
Latissimus dorsi
External oblique
Gluteus medius
Gluteus maximus
Iliotibial band
Adductor magnus
Gracilis
Semitendinosus
Biceps femoris long head
Vastus lateralis
Semimembranosus
Biceps femoris short head
Sartorius
Peroneus longus
Soleus
Achilles tendon
Peroneus longus (T)
Peroneus brevis
Extensor digitorum longus (T)
Extensor digitorum brevis
Spine of scapula
Rhomboid
Infraspinatus
Teres minor
Teres major
Triceps long head
Triceps lateral head
Serratus anterior
Sacrospinalis lateral head
Triceps tendon
Sacrospinalis medial head
Brachialis
Triceps medial head
Brachioradialis
Extensor carpi radialis longus
Anconeus
Extensor carpi ulnaris
Extensor digitorum
Flexor carpi ulnaris
Palmaris longus
Gastrocnemius lateral head
Gastrocnemius medial head
Flexor digitorum longus
Hetiam Duan

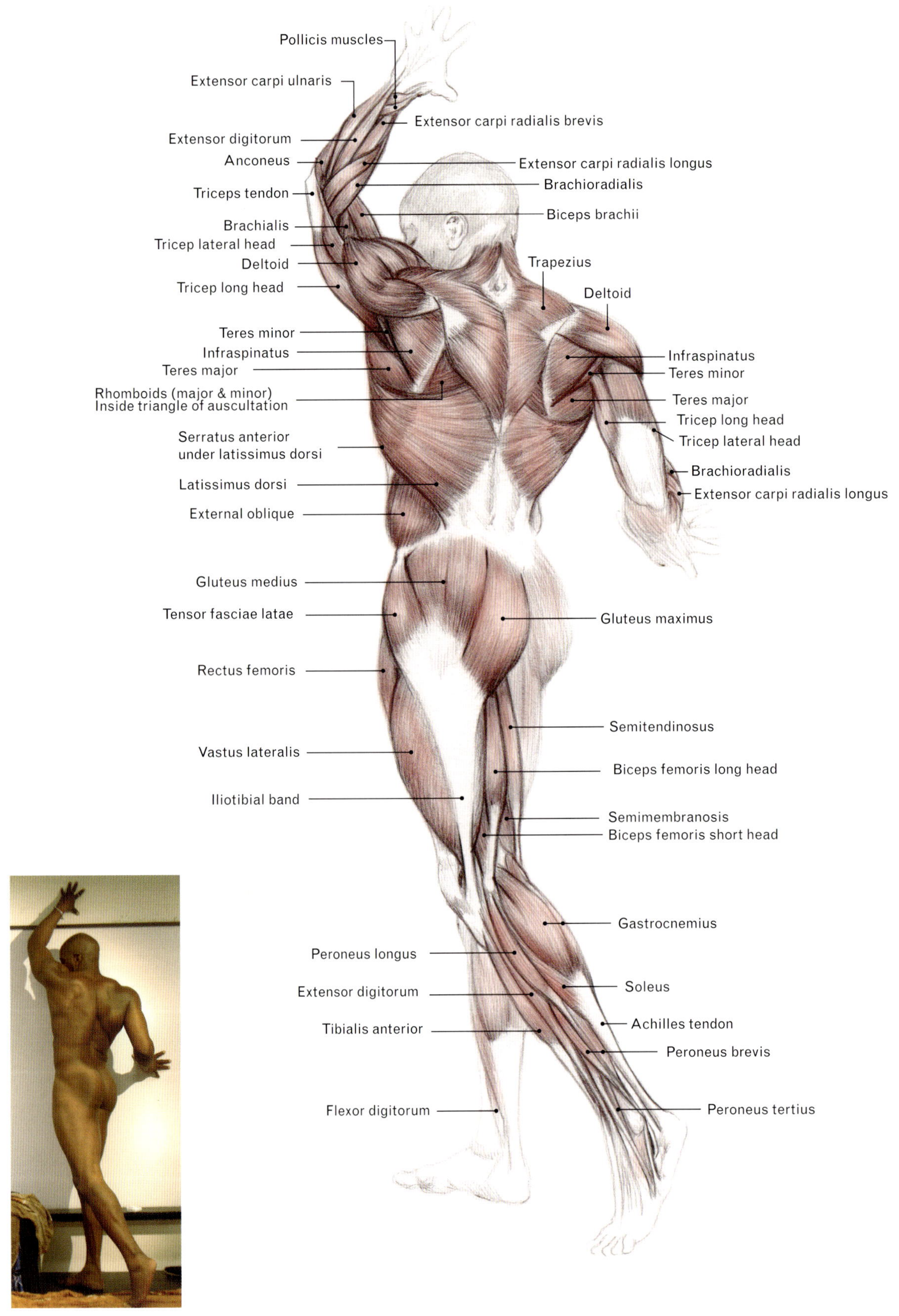

Pollicis muscles
Extensor carpi ulnaris
Extensor carpi radialis brevis
Extensor digitorum
Extensor carpi radialis longus
Anconeus
Brachioradialis
Triceps tendon
Biceps brachii
Brachialis
Tricep lateral head
Deltoid
Trapezius
Tricep long head
Deltoid
Teres minor
Infraspinatus
Teres major
Infraspinatus
Teres minor
Rhomboids (major & minor)
Inside triangle of auscultation
Teres major
Tricep long head
Tricep lateral head
Serratus anterior
under latissimus dorsi
Brachioradialis
Latissimus dorsi
Extensor carpi radialis longus
External oblique
Gluteus medius
Tensor fasciae latae
Gluteus maximus
Rectus femoris
Semitendinosus
Vastus lateralis
Biceps femoris long head
Iliotibial band
Semimembranosis
Biceps femoris short head
Gastrocnemius
Peroneus longus
Extensor digitorum
Soleus
Tibialis anterior
Achilles tendon
Peroneus brevis
Flexor digitorum
Peroneus tertius

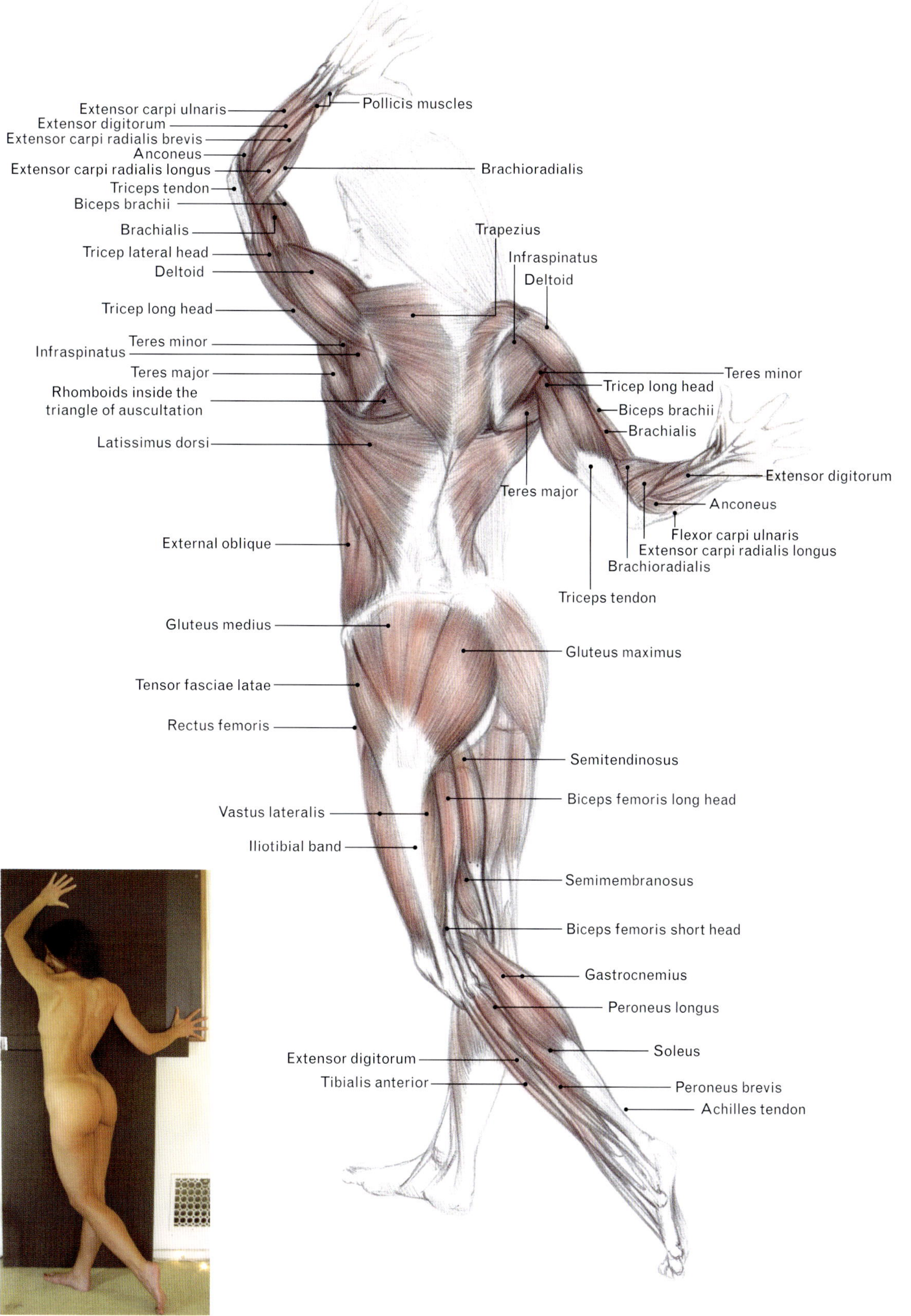

Extensor carpi ulnaris
Extensor digitorum
Extensor carpi radialis brevis
Anconeus
Extensor carpi radialis longus
Triceps tendon
Biceps brachii
Brachialis
Tricep lateral head
Deltoid
Tricep long head
Teres minor
Infraspinatus
Teres major
Rhomboids inside the triangle of auscultation
Latissimus dorsi
External oblique
Gluteus medius
Tensor fasciae latae
Rectus femoris
Vastus lateralis
Iliotibial band
Extensor digitorum
Tibialis anterior
Pollicis muscles
Brachioradialis
Trapezius
Infraspinatus
Deltoid
Teres minor
Tricep long head
Biceps brachii
Brachialis
Teres major
Extensor digitorum
Anconeus
Flexor carpi ulnaris
Extensor carpi radialis longus
Brachioradialis
Triceps tendon
Gluteus maximus
Semitendinosus
Biceps femoris long head
Semimembranosus
Biceps femoris short head
Gastrocnemius
Peroneus longus
Soleus
Peroneus brevis
Achilles tendon

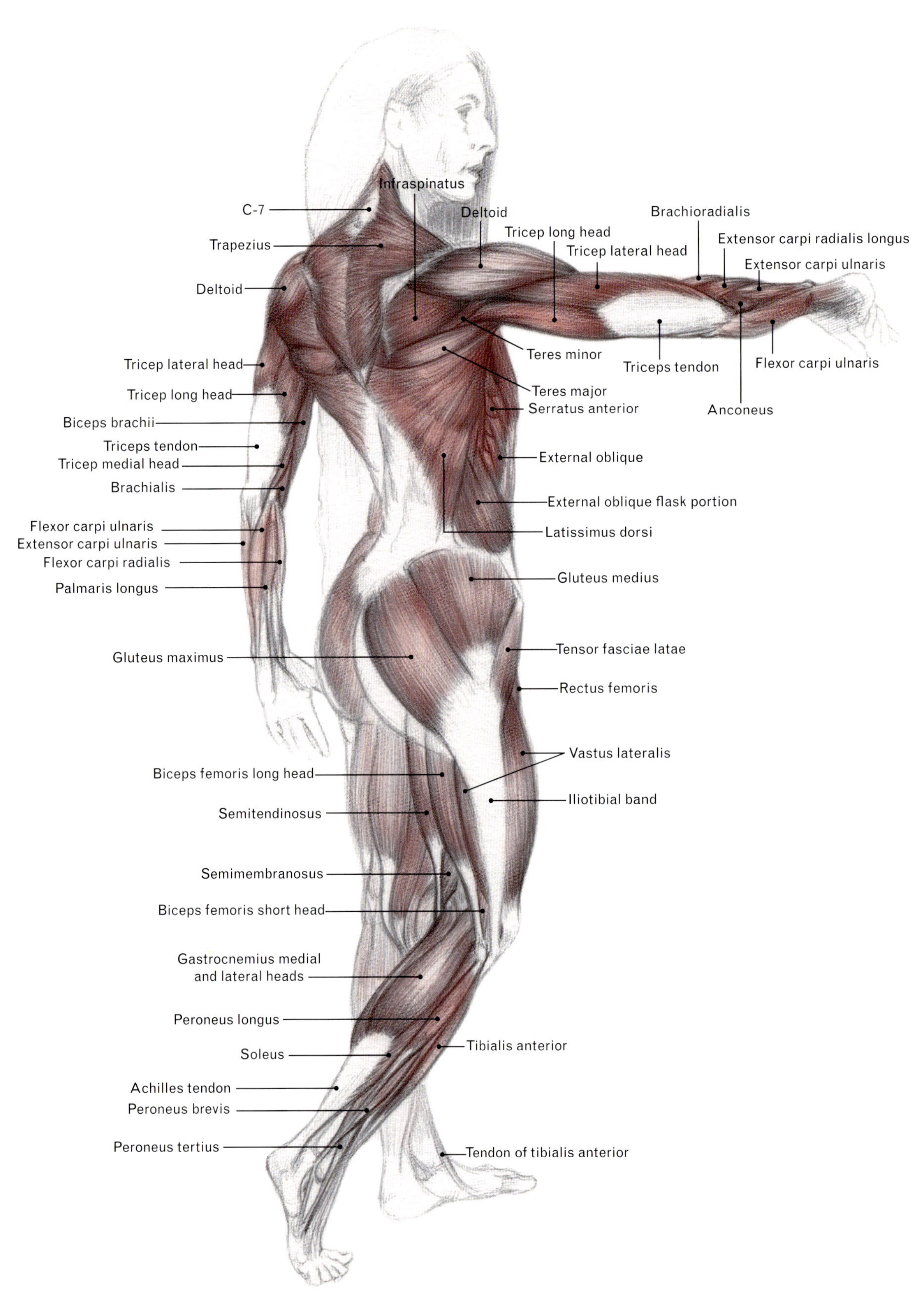

Intraspinatus
C-7
Deltoid
Tricep long head
Brachioradialis
Trapezius
Tricep lateral head
Extensor carpi radialis longus
Deltoid
Extensor carpi ulnaris
Teres minor
Tricep lateral head
Triceps tendon
Flexor carpi ulnaris
Tricep long head
Teres major
Biceps brachii
Serratus anterior
Anconeus
Triceps tendon
Tricep medial head
External oblique
Brachialis
External oblique flask portion
Flexor carpi ulnaris
Latissimus dorsi
Extensor carpi ulnaris
Flexor carpi radialis
Gluteus medius
Palmaris longus
Tensor fasciae latae
Gluteus maximus
Rectus femoris
Vastus lateralis
Biceps femoris long head
Iliotibial band
Semitendinosus
Semimembranosus
Biceps femoris short head
Gastrocnemius medial
and lateral heads
Peroneus longus
Tibialis anterior
Soleus
Achilles tendon
Peroneus brevis
Peroneus tertius
Tendon of tibialis anterior

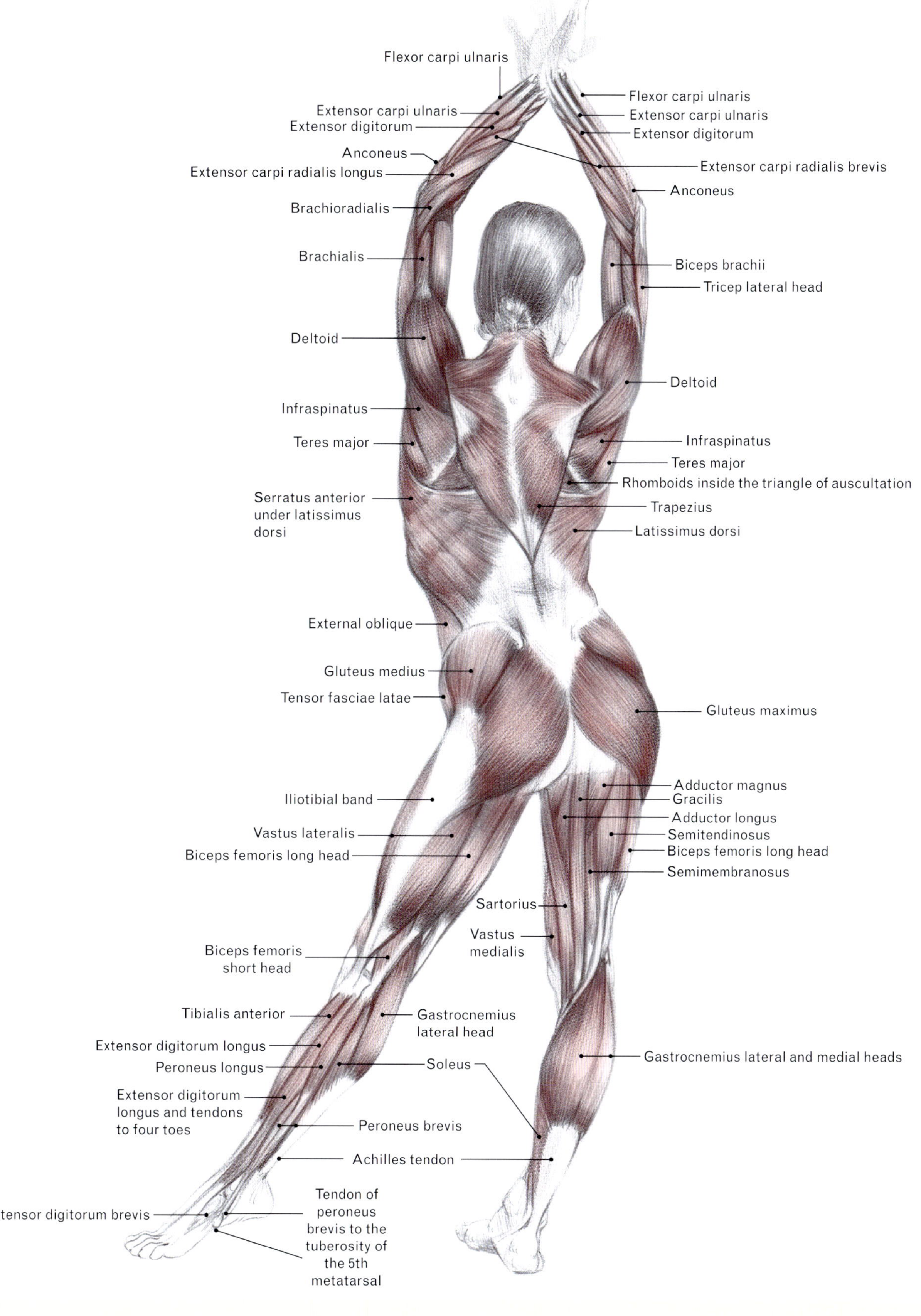

Flexor carpi ulnaris
Extensor carpi ulnaris
Extensor digitorum
Anconeus
Extensor carpi radialis longus
Brachioradialis
Brachialis
Deltoid
Infraspinatus
Teres major
Serratus anterior under latissimus dorsi
External oblique
Gluteus medius
Tensor fasciae latae
Iliotibial band
Vastus lateralis
Biceps femoris long head
Biceps femoris short head
Tibialis anterior
Extensor digitorum longus
Peroneus longus
Extensor digitorum longus and tendons to four toes
Extensor digitorum brevis
Flexor carpi ulnaris
Extensor carpi ulnaris
Extensor digitorum
Extensor carpi radialis brevis
Anconeus
Biceps brachii
Tricep lateral head
Deltoid
Infraspinatus
Teres major
Rhomboids inside the triangle of auscultation
Trapezius
Latissimus dorsi
Gluteus maximus
Adductor magnus
Gracilis
Adductor longus
Semitendinosus
Biceps femoris long head
Semimembranosus
Sartorius
Vastus medialis
Gastrocnemius lateral head
Gastrocnemius lateral and medial heads
Soleus
Peroneus brevis
Achilles tendon
Tendon of peroneus brevis to the tuberosity of the 5th metatarsal

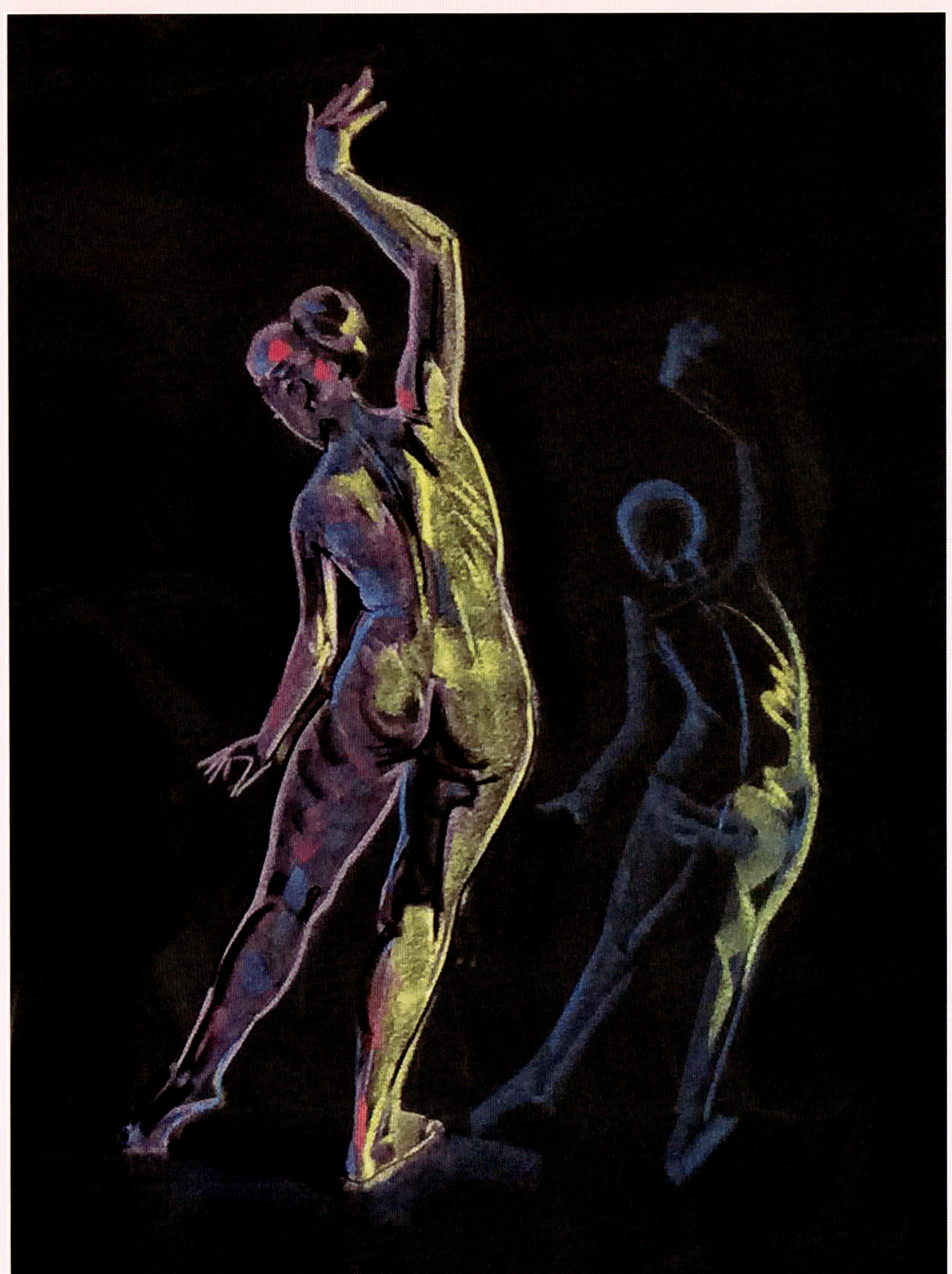

PART II
ANATOMY APPLIED

"Creativity takes courage." —Henri Matisse

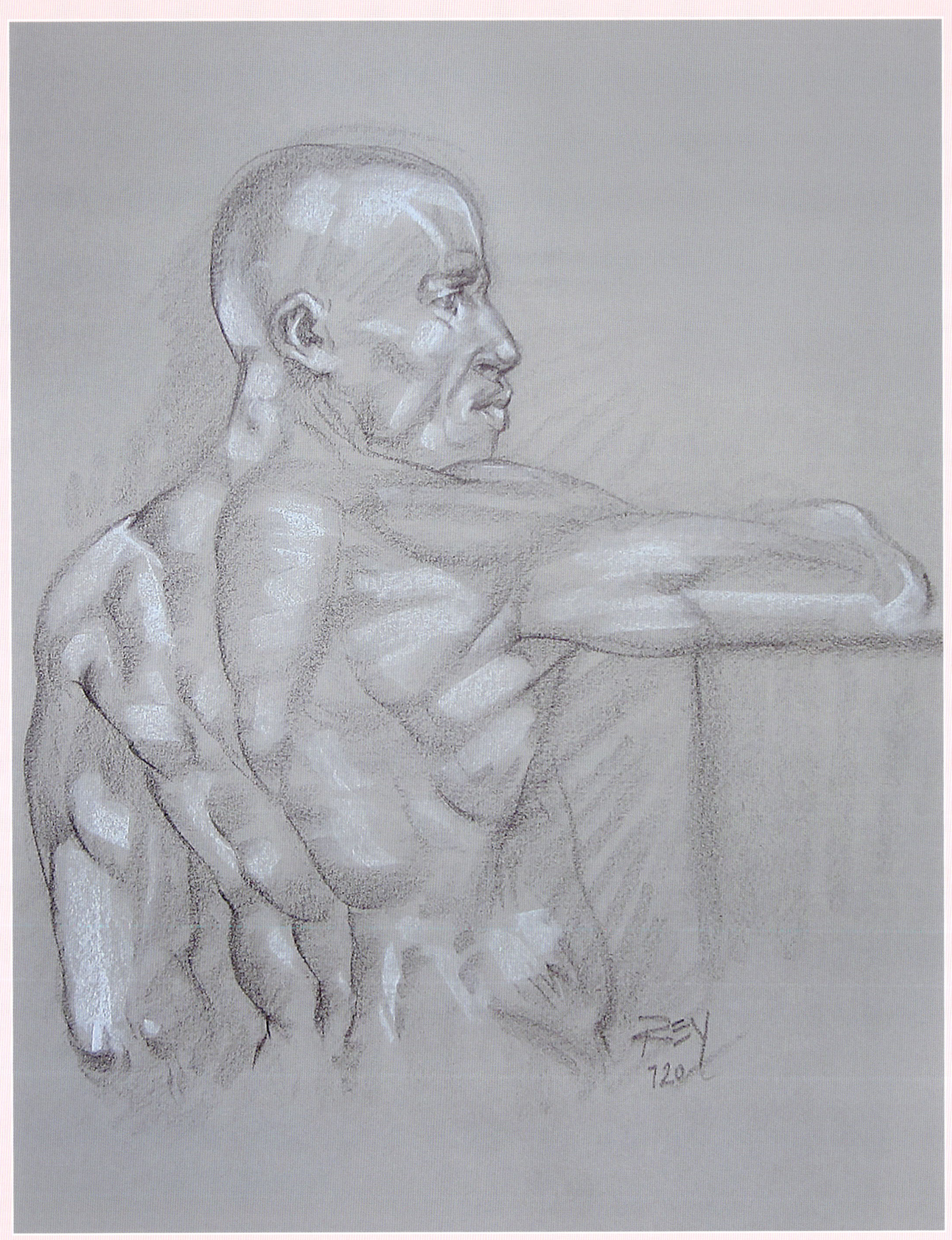

FIGURATIVE ART

I believe that every decision an artist makes is derived from an innate desire to communicate, to be heard. Figurative art has the potential for infinite variation and therefore also for vast individual expression. In this section of the book, I will lay out ways for you to use the anatomical knowledge you have acquired and put it into practice.

Literal/Classical and Interpretive Approaches

"I don't draw what I *see,* I draw what I *feel.* This is my philosophy about drawing the figure. As I said, figure drawing is like handwriting, unique and highly personal."

First, I will address two categories, of the many possibilities, in which figurative art can be generally placed. The first category is the literal depiction of the human form or the classical approach to figurative drawing. Some of my favorite examples in art history are by Jean-Auguste-Dominique Ingres and Jacques-Louis David. Their clear and meticulous rendering of the human form is the epitome of neoclassicist realism. Today, there are many examples of this type of tightly controlled and faithfully depicted figure drawing from talented artists. The literal depiction of the human form takes countless hours and the patience of Job. Not all of us have that much patience built into our DNA. I know I don't, but I also love to draw the figure. And hopefully the knowledge you have gained so far in this book about the human anatomy, will excite you to draw even more.

The second category is the interpretive depiction of the human form. A good analogy might be that if the first category of drawing is calligraphy, then this second category is one's signature. As a teacher, I try to allow my students' style, their signatures, to evolve naturally through disciplined and restrained exercises. To facilitate this approach, my anatomy classes are pedantic and in many cases I teach without a model. I teach what the body is; not how to draw it. That part I leave up to the individual.

Both types should be explored as you hone your drawing skills. Remember to think about what your goals are, whether it's mastering drawing hands (see pages 60–64) or depicting a person in motion (see page 138), and review these body areas and their muscular and skeletal structure in order to accomplish those goals. And then make new ones!

As for my own work, it tends to be interpretive. I don't draw what I *see*, I draw what I *feel*. This is my philosophy about drawing the figure. As I said, figure drawing is like handwriting, unique and highly personal. I did not master this as a young art student, as I did not quite know what I was doing or where I was going.

Finding Your Style

At ArtCenter College of Design in Pasadena, California, I remember watching my instructor Harry Carmean, an amazing draftsman, draw at his easel. During breaks, I was among the students who would stare in awe at the marks he had made on that pad. We would pick up one of his pencils, look at it as if it possessed some magic that we did not have, but it was the same exact pencil that we were using. His strokes were fluent and graceful, yet powerful and deeply emotional. How did he do this? We tried to emulate the master to no avail. Carmean once told me that the reason was that it was his handwriting, not mine. So, I stopped trying to imitate him and started my quest to discover my own handwriting. Granted, when viewing my figures now I see his influence. I see some of my other teachers or masters of the past in my strokes as well, but when you know what you are doing and combine all that you have felt, learned, and explored on your journey, you will ultimately find your own signature and thus your artistic voice.

Young students often ask me, "How do I find my style?" The answer is not to look for it, your style will gradually reveal itself, but you do have to put in the pencil mileage. You do have to keep moving. Like the great humorist, Will Rogers once said, "Even if you are on the right track, you'll get run over if you just sit there."

When studying the figure, it is important to be careful not to get too caught up in any popular new way of drawing it. This is something that I see often with my young students. They emulate styles that may be flashy and shiny but ultimately may not be true to who they are as artists. They might emulate the way car designers draw cars, but I think more highly of the human form, too much to make it seem shiny or plastic. I can emphasize because I, too, had to resist this when I was a young student.

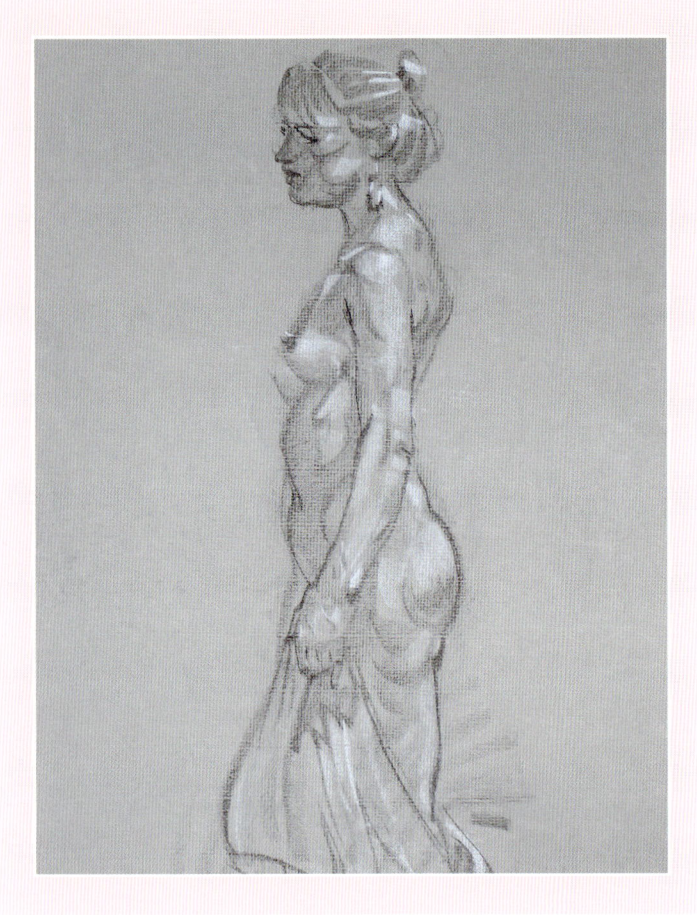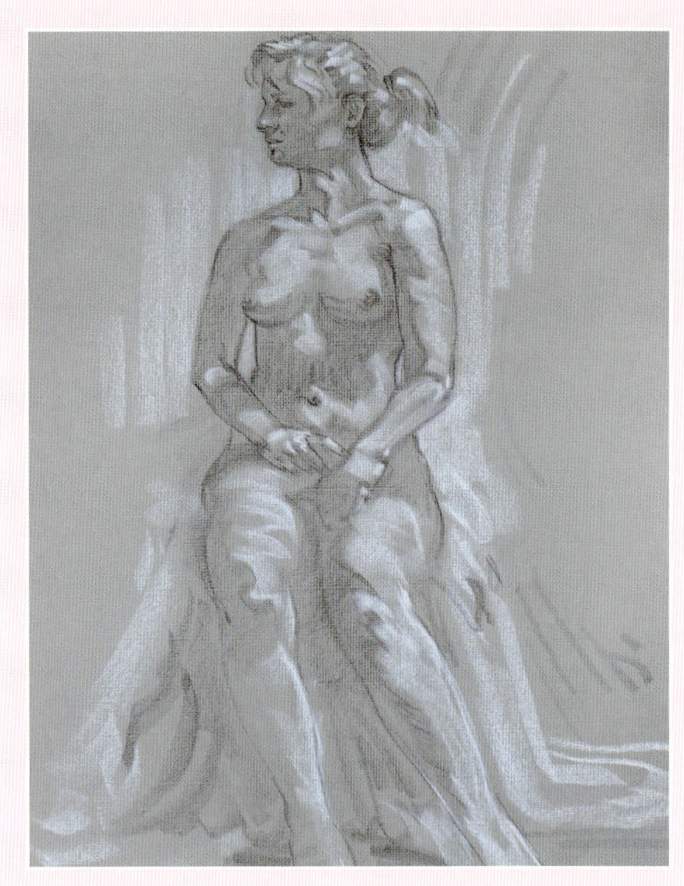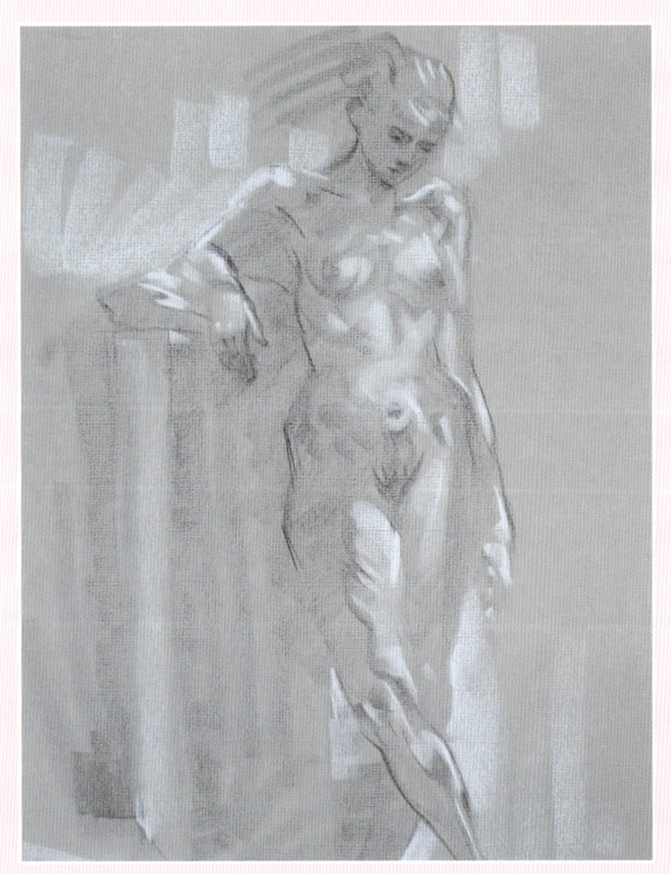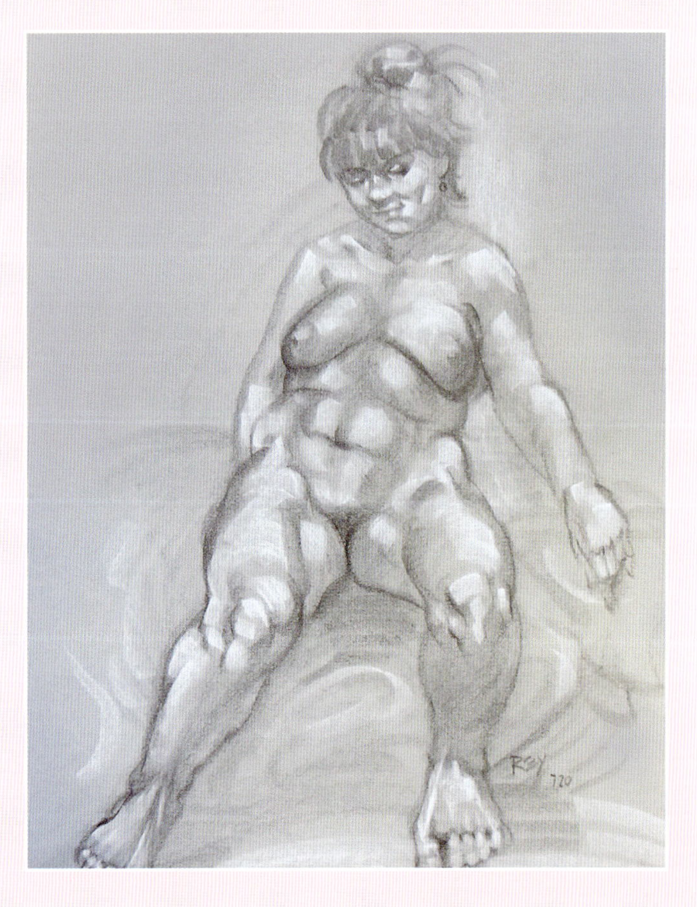

Is Copying Ever Okay?

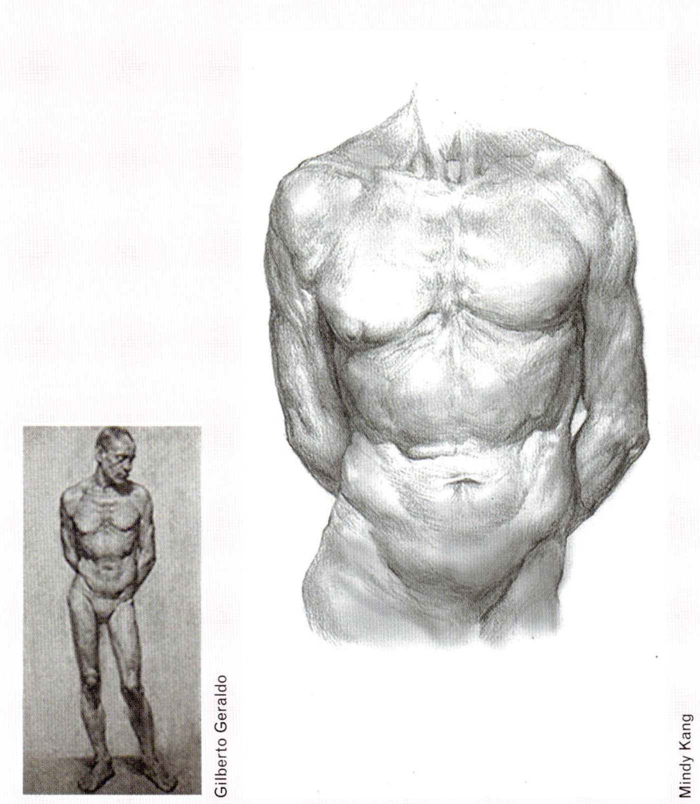

Gilberto Geraldo

Mindy Kang

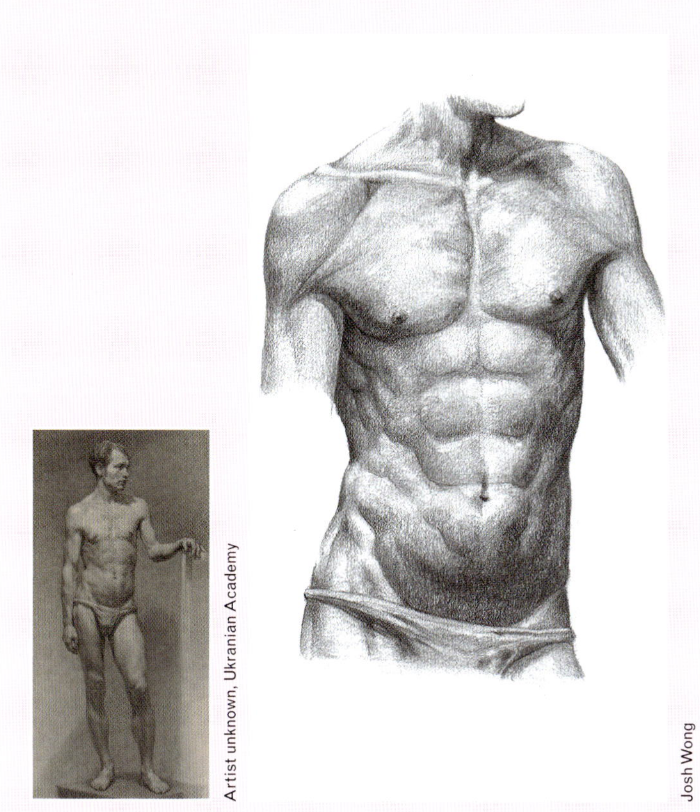

Artist unknown, Ukranian Academy

Josh Wong

Copying is the best way for any artist to get better. Most young artists do not have the luxury of having a model to draw, but they can always copy from one of the masters.

By "copy," I mean practice, just as if you were taking a piano class. Music students are often asked to work out of lesson books and songbooks at the level needed at each stage. In regard to drawing the figure, this is the same approach.

Look for images on the Internet and copy them. I choose artists I am familiar with: Iliya Mirochnik, Gilberto Geraldo, Sergey Chubirko, or any academic artist. Use artists of the past such as Pierre-Paul Prud'hon or Pontormo. Observe their subjects and draw them as if they were models in the room but depicted in your style of drawing. It is not plagiarizing since you are using them to help you. This is also true when you are learning a piano piece composed by Frédéric Chopin. Plagiarizing means passing off someone else's work as your own.

When my students use any image by someone else when doing their homework, they have to credit them as we do here in this book. (Review "Analysis of Form in Four Steps" on pages 38–39.) So, have fun, use the masters of yesterday and today to help you get masterful as well! Draw the same image over and over again as if it were a piece of music. This will aid you in drawing the figure from life.

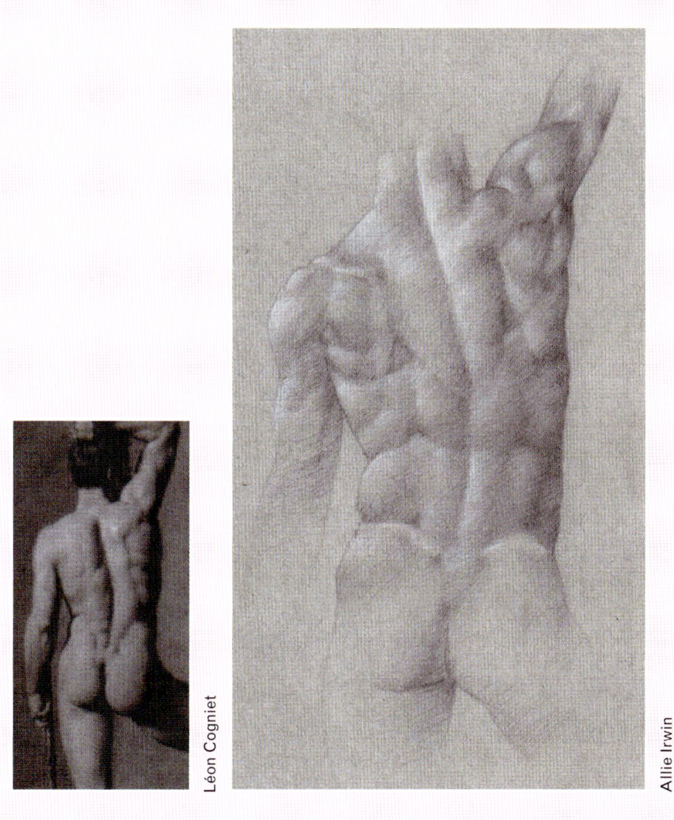

Léon Cogniet

Allie Irwin

HOW TO MAINTAIN PROPORTIONS

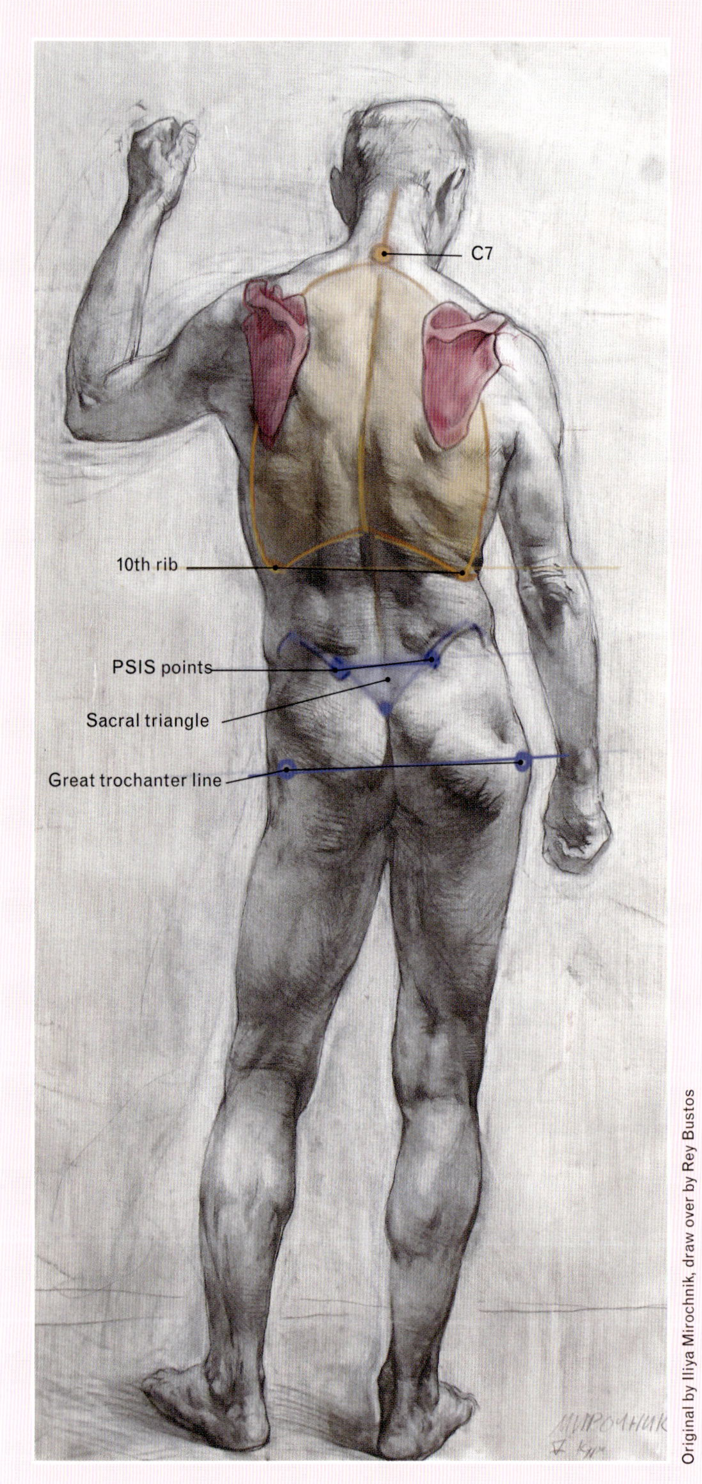

Original by Iliya Mirochnik, draw over by Rey Bustos

The proportion of the human figure in art is often a topic of debate. Of course, in the history of art there have been many depictions of the human form for a myriad of different reasons. The Renaissance, roughly spanning the 14th to 16th centuries, was a formal period of strictly classic art, highly conservative, intellectual, and restrained from emotion. Mannerism is an artistic style that followed and flowed from the Italian High Renaissance, from 1520 to the end of that century in Italy, and even longer in some parts of Europe; characterized by elongated, flowing figures, and more emotionally charged compositions as seen by many artists, such as Jacopo Pontormo (1491–1557). Even Michelangelo was a master of the High Renaissance and Mannerism.

The Baroque period is characterized by exaggerated, dynamic motion, complicated compositions, and a focus on grandeur in painting, sculpture, and music. Gian Lorenzo Bernini and Peter Paul Rubens are great examples of this. Why is this important to know? These masters were able to change the human proportions compared to how we see them in real life and still have their work look "right."

If you were to observe a standing Leonardo figure, Pontormo figure, and Peter Paul Rubens figure, you would notice the main landmarks all still fall in their proper places. Let me explain. When I stand up, my wrist is at my great trochanter. The length of my thigh equals the rest of my leg and heel down to the ground. If I continued to bend my knee, eventually I would be sitting on my heel; the heel would be at my great trochanter. The same is true for any of the figures from the artists in these periods! Examine the work of Leonardo, Raphael, Pontormo, and John Singer Sargent. Nothing is ever absolute; there will always be exceptions but generally this statement is true. A common mistake that my students make, for example, is that the thighs on their figures are often too long. Once they make the length of the leg/heel equal to the thigh, *voilà!* Problem solved.

Another way of looking at it: if I were to take the average male figure and draw it as a proportional diagram (the eight-head Greek proportion) on my blackboard, the following would be observed: the elbow bend hits the same horizontal line as the 10th rib, above the navel; the wrist hits the great trochanters and pubic bone; and, most importantly, the length of the femur, thigh, equals the rest of the leg and foot as that foot hits the ground.

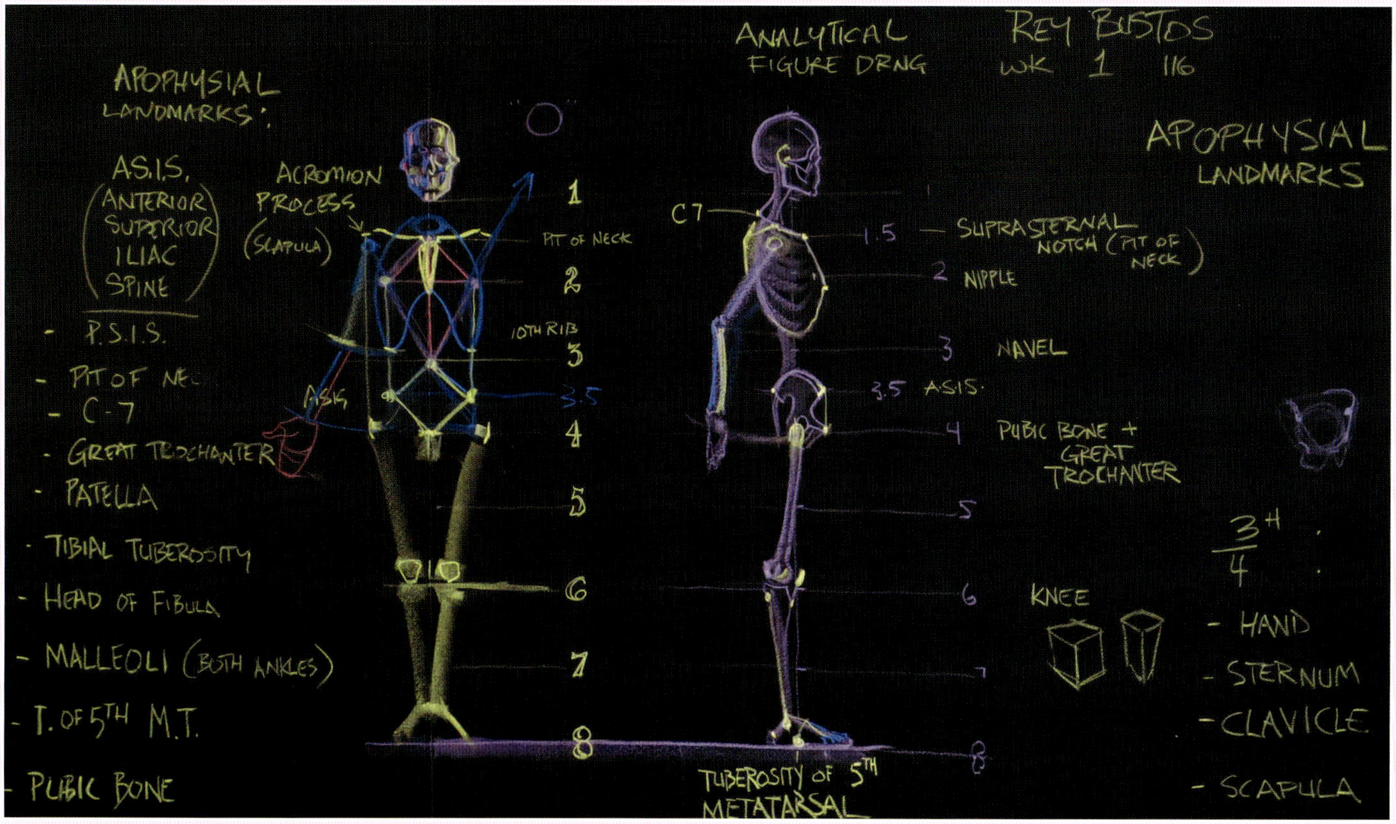

APOPHYSIAL LANDMARKS:

- A.S.I.S. (ANTERIOR SUPERIOR ILIAC SPINE)
- P.S.I.S.
- PIT OF NECK
- C-7
- GREAT TROCHANTER
- PATELLA
- TIBIAL TUBEROSITY
- HEAD OF FIBULA
- MALLEOLI (BOTH ANKLES)
- T. OF 5TH M.T.
- PUBIC BONE

ACROMION PROCESS (SCAPULA) — PIT OF NECK — 10TH RIB — ASIS

ANALYTICAL FIGURE DRNG — REY BUSTOS — WK 1 — 116

APOPHYSIAL LANDMARKS

C7 — 1.5 SUPRASTERNAL NOTCH (PIT OF NECK) — 2 NIPPLE — 3 NAVEL — 3.5 ASIS — 4 PUBIC BONE + GREAT TROCHANTER — 5 — 6 KNEE — TUBEROSITY OF 5TH METATARSAL

3 3/4 — HAND — STERNUM — CLAVICLE — SCAPULA

I once asked my then 10-year-old daughter to stand at attention, and those points hit the same way on her own body as well. With her hands at her sides, her wrists were at exactly the same points on her body as my wrists were on mine, at the great trochanter. And the bends of elbow were at the 10th rib. Isn't that amazing?

So, if you want to change your proportions and still make them look "correct," remember these points and where these parts of the body lie in relation to their corresponding placements. Your work will look graceful and you will be better able to create more pleasing rhythms. Or tweak the proportions depending on your needs.

The Greeks of antiquity used the familiar eight-head proportion for their figures. Comic artists use eight or nine for their superheroes. If you measure your own head and count your head down to the ground, it might only be seven and one quarter. The Greeks created the idealized eight-head proportion for the simple fact that their art was about honoring their gods. They were not depicting an average Joe. Their gods had to be "perfect," larger than life, much like superheroes. Captain America was not supposed to look like you and me, nor were Apollo or Zeus.

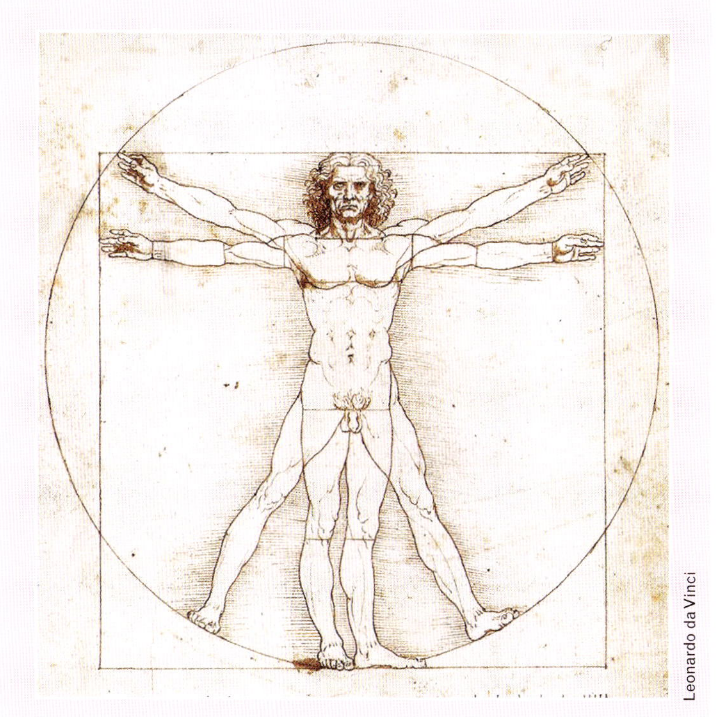

Leonardo da Vinci

Depicting Different Body Types

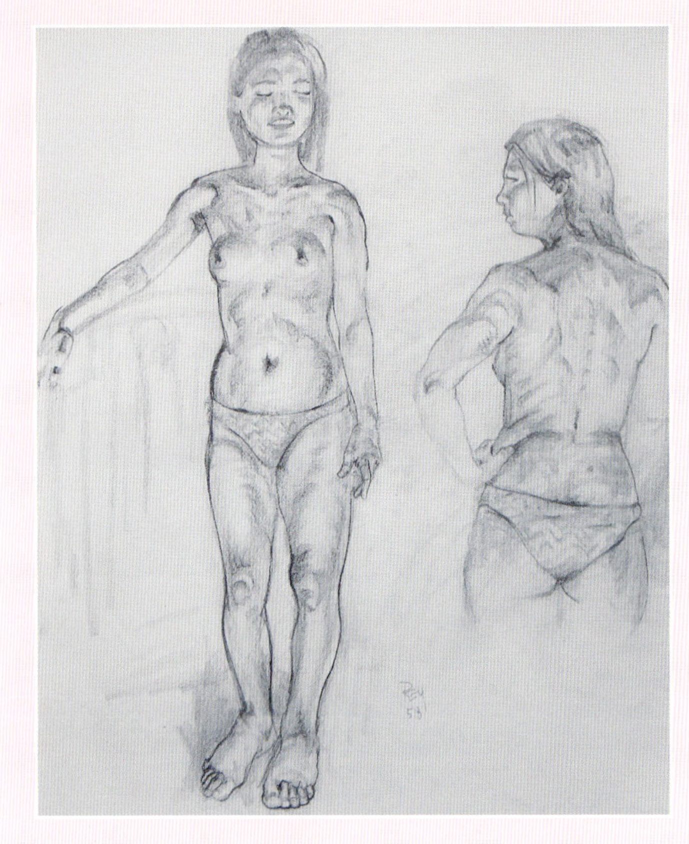

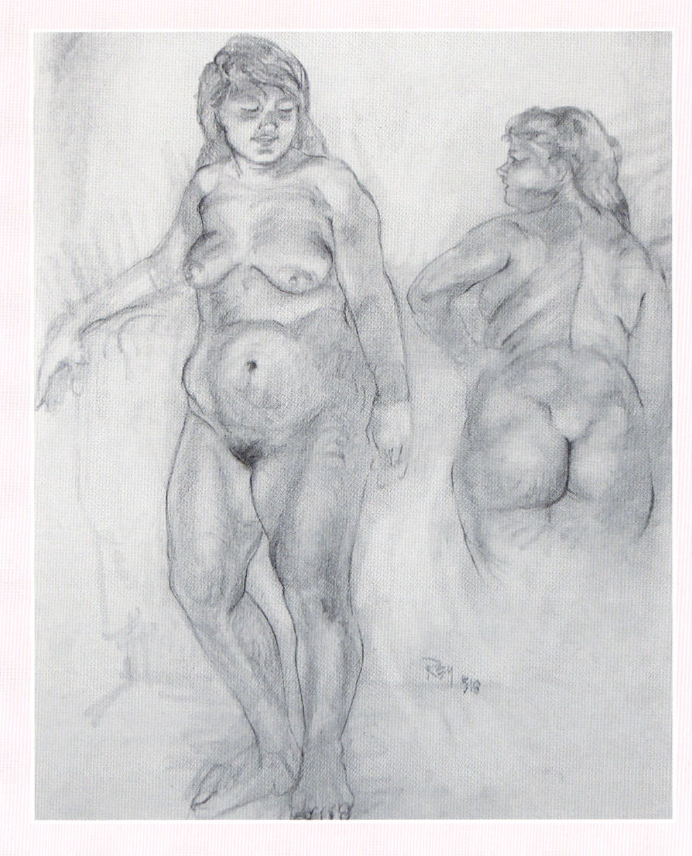

There are numerous body types, but American psychologist and physician William Sheldon narrowed them down to three shapes: endomorphic, mesomorphic, and ectomorphic. Obviously, there are many variations within this spectrum model. He was looking for correlations between physiques and personality/deliquency traits, if any. It's odd and even a bit uneasy to study, but I still find it is useful to learn from these three basic forms. Here is an overview:

• Ectomorphs are slender, their skeletons are more clearly visible, and they have a faster metabolism.

• Mesomorphs tend to be stockier and more muscular.

• Endomorphs have a slower metabolism and tend to be soft with more fat throughout their bodies.

Remember, women and men carry body fat differently, (see pages 89 and 90). Women generally have it at the buttocks, thighs (specifically around the great trochanters), breasts, and on their ilia (waist to rib cage). Men tend to have proportionately less body fat and carry it around their waist covering the flank portion of their external obliques and abdominal area.

As artists we have to pay attention to these different body types and take time to understand how the skeleton, for example, can manifest itself in each. So, let's say, a fuller figured model will show dimples where a thin model will show bony prominences.

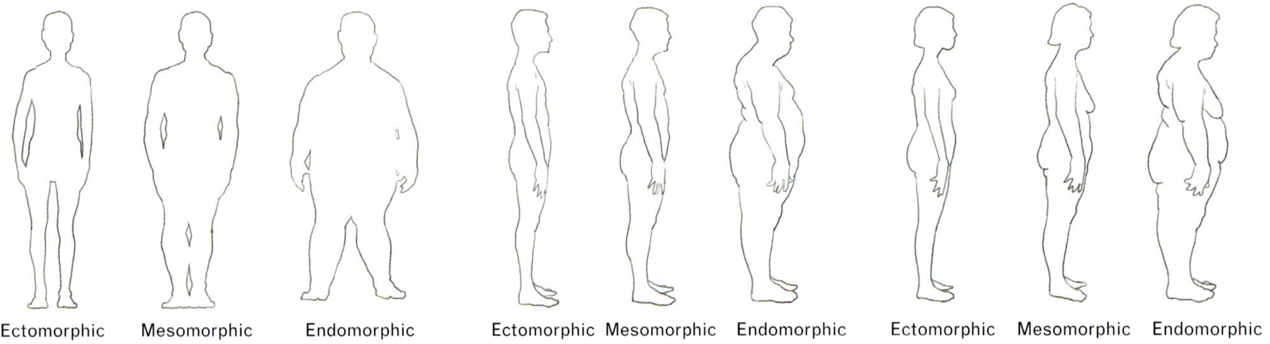

DRAWING FROM CADAVERS

"Art is science made clear." —Jean Cocteau

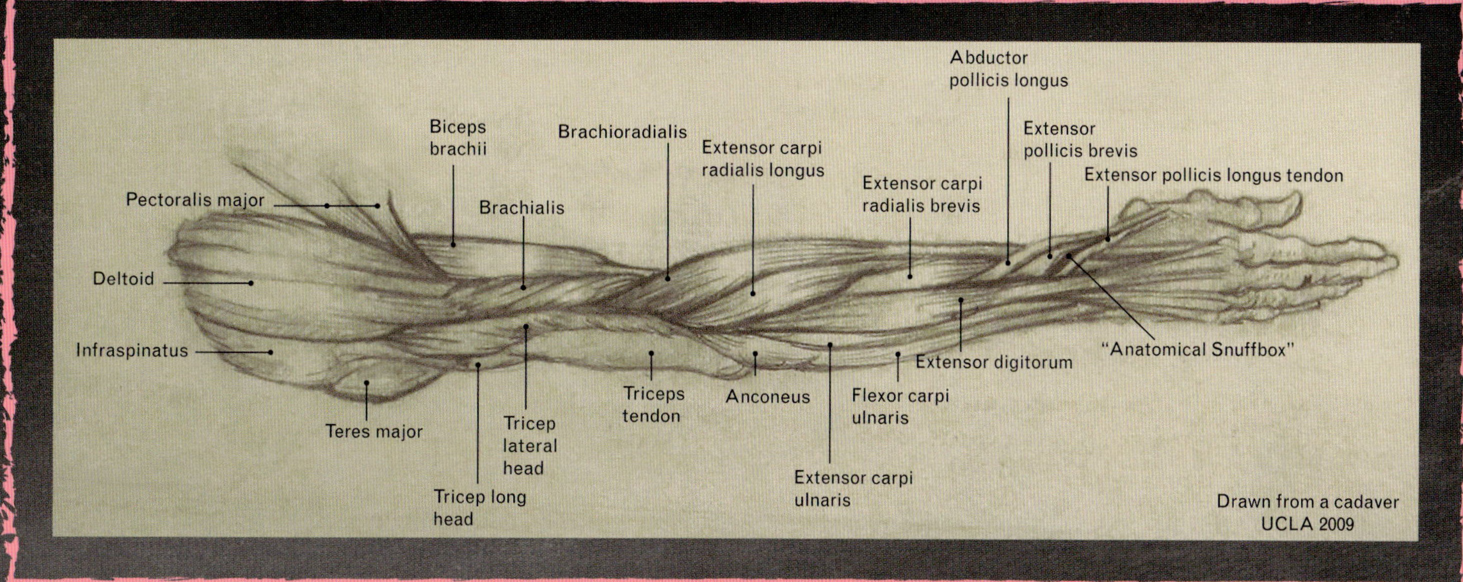

For the past decade, I have been able to take each of my classes to the anatomy lab at UCLA to view and touch cadavers and use them as reference for their drawings. My students are given smocks and surgical gloves so that they can have that tactile experience and not simply be spectators. The value of this day at the lab is immense. It is a hands-on, amazing, and transcendent experience that I never tire of, and one my students never forget. It is a way for my students to get many of their anatomy questions answered, and to feel what they have been learning. If I want to teach them about a certain muscle in the body, they can take their time to really feel and examine it.

For example, my favorite area to share is the iliotibial band. I often ask one of my students to place his or her hand in between the vastus lateralis on the side of the thigh, and the area of the iliotibial band by the knee and pull upward to feel its tautness and surprising strength. The iliotibial band is often difficult to illustrate in artistic anatomy books, mine included, because it is hard to depict its complex form. I describe it in class as something like packing tape or tough plastic wrap, translucent and somewhat milky white. That is just one example of the many things to explore on the body.

Drawing from cadavers is not only a rare opportunity, it also takes you right back to the time of Leonardo, and those who came centuries before, artists who learned from direct contact with this beautiful subject. While it is no longer necessary for the artist to study directly from cadavers, I myself have learned a lot from doing this.

While the cadaver lab, unfortunately, is not available to most artists, there are now many resources online to look at cadaver specimens. On pages 26, 53, and 69, I have included casts created by my friend and colleague Eliot Goldfinger to give you an idea of what my students get to see.

You may contact your local college or university and ask if it may be possible to sit in on a lecture in a physiology class. You may also look through medical anatomy books with photos of cadavers. It is important to view the drawings and work of Leonardo da Vinci since he has many drawings done from cadavers.

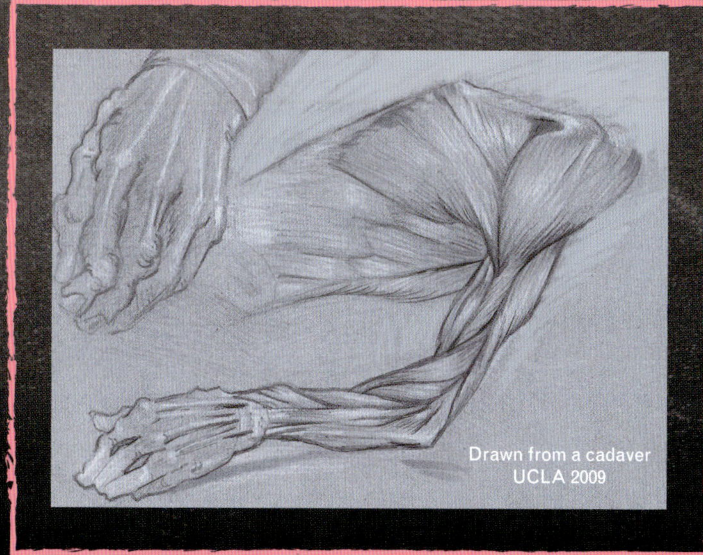

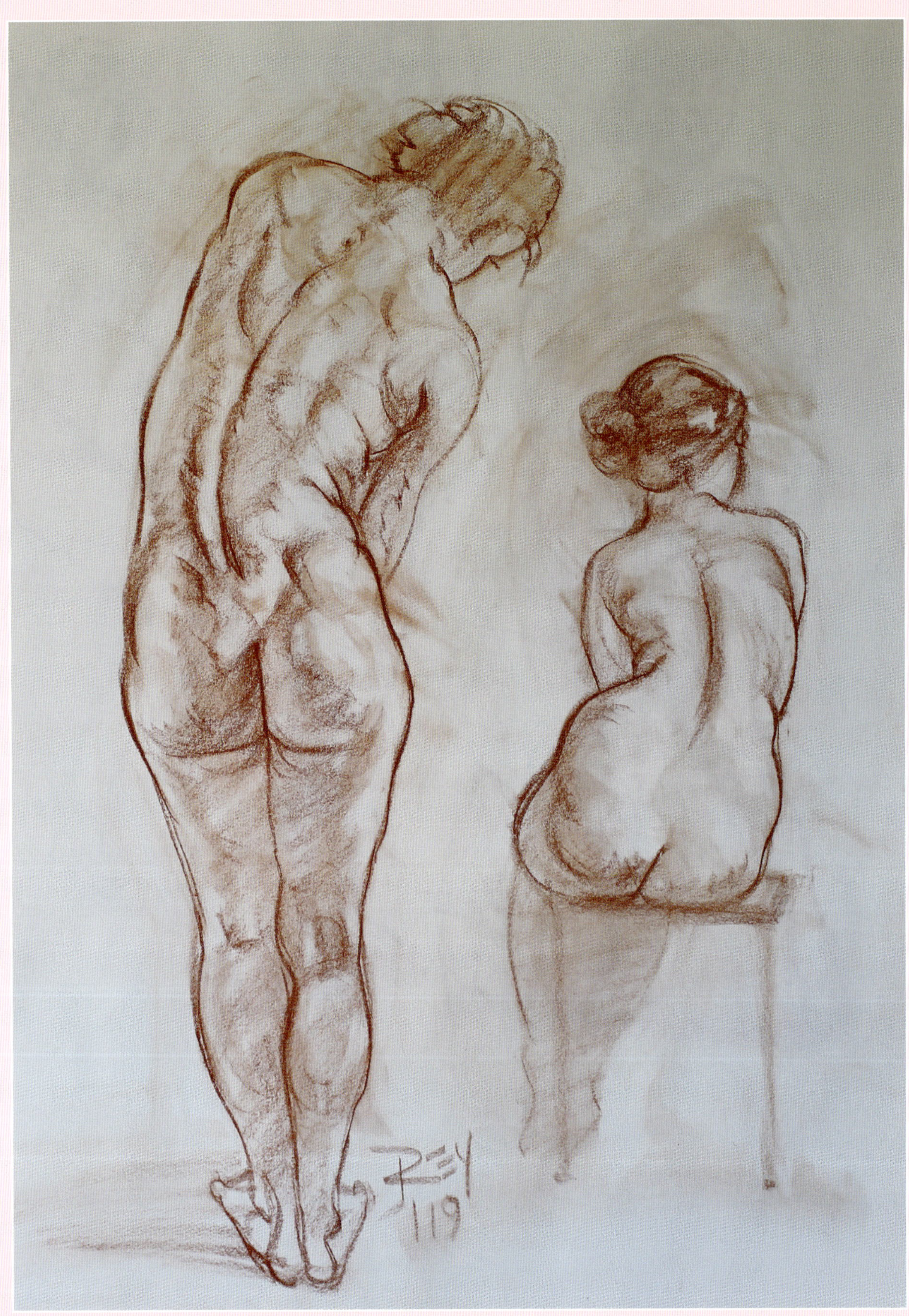

PUTTING THE "LIFE" IN LIFE DRAWING

"Every child is an artist. The problem is how to remain an artist once we grow up." —Pablo Picasso

We as teachers are somewhat like a Rosetta Stone or GPS that makes it easier to navigate through a subject that is fraught with complexity and challenges. In any figure class or workshop, the teacher or facilitator will often suggest poses depending on the class and the lesson's objective, and will choose a period of time for each, often organized from short to long poses. For example, 2-minute "warm-ups" or gesture poses followed by a series of 5-minute poses, with times increasing to 10, 15, and 20 minutes. Anything past this is usually split up so that the model can take stretch breaks. Every teacher I know has a series of times that they like to give to their classes but please note that this is often very dependent on that day's particular focus or general objective of the class itself. If it is an academic class like those in traditional ateliers, the pose may last for hours and even go into separate days!

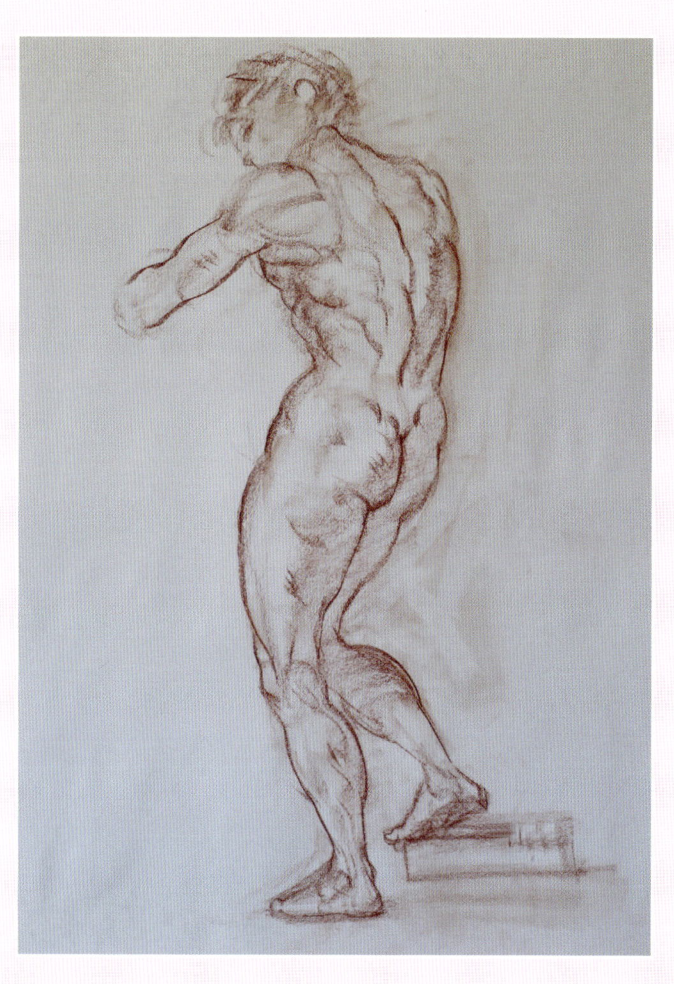

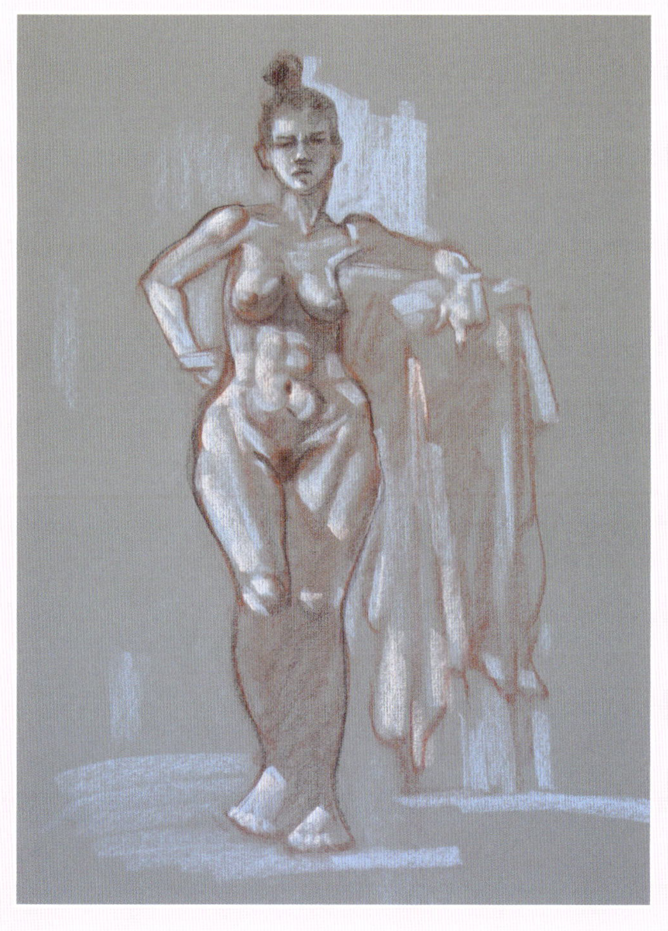

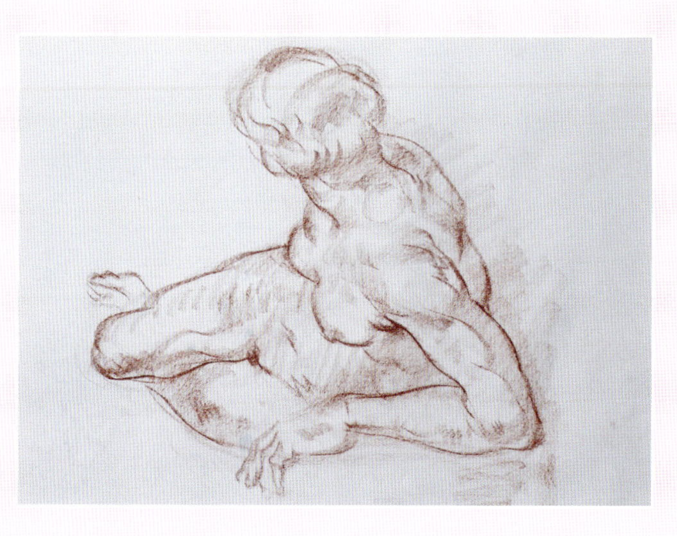

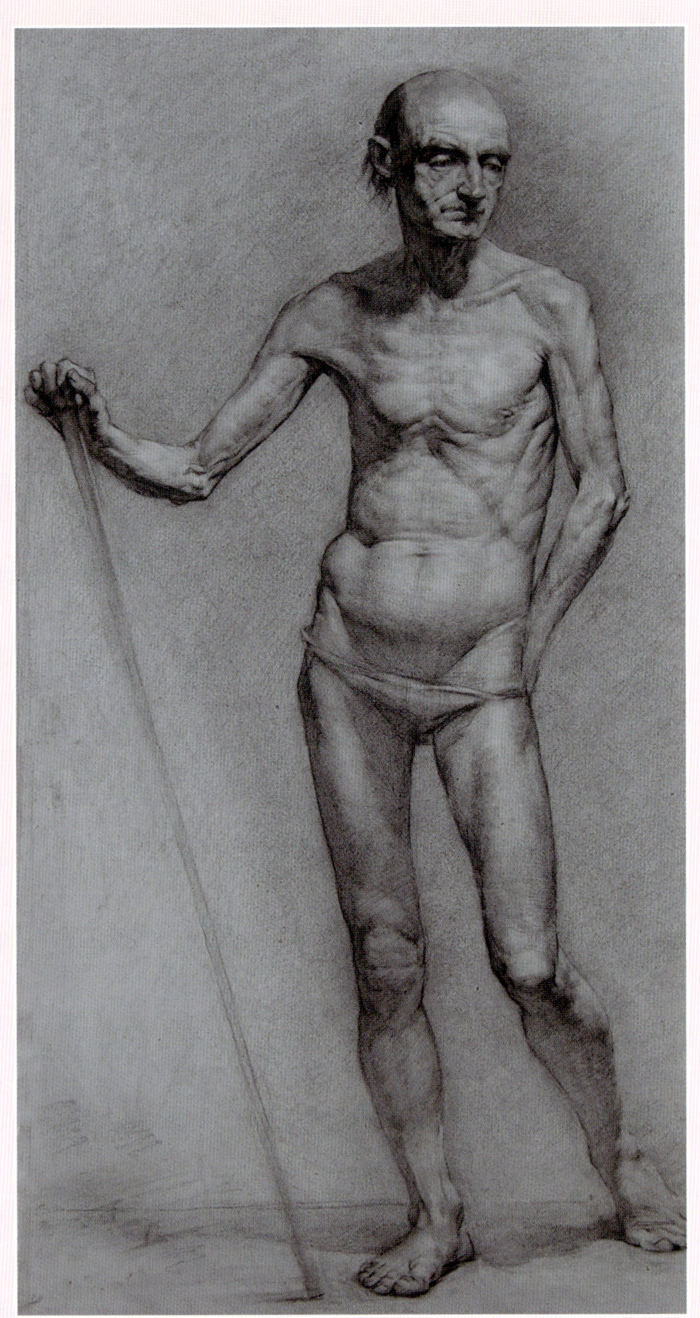
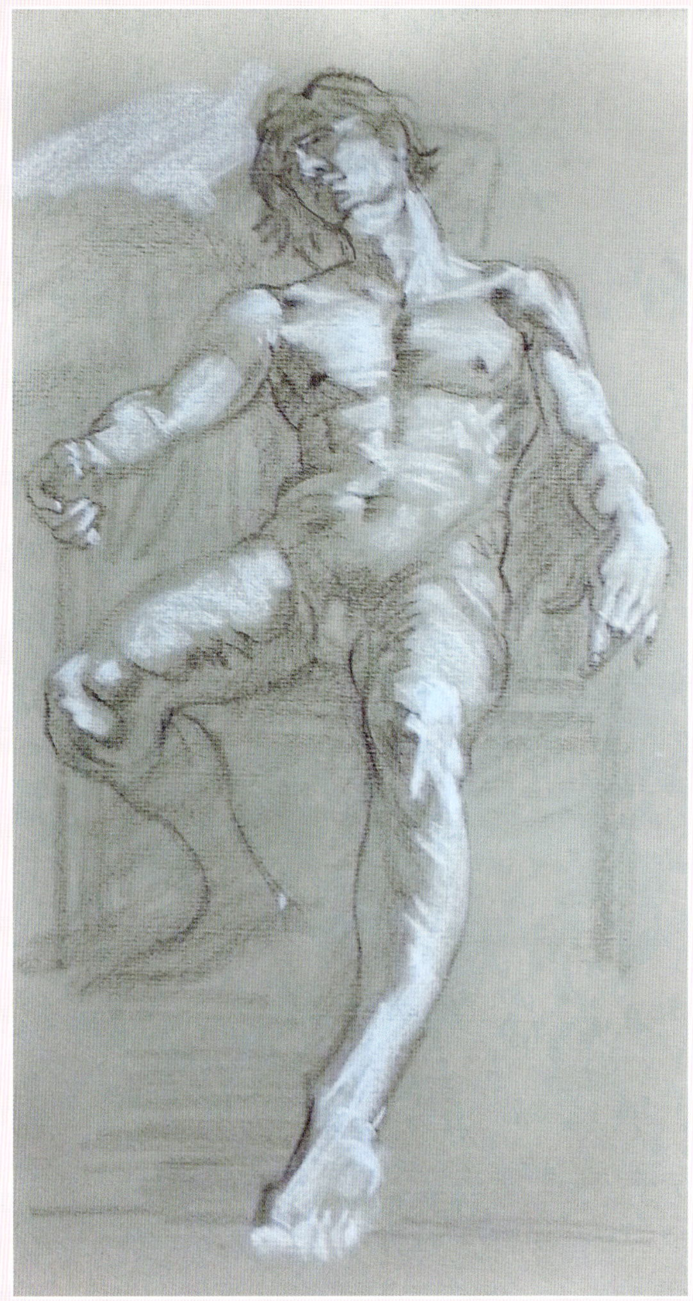

For my classes and for me personally, the perfect amount of time for a pose is 20 minutes, long enough to do a fluent, rhythmic, and graceful drawing without feeling hurried. If you can't get to the entire figure in 20 minutes, then you are thinking too much, stuck in the details that do not matter. I tell my students that the objective of the "Ideal 20," as I call it, is to try to capture the feeling of the pose rather than the (less important) representation of the pose. Certainly the academic pose (left) is more studied and truer to real-life than mine (right), which captures a feeling or gesture rather than a literal representation.

To Commit or Not to Commit to a Pose?

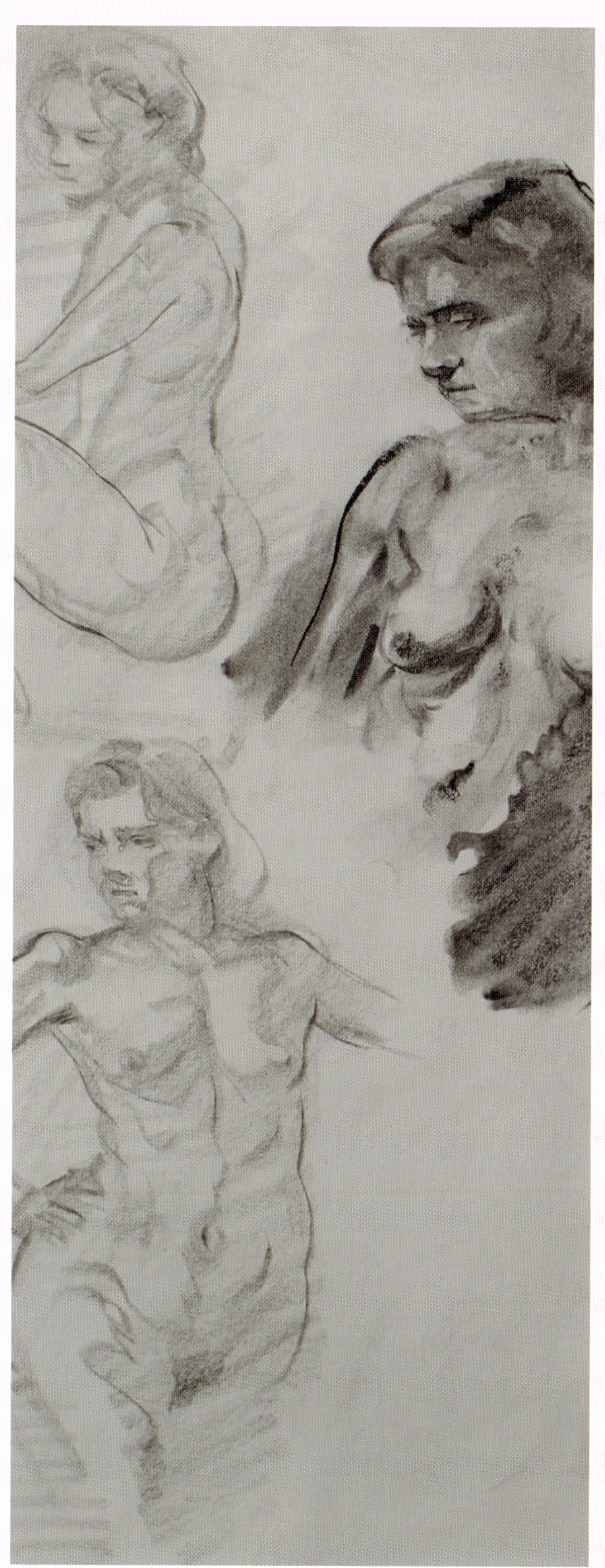

You should not feel stuck by or committed to a model's pose when you're doing life drawing. Often when models get themselves into a timed pose, unless specifically directed by the instructor, they will simply get into a pose of their choice. And depending on the model's experience or natural grace, he or she may give you a wonderful pose to draw from. But as with most workshops or classes, there are usually so many people in the room, you cannot control your vantage point.

What I do, and what I tell my students, is that it is ultimately up to us to create with the model merely being the muse. If, for example, the model's hand is in an awkward position relative to your eye, then do not draw it as you see it. Instead, draw the hand *as you would like it to appear.* This will create more personal and graceful drawings. Just look at the Old Masters' works. They tended to make everything more dramatic, like being at an opera.

"It is drama that sets works of art apart from the mundane reality of how things really are."

No one speaks to one another in song across balconies, nor do we signal with our fingers in that "over yonder" way that the Old Masters depict in paintings when pointing or making hand gestures. It is drama that sets works of art apart from the mundane reality of how things really are. Have fun and remember this advice: when drawing from a live model, pretend that you are making up a figure but with a figure in front of you.

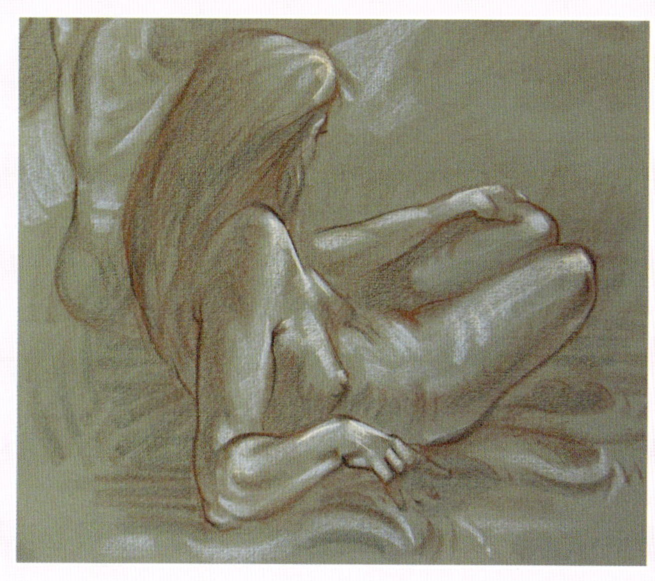

Tutorial: Analytical to Gestural Drawing

The ultimate goal of my classes—and this book—is for students to be able to draw the human figure with anatomy infused into each drawing, which is to say, each will possess the ability to hide the anatomy behind a more dynamic, soulful, and personal expression. The anatomy is merely the underlying structure that creates the power and the method with which to achieve all the other goals of personal expression. This tutorial will explain the steps to take to go from an empty page, to viewing a model, to creating a drawing with a life of its own. This will prepare you for all the anatomy exercises to come in Section III of the book.

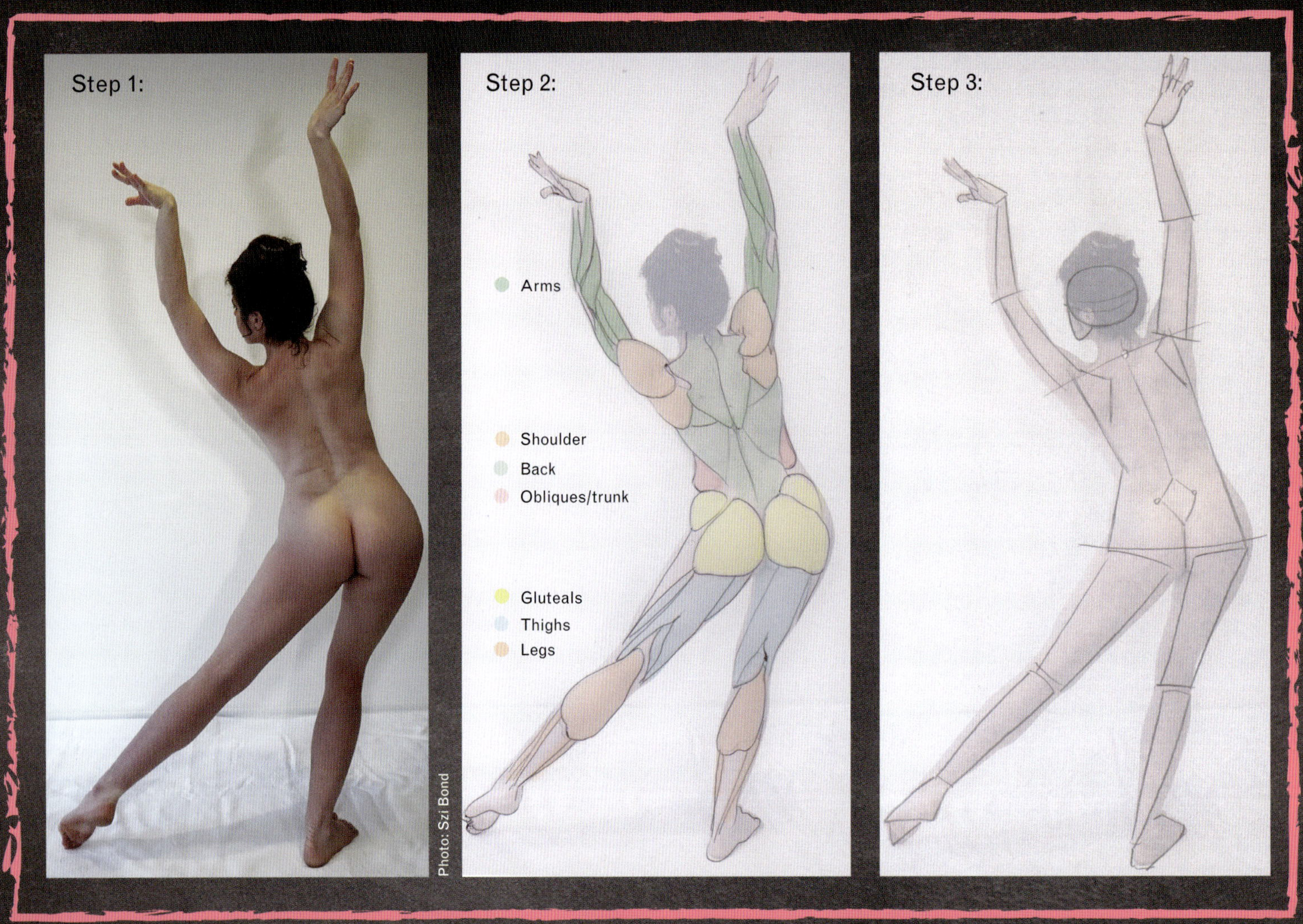

STEP 1: SELECT REFERENCE

First, ask the model to pose in dynamic ways. Take photographs, print the images and choose a favorite as reference.

STEP 2: DRAW THE MUSCLE GROUPS

Next, place tracing paper over the image. An easy alternative is to reduce the opacity of the image using Photoshop so that it looks like it has tracing paper over it, and print the image. Then on the tracing paper (or Photoshop printout), draw the major muscle groupings and label them to better "see" what is not always seen. You must know before you interpret.

STEP 3: SIMPLIFY THE FORMS

After doing analytical study, proceed to the simplification step. There are many ways to do this. In these examples, I got fresh tracing paper for the images and used the **main frame method**, whereby I located the acromion process of the scapula (the shoulder), down to the great trochanters of the femurs, using only two movements: one to show the stretched side of the torso and one for the compressed or bent side. This works well for poses that are mostly front or mostly back views. For side views, I suggest more organic forms like ovals. Once the structure is ready, then it is time to draw.

STEPS 5 AND 6: TRANSFER REFERENCE AND BLOCK-IN THE DRAWING

Draw the reference on the large format paper, 18 x 24 inches as if you were in a drawing workshop. Refer to the tracing paper overlay. Do not worry too much about being exact unless you have a lot of patience. I do not. Get the gist of the pose, that is what matters.

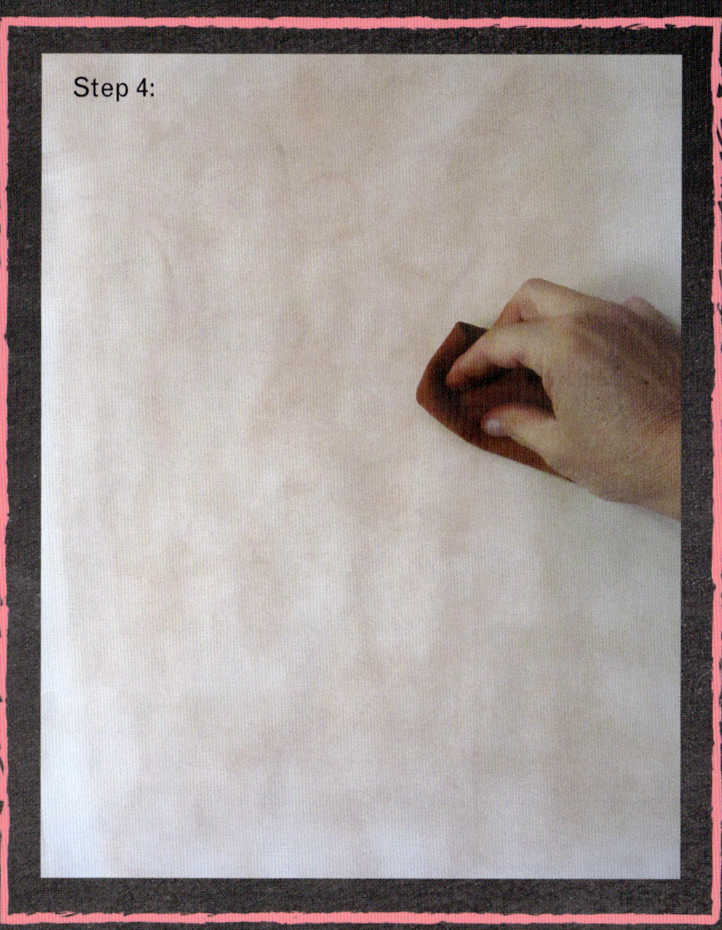

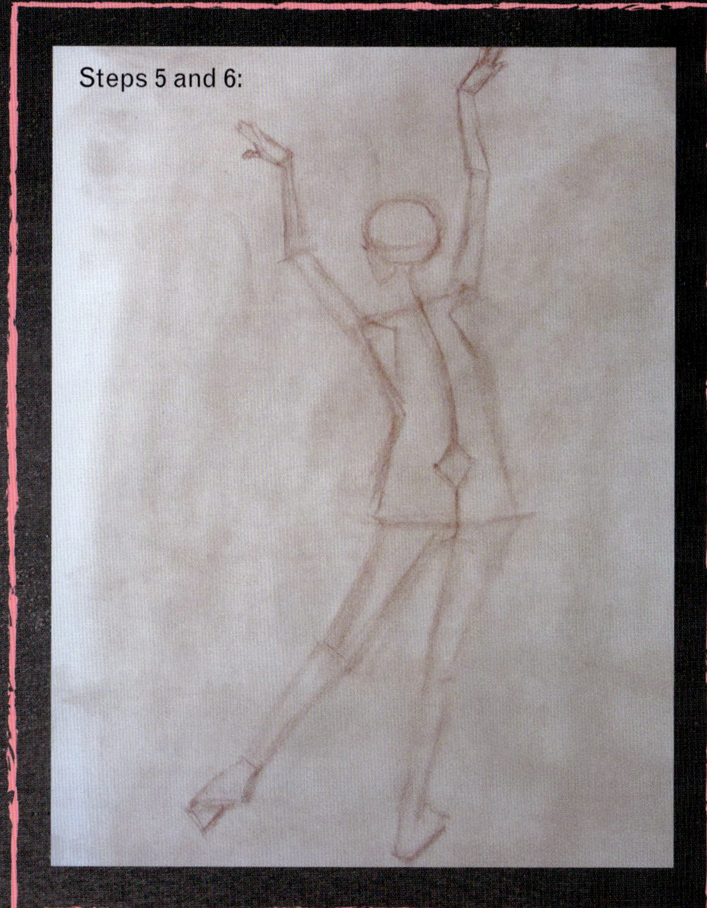

STEP 4: PREP THE DRAWING PAPER

For this drawing, I chose large format, 18 x 24 inch paper. I then use a chamois that has been dusted with conté pencil powder that is gotten by sanding the pencil. This is easy since you have to sharpen the point of the pencil anyway. This pad has felt under it as well as about ten sheets of white sketch paper under the top drawing surface paper (see page 145). I do not worry about the tone being uneven, I like the painterly look of this.

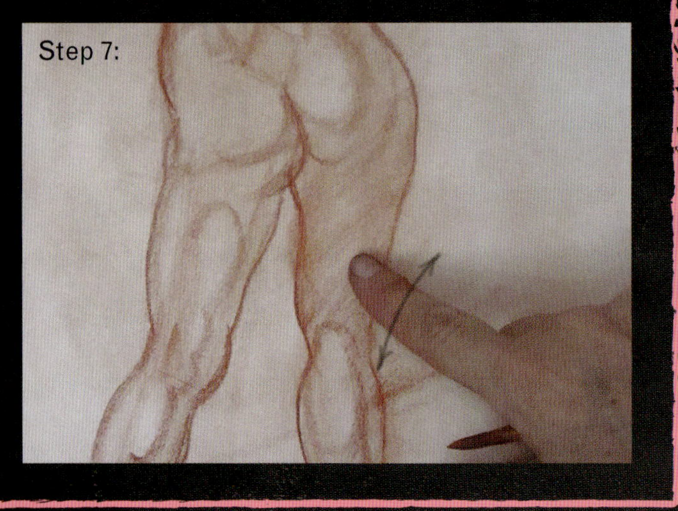

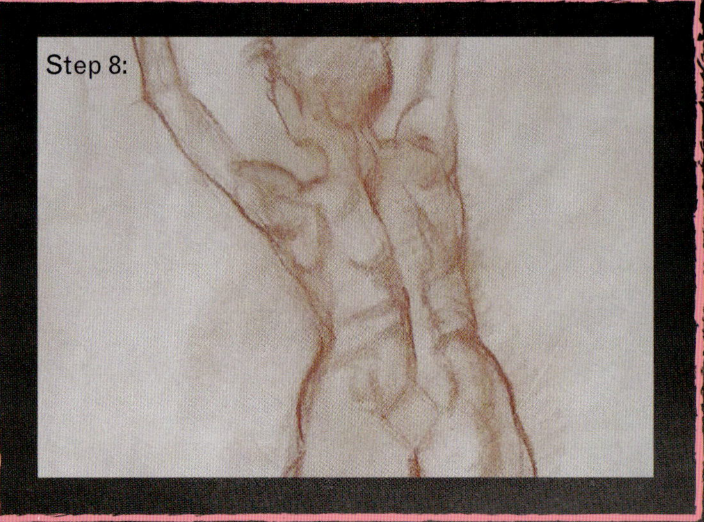

STEP 7: BLEND THE DRAWING

This image illustrates how I love to use my finger to blend and soften the drawing. In this case it made the shadow areas smoky and less sketchy, more painterly.

STEP 8: SEPARATE THE LIGHT

Separate the light sides from the shadow sides of the body. Accentuate certain lines to create **visual foci.** Try to guide the eye by making harder, darker strokes in the areas you like best, in this case, the hips. I wanted the model to look even shapelier, something the Old Masters did often.

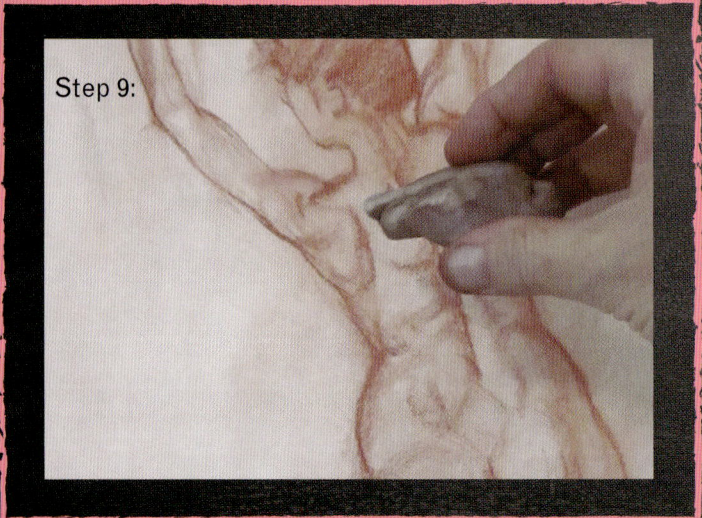

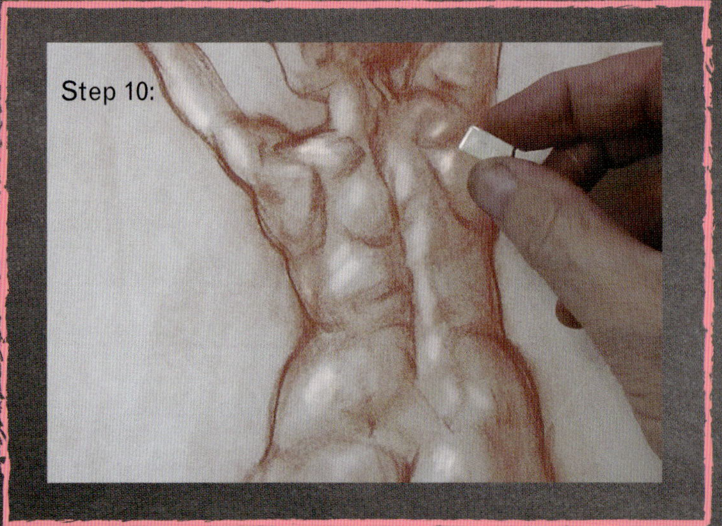

STEP 9: PULL LIGHT OUT MORE

Use a kneaded eraser to start to pull out the light areas from each form. This is why I like to prepare or tone the paper before starting, in order to erase later; the darker the tone, the more effective the eraser is in creating highlights.

STEP 10: ADD BRIGHTER HIGHLIGHTS

Erasing was not enough to create the contrast that I felt the drawing needed for better impact, and drama. So I used a broken piece of Nupastel white to add brighter highlights. Using the side edge of the piece feels more like a flat brushstroke. This also complemented the accent marks and lines that I spoke of earlier. Be careful not to overuse the white. This is common with students and can be distracting or ineffective by drawing attention to the white rather than the figure. Too much white, or spotty white, can also make the model look oily, so be careful.

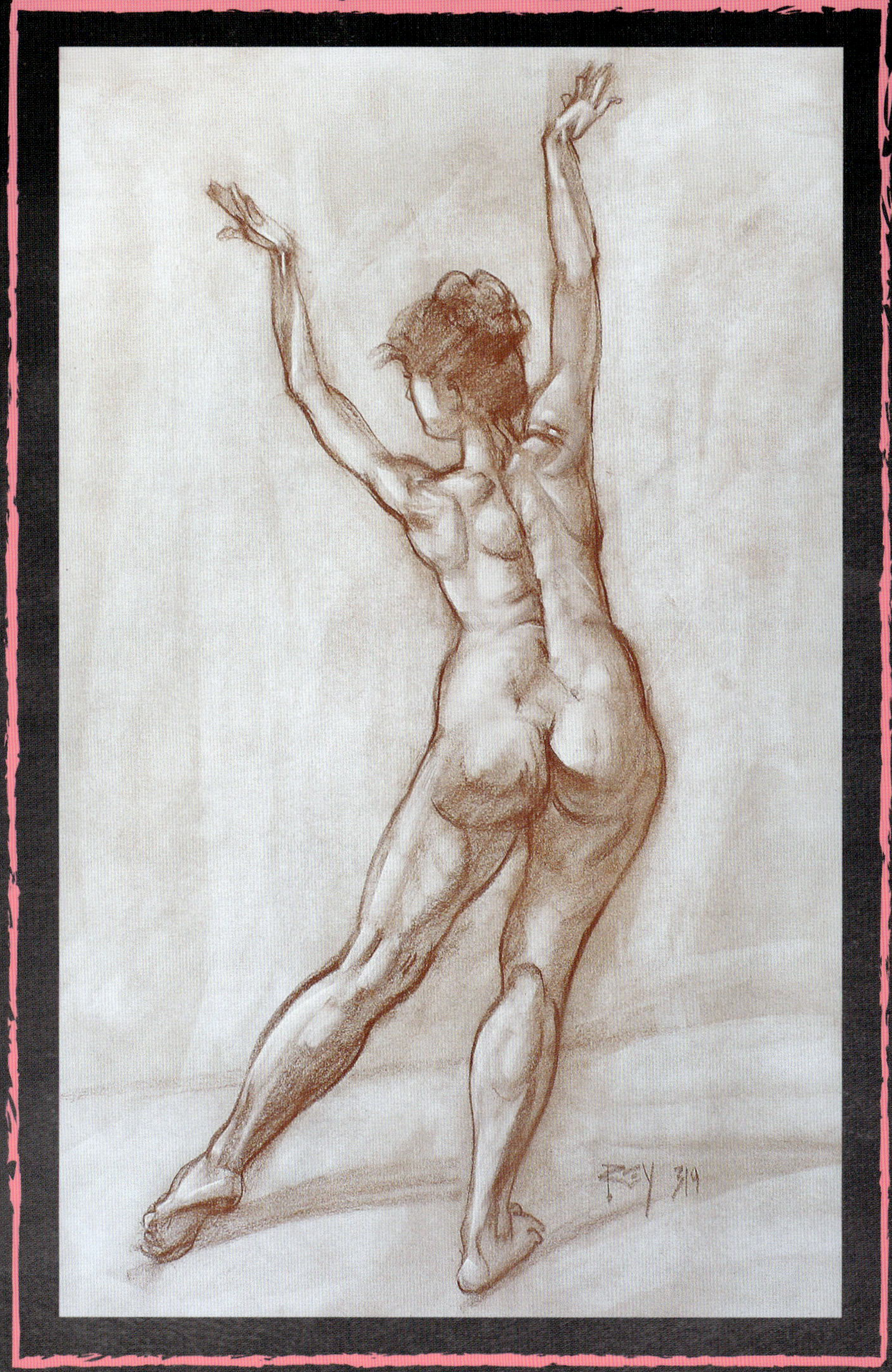

I now know well what my teachers were trying to tell me long ago: do not worry so much about the details of a figure drawing and instead find out the secret to being able to draw the overall figure well and, more importantly, to enjoy the process with a full heart. I have that enjoyment now and it is my greatest desire to share that feeling with all of my students. With patience, time, and anatomical knowledge, there will be a freedom that is given as the gift for those who stay on course and never give up. The journey is tough but worth it.

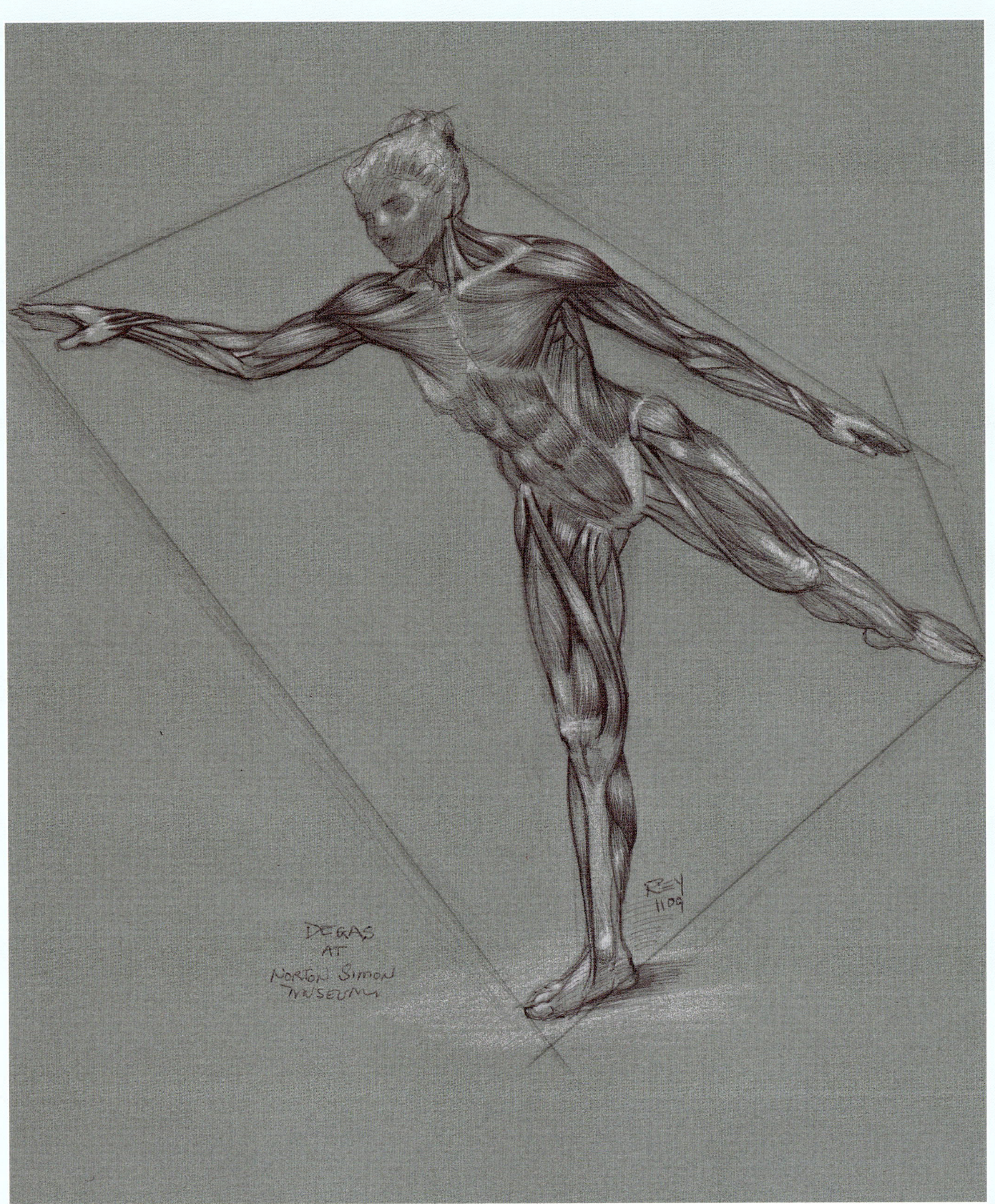
DEGAS
AT
NORTON SIMON
MUSEUM
REY
1109

PART III
MORE ANATOMY EXERCISES

EXERCISE DAILY

Daily exercise is integral to improving your skills as an artist and testing your knowledge of human anatomy. This section includes more of my favorite drawing techniques and exercises used in classrooms—where I have been a student or a teacher—to assist you on your journey.

While these exercises are in order of complexity, starting with more exploratory tasks to more complex challenges, they may be done in any order based on your specific needs and circumstances.

Whether you have two minutes to sketch the silhouette of someone on the bus, or fifteen minutes to draw from a live model at a workshop, each exercise is worthwhile. The accomplished student artwork featured throughout this book is a testament to the value of these approaches, and I hope they will prove effective in your own work.

Before you even start drawing the human figure, try this exceptional exercise to better depict the direction of forms.

Draw a Tree

In my first-figure drawing class at Glendale Community College in Southern California, the instructor took us across the street to the park, which confused me. I thought, *"The park? Are we going to have a model right out in the open?"* To my surprise we were asked to draw the many old trees around us. The point was to observe the direction of the limbs, how they moved toward or away from us. The best trees were ones that were bare or close to bare so as to see the limbs more clearly. I learned how to draw marks illustrating their direction. Look at the joints, where limbs branch off and bulbous knots form, resembling our own joints.

Visit your local park or observe trees in your neighborhood and take time sketching them for ten minutes. Pick a tree that you like. Yes, one will call to you...its grandeur and elegance tells your inner self, it wants to be your model today. Start by simply taking the view in: how textured it is, how its limbs flow in and out, up and twisting. Then draw the trunk and truly feel with your eyes the direction of the tilt of the trunk, even if it is subtle; it is either falling away or falling toward you and this may change as you move up the trunk on "your" tree. As you move up, notice how the branches sprout out from their base and move outward, and then they themselves sprout smaller branches and so on. Be aware that your strokes will illustrate the angle and direction of the limbs and branches.

It helps to visualize (or observe) a threaded screw. If you were to draw it as it tilts away from you and upward, the threads will be arced in that direction and so on. As you sketch the tree, do not worry about erasing; this is an exercise that is meant to make you more sensitive to form direction. Drawing a tree can serve as a nice warm-up session before you start drawing a figure. When I did finally get to draw my first figure in class, I had a better idea as to how to tackle the challenges of the figure. These days I find it enjoyable to make up my own trees to keep this lesson clear in my head, plus it's fun and always helpful.

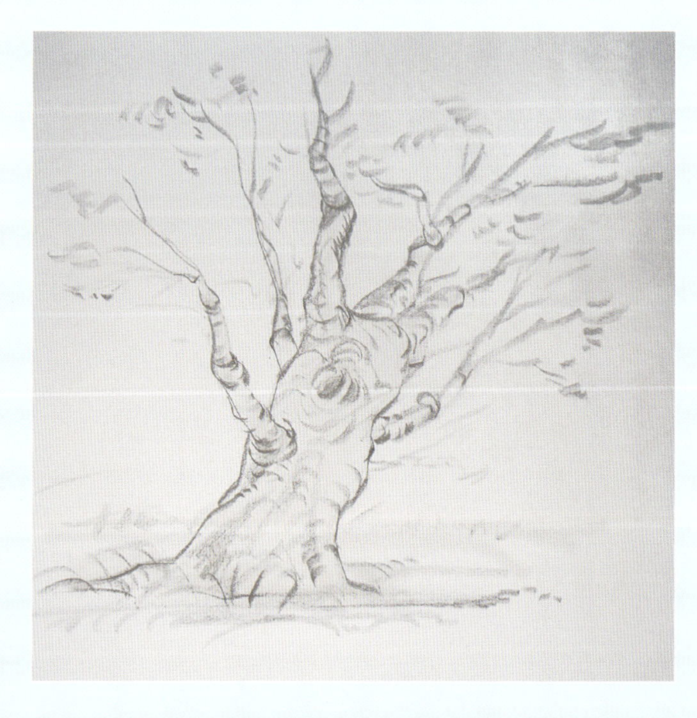

Switch Drawing Hands

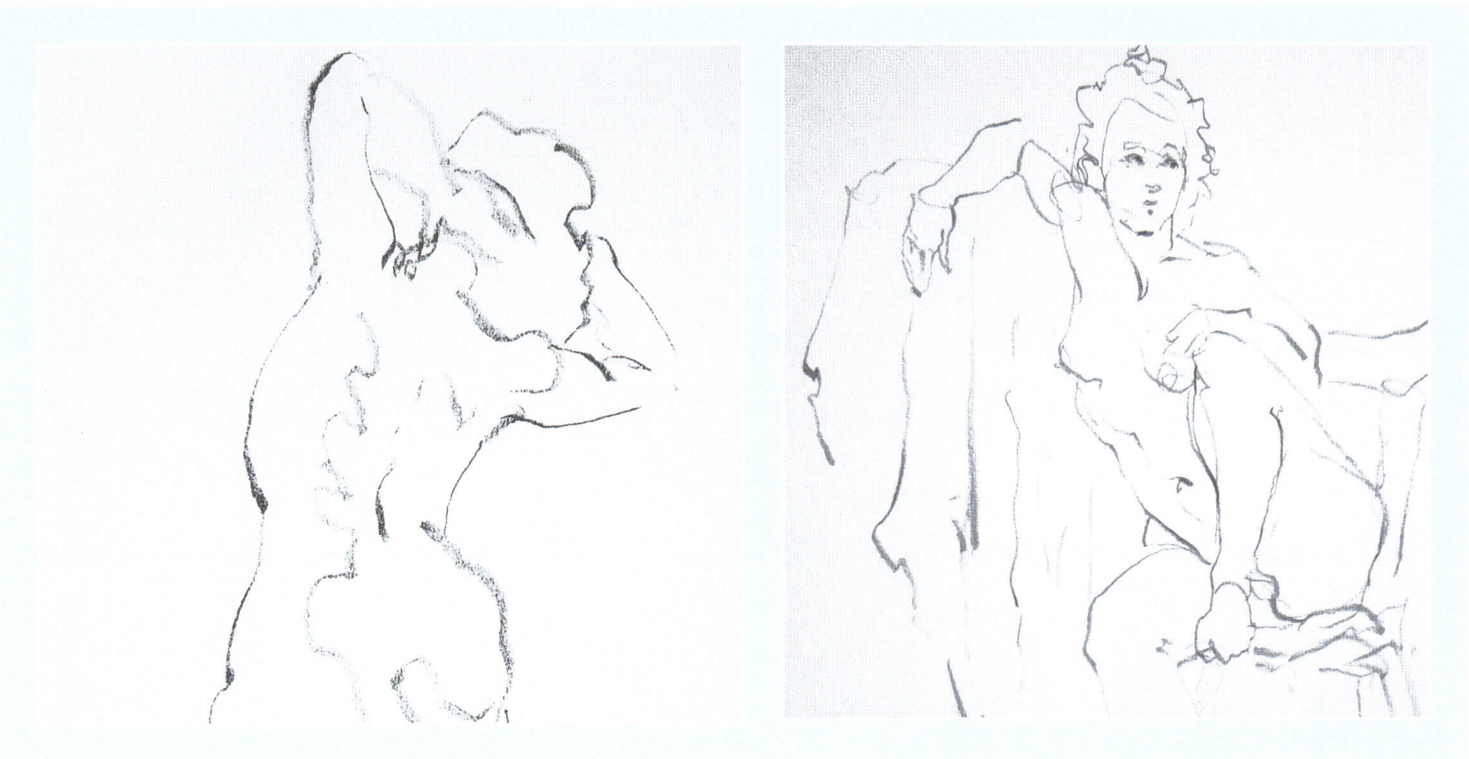

This is a favorite exercise among drawing instructors. I personally love doing this. Simply use your less dominant hand for drawing, whether you're doing quick sketches or have the benefit of a live model for an extended amount of time.

It increases your focus because the control that you have relied on is no longer at your disposal. It is humbling and fun but, more importantly, it wakes up a part of your thinking that was not being used. This exercise surprises students in that they can often get the rhythm of the pose much better when they do not have the automatic use of the dominant hand.

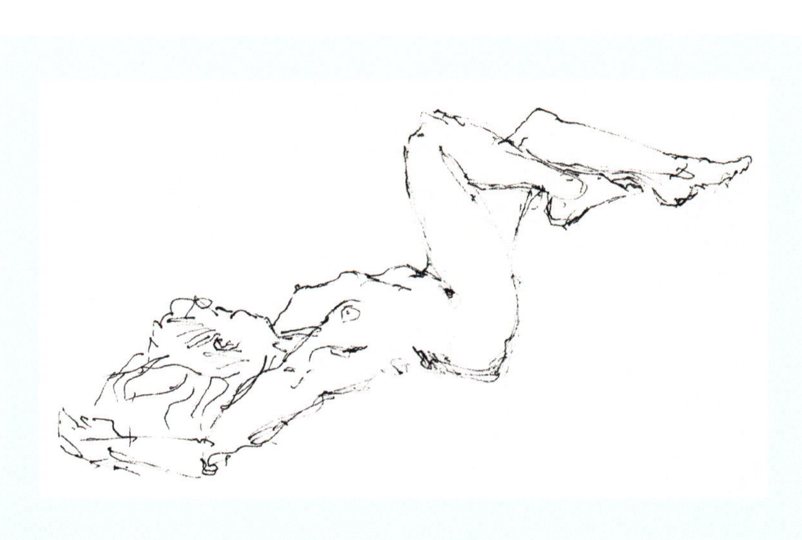

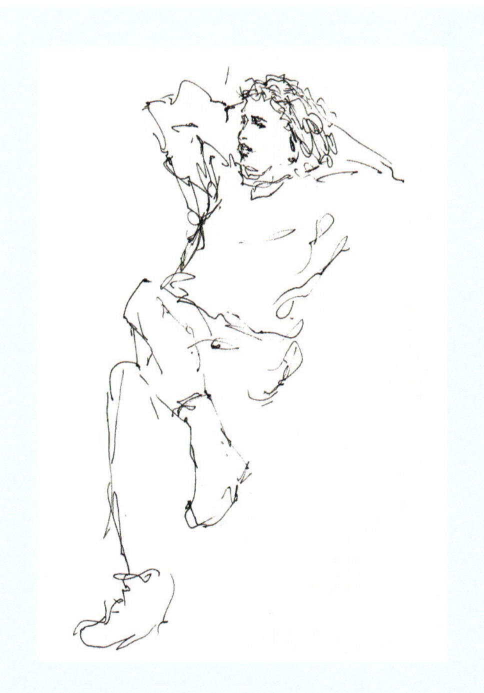

Draw from TV: Control Your Model

Sketch often and experiment with different styles and techniques. Use reference or draw from life. I often sketch when I watch TV alone, pausing a program to draw the faces onscreen. This allows me to sit and relax, pause when there is an interesting person to draw, and then stop the person while in action to sketch various positions. The great thing about modern televisions is that when they pause, the image is perfectly clear, sharp, and still for exactly five minutes, which is the maximum time required for these sketches. The drawings below were done on a single page from various programs that I watched. From news to sports, it's a wealth of material to draw from. This is one of my favorite exercises since the people on TV are not posing per se, so their movements are more natural.

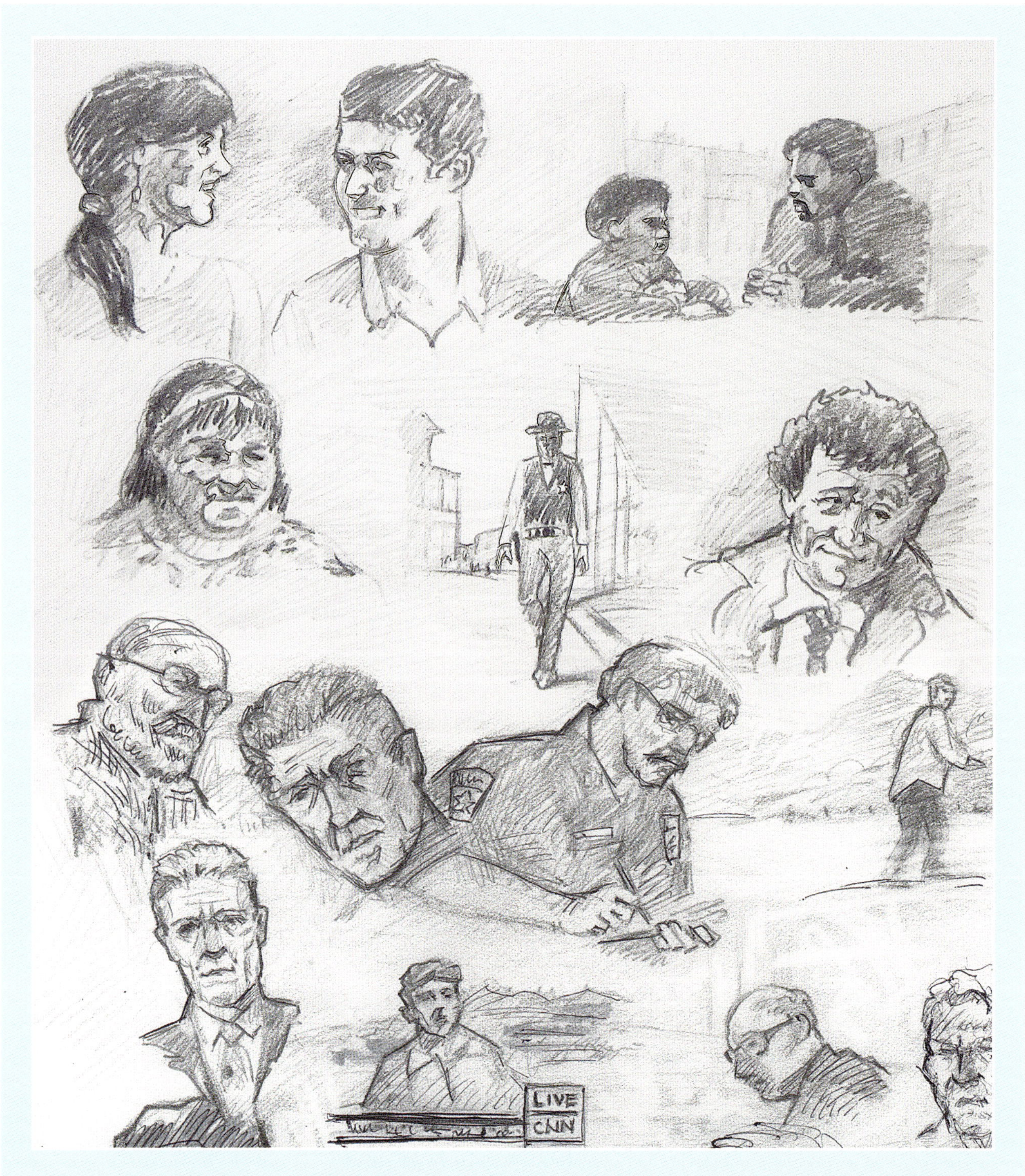

FOCUS ON BODY PARTS

Now you are ready to draw. Drawing the figure requires a combination of many elements, and can be as challegnging as learning music and language. It requires study and practice. Anyone who has learned to play a musical instrument or speak a second language (or even your first language) can relate.

The reality is that there are no easy paths to great drawing, especially when it comes to the most formidable subject for any artist of any century: the human figure. Pencil mileage is going to be reiterated by every drawing teacher and there is no shortcut. It is like walking 2,000 miles (approximately 3,200 km) on foot—you just have to keep taking each step forward, and eventually you will get there. You must learn the basics of drawing forms, valuing the lights and darks to create depth, and honning your vision to see every angle, every mark, and how each one relates to the other.

I remember in drawing class the professor would have us do homework that entailed drawing tabletop objects, such as a pencil sharpener, spoon, eraser, or coffee cup. All of these were done with very sharp 2H and HB graphite pencils. To train us to create visual communication more effectively, we could not use any shading, no values to create form or depth. Instead, they had to be achieved with lines and line weight. Edges of a box, for example, would be drawn slightly differently; the closest edge would be drawn slightly darker to have it visually advance and seem closer.

At first, my classmates and I wondered why we were drawing our pencil sharpener for a head-drawing class... until we started to draw the models in class. Once again, our teacher would have us draw the head without any value, purely with line. We relied on slight overlapping and darker accents to simulate depth and volume. All of us were amazed at how much better we saw every little change of every aspect of the head: the slight slants of the eyes and nose—everything became clearer to us.

Drawing is also about building on simple shapes. The basic ABCs of drawing are cylinders, spheres, cubes, and cones. These forms are used to help you practice making the forms three-dimensional. Value is one of the most important aspects of all of art whether you draw, paint, or work digitally. The relationship between lights and darks are crucial in creating believable forms.

One of the least talked about aspects when you are learning to draw is that personal preferences matter. We do not all like the same food, the same shoes, or have the same tastes when viewing art. Identify what you like when you are perusing art books or walking through a museum or gallery. You can only get better at art when you know what you are drawn to. Follow your heart but also know that what you may be faced with when you are in a professional setting. As an illustrator I often had to conform to what an art director had in mind or what the job called for. Fortunately, this direction can be the best friend for any artist—and deadlines. To create art for a specific purpose beyond your own wants and needs and being confined to a time frame actually helps you grow.

The one thing that you should do as a student and artist is know what you like, by trying every kind of pencil that you can get your hands on as well as paper. See, there is a perfect combo out there for each of us: that "right" pencil with the "right" paper and for the right reason. This reminds me of professional guitarists; they never just own one guitar. When playing live it is common to see a musician change guitars between songs, because each guitar has a different sound, and the artist chooses one based on which best matches the feel of a particular song. I know that I love using one pencil with a specific type of paper; even the hardness of the surface under my paper makes a huge difference. You can only discover your preference combination through trial and error.

When you first start to draw a figure, keep the forms simple. The human body is complicated. Anatomy needs to be studied, but remember that it will make your drawings stiff and harsh. They will remain like this until your knowledge of human anatomy is so comprehensive that you do not have to think about anatomy any longer. Remember that gesture drawings happen in time; it takes years to see your gestural drawing emerge. I have all of my students start with longer poses first, and then gradually move toward shorter poses. For instance, in my classes, I start with 40-minute poses, then decrease to 15-, 10-, and 5-minute poses, and finally, but not always, 2-minute poses. Study comes first, then speed. Be patient and do not lose heart, once the elements of drawing become second nature, all of your hard work will be worth it.

Tutorial: Female vs. Male Standing Figure

As noted in previous chapters, there are some basic physical characteristics that set apart a male from a female: men have a longer torso, broader shoulders, and smaller hips. This tutorial shares four easy steps to depicting a male and female in standing position from the rear. Once you have nailed the general form, you will be able to start positioning your figure in other ways with more ease. You can repeat this exercise with varying body types, including people of different ages, to train yourself to better place underlying bones in your sketches.

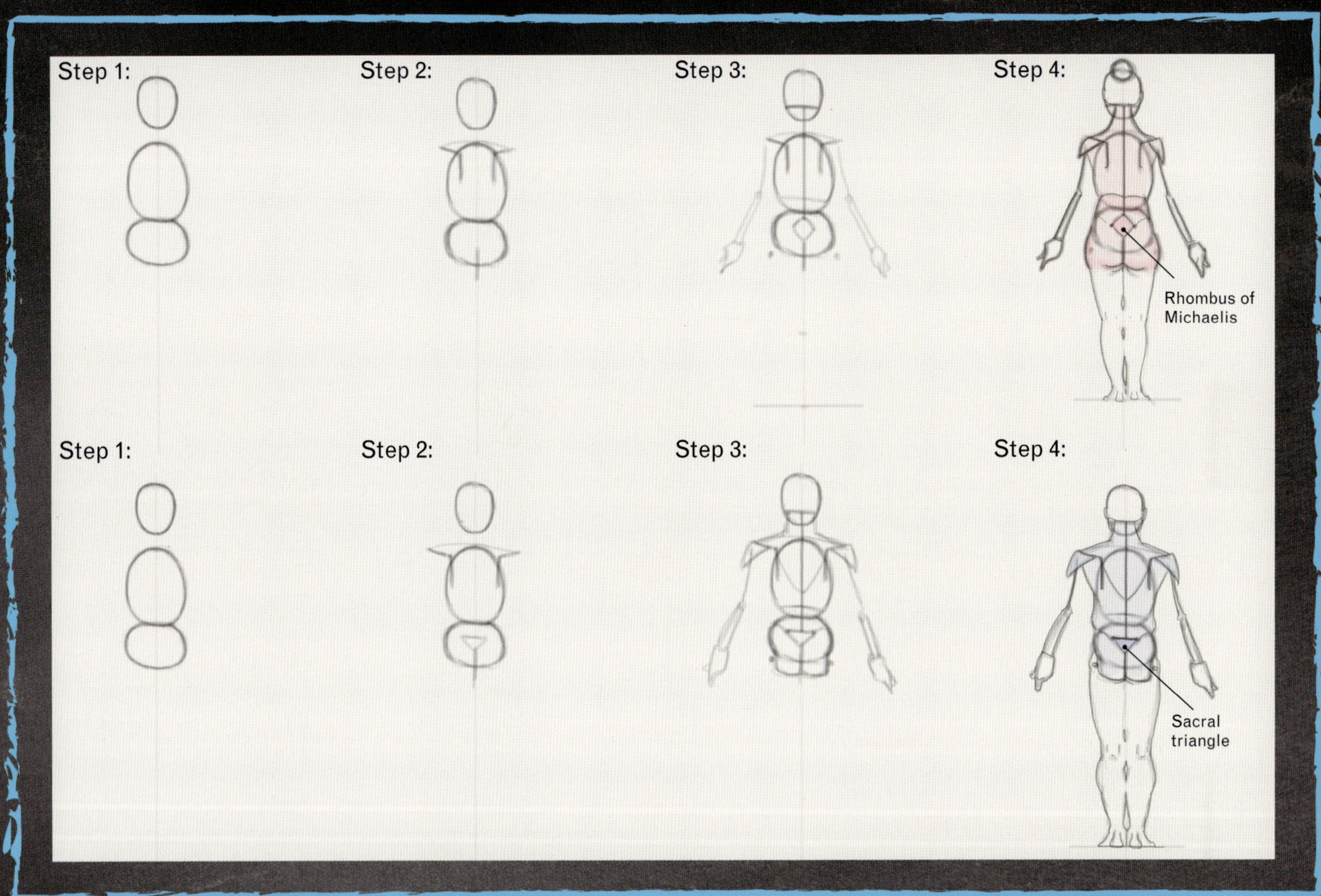

STEP 1:

Start with the very simple "snowman" sketches by drawing the head, torso, and lower torso. Do not designate the gender yet.

STEP 3:

On the female, place the Rhombus of Michaelis, making the spine appear shorter. Then, place the great trochanters on both genders, but wider on the female since women's hips are wider than men's.

STEP 2:

Next, draw the scapulae: closer together on the female torso and farther apart for the male. On men, the distance between the scapulae is greater due to thicker underlying muscles, not necessarily because of a larger frame or rib cage. Then, place the sacral triangle on the male figure just above the gluteal cleft.

STEP 4:

Draw the lumbar fat pads on the female that bridge the area between the ilium of the pelvis and the thorax (rib cage). Fat covers the great trochanters as well on the female. On the male the flank portion of the external oblique is much more clearly defined.

Capturing the Main Frame

The main frame is basically the chassis of the body, like a tree without any branches. It is the area between the acromion processes of the scapulae and each great trochanter of the femurs, seen here in the colored area of a simplified figure in action. It is easy to see the shoulders and hips, so the main frame works well as a malleable rectangle. but it can also be a peanut shape that can fit into that rectangle. It is essential in capturing the rhythm and flow of the figure. Note the angles of both the shoulders and the hips. I cannot stress enough how important it is for you to see both of these critical angles and how they relate to each other; it is the essence and poetry of any pose.

When looking at a posed figure, identify the main frame by locating the spine of each scapula and the medial border. The spine is the slanted protruding bony aspect of the scapula that ends at the shoulder, (acromion process to be exact). The medial border is the edge of the scapula that roughly parallels the spine. Notice how these two lines can be viewed as hands on a clock. At neutral, when the arms are relaxed at the sides, the right scapula is at 2:30, the hour hand is the spine of the scapula and the minute hand the medial border. The left scapula is at 9:30, the hour hand being the spine of the scapula and the minute hand being the medial border that roughly parallels the spine. Remember that the horizontal line crossing the great trochanters is also the one that crosses the pubic bone on the front, as illustrated on the next page.

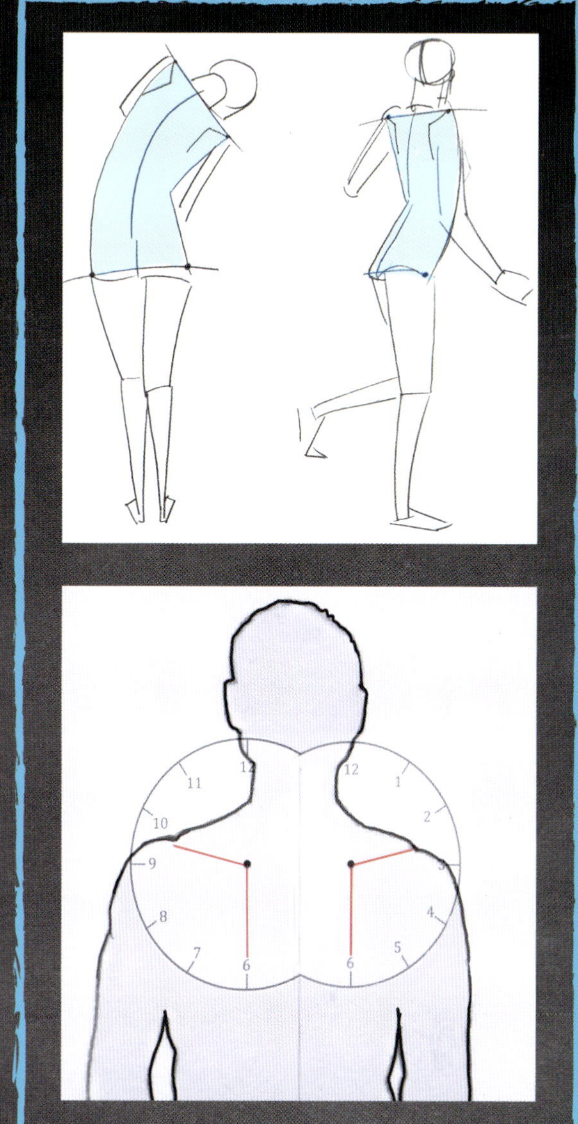

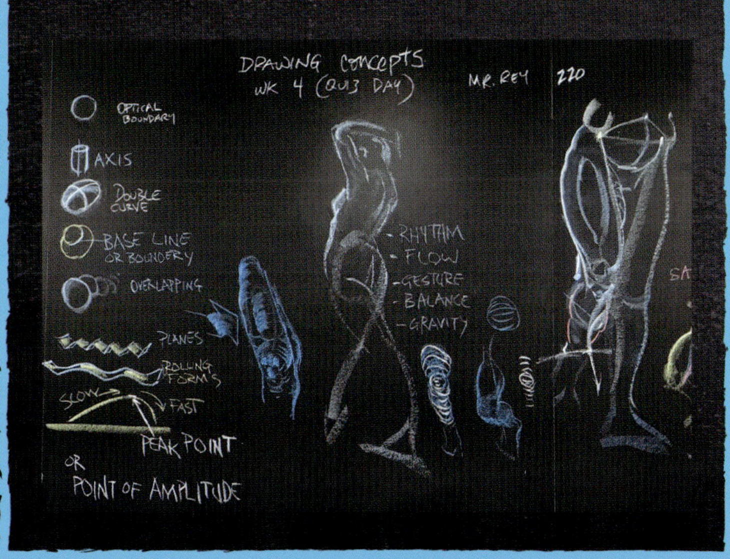

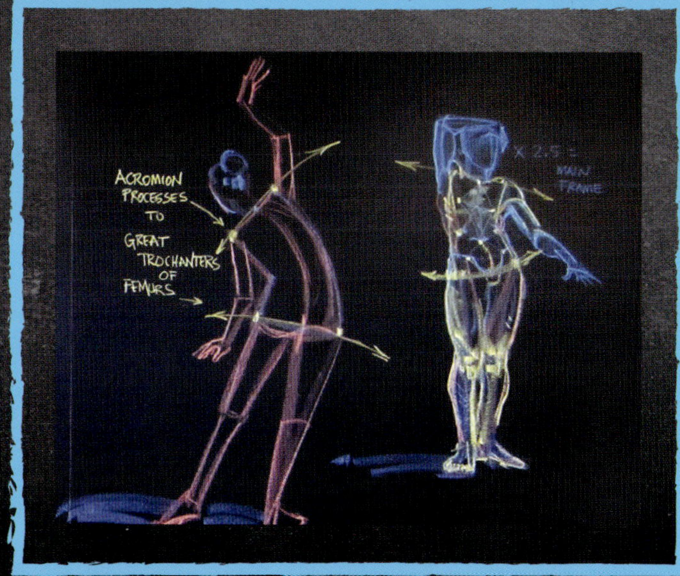

Draw Skeletal Armature

One of the biggest mistakes my students make is elongating torsos, which leads to making the lower limbs too long as well. One way to keep the thorax (rib cage) and the pelvis from straying too far apart from one another is by chaining the two with the lumbar vertebrae. This is also a good way to practice twisting of the two. These can be done from the imagination or with reference. At times I have my students use tracing paper over a selected figure from art or from stock model photos to assist with this exercise.

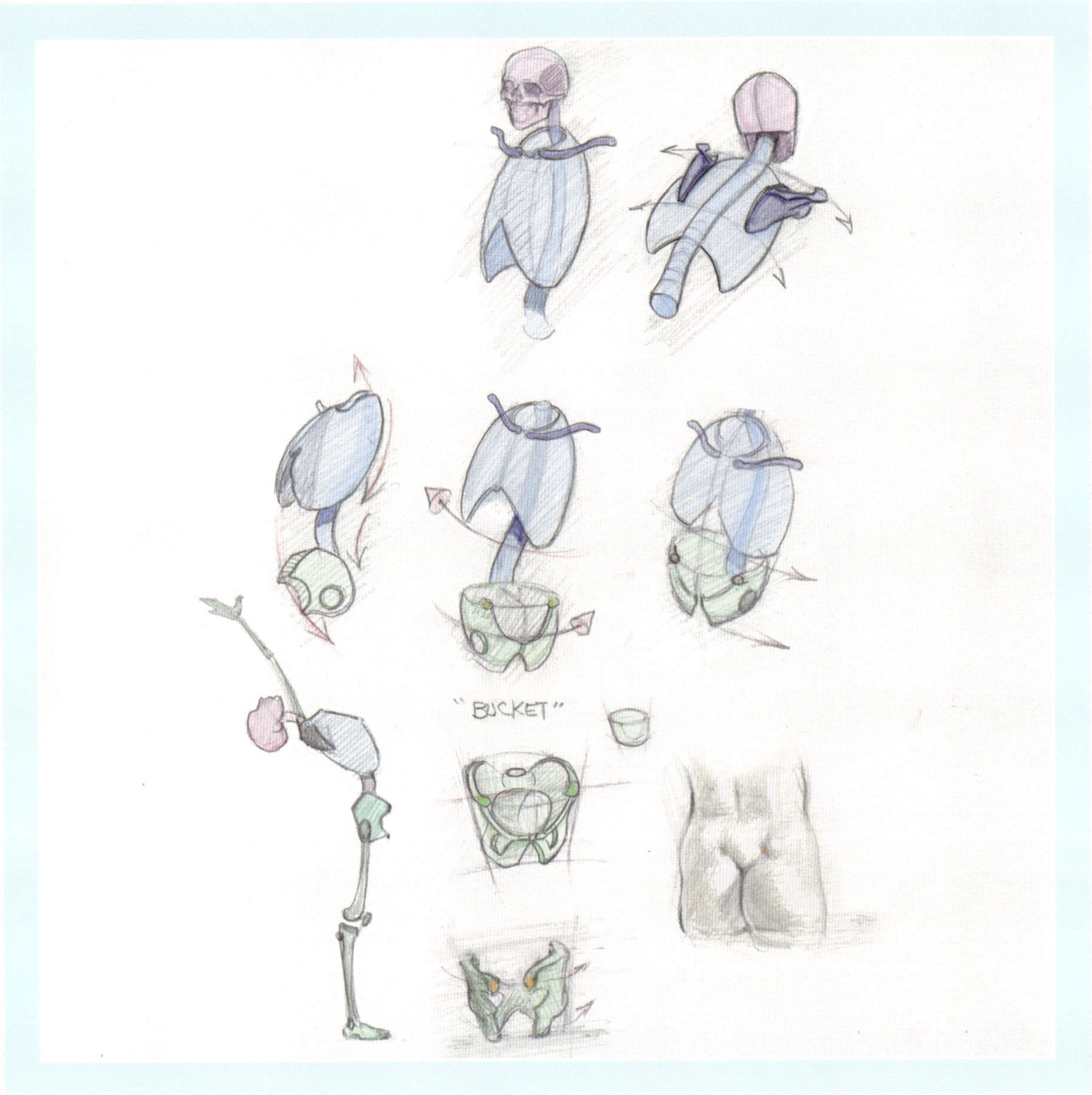

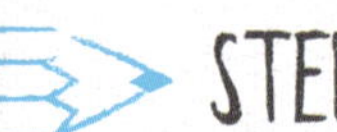

STEP 1:

Start by sketching the head, as it will establish the scale.

STEP 2:

Draw the thorax and rib cage, which is roughly one and a half times larger than the head. Keep it simple, like an egg.

STEP 3:

When you add the pelvis, keep it as a rounded form, or very simplified, and then link the thorax and pelvis with the spine.

Origin and Insertion: The Drumstick Form

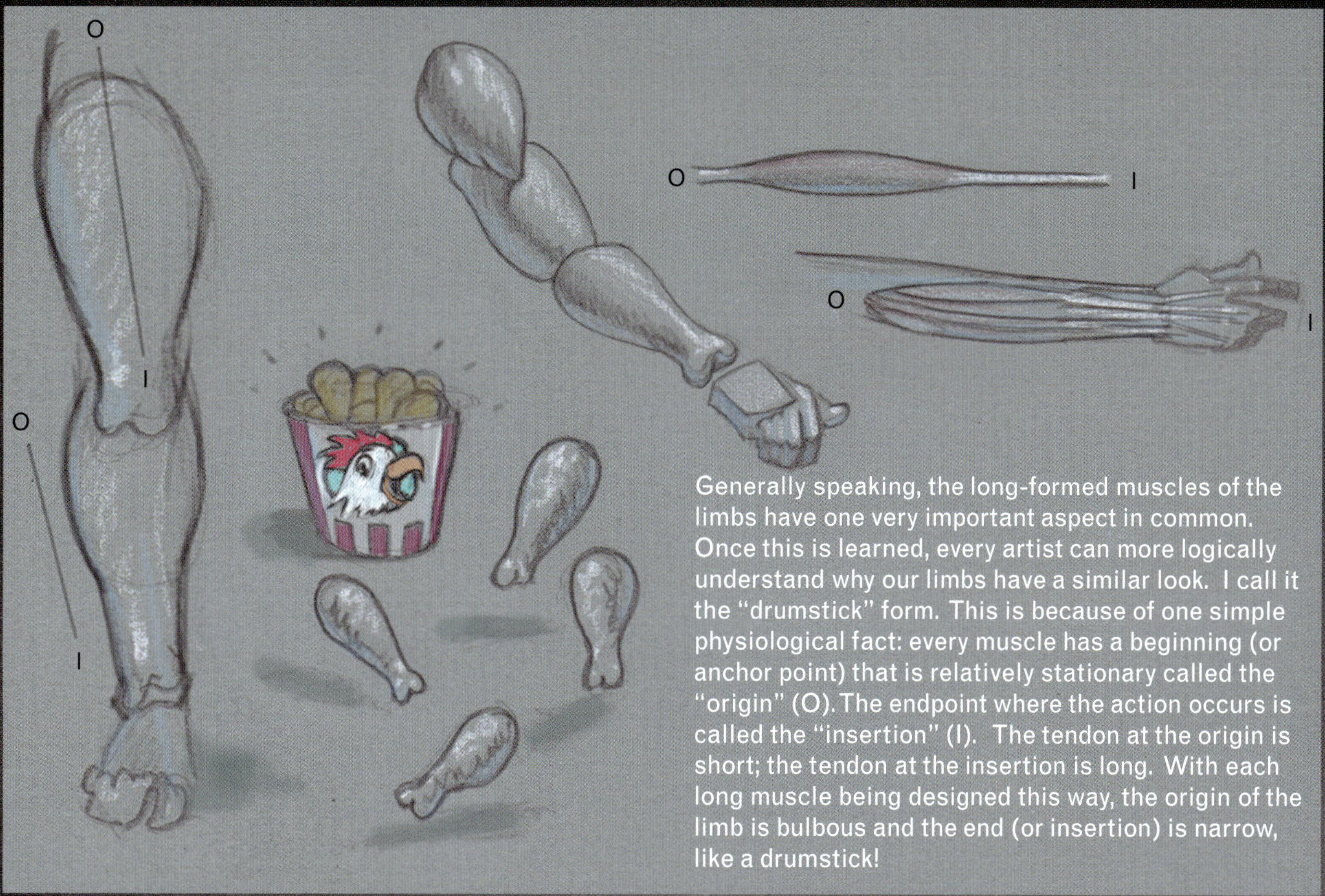

Generally speaking, the long-formed muscles of the limbs have one very important aspect in common. Once this is learned, every artist can more logically understand why our limbs have a similar look. I call it the "drumstick" form. This is because of one simple physiological fact: every muscle has a beginning (or anchor point) that is relatively stationary called the "origin" (O). The endpoint where the action occurs is called the "insertion" (I). The tendon at the origin is short; the tendon at the insertion is long. With each long muscle being designed this way, the origin of the limb is bulbous and the end (or insertion) is narrow, like a drumstick!

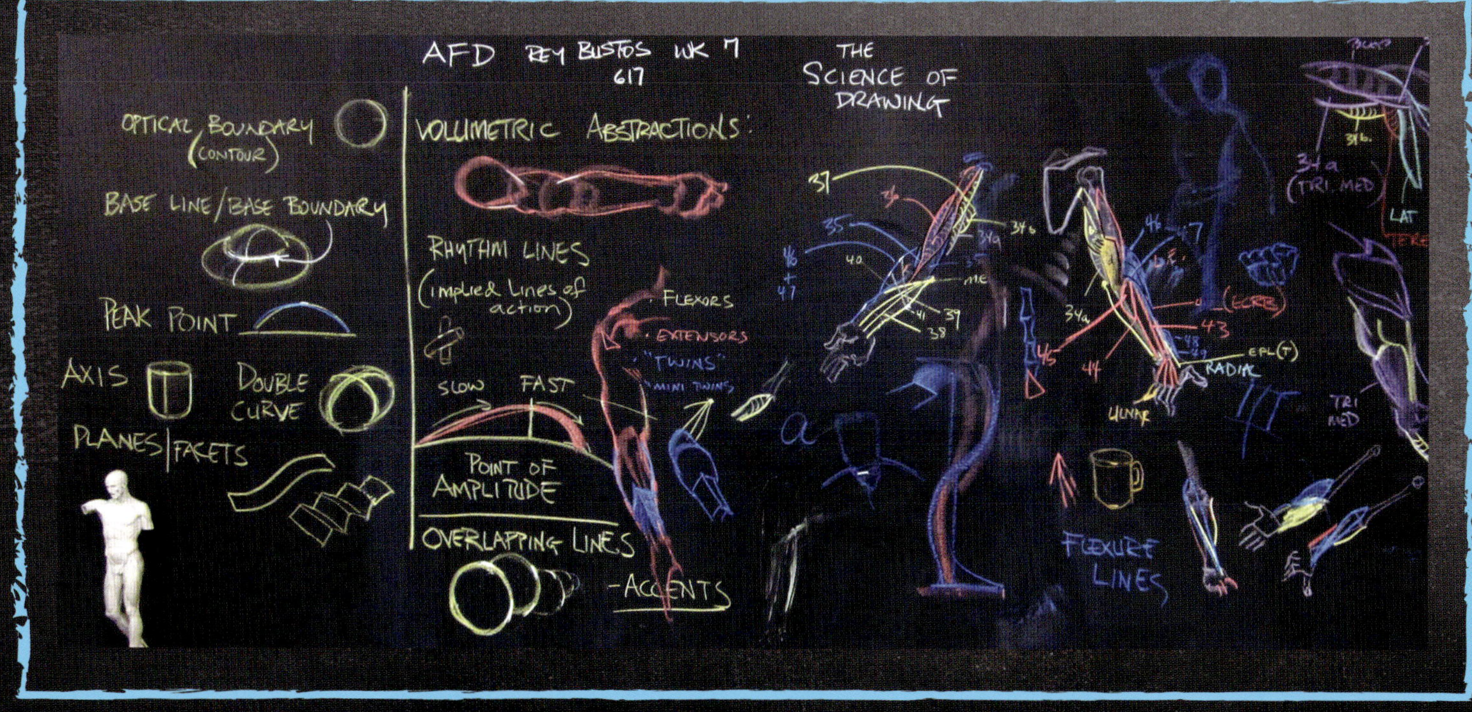

Constellation Drawing

Constellation drawing is my favorite method to teach my students how to construct the body. Using our innate human tendency to visually connect the dots we see in our mind makes this method the easiest for people of all ages to use when figure drawing. From the earliest of times people have looked into the heavens and created objects, animals, and even people by imagining that the stars are connected. Our internal imagery makes it look as if a group of dots represents whatever the viewer's imagination sees.

I teach many very young students as well as college-aged and older professionals, so I have seen firsthand that even at a very early age, if I draw a series of dots—let's say eight in an area that is sixteen inches in diameter—and ask the young children what it is, they immediately blurt out "a circle." Making use of this natural tendency, I started playing with having all my students, young and old, see the model or reference as a constellation. The "stars" in this case being placed at the major joints and landmarks of the body. This is a variation on methods used in countless classrooms, which I learned in Harry Carmean's class when I was a young art student. It was the single most valuable lesson that I'd had up to that point.

Burne Hogarth at ArtCenter College of Design taught another helpful variation in which he saw the torso and pelvic area as a peanut shape within the rectangular main frame; basically the egg-shaped area of the rib cage and the rounded are of the pelvic region. This works best in side view.

As you can see from the overlays in the following images, the basic body is plotted out as if it were the armature wire frame of a clay sculpture.

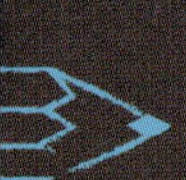

> **Exercise:** Take this pose as an example and plot the positions of the major joints and points as though they were stars in a constellation. Start with the head, then the bottom tip of the chin and then its relative position to the pit of the neck, nipples, navel, shoulders, and all the joints. Plot as many stars as you like or that you see.
>
> 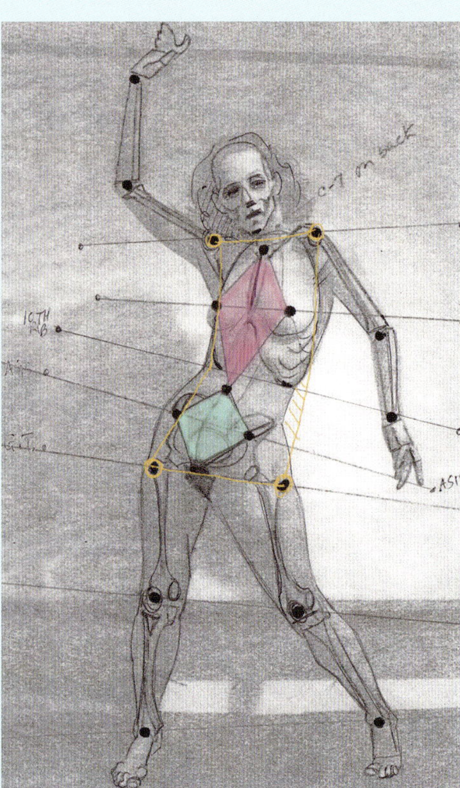
> 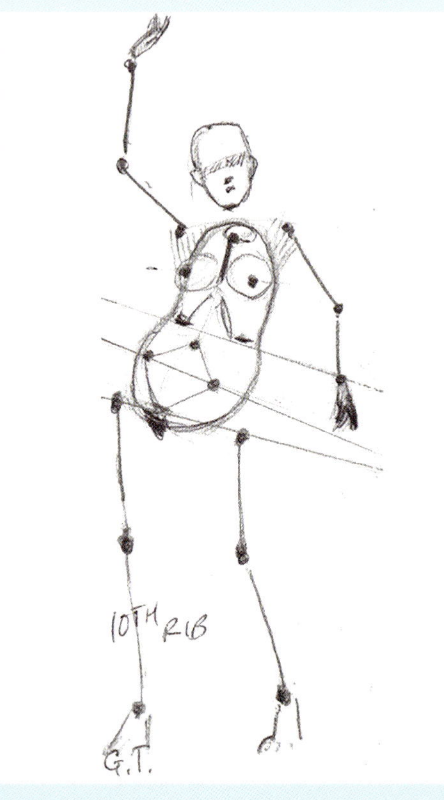
>

Proportion Check: Main Frame and Constellation Drawing

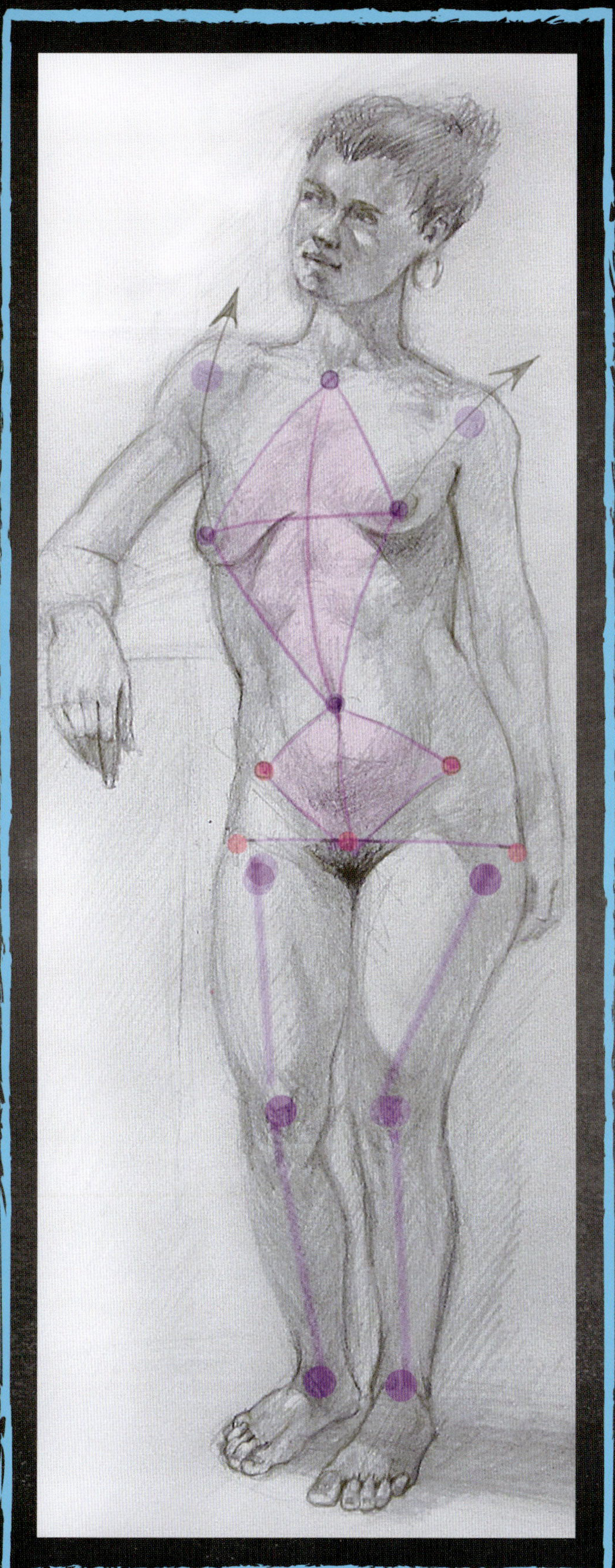

Everyone has their own unique "kite." Many times this can look more like a diamond shape. The next most important series or "stars" are the navel to the ASIS points of the pelvis to the pubic bone. As discussed on page 45, when perfectly arranged on a fictitious model, these are what I call the "baseball diamond." These are rarely as exact as a baseball diamond, but it always gives the artist a clear guideline for that particular model's constellation points. The two areas, the kite and the baseball diamond combined, create an easy method for any artist to keep their proportions in check since they are linked together at the navel.

Exercise: Using tracing paper, draw the main frame over whatever reference you like, and then try it with a live model. Identify the body's "stars." It is amazing how much easier it will be to depict this part of the body with these useful tools. The most important stars are the ones that create the "kite" of the front of the body. The kite is formed by the landmarks of the pit of the neck to each nipple and then to the navel.

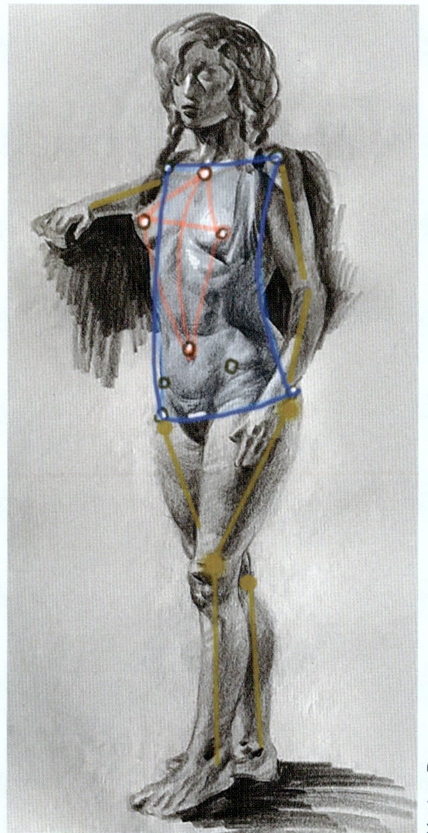

Hetian Duan

CREATING SILHOUETTES

Before moving on to detailed drawings of the human figure, let's continue our warm-up with some fun silhouette exercises.

Quick Thumbnails

Whether you are in a workshop or coffee shop, this is a great way to quickly jot down the main gist of each figure. Working small and quickly, simply sketch in the space that the figure takes up. Without the interior smaller forms (details), you are forced to reduce the figure to its mere essence.

These silhouettes span across one of the pages in my 9 x 12 inch sketchbook, so each one of these figures is about 2 inches tall. This is an excellent way to improve your visual skills by eliminating all of the details. This is also effective in capturing people who are not posing for you and move while you are drawing. I did this at my local café, and they took about two minutes each—just enough to capture the pose and even attitude. You'll be surprised how much you can learn from this exercise.

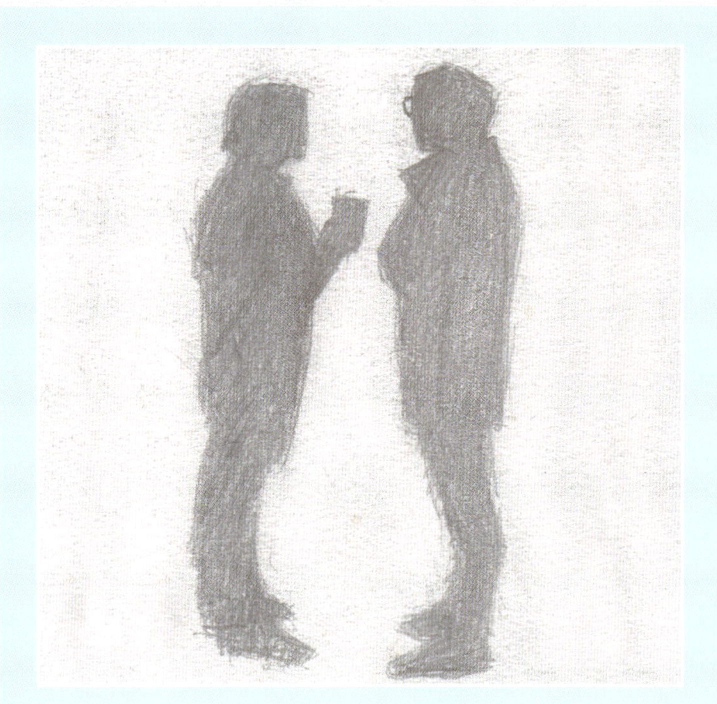

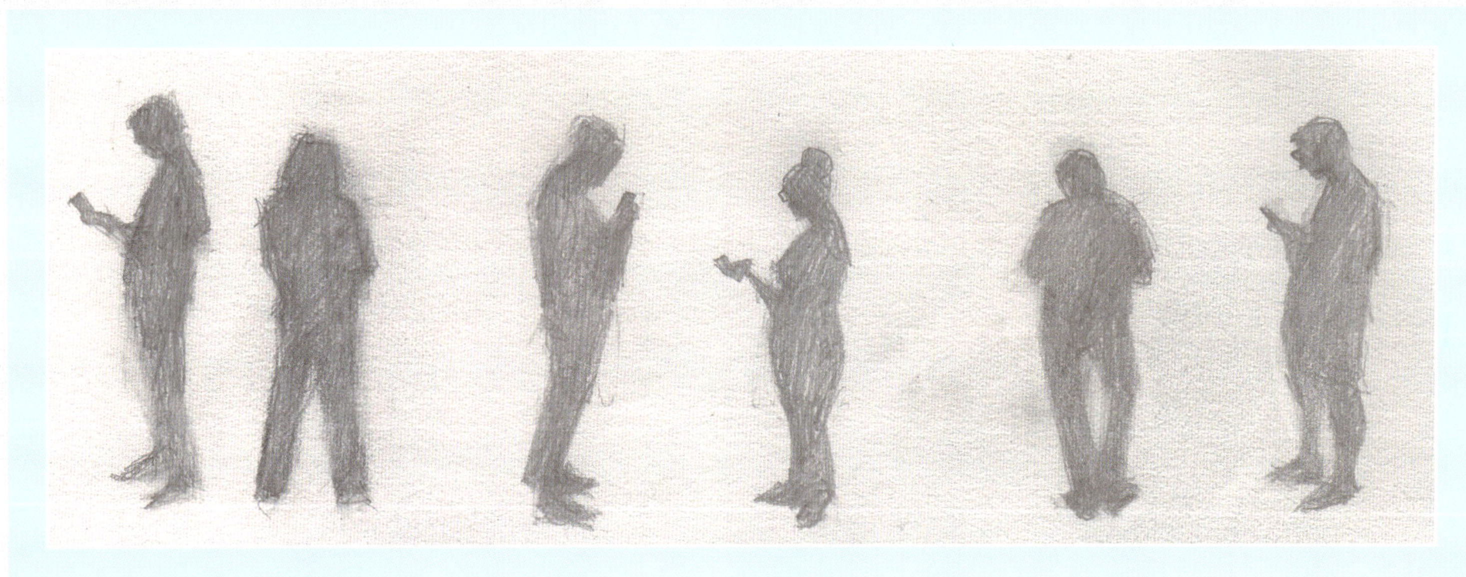

Cutting vs. Drawing

One fabulous exercise that I do in some of my classes does not require drawing at all—in the conventional sense—it involves cutting. I have my students carefully cut the outline of the model out of black paper using an X-Acto knife. It works best with a thinner type of paper, like wrapping paper.

A 15-minute pose would be ideal to capture, if possible. Place the paper on the cardboard back of your 18 x 24 inch pad to avoid damaging your drawing board. Cut the figure out by starting at one point (for instance, the head) and then traveling around the body, cutting out the negative shapes, such as the triangle that occurs with a bent arm, hand on hip. Aim for the figure to be around 12 to 18 inches tall so as not to be too small or too large. This is a great exercise because it uses a different part of your brain and gives the detail-focused part of your brain a break!

What you will discover from doing this exercise is fascinating and important. Your brain will naturally see the spaces between the body better, and you will learn to see more carefully the space that the model takes in the room. Since there are no details to draw, you get a better view of the overall composition. This exercise is best with standard standing poses, what I call "Waiting for the Bus" poses. The next exercise is a variation of this and a natural progressive step.

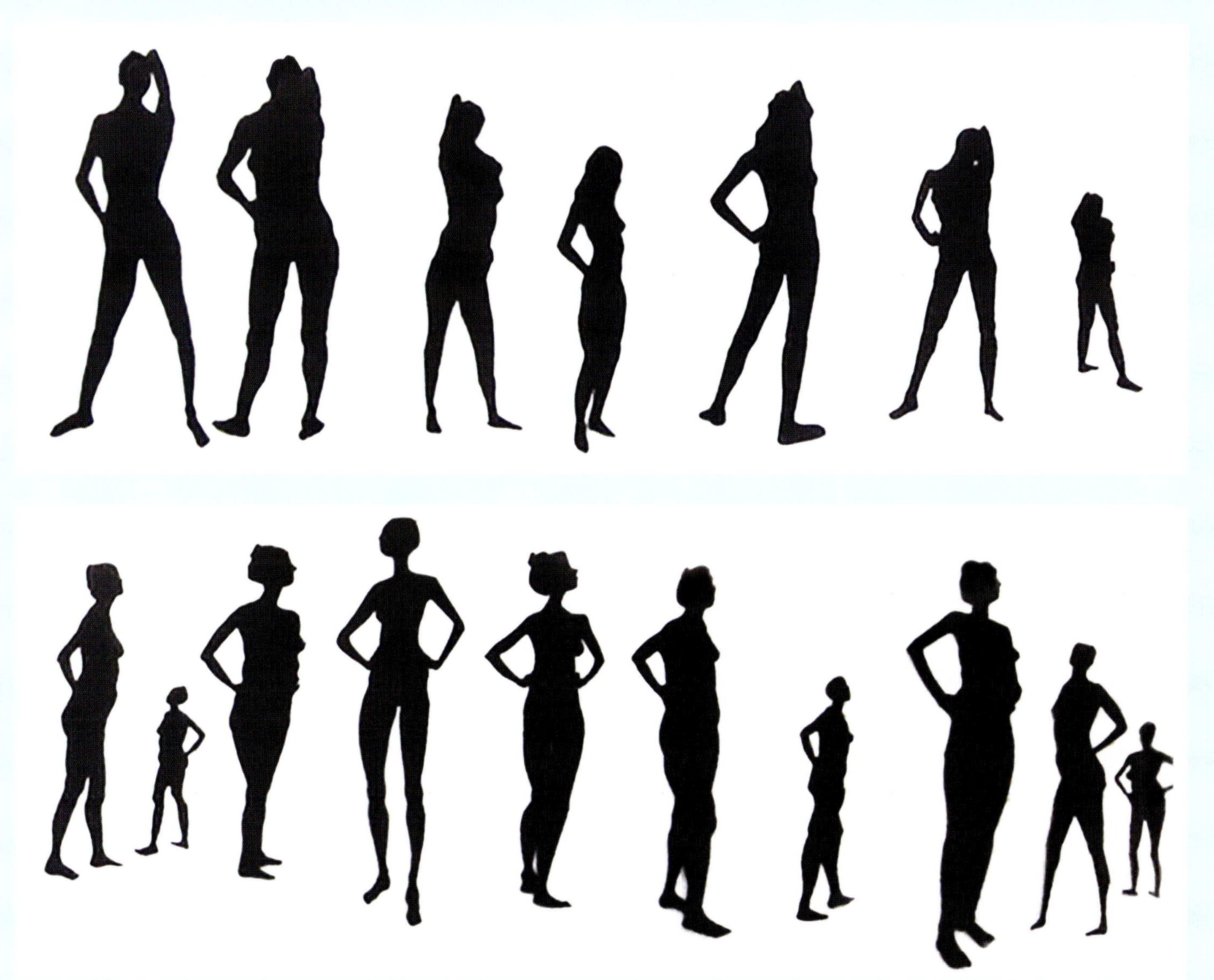

Drawing with a Chamois

In this exercise, take a well-blackened chamois (or even a cotton pad), use your index finger or index and middle fingers inside the chamois, and draw. Like the basic principle of the earlier quick thumbnail exercise, once again you can't really create details, which forces you to focus more on the silhouette, a smoky version of the pose. Once you get the hang of drawing this way, after two or three 10-minute poses, take an eraser to refine the edges and contours. It is best to use a retractable pen-shaped eraser or kneaded eraser. This is an amazing way to learn how to draw better by only depicting the essence of the pose without the added burden of details. I have had kids draw this way with amazing results! The silhouette and cutout below were both done by a 13-year-old.

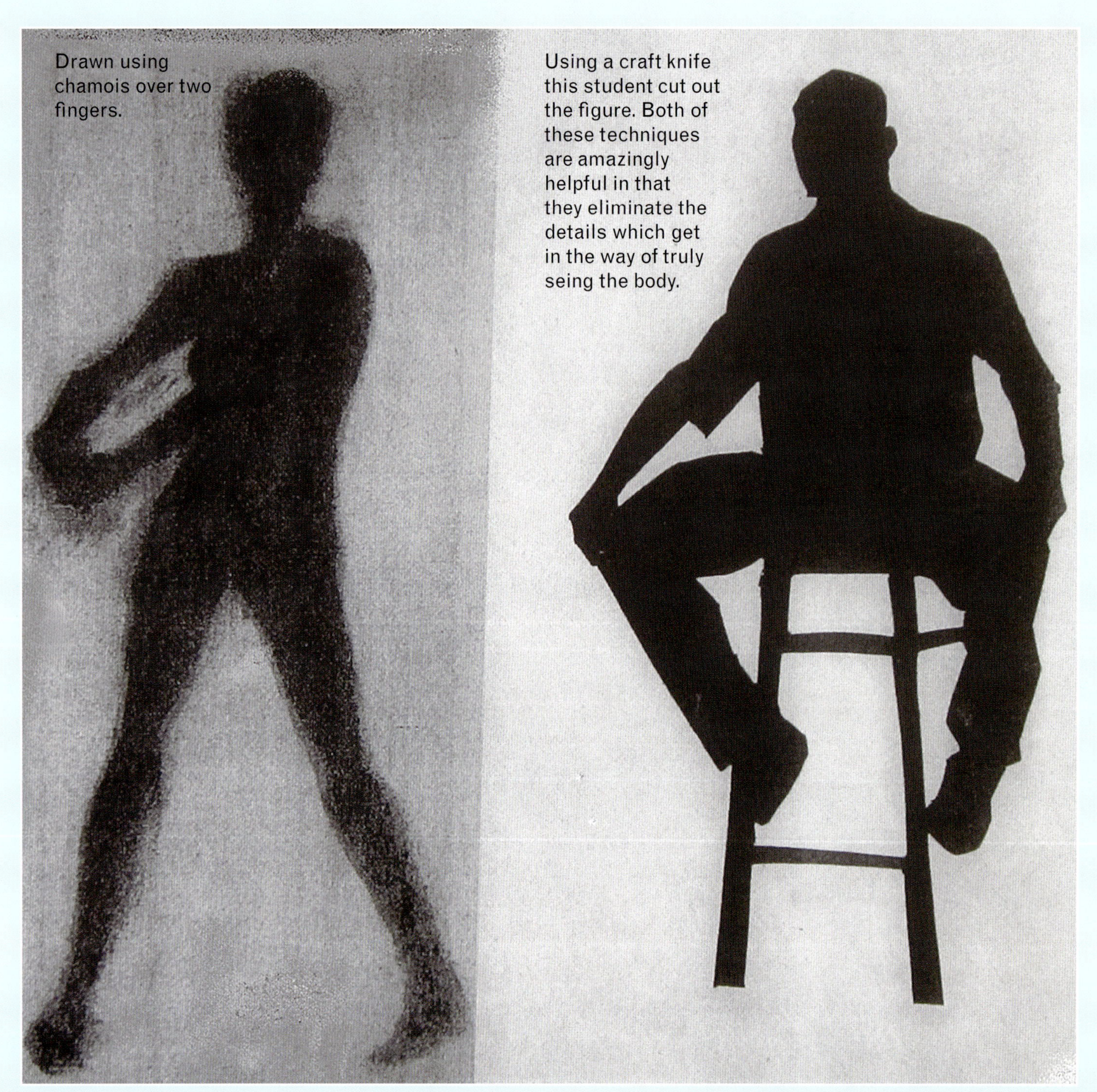

APPLYING SHADOWS

When tackling shadows, one of the best tools at your disposal is the ability to squint. View the model and squint to lessen the values, then while you draw, simplify the shapes created by the shadows (see image below). I often use the example of a Beatles T-shirt I have with the Fab Four presented in two values: their faces in white against the black shirt. It only takes two values to create a likeness of a person. This illustrates just how important it is to squint and see the figure or face in two values.

Exercise: On white paper, draw the shadows that you see on a face, for instance, the shadows under and around the brow and eyes, under the nose, under the upper lip, under the lower lip, and under the chin onto the neck. As with anything else, practice, and the payoff is more enjoyment as you continue to learn and grow.

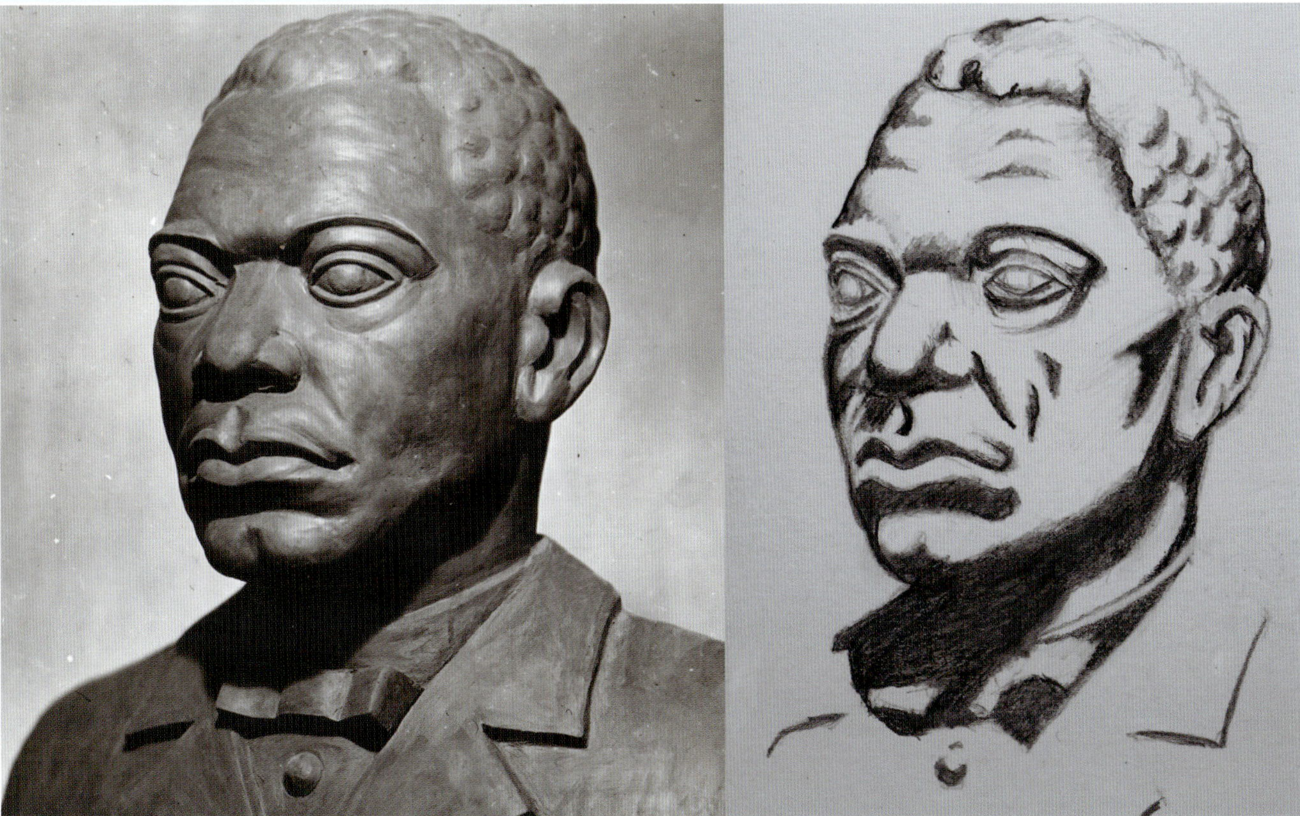

Selma Burke, circa 1935, Booker T. Washington

On the next page, let's apply shadows to an object. Using a red rubber ball, the relationship between the darkest area of the form, the core, and the direction of the main light source can be explained.

The ball has a factory seam that I will use to illustrate the core shadow in all of the forms.

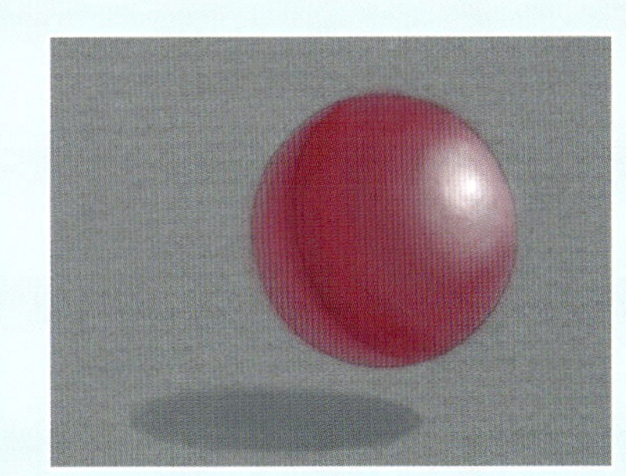

Parts of the sphere are labeled, indicating shadows and light. This simple, direct side view shows that when light hits the ball, it creates a highlight, or hot spot, of light.

The core (dark band) runs perpendicular to the direction of the light beam, and is the area on the form that gets the least amount of direct light and the least amount of bounced backlight (reflected light).

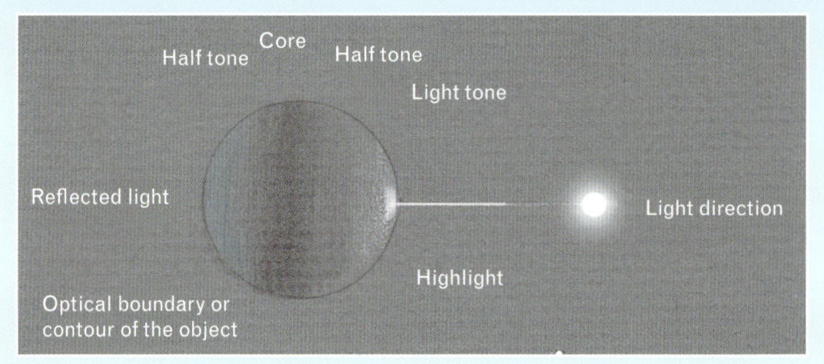

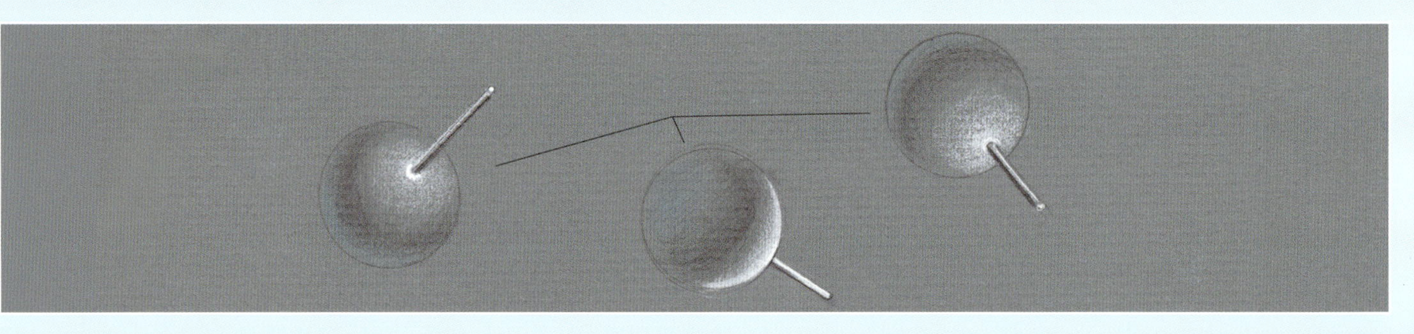

This illustration shows a dowel in the ball to simulate the light direction. The entry point of the dowel is the highlight; the core shadow turns as you shift the dowel around.

The image on the immediate right shows a dowel resting on a ball, casting a shadow. The cast of the dowel is darkest where it touches the ball and it softens as it goes further on its way around the ball. It ends at the core and it is the exact same value as the value of the core! It will never be visible in the reflected light area. The image on the far-right shows how shadows change on a form that has many forms within it, a head and face.

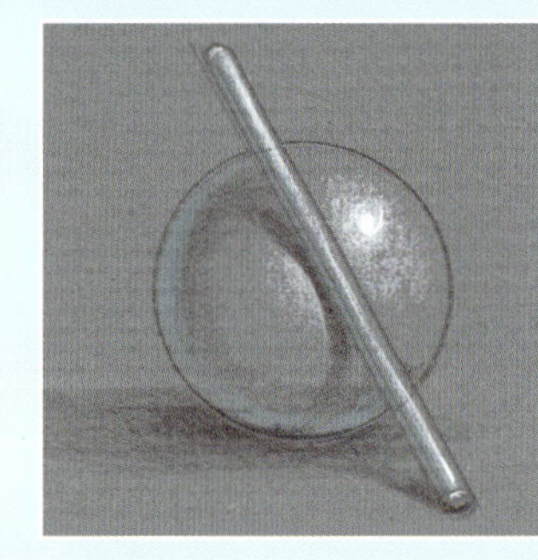
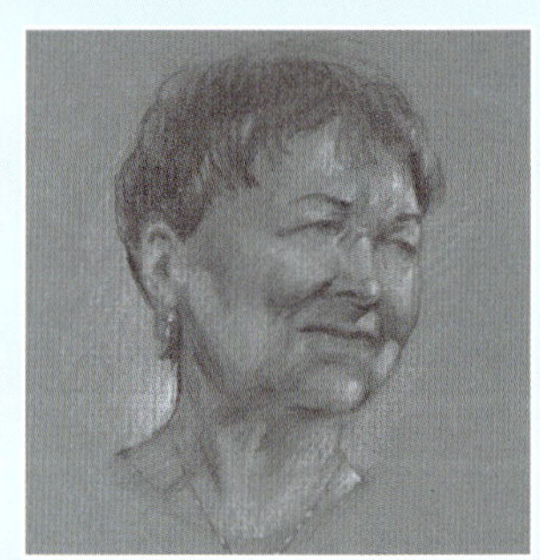

Exercise: Make up random shapes and chain them together, almost like balloon animals. Make up the light position as best that you can and draw from imagination. If imagining this is too challenging, set up objects on a table, light them (preferably with a single light source like a desk lamp), and then draw.

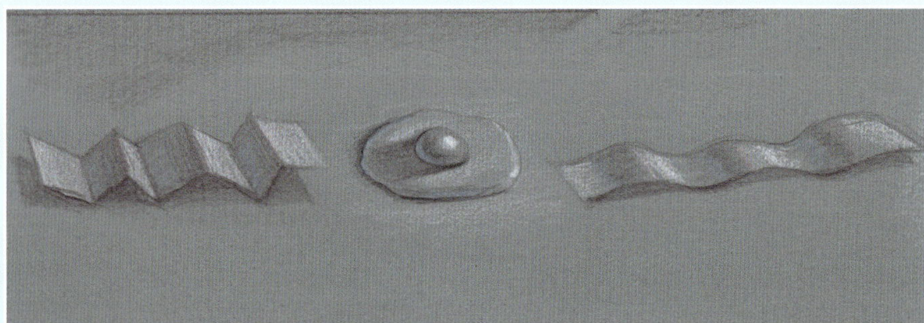
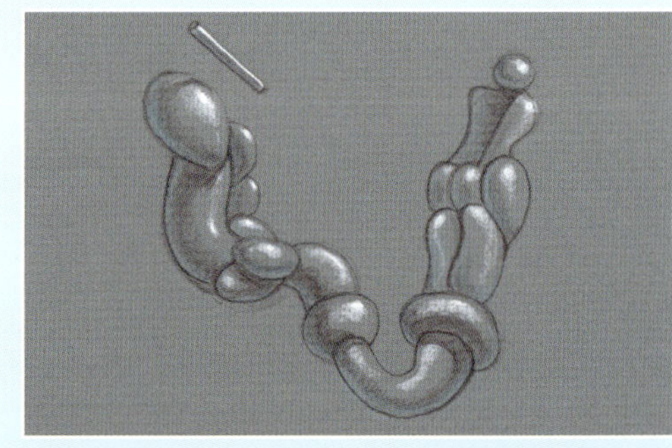

MASTERING POSES: CHOOSING YOUR REFERENCE

First of all, know that these are my opinions; other teachers have their own. Everyone can teach you something, even if it is something that does not suit you, including my own opinions and suggestions in this book. As I have said many times, education is a buffet full of options. Try new things when possible and do this often, and you will continue to know yourself as an artist. If you are like me, the learning never ends, nor does exploration.

I suggest my students draw the human figure often, and not wait for class or a figure-drawing workshop. When I do not have a model—which is almost always—I use art reference. I do that more than I use photos of models. The reason being—and this is more important for students—that when art is created, good art, the artist has already imbued the drawing with their knowledge, therefore there is a more direct connection to the figure since it has already been drawn, sculpted, or painted with the artist's knowledge. I also look for work that is similar to my own style. I love the Mannerists, and I consider myself a Mannerist in drawing style, so I often use drawings by Pontormo or Tiepolo. I also love the drawings of Andrea del Sarto, Michelangelo, Artemisia Gentileschi, Judith Leyster, Peter Paul Rubens, Sofonisba Anguissola, and Dean Cornwell, to name just a very few.

When I was teaching myself to draw better—which continues to this day—I often placed tracing paper over the printed reference. I broke it down, as on page 126, and studied the simple shapes and rhythm of each figure and captured it on the paper. I would then take the tracing paper without the reference and place it next to the large-format pad on my easel. I would redraw the simplified forms and take it to whatever degree of finish that I desired. The key is to pick images that inspire you, period.

It's like being a musician; people who become jazz musicians, for instance, generally choose to be because that is the genre that inspired them the most. They likely studied jazz and specific jazz artists and played their music until they memorized it without looking at the sheet music. Eventually, those artists could create their own music or interpretations of it. I personally love redrawing a Pontormo drawing, for example, but I do not copy it—I reinterpret it. Since he interprets the body, his figures are not realistic; they are better, in my opinion. In essence, I am interpreting an interpreter. It's a hoot and it gives me endless pleasure, and I think it will bring the same for you as well.

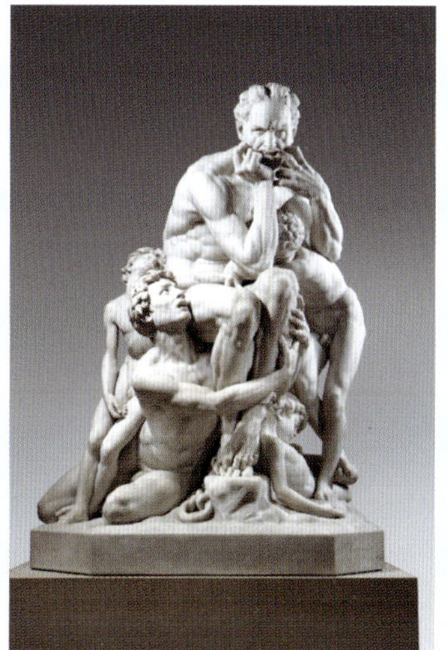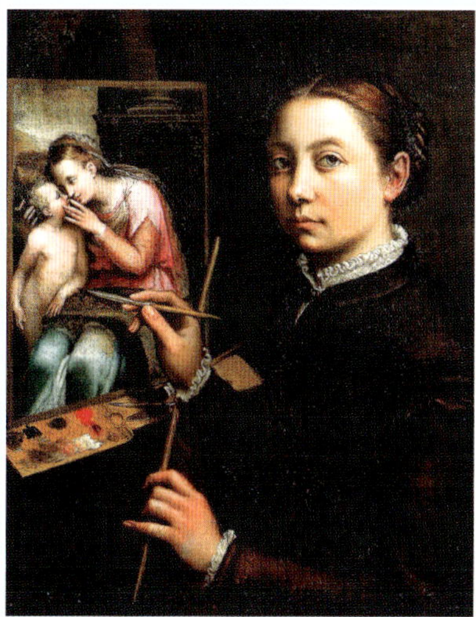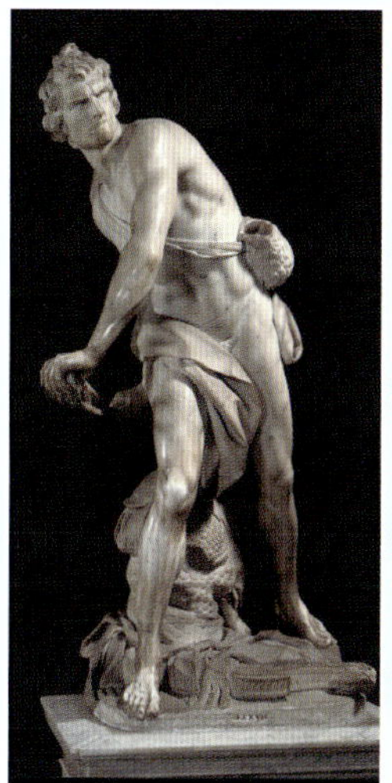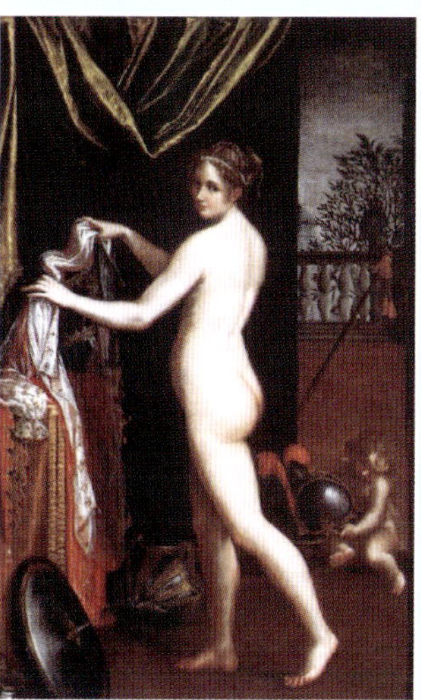

Jean-Baptiste Carpeaux, *Ugolino and His* Sons, 1867 | Sofonisba Anguissola, *Self-Portrait at Easel*, 1556 | Gian Lorenzo Bernini, *David*, 1624 | Lavinia Fontana, *Minerva Dressing*, 1612

Tutorial: Standing Poses

Now let's apply some of the tools I've given you to draw a man in a standing pose from reference.

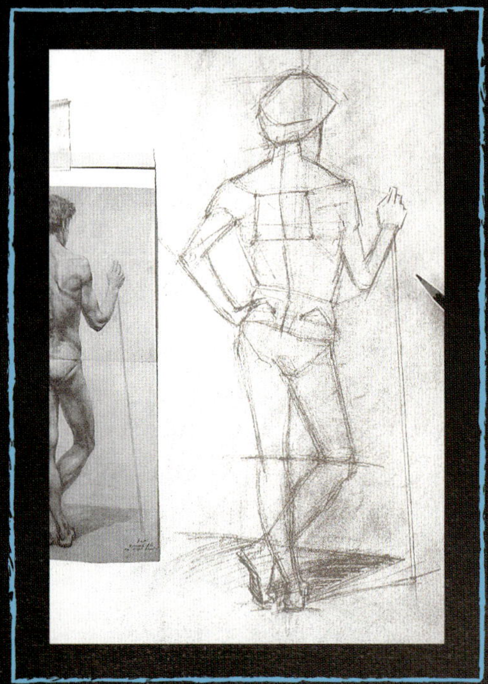

STEP 1:

I drew from reference using a graphite pencil, plotting the figure, and blocking it in.

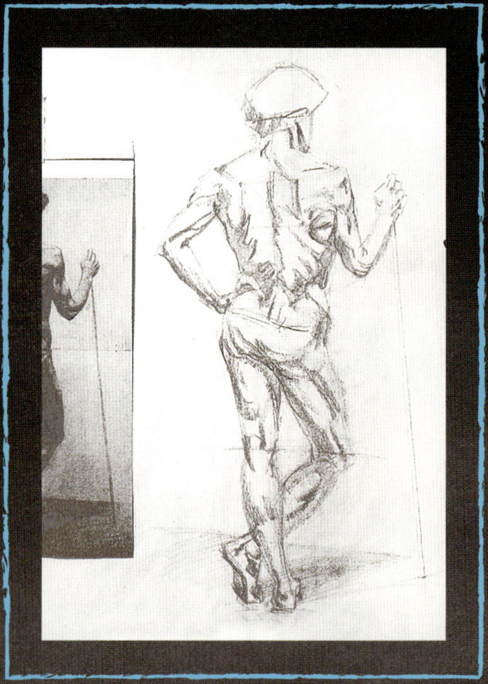

STEP 2:

With this drawing I decided to use soft vine charcoal for placing the shadow borders.

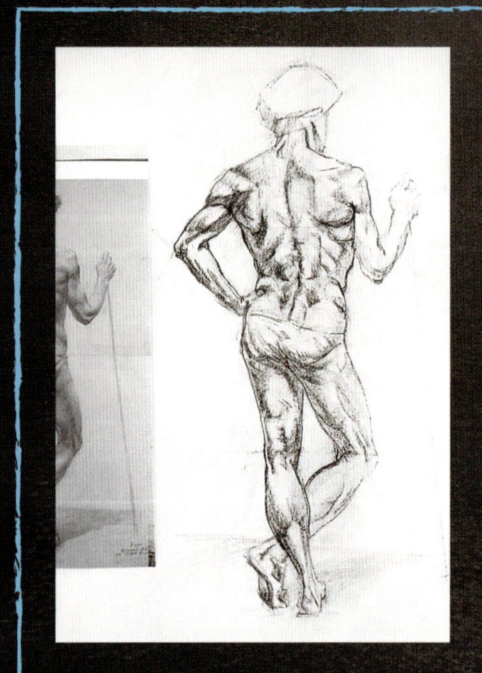

STEP 3:

Using my finger, I pushed the charcoal around to blend it and then defined contours as well as other inner forms with graphite again, this time with a softer pencil, such as a 3B.

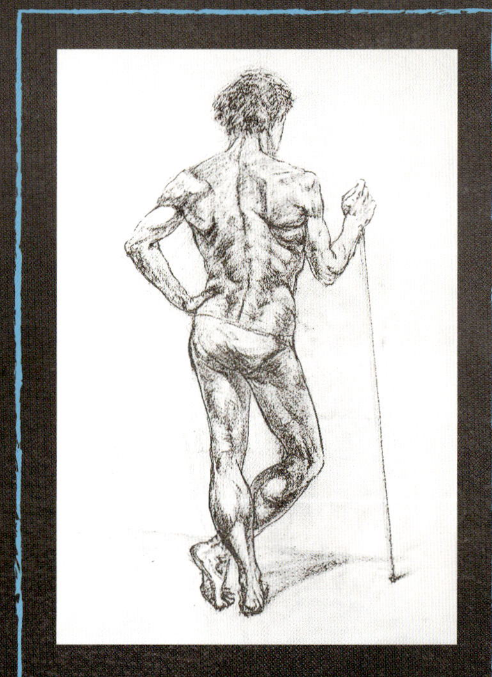

STEP 4:

I started (top left) with the hard graphite pencil for the blocking in, 2H or HB, then the vine charcoal. This finish was all graphite pencils, changing hardness as needed: 3B, 6B, etc.

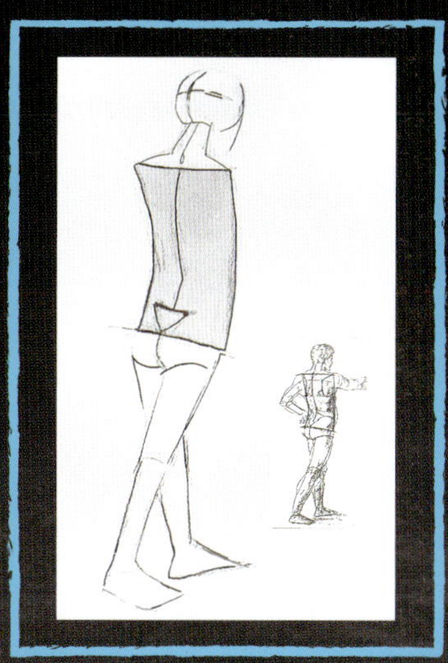

STEP 1:

Again, first, block in the main frame, capturing the angle of the torso in this case, and outline the shape of the body.

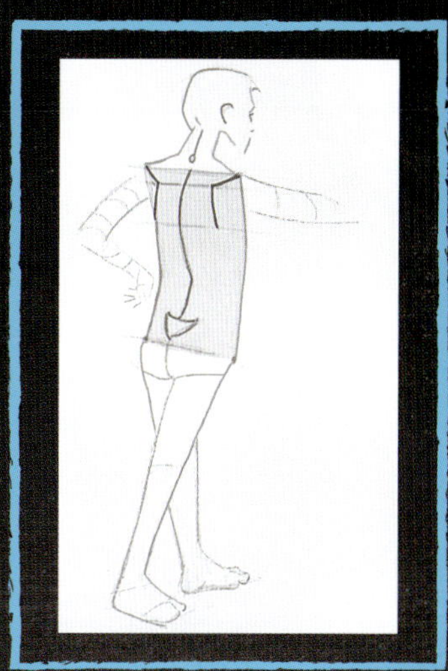

STEP 2:

Next, locate the scapulae and simplified limbs using straight lines. Remember the clock hands from page 127?

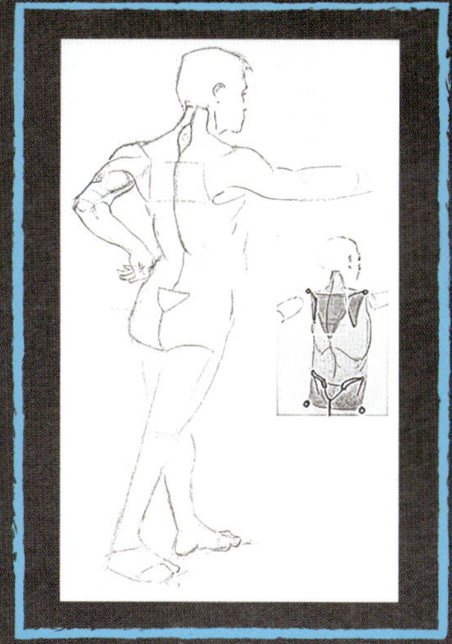

STEP 3:

Look for large muscle masses like the trapezius and start to fill out the forms.

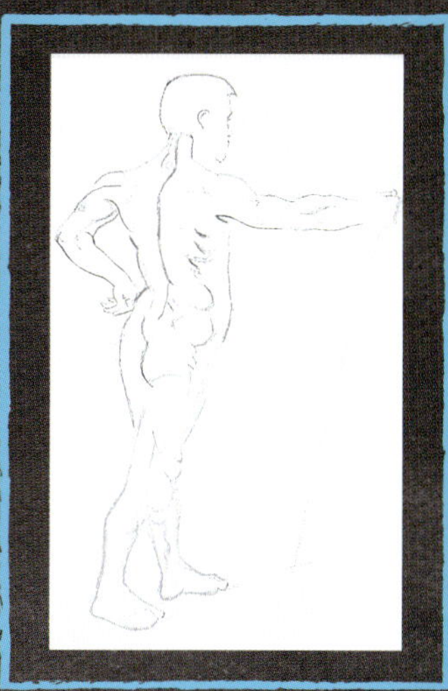

STEP 4:

Separate the light from the shadow sides; squinting is a great tool for this.

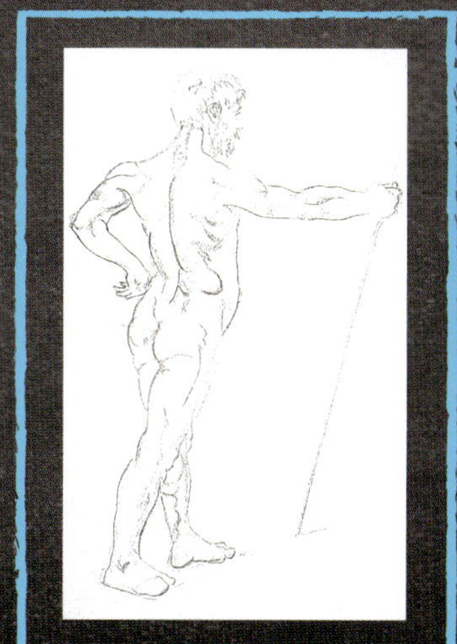

STEP 5:

Start to add more details without overworking your drawing. Try to use as few strokes as possible.

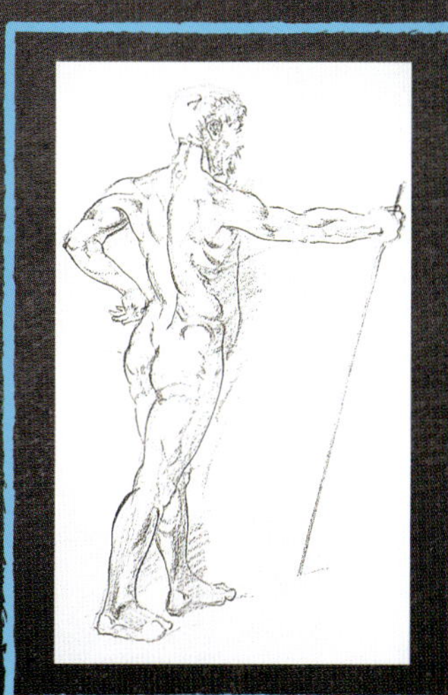

STEP 6:

When do you know the drawing is finished? That is up to you! This drawing took about fifteen minutes using a black Progresso pencil stick.

Tent Drawing

Great for practicing reclining and compact poses

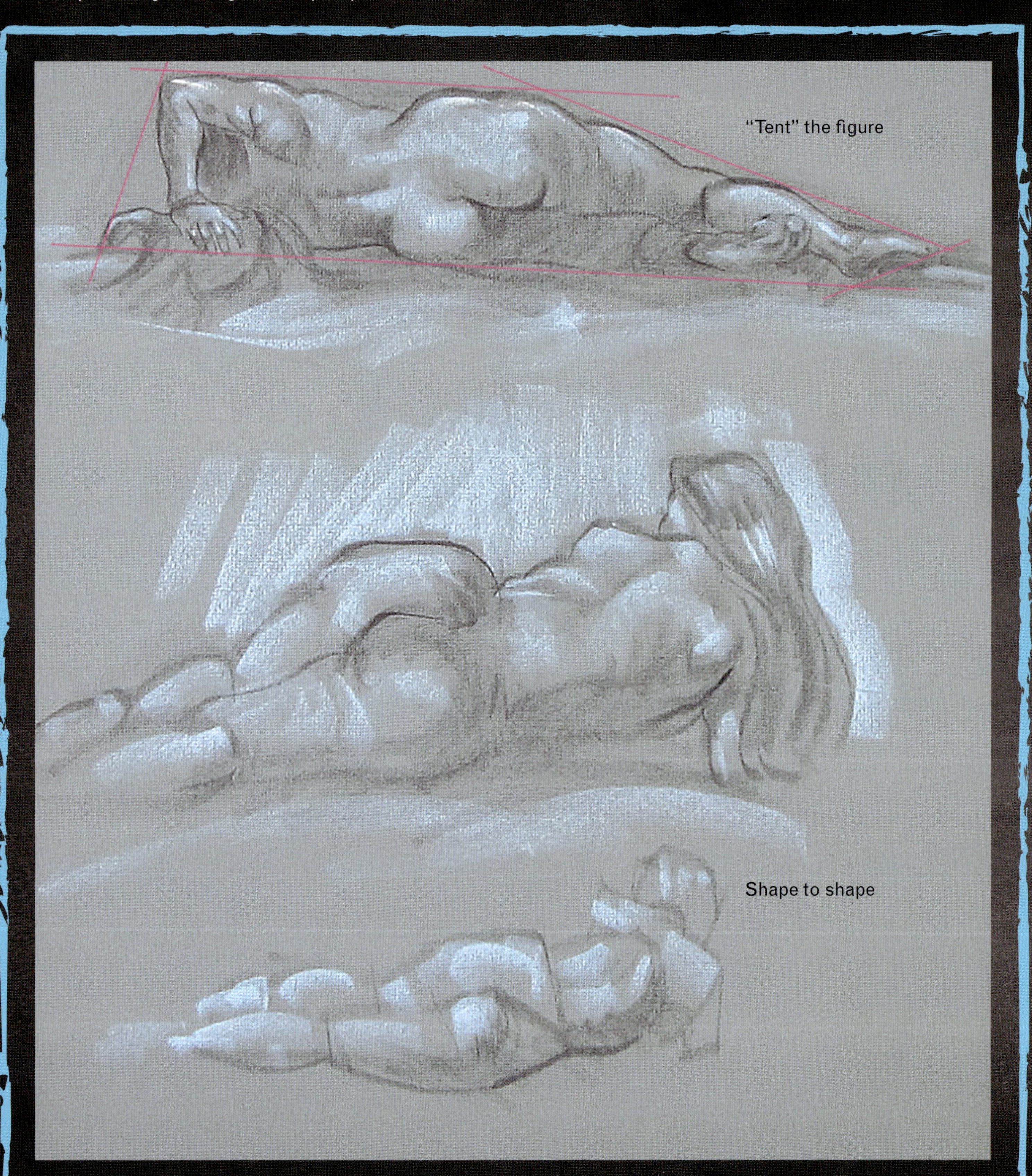

Tent drawing is the second major drawing method that I employ in my classroom after constellation drawing. There are many variations of this method and different names for it, such as envelope or box plotting. When viewing the model, whether from life or drawing from reference, visualize and draw where the lines would be as if placing a taut string across two peaks or points. In the reclining image shown on the opposite page, I used the elbow-to-hip peaks as a starting point as if this model were a mountain range. From there I made another beeline to the toes. Once you have the enclosed box with the fewest sides—let's say five, as shown—then your figure will fit in that box. It is as if you were sculpting the figure out of the box. This is by far the most effective method in tackling the daunting task of drawing the reclining figure but can be used with any pose. The approach is brilliantly simple to understand, but it can also be frustrating. This method forces you to contain most of the body within boundaries to train you to better depict reclining poses. It does take more patience and a more careful eye, but it is worth it. This method can also be applied to standing poses.

Exercise: Draw straight lines, as few as possible, that hit the furthermost forms of the body. Think of it as putting the model in a carefully fitted box. I recommend this method when one of my students is challenged with an awkward reclining pose. No longer will you run out of room at the bottom of your paper and be forced to crop out a foot.

Exercise: Try putting tracing paper over any reference, then pencil in the envelope (the space created when drawing straight lines that touch the outermost projections of the body). Use the fewest possible lines; often it only requires five. It's a method that is, in a way, sculpting. The envelope can be seen as the rock or marble with the figure inside. You merely start with the envelope or box around the figure and chip away until you refine the contours and gradually reveal the figure. After establishing the envelope around the reference, transfer the envelope to another piece of paper and begin your sketch. Finally try drawing the envelope freehand from a live model and then begin chipping away at the spaces.

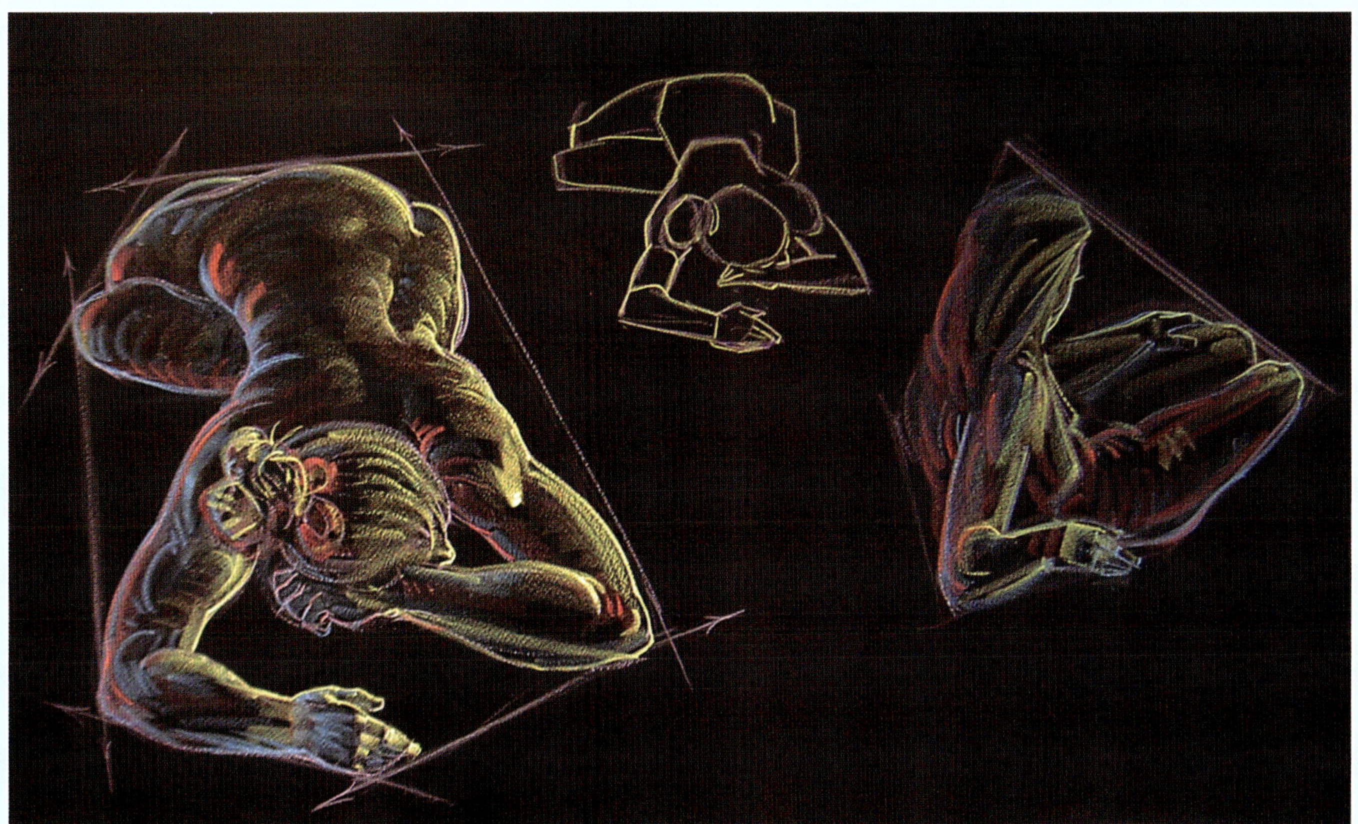

Tutorial: Reclining Poses

The more you practice the tent-drawing exercise, the less difficult reclining poses will be. Another approach I use is to isolate different sections of the body to make the task more manageable.

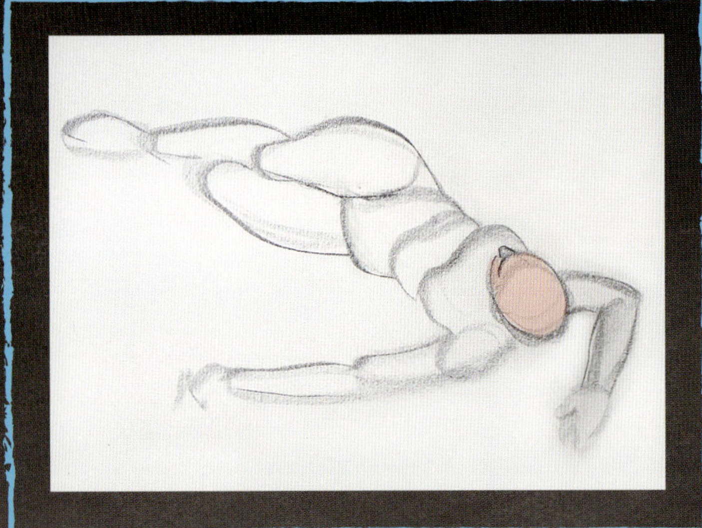

STEP 1:

First, start with the general outline of the body, laying down initial strokes and shapes.

STEP 2:

Next, move onto the chest, shoulders, and thorax (rib cage). This method often reminds me of a road trip, the centerline of the body being the road as it flows over the upcoming hills.

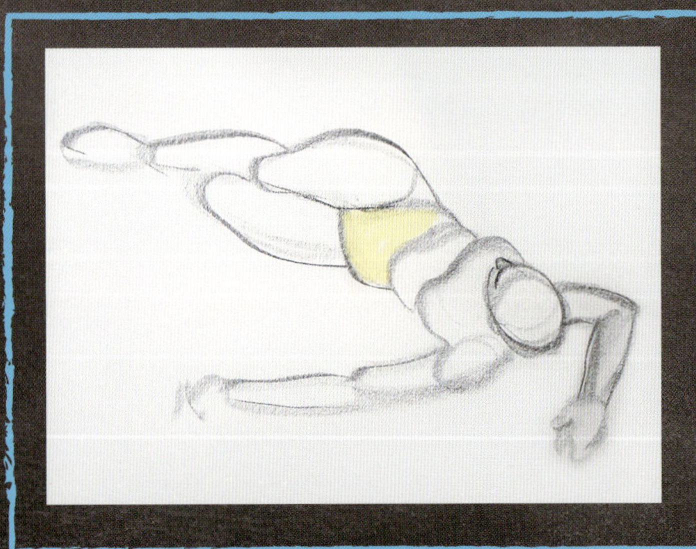

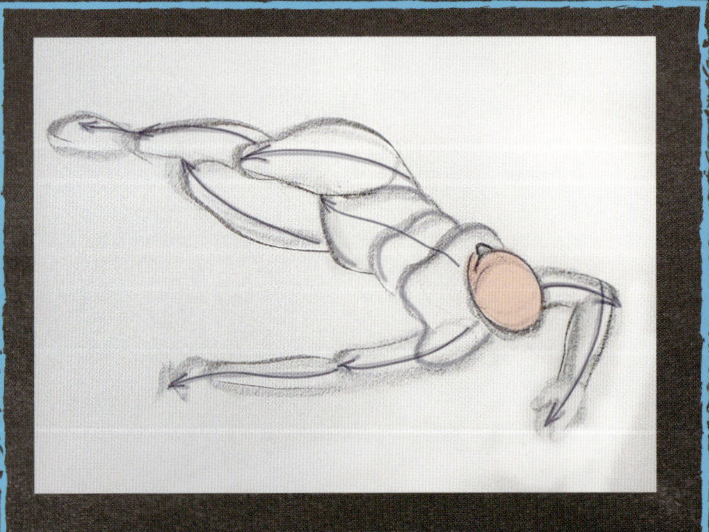

STEP 3:

Draw the next shape, the abdomen and navel, to help with placing the center of the body as it twists toward the pubic bone.

STEP 4:

It is important to make swooping arcs for the rhythms of the limbs. This will make your figure look more lifelike.

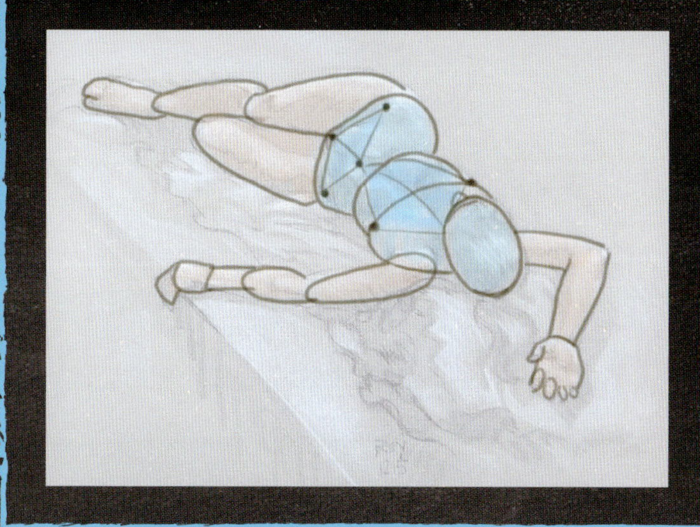

STEP 5:

Now that the general flow and outline of the figure is set,
start to add more details.

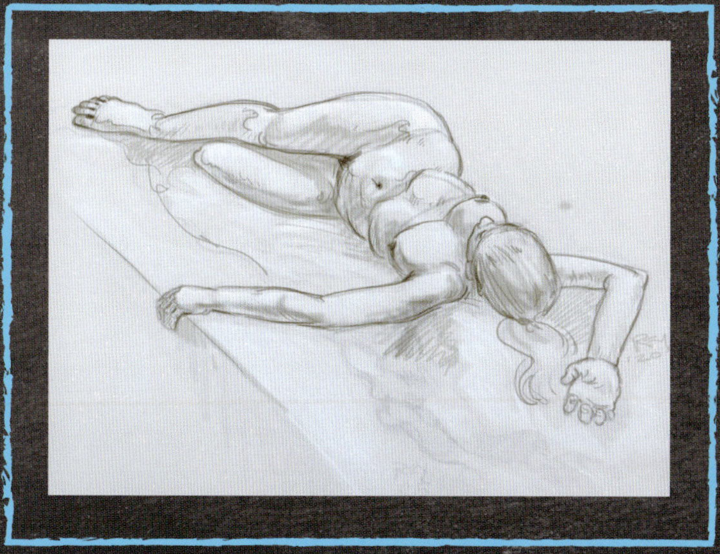

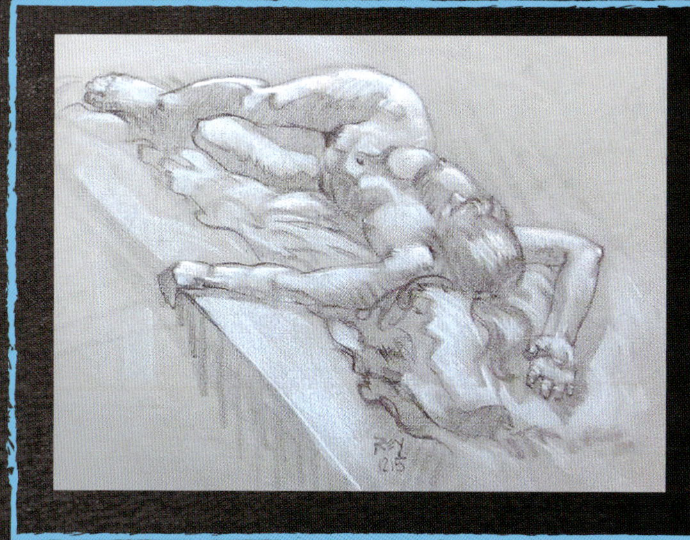

STEP 6:

Continue to finesse your drawing until you are satisfied with the results.

ANIMATING THE BODY

This assignment will help you visualize how the body's position might change during any given series of movements. It may be helpful to act it out. This can be a fun and challenging way to gauge where you are in your artistic development.

Exercise: Do a series of drawings of a figure in action. The series can follow one particular action, such as throwing a ball, or be of several movements, for instance, a ballerina performing a routine. Start by drawing the initial constellation and then shifting each star to follow the action through. The drawings can be as simple or detailed as you wish. This is an exercise so do not expect it to look fluent at first. It does take practice. This will be a clear indicator of what you need to work on to fine-tune the weaknesses you might still have at this point.

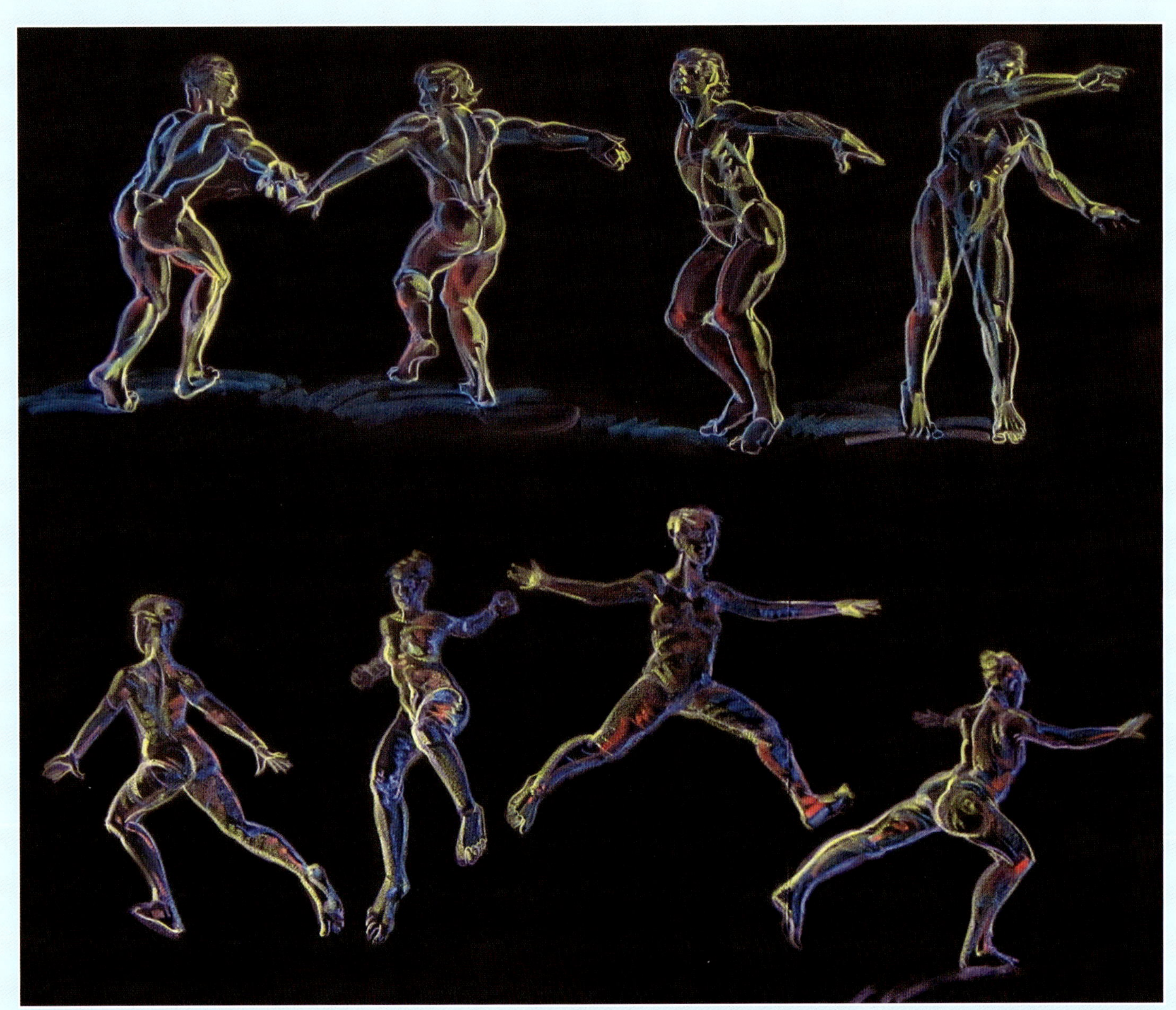

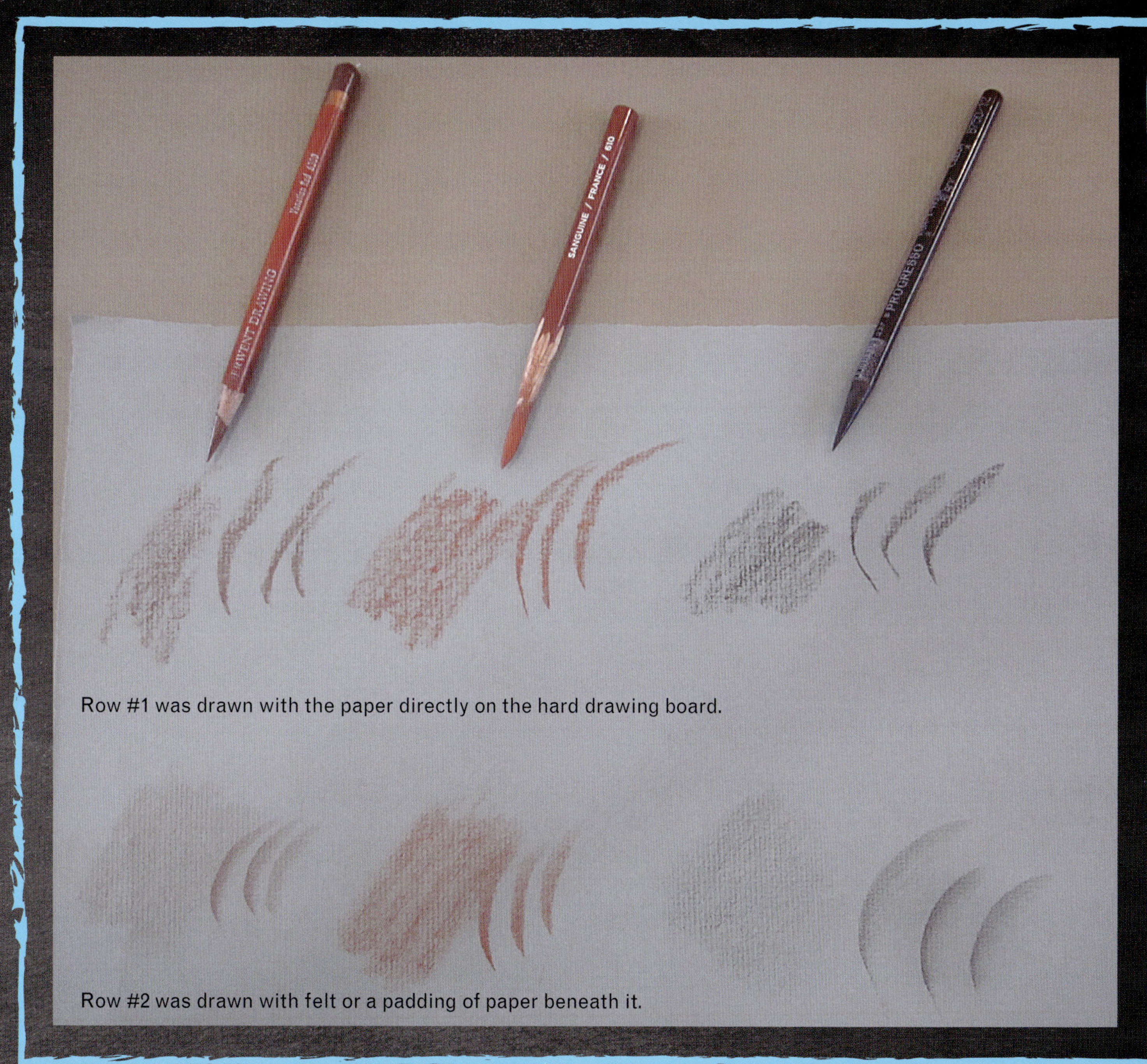

Row #1 was drawn with the paper directly on the hard drawing board.

Row #2 was drawn with felt or a padding of paper beneath it.

You have reached the last page of our exercises, and to close, I have one last tip for you. Turn over your sketch pad, and place a piece of 18 x 24 inch felt on the back to soften the surface, or take twenty or so pages from the front of the pad and do the same. This softness allows the pencil to gently move around the surface creating a smokier line, especially when using the side of the lead. This allows for more line variety and expression on future projects!

GALLERY

"Rey is quite an amazing painter. He is a great teacher, but also a talented practicing artist."

— Eliot Goldfinger

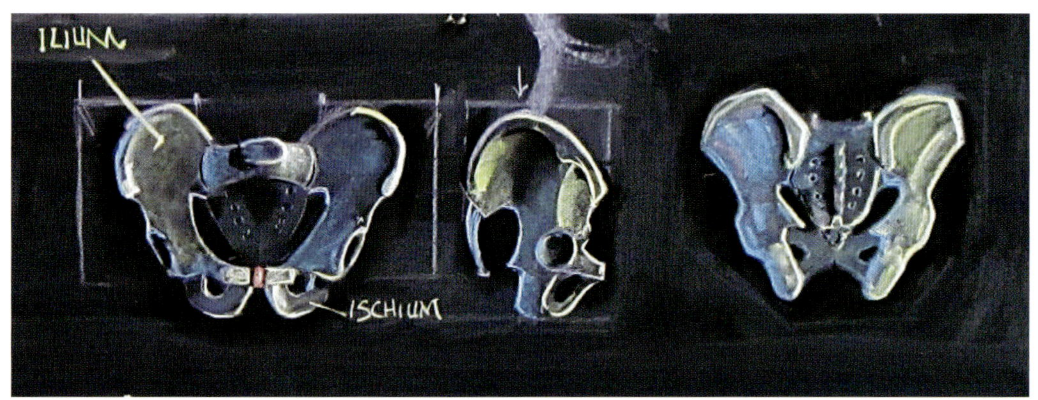

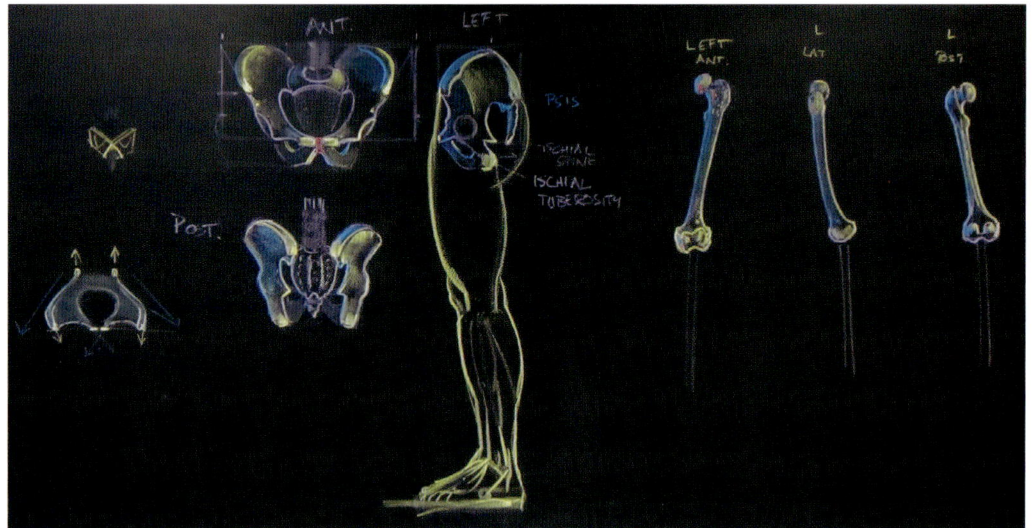

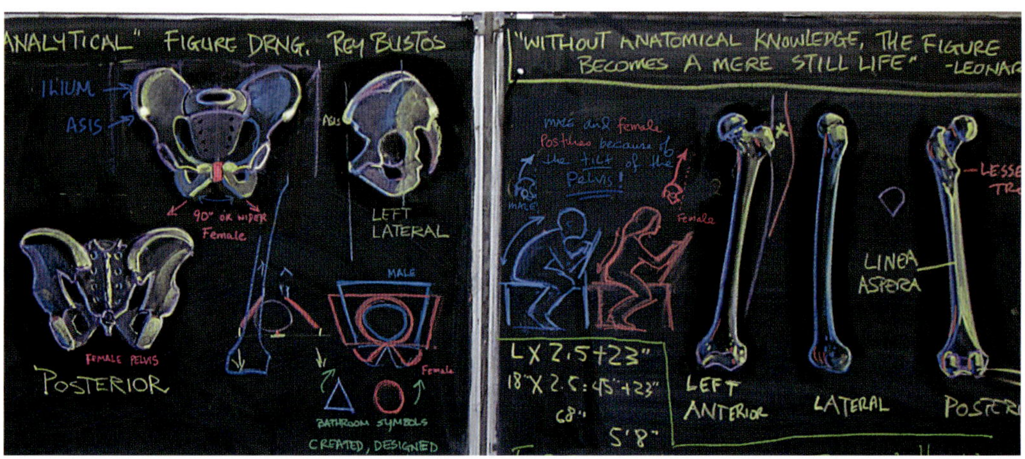

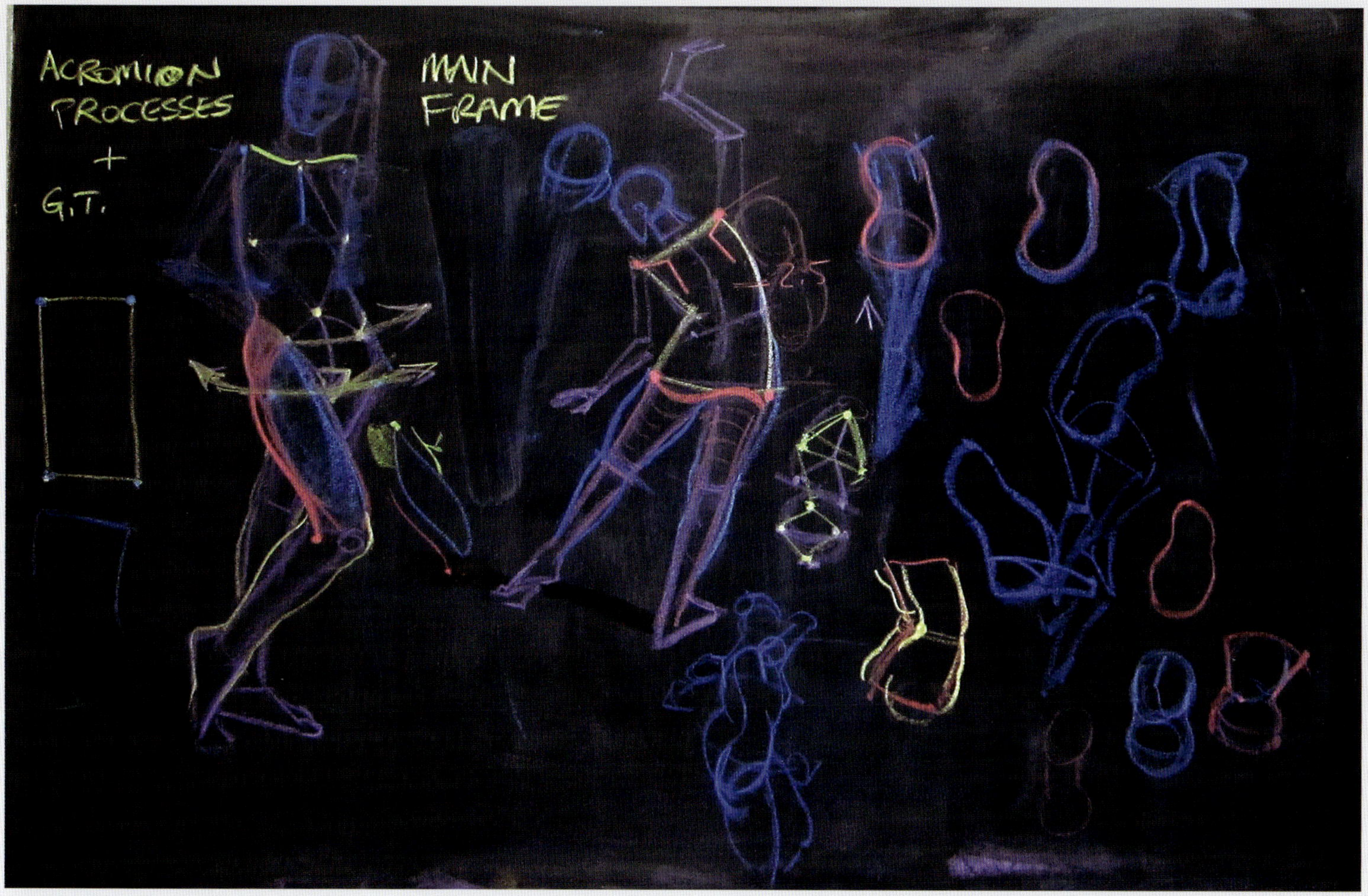

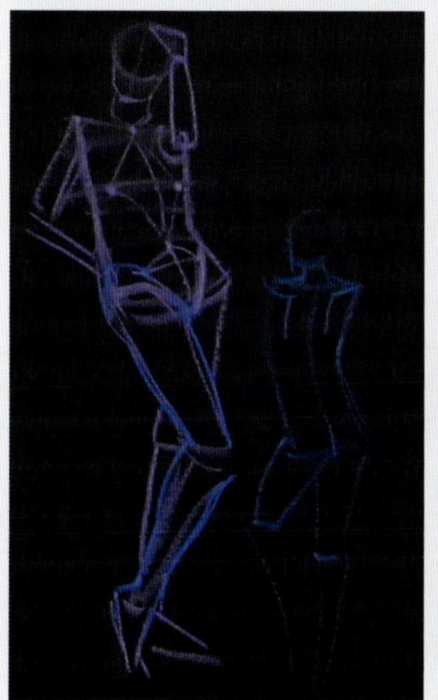

ACROMION PROCESSES
+
G.T.
MAIN FRAME

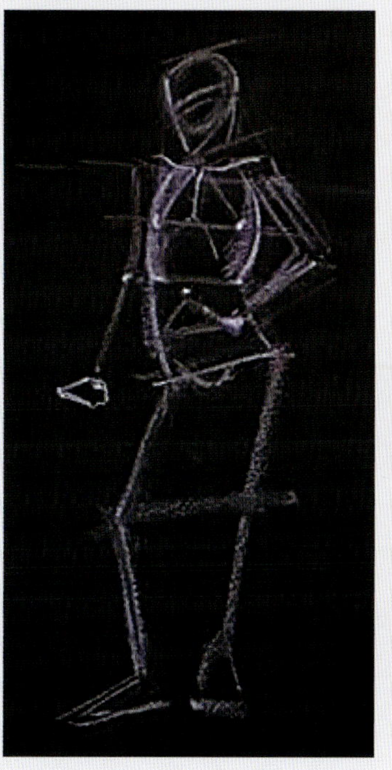

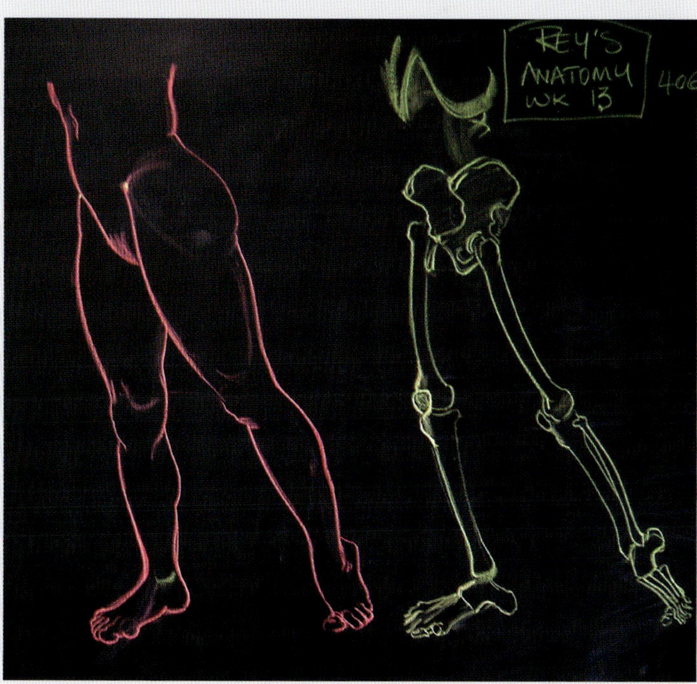

REY'S ANATOMY WK 13
406

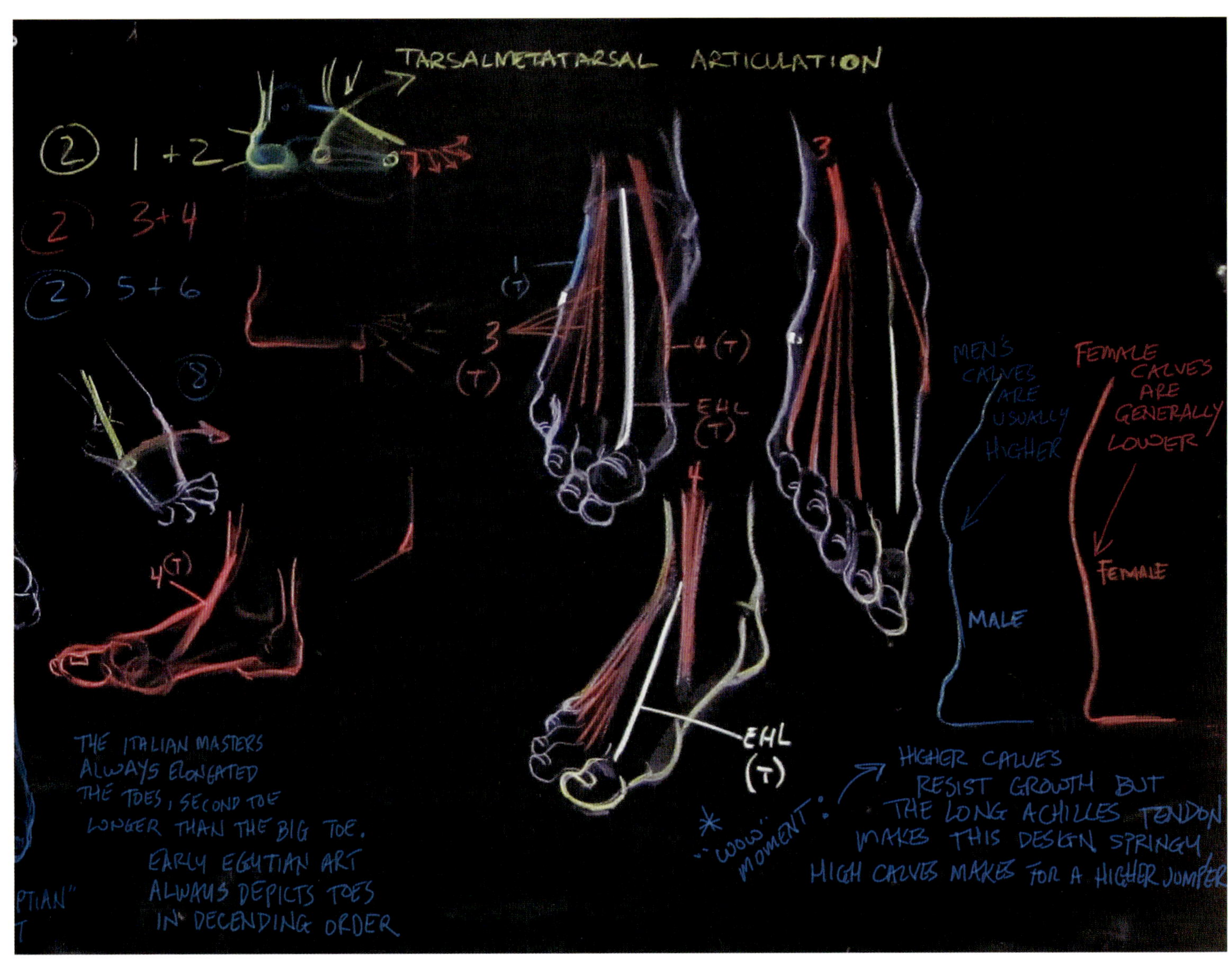

TARSALMETATARSAL ARTICULATION
② 1 + 2
② 3 + 4
② 5 + 6
⑧
1 (T)
3 (T)
4 (T)
EHL (T)
3
4
4 (T)
EHL (T)
THE ITALIAN MASTERS
ALWAYS ELONGATED
THE TOES, SECOND TOE
LONGER THAN THE BIG TOE.
EARLY EGYTIAN ART
ALWAYS DEPICTS TOES
IN DECENDING ORDER
MEN'S CALVES ARE USUALLY HIGHER
FEMALE CALVES ARE GENERALLY LOWER
MALE
FEMALE
* "WOW" MOMENT:
HIGHER CALVES RESIST GROWTH BUT
THE LONG ACHILLES TENDON
MAKES THIS DESIGN SPRINGY
HIGH CALVES MAKES FOR A HIGHER JUMPER

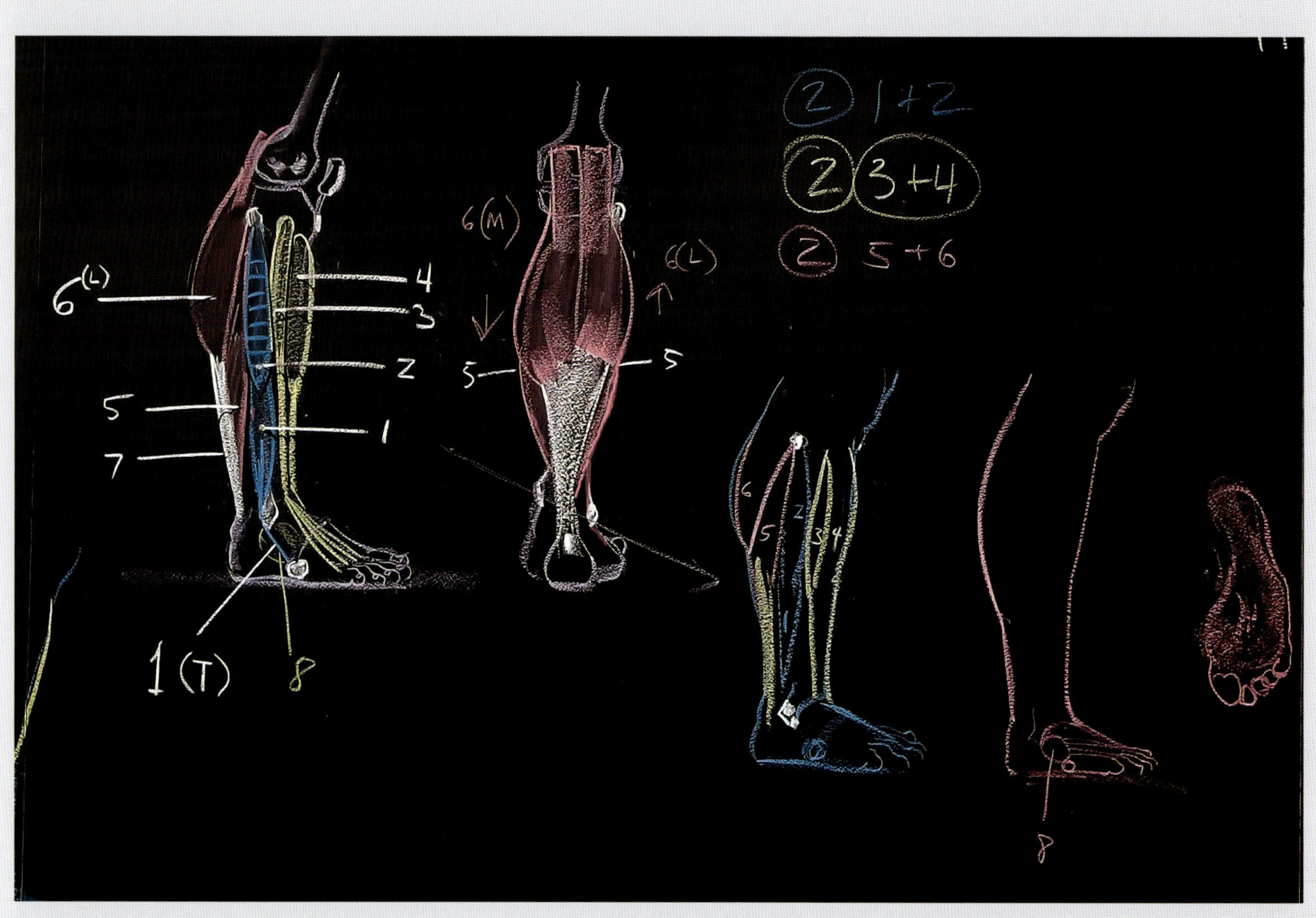

6(L)
4
3
2
1
5
7
1 (T)
8
6(M)
6(L)
5
5
2 1+2
2 3+4
2 5+6
6
5
2
3 4
8

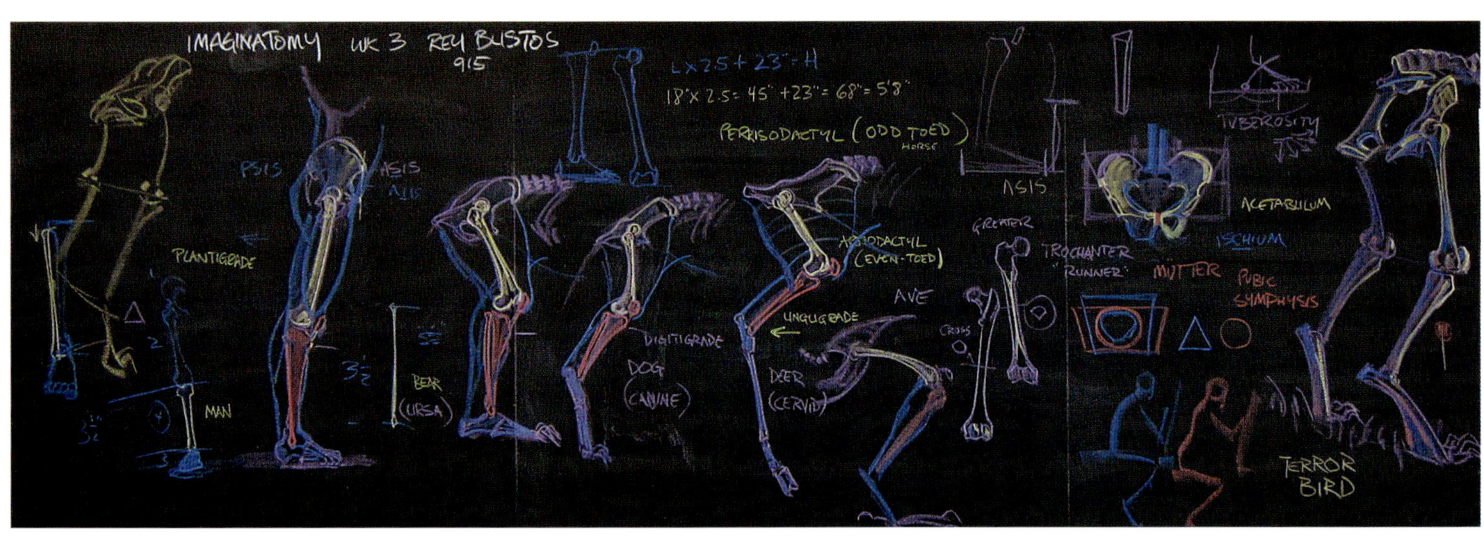

IMAGINATOMY WK 3 REY BUSTOS 915
L x 2.5 + 23" = H
18" x 2.5 = 45" + 23" = 68" = 5'8"
PERRISODACTYL (ODD TOED) HORSE
TUBEROSITY
ASIS
PSIS
ASIS AIIS
PLANTIGRADE
ACETABULUM
GREATER
ARTIODACTYL (EVEN-TOED)
TROCHANTER "RUNNER"
ISCHIUM
MUTTER
PUBIC SYMPHYSIS
MAN
BEAR (URSA)
DIGITIGRADE
DOG (CANINE)
UNGULIGRADE
AVE
DEER (CERVID)
CROSS
TERROR BIRD

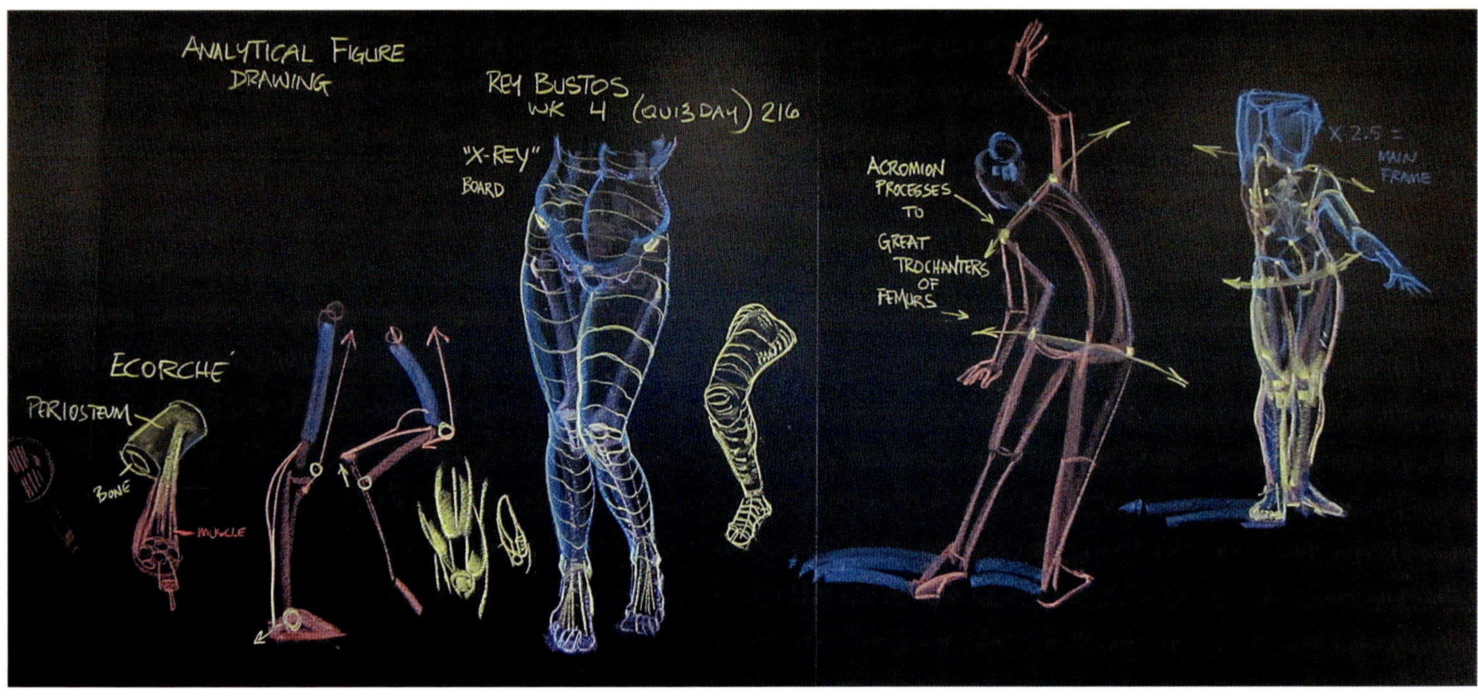

ANALYTICAL FIGURE DRAWING
REY BUSTOS WK 4 (QUIZ DAY) 216
"X-REY" BOARD
ECORCHE
PERIOSTEUM
BONE
MUSCLE
ACROMION PROCESSES TO GREAT TROCHANTERS OF FEMURS
X 2.5 = MAIN FRAME

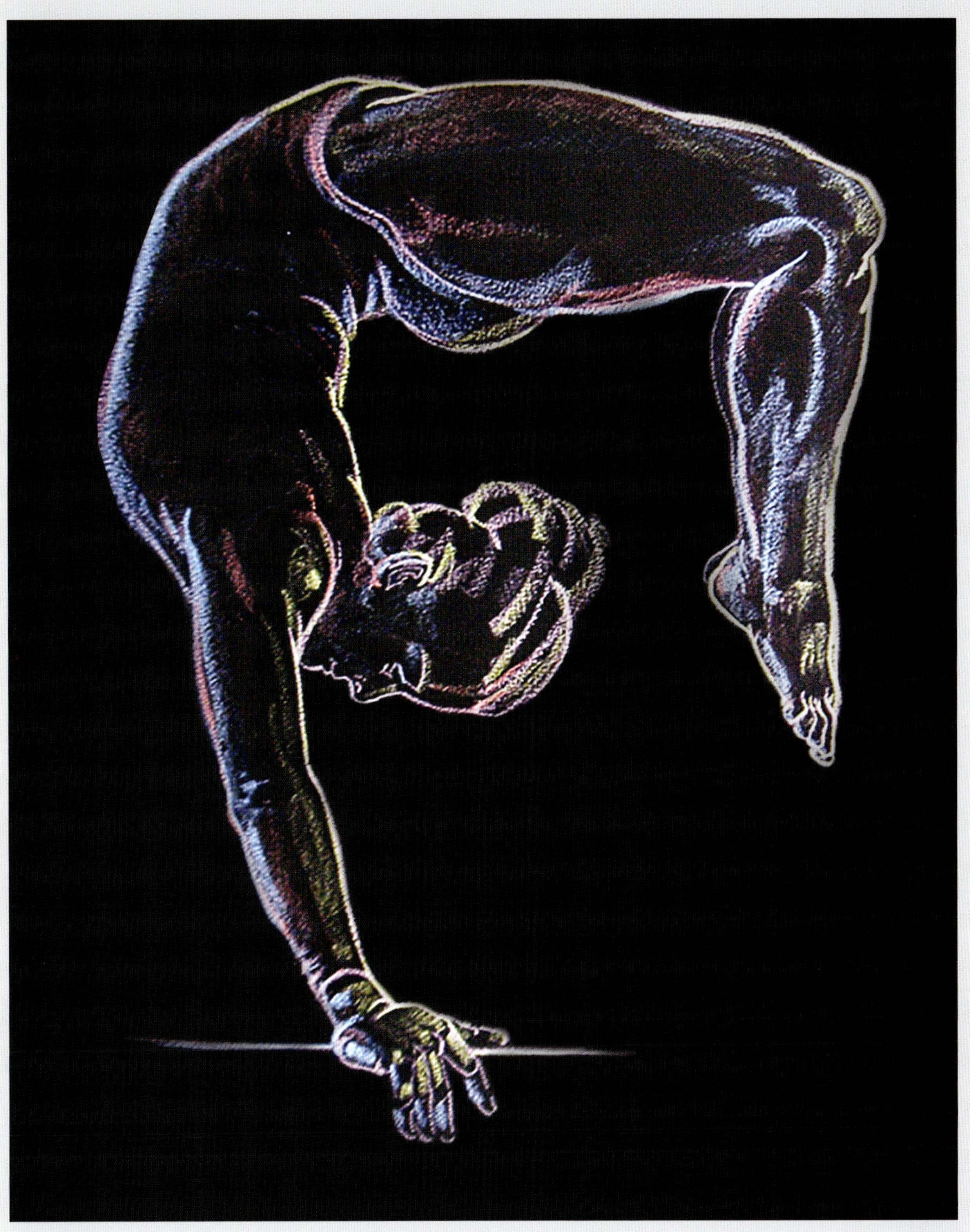

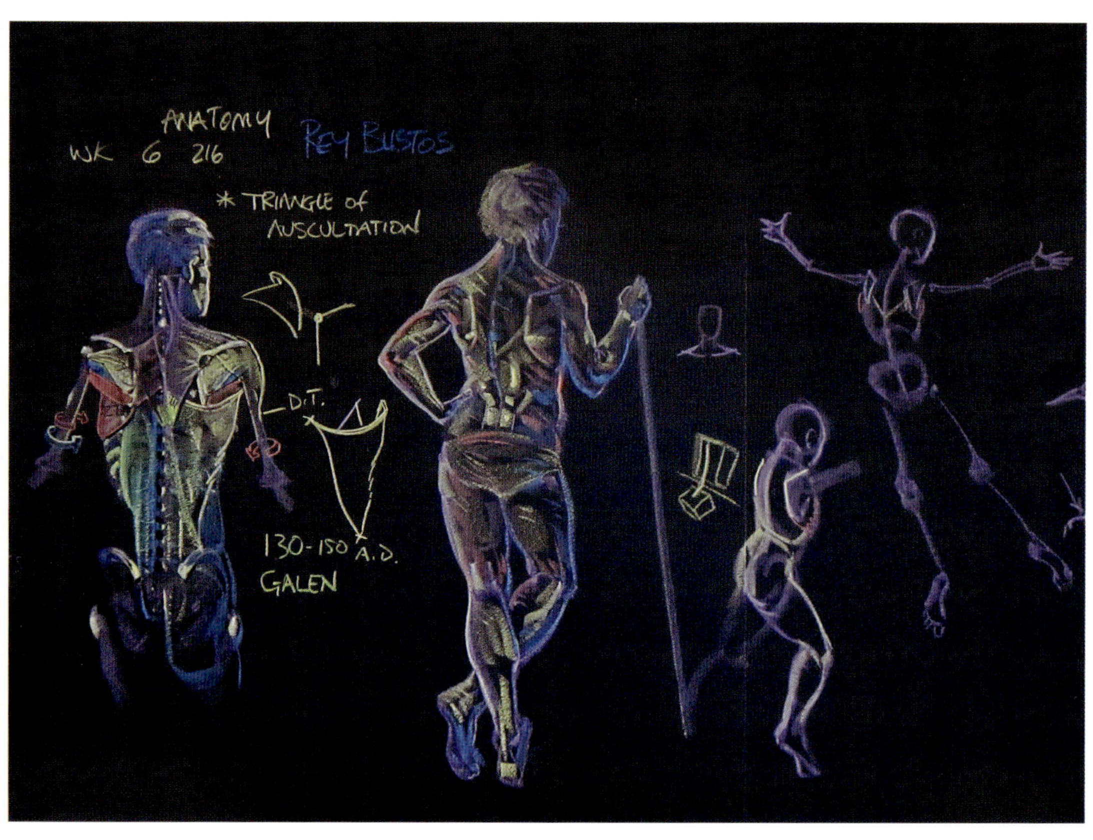

ANATOMY
REY BUSTOS
WK 6 216
* TRIANGLE OF
AUSCULTATION
D.T.
130-150 A.D.
GALEN

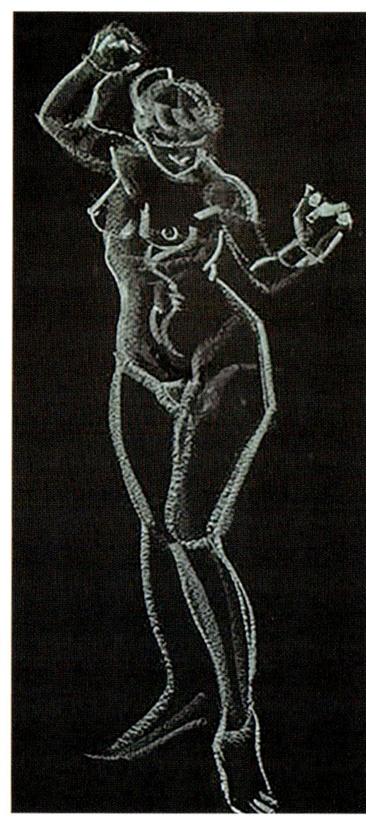

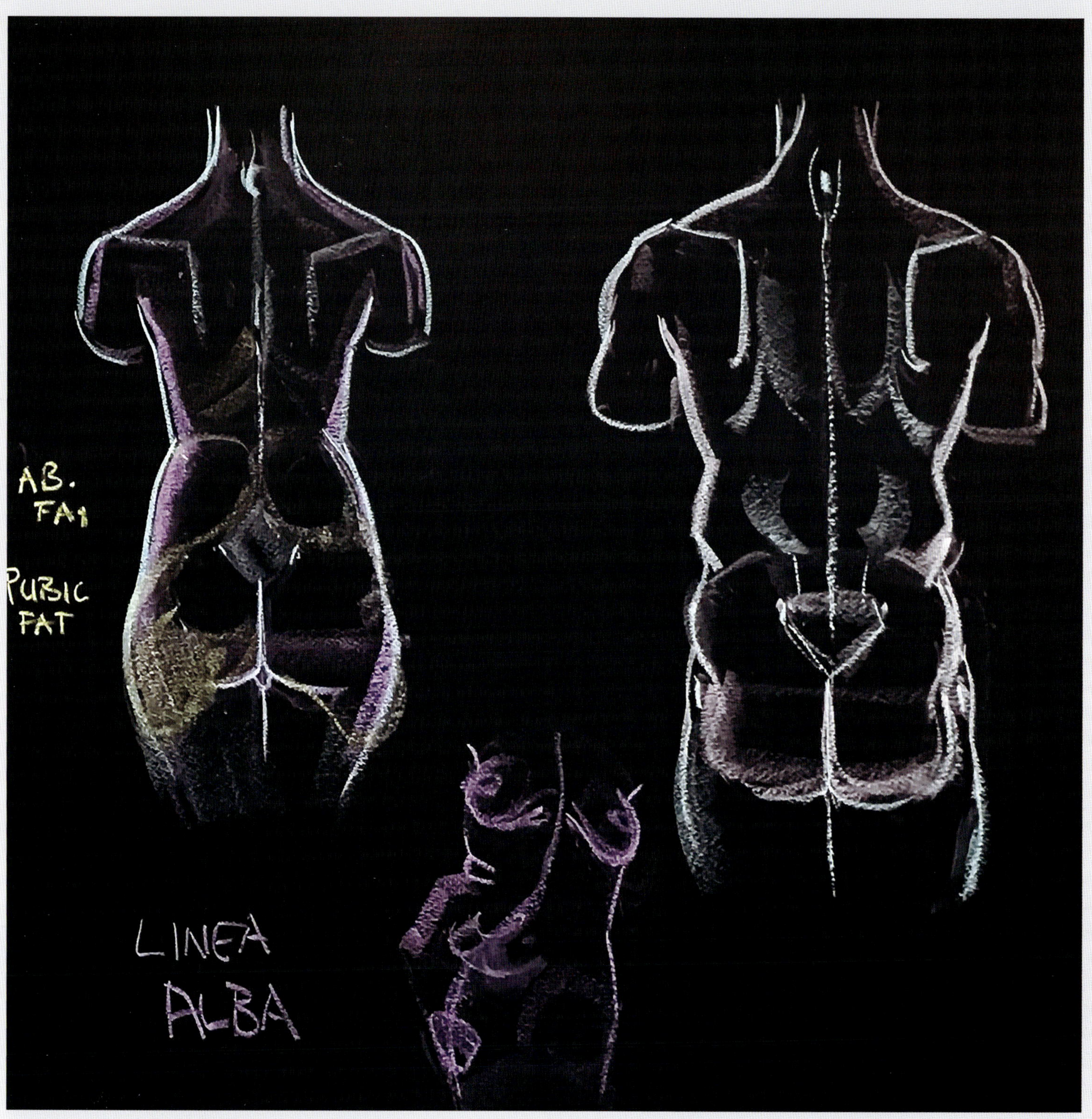

AB.
FAT

PUBIC
FAT

LINEA
ALBA

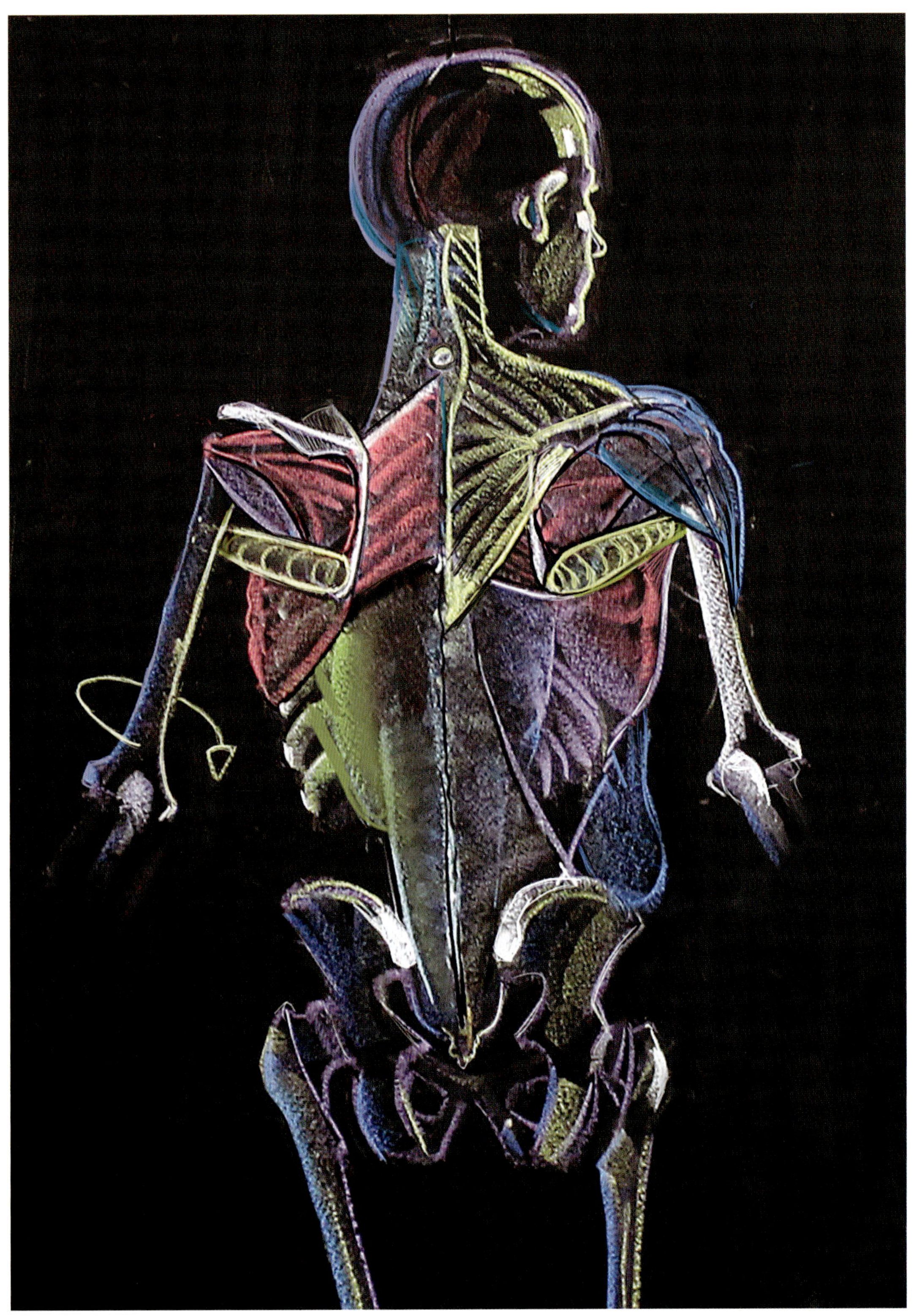

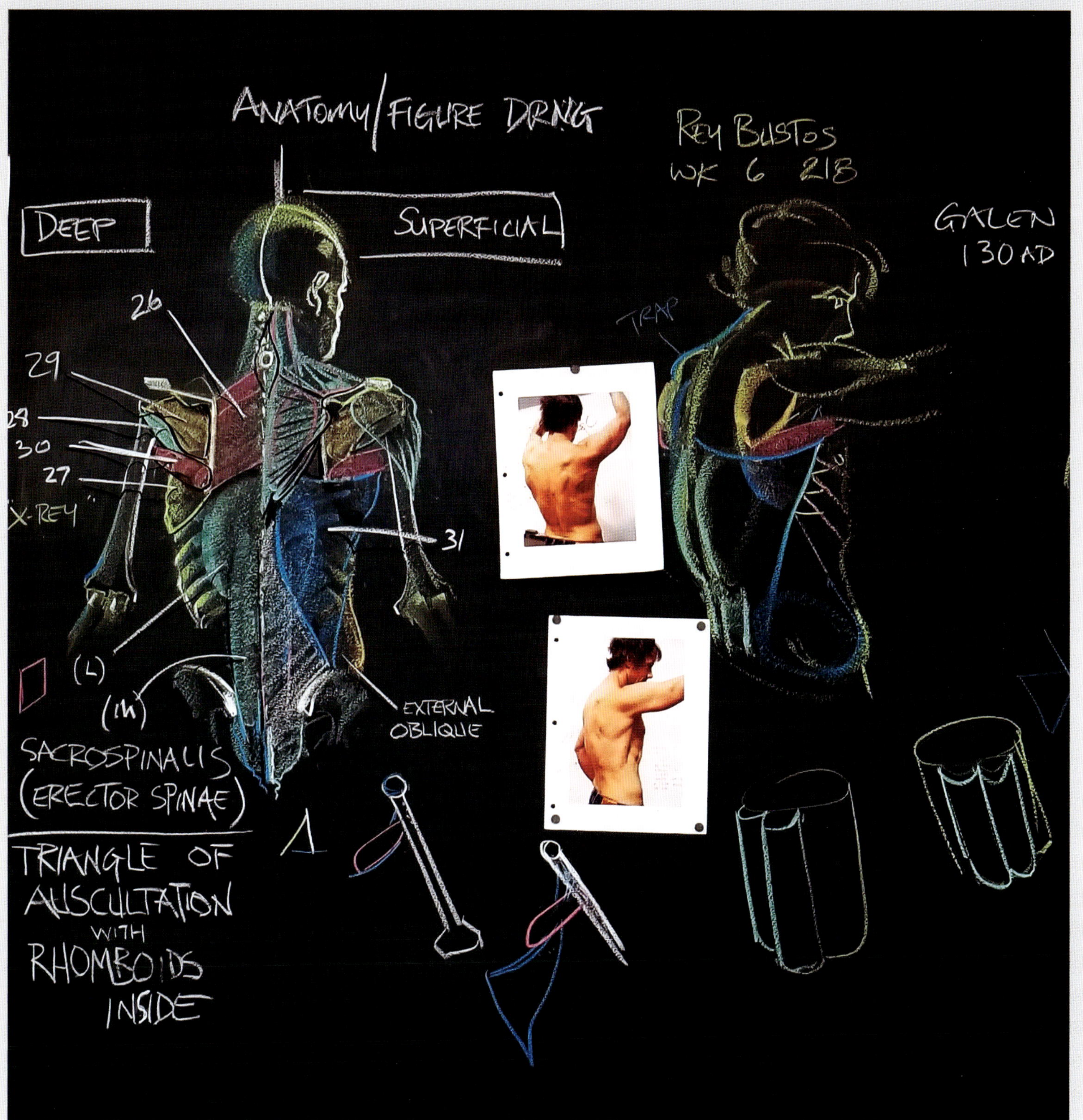

ANATOMY/FIGURE DRNG
SUPERFICIAL
DEEP
REY BUSTOS
WK 6 218
GALEN
130 AD
26
29
28
30
27
X-REY
TRAP
31
(L)
(m)
SACROSPINALIS
(ERECTOR SPINAE)
TRIANGLE OF
AUSCULTATION
WITH
RHOMBOIDS
INSIDE
EXTERNAL
OBLIQUE

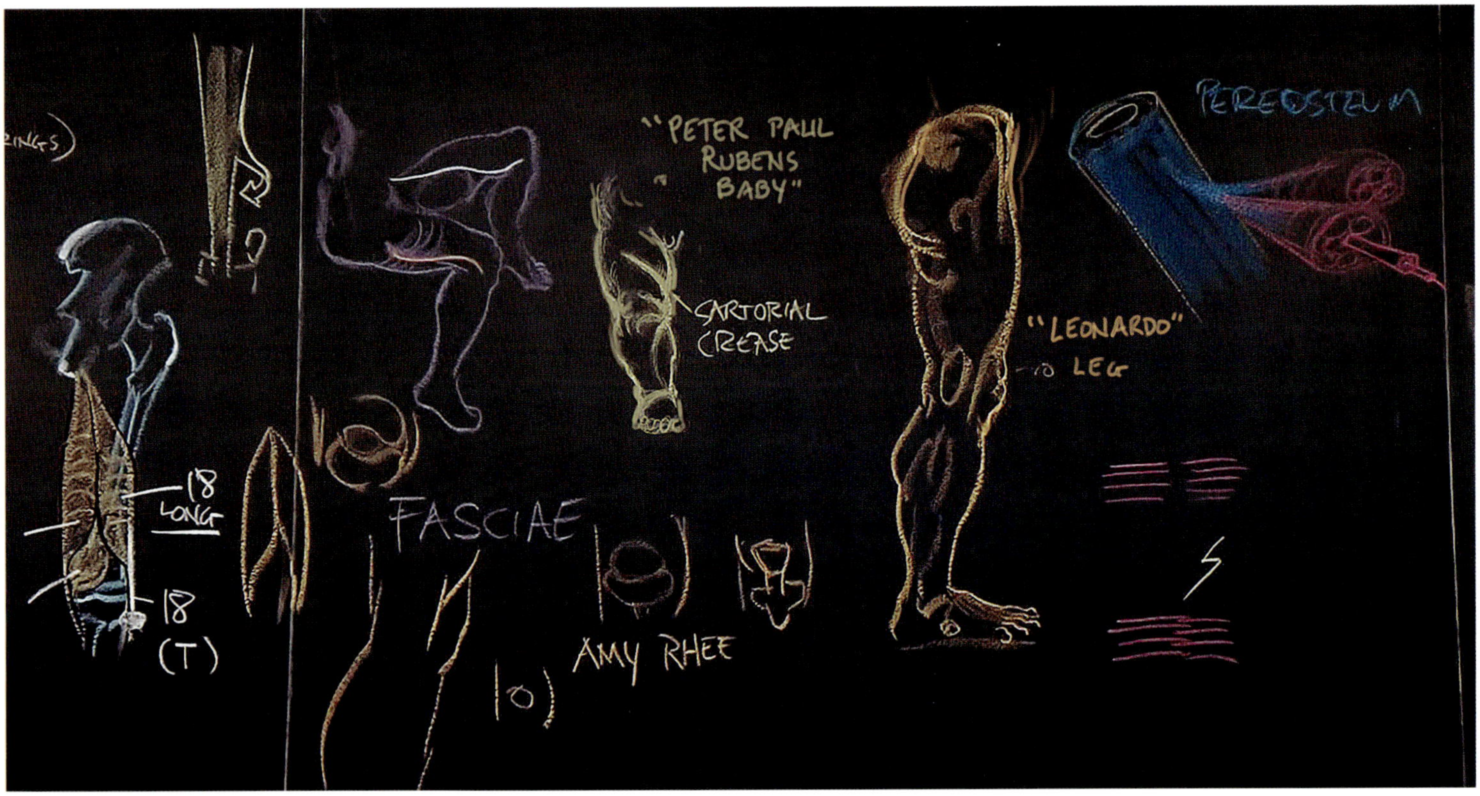

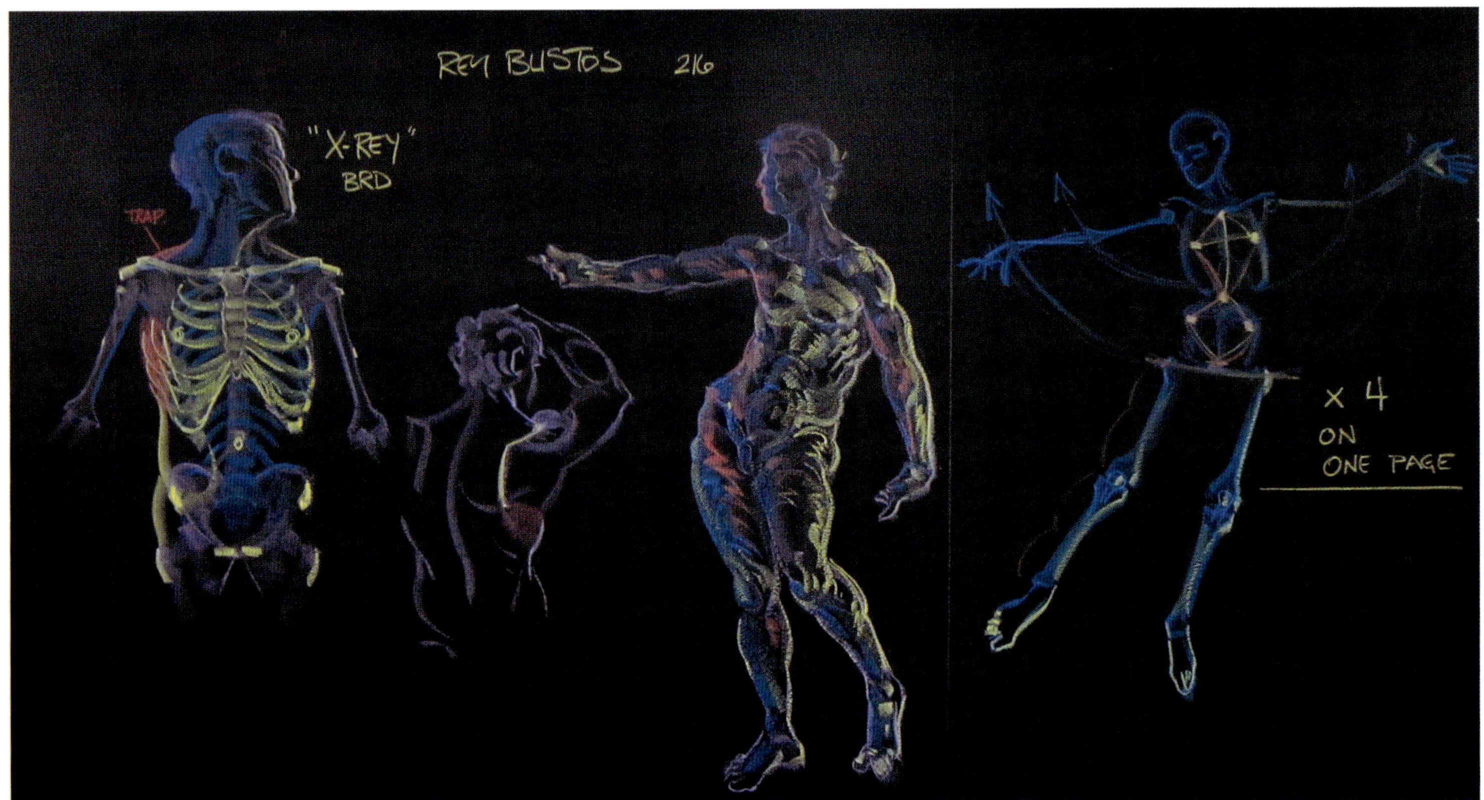
RINGS)
"PETER PAUL RUBENS BABY"
SARTORIAL CREASE
PERIOSTEUM
"LEONARDO" LEG
FASCIAE
AMY RHEE
18 LONG
18 (T)
REY BUSTOS   216
"X-REY" BRD
TRAP
X 4
ON
ONE PAGE

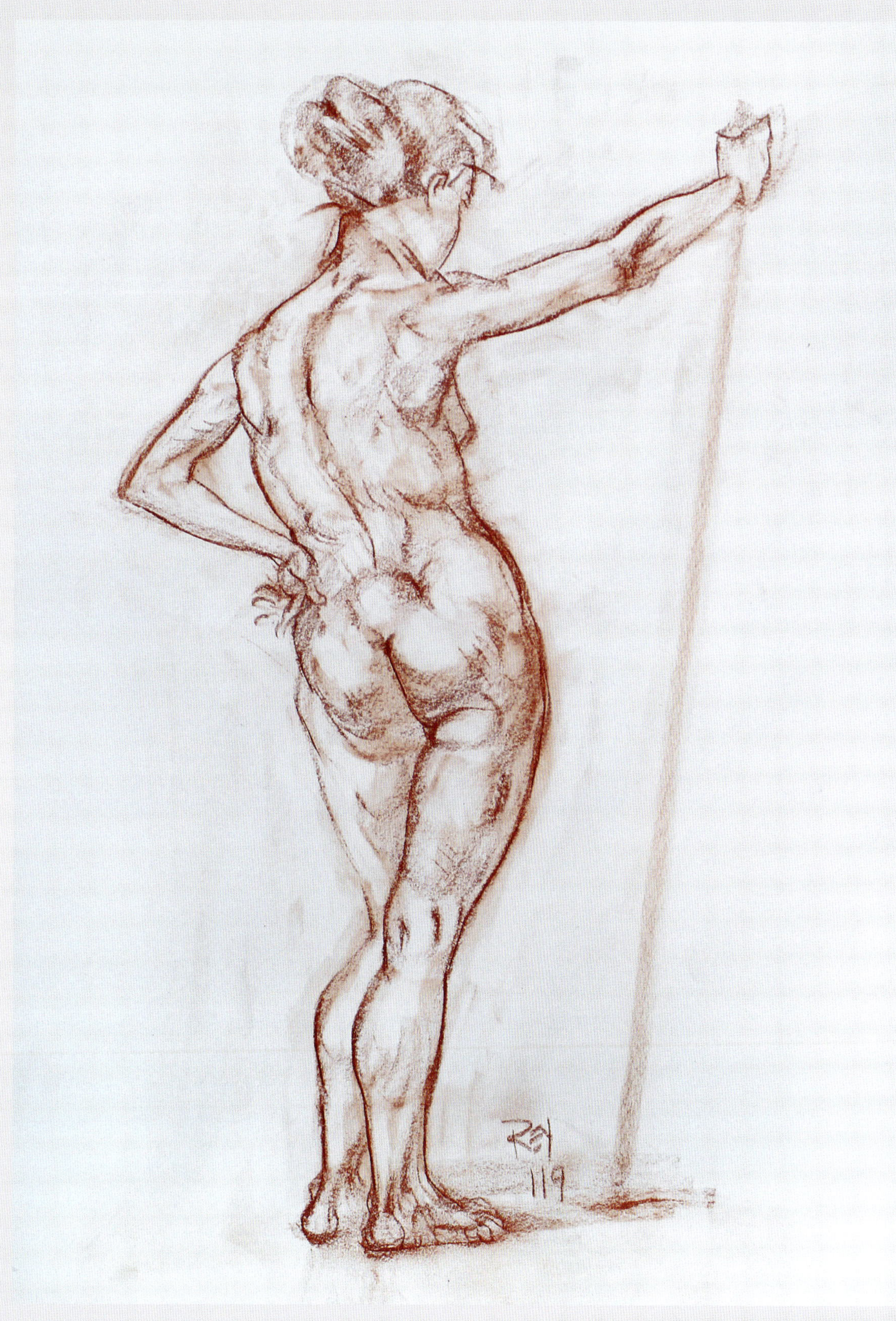

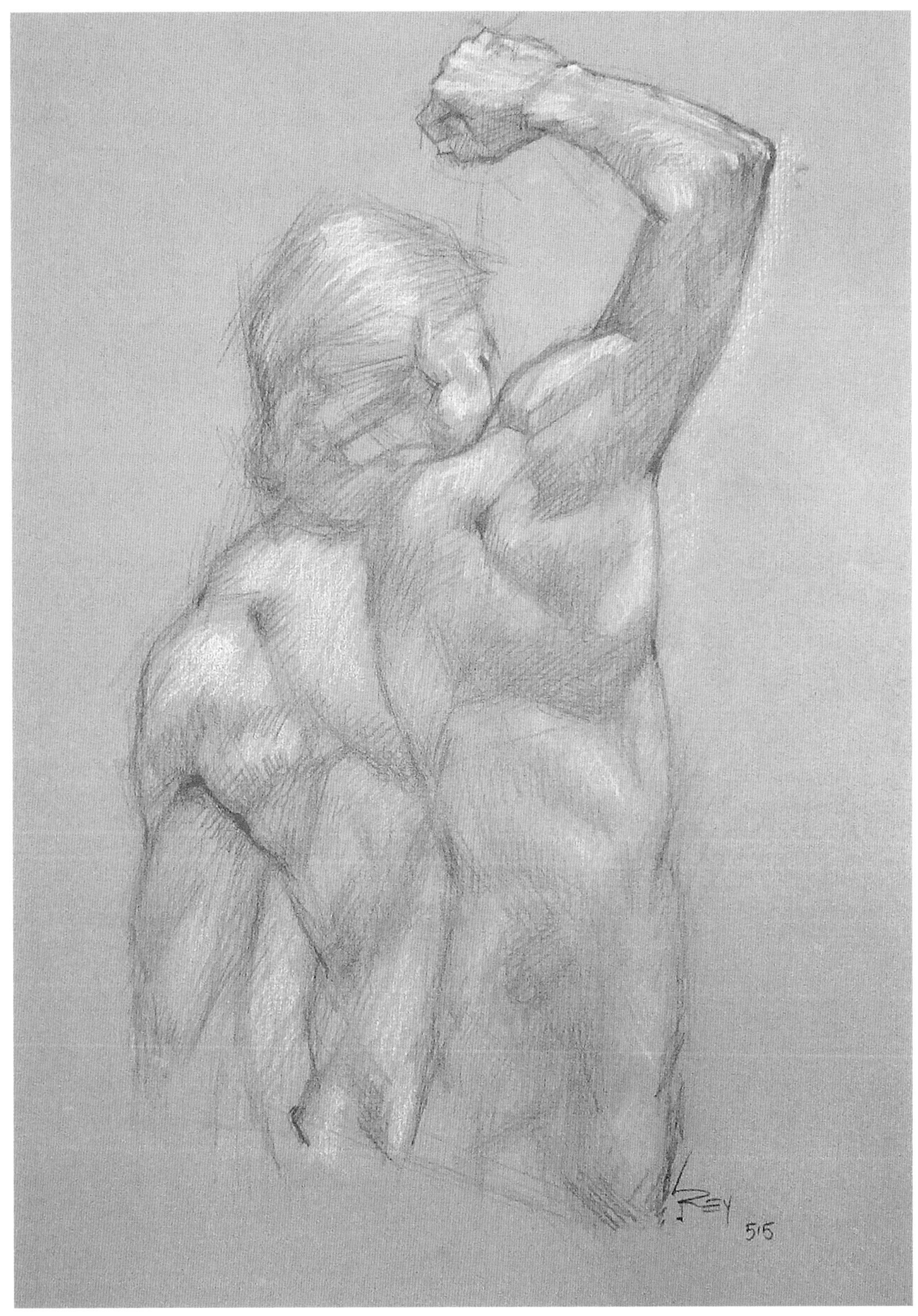

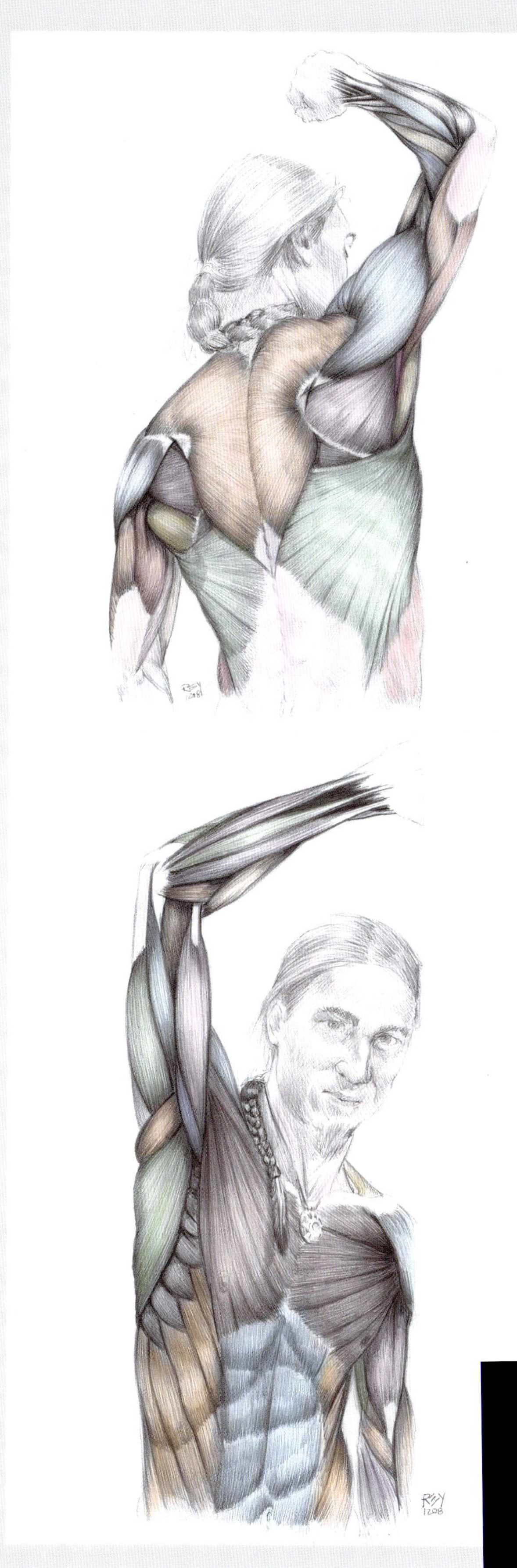

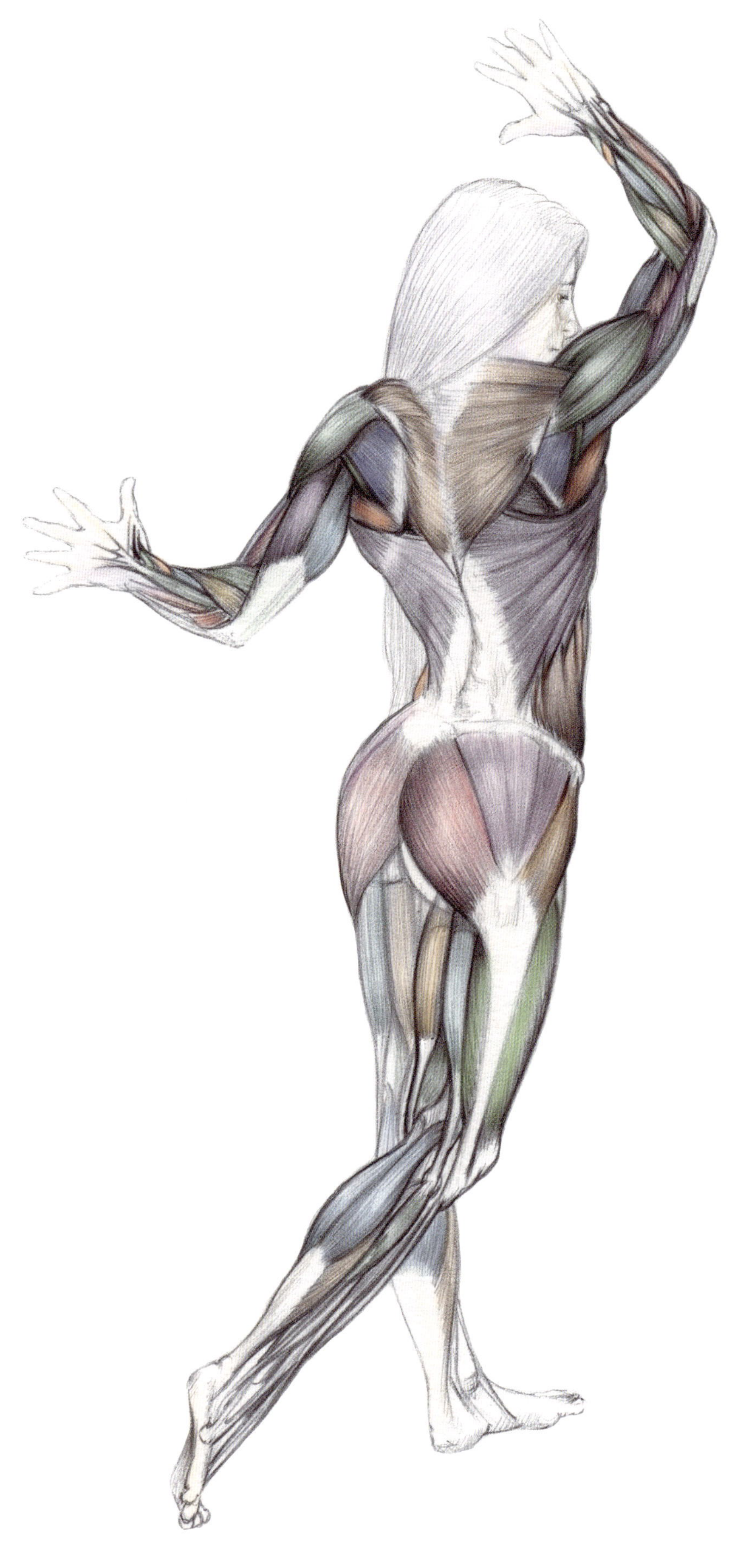

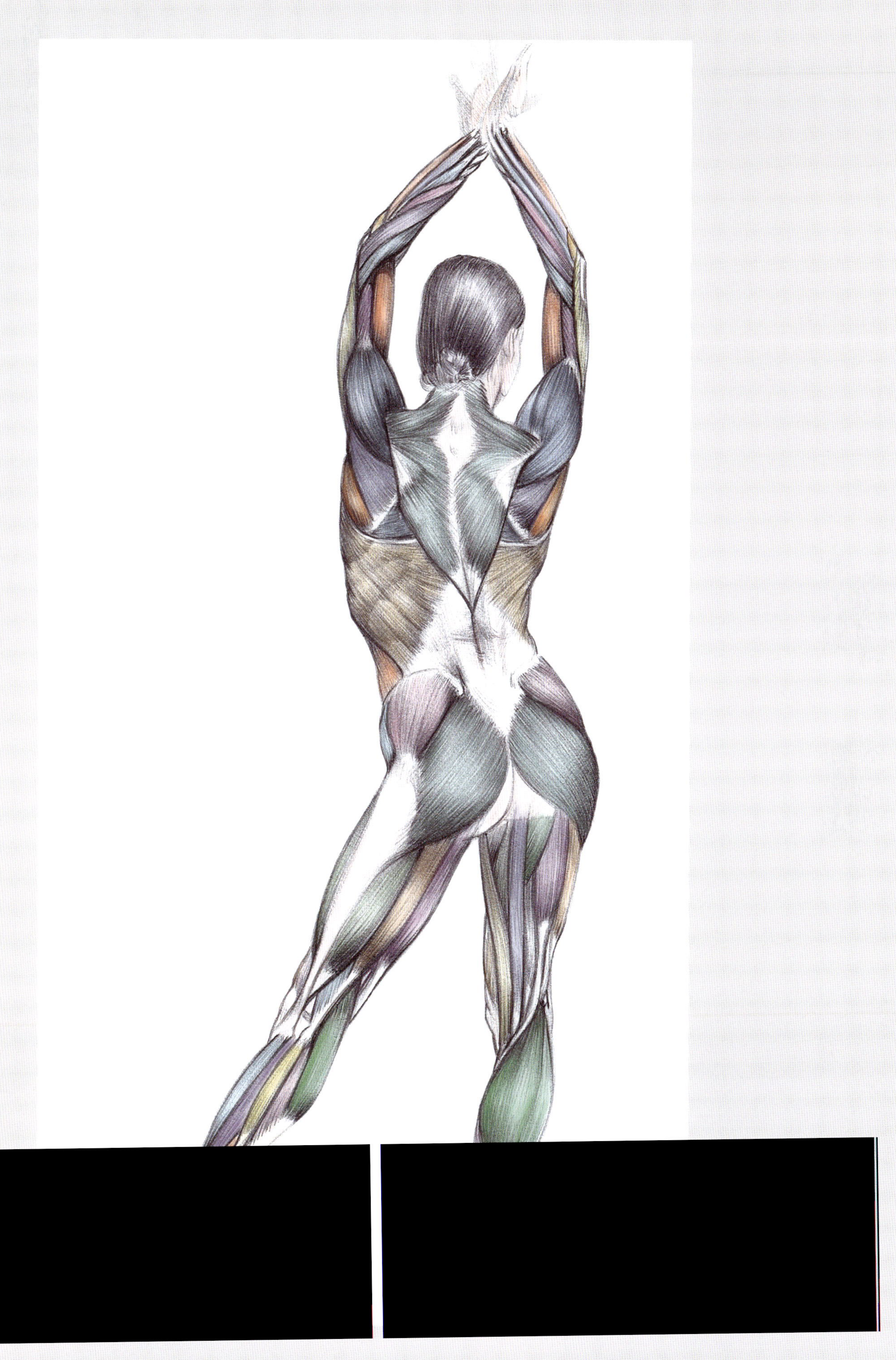

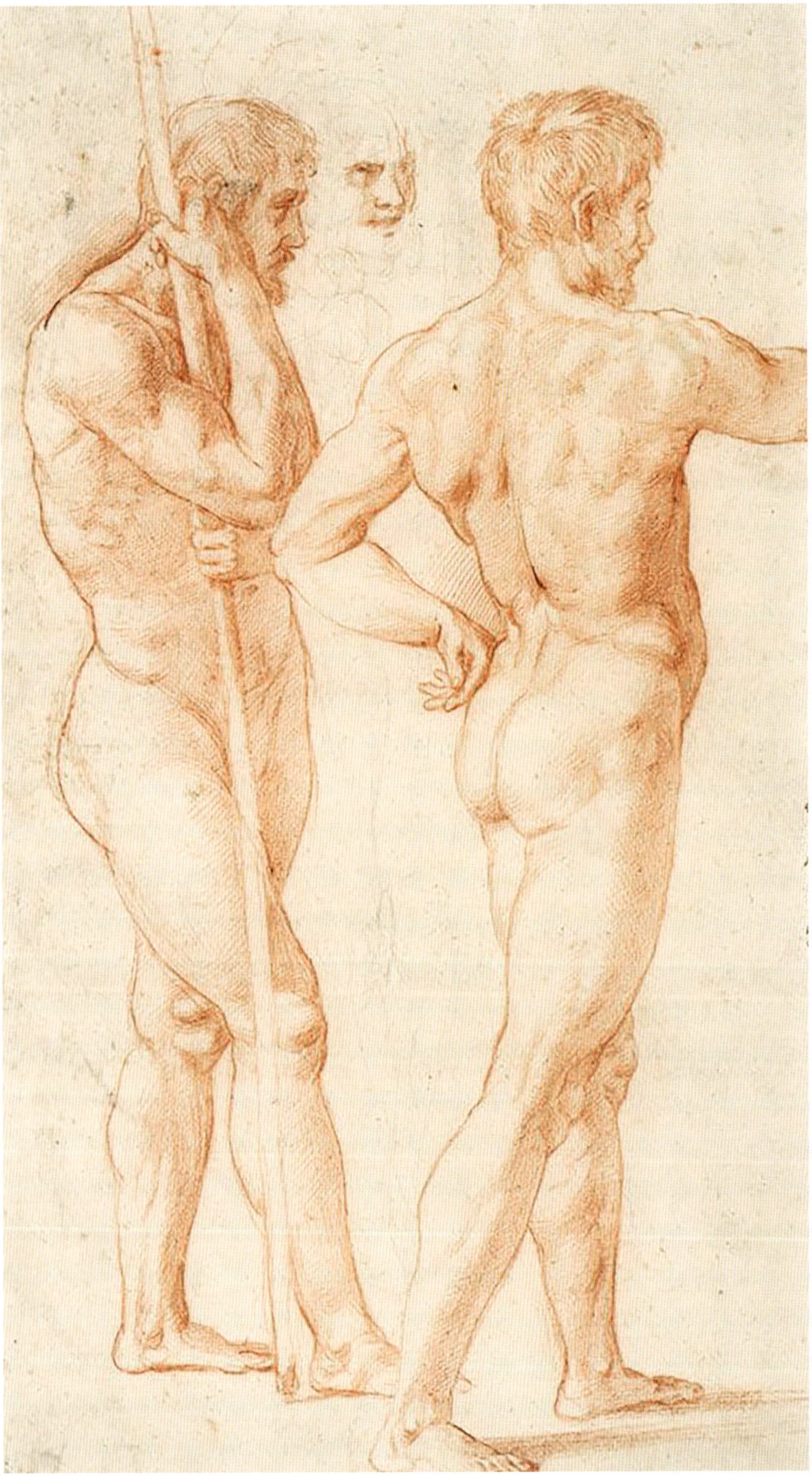

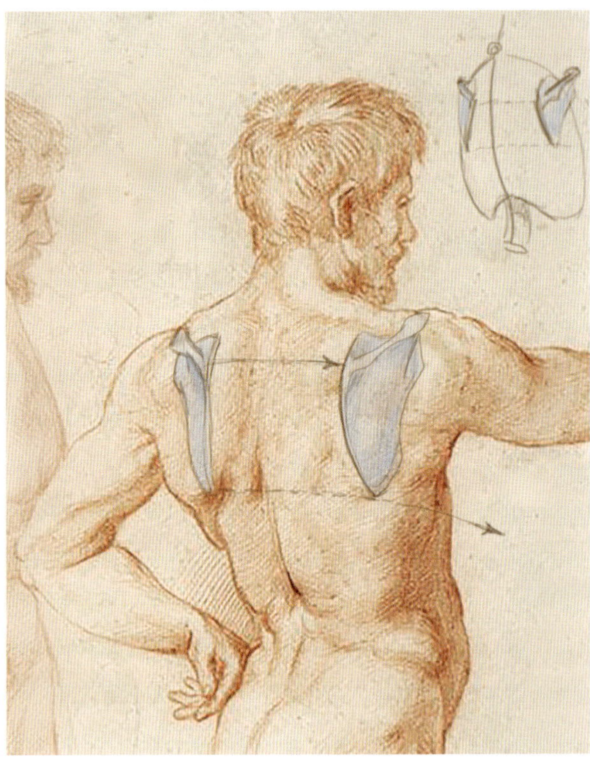

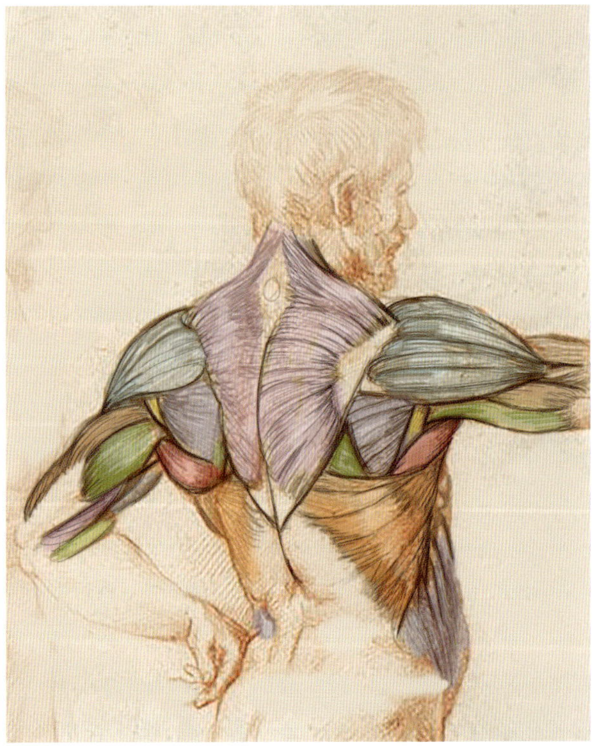

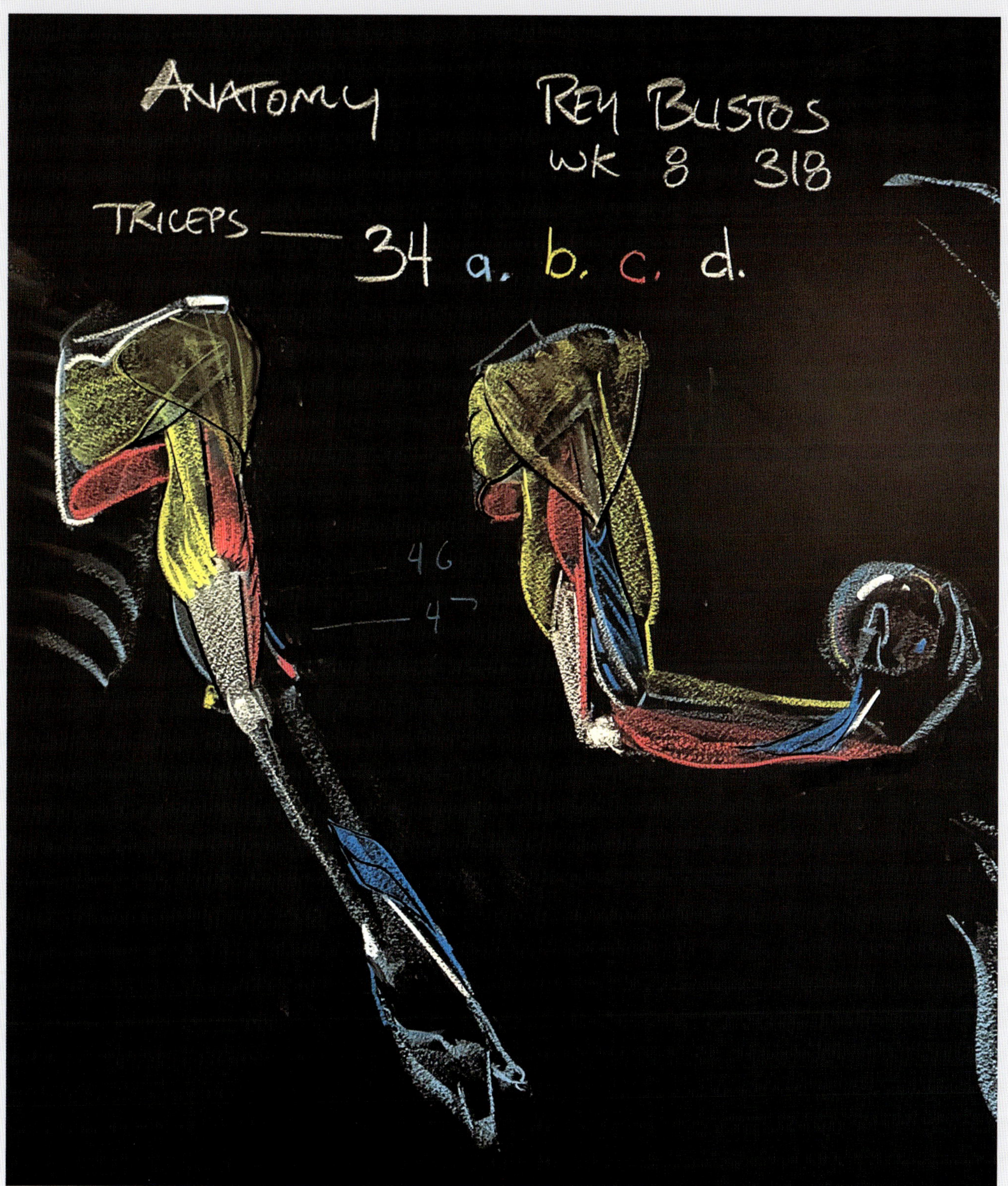

ANATOMY
REY BUSTOS
WK 8   318
TRICEPS — 34 a. b. c. d.

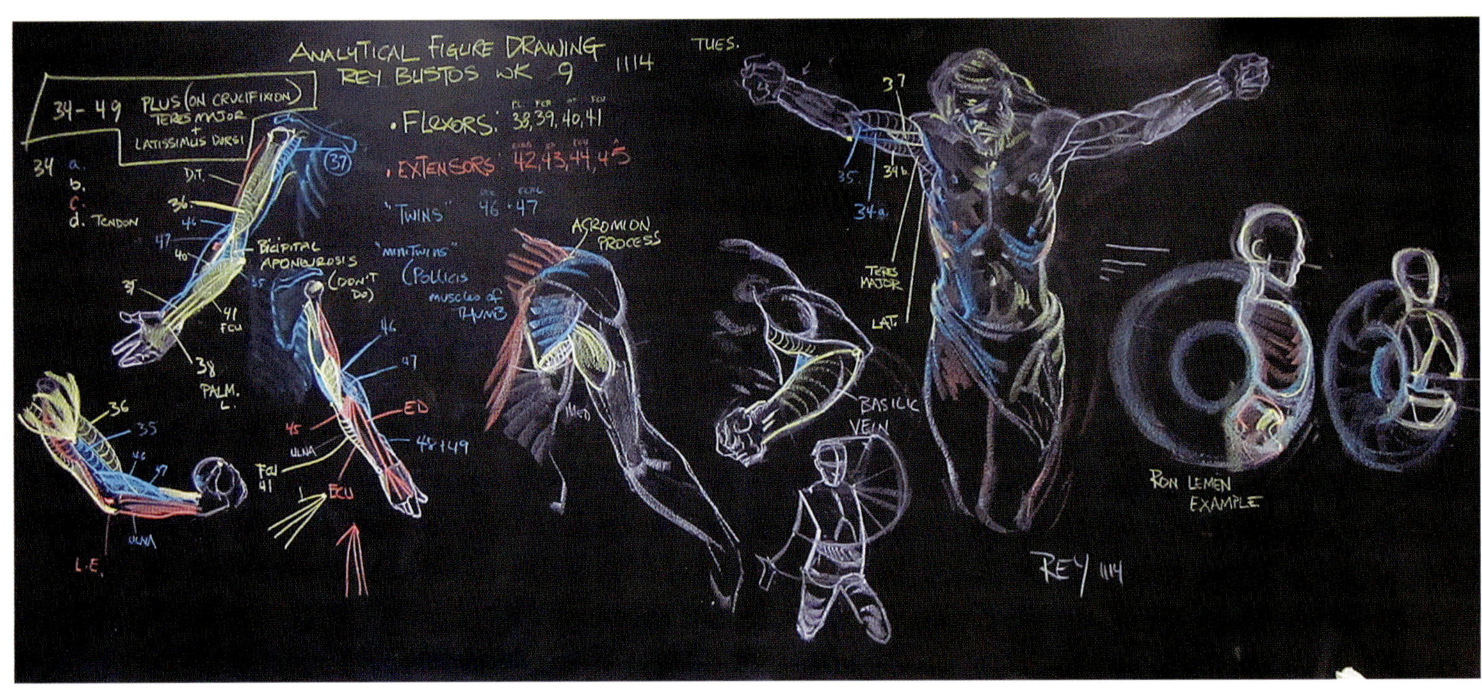

ANALYTICAL FIGURE DRAWING
REY BUSTOS WK 9 1114
TUES.
34-49 PLUS (ON CRUCIFIXION) TERES MAJOR + LATISSIMUS DORSI
FLEXORS: 38, 39, 40, 41
EXTENSORS: 42, 43, 44, 45
"TWINS" 46 · 47
"MINI-TWINS" (POLLICIS muscles of THUMB)
BICIPITAL APONEUROSIS (DON'T DO)
ACROMION PROCESS
BASILIC VEIN
TERES MAJOR
LAT.
RON LEMEN EXAMPLE
REY 1114

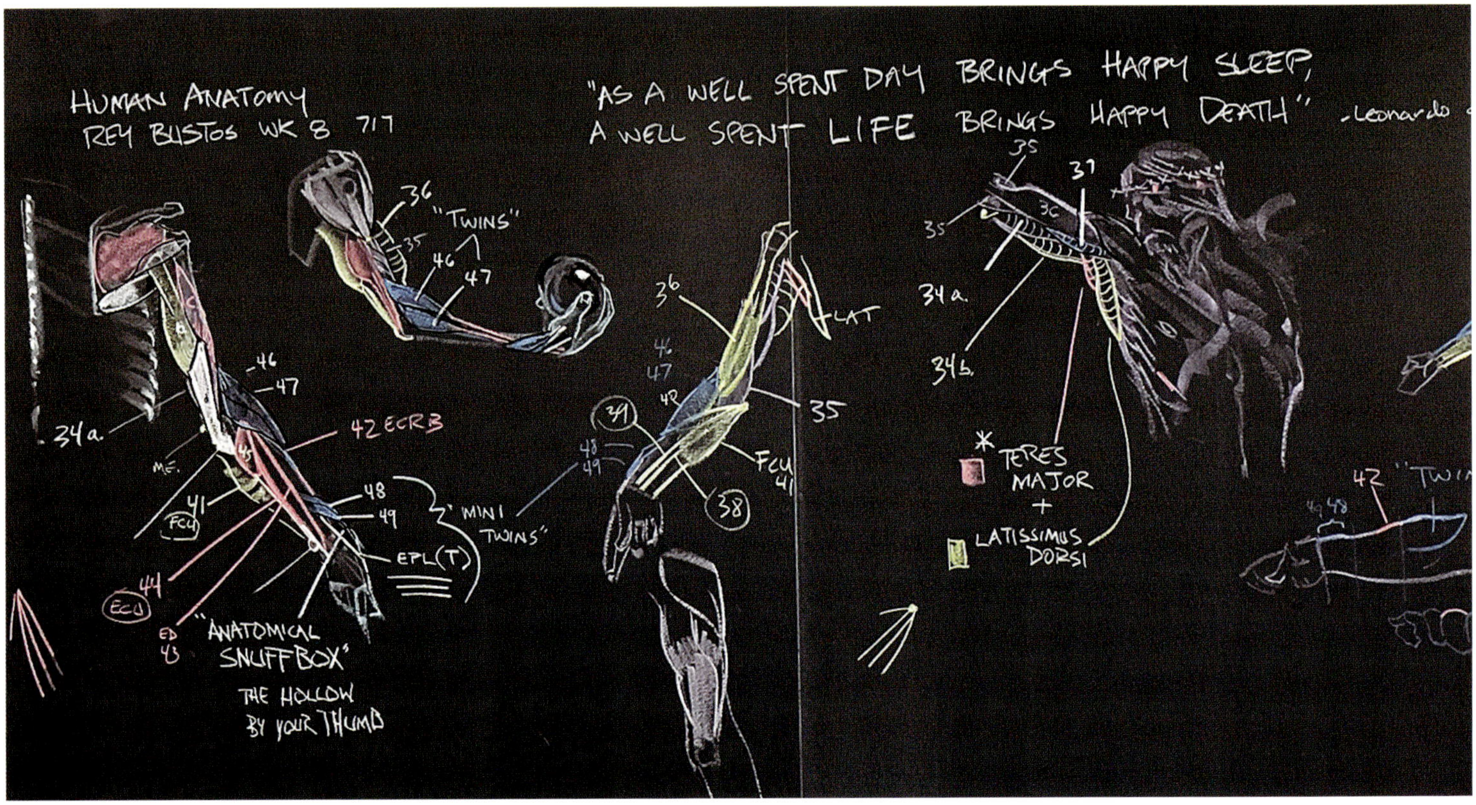

HUMAN ANATOMY
REY BUSTOS WK 8 717
"AS A WELL SPENT DAY BRINGS HAPPY SLEEP, A WELL SPENT LIFE BRINGS HAPPY DEATH" -Leonardo
"TWINS"
42 ECRB
"MINI TWINS"
EPL (T)
"ANATOMICAL SNUFFBOX"
THE HOLLOW BY YOUR THUMB
TERES MAJOR + LATISSIMUS DORSI
LAT
FCU

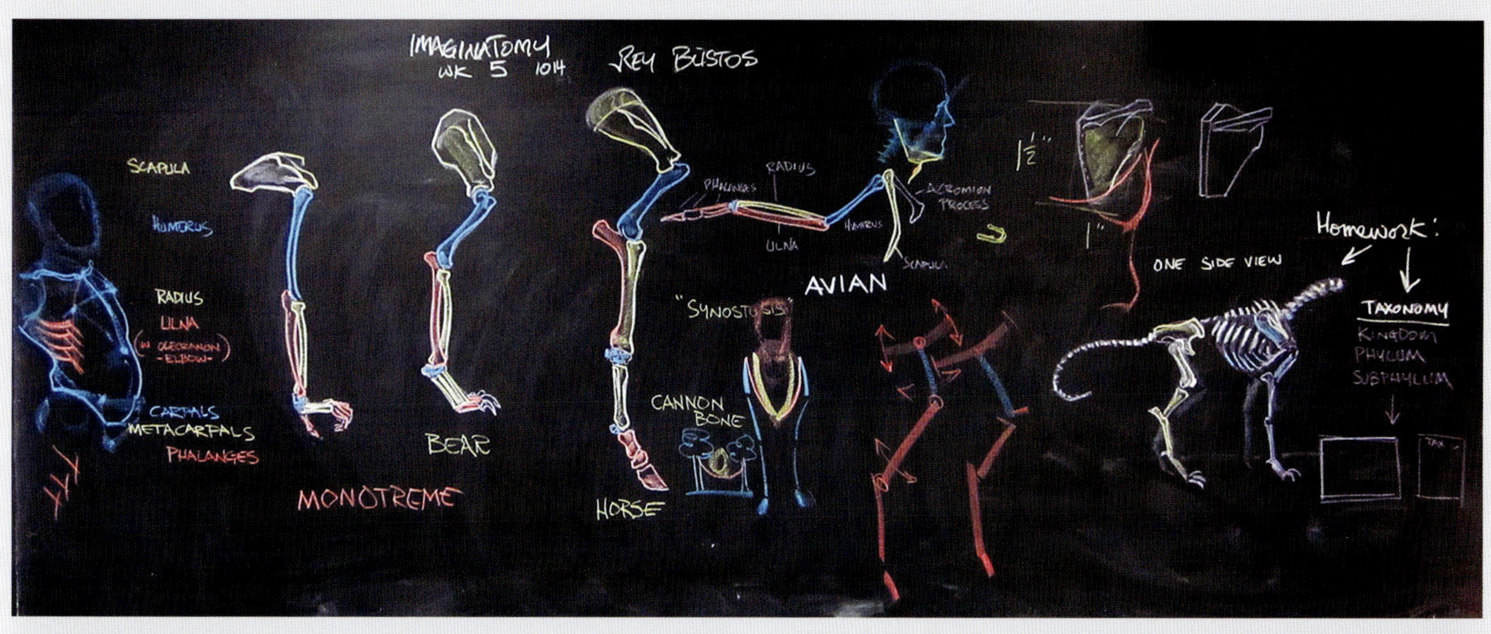

IMAGINATOMY
WK 5   1014
REY BUSTOS
SCAPULA
HUMERUS
RADIUS
ULNA
(w/ OLECRANON)
-ELBOW-
CARPALS
METACARPALS
PHALANGES
MONOTREME
BEAR
PHALANGES
RADIUS
ULNA
HUMERUS
ACROMION PROCESS
SCAPULA
AVIAN
"SYNOSTOSIS"
CANNON BONE
HORSE
1 1/2"
1"
ONE SIDE VIEW
Homework:
TAXONOMY
KINGDOM
PHYLUM
SUBPHYLUM
TAX

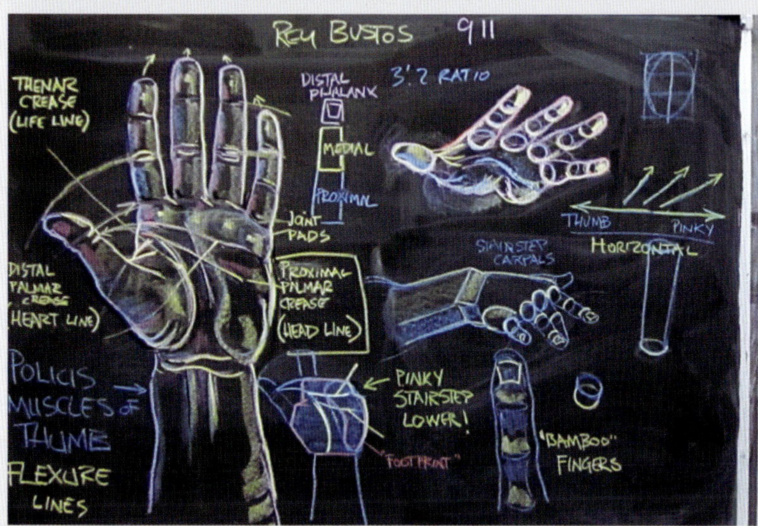

REY BUSTOS   911
THENAR CREASE
(LIFE LINE)
DISTAL PHALANX
3':2 RATIO
MEDIAL
PROXIMAL
JOINT PADS
DISTAL PALMAR CREASE
(HEART LINE)
PROXIMAL PALMAR CREASE
(HEAD LINE)
POLICIS MUSCLES OF THUMB
FLEXURE LINES
PINKY STAIRSTEP LOWER!
"FOOT PRINT"
STAIRSTEP CARPALS
THUMB
PINKY
HORIZONTAL
"BAMBOO" FINGERS

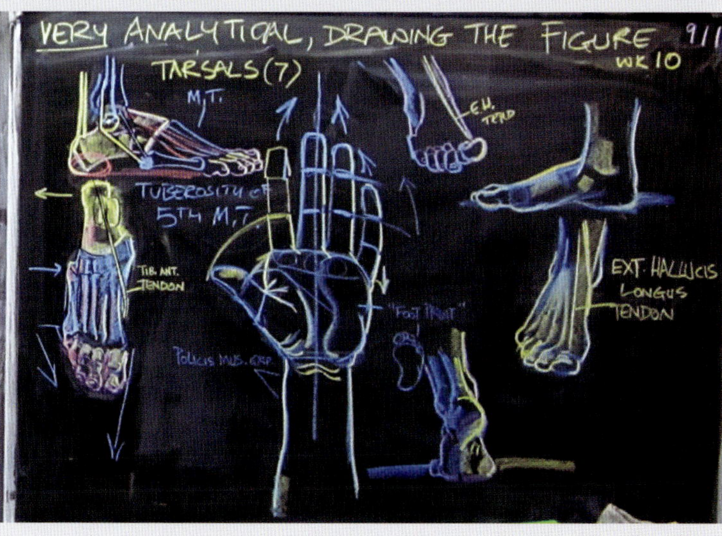

VERY ANALYTICAL, DRAWING THE FIGURE   911
WK 10
TARSALS (7)
M.T.
E.H. TEND
TUBEROSITY OF 5TH M.T.
TIB. ANT. TENDON
POLICIS MUS. GRP
"FOOT PRINT"
EXT. HALLUCIS LONGUS TENDON

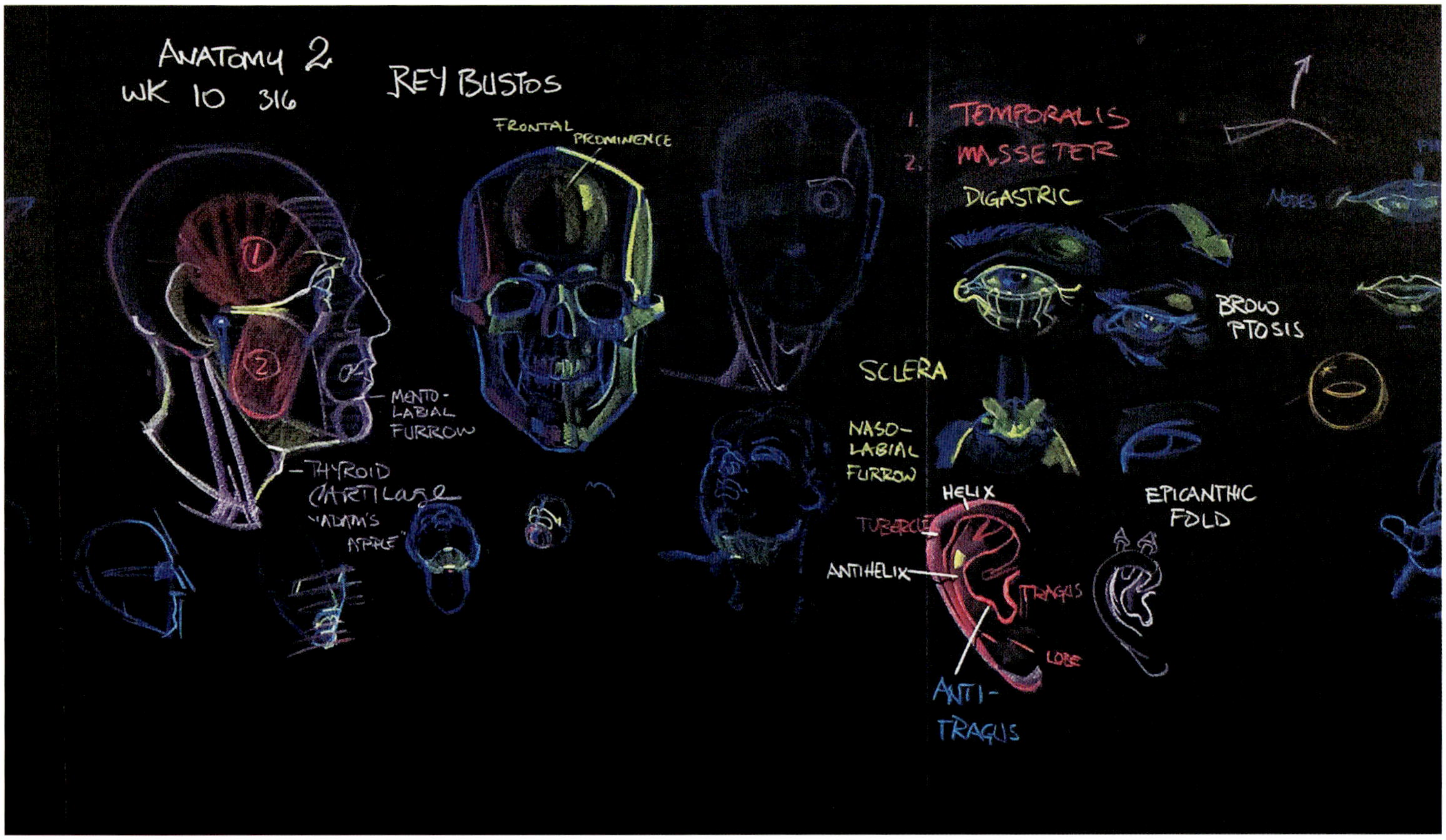

ANATOMY 2
WK 10 316
REY BUSTOS
FRONTAL PROMINENCE
1. TEMPORALIS
2. MASSETER
DIGASTRIC
NOTES
BROW PTOSIS
SCLERA
MENTO-LABIAL FURROW
NASO-LABIAL FURROW
THYROID CARTILAGE "ADAM'S APPLE"
HELIX
TUBERCLE
ANTIHELIX
TRAGUS
LOBE
ANTI-TRAGUS
EPICANTHIC FOLD

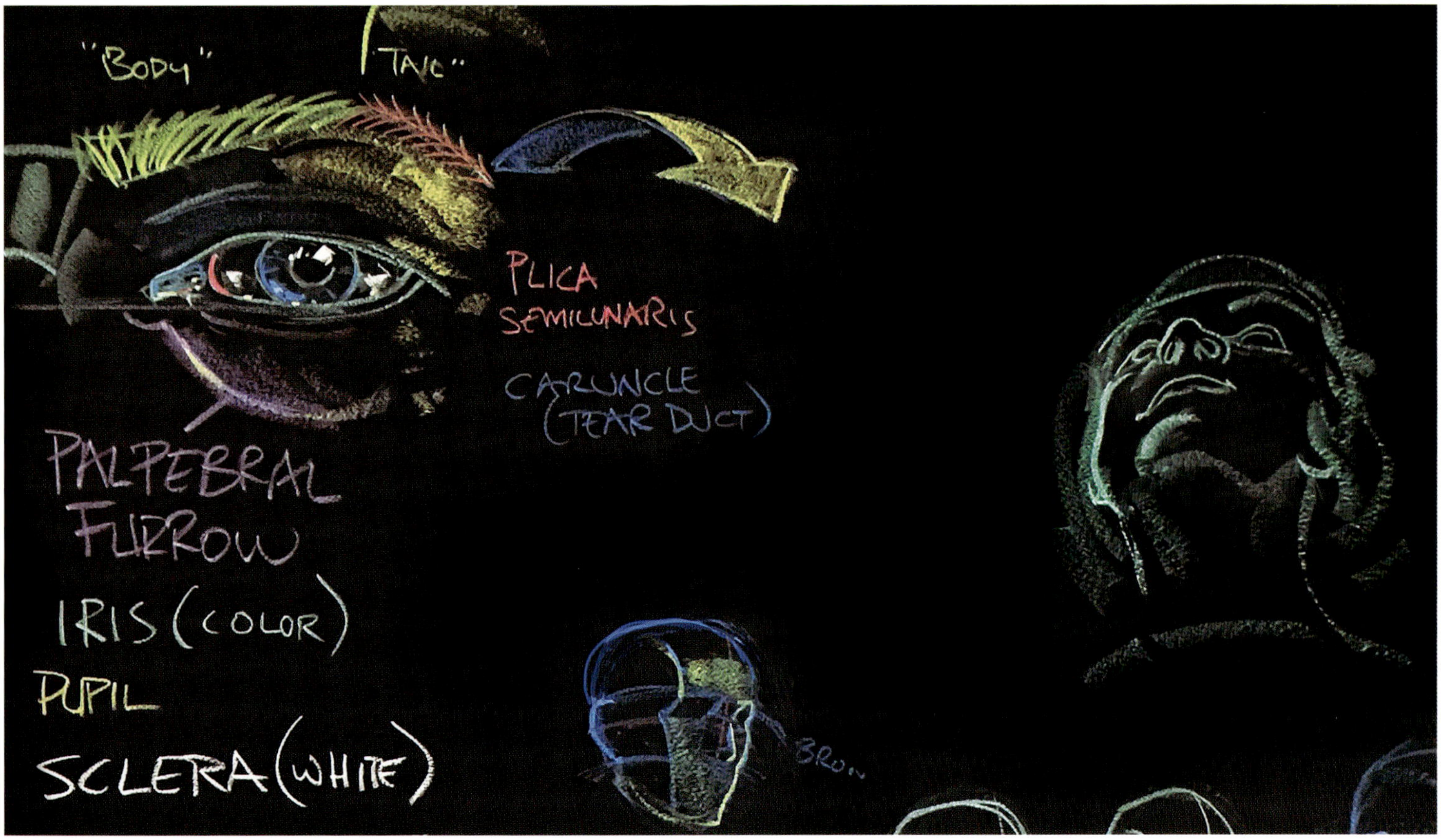

"BODY"
"TAIL"
PLICA SEMILUNARIS
CARUNCLE (TEAR DUCT)
PALPEBRAL FURROW
IRIS (COLOR)
PUPIL
SCLERA (WHITE)
BROW

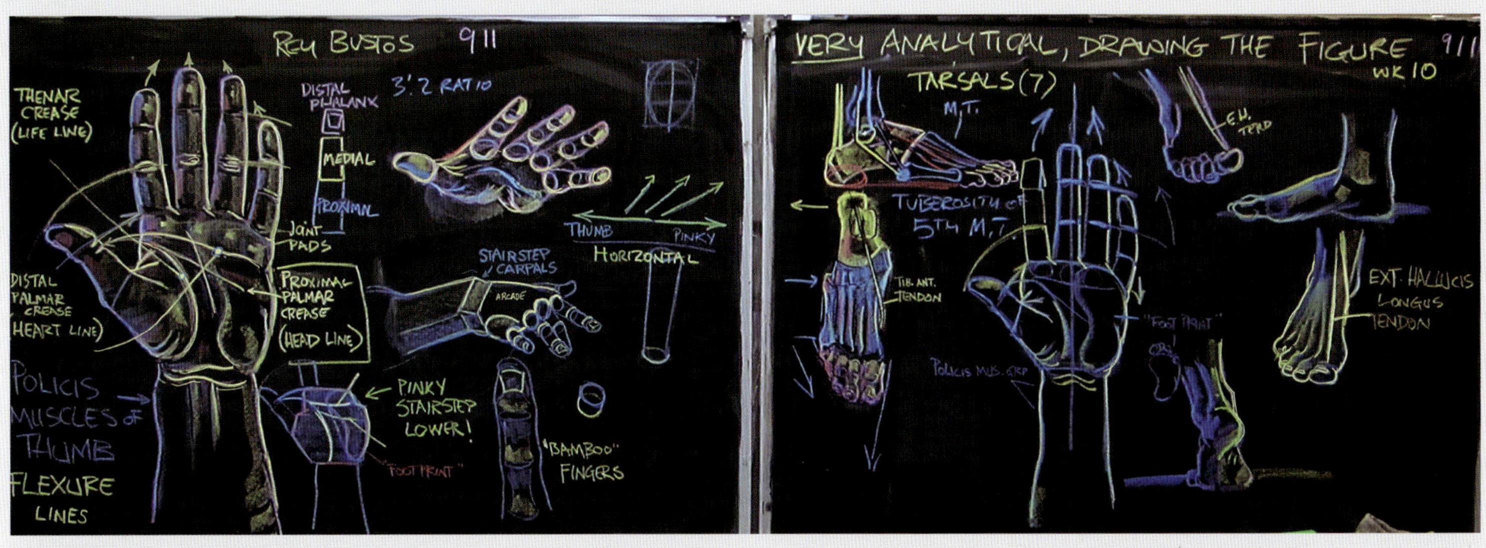

REY BUSTOS   911
THENAR CREASE (LIFE LINE)
DISTAL PHALANX
3:2 RATIO
MEDIAL
PROXIMAL
JOINT PADS
DISTAL PALMAR CREASE (HEART LINE)
PROXIMAL PALMAR CREASE (HEAD LINE)
STAIRSTEP CARPALS
ARCADE
THUMB
PINKY
HORIZONTAL
POLICIS MUSCLES OF THUMB
FLEXURE LINES
PINKY STAIRSTEP LOWER!
"FOOT PRINT"
"BAMBOO" FINGERS
VERY ANALYTICAL, DRAWING THE FIGURE   911   WK 10
TARSALS (7)
M.T.
E.H. TEND
TUBEROSITY of 5TH M.T.
TIB. ANT. TENDON
"FOOT PRINT"
EXT. HALLUCIS LONGUS TENDON
Policis Mus. EXP

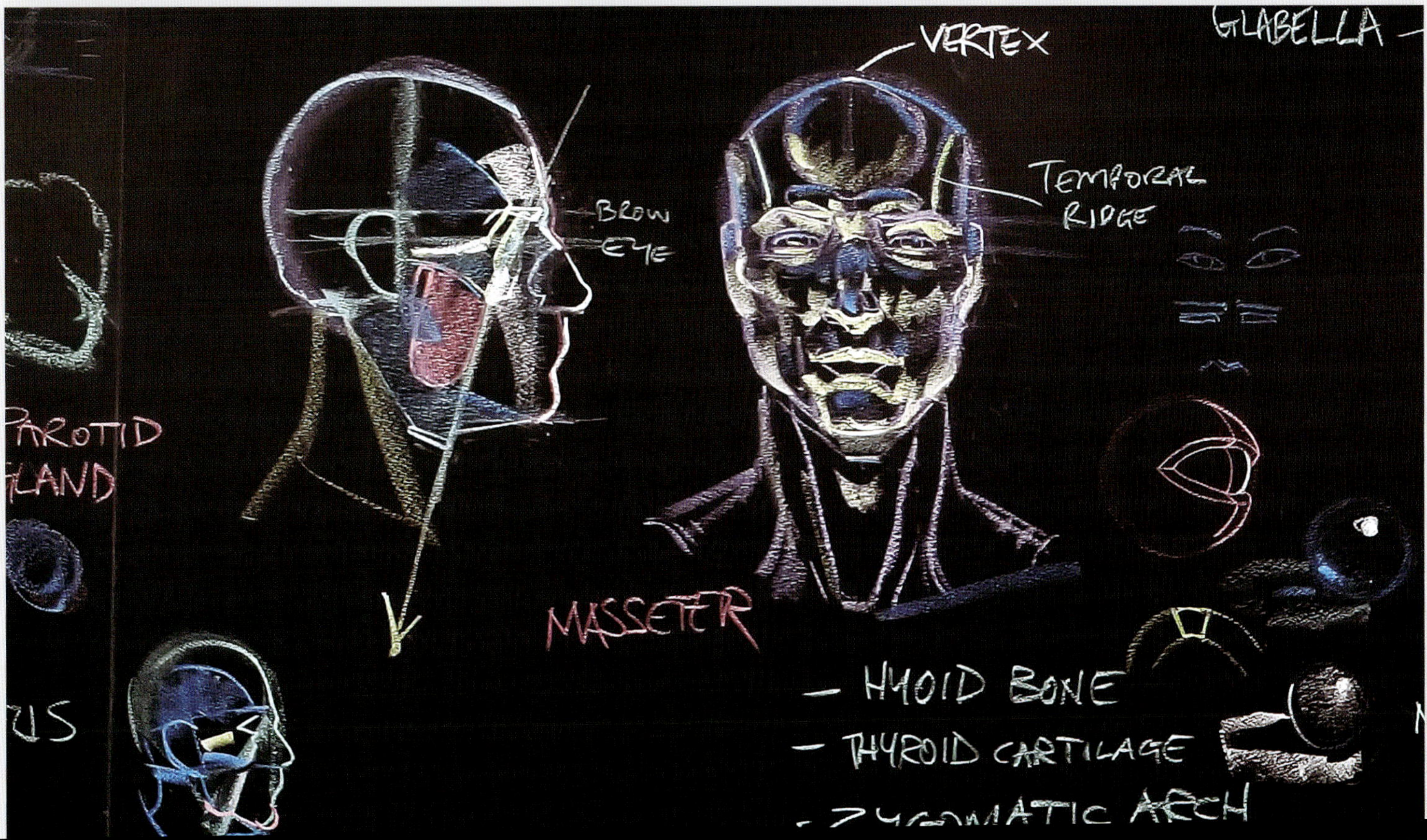

VERTEX
GLABELLA
BROW
EYE
TEMPORAL RIDGE
PAROTID GLAND
MASSETER
— HYOID BONE
— THYROID CARTILAGE
— ZYGOMATIC ARCH

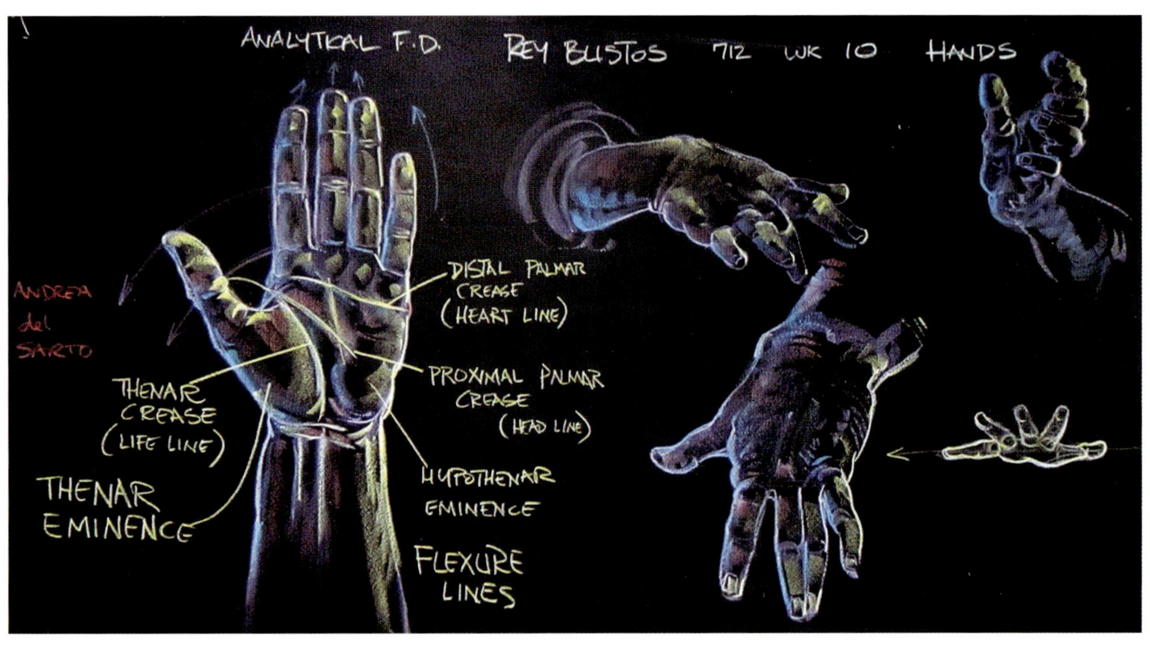

ANALYTICAL F.D.   REY BUSTOS   712   WK 10   HANDS
ANDREA del SARTO
DISTAL PALMAR CREASE (HEART LINE)
PROXIMAL PALMAR CREASE (HEAD LINE)
THENAR CREASE (LIFE LINE)
THENAR EMINENCE
HYPOTHENAR EMINENCE
FLEXURE LINES

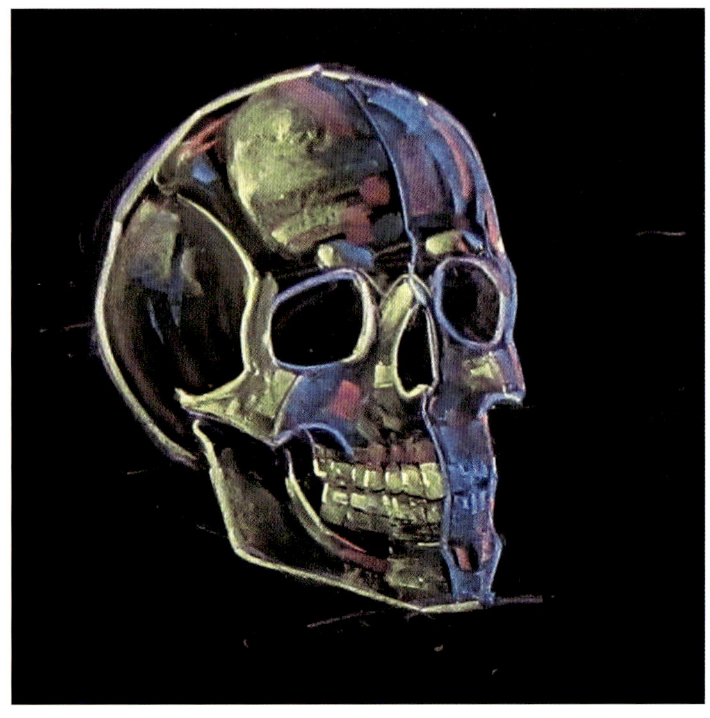

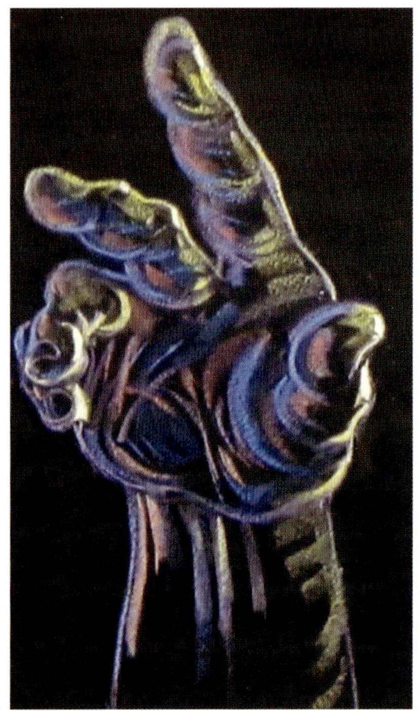

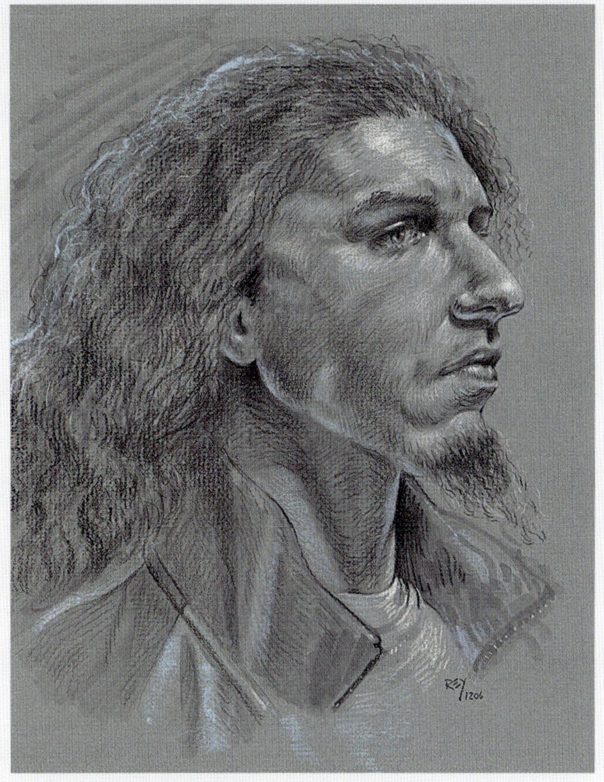

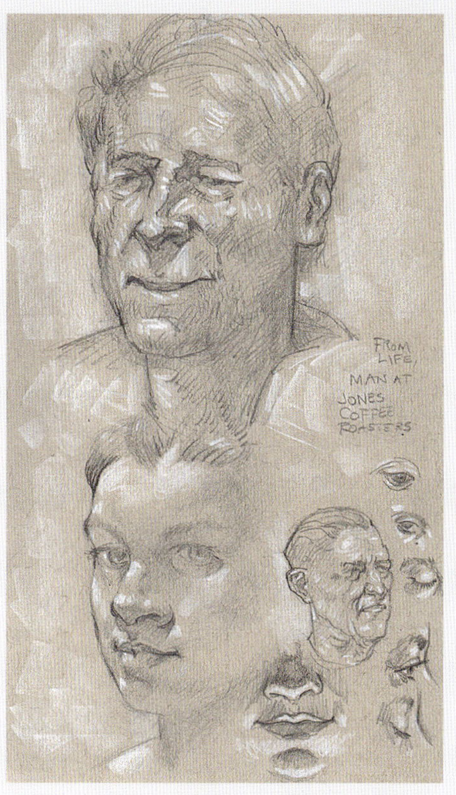
FROM
LIFE,
MAN AT
JONES
COFFEE
ROASTERS

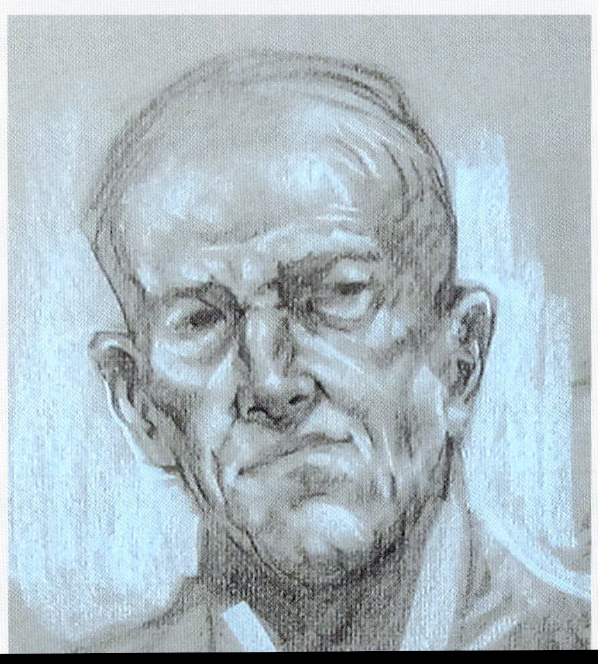

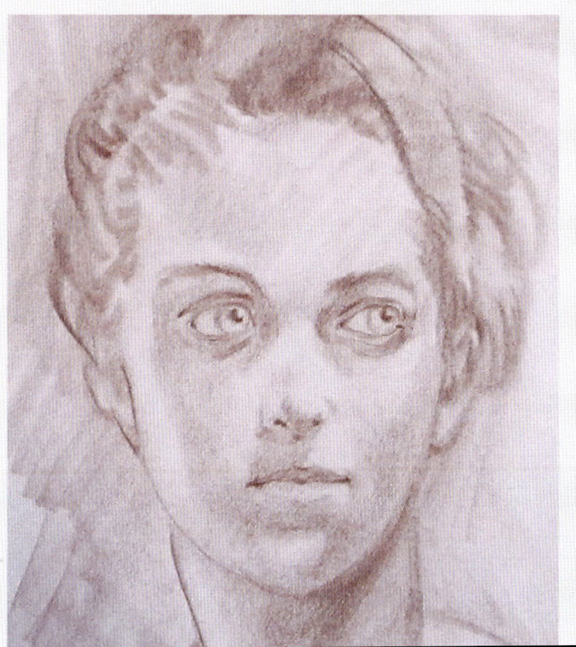

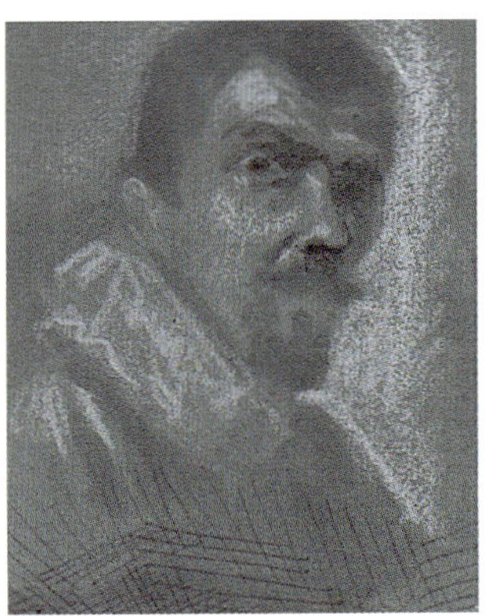

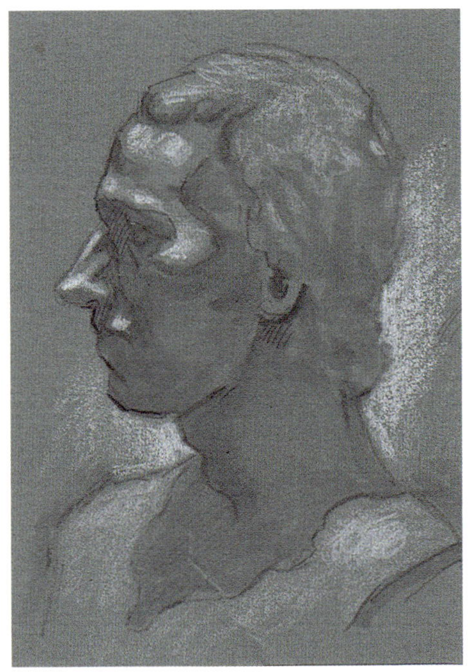

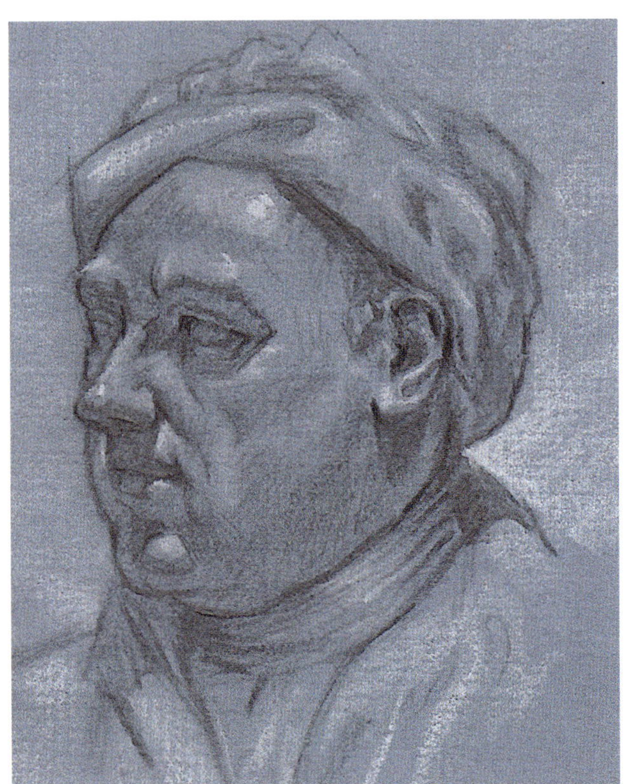

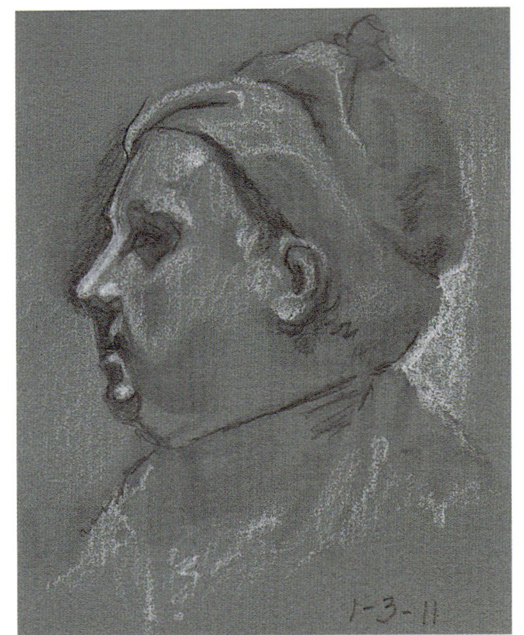

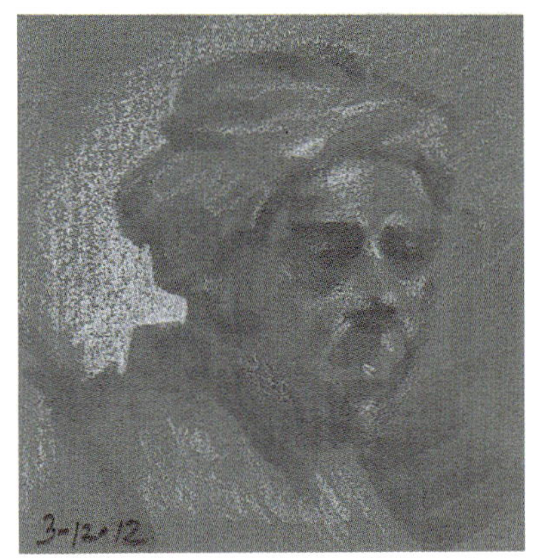

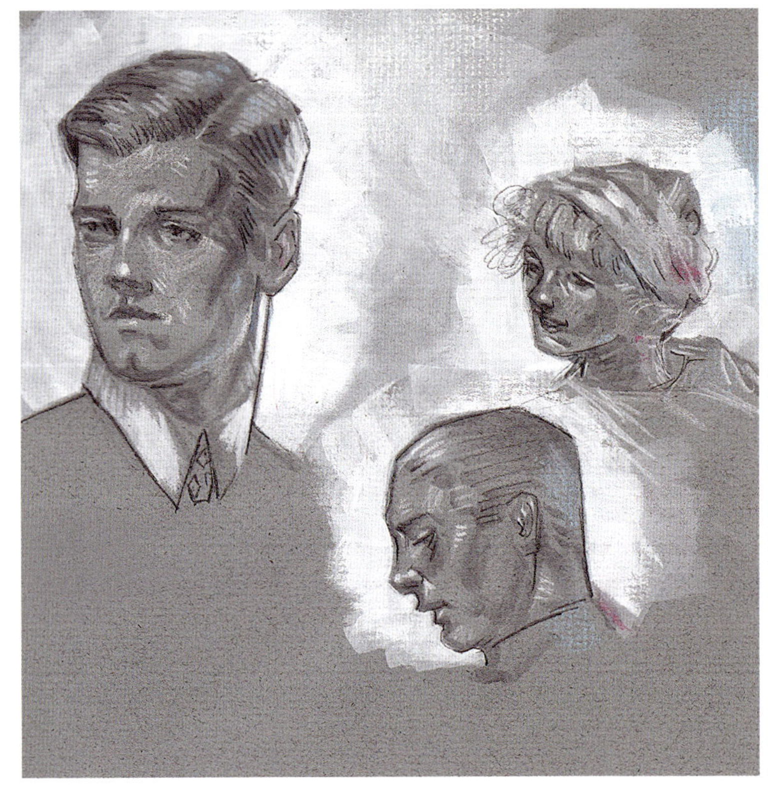

Studies in pen and gouche of J. C. Leyendecker portraits

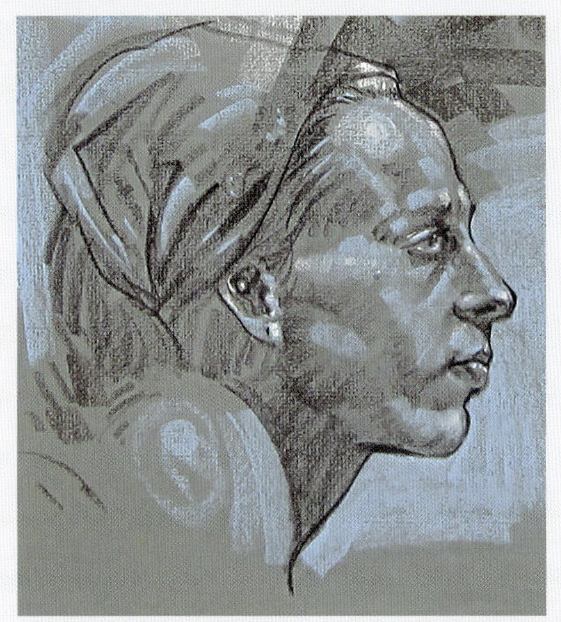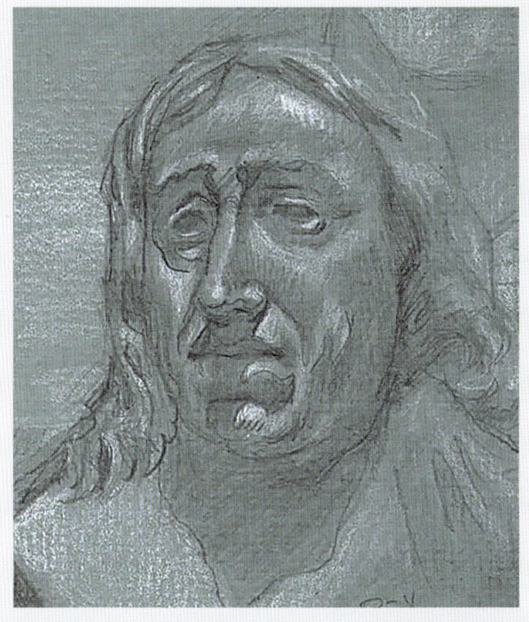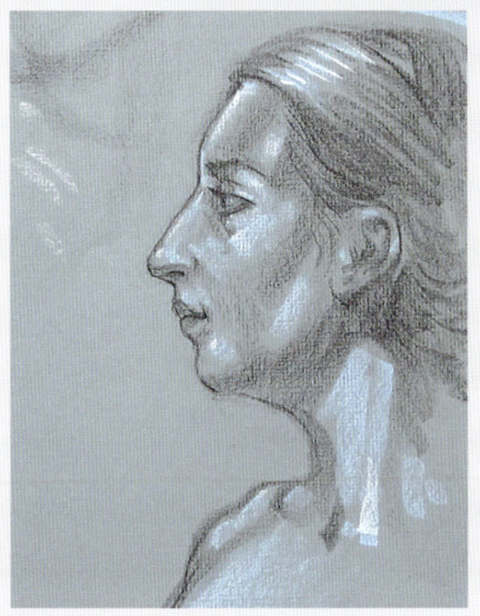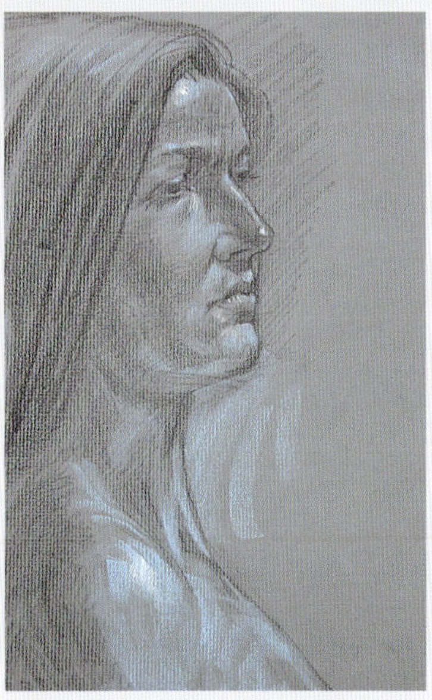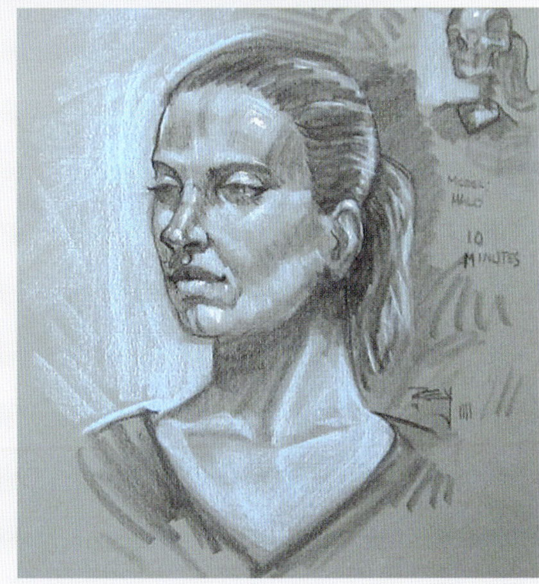
MODEL
HALO
10
MINUTES

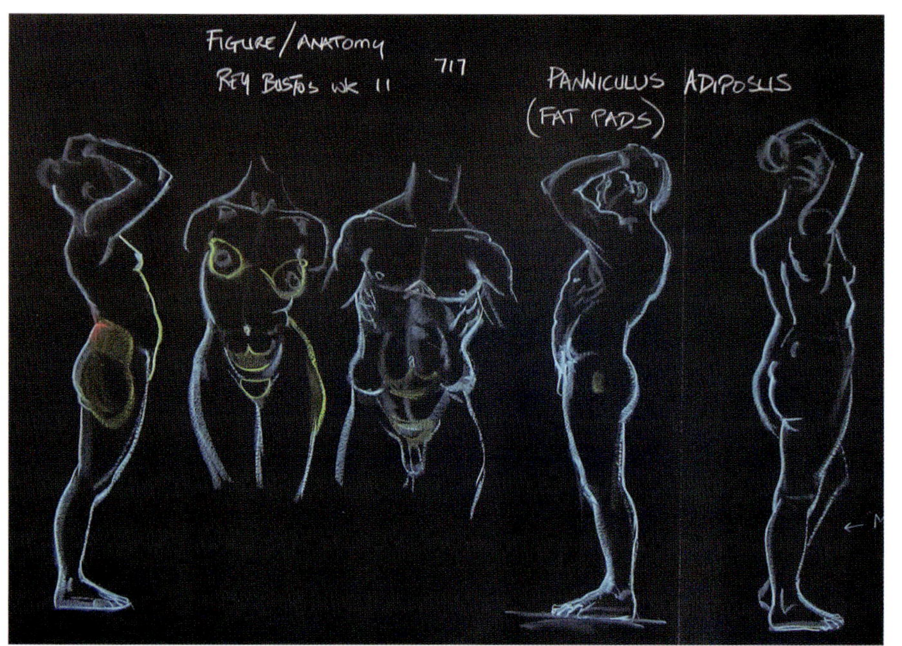

FIGURE / ANATOMY
REY BUSTOS WK 11   717
PANNICULUS ADIPOSIS
(FAT PADS)

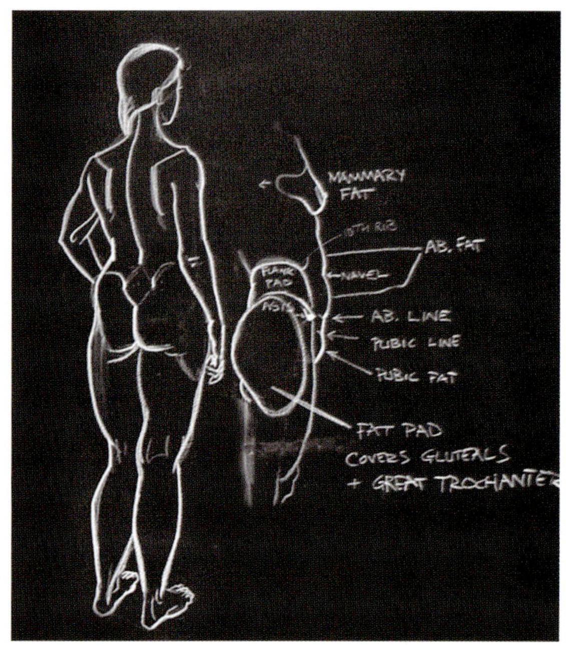

MAMMARY FAT
10TH RIB
AB. FAT
FLANK PAD
NAVEL
PSIS
AB. LINE
PUBIC LINE
PUBIC FAT
FAT PAD
COVERS GLUTEALS
+ GREAT TROCHANTER

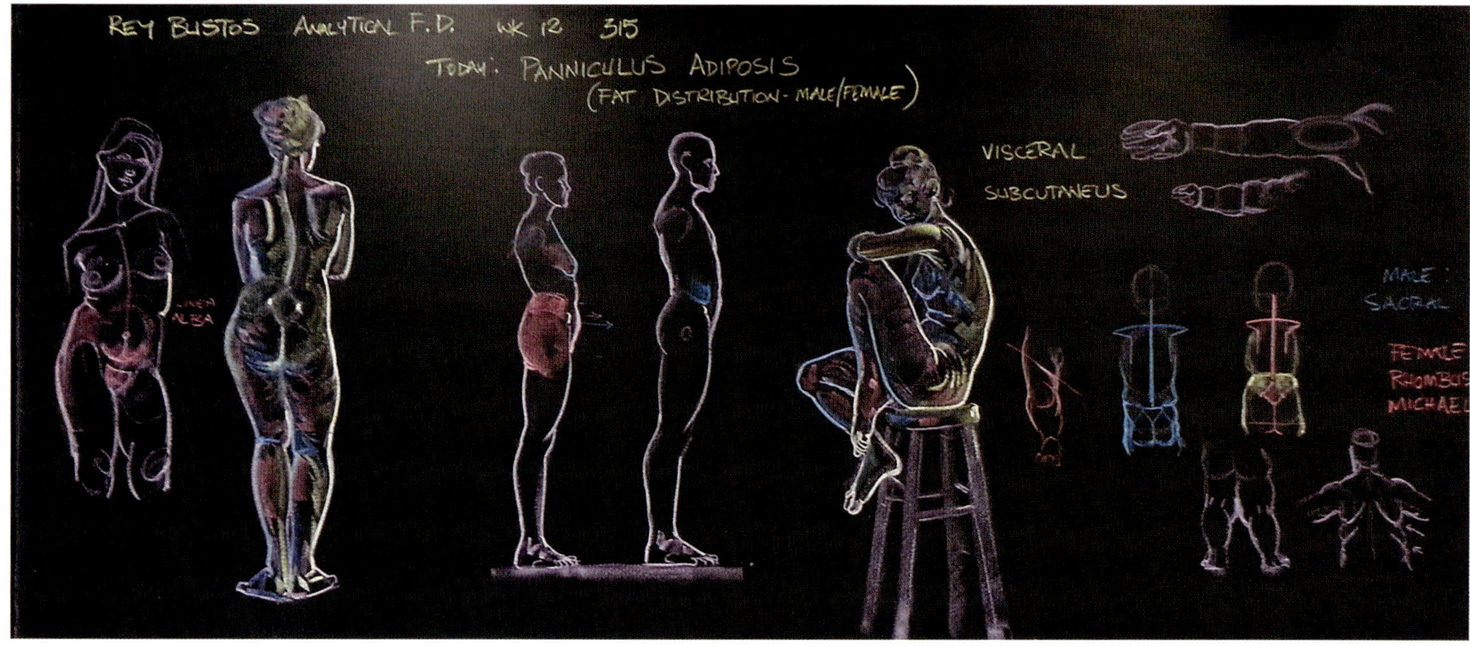

REY BUSTOS   ANALYTICAL F.D.   WK 12   315
TODAY: PANNICULUS ADIPOSIS
(FAT DISTRIBUTION - MALE/FEMALE)
LINEA ALBA
VISCERAL
SUBCUTANEUS
MALE SACRAL
FEMALE RHOMBUS MICHAEL

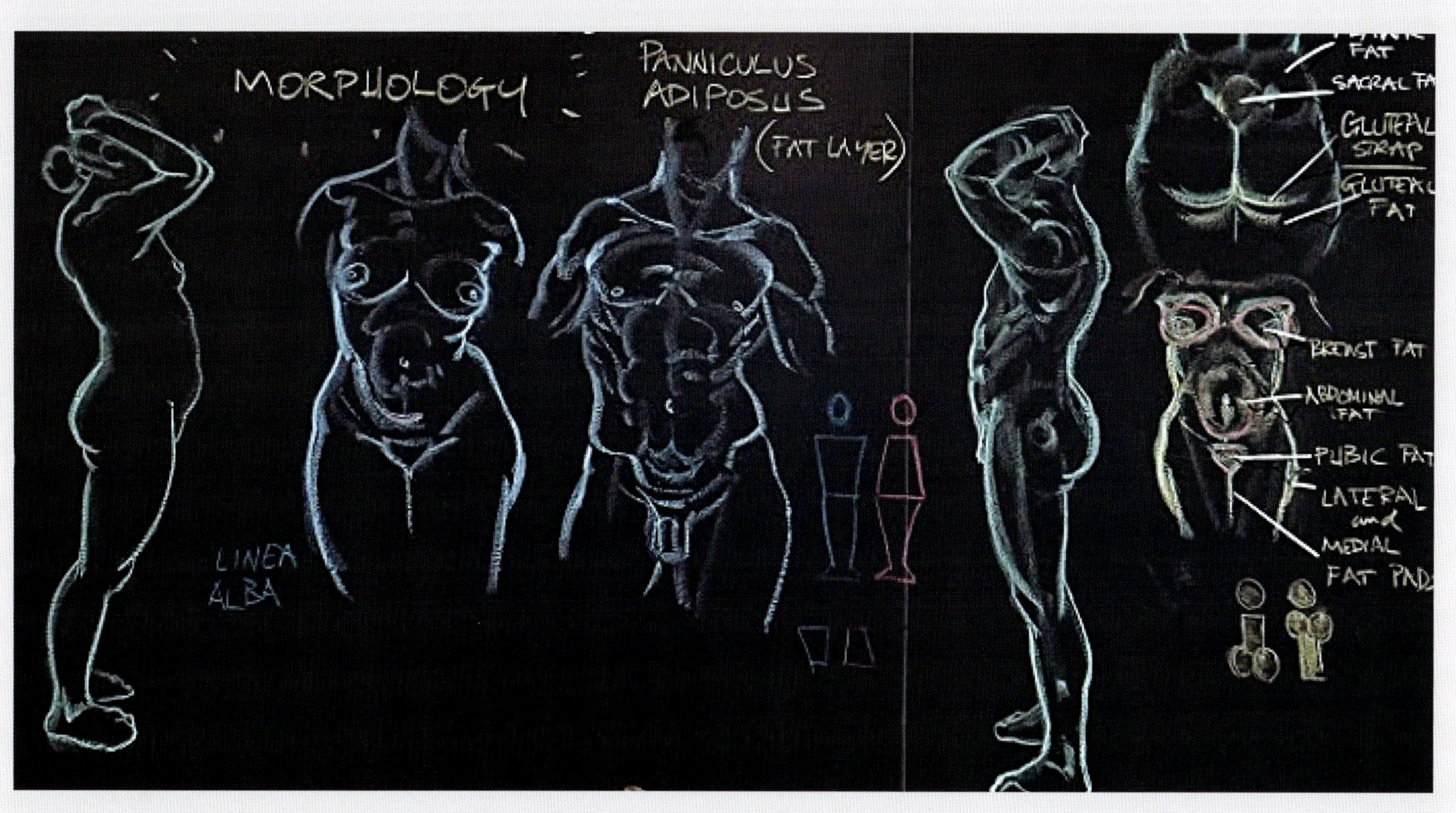

MORPHOLOGY
PANNICULUS
ADIPOSUS
(FAT LAYER)
LINEA
ALBA
FAT
SACRAL FAT
GLUTEAL
STRAP
GLUTEAL
FAT
BREAST FAT
ABDOMINAL
FAT
PUBIC FAT
LATERAL
and
MEDIAL
FAT PADS

ADDITIONAL REFERENCE IMAGES

In my thirty years of teaching, I have been fortunate to instruct—but also learn from—exceptional students. It gives me great joy to discover helpful educational tools that I can then introduce to others. This section contains more artwork and image references that you may find useful while perfecting your own figurative art skills.

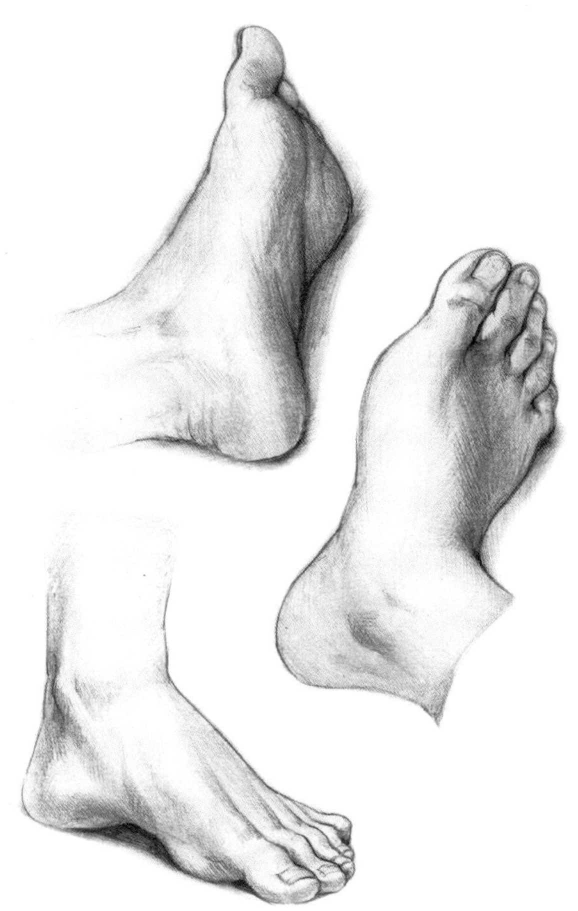

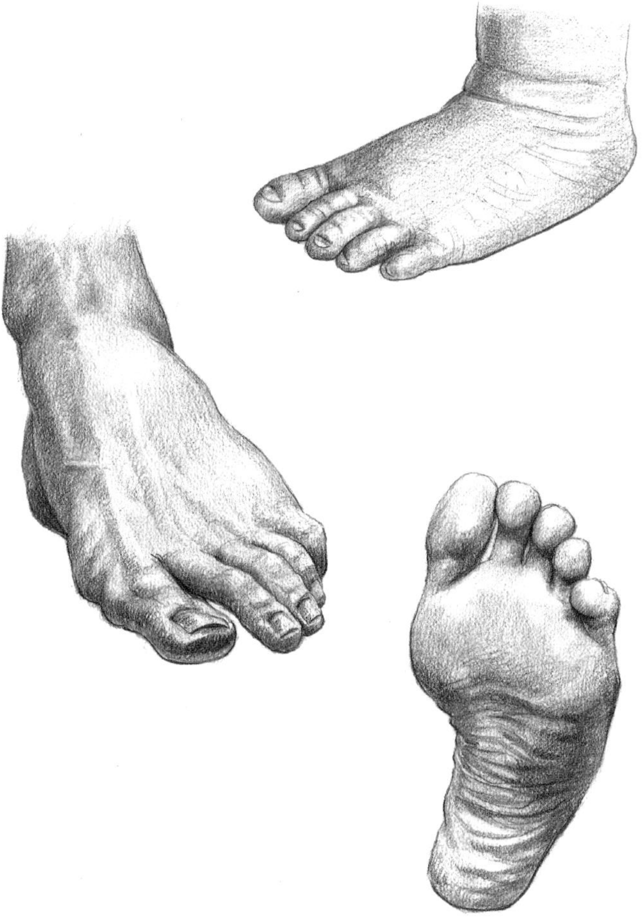

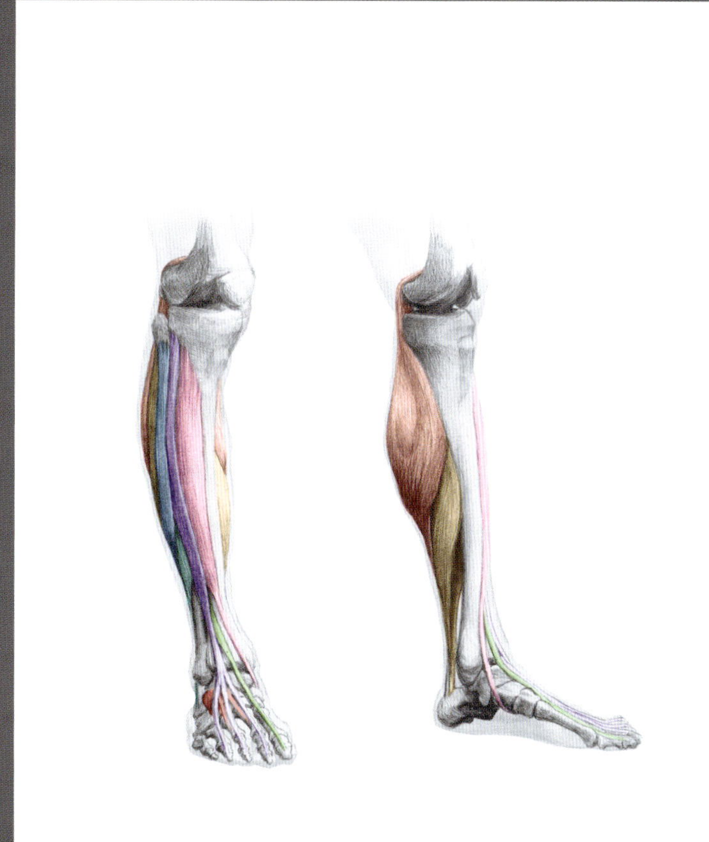
Amaro Koberle

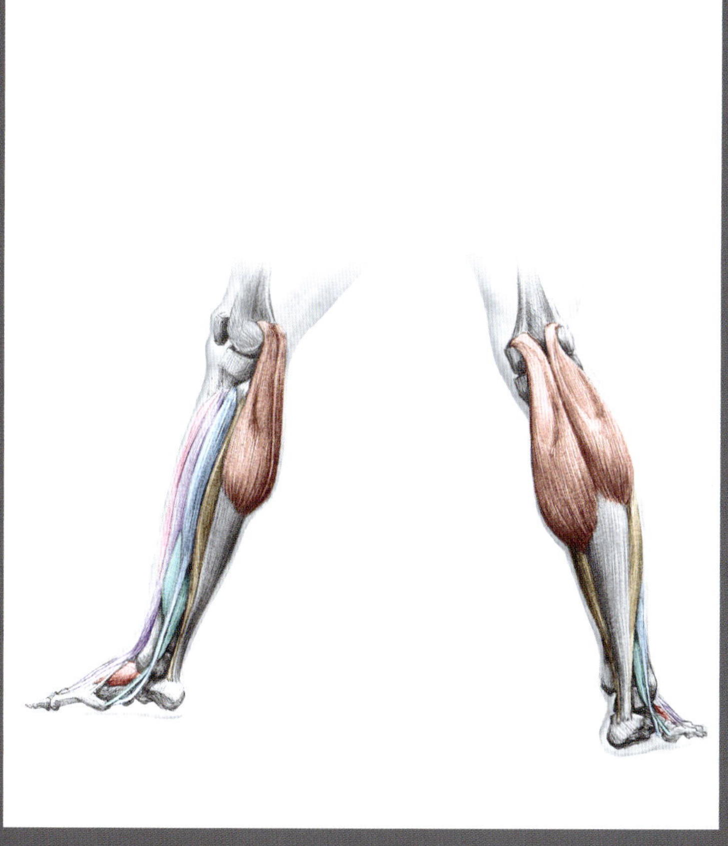
Amaro Koberle

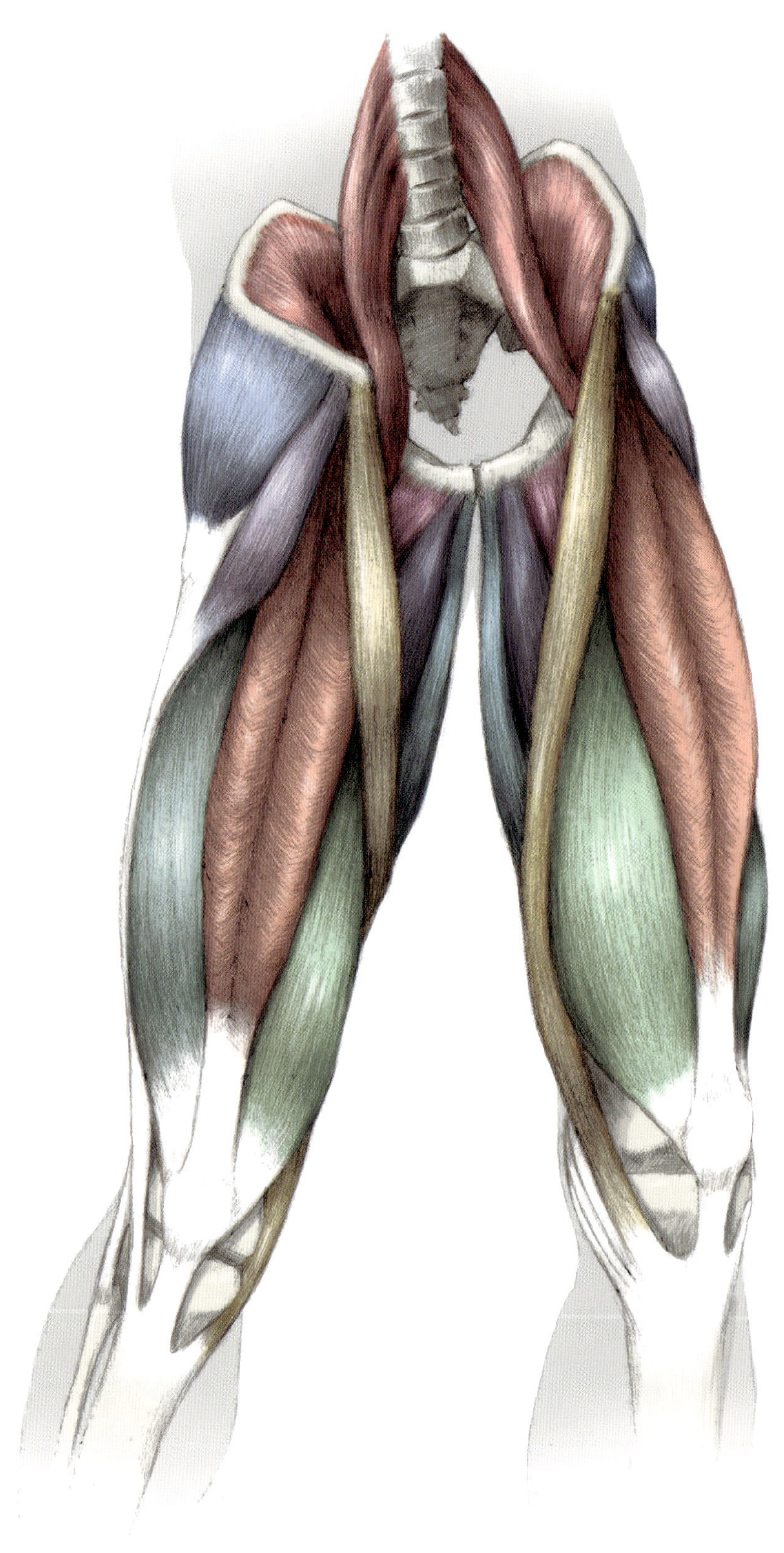

Allie Irwin

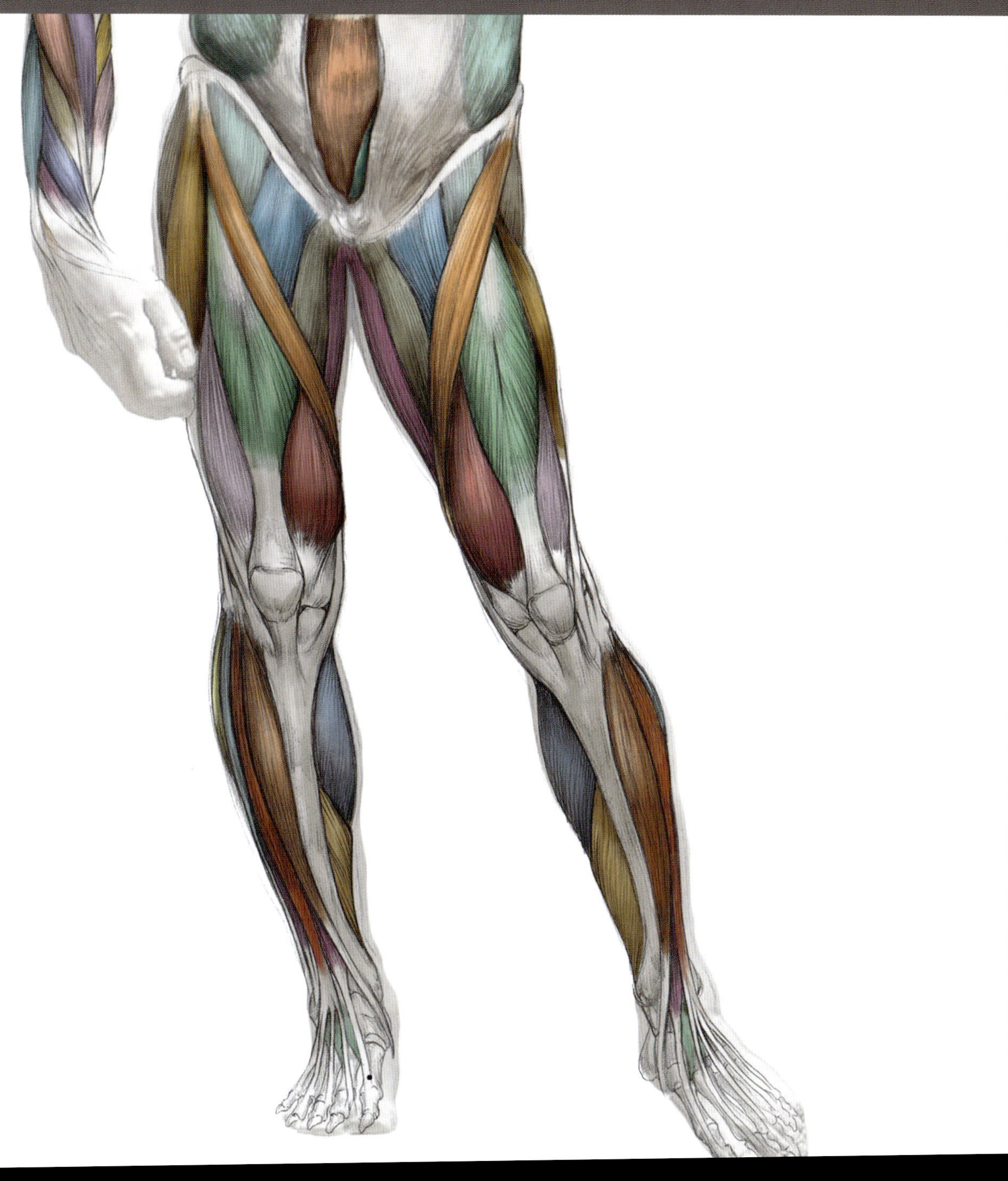

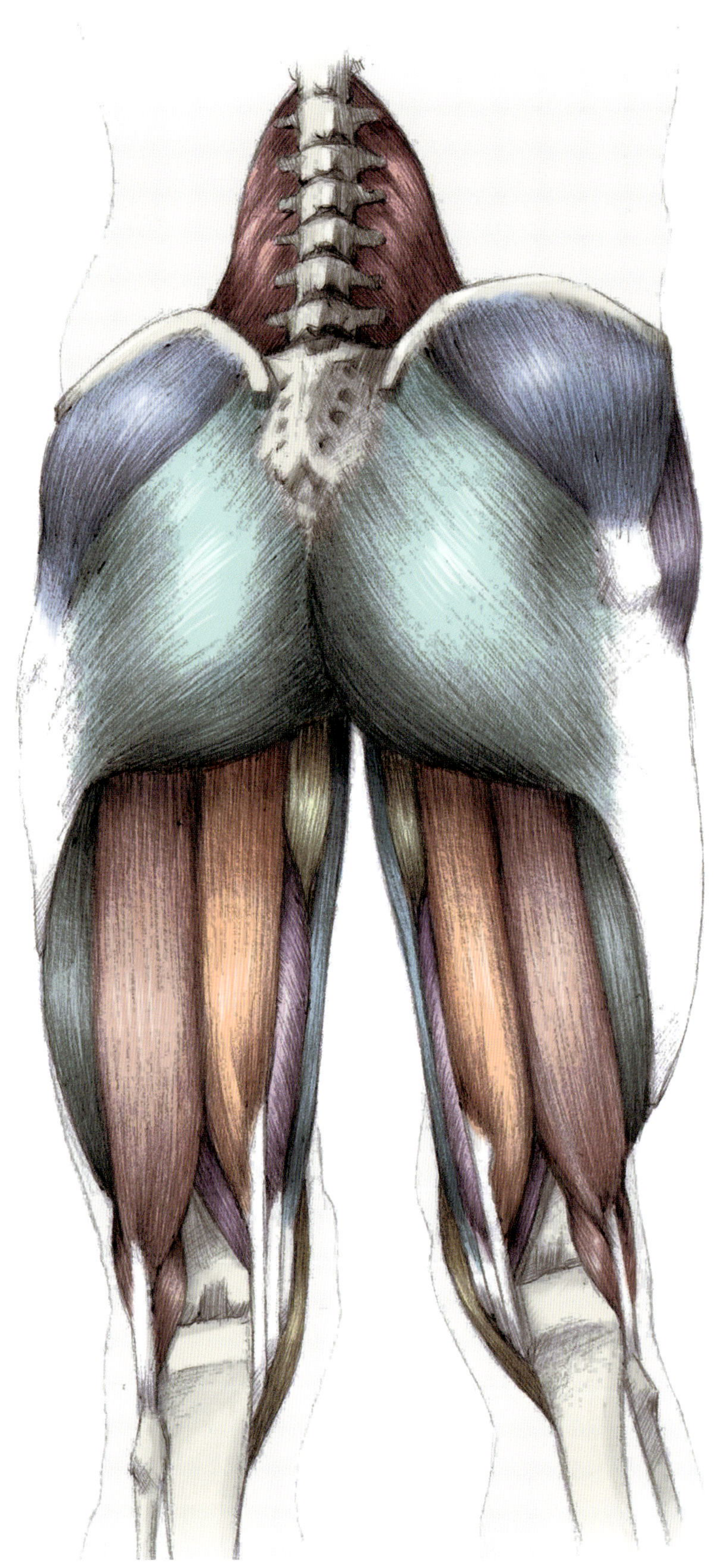

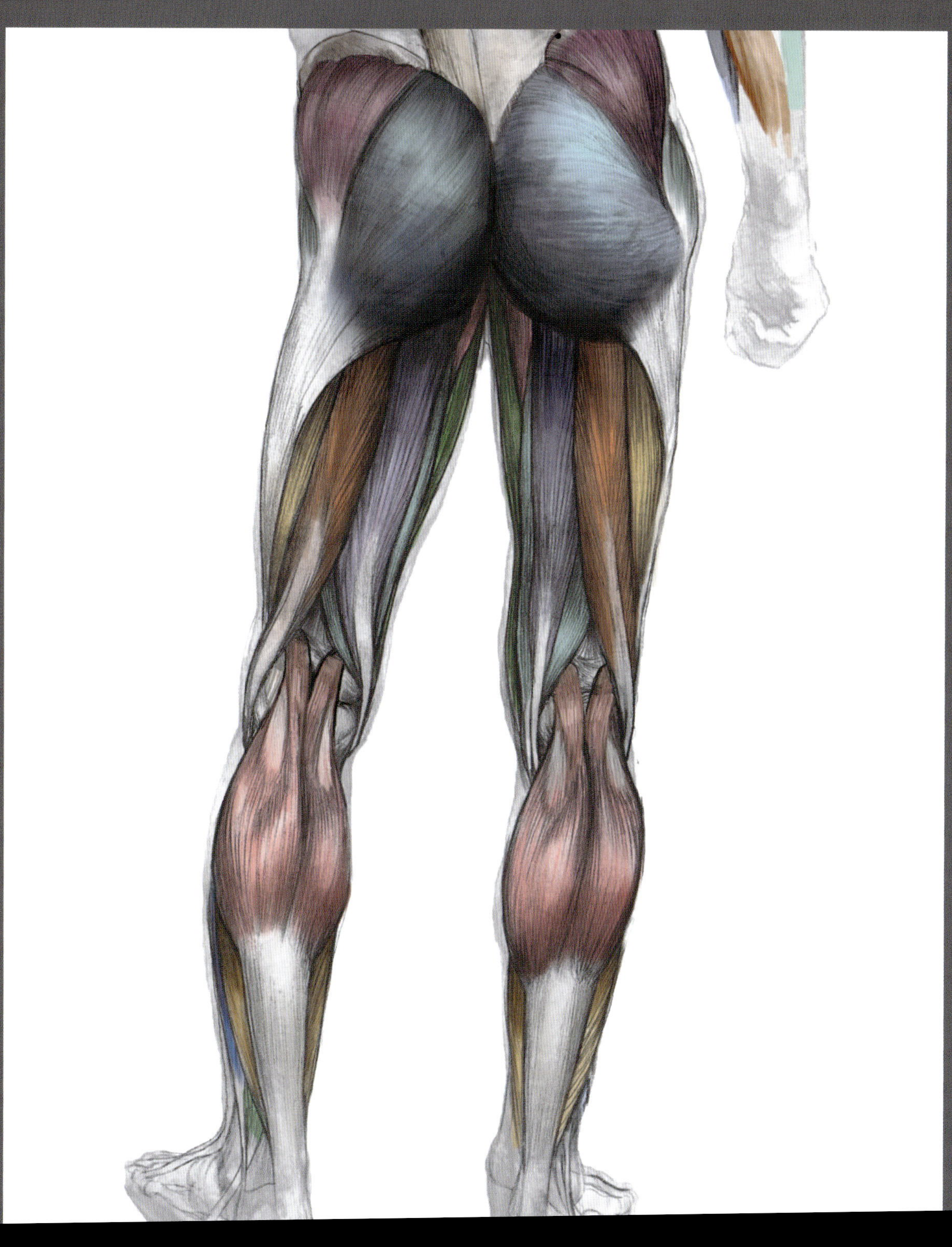

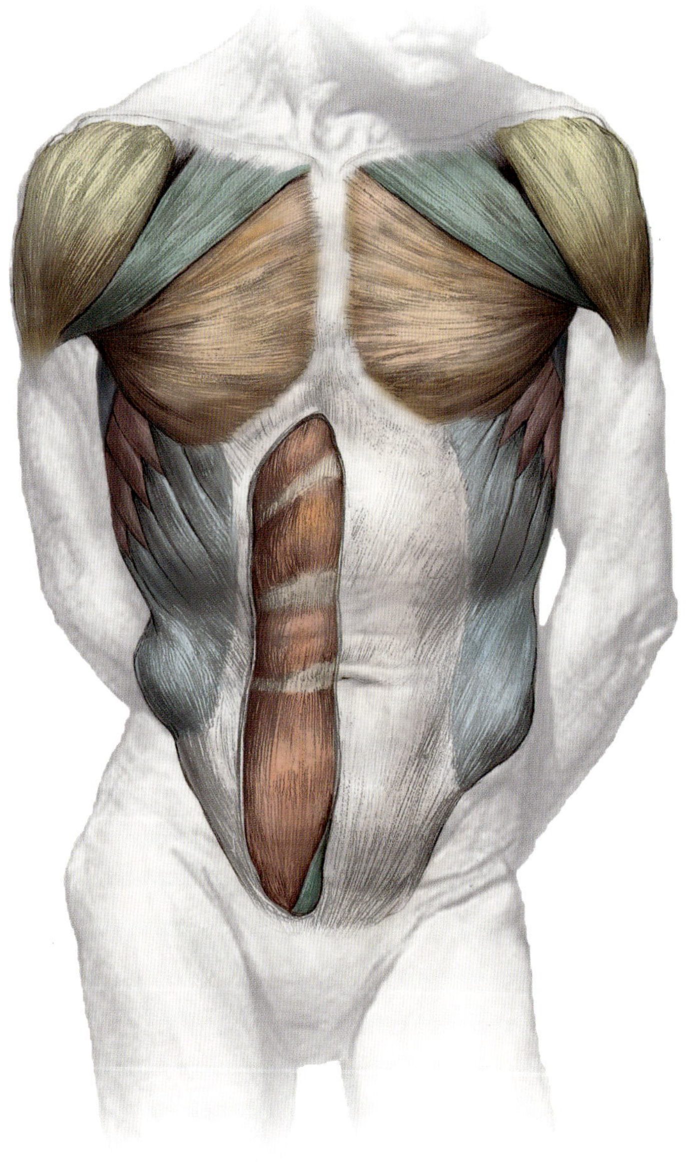

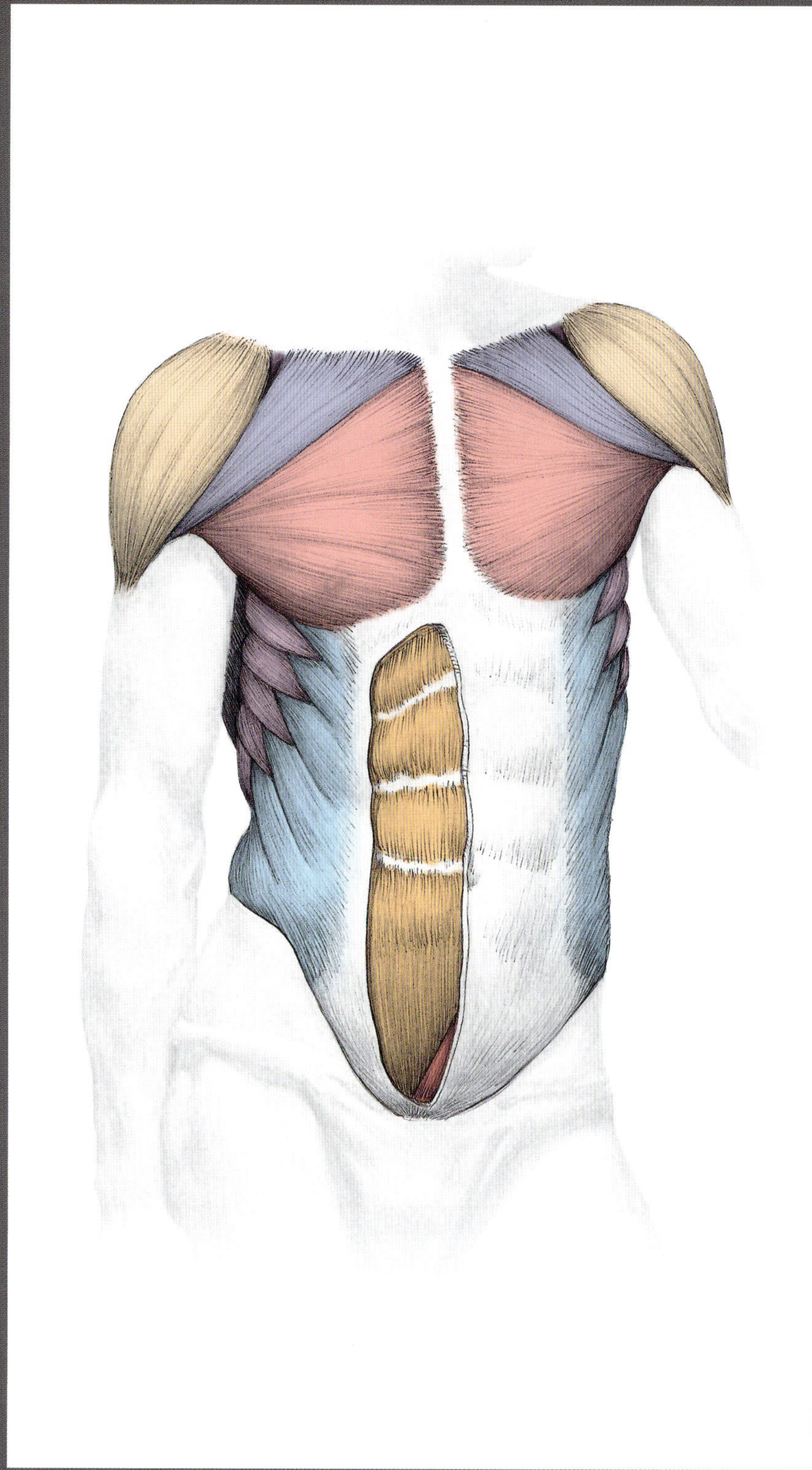

Josh Wong

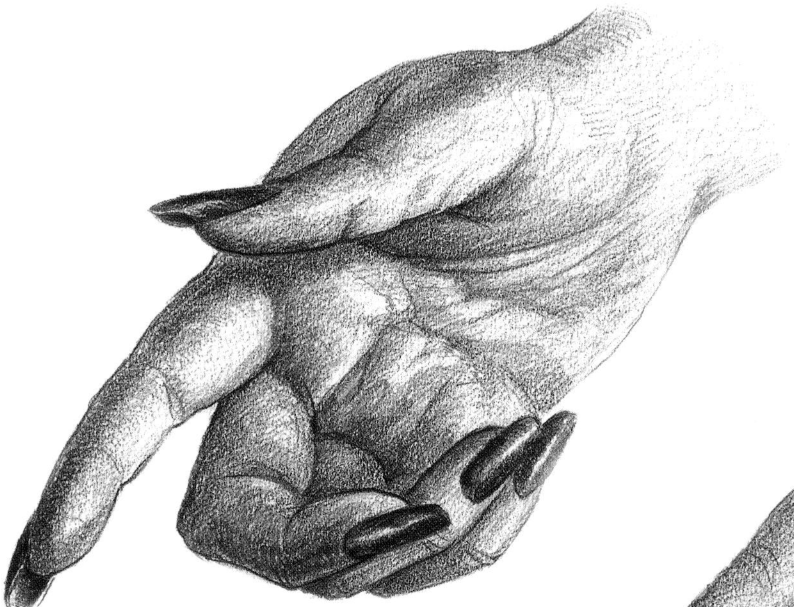

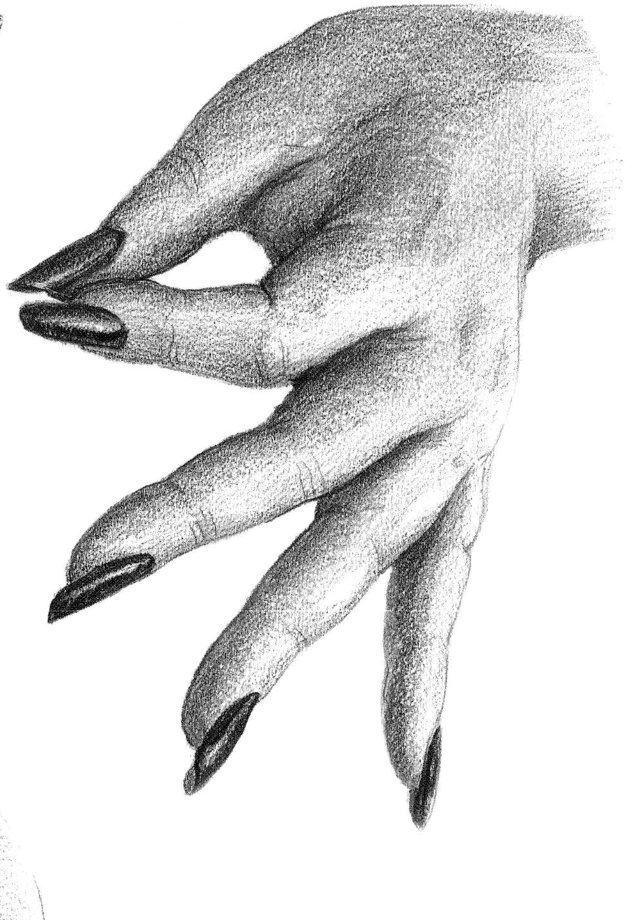

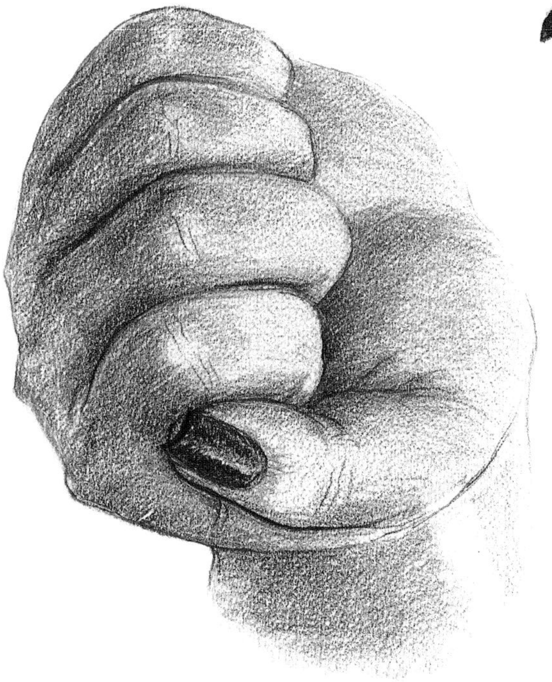

Josh Wong

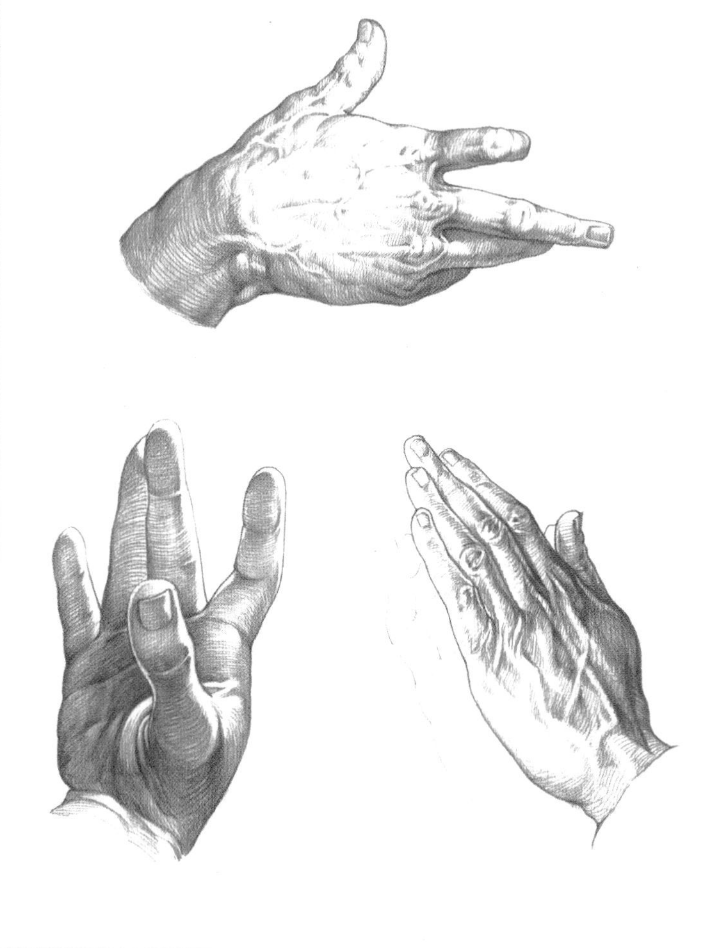

Kendrick Wang

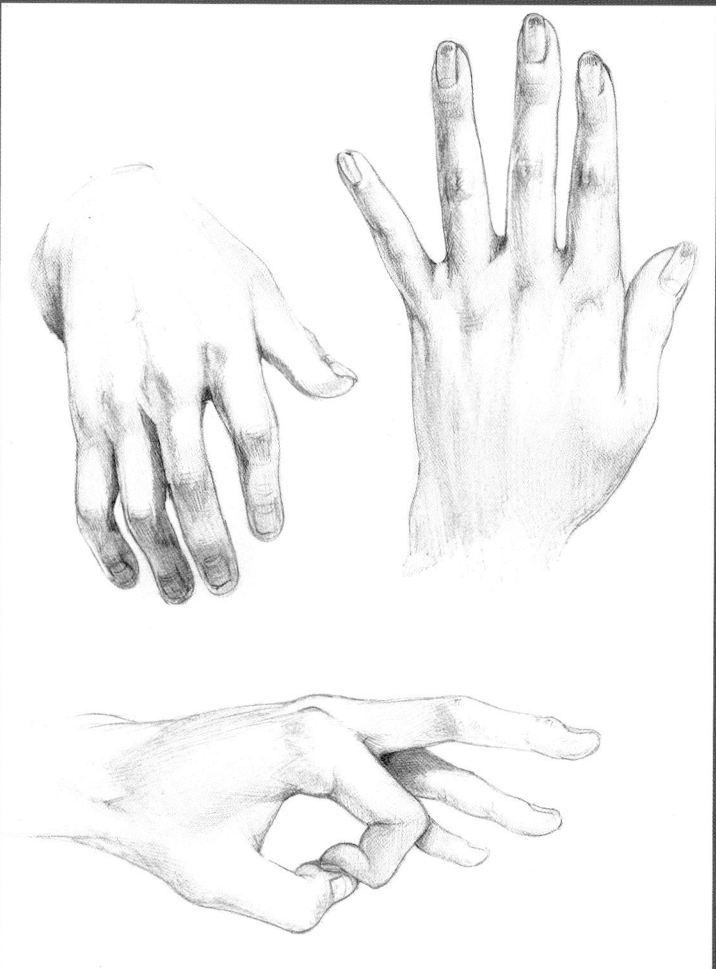

Erin Shin

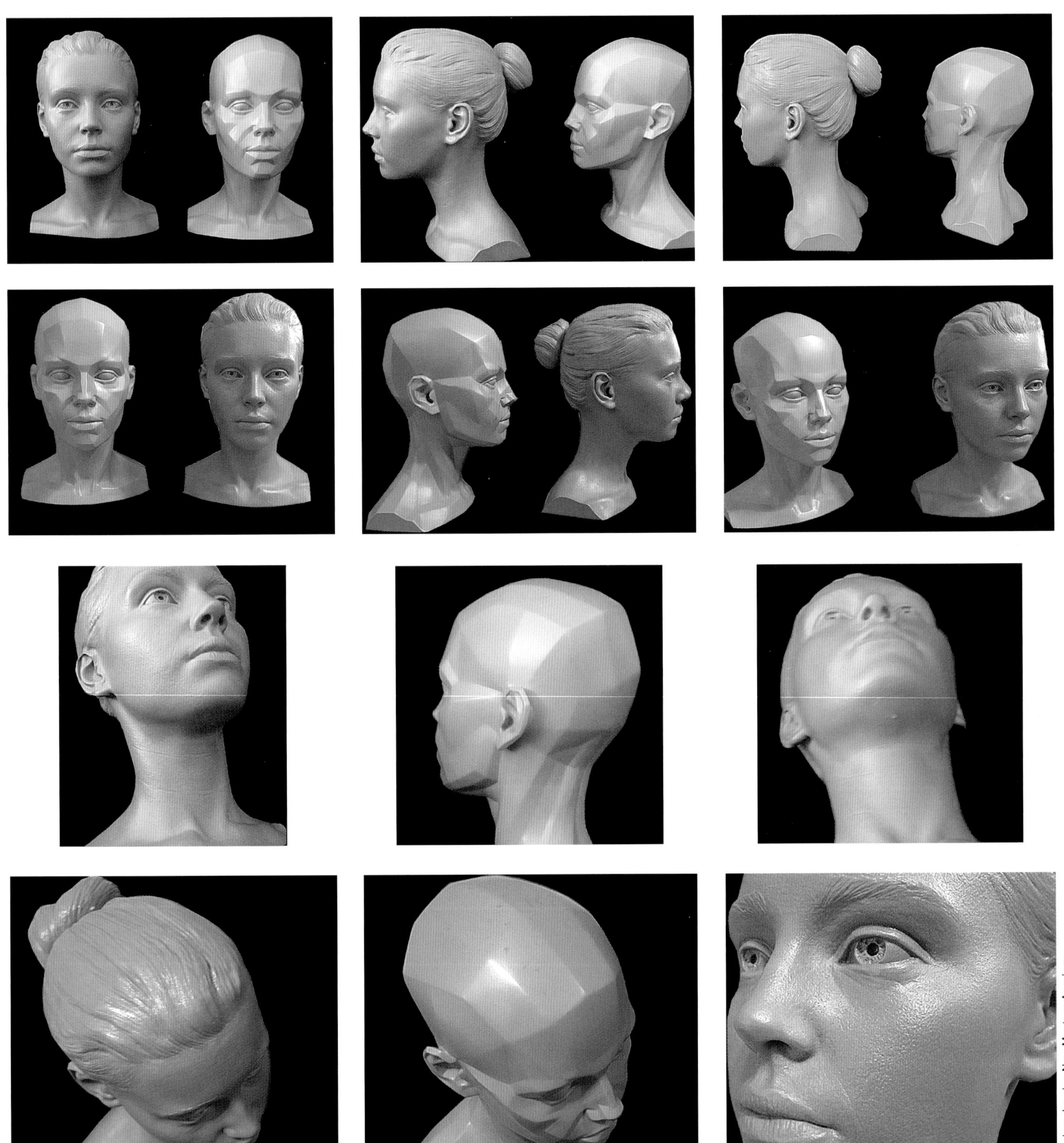

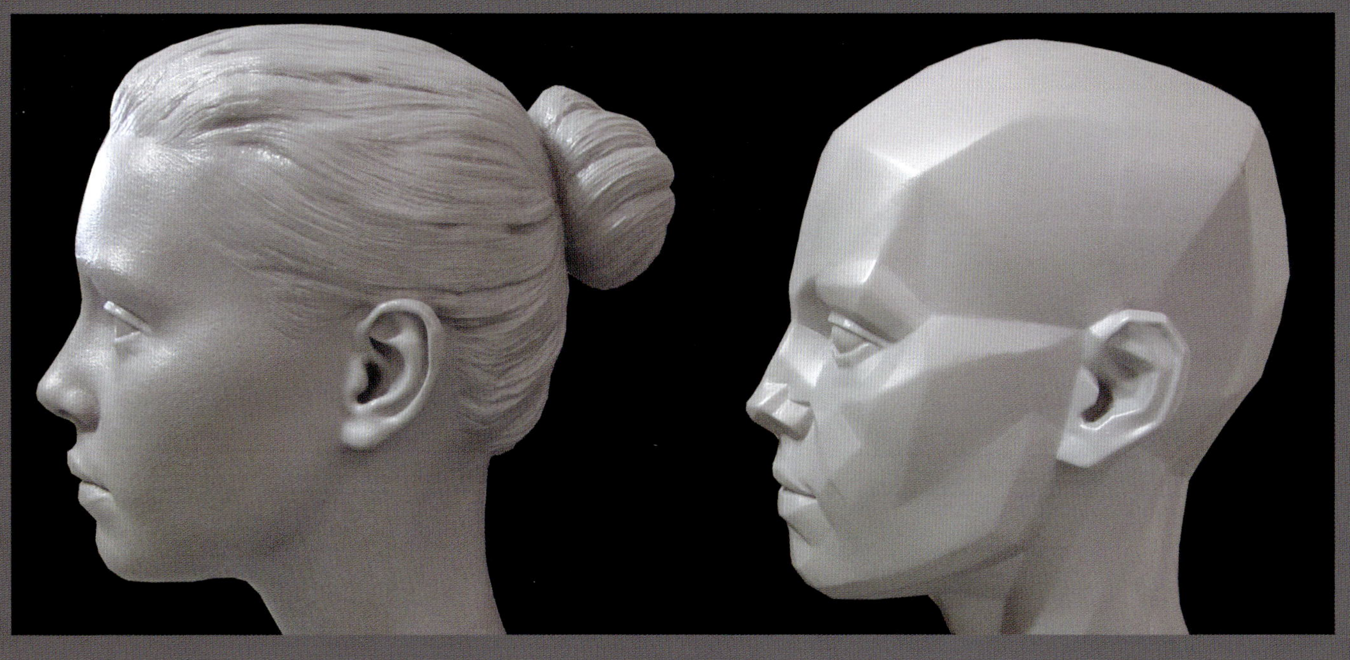

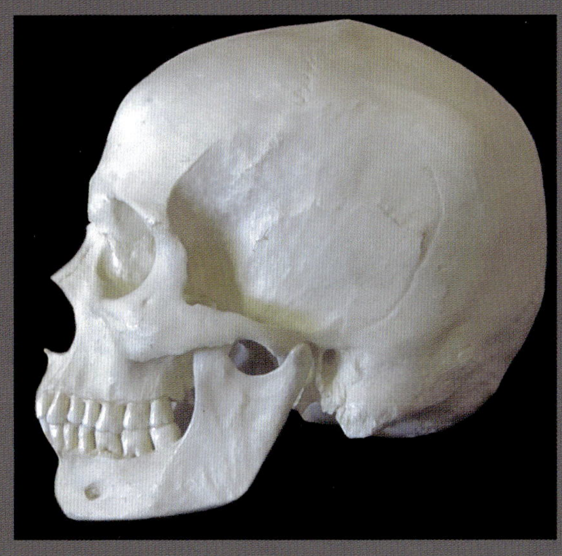

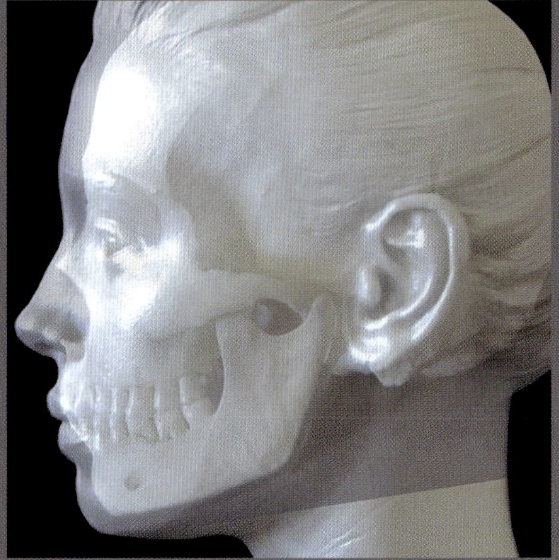

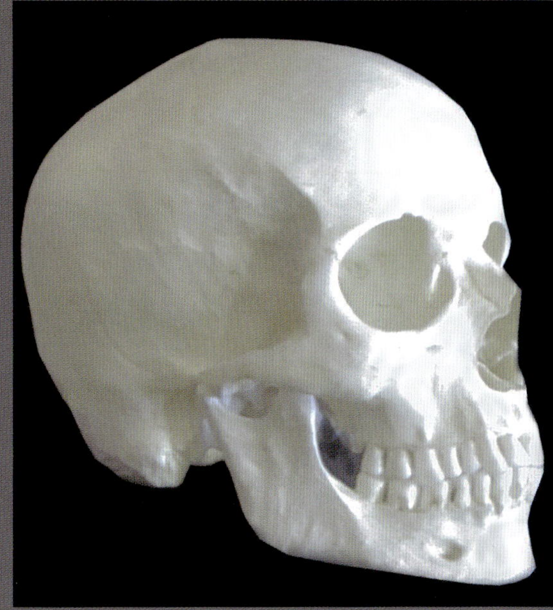

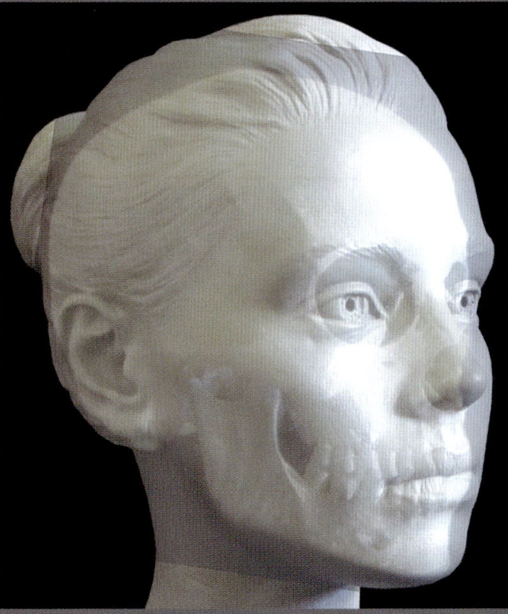

Joshua Jacobo, New Masters Academy

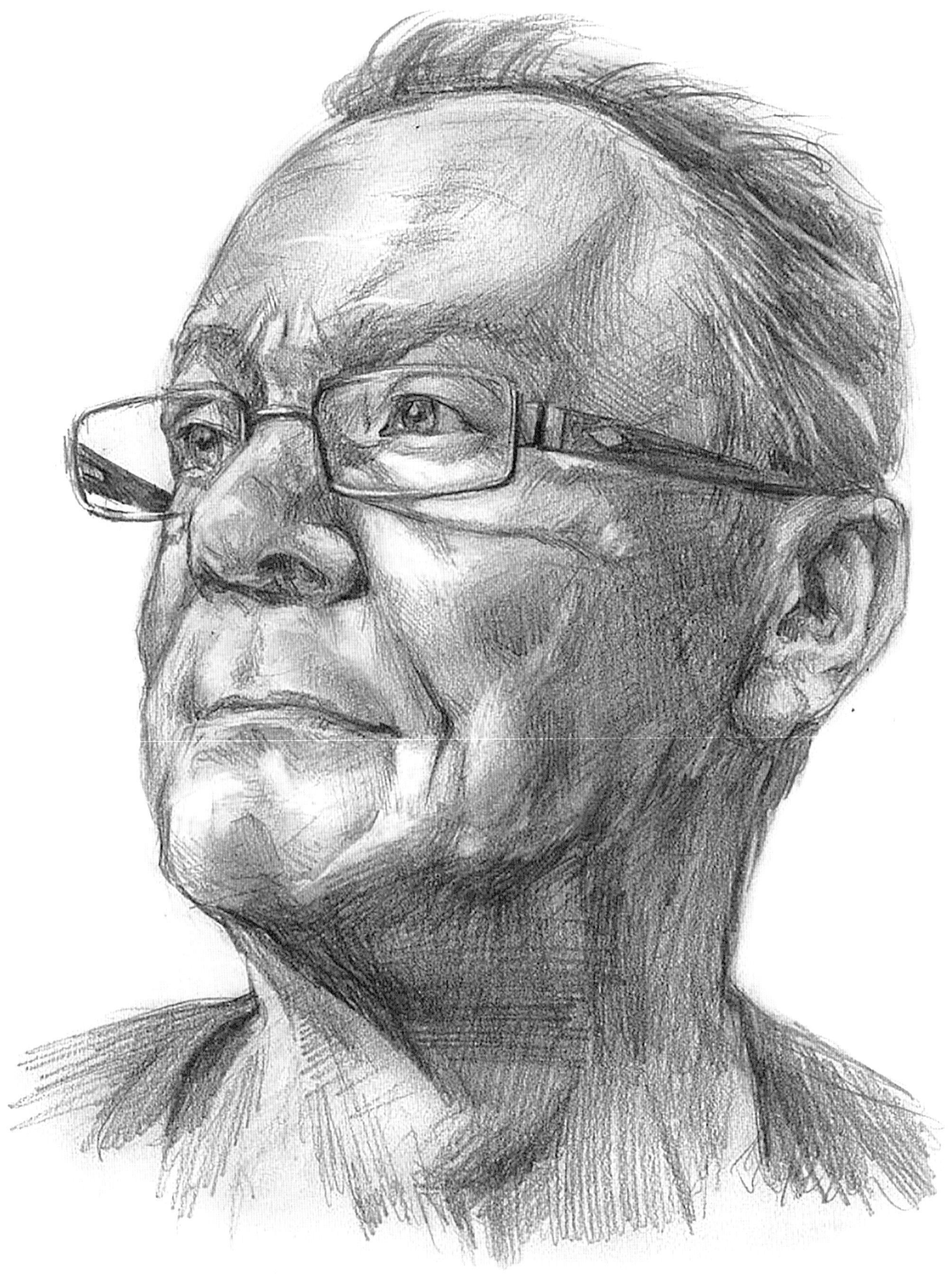

Jenelle Yuan

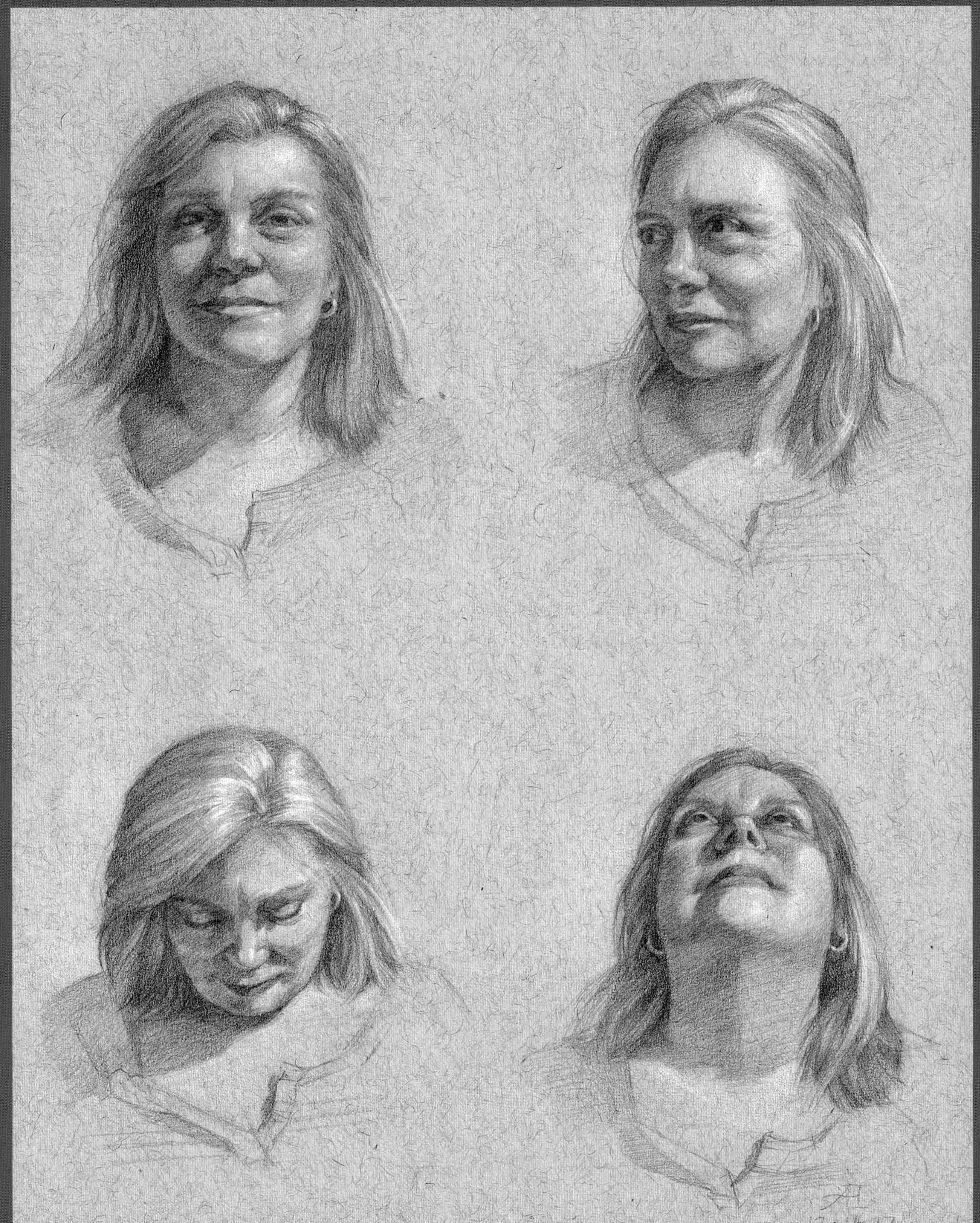

Allie Irwin

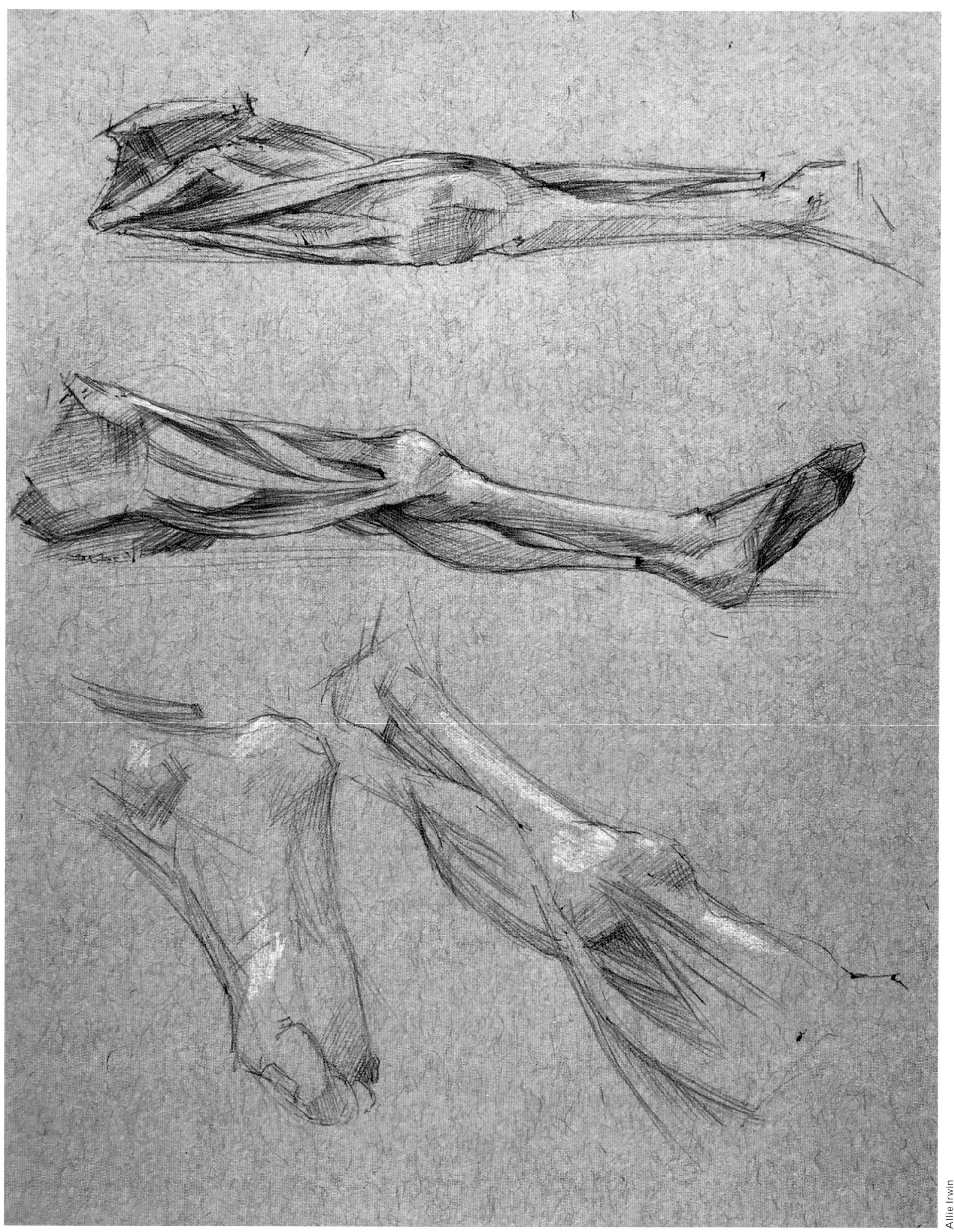

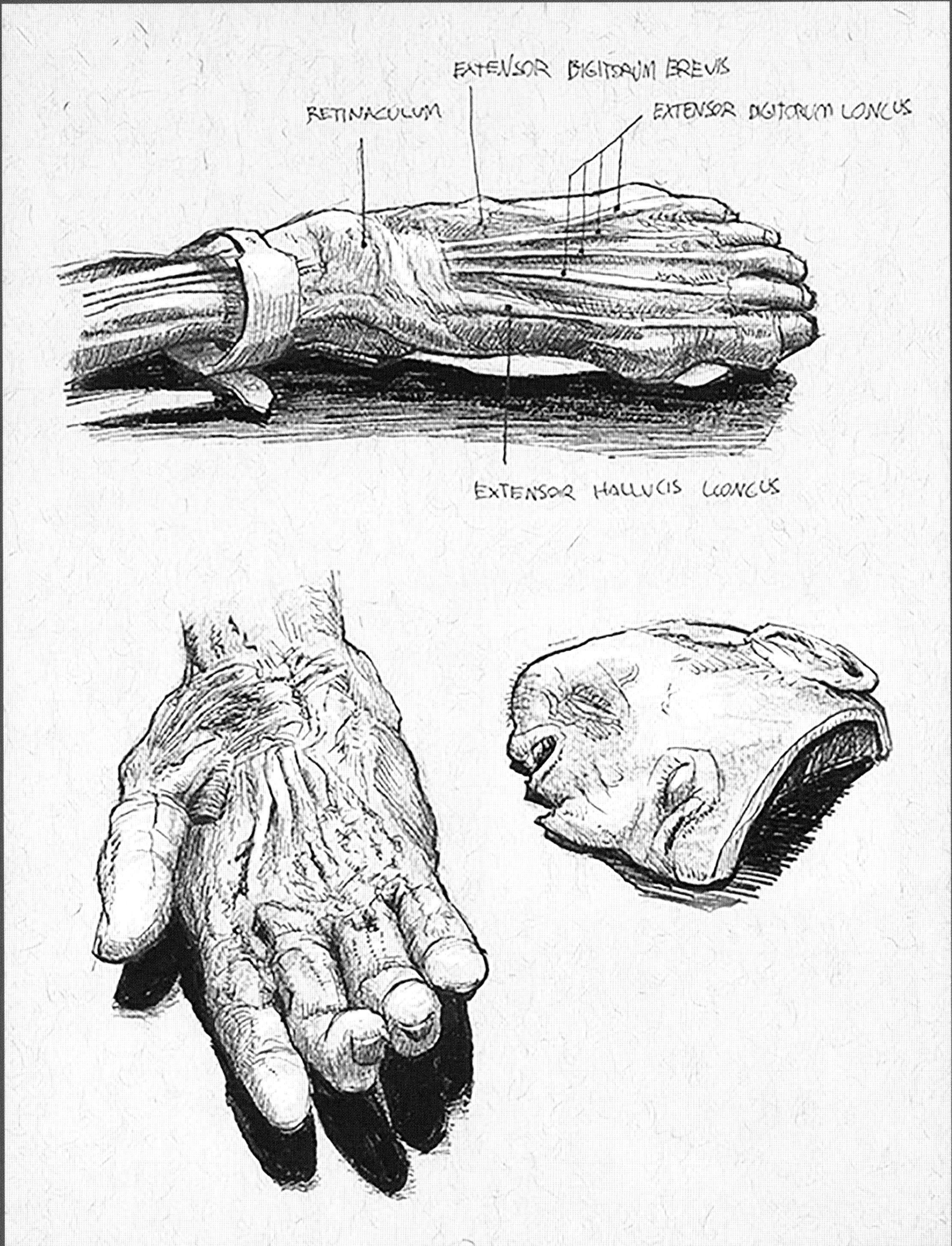

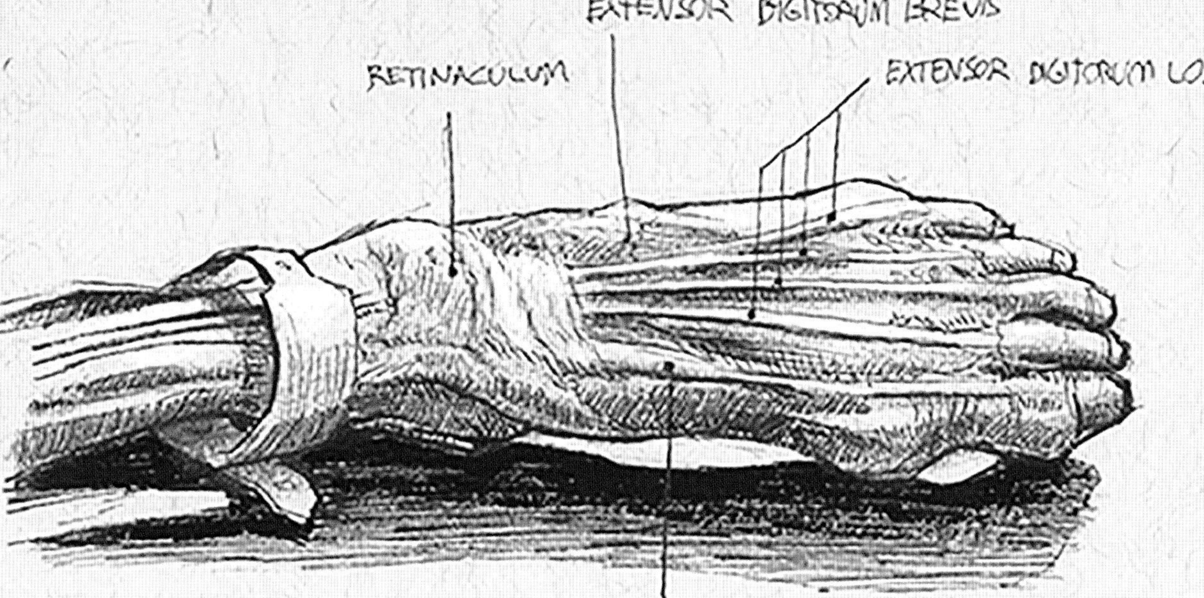

EXTENSOR DIGITORUM BREVIS
RETINACULUM
EXTENSOR DIGITORUM LONGUS
EXTENSOR HALLUCIS LONGUS

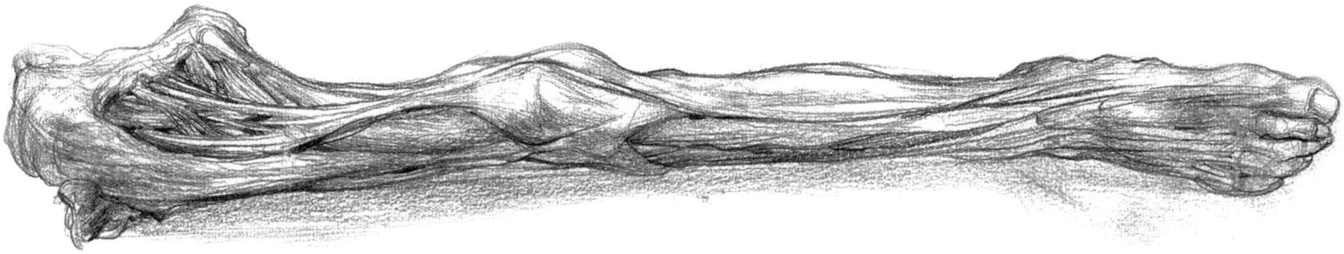

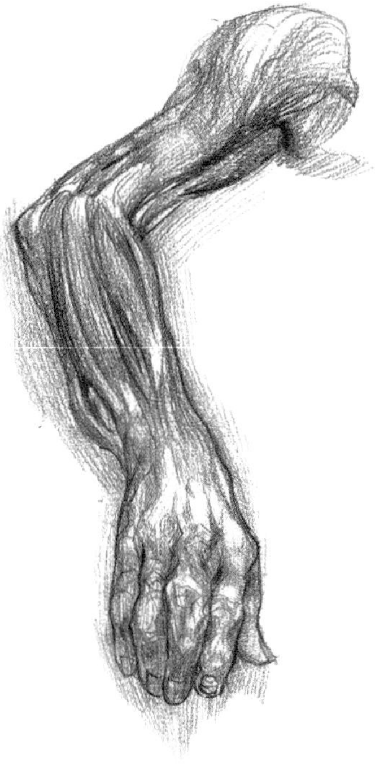

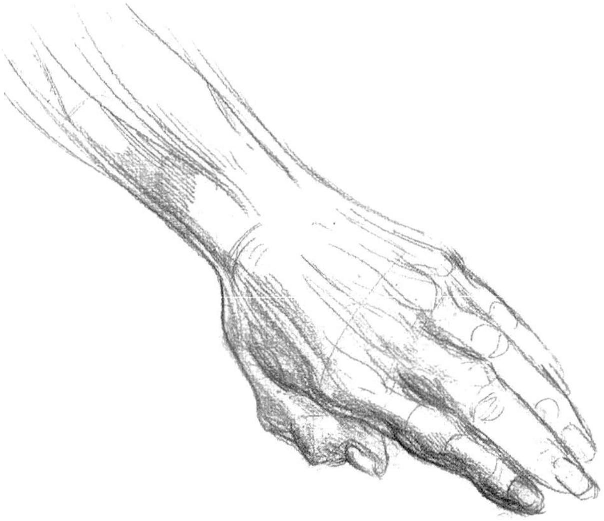

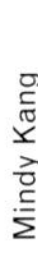

Mindy Kang

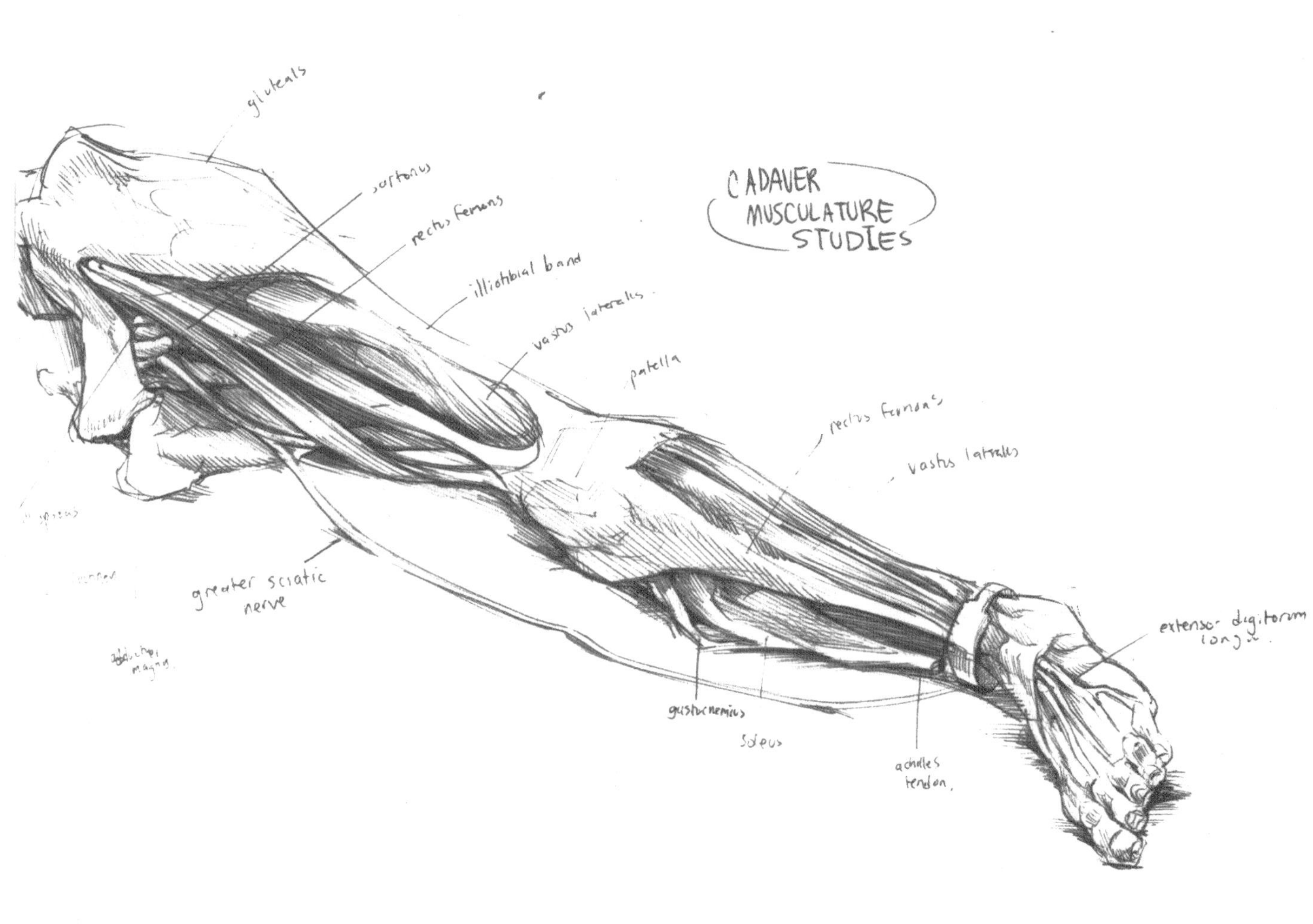

gluteals
sartorius
rectus femoris
illiotibial band
vastus lateralis
patella
CADAVER MUSCULATURE STUDIES
rectus femoris
vastus lateralis
greater sciatic nerve
gastrocnemius
soleus
achilles tendon
extensor digitorum longus
Erin Shin

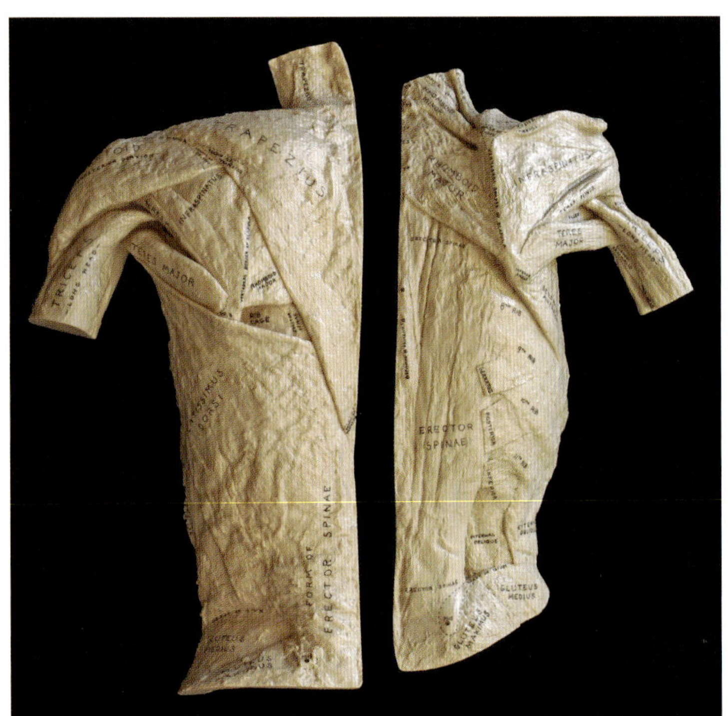

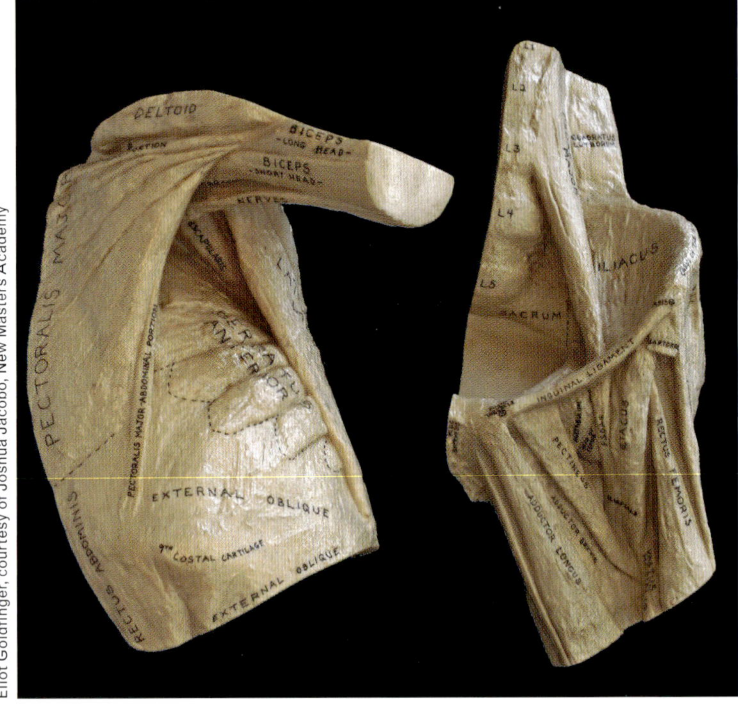

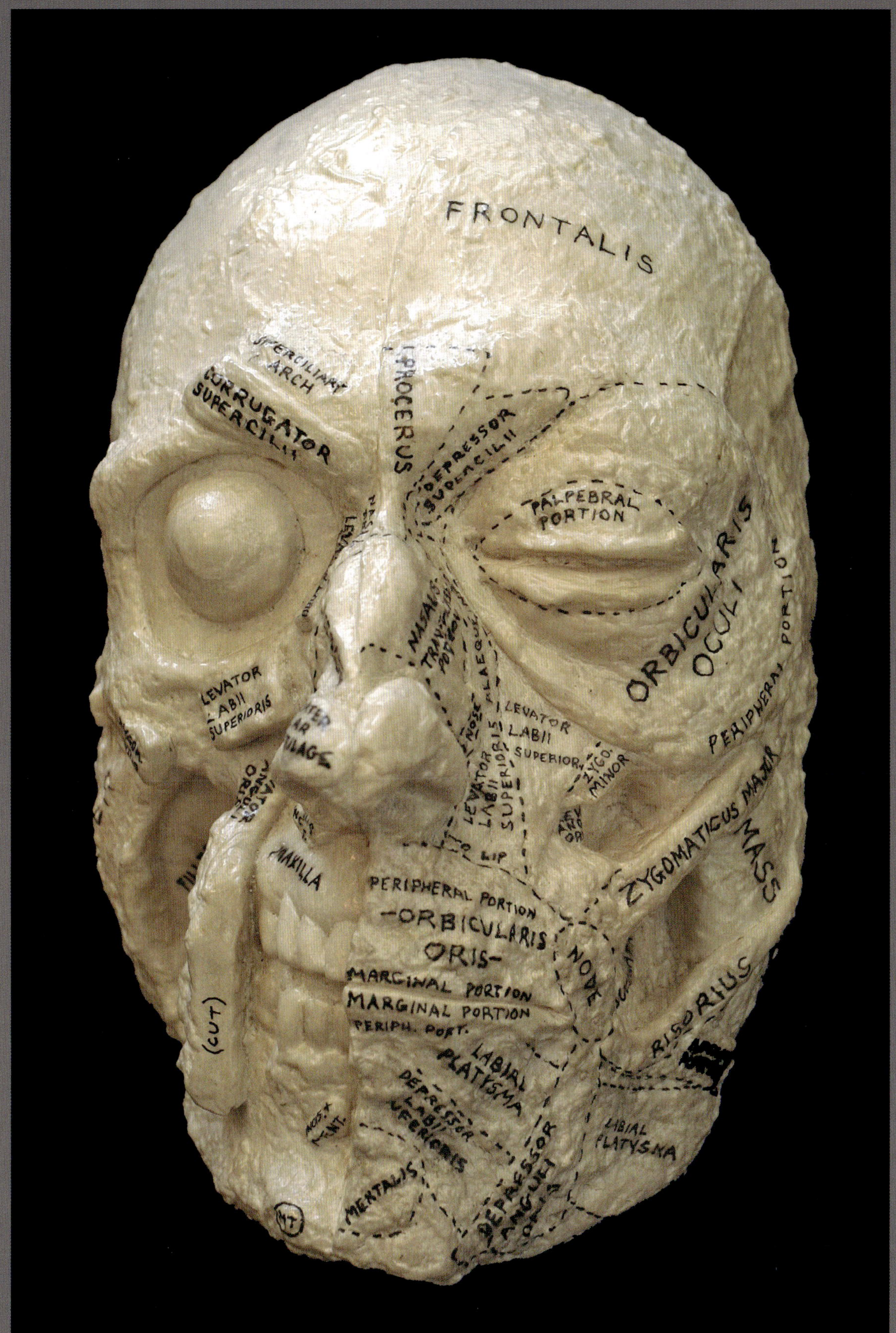

Eliot Goldfinger, courtesy of Joshua Jacobo, New Masters Academy

GLOSSARY

— A —

abduct (ab-**duhkt**) To move away from midline.

abduction (ab-**duhk**-sh*uh*n) The action of moving away from midline.

abductor (ab-**duhk**-ter) A muscle that moves a body part away from midline.

abductor hallucis longus (ab-**duhk**-ter **hæl**-*uh*-sis lon-*guhs*) A muscle that pulls the big toe up toward the head.

abductor pollicis longus (ab-**duhk**-ter p*uh*l-**ee**-sis **lon**-guhs) A forearm muscle that pulls the thumb out to the hitchhike position. This belongs to the "anatomical snuffbox" group, described on page 64.

acetabulum (as-i-**tab**-y*uh*-l*uh*m) The hip socket on the pelvis into which the head of the femur fits.

Achilles tendon (*uh*-**kil**-eez) The large tendon that attaches the calf muscle (gastrocnemius) and soleus to the heel (calcaneus).

acromion process (*uh*-**kroh**-mee-*uh*n) The bony mass at the end of the spine of the scapula. This is where the shoulder muscle, the deltoid, surrounds the spine of the scapula.

adduct (*uh*-**duhkt**) To bring closer to midline.

adduction (*uh*-**duhk**-sh*uh*n) The action of bringing closer to midline.

adductor group (*uh*-**duhk**-ter) The muscles on the inner thigh that bring the legs together. The ones studied in this book are: adductor magnus, adductor longus, pectineus, and gracilis; not included is the adductor brevis.

adductor longus (*uh*-**duhk**-ter **lon**-g*uh*s) A large, flat, triangular muscle that helps bring the thigh closer to the midline of the body, bringing the knees together.

adductor magnus (*uh*-**duhk**-ter **mæg**-n*uh*s) The largest of the adductor group but not easily seen. It is at the inner part of the thigh and under other muscles, making it difficult to point out on a model.

anatomical snuffbox A hollow at the top of the wrist just before the thumb, created by three tendons: abductor pollicis longus, extensor pollicis brevis, and the extensor pollicis longus. Fun fact: this is where, in the distant past, people would place snuff (powdered tobacco) and sniff it.

anconeus (an-**ko**-nee-*uh*s) A triangular muscle close to the elbow that helps in extending the arm.

anterior (an-**teer**-ee-er) Front, or toward the front.

anterior superior iliac spine, or ASIS (an-**teer**-ee-er *suh*-**peer**-ee-er **il**-ee-ak) The pointy and protruding tips of the pelvis at the belt line, at the front ends of the ilia of the pelvis.

axilla (ak-**sil**-*uh*) The armpit, created by the walls of the latissimus dorsi and the pectoralis major.

axis (**ak**-sis) An imaginary centerline running vertically through the body or form.

— B —

belly of muscle The fleshy center part of a muscle made of contractile tissue.

biceps brachii (**bahy**-seps **brey**-kee-ahy) A prominent, two-headed muscle that lies at the front of the arm. It flexes and supinates the arm.

biceps femoris (**bahy**-seps fee-**mohr**-is) A two-headed muscle of the hamstring group or thigh flexors. It helps bend the knee.

bipennate muscle (bahy-**pen**-eyt) A muscle with fiber arrangements that are attached at an angle from two different directions, resembling a feather. *Penna* means feather in Latin.

body types *See ectomorph, endomorph, and mesomorph.*

bone Hard tissue made of collagen and calcium phosphate. There are approximately 206 bones in the human adult. At birth there are about 270 because many of these bones have not yet fused together.

bony landmark Areas on the body where a bone or part of

a bone lies close to the surface of the skin and can be felt or seen.

brachialis (brey-**kee**-æl-is) A flat muscle of the upper arm that creates a bed for the biceps brachii and helps flex the elbow.

brachioradialis (brey-kee-oʊ-rey-dee-**æl**-is) A prominent muscle that starts at the side of the upper arm and spirals toward the thumb. It helps flex the elbow and supinates the forearm.

bridge of the nose The bony ridge of bone that protrudes in some individuals.

brow ridges The two protruding bones over the eyebrows, usually more prominent on men.

— **C** —

calcaneus (kal-**key**-nee-*uh*s) The large heel bone of the tarsal group of the ankle.

canon of the body The mathematical proportional system used to measure the body.

carpal bones (**kahr**-p*uh*l) The eight bones of the wrist. These are: capitate, hamate, lunate, pisiform, scaphoid, trapezium, trapezoid, and the triquetral bone.

carpal tunnel An area at the palmar side of the wrist that has a strong strap, the retinaculum ligament, that creates a passageway for the many flexor tendons of the forearm. This area can become aggravated from misuse and create pain in an individual.

cartilage (**kahr**-tl-ij)

1. Connective tissue found in joints that acts as a shock absorber.

2. Tissue that creates the shapes of the ear and nose.

3. Tissue attached to the ribs that acts like bone, protecting the organs.

cervical vertebrae (**sur**-vi-k*uh*l **vur**-t*uh*-brey) The seven bones of the spine that are located in the neck.

clavicle (**klav**-i-k*uh*l) Either of the two slender bones that form the anterior part of the shoulder, commonly called the collar bones.

coccyx (**kok**-siks) The four small bones and the bottom of the sacrum of the pelvis, forming the lower extremity of the spinal column.

concha (**kong**-k*uh*) The bowl-shaped area of the ear.

connective tissue Tissue that holds, supports, or connects various structures of the body. Connective tissue includes bone, cartilage, ligaments, tendons, aponeuroses, fascia, and subcutaneous fat.

contraction The shortening of muscle fibers creating movement in the skeletal system.

— **D** —

deltoid (**del**-toid) A large triangular muscle covering the shoulder joint, used for raising the arm away from the body. This muscle is broken up into three parts: the rear or scapular portion, the front or clavicular section, and the center or acromial portion.

digastric muscles (dahy-**gas**-trik) A muscle of the lower jaw, which assists in lowering the jaw.

digit (**dij**-it) A finger or toe.

distal (**dis**-tl) Situated away from the point of origin or attachment of a limb or bone.

dorsal (**dawr**-s*uh*l) Situated on or near the back. It is also used to describe the top of the foot.

dorsiflexion (dawr-s*uh*-**flek**-sh*uh*n) The foot flexed at the ankle up toward the head.

— **E** —

ectomorph (**ek**-t*uh*-mawrf) A person who has a thin body type with noticeable skeletal protrusions.

endomorph (**en**-d*uh*-mawrf) A person with a heavy body build, ranging from stout to obese.

epicanthus (ep-i-**kan**-th*uh*s) A fold of skin that covers the inner corner of the eye.

epicondyle (ep-i-**kon**-dahyl) A rounded protuberance at the end of a bone, where tendons, ligaments, and muscles attach.

eversion (ih-vur-zh*uh*n) The action of turning the foot outward.

extend To straighten an area like the torso, limb, finger, or toe from a bent or flexed position.

extensor (ik-**sten**-ser) A muscle that serves to straighten a part of the body.

extensor carpi radialis brevis (ik-**sten**-ser **kahr**-pahy rey-dee-æl-is **brev**-is) A muscle in the forearm that serves to extend and bend the wrist.

extensor carpi radialis longus (ik-**sten**-ser **kahr**-pahy rey-**dee**-æl-is **lon**-g*uh*s) One of the five main muscles that moves the wrist.

extensor hallucis longus tendon (ik-**sten**-ser **hæl**-*uh*-sis **lon**-g*uh*s) The prominent tendon that pulls up on the big toe. *Hallux* is Latin for "big toe."

— F —

facet (**fas**-it) The flat area of a bone, or a visualization of an area as flat areas or planes, to show the major changes of form.

fascia (**fash**-ee-*uh*) Thin, fibrous, connective tissue that surrounds muscles and muscle groups.

femur (**fee**-mer) A bone extending from pelvis to knee; the thighbone. The longest bone of the human body, it is the major bone in determining a person's height. The forensic formula is length of the femur in inches, multiplied by 2.5, plus 23 inches.

fibula (**fib**-yuh-l*uh*) The outer and thinner of the two bones of the leg, extending from knee to ankle. The tibia being the larger bone.

flexion (**flek**-sh*uh*n) The action of bending a limb. The position of a limb while bent.

flexor carpi radialis (**flek**-ser **kahr**-pahy rey-dee-**æl**-is) One of the muscles on the anterior side of the forearm that serves to bend and straighten the hand.

foramen (fu*h*-**rey**-m*uh*n) An opening, or short passage, in a bone; (plural, foramina).

fossa (**fos**-*uh*) A shallow depression on a bone, but it can also be on the body's surface.

frontalis (fruhn-**tey**-lis) The muscle on the forehead.

— G —

gastrocnemius (gas-truh-**nee**-mee-*uh*s) The calf muscle.

glabella (gluh-**bel**-uh) The small, flat area of bone between the eyebrows. Sometimes referred to as the keystone.

glenoid fossa (**glee**-noid **fos**-*uh*) The shallow socket on the scapula where the head of the humerus attaches.

gluteal cleft (**gloo**-tee-*uh*l) The vertical division between the two gluteus maximus muscles.

gluteal fold The prominent horizontal fold at the bottom of the gluteus maximus.

gluteal muscles There are three major muscles that make up this group: the gluteus medius, gluteus maximus, and the tensor fasciae latae.

gluteus maximus (**gloo**-tee-*uh*s **mak**-suh-m*uh*s) The very large muscle of the gluteal group that extends the thigh backward and helps maintain an upright posture.

gluteus medius (**gloo**-tee-*uh*s **mee**-dee-*uh*s) Large abductor on the side of the gluteal group.

gracilis (**gras**-*uh*-lis) Long, belt-like muscle of the inner thigh that helps pull the leg inward and bend the knee.

great trochanter, or **greater trochanter** (troh-**kan**-ter) The large, prominent, and protruding process of the upper femur.

— H —

hallux (**hal**-*uh*ks) Big toe

hamstring group Also called the thigh flexors, these are the muscles of the back of the thigh that bend the knee joint.

head of the femur (**fee**-mer) The round ball that fits into the acetabulum (the hip socket).

head of the fibula (**fib**-yuh-l*uh*) The expanded part of the top of the fibula.

head of the humerus (**hyoo**-mer-*uh*s) The ball of the upper part of the arm bone that articulates with the glenoid fossa of the scapula.

humerus (**hyoo**-mer-*uh*s) The upper arm bone, extending from shoulder to elbow.

hyoid bone (**hahy**-oid) The U-shaped bone that is just above the Adam's apple, under the jaw.

— I —

iliac crest (**il**-ee-ak) The top curved edge of the pelvis.

iliotibial band (**il**-ee-oh-**tib**-ee-*uh*l) A strong, flat, fascia strap that attaches from the gluteal muscles all the way up to the ilium and down to the upper, lateral area of the tibia. Also called the **IT band.**

ilium (**il**-ee-*uh*m) The widest of the three bones that form the pelvis, located in the upper portion.

inferior Below; closer to foot.

infraclavicular fossa (in-fr*uh*-klav-**i**-kyoo-ler **fos**-*uh*) Literally means "shallow depression below the clavicle." This is a small dip or depression under the clavicle and in between the deltoid and the clavicular portion of the pectoralis major.

infraspinatus (in-fr*uh*-spahy-**ney**-t*uh*s) The large muscle on the shoulder blade attached under the spine of the scapula. Hence its name, which means "under the spine."

inguinal ligament (**ing**-gw*uh*-nl) The strappy, fibrous band that spans from the anterior superior iliac spine (ASIS) to the pubic bone.

insertion of a muscle The attachment of a muscle at the end where it moves.

inversion (in-**vur**-zh*uh*n) The movement of the foot turning inward, medially.

iris (**ahy**-ris) The colored portion of the eye with the pupil at its center.

ischial tuberosity (**is**-kee-*uh*l too-buh-ros-i-tee) The lower protuberance of the ischium, sometimes referred to as the "sit bone." The hamstring muscles attach here.

ischium (**is**-kee-*uh*m) The lower portion, or loops, of the pelvis.

— J —

joint The connection point of two bones, where they meet.

— L —

lacrimal caruncle (**lak**-ruh-m*uh*l **kar**-uhng-k*uh*l) The pinkish, fleshy tear duct on the inner corner of the eye.

lateral malleolus (muh-**lee**-uh-l*uh*s) The outside ankle, the distal or bottom end of the fibula.

latissimus dorsi (l*uh*-**tis**-*uh*-m*uh*s **dawr**-sahy) A broad, triangular muscle on each side of the midback that helps in extending the arm and medial rotation.

leg In anatomy, this is the area between the knee and the ankle, including the shin and calves.

lesser trochanter (troh-**kan**-ter) The small, protruding bone on the inside of the femur, at the top.

ligament (**lig**-*uh*-m*uh*nt) A band of tissue that connects bone to bone. (Tendons attach muscles to bone).

linea alba (**lin**-ee-ah **ahl**-b*uh*) The white, fibrous structure that runs down the centerline of the front torso from the bottom of the sternum to the pubic bone.

linea aspera (**lin**-ee-ah **as**-per-*uh*) The prominent, longitudinal ridge on the back of the femur.

lumbar vertebrae (**luhm**-bahr **vur**-t*uh*-brey) The five spinal bones of the lower back between the thorax and the pelvis.

— M —

mandible (**man**-duh-b*uh*l) The bone of the lower jaw.

manubrium (muh-**noo**-bree-*uh*m) The upper part of the sternum.

masseter (ma-**see**-ter) The prominent chewing muscle on the side of the jaw.

mastoid process (**mas**-toid) The prominent bony protrusion behind the ear at the base of the skull.

medial (**mee**-dee-*uh*l) Closer to midline.

medial line The imaginary, vertical centerline of the body of limbs.

medial malleolus (m*uh*-**lee**-uh-l*uh*s) The bump on the inside ankle; the lower inside end of the tibia.

meniscus (mi-**nis**-k*uh*s) A crescent-shaped cartilage pad in between the tibia and femur; (*plural*, menisci).

mentalis (men-**tay**-lis) A small muscle at the tip of the chin that allows the lips to pout and raises the chin. When engaged, it may have many little dimples, as when biting a lemon.

mental protuberance The chin area of the mandible. Humans are the only primates that have this; therefore, humans are the only primates with a chin.

mesomorph (**mez**-*uh*-mawrf) One of the three body types characterized by a naturally muscular, sturdy build.

metacarpal bones (met-uh-**kahr**-p*uh*l) The bones of the hand between the wrist and the fingers. *Meta* means beyond, and *carpus* means wrist; therefore, this literally means "beyond the wrist" bones.

metacarpophalangeal joints (met-*uh*-**kahr**-poh-f*uh*-**lan**-jee-*uhl*) Literally, this means the joint between the body of the hand and the fingers; the knuckles.

metatarsal bones (met-*uh*-**tahr**-s*uh*l) The bones of the top of the foot, between the ankle and toes.

multipennate muscle (**muhl**-tee-**pen**-eyt) A muscle with multiple tendon branches, with muscle fibers attached along both sides of each tendon, resembling a feather. The side of the deltoid has this very clearly visible on a cadaver.

muscle (muhs-*uh*l) Soft tissue made up of contractile cells.

— N —

nasal bones The bones on the face that form the bridge of the nose.

nasolabial fold (**ney**-zoh-**ley**-bee-*uh*l) A crease that runs from the nostril wings to the lateral edges of the mouth. Naso means nose, and labial means related to or near the lips.

navel (**ney**-v*uh*l) Belly button. Also called the umbilicus.

nose The external bony and cartilaginous structure over the nasal cavity.

nostrils The two small openings formed by the cartilage of the wings of the nose.

nuchal ligament (**nu**-k*uh*l) This is the strong ligament that attaches at the base of the skull and down along the spinous processes of the cervical vertebrae of the neck. You can feel this by placing your finger on the back of your neck, and then dropping your head down to your chest. The nuchal ligament will be felt very easily as if it were a cable stretching down the center of the back of the neck.

— O —

oblique (oh-**bleek**) In anatomy this means at a slant or diagonal.

occipital bone (ok-**sip**-i-tl) The bone at the back of the skull.

olecranon (oh-**lek**-r*uh*-non) The proximal, prominent bump on the ulna, at the elbow.

orbicularis oris (or-**bik**-y*uh*-ler-is **awr**-is) The large, flat muscle that surrounds the mouth.

— P —

palm The anterior surface of the hand.

palmaris longus (pahl-**mar**-is **lon**-g*uh*s) One of the flexor muscles of the forearm that originates at the medial epicondyle (funny bone) and extends to the palm.

parotid gland (p*uh*-**rot**-id) The largest of the salivary glands, and because it sits on top of the masseter (chewing muscle) by the ear, it softens the jaw line by the earlobe.

patella (p*uh*-**tel**-*uh*) The kneecap; the largest of the sesamoid bones.

patellar ligament (p*uh*-**tel**-*uh*r) The prominent ligament that connects the patella to the tibial tuberosity.

pectineus (pek-**tin**-ee-*uh*s) The relatively rectangular adductor muscle of the inner thigh.

pectoralis major (pek-t*uh*-**ral**-is **mey**-jer) The large muscle on either side of the chest that assists in drawing the shoulder forward and rotating the arm inward. In this book it is divided into two parts: the pectoralis major sternal head and the clavicular head.

pelvic brim (**pel**-vik) The large opening in the pelvis basin.

pelvis (**pel**-vis) The main bony structure of the lower torso. Latin for "basin."

pennate muscle (**pen**-eyt) A muscle arrangement that

has muscle fibers coming at an oblique or slanted angle. *Penna* means "feather" in Latin. *See also bipennate and multipennate muscles.*

peroneus brevis (per-*uh*-**nee**-*uh*s **brev**-is) The muscle on the outer leg, by the ankle, which assists in extending the foot and turning it outward. The tendon is very prominent as it uses the lateral malleolus of the fibula as a pulley and then inserts at the tuberosity of the fifth metatarsal on the side of the foot.

peroneus longus (per-*uh*-**nee**-*uh*s **lon**-g*uh*s) This muscle partners with the peroneus brevis on the fibular side of the leg to help flex the foot and move it outward.

pes anserinus (**pes eyn**-*suh*-**rahy**-n*uh*s) The tendinous bundle that creates a large mound on the inside of the knee. Latin for "goose foot."

phalanx (**fey**-langks) The fingers and toes. It means "a row of soldiers" in Greek; *plural*, phalanges (fuh-**lan**-jeez).

philtrum (**fil**-tr*uh*m) The vertical depression or trough above the upper lip, just below the septum of the nose.

pit of the neck This is the hollow created between the proximal ends of the clavicles and above the sternum. It is also called the suprasternal notch, meaning the notch above the sternum.

plantar flexion (**plan**-ter **flek**-sh*uh*n) An action at the ankle joint, moving the foot up toward the head.

posterior (po-**steer**-ee-er) On the back of the body, or the back surface of body part.

posterior superior iliac spine, or **PSIS** (po-**steer**-ee-er s*uh*-peer-ee-er **il**-ee-ak) The protruding bony bumps on the back of the pelvis that create the two dimples on the rear of the lower torso.

process (**pros**-es) A bony projection on a bone that can often be seen or felt.

pronate (**proh**-neyt)

1. To rotate the hand with the palm down or toward the back.

2. To rotate the foot inward so that the inner edge of the foot bears the weight when standing.

pronator teres (**proh**-ney-ter **ter**-eez) This muscle is on the flexor area of the forearm and originates at the medial epicondyle (funny bone) in the same area as the major flexors of the arm. It is obliquely placed and pronates the arm as it inserts onto the lateral aspect of the ulna.

protuberance (proh-**too**-ber-*uh*ns) A bump or outgrowth on a bone.

proximal (**prok**-s*uh*-m*uh*l) Situated toward the point of origin or attachment of a limb or bone.

pubic arch (**pyoo**-bik **ahrch**) The space between the ischia on the pelvis; it is a good indicator of the sex of the person. On a male, it resembles the angle of a capital "A." On a woman, it is wider, at a 90-degree angle or more. The genitals lie in the area.

pubic bone (**pyoo**-bik) The bridge of bone at the front of the pelvis.

pubic symphysis (**pyoo**-bik **sim**-f*uh*-sis) The joint between the pubic bones; a fibrocartilage pad lies in this space.

pupil (**pyoo**-p*uh*l) The small black opening or aperture of the iris of the eye.

pyramidalis (pir-*uh*-mi-**dal**-*uh*s) The small triangular muscle just above the pubic bone at the top of the lower end of the rectus abdominis. It is present in 80% of humans.

— **Q** —

quadriceps group (*kwod*-r*uh*-seps) The muscles of the front of the thigh. There are four—as quad implies—but only three are visible: vastus medialis, vastus lateralis, and rectus femoris. The fourth is vastus intermedius, which is underneath the rectus femoris.

— **R** —

radius (**rey**-dee-*uh*s) One of the two bones of the forearm. The ulna is the other. The radius basically follows the thumb.

rectus abdominis (**rek**-t*uh*s ab-**dom**-*uh*-nis) The large, flat "six-pack" muscle of the abdominal region.

rectus femoris (**rek**-t*uh*s fee-**mor**-*uh*s) The trout-shaped, bipennate muscle of the front of the thigh.

retinaculum (ret-n-**ak**-y*uh*-l*uh*m) Any of the bands that pass over and under tendons to hold them together, such as at the wrists and ankles. They are like nature's duct tape.

rhomboids (**rom**-boids) There are two: rhomboid major and minor. They are both attached to the spine and insert on the inner edge of the scapula. They have an oblique angle, or upward slant. The top edge is at the inner spine of the scapula and toward the seventh cervical vertebra.

rhombus of Michaelis (**rom**-b*uh*s of **mahy**-k*uh*l-is) An area created by subcutaneous fat on a woman that covers the sacrum and therefore creates a soft, diamond-shaped rhombus at the lower back. It makes women's backs look more feminine. Men have the sacral triangle.

rib cage The bones and thoracic cartilage that protect the organs. Also called the thorax. There are fourteen true ribs, six false ribs and four floating ribs; twenty-four total.

— S —

sacral triangle (**sey**-kr*uh*l) The triangular area seen at the sacrum of the pelvis.

sacrospinalis (sey-kroh-**spahy**-nal-is) or also called the erector spinae muscles. A group of nine muscles along the length of the back that create two major forms. The medial form is at the base of the spine and is narrow and tubular. The lateral form is seen around the bottom of the rib cage on the back and has larger bellies that can be seen all the way up the spine in some poses but are more pronounced at the base of the rib cage up to the lower part of the scapulae.

sacrum (**sey**-kr*uh*m) The shield-like bone on the back, in between the two pelvic halves.

sartorius (sahr-**tawr**-ee-*uh*s) The longest muscle of the human body, it originates at the anterior superior iliac spine (ASIS) of the pelvis, at the beltline, and winds toward the inside of the knee, attaching at the top of the tibia. It separates the quadriceps and the adductors of the thigh.

scapula (**skap**-yuh-l*uh*) Either of the two, flat, South America-shaped bones that glide on the back. Commonly known as the shoulder blades.

sclera (**skleer**-*uh*) The white of the eye.

semimembranosus (sem-ee-mem-bruh-noh-suhs) One of the hamstring or flexor muscles of the back of the thigh.

semitendinosus (sem-ee-ten-d*uh*-**noh**-s*uh*s) One of the hamstring muscles of the back of the thigh. Its tendon is

remarkably long and very prominent on the back medial of the knee.

septum (**sep**-t*uh*m) A wall of connective tissue that divides an area of the body into two sections, like the nose.

serratus anterior (s*uh*-**ray**-t*uh*s) A fingerlike, fan-shaped muscle, with eight or nine paw-like fingers, that originates on the front under the nipple and inserts at the lower edge of the scapula.

sesamoid bone (**ses**-*uh*-moid) A pebble-like bone embedded in a tendon to create mechanical advantage. The patella (kneecap) is the largest of the sesamoids. There are also a couple behind the joint of the big toe and thumb.

seventh cervical vertebra (C-7) The pronounced and last bone of the neck vertebrae.

shoulder girdle The bony ring around the neck area created mostly by the clavicles and the spines of the scapulae.

skeleton The bony framework of the body. The human skeleton is made up of 206 bones in an adult, 220 in young children. The number lessens as bones fuse together.

skull The entire set of bones that create the head and face of the skeleton.

soleus (**soh**-lee-*uh*s) The large muscle under the two gastrocnemius heads that share the Achilles tendon. It helps extend the foot forward.

spine A sharp, pointy process of a bone. It is also the common name for the vertebral column.

spine of the scapula The prominent, bony shelf of the scapula. Sometimes I call these the clavicles of the back. They help create the shoulder girdle.

spinous process (spahy-nuhs) The pointy protruding part of each of the vertebrae.

sternocleidomastoideus (**stur**-noh-cli-doh-mas-**toid**-ee-*uh*s) The prominent muscle of the neck that can be more easily seen when turning the head to one side. It attaches to the sternum, clavicle, and the mastoid process, hence its name.

sternum (**stur**-n*uh*m) The necktie-looking bone on the front of the chest. Commonly called the breastbone.

subcutaneous fat (**suhb**-kyoo-tey-nee-*uh*s) The fat layer under the skin.

superficial muscles The muscles closer to the surface of the body that create the visible forms.

superior (s*uh*-*peer*-ee-er) Higher, or closer to the head.

supination (soo-puh-**ney**-sh*uh*n) The movement of the hand as it rotates the palm upward.

symphysis (**sim**-f*uh*-sis) A slightly moveable cartilaginous joint, such as the prominent one at the pubis. *See pubic symphysis.*

— T —

tarsal bones (**tahr**-s*uh*l) The seven bones that make up the ankle and heel. They are: calcaneus, talus, navicular, cuboid, and the three cuneiform bones.

temporalis (tem-p*uh*-**rahl**-is) The muscle on the side of the skull, on the temple.

tendon (**ten**-d*uh*n) Connective tissue that attaches muscle to bone. (Ligaments connect bones to other bones).

tensor fascia latae (**ten**-sawr **fash**-ee-*uh* **lah**-tee) One of the gluteal muscles, it is shaped like a teardrop and is seen at the area of one's jeans pocket.

teres major (**ter**-eez) A long, round muscle prominent at the lower tip of the scapula and visually moving toward the underarm.

teres minor (**ter**-eez) A small, cigar-shaped muscle that is tucked in between the infraspinatus and the teres major. It is not easily seen on most people.

thigh (thahy) The upper leg.

thoracic vertebrae (thoh-**ras**-ik **vur**-t*uh*-brey) The twelve vertebrae that compose the middle segment of the spine where the ribs attach, between the cervical vertebrae and the lumber vertebrae.

thorax (**thawr**-aks) The rib cage.

thumb The opposable first digit of the hand. The Latin word for thumb is *hallux*.

thyroid cartilage (**thahy**-roid **kahr**-tl-ij) The cartilage that lies at the front of the neck. It is prominent on men and often called the "Adam's apple."

tibia (**tib**-ee-*uh*) The larger of the two bones of the shin.

tibialis anterior (tib-ee-**ahl**-lis an-**teer**-ee-er) One of the contour muscles of the front of the shin. It helps to raise the foot up toward the head and also to help invert it. Its tendon is very prominent at the foot and appears to move toward the arch of the foot.

tibial tuberosity (**tib**-ee-*uh*l too-buh-**ros**-i-tee) The prominent "nose" of the tibia just below the patella and where the patellar ligament is attached.

tip of the nose The end of the nose that is made up of two pieces of cartilage. Also called the apex of the nose.

torso (**tawr**-soh) The trunk of the body; everything but the limbs and head.

tragus (**trey**-g*uh*s) The cartilaginous bump by the ear hole that can be pushed in to shut out sound.

trapezius (tr*uh*-**pee**-zee-*uh*s) The large back-and-shoulder muscle that takes up a major area of the back. Its muscle fibers radiate in many different directions, making this an amazingly active muscle in a large variety of movements.

triceps brachii (**trahy**-seps **brey**-kee-ahy) The three heads of the upper arm that extend the forearm. The three heads are: long head, lateral head, and medial head; and all three are attached to the elbow (olecranon) by the triceps tendon.

true ribs The fourteen ribs, or seven pairs, that attach most directly to the sternum. The three pairs of false ribs attach to the costal cartilage and the two pairs of floating ribs do not attach to anything at the front.

tubercle (**too**-ber-k*uh*l) A bump on a bone or cartilage.

tuberosity (too-buh-**ros**-i-tee) A rough protuberance on a bone where a tendon or ligament is attached.

— U —

ulna (*uh*l-n*uh*) One of the two forearm bones, the other being the radius. The ulna follows the pinky finger.

ulnar furrow The furrow created by the crest of the ulna due to the attachment of the flexors and extensors, with the crest being the meeting of the two, creating a furrow or linear indentation.

— V —

vastus lateralis (**vas**-t*uh*s lat-er-**ahl**-is) The largest of the quadricep group of muscles that extends the leg. It runs down the lateral aspect (outside) of the thigh and rolls toward the front, close to the knee. It shares the quadriceps tendon with the other three muscles of this group: the vastus medialis, rectus femoris, and the hidden quadricep, the vastus intermedius. The tendon surrounds the patella and becomes the patellar ligament, which attaches to the tibial tuberosity.

vastus medialis (**vas**-t*uh*s **mee**-dee-ahl-is) One of four quadriceps, this muscle appears to be teardrop-shaped and is the lowest of the group by the patella on the front, inside area of the knee.

vertebra (**vur**-t*uh*-br*uh*) The singular of the bones that make up the spinal or vertebral column. vertebrae (vur-tuh-brey) The plural form of vertebra.

vertebral column (**vur**-t*uh*-br*uh*l) The spine of the back of the skeleton. Also known as the backbone.

vomer bone (**voh**-mer) The wall of bone that forms a large part of the septum between the right and left cavities of the nose.

— W —

wing of nose The cartilaginous area flanking the side of the nose that creates each nostril.

wrist bones See carpal bones.

— X —

xiphoid process of the sternum (**zif**-oid) The small bone at the very bottom of the sternum. Xiphoid means "sword-like" in Greek.

— Z —

zygomatic arch (zahy-*guh*-**mat**-ik) The arch on the side of the skull; the cheek bone.

zygomaticus muscles (z*ah*y-g*uh*-**mat**-ik-is) Two thin, strap-like muscles, major and minor, that attach on the zygomatic arch and the corners of the mouth and upper lip.

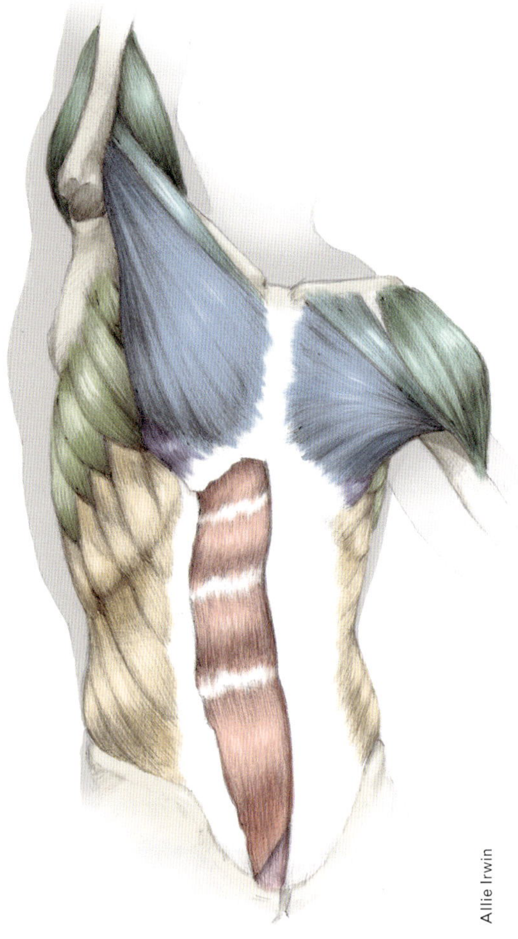

Allie Irwin

INDEX

— A —

Aging
    arm of an old man, 61
    changes in hands of women, 63
    facial changes occurring with, 71, 73, 79, 87
    overall changes occurring with, 50, 91
Anatomy applied, 103–120
    committing to poses, 115
    copying, 107
    depicting different body types, 110
    drawing from cadavers, 111
    figurative art, 105–106
    finding your style, 105
    literal/classical and interpretive approaches, 105
    maintaining proportions, 108–109
    putting "life" in life drawing, 113–114
    tutorial of analytical to gestural drawing, 116–119
Anatomy in art, 7, 9, 11–13
Apps, 20
Arcade Method of drawing hands and feet, 30, 65
Arms, 54–61
    forearm muscles, 54–61
    muscles, 44
    overview of, 54
    reference images for, 188
    skeleton of, 56
    tendons of, 60
    upper arm musculature and tendons, 55, 57–61
Artists
    author's favorite, 8, 77, 87, 105, 137
    Claude Monet, 8
    Eliot Goldfinger, 26, 53, 69, 111
    Illya Mirochnik, 95, 97
    Leonardo da Vinci, 87, 108–109, 111
    Louis-Léopold Boilly, 85
    Michaelangelo, 18, 28, 83, 94, 108
    Old Master's works, 54, 115
    period examples, 8, 108
    sample illustrations of, 107–109
    William-Adolphe Bouguereau, 8, 31

— B —

Babies, 35, 61, 80, 87–88
Baroque period, 108
Blending technique, 118
Blind persons, 78
Body types, 110
Boilly, Louis-Léopold, 85
Bones, 12–13, 19, 33. *See also* Skeleton; *specific body parts*
Bouguereau, William-Adolphe, 8, 31
Bustos, Rey
    approach of, 7, 105
    background of, 8
    favorite artists of, 8, 77, 87, 105
    photo of, 9
    sketch of, 184

— C —

Cadavers, 111, 189
Carmean, Harry, 105, 130
Cellini, 18
Communication via art, 8
Copying, 107
Corpses, 78
Crediting artists, 107

— D —

Digital tools for art, 14
Digitized art, 51
Directional terms in anatomy, 11
David 18, 83

— E —

Écorché, art of, 92–93
Emotional expression in art, 8, 9
Etymology of bone terms, 12–13
Exercises and tutorials
    analysis of form in four steps, 38–41
    Analytical to Gestural Drawing tutorial, 116–119
    animating the body, 144
    applying shadows, 135–136
    bamboo shoot approach to drawing fingers, 65
    Capturing the Main Frame, 127
    Constellation Drawing, 130
    creating silhouettes, 132
    Cutting *vs.* Drawing, 133
    Draw a Tree, 122
    Draw from TV, 124
    for drawing a skeleton, 22–23
    Drawing with a Chamois, 134
    Draw Skeletal Armature, 128
    Female *vs.* Male Standing Figure, 126
    focus on body parts, 125
    frequency of, 122
    globe method of drawing head and neck, 84–86
    mastering poses, 137
    for mouth drawing, 82
    for nose drawing, 81
    Origin and Insertion/Drumstick Form, 129
    Proportion Check: Main Frame and Constellation Drawing, 131
    Reclining Poses tutorial, 142–143
    section slices on a foot, 29
    Standing Poses tutorial, 138–139
    Switch Drawing Hands, 123
    Tent Drawing, 140–141
Eyes, 78–79

— F —

Faces. *See* Head (face)
Facial features, 77–88
    ears, 83
    eyes, 78–79
    mouths, 82–83
    noses, 80–81
    overview of, 77
Far East art, 8
Fat, 89–91, 110
Feeling, 8, 114
Feet, 27–31, 172, 186–189
Figurative art, 105–106

— G —

Galen, 52
Gallery, 146–191
Gluteals, 37
Goldfinger, Eliot, 26, 53, 69, 111 52, 89, 92, 95, 108, 109, 110, 117, 126, 127
Greuze, Jean Baptiste 65

— H —

hand 9, 28, 30, 47, 54, 59, 62, 123, 125
head 84, 86, 87, 125, 126, 128, 130, 133,
     136
Hogarth, Burne 53, 72, 130, 163

— I —

Impressionism, 8

— K —

"Kite" method of drawing front torso
     views, 45, 131
Knees, 34

— L —

Leg muscles and tendons
     adductors, 35
     exercise of form analysis in
     four steps, 38–39
     flexors, 36
     gluteals, 37
     knees, 34
     lower leg, 24–26, 28
     quadriceps, 33
     reference images for, 173–177,
     186, 189
     thigh and gluteal area, 32–37
Leonardo da Vinci, 87, 108–109, 111
Light, 118

— M —

Main frame method, 43, 127, 131
Male and female characteristics
     of bony landmarks, 19
     of external obliques, 46
     in facial muscles, 69
     fat distribution variations,
     89–90, 110
     female *vs.* male standing figure
     exercise, 126–127
     of hands, 63
     of the leg, 25
     in neck muscles, 72–73
     of the pelvis, 47
Mannerism period in art, 108, 137
Materials and suggested usage,
     14–15, 125
Michelangelo, 18, 28, 83, 94, 108
Mirochnik, Illya, 95, 97
Monet, Claude, 8
Mouths, 82–83
Muscles, 10–12, 33, 94–102. *See also*
     specific body parts

— N —

Necks, 71–73
Noses, 80–81

— O —

Orwell, George, 71

— P —

Panniculus adiposus, 89
Paper, 15, 117, 145
"Peasant toe," 31
Pelvis, 47
Photoshop, 22–23
     116
Portrait artists, 77
Proportions, 20, 108–109, 131

— R —

Realism, 8
Reference images, 172–191
Renaissance, 108
Richer, Paul, 31

— S —

Sartorial crease, 35
Sculptures, 18, 92–93
Shadows, 135–136
Sheldon, William, 110
Silhouettes, 132–134
Skeletons, 18–23. *See also* Bones
     arm skeleton, 56
     axial and appendicular, 21
     drawing exercises of, 22–23
     in écorché illustrations, 92–93
     full figure illustrations, 16,
     18–23
     importance of, 18, 20
     leg bones, 35
     pelvis of, 47
     proportional guide for, 20
     scapula of, 51
Skills that breathe life into figurative
     art, 9, 69, 115–119
Skulls, 74–75

— T —

Tendons. *See specific body parts*
Terminology related to anatomy,
     11–13
Tips, 145
Toes, 28–31
Tools of the trade, 14–15
Torsos, 42–53
     back torso and shoulder mus-
     culature, 48–50, 52–53
     front view musculature, 43–46
     how to draw, 45
     method for learning back torso
     and shoulder musculature, 53
     overview of, 43
     the pelvis, 47
     reference images for, 178–179,
     190
     scapula movements, 51
Tutorials. *See* Exercises and tutorials

— U —

Ukiyo-e genre, 8

— W —

White, technique for using, 78
Women. *See* Male and female charac-
     teristics
Wrinkles, 30, 69

CREDITS

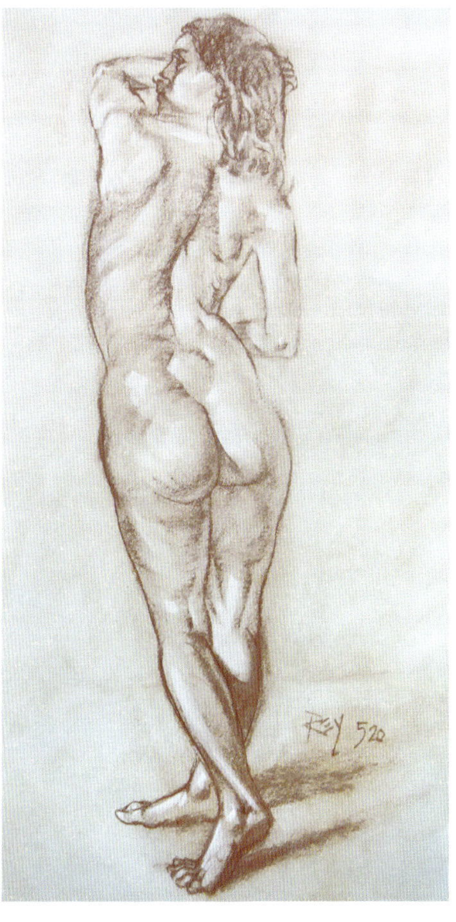

Artist Credits:

Allie Irwin 🌐 www.allieirwinart.com 📷 allie.irwin

Amaro Koberle 🌐 www.amarokoberle.com 📷 amarokoberle

Joel Lee 🌐 www.joelleeart.com 📷 joelleezj

Eddie Hsu 🌐 www.hantine.com

Erin Shin 🌐 www.erinshin.com 📷 enshiart 🐦 enshiart

Hetian Duan	Mindy Kang	Josh Wong
Jinwen Hui	Minji Kim	
Julia Hui	Grace Park	

Photography Credits:

Victor Beltran
Nikhil Hume
Jason Mendoza

Model Credits:

Bambi Corso	Quantae Love	Yuki Toy
Michelle Gibson	Ryder Palmere	Eric Underwood
Rajiv Jain	Michael Ravenwood	Cristie Wilson

RESOURCES AND ONLINE SCHOOLS

New Masters Academy: www.nma.art
3d models, anatomy courses, photos, and resources including The Goldfinger Cadaver casts produced by Jacobo Workshop.

www.anatomytools.com
Andrew Cawrse - Fine Art Sculptor & Anatomist, Founder

www.gallerygirls.com sketching and painting references for artists

L' Écorché' by MD3D Inc. App showing skeleton and muscle reference using the Jean Houdon écorché and a remake of this sculpture by Scott Eaton.

LA Academy of Figurative Art

Gnomon School of Visual Effects

THE ART OF PURSUIT

Any endeavor worth pursuing has its challenges, but they are always worth it. The main thing to remember is that with great desire and persistence there are great rewards. The joy of any creative endeavor is the liberation of the soul, the exaltation of the human spirit. The power of art in life and in any society can never be overstated—it is the essence of the heart and soul of a culture.

In whatever manner that you pursue art, whether it is as a profession or as a hobby, do it with reverence, appreciation, and understanding. Everyone learns at different rates and in a variety of ways. In this book, I gave you options, like a buffet of sorts, for you to pick and choose from to help you reach your particular goals.

The last piece of advice I have for you is to be patient with yourself. Find joy every time that you draw or make art. Feed the inner child and treat that little kid with gentleness and kindness. We say things to ourselves that you would never say to a child in your care, so do not do that to yourself.

Be patient, find inspiration in all that is around you, and keep making art!

ABOUT THE AUTHOR

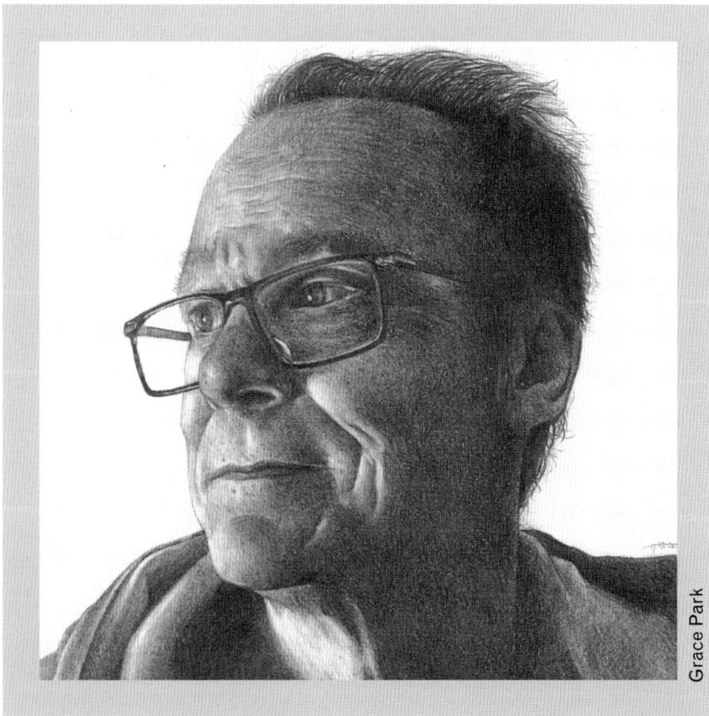

Rey Bustos received his BA in Illustration from ArtCenter College of Design in 1989 with honors. Since 1990 he has taught figure drawing, composition, and 2D and 3D anatomy, and today is considered one of the preeminent artistic anatomy teachers in the country. Bustos is a teacher at the Animation Guild who also teaches at ArtCenter College of Design in Pasadena, CA, Los Angeles Academy of Figurative Art, and Kline Academy of Art in Culver City, CA and conducts online classes for Computer Graphics Masters Academy (CGMA), New Masters Academy, Vertex School, and Gnomon School of Visual Effects.

reybustos.com

ACKNOWLEDGMENTS

For my wife, Fiona, for her help with this project, but most importantly for her support and love. To our daughter, Catherine, the reason for everything that we do; the purity of her soul and love keeps us focused and reminded of the most important things in life.

Many thanks to the countless people who have made this book possible: my students past, present, and future; and the students who have lent their talents to the pages of this book, allowing me to include their classroom homework. To all of my models, the muses in the classroom, your presence in the room inspires all of us to try to capture the beauty of not only your physical beings but, more importantly, your inner spirit. Thank you especially to the models who graciously allowed me to use their images to better illustrate lessons taught in my classes and in the chapters within. I am very grateful to Dr. Anthony Friscia and UCLA for allowing my classes to learn from their cadavers; the experience has been invaluable for me and my students, who have benefitted from it tremendously. It is impossible to calculate what a gift it has been to learn from this most direct manner.

To the many teachers who made the biggest difference in my life and work, and specifically to those who made the most impact in my knowledge of the human form, thank you: Burne Hogarth, Harry Carmean, Vern Wilson, Mark Strickland, and Lorri Madden. I am privileged to be surrounded by amazing colleagues; I am humble because of the greatness that I have all around me. To all of the brothers and sisters who I did not know, those who lived long before I was born, the history of figurative art has been and is an amazing example of the greatness of human beings when stretched to their most exalted selves. The genre of figurative art has always been and will always be a humbling art form for all of us that are immersed in it. It has been a passion and an honor for me personally to study the masters of the past as well as those of today; many examples from them were used in this book.

I would also like to thank my parents, Reinaldo and Marina Bustos, for the sacrifices that it took to bring our family to this great country. They knew that our lives would be better here and that their children would have the opportunity to become whatever they wanted to be and reach their highest potential. They were right. I owe everything to these two humble, unassuming people.

I am incredibly grateful to the team at Design Studio Press: Scott Robertson, Tinti Dey, and my fabulous editor, Teena Apeles. The greatness of every culture can be defined by its art and how it sponsors it. The quality of their work will add to the art of our culture. Let's keep art flowing and continue to keep the bar high. We can only do this through knowledge and understanding and that requires continued study and searching for the truth that lies in all great art.

This book is dedicated to the loving memory of these individuals:

Reinaldo Bustos, Sr.

Sue McCarthy Bustos

Steven "Rivets" Rivera

May they rest in peace.

I know that you believed in me and I hope that I made you proud.

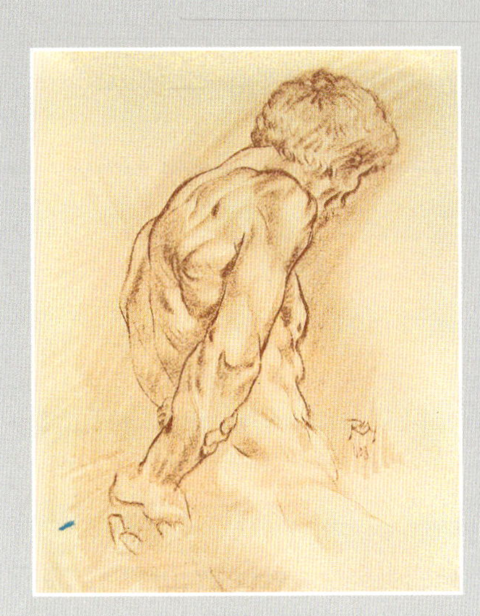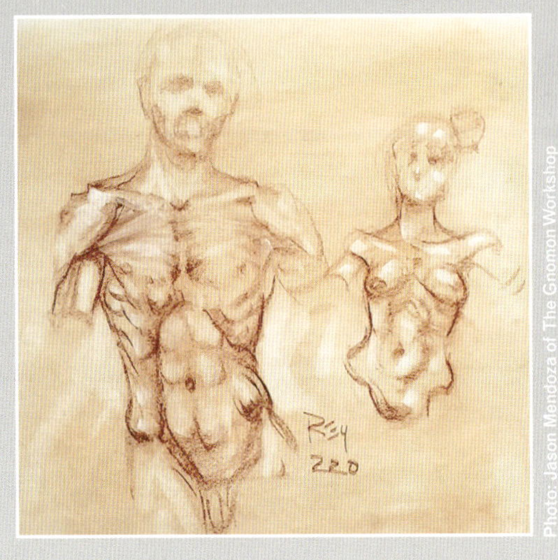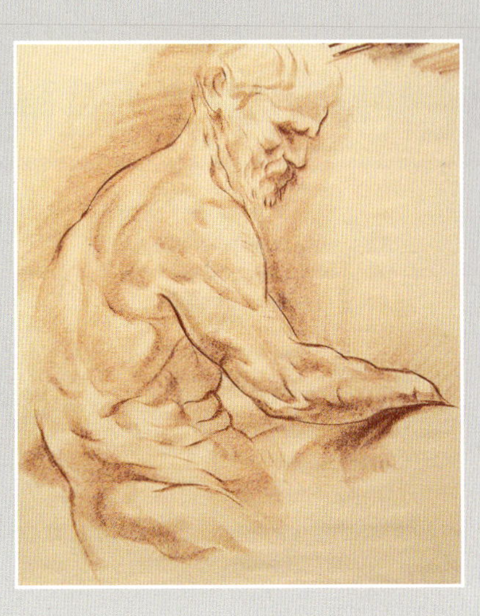

ALSO FROM DESIGN STUDIO PRESS

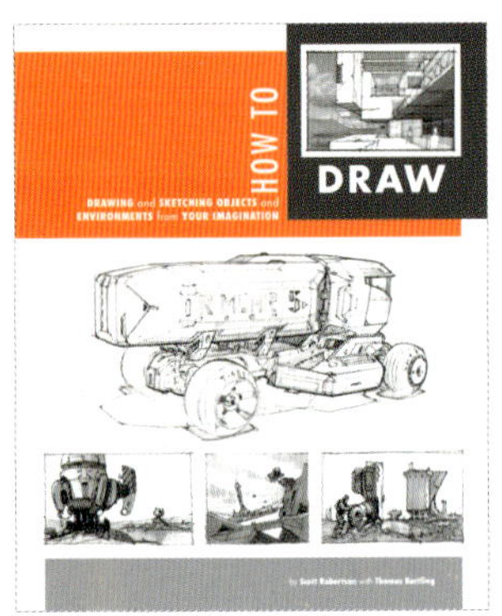

Paperback ISBN: 978-193349273-5
Hardcover ISBN: 978-193349275-9

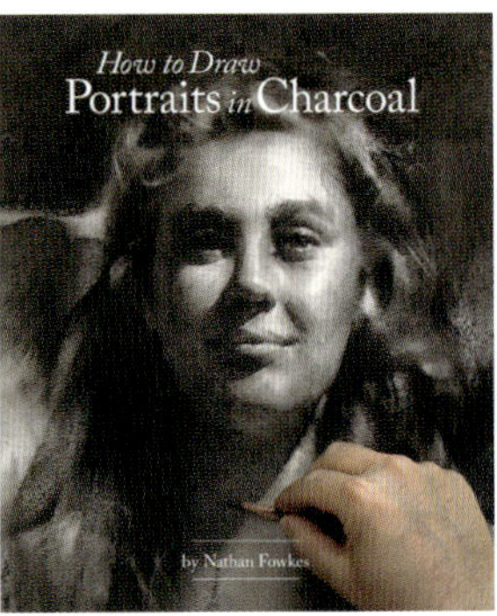

Paperback: 978-162465031-4

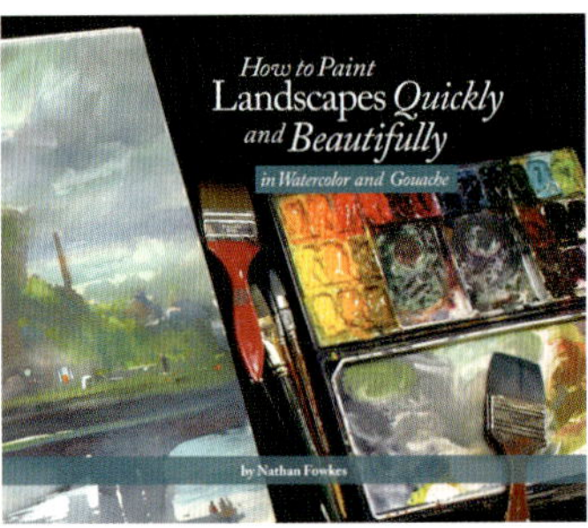

Paperback: 978-162465049-9

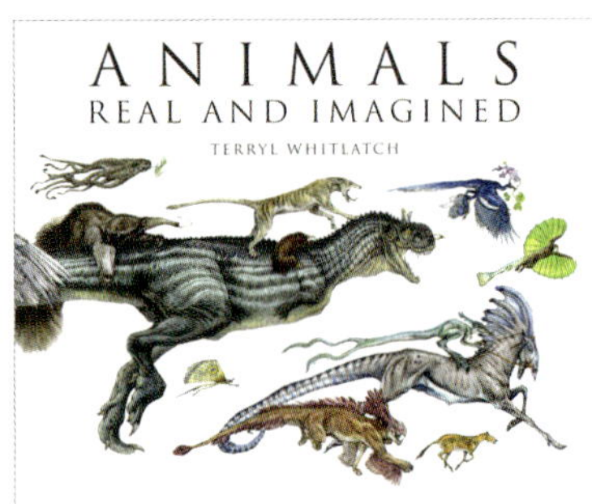

Paperback: 978-193349292-6

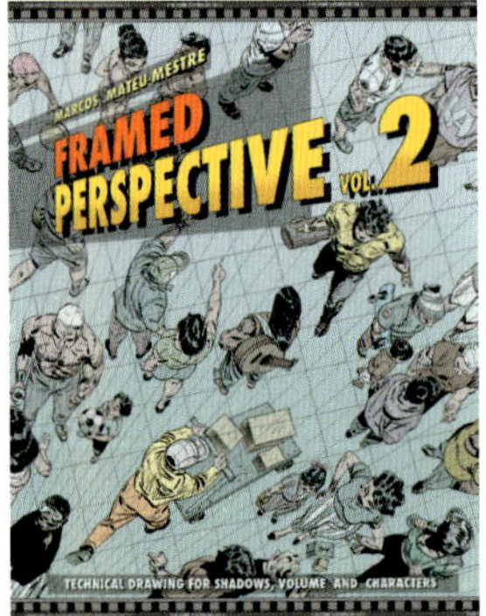

Paperback: 978-162465032-1

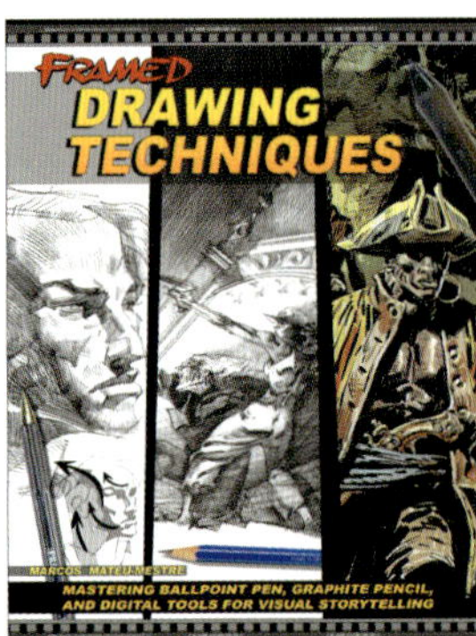

Paperback: 978-162465040-6

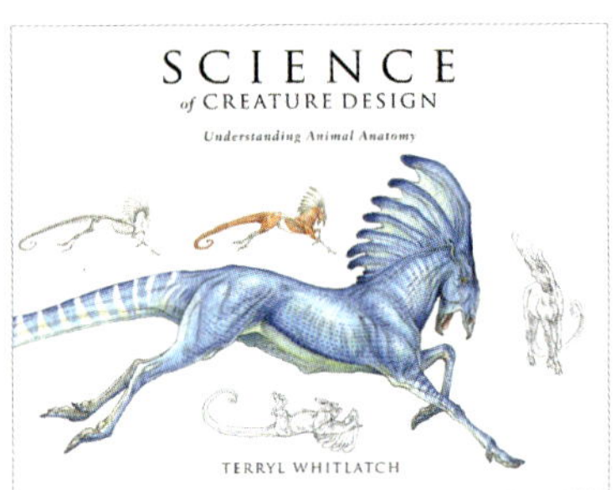

Paperback ISBN: 978-193349256-8
Hardcover ISBN: 978-162465029-1

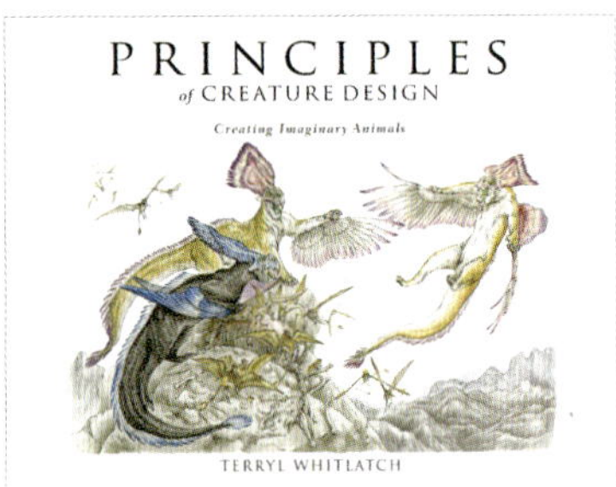

Paperback ISBN: 978-162465021-5
Hardcover ISBN: 978-162465028-4

To order additional copies of this book and to view other books we offer, please visit:
www.designstudiopress.com

For volume purchases and resale inquiries, please email:
info@designstudiopress.com

To be notified of new releases, special discounts and events, please sign up for the mailing list on our website, join our Facebook page, or follow us on Twitter:

facebook.com/designstudiopress
twitter.com/DStudioPress